Encyclopedia of World Stamps, 1945–1975

James A. Mackay

Encyclopedia of World Stamps 1945-1975

1945-1975

McGraw-Hill Book Company
New York   St. Louis   San Francisco

Published in the United States
by McGraw-Hill Book Company 1976

By the same author:

World of Stamps
Money in Stamps
The Tapling Collection of Postage Stamps
Commonwealth Stamp Design, 1840–1965
The Story Of Malta and her Stamps
The Story of Great Britain and her Stamps
The Story of Eire and her Stamps
The Story of East Africa and its Stamps
Airmails, 1870–1970
Cover Collecting
The World of Classic Stamps
The Dictionary of Stamps in Colour
A Source Book of Stamps
St. Kilda: Its Posts and Communications

With George F. Crabb:

Tristan da Cunha: Its Postal History and Philately

Encyclopaedia of World Stamps, 1945–1975 is published
simultaneously by

Australia: Rigby Limited.
Canada: Methuen Publications.
Germany: Ebeling Verlag.
Norway: Wennergren-Cappelen A/S.
Spain: Editorial Noguer S.A.
Sweden: Bokförlaget Forum A.B.
United Kingdom: Lionel Leventhal Limited.
United States of America: McGraw-Hill Book Company.

Acknowledgments

The author wishes to thank the following for specimens of stamps and
data used in the compilation of this book: the Crown Agents for Overseas
Territories and Administrations of Sutton, England; the Inter-
Governmental Philatelic Corporation of New York; Agence Philatélique
d'Outremer of Brussels; Artia of Prague; Philatelia Hungarica of
Budapest; Chulpanmul of Pyongyang; Cartimex of Bucharest;
Cubartimpex of Havana; Mezhdunarodnaya Kniga of Moscow and the
Philatelic Bureaux of Australia, Austria, Belgium, Bhutan, Bulgaria,
Burundi, Canada, the Cook Islands, Denmark, Finland, France, the
German Democratic Republic, the German Federal Republic, Guinea,
Greece, Ireland, Israel, Liberia, Mexico, the Netherlands, New Zealand,
the Condominium of the New Hebrides, Nicaragua, Papua–New Guinea,
Poland, Portugal, Rhodesia, Rwanda, Samoa, South Africa, Spain,
Sudan, Sweden, Switzerland, Taiwan, Turkey, the United Nations, the
United States of America, Venezuela and Vietnam.

The author is also indebted to the many dealers who helped with the
location of the more elusive items, but a special mention is due to
G. Vincent Base of the Camberley Stamp Centre; A. Constantine; Dr. O.
Bacher of the Westminster Stamp Company; Theodore Champion of Paris;
M. A. Bojanowicz of Arthur Boyle Ltd.; Campbell Paterson, Ltd.; Ian
Fine of the Harrow Coin and Stamp Company; the staff of A. D. Hamilton
Ltd. of Glasgow; Sam Malin of the Suburban Stamp Company; Peter
Rickenback of the Waltham Stamp Company; Stanley Gibbons
International Ltd.; J. Uttley of Sutton Coldfield.

Thanks are also due to Arthur Blair, who read the manuscript and
offered much helpful and constructive criticism, and to Michael Boxall
and the late Irving Farren who edited the manuscript.

Library of Congress Cataloging in Publication Data
Mackay, James Alexander.
  Encyclopedia of world stamps, 1945–1975.

  1. Postage-stamp—Dictionaries.   I. Title
HE6196.M34 1976   769'.56'03   76–17283
ISBN 0–07–044595–8

This book was designed and produced by
Lionel Leventhal Limited, 2–6 Hampstead High Street,
London NW3 1PR.

Edited by Irving Farren and Michael Boxall.
Designed by David Gibbons.
Colour reproduction by Nefli, Haarlem, Netherlands.
Colour printing by Drukkerij de Lange/van Leer B.V., Deventer,
  Netherlands.
Text printing and binding by Cox & Wyman, Fakenham, England.

Introduction

This book traces the development of postage stamps throughout the world during the three decades from the end of the Second World War – the most interesting and prolific period since stamps first appeared, largely as a result of changes in official attitudes towards stamp-collecting. Before the war, with relatively few exceptions, postal administrations regarded philatelists as a nuisance and made little effort to cater for their needs. By contrast, no postal authority today can afford to ignore the philatelic market. To be sure, there have always been countries that derived a large part of their revenue from philatelic sales; but nowadays even the most conservative administrations appreciate that the income from stamps sold to collectors helps to defray the cost of their postal services. As a result, a great deal of money is spent by philatelic bureaux in promoting the hobby and it has been estimated that the number of collectors throughout the world has trebled since 1945.

In an age when the global output of stamps is so vast, there are few who could ever hope to encompass the entire field of stamps from 1840 onwards. Some collectors restrict their interests to the stamps of one country or a group of countries studied in depth from the first issues onwards, but even this limited goal becomes increasingly difficult as the prices of so many pre-war stamps escalate and material becomes much more elusive.

The supply of older stamps fell far short of the demand years ago, and this has forced more and more collectors to concentrate on post-war issues. Even in this relatively brief period, however, it has become virtually impossible to collect the stamps of the whole world and some degree of specialisation is inevitable. The current output of new issues is estimated at about seven thousand stamps a year and, as postal rates inexorably rise, the cost of keeping up with contemporary stamps alone is increasingly exorbitant.

The dedicated stamp collector is obsessed by the desire to own complete sets. Nothing annoys him more, therefore, than a collection with gaps he has little hope of filling. But this situation is bound to arise with the stamps of any country that issued them a century ago, and also with a high proportion of those from countries that began issuing within the past fifty years. The collector of post-war stamps, on the other hand, has a wide range of countries from which to choose: former colonies that changed their name on attaining independence; old countries fragmented by the misfortunes of war; and entirely new countries carved out of the remnants of former empires. All of these offer the prospect of starting at the beginning and – with patience, persistence and luck – reaching a reasonable state of completion. The same prospect attracted many newcomers to the hobby after the First World War, when the political changes were mainly confined to Europe; but the scope is infinitely greater for the collector of post-1945 stamps – for throughout the world the end of the Second World War had tremendous social, political and economic impacts that are reflected in the stamps of the ensuing period (a period for which the collector often equates the term 'post-war' with 'modern').

The thirty years covered by this book conveniently divide themselves into three clear-cut decades. Politically, they are readily identifiable as the decade of the aftermath of war, the decade of the emergent nations and the decade of Détente and Ostpolitik. These aspects of global history have each had a major effect on philately; but from the purely philatelic point of view, each period may be said to have had its distinctive character highlighted by, respectively, the beginnings of 'incidental' philately, the development of thematic or topical issues and the rise of commercial philatelic agencies. There are, of course, many other trends and developments woven into the pattern of post-war philately, some of which can be clearly pinpointed while others are, as yet, ill-defined.

In this book, the countries are arranged alphabetically within continents or recognisable country-groups for each period, and each period is preceded by an introductory section giving an overall survey of the salient points in that decade, discussing both the aesthetics and the mechanics – design and printing processes – as well as the trends in stamp-collecting that have had important repercussions on stamp-issuing policy.

Over 4,500 stamps have been selected to illustrate the three decades. Relatively more space has been allocated to the stamps of the most recent period, partly because it is the most prolific and partly because the stamps have shown a disconcerting tendency to become larger in size in recent years.

The value of this encyclopaedia is greatly enhanced by showing the stamps in full colour, reproduced in their original size. It is only in very recent years that it has been permitted to reproduce stamps in this manner and this volume is, we believe, the first major work to do so. The stamps shown are all postally-used specimens and their postmarks provide some insight into the types of cancellation used in different parts of the world.

Contents

1945-1954
General Survey of the Decade

In many respects the end of the Second World War in Europe had a more dramatic impact on philately than the course of the war itself. One of the final acts of the Nazi régime, as the Red Army was fighting its way through the streets of Berlin, was to issue two stamps depicting S.A. and S.S. troopers and marking the 12th anniversary of the Third Reich. A few hours later Berlin had fallen, Hitler was dead and the unconditional surrender of Germany was imminent. Miraculously, a postal service of some sort continued to function as the country was overrun by the victorious armies of the four major Allied powers. Germany was swiftly partitioned into four zones of occupation, and Berlin was similarly divided. Thereafter, the smooth operation of the postal services was at times bedevilled by the animosities and differences that arose among the Allies; and the chaos was compounded by the fact that none of the stamps of the erstwhile régime was acceptable to the Allies.

Only the British and Americans had made any provision for filling the philatelic vacuum, based on their previous experiences in the liberation of Ethiopia in 1942 and the invasion of Italy in 1943, and stamps inscribed 'AM POST DEUTSCHLAND' were prepared for the Allied Military Government at the Bureau of Engraving and Printing in Washington and, subsequently, by Harrison and Sons in England. These stamps were produced by letterpress and photogravure respectively. After the occupation had begun, they were lithographed by Westermann of Brunswick. Thus three countries and three distinct printing processes were involved in their manufacture. The 'AM Post' stamps circulated mainly in the Anglo–American zones, but to a limited extent they seem also to have been available in the French and Soviet zones. Neither of these latter powers had made provision for the postal services in their spheres and it was left largely to the postal authorities at regional or local levels to improvise.

Immediately after the Nazi collapse, the stocks of Hitler Head definitives and 'Grossdeutsches Reich' commemoratives were withdrawn from sale. Mail was prepaid in various ways: by manuscript endorsement, by 'Paid' handstruck markings, by Nazi stamps with the Hitler profile heavily defaced, or by a combination of these methods. Even in the relatively orderly Anglo–American zones, local makeshifts of this type occurred from time to time. New issues of a more sophisticated nature, including local charity or semi-postal stamps, continued to appear well into 1946. By December 1945 the French had introduced a general Arms series of stamps in their zone. The Russians at first divided their zone into six postal districts, each with its own stamps, and then adopted the general series of the Anglo–American zones. As a result of the currency reform in the Anglo–American zones in 1948, separate issues were resumed in the respective zones. Throughout this period the French remained aloof from their Allies and produced a set of stamps for use in their own zone. This general series was replaced by individual sets for Baden, Rhineland Palatinate, Württemberg and the Saar in 1947.

The pattern of events was rather similar in Austria, though of much shorter duration: the country was divided into four zones, and Vienna was partitioned. Stamps of Nazi Germany were overprinted 'Österreich' and the features of Adolf Hitler were defaced. These stamps were rapidly superseded by distinctive sets of the Soviet zone and the British, French and American authorities acting in concert. Austria differed in status from Germany in that the country was liberated rather than occupied, and steps were accordingly taken to transfer the administration to a civil government. The Austrian republic, which had disappeared in 1938, was formally resurrected on 14th May 1945 and a unified postal service was resumed in October. Thereafter, the zonal issues were superseded by the stamps of the Austrian government.

At the end of the Second World War the countries of Europe fell into several broad categories depending on their belligerent, neutral or victim status, and this affected their stamps to a large extent. As might be expected, the changes were least obvious in Russia and Britain, where the termination of the war meant no constitutional alterations that would be reflected in issues of stamps; and the same was true of the neutral countries – Switzerland, Portugal, Spain and Sweden. Of the rest, seven countries had continued to exist with more or less their separate identities although under enemy occupation, and a further four had been dismembered or had ceased to exist for the duration of hostilities.

While the war was still in progress, France had had various makeshifts as parts of the country were liberated. As early as 1943 the French Committee of National Liberation had produced distinctive stamps for use in Corsica, following the Allied landings, and a series typographed in Washington was released on the French mainland after the Normandy invasion of June 1944. Stamps produced by De La Rue in London were used during the period of the provisional government, after the occupation of Paris and the collapse of the Vichy régime. Appropriately, the first stamp issued in 1945 was one commemorating the liberation (2:16).

Characteristically, the first commemoratives issued by Greece after the war were a pair inscribed 'OXI' (no) marking the fifth anniversary of resistance to the Italian ultimatum that brought Greece into conflict with the Axis powers. Otherwise, Greek stamps made the transition to peacetime conditions – if raging inflation and a bloody civil war can be regarded as peacetime conditions – without any change in their design. After liberation, the country was under the regency of Archbishop Damaskinos until the restoration of the monarchy in September 1946, which was marked by an overprint (plus inflationary surcharge) on pre-war stamps portraying King George II.

Of the other European monarchies, Belgium alone suffered a constitutional crisis that threatened to split the country in two. The alleged collaboration of King Leopold III with the Germans during the war meant that he could not resume his throne, and a regency continued until his son Baudouin came of age in 1951 and was proclaimed king. None of these upheavals was reflected in the stamps of the immediate post-war decade. The pre-war definitives portraying King Leopold continued in circulation, and new values were added to the set as late as 1956. Even at the end of 1944 some of these stamps were released, with the addition of a 'V' emblem denoting Victory, and they survived well into the 1950s. The only philatelic references to the grim realities of the war were the various sets of semi-postal stamps with premiums in aid of war victims and former prisoners of war, issued in 1945–6.

Both Norway and the Netherlands had stamps printed in Britain during the war for the use of their governments in exile and naval and military personnel serving with the Allied forces. In both countries, new denominations were added to the series after liberation. In fact, the Dutch series was not valid for postage within the Netherlands until after 1st April 1946. Holland's first post-war issue was a symbolic 7½-cent stamp celebrating liberation, but Norway's only reference to the war consisted of a charity set, portraying Crown Prince Olav, and a stamp of 1946 referring to the training of the Royal Norwegian Air Force in Canada. Pre-war definitive issues continued to appear in both countries long after the war had ended.

In this respect, Denmark was even more conservative, continuing to add new values or changes of colour to the Caravel definitive series – in use since 1933 – to the present day. A series portraying King Christian X, released during the Nazi occupation in 1942, continued to appear until 1948. Little note was taken of the war other than a belated Liberation series in 1947, and the first post-war commemoratives characteristically celebrated the 75th birthday of the King, who had remained doggedly at his post throughout the German occupation.

In Eastern Europe the end of hostilities had a more noticeable impact on stamps. Albania had endured Italian and, latterly, German occupation before emerging in October 1944 as a 'democratic state'. Amid a spate of commemorative overprints on issues of the Fascist régime came a pictorial definitive series in November 1945, overprinted subsequently to mark the Constitutional Assembly and then to signify the proclamation of the People's Republic in July 1946. Albanian stamps thereafter settled down to an unvarying diet of commemoratives extolling the exploits of the partisans or promoting the desired image of the Communist way of life.

The Grand Duchy of Luxembourg, occupied in 1940, was absorbed into the Third Reich a year later as part of the Moselland region. With the restoration of independence in 1944 came a series, recess-printed by the American Bank Note Company, portraying the Grand-Duchess Charlotte. Like France and the Netherlands, the first distinctive post-war issue referred to the liberation and paid tribute to the Four Powers. Several issues in the immediate post-war years paid homage to the resistance fighters, and a 1947 set honoured the late General George S. Patton.

Czechoslovakia, Poland and Yugoslavia were dismembered by the Nazis before or during the war and had to be re-constituted after their liberation in 1944–5. Both Poland and Yugoslavia had continued to maintain a precarious philatelic identity during the war, however, with sets of stamps produced in England for the use of their exiled governments and military personnel; but in neither case were these stamps put into circulation after the liberation. Stamps produced locally, in areas under the the control of partisan units or in those districts liberated by the Red Army, were used instead. Curiously enough, Czechoslovakia, without having had the benefit of an emigré series during the war, used a set printed by De La Rue in London in the immediate post-war period. Various other sets were issued in Kosice, Bratislava and Prague under Russian auspices, including a series portraying Jan Masaryk that had been produced at the State Printing Works in Moscow. Apart from a series of August 1949 marking the first anniversary of the Slovak rising, the war had little impact on Czech stamps until the series of 1947 marking the fifth anniversary of the destruction of Lidice. The transition from a democracy to a Soviet satellite was gradual and President Beneš continued to grace the definitives until 1948, when his death brought the Communist leader Klement Gottwald to power.

Poland's post-war stamps, by contrast, were largely preoccupied with the horrors and hardships of the recent war – first with stamps celebrating the liberation of successive towns and then emphasising the grim realities, with the spectre of death over Majdanek concentration camp and a series of before-and-after views of Warsaw. Other stamps referred to the Battle of Grunwald, in which the Poles had defeated the Teutonic Knights in the fifteenth century, or commemorated the anniversary of the 1863 uprising against Tsarist Russia.

Four countries formerly in the Axis camp – Italy, Hungary, Bulgaria and Romania – switched allegiance before the war ended. In Italy, the 1929 definitive series was reissued in 1945 with the Fascist emblems removed. Hungarian stamps were overprinted 'FELSZABADULAS' (liberation) and surcharged with new values after Admiral Horthy abrogated his powers to a provisional government under Soviet auspices. The astronomical hyper-inflation that engulfed Hungary soon afterwards, rendered the Horthy stamps obsolete more swiftly and effectively than any political change could have done. In the monarchies of Bulgaria and Romania, the switch from Fascist to Communist domination was achieved without any apparent change in the stamps. In both cases the respective monarchs, Simeon II and Michael, were portrayed on stamps; and the prolific issues of the latter continued to the end of 1947, giving no hint of the realities of power. Only the occasional stamp of this period marking Romanian–Soviet amity indicated that Romania was rapidly moving into the Russian orbit. Bulgarian stamps – with the exception of definitives featuring the old royal emblem of a crowned lion – bore the unmistakable character of contemporary Soviet graphic design, with ponderous allegories of freedom and the Fatherland Front.

Of the neutral countries of Europe, Switzerland alone took note of the war with a pair of semi-postals of 1945 whose premiums went to a war relief fund. The stamps of Spain continued to hark back to the tragic civil war of 1936–9, and those of Portugal and Sweden continued to glorify the exploits of medieval seafarers or commemorate the anniversaries of such worthy bodies as the Swedish press, the savings movement and the agricultural show. If stamps are anything to judge from, Turkey's sole preoccupation in 1945 was the national census, though an indication of that country's adjustment to the post-war world was the set of three stamps in 1946 marking the visit of the U.S.S. *Missouri* to Istanbul. Finland was Europe's odd-man-out in 1945, having been allied with Germany against Russia while managing to maintain tenuous links with the free world. The recent conflict was ignored in the annual Red Cross issues, and the main themes for philatelic commemoration in 1945 were the birthdays of two octogenarians – President Stahlberg and the composer Sibelius.

The Second World War also had repercussions in Asia, where the dominant Axis power had been forced into unconditional surrender by the use of atomic weapons. Compared to Germany, however, Japan made the transition from war to peace with very little effect on the nation's stamps. The changes were much more subtle: the militaristic subjects (fighter-pilot, munitions-worker, and the slogan 'The enemy will surrender') were replaced by views of temples and a mask from the Noh dramas – but the depreciation of the yen would have made additions to the series inevitable in any case. More significant was the fact that the definitives were often released either imperforate or with a roulette form of separation when the perforating machines broke down and could not be repaired. The secularisation of imperial power, as a result of the Constitution of 1947, was reflected in the removal of the chrysanthemum emblem from Japanese stamps issued from 1948 onwards. By contrast with the plethora of Allied issues in Germany, only one occupying force issued special stamps in Japan. Australian stamps overprinted 'B.C.O.F.' (British Commonwealth Occupation Force) were issued on 11th October 1946. They were withdrawn two days later, following protests from the Japanese government, and were reissued the following May (13:49). In March 1949 they were finally withdrawn. Exceptional were the Ryukyu Islands, which were detached from Japan and governed by the United States military authorities until 1952, from which time they came under an American civil administration until they reverted to Japan in 1972. Distinctive stamps were released throughout this period.

The surrender of the Japanese in the Pacific and South-East Asia left a vacuum that the former colonial powers confidently intended to fill. The defeat of European and American powers by an Asian country ensured that the old order could never be resumed, and the entire decade after the Second World War – from Java to Dien Bien Phu – is a saga of European imperial decline in the face of determination by the once-subject peoples to attain full independence. Philatelically, it was marked by the stamps of the erstwhile Netherlands Indies and French Indo-China to denote their usage in Indonesia and Vietnam respectively. The situations in the two areas were quite different. At first the régime established by Ho Chi-minh was tolerated by the French, who overprinted Indo-Chinese stamps 'Viet-Nam Dan-Chu Cong-Hoa' (Vietnam Democratic Republic); but when fighting broke out between the French and the Viet-Minh in December 1946, Ho Chi-minh withdrew his forces to northern Tongking and established a separate régime, subsequently known as North Vietnam or the Vietnam Democratic Republic. The French subsequently established the Annamese ruler Bao Dai as head of the state of Vietnam. Stamps thus inscribed were introduced in 1951 and similar issues made at the same time for Cambodia and Laos, the other components of Indo-China.

At the time of the Japanese surrender in Java and Sumatra, an Indonesian republic was proclaimed by Dr. Sukarno in defiance of the Dutch. Rather crude stamps were issued by the republicans in those parts of Java and Sumatra under their control, but stamps of the Netherlands Indies continued to circulate in the remaining islands. In a bid to counter Sukarno, the Dutch established an autonomous régime in their area and renamed it Indonesia in September 1948, the contemporary Indies stamps being thus overprinted. In December 1949 the Dutch yielded further, permitting the territory under their control to be amalgamated with the republican area under the title of the United States of Indonesia. The country was nominally an independent state within the Netherlands-Indonesian Union, but the last remnants of Dutch control were progressively shaken off and the United States of Indonesia became a unitary republic in 1950. It dissolved the union with the Netherlands in 1954. The various changes of status are reflected in the inscriptions found on the stamps of the period. In the same year, the Viet-Minh decisively defeated the beleaguered French in Dien Bien Phu and the independent republics of North and South Vietnam were created, with the Seventeenth Parallel as their common boundary.

Divisiveness was to be the keynote in other parts of post-war Asia. Korea, which had been under Japanese domination since the end of the nineteenth century, was liberated in 1945 but was almost immediately partitioned between the Americans and the Russians (the latter having declared war on Japan in the closing weeks of the war). Distinctive stamps were issued by the occupying forces in their respective spheres. Those of the Soviet zone portrayed Marshal Kim Il-sung, a theme that continues to this day. The Americans handed over power to a civil government in South Korea in July 1948 and shortly afterwards, the Russians established the People's Democratic Republic of Korea in the area north of the Thirty-eighth Parallel. From the outset, there was a strong ideological tendency in the design of both republics – less obvious in the Syngman Rhee issues of the South than in the crude allegorical designs of the North.

The political and economic disintegration of China had been chronic since the foundation of the republic in 1912, and the long war with Japan had merely aggravated the situation. Philatelically, the situation was marked by a wide variety of provincial issues – some necessitated by regional fluctuations in the value of the yuan and others by authority of the Communists for use in those districts under their control. As the Japanese withdrew, the Communists seized power in large areas of Manchuria – substantially aided by the Russians, who had invaded the Japanese puppet empire of Manchukuo towards the end of the Second World War. The stamps issued by the Communists in the post-war period fall into two categories: those of a local validity, prepaying the postage on mail within areas captured from the Nationalists between 1945 and 1949; and those produced in 1949 for use in the so-called Liberation Areas of Central, East, North, North-west, South and South-west China. These stamps, with their battle scenes, symbols of liberation and portraits of Chairman Mao, foreshadowed the stamps issued by the People's Republic of China in the early 1950s.

The post-war stamps of the Nationalists continued the previous pattern of interminable sets portraying Dr. Sun Yat-sen (eight sets between 1929 and 1945 and a further four between 1945 and 1949), interspersed by portrait sets honouring President Chiang Kai-shek. The most striking feature of post-war Nationalist stamps was their enormous values as the currency was reformed and revalued in a vain bid to stem rocketing inflation. Separate issues were made for Formosa, under Japanese control since 1895 and returned to the Nationalists in 1945. Chinese stamps surcharged in Japanese currency were introduced after the war. Subsequent stamps were similar to those used on the mainland, distinguished merely by minor differences in the characters of the inscriptions. When Formosa (Taiwan) was elevated in 1949 from being just an offshore island to becoming the home of the Nationalist government, the change was scarcely noted in its stamps, distinguished only by their surcharge in silver yuan currency. Subsequent issues were inscribed 'REPUBLIC OF CHINA', implying a currency in an area much larger than Formosa and a handful of offshore islands.

In the Asiatic parts of the British Empire that had been occupied by the Japanese, stamps signposted the slow return to normality. The pre-war stamps of Hong Kong were resurrected without any distinguishing overprint; but in Malaya and Burma the stamps were overprinted 'BMA' or 'MILY ADMN' to signify the British Military Administration. Pre-war stamps of the Straits Settlements with the 'BMA' overprint were used throughout the Malay States, being gradually superseded, from 1948 onwards, by issues in uniform designs for each state. The former Straits Settlements were broken up and individual issues were made for Malacca, Penang and Singapore. The Malay state of Perlis joined the ranks of the stamp-issuing states in 1948. In Burma the stamps were reissued in 1946 minus the Military Administration overprint and in new colours, to distinguish them from the demonetised pre-war series. In October 1947, pending the granting of full independence, the series was overprinted in Burmese to signify 'Interim Government'. These rapid political developments, reflected in frequent changes of stamps, stimulated speculation in Burmese philately to such an extent that the stamps of the immediate post-war period have been a drug on the market ever since.

Although Burma had opted for complete independence, Ceylon and the Indian sub-continent had settled for dominion status within the British Commonwealth. In 1947, India was partitioned into the dominions of India and Pakistan, which very roughly corresponded to the predominantly Hindu and Moslem areas of the sub-continent. The contemporary King George VI stamps of India were overprinted for use in Pakistan; but the stamps of the British Raj continued unchanged in India until 1949, when a series depicting antiquities and architecture was released. These stamps, together with the independence commemoratives, were produced in letterpress or offset lithography. A refreshing diversion was provided by the series of 1948 honouring Mahatma Gandhi, produced in photogravure by Courvoisier of Switzerland. Four years later, the Indian Post Office installed its own photogravure equipment and, from 1952 on, the majority of Indian stamps have been printed by that process. India became a republic in 1950, with suitably symbolic stamps, but Pakistan continued as a dominion until 1956.

Ceylon did not become a dominion until 1948, though the Constitution of 1947 had resulted in greater autonomy than had previously been the case. The set of four stamps celebrating the new constitution was recess-printed by Bradbury Wilkinson in the prevailing two-colour colonial genre – a full-face portrait of King George VI inset in pictorial designs. By contrast, the dominion series of 1949 by the same printers, marking the first anniversary of independence, broke away from the colonial pattern with its flag motif and portrait of Prime Minister Senanayake. Nevertheless, Ceylon continued to be the most 'British' of the new dominions – philatelically, at least. The George VI pictorial definitives continued in use until 1951; and it was the only post-war dominion to portray Queen Elizabeth on its stamps.

The transition to independence was less smooth in other areas under British control. In Western Asia the former British and French mandates in Syria, Lebanon and Palestine came to an end. The French-controlled territories became fully independent while the war was still in progress, though the post-war stamps of Syria and Lebanon showed little outward change in design or inscription. Palestine had managed with a pictorial definitive series that had remained unchanged since 1927, but the conservatism of these stamps – with their biblical vignettes of Rachel's Tomb and the Sea of Galilee – belied the deep communal unrest between Arab and Jew as British control disintegrated. The end of the British mandate and the emergence of the Jewish national state of Israel in May 1948, was marked by bloody fighting that was to develop into a full-scale war between the infant state and its Arab neighbours. The interim period was marked by numerous emergency issues and local makeshifts prior to the Doar Ivri (Hebrew Post) series depicting ancient coins from the period of the two Jewish revolts against Roman domination. Israel's birth pangs stirred the imagination of the world, and its stamps were avidly collected, not only by Jews all over the world but also by many philatelists whose interest was captured by the biblical allusions of the commemorative issues.

To the east of Palestine lay the Arab state of Transjordan, under British mandate until 1946. Here the transition to complete independence was relatively peaceful. The stamps continued to bear the name 'TRANSJORDAN' until 1949, when the inscription 'THE HASHEMITE KINGDOM OF JORDAN' was adopted. As British control in Palestine collapsed, Jordan and Egypt seized the predominantly Arab portions – on the west bank of the River Jordan and in the Gaza district respectively – and both countries issued stamps overprinted or inscribed 'PALESTINE' for use in their own districts. Ordinary Jordanian stamps had been substituted by 1949, but Palestinian stamps continued to be released by Egypt until 1967.

Elsewhere in Asia there was remarkably little change in the stamps issued in the late 1940s. Comparatively few stamps were issued in that period by Iraq, Iran or Afghanistan. The post-war stamps of Saudi Arabia were virtually confined to occasional sets commemorating visits of other Arab rulers to Riyadh; and the neighbouring kingdom of the Yemen continued to produce infrequent stamps in non-figurative motifs, following a trend established with the first stamps in 1926. At the same time, however, there were occasional issues of stamps purporting to come from the Yemen but available only from a philatelic agency in New York – an ominous portent of things to come.

Africa

Philatelic activity in Africa in the 1940s mirrored the largely colonial status of the continent. Foreign control was reflected in the choice of subject on the stamps of even those countries that were nominally independent. Thus Liberia, then virtually a plantation of the giant U.S. Rubber Corporation, was one of the first countries anywhere in the world to issue stamps in memory of the late President Roosevelt and followed this in 1947 with a set celebrating the centenary of the first American stamps. In Egypt, special stamps were still being provided for the use of British troops occupying the Suez Canal zone – although King Farouk was beginning to assert himself against British power. The early post-war stamps reflected the growing spirit of independence and Arab consciousness with such themes as Arab union in 1945 and the evacuation of the British from Cairo in 1946–7, culminating in Egyptian participation in the first Arab–Israeli war in 1948. Farouk had even more grandiose ideas. His self-proclaimed sovereignty over the Sudan was marked in 1952 by an Arabic overprint on all the stamps then current; but these ambitions were short-lived, and the revolution that led first to his abdication and then to the overthrow of the monarchy in 1953, was reflected in the overprint of the self-same stamps with sets of bars that obliterated his portly features.

The only other fully independent African country, Ethiopia,

had only recently been liberated after six years of Italian rule. Appropriately, one of the first post-war issues was a series of Red Cross stamps – prepared initially in 1936 but unissued because of the Italian invasion. The stamps were overprinted with a large 'V' for Victory. The majority of post-war Ethiopian stamps were recess-printed in England and closely resembled contemporary British colonial stamps, with pictorial vignettes in contrasting colours and inset portraits of the Emperor Haile Selassie.

In the immediate post-war period, the French territories in Africa were grouped into vast administrative areas known as French West Africa and French Equatorial Africa. Together with the outlying territories of the Somali Coast and the islands of Madagascar and Réunion, they abandoned the pre-war penchant for garish letterpress stamps and chose sensitively engraved pictorials instead. The stamps produced in London (mainly in photogravure or offset-lithography) for the Free French authorities in these overseas territories remained in use for some time after the war. In the British part of Africa there was very little philatelic progress. South Africa abandoned the 'War Effort' and 'bantam' sets (the latter being a commendable attempt to save paper by drastically reducing the size of the stamps) and reverted to the pre-war pictorial issues, printed in bilingual pairs. The practice of releasing commemorative stamps with inscriptions alternately in English and Afrikaans continued until 1953 – to the annoyance of philatelists, who objected to having to pay twice over. The situation was aggravated by the fact that the same commemoratives were also overprinted for use in neighbouring South West Africa.

The British colonies in Africa continued to use the George VI definitives that had been introduced in 1938, enlivened only by occasional changes in colour or perforation. Very few distinctive commemoratives appeared in this decade, though the monotonous colonial omnibus issues more than compensated. Of the four West African countries, the Gold Coast alone produced a new pictorial definitive series, in 1948, and none of them issued commemoratives other than the colonial omnibus sets. Nyasaland issued a pictorial series in 1945, replacing a semi-heraldic set, but the Rhodesias clung to their 1938 issues; and all three territories produced a mini-omnibus issue in 1953 marking the Rhodes Centenary Exhibition. The royal visit to Africa in 1947 provided the opportunity for a mini-omnibus issue in the High Commission Territories of Basutoland, Bechuanaland and Swaziland as well as distinctive designs in South Africa and the Rhodesias. The visit of Princess Elizabeth and the Duke of Edinburgh to East Africa in 1952 was marked by two definitive stamps re-engraved with a commemorative inscription. It was during this visit that King George VI died and the Elizabethan era was ushered in, though the philatelic implications of the new reign were not felt until the mid-fifties.

America

Politically and economically, the American continent was least affected by the Second World War and, not surprisingly, there was little evidence in the stamps of the late forties of any sudden transition from wartime to peacetime conditions. In the United States there was a noticeable increase in the number of commemorative stamps in the late forties, reaching a peak in 1948 when a wide range of worthy causes – from Gold-Star Mothers to the poultry industry – were philatelically honoured. Thereafter the number of new issues declined and related mainly to state anniversaries and similar occasions. The Presidential series of definitive stamps, introduced in

1938, continued without change throughout the first post-war decade and was only gradually phased out from 1954 when a series portraying famous Americans and depicting national landmarks was inaugurated.

The United States produced several stamps paying tribute to the armed services, and a few Latin-American countries issued victory stamps, but the most significant event of 1945 with long-term philatelic repercussions was the death of Franklin D. Roosevelt. The United States departed from the usual practice of confining commemorative issues to single stamps by producing a series of four. Other countries of the American continent were much more prolific, with particularly lengthy sets from Nicaragua and El Salvador. The memorial stamps for Roosevelt continued to appear at intervals for several years; and it should be noted that commemoration of the late President extended farther afield, with Greece, Hungary, Liberia, Monaco and San Marino contributing sets. With the exception of Greece, whose sober black-edged pair was inspired by a genuine feeling of loss, the others seem to have been motivated by a desire to earn dollars from philatelic sales – a trend that gathered momentum in the 1950s.

The return to peacetime conditions had its main impact on the stamps of Canada, where there had been a definitive series publicising the national war effort. In 1946 the higher denominations in the series were replaced by pictorial stamps marking the return to peacetime occupations; but the lower values, portraying King George VI in various uniforms, remained current until 1949 when a series based on recent photographs of the King was adopted.

The British colonies in the Americas followed the conservative policy towards new issues that prevailed throughout the British Empire at that time; but the economic crises that beset Britain in the aftermath of war had a profound effect on the Caribbean islands, which opted out of the sterling area in 1949 and adopted the Caribbean dollar of 100 cents in place of pounds, shillings and pence. The colonies that made up the Windward and Leeward Islands were slow to change their definitive stamps. Although St. Lucia had a decimal series in 1949, adapting the designs of the 1938 set, other territories did not introduce decimal stamps until 1951–2 when the opportunity was taken to use entirely new designs with a more mature portrait of the King inset.

The West Indian colonies of France became overseas *départmements* of metropolitan France in 1949 and thenceforward used ordinary French stamps. Guadeloupe and Martinique, together with French Guiana, issued new definitives in 1947, printed by the intaglio process and using a standard formula of native types, wildlife and scenery.

The stamps of the Dutch West Indies continued to bear the name of the principal island, Curaçao, until 1949 when the more accurate name Netherlands Antilles was introduced. In the Curaçao period there were lengthy semi-postal sets with premiums in aid of reconstruction in war-torn Holland and for the relief of refugees from the East Indies who had been uprooted by the Indonesian struggle for independence. The definitives of Curaçao and the Netherlands Antilles conformed to the standard Dutch pattern – as did the definitives issued by Surinam (Dutch Guiana), which replaced a pictorial series printed by the American Bank Note Company with a standard Dutch set in 1948.

Australasia

In Australasia the main philatelic activity of the post-war decade was in Australia and New Zealand, both of which continued to use definitives introduced before or during the war while increasing their output of commemorative stamps. Increases in postal rates in 1948 and 1950 led to the introduction of many new designs in the Australian series as well as some unusual denominations, including the shilling-half-penny (1/0½d). A curious innovation of 1950 was the release of commemorative stamps of different designs but of the same denomination printed alternately in the same sheet. Although this practice was prevalent in the early 1950s, culminating in strips of three designs side by side in a food-production propaganda set of 1953, Australia abandoned the idea soon afterwards. Although most other countries have since adopted the principle of composite issues, Australia has used it only rarely. Papua-New Guinea, which had issued stamps before the war, used ordinary Australian stamps until 1952 when stamps for the joint territory were introduced.

The British colonies in the Pacific area produced no distinctive stamps in the immediate post-war years; but Tonga, which has earned an unenviable reputation for philatelic prodigality in more recent years, introduced a modern pictorial definitive series in 1953 – replacing designs which, in some instances, had been current since 1897.

Omnibus issues

It would not be true, however, to suppose that the numerous colonies and protectorates that then composed the British Empire had not given the collector plenty to think about. Variety in definitive and individual commemorative issues was lacking, perhaps; but the period from 1946 to 1953 was marked by a succession of lengthy omnibus issues. In 1946–7 the colonies each issued two stamps belatedly celebrating victory in the Second World War and featuring a view of the Houses of Parliament in London. In 1948–9 they astounded the philatelic world by producing two stamps apiece to mark the silver wedding of King George VI and Queen Elizabeth. Standard designs were used for a low value, usually representing the letter rate, and a very high value – in many cases of £1 or its equivalent in local currencies. Sales of the silver wedding stamps from the Crown Agents bureau in London alone exceeded £900,000 – an incredible sum for that period. Hard on the heels of the silver wedding stamps came sets of four stamps from each colony in 1949 to mark the seventy-fifth anniversary of the Universal Postal Union. The series was relatively unpopular with collectors, which might explain why the next omnibus series did not appear until 1953 and was then confined to a single stamp per territory to mark the coronation of Queen Elizabeth II.

Great Britain and the independent dominions also acknowledged these occasions to a greater or lesser extent, the U.P.U. anniversary being of such world-wide importance that the majority of postal administrations took part in the philatelic celebration. Although a sizeable collection could have been formed of the colonial omnibus and individual commemoratives of 1945–6 celebrating victory, peace and liberation, the Universal Postal Union anniversary was the first truly global event to merit commemoration everywhere. Other events might have been of world-wide interest but their philatelic recognition was usually confined to those countries most directly concerned. In this category were the Olympic Games of 1948 and 1952, heralded by stamps from the host countries, Britain and Finland (with Switzerland and Norway covering the respective Winter Olympics). In both Olympic years Austria issued stamps to raise funds for its national team and thus established the precedent for the numerous countries in more recent years issuing a multitude of Olympic stamps even though they were not directly involved.

The Cold War

The 'Cold War' of the late forties and early fifties exercised a subtle influence on the philately of the period. The iron curtain that descended on Europe – to use Churchill's memorable phrase – affected the subject matter of the stamps issued by the countries in the Soviet camp, ranging from interminable propaganda issues extolling the virtues of economic reforms and five-year plans, to the spate of mourning stamps in 1953 following the death of Joseph Stalin. Nevertheless, there was none of the anti-American or anti-imperialist sentiment that was to be found in stamps of the sixties, and it was in Germany alone that specific aspects of the cold war found expression in stamps. The Soviet blockade of West Berlin resulted in 'Help Berlin' stamps from the Anglo–American zones, together with diminutive stamps denoting a compulsory levy on correspondence in West Germany to raise funds for the air lift. In Berlin, semi-postal stamps raised money for the same purpose. Significantly, West Berlin issued stamps in 1953 to commemorate the anti-Soviet uprising in East Berlin in June of that year. The Korean war produced relatively few stamps apart from those issued by the Koreans themselves. Subsequently, India produced special stamps for the use of Indian custodian forces supervising the cease-fire in Korea, and similar sets were issued in 1954 for use by Indian troops serving with the International Commission in Cambodia, Laos and Vietnam.

The end of an era

King George VI died in February 1952, but the first British stamps portraying his successor did not appear until the following December, the series of low values was not completed until 1954, and the 'Castles' high values did not appear until eighteen months after that. In 1953 Elizabethan definitives gradually appeared in Canada, Australia and New Zealand; and by the end of that year a sprinkling of definitives had been released in several of the colonies, generally retaining the basic designs of the Georgian stamps but with a new portrait substituted. In many cases, however, Georgian stamps were retained until 1956 and often the only indication of a change of ruler consisted of the coronation stamps released in June 1953. A dozen countries issued commemoratives in 1953–4 to mark the round-the-world royal visit – but with the exceptions of Australia, New Zealand and Ceylon the stamps consisted of definitive designs suitably re-engraved to include a commemorative inscription.

Printing processes

In 1954 recess-printing (also known as intaglio) was still the dominant process by which the bulk of the world's stamps were produced. Britain, Norway, Switzerland, Russia and Japan were notable pioneers of photogravure before the war, but only the Swiss firm Courvoisier had made any serious attempt to explore the possibilities of multicolour combinations. Before the war, a few British colonies had produced definitives in photogravure, but this practice was not extended to other territories (Mauritius and North Borneo) until 1950, and the familiar two-colour intaglio continued to be the standard colonial process for a further decade. Lithography was sparingly used. It was employed only when necessary to inject additional colour into stamps for which the basic process was intaglio. The Dominican Republic had pioneered multicolour lithography in 1944 but the results were so garish as to be unlikely to encourage experiment elsewhere. Postage stamps, the most conservative form of graphic design, continued to promote the styles and lettering established in the late 1930s until the end of the first post-war decade.

1945-1954
Philatelic Survey by Country

Europe

Albania
The partisans of Enver Hoxha proclaimed an independent state in October 1944, though the Germans were not expelled from Albania until the end of the year. The majority of stamps produced in 1945 consisted of overprints on the issue of the Nazi occupation, but a pictorial definitive series (*I*:1) was released in November of that year. It was subsequently overprinted in 1946 – first to commemorate the Constituent Assembly and then to celebrate the proclamation of the People's Republic (*I*:2). The stamps of the ensuing period were almost entirely ideological in character and were produced in Belgrade, Prague or Budapest by a surprisingly wide range of processes – typography, lithography, photogravure and recess (*I*:3).

Andorra
With the exception of a 100-franc airmail stamp in 1950, featuring chamois and the Pyrenees, the French Post Office produced no stamps distinctive of the period, although increases in postal rates between 1946 and 1951 resulted in new values and changes in colour in the definitive series adopted in 1944. The Spanish Post Office, however, introduced a new series between 1948 and 1953. Stamps in the Edelweiss design (*I*:4) were produced in photogravure, and the remaining pictorials were recess-printed.

Austria
Postal services were resumed in the Soviet zone on 2nd May 1945, stocks of the Hitler Head definitives of Nazi Germany being overprinted in Vienna and valid for postage in Lower Austria only (*I*:5). Similar stamps with a vertical overprint (*I*:6) were issued in Graz for use in the province of Styria. A series lithographed at the United States Bureau of Engraving and Printing in Washington (*I*:7) was released in the British, French and American zones at the end of June, and a series depicting the national arms (*I*:8) was issued in the Soviet zone a week later. The pfennig values of the Soviet series were printed in letterpress – though several are also known to have been lithographed – and the mark values were recess-printed.

The Austrian civil government assumed control of the postal services in all four zones of occupation on 1st October 1945, introducing a series featuring scenery the following month. The schilling values exist in flat-plate and rotary printings, the former having a pronounced screened background to the inscriptions whereas the latter show little sign of screening (*I*:9). This series was superseded in 1948 by definitives depicting provincial costumes (*I*:10). During a life of almost twenty years, the series underwent numerous changes of colour. Thinner, whiter paper replaced the original greyish paper in 1958–9, and in 1964 the 3-schilling and 5-schilling values were released on fluorescent paper in connection with automatic letter-sorting experiments.

The pre-war policy of charity or semi-postal stamps was expanded in the post-war period with sets raising funds for reconstruction, prisoner-of-war relief and the restoration of architecture and national art collections (*I*:11, 13, 14, 16). Regular issues were also made on behalf of the Vienna Prize and other racing funds (*I*:19). The majority of commemoratives were confined to famous Austrians (*I*:12, 17), but important anniversaries such as the telegraph centenary (*I*:15) were also remembered, invariably by single stamps printed in recess. The practice of issuing Christmas stamps, pioneered by Austria in the 1930s, was revived in 1953 (*I*:18). Two- or three-colour recess, introduced in 1948, was used increasingly for commemoratives from 1954 onwards (*I*:20).

Belgium
An ultra-conservative policy was pursued in respect of definitive stamps, the Leopold III series of 1936 being used throughout the first decade after the war. A victory-V emblem was added to the design in 1944, and stamps of this series were surcharged '−10%' in 1946 to denote a reduction in postal rates (*I*:22). The Leopold series continued in use long after the introduction of stamps portraying King Baudouin in 1952. The first Baudouin series (*I*:30), which was recess-printed, depicted the king without his spectacles. A new series showing a bespectacled king was released the following year and it remained current until 1970 (*I*:31).

Since 1910 Belgium has been one of the most prolific producers of charity stamps, and the post-war period was no exception. In addition to such perennial favourites as winter relief and anti-tuberculosis funds, came stamps with premiums in aid of prisoners-of-war and victims of Nazi oppression (*I*:21). The first of the post-war commemoratives appeared in June 1946 and consisted of three stamps marking the centenary of the Ostend–Dover mail-boat service (*I*:23). Relatively few commemorative stamps in the strict sense, without a charity premium, appeared in the immediate post-war decade. Stamps of 1947 marked an international film festival and the golden jubilee of Belgian Antarctic exploration (*I*:24, 25). Important postal events included the centenary of Belgian stamps in 1949 and the 13th Universal Postal Union Congress in 1952, both marked by expensive sets (*I*:27, 29). The portrait definitives were augmented by a small-format series featuring the Belgian lion and the numerals of value (*I*:28), introduced in 1951 and periodically up-dated ever since. A lengthy series devoted to industries and occupations (*I*:26) appeared in 1948–9 to complement the Leopold definitives.

Bulgaria
Technically a kingdom at the end of the war, Bulgaria became a People's Republic in September 1946. Nevertheless, stamps such as the official series of 1945 (*I*:32), featuring the royalist crowned lion, remained in use until 1950. The rather crude letterpress of the stamps printed immediately after the war gave way to photogravure in 1948. The majority of commemoratives honoured such famous Bulgarians as the writer Blagoev (*I*:35) or Russians such as the radio pioneer Popov (*I*:33). Other stamps publicised the industrialisation and mechanisation of the country; the series of 1951 featured the first trucks, steam-rollers and tractors of Bulgarian manufacture (*I*:34).

Cyprus
With the exception of changes in the colour of two denominations of the 1938 George VI series and the introduction of a new denomination in 1951 as a result of increased postal rates, Cyprus produced no distinctive stamps in the first post-war decade. Four commemorative sets appeared in this period, all conforming to the colonial omnibus designs, celebrating victory (*I*:36), the royal silver wedding, the 75th anniversary of the UPU and the coronation of Queen Elizabeth.

Czechoslovakia
The liberation and reunification of Czechoslovakia in 1945 was reflected in the spate of stamps issued in Kosice, Bratislava and Prague. The first Prague issue (*I*:37) was adapted from the series

issued under Nazi auspices in Bohemia and Moravia, and the War Heroes set was recess-printed by De La Rue in London (*1*:38). Jindra Schmidt (who was responsible for many post-war issues) designed and engraved the series of 1945–7 portraying Masaryk, Beneš and Stefanik (*1*:39, 40). President Beneš appeared on many other stamps up to the time of his death in 1948 (*1*:42), but thereafter his Communist successors, Gottwald and Zápotocký, were featured on the definitives of 1948–53 (*1*:43, 49). The sets for ordinary postage were augmented by airmail issues featuring scenery (*1*:41) and the small-format view of Zvolen Castle in 1949 (*1*:46). A lengthy series devoted to industries and occupations appeared in 1954 (*1*:51).

By contrast with the other Soviet satellites Czechoslovakia toned down the political character of its stamps, confining it to the annual Labour Day (*1*:50) and occasional Soviet Friendship issues. Famous Czechs, such as the poet Fucik and the writer Neruda (*1*:44, 52), formed the subject of many of the commemoratives; but Czechoslovakia was also one of the earliest countries to pay tribute to distinguished foreigners, such as Chopin and Beethoven (*1*:45, 48). Other stamps publicised such current events as Miners' Day and Agriculture Day (*1*:47).

Apart from a few photogravure stamps, Czechoslovakia relied heavily on the intaglio process and produced many delicate masterpieces of line-engraving.

Denmark

Danish definitives of this period formed a tripartite series. The numeral stamps introduced in 1933 continued to provide the lowest denominations, and a series of kroner values with an armorial motif was released in 1946 (*2*:3). The middle values portraying King Christian X were superseded in 1948 by a series depicting King Frederick IX. The 30-öre value of this series was surcharged 10-öre in aid of the Netherlands Flood Relief fund of 1953 (*2*:6).

The few commemoratives released in the immediate post-war period consisted mostly of single stamps, such as the Tycho Brahe and Royal Academy issues of 1946 and 1954 respectively (*2*:2, 8), but pairs were released in 1951 for the anniversary of the Naval Officers' College and the centenary of Danish postage stamps (*2*:4, 5). The 75th anniversary of the birth of King Christian was marked by three stamps designed by Viggo Bang of Denmark but engraved by Sven Ewert of Sweden (*2*:1). The most important event of the decade was the millennium of Denmark, celebrated by two sets of five stamps issued between September 1953 and January 1956 with subjects each representing a century of Danish history (*2*:7).

Finland

Scandinavian conservatism ensured a long life for the definitives designed by Miss Hammarsten Jansson, first released in 1930. Post-war inflation necessitated new values and changes of colour in 1945–6 and 1947–52 (*2*:9). The typographed series was superseded in 1954 by similar designs by Bengt Ekholm (*2*:14) printed in recess.

The same process was used exclusively for the commemorative stamps of the period, confined mainly to single stamps or pairs (*2*:10, 11). Sets with charity premiums were produced annually in May and September in aid of the Red Cross and anti-tuberculosis funds respectively (*2*:12, 15). Aspects of health were the keynote of the TB stamps, but the Red Cross issues covered a wide range of themes connected with flora and fauna.

France

Appropriately, the first French stamp of 1945 was a 4-franc-denomination by Pierre Gandon celebrating the Liberation (*2*:16). The allegorical motif of Marianne on Pegasus, exhorting the Resistance forces, was in the heroic mould of French public murals and sculpture of the nineteenth century – a genre that lingered on in postage stamps until the late 1940s. The same allegorical approach is evident in Gandon's designs for the airmail series of 1946–7 (*2*:20) and the Peace Conference of 1946 (*2*:23). The post-war definitive series portraying Marianne (*2*:18) also included a design featuring the Cross of Lorraine and broken chains (*2*:17), setting a precedent for typographed stamps reproducing coats of arms in full colour (*2*:21). The arms series of 1946 was followed by many others (*2*:42), that provide the lowest denominations of the definitive range to this day.

In 1946, France resumed the practice of devoting the higher denominations of the definitive range to large-format stamps featuring scenery and landmarks (*2*:22). At regular intervals since then, new designs have made every aspect of the French landscape familiar to the philatelist (*2*:34, 37, 39) – use of the multicolour Giori recess method enhancing them from 1953 onwards (*2*:45). High-denomination airmail stamps likewise featured scenery, a series depicting aerial views being released in 1949–50 (*2*:26). Four years later, a set featuring modern French aircraft was issued (*2*:44). Small stamps with allegorical themes were introduced in 1954, the majority being pre-cancelled 'AFFRANCᵗˢ POSTES' prior to release (*2*:46). Between 1953 and 1955 the arms, scenes and allegories of the definitive range were augmented by a set of eleven stamps featuring characters from French literature and national industries connected with the applied arts.

In the aftermath of the war, several French charity stamps bore premiums in aid of devastated cities (*2*:19) and war victims; but the annual series devoted to the National Relief Fund was reintroduced in 1946, after a gap of one year, and has continued to this day. The subjects have invariably been famous men and women, the series of 1948 being devoted to participants in the 1848 Revolution (*2*:28). The commemoratives of the immediate post-war period continued the previously adopted formula of paying tribute to important current events as well as celebrating historic anniversaries. In the former category came the stamps marking the UNESCO conference of 1946 and the convening of the General Assembly of the United Nations at the Palais de Chaillot in 1951 (*2*:24, 33). Sets marking the 12th UPU Congress in 1947 and the International Telephone and Telegraph Conference in 1949 included an outsize airmail stamp depicting views of the River Seine (*2*:25). Other stamps in this group ranged from the 5-franc of 1947 that marked the Scout Jamboree (*2*:25) to the 30-franc of 1954 that commemorated the First Conference of Romanesque Studies at Tournus in 1954 (*2*:48).

Famous persons provided the bulk of the subjects for the historic stamps, generally confined to single stamps – although Madame Récamier (*2*:30) was paired with Madame de Sévigné, her contemporary, on stamps of 1950. The solid backgrounds that characterised so many of these portrait stamps (*2*:31) gave way to lighter, often unshaded grounds typified by the Laennec stamp of 1952 (*2*:38) and many later issues; and a more imaginative treatment of the subject began with the bi-coloured 12-franc stamp of 1951 commemorating the aviator Maurice Noguès (*2*:35). The stamp portraying Maréchal de Lattre de Tassigny (*2*:36) appeared in monochrome in 1952 but was reissued two years later recess-printed in two colours. By contrast, the black stamp of 1948 in memory of General Leclerc was reissued with a new inscription promoting him to Marshal of France – first in red-brown in 1953 and then in blue and green in 1954. Other early trends towards more colourful stamps were demonstrated by the Franco–American friendship issue of 1949 and the 15-franc of 1951 publicising the Popular Pictorial Art Exhibition (*2*:29, 32).

The first French series of a purely thematic nature appeared in November 1953 and consisted of six stamps devoted to sports (*2*:41). Occasional scenic stamps that were neither commemorative nor definitive were also issued, such as the Versailles Gateway stamps of 1952–4, after Utrillo (*2*:39). The 18-frac stamp of 1954 (*2*:47), in fact, commemorates four centuries of Renaissance gardens, although no mention of this was made in the inscription.

Germany

Following the defeat of the Nazi régime, stocks of the Hitler Head definitive stamps were overprinted in various ways to obliterate the features of the late Führer – ranging from patterns made with corks or rubber erasers (*3*:1) to the armorial designs of Würzen and Bad Gottleuba. Makeshifts of this type were mainly confined to the Soviet zone, the British and Americans having made provision for a postal service under Allied military auspices prior to the invasion of Germany. A series designed by W. A. Roach and engraved by E. H. Helmuth was initially typographed in Washington, and a subsequent printing was made of some values by Harrison and Sons in England, using the photogravure process. Finally, between August 1945 and January 1946, the series – with some entirely new denominations – was lithographed by G. Westerman of Brunswick. The stamps featured a Teutonic 'M', symbolising the military occupation, and were simply inscribed 'AM POST' (Allied Military Post) with 'DEUTSCHLAND' at the foot (*3*:2).

They were superseded in February 1946 by a numeral design

(3:3) intended for use in all four zones of occupation. The French, however, had issued their own stamps featuring coats of arms of German provinces (3:7), and they followed this by releasing distinctive sets for use in Baden, the Rhineland-Palatinate and Württemberg (3:8–10) that remained current until the end of 1949. For a period of two years, joint issues of stamps appeared in the British, Russian and American zones.

The numeral series was followed in March 1947 by a set depicting workers (3:4). Commemoratives of the tri-zonal period marked the Leipzig and Hannover trade fairs and the 50th anniversary of the death of Heinrich von Stephan, founder of the Universal Postal Union (3:5).

The disintegration of Allied co-operation began in June 1948 when the currency in the American, British and French zones was reformed. The workers definitives of the Anglo–American area were overprinted with a continuous post-horn motif (3:18) and those in the Soviet zone were overprinted first with district names and numbers (3:6) and then with 'Sowjetische Besatzungs Zone' (Soviet Occupation Zone). Thereafter, the Western Allies and their Soviet partner drifted farther and farther apart.

At the beginning of the occupation period the Russians had divided their zone into six Oberpostdirektion (postal districts), each of which issued its own stamps between August 1945 and March 1946. Stamps were released in Berlin–Brandenburg, Mecklenburg–Vorpommern and Thuringia, and Saxony was divided into districts under Halle, Leipzig and Dresden (3:11–14). The stamps of Berlin–Brandenburg were subsequently overprinted early in 1948 for use throughout the Soviet Zone, and this overprinted series was replaced in October 1948 by a set portraying famous Germans (3:16). The large-sized Leipzig Fair stamps – begun under Allied auspices in March 1947 – continued until 1950 (3:17).

The Russians withdrew from the four-power control of Berlin on 1st July 1948, and the three western sectors of the city eventually formed a Land (province) of the German Federal Republic. The 'workers' series, diagonally overprinted 'BERLIN', was released in West Berlin in September 1948 (3:22) and was superseded by a pictorial series in 1949 (3:23). Also in September 1948, the Anglo–American zones adopted a definitive series featuring prominent buildings (3:20) and released several commemorative sets including stamps for the 700th anniversary of Cologne Cathedral and the bicentenary of Goethe (3:19, 21). A semi-postal pair raised funds for aid to Berlin during the Soviet blockade, and all mail in the Western zones had to bear a 2-pfennig tax stamp (3:24) to help finance the Berlin airlift. The stamp was overprinted in 1949 and was used to raise money for house-building funds in the French province of Württemberg (3:25).

Philatelically, Germany has existed in three parts, since 1949, with separate issues in West Berlin, West Germany (the Federal Republic) and East Germany (the Democratic Republic). The stamps used in West Berlin up to 1952 were merely inscribed 'DEUTSCHE POST' (3:26, 27, 29), but from then until 1955 they bore the legend 'DEUTSCHE POST BERLIN' (3:28, 30–32). Noteworthy among the special issues of this period are the pair of August 1953 commemorating the uprising against Soviet power in East Berlin on 17th June of that year (3:31).

The Federal Republic was established on 23rd May 1949 from the former American, British and French zones, and its first distinctive stamps – released in September 1949 – marked the opening of the Federal parliament (3:33). The 'buildings' definitives were gradually replaced in 1951–2 by a post-horn and numeral design (3:34), and this was superseded in 1954 by a series portraying President Heuss (3:45). Relatively few charity stamps were issued in the ensuing period other than the annual set portraying 'helpers of mankind' (3:37, 44), which evolved out of a refugees-relief-fund series of 1949. Stamps marking the 700th anniversary of St. Mary's Church, Lübeck, the Wuppertal Stamp Exhibition and the jubilee of the Munich Science Museum (3:35, 36, 38) also bore charity premiums. The starkly realistic 10-pfennig stamp of 1953, with the inscription 'Remember our Prisoners of War', was an oblique reminder of the Germans still languishing in Soviet camps; but for the most part, federal commemoratives eschewed any political message and concentrated on the anniversaries of famous Germans (3:40–42, 46) or contemporary exhibitions (3:43).

Not surprisingly, the stamps of the Democratic Republic –

established in October 1949 – reflected East Germany's alignment with the Communist bloc. Several sets of this period publicised German friendship with other Communist countries (3:49). Apart from the Famous Germans series of the former Soviet zone, which continued in use until 1953, definitives of 1950–51 portrayed President Pieck (3:51). A series featuring workers and buildings appeared in August 1953. The original version was lithographed, but a letterpress version was issued the following November (3:54). A commemorative series of 1950 marking the 250th anniversary of the Berlin Academy of Sciences was also retained as a quasi-definitive set (3:53). Special stamps for official use (3:57) were introduced in 1954 and can be found either lithographed or typographed. The commemoratives of this period (3:47–50, 52, 55–56) were invariably lithographed by the German Bank Note Printers, in Leipzig.

Gibraltar

With the addition of a 5-penny denomination in 1951, the George VI pictorial series of 1938 continued in use until 1953, when an entirely new Elizabethan series was adopted (4:2). The inauguration of a legislative council was marked by overprinting four values of the Georgian series 'NEW CONSTITUTION' in 1950 (4:1), apart from which, Gibraltar's only commemoratives in this period consisted of the colonial omnibus sets. The 3-penny stamp of the Elizabethan series was re-engraved with an inscription commemorating the royal visit of May 1954.

Greece

The early post-war stamps of Greece reflected the turbulent conditions that had prevailed during the Axis occupation. Appearing in October 1945, the first commemorative issue consisted of two stamps celebrating the 5th anniversary of the resistance to the Italian ultimatum (4:3). The wartime pictorial series was retained, but it was surcharged with astronomical amounts as a result of the hyper-inflation that had been chronic since 1943 (4:4). Even the pre-war stamps portraying King George II, resurrected with an overprint marking the restoration of the monarchy, had to be additionally surcharged (4:5).

The Dodecanese Islands, formerly an Italian colony, were transferred to Greece in March 1947 and used Greek stamps overprinted in Greek capitals 'S.D.D.' to signify military administration (4:12). Ordinary Greek stamps were substituted in November 1947.

A new definitive series depicting scenery and artifacts of the islands (4:6) was introduced in Greece at the same time. Ancient Greek art provided the inspiration for the series of 1954, featuring sculpture, pottery and coins (4:10). Commemorative stamps of the early 1950s recalled the Battle of Crete and other recent campaigns (4:9), publicised the reconstruction programme of 1951 and recorded membership of NATO (4:8, 11). In many cases, the subjects were derived from classical art. By contrast, the church restoration fund stamp of 1948 (4:7) depicted a fresco of St. Demetrius from the Byzantine era.

Great Britain

British stamps of the post-war decade form two groups divided by the death of King George VI and the accession of Queen Elizabeth II in February 1952. Stylistically, the main difference was the use of a medallic profile for the Georgian stamps and the adoption of a 'proper' portrait of the Queen, based on a photograph by Dorothy Wilding. The contrast between the definitives of each reign (4:17, 21) can be seen in the less obtrusive lettering and neater arrangement of the heraldic flowers in the newer series.

The few commemorative stamps of 1946–51 concentrated on symbolic elements (4:13, 16, 18, 19), notable exceptions being the naturalistic silver wedding issue of 1948 (4:14) and the curious pair of the same year, marking the third anniversary of the liberation of the Channel Islands (4:15), the obscure vignette of which shows islanders carting seaweed for manure.

A major concession to those who had long clamoured for more pictorial stamps for Great Britain was the release of four high values in 1951, two of which featured H.M.S. *Victory* (4:20) and the white cliffs of Dover. But the coronation series of June 1953 – the only commemoratives of the new reign in this period – continued the previous formula of symbolism and heraldic motifs dominated by the royal portrait (4:22).

Hungary

During the period of the provisional government, established between October 1944 and February 1946 under Soviet auspices, Hungary produced a spate of surcharges on earlier definitives and commemoratives as the pengö plummeted in value. By January 1946, money was depreciating so rapidly that it was no longer possible to issue stamps to keep up with the changes in postal rates. Instead, stamps were overprinted to denote the various duties and were sold at the rate current on the day of sale (4:24).

Prior to the establishment of the People's Republic in August 1949, the majority of stamps bore symbolic designs typifying reconstruction and currency reform (4:23, 25). Among the commemoratives of the late 1940s was the Liberty issue of 1947, portraying patriots of earlier periods (4:26); and in common with many other European countries, Hungary celebrated the centenary of the 'Year of Revolutions' with a set in 1948, honouring the Magyar insurrection against Habsburg rule (4:27).

After the proclamation of a new constitution on Soviet lines, however, the familiar pattern of Five-Year-Plans and May Day rallies (4:28, 30) was imposed on Hungarian stamps. Two versions of the 60-filler Youth stamp of 1950 exist: the first contains a reference to Scouts (Harcaihoz) in the caption, which was hastily replaced in the second (4:29) – the amended caption referring to Young Pioneers. The Rebuilding Plan of 1951 was the theme of the definitive series (4:32), which continued – with changes in designs and a slight reduction in format – into the 1960s. By 1952, however, lengthy thematic sets featuring birds, insects, scientists (4:31) and other subjects were beginning to appear, and the ideological emphasis was reduced.

Iceland

The first post-war series was designed for airmail, featuring aircraft over Icelandic scenery (4:33). A series for ordinary postage was released between 1950 and 1954. It depicted scenery and occupations (4:35). Few commemoratives were issued, the most unusual being the set of 1948, marking the eruption of Mount Hekla in the previous year (4:34). A series of October 1953 reproduced medieval manuscripts with frames ornamented in the style of the *Reykjabók* and the *Skarosbók* (4:36).

Ireland

The immediate post-war decade was one of transition in Irish stamps, not only in the process used but also in the subject matter and presentation of the commemoratives. The political dividing line – the proclamation of the republic in April 1949 – had little effect on stamps, though the James Mangan and Holy Year stamps of 1949–50 (4:41, 42) bore the inscription 'Poblact na hEireann' (and broke with tradition by including the English equivalent – 'Republic of Ireland'). Thereafter, the earlier form 'Eire' (Ireland) was resumed. But although the Young Ireland and Parnell–Davitt issues of 1945–6 (4:37–8) were captioned exclusively in Gaelic, there was a greater tendency after 1950 to relax the ban on the use of English – not only in the names of those commemorated, such as Thomas Moore and Robert Emmet (4:43, 45), but also in the pair publicising An Tostal, the Ireland-at-Home Festival of 1953 (4:44). A curious exception was the set of 1948, portraying Wolfe Tone and bearing no caption at all, it being assumed that the date '1798' would immediately identify the subject as the 150th anniversary of insurrection (4:40).

The use of religious subjects was understandable in the Holy Year stamps of 1950 and the Marian Year stamps of 1954 (4:42, 46); but it was also extended to secular subjects, as in the airmail series of 1949–54 depicting the Angel Victor over landmarks associated with St. Patrick (4:39), which broke another tradition by being recess-printed instead of typographed. Recess-printing was used increasingly from 1952 onwards, the printers being De La Rue's Dublin subsidiary.

Italy

During the regency of Crown Prince Umberto, from 1944 to 1946, the stamps of the Mussolini era were reprinted without their Fascist emblems (5:1). Some stamps of the erstwhile Italian Social Republic (the puppet régime in northern Italy nominally ruled by Mussolini from 1943 to 1945) were issued between March 1945 and May 1945 with the Fascist emblems and inscriptions obliterated (5:2). These

makeshifts were replaced in October 1945 by a photogravure series symbolising freedom, peace and enlightenment (5:3). A recess-printed 100-lira value symbolising work, justice and the family (5:5) was introduced in 1946, and an airmail series with suitable allegory combined with an aeroplane motif (5:4) was issued between October 1945 and April 1947. Subsequent definitives adopted a more thematic approach: a series of 1946 featured medieval Italian republics – an oblique reference to the establishment of the republic in June 1946 (5:6) – and the lengthy series of 1950 featured provincial occupations (5:9). An aircraft over Rome was the subject of the 1948 airmail set (5:7).

The output of commemoratives continued at the pre-war pace, with a tendency towards the release of shorter sets at more frequent intervals. Famous men such as Mazzini and Corelli (5:8, 17) vied with important current events for philatelic honour. The Milan Fair, the Triennale (5:10, 15) – this being given an unusually modernistic treatment – the Bari Levant Fair and the World Cycling Championship (5:11, 16) typify the events and the range of designs used in this period.

The range of subjects covered by special issues was diverse. Two stamps of 1951 featured views of Montecassino Abbey before and after its restoration (5:12), and continuing interest in North Africa was evident in the 25-lira stamp of 1952 marking the centenary of the Italian Mission to Ethiopia (5:14). Other stamps of the early 1950s included a set of three for Armed Forces Day, a pair commemorating Interpol and a single featuring Pinocchio (honouring Carlo Collodi, the writer of books for children) (5:13, 18, 19).

A new definitive set was introduced in 1953 and has remained current. Known as 'La Siracusa', the design was based on Syracusan dekadrachms of the fifth century B.C. (5:21). In 1954–5 the motif was incorporated in the design of two stamps bearing slogans exhorting taxpayers (5:22). The definitive range was augmented in 1953–4 by a set of six that featured views of tourist resorts (5:20).

Liechtenstein

Although it had acquired a reputation for balancing its budget by sales of stamps, the tiny principality of Liechtenstein moderated its output to an average of eight stamps a year in the post-war decade. One of the last of the lengthy thematic sets was devoted to pioneers of flight, issued in 1948 (5:23). A new definitive series was launched in 1951, depicting peasants with agricultural produce (5:25).

Commemorative sets of the early 1950s tended to be much shorter, a typical example being the three stamps marking the termination of the Marian Year in 1954 (5:24).

Luxembourg

The first stamps released after the liberation in 1944 were definitives recess-printed by the American Bank Note Company – a simpler and up-dated version of the 1926 series by the same printers. Increases in postal rates led to several changes of colour and new values in March 1946 (5:26). Courvoisier produced a photogravure airmail series in 1946 (5:27), and the same firm recess-printed a new definitive series in 1948, with a more mature portrait of the Grand-Duchess (5:28).

Annual charity issues were reviewed in 1945 with a war-victims relief fund set, but in subsequent years these semi-postals raised money for the national welfare fund. A tourist propaganda series was released gradually between 1948 and 1955, supplementing the definitive range (5:30).

Although Courvoisier continued to produce the majority of Luxembourg's stamps (5:29), from 1952 an increasing number was printed by Enschedé of Holland, including the 2-franc stamp marking the World Fencing Championships of 1954 (5:31).

Malta

Self-government, withdrawn during the political troubles of the 1930s, was returned to Malta in 1947. It was signalised by the overprinting of the Georgian definitives (5:32). The award of the George Cross to the island fortress in 1942 referred to in many of the post-war issues, including the set of three celebrating the visit of Princess Elizabeth in 1950 (5:33) and the various omnibus issues. The only other distinctive issues in this period were two sets of three – one set in 1951, commemorating the 700th anniversary of the Scapular (5:34), and one set in 1954 for the centenary of the dogma of the Immaculate Conception (5:36). For the royal visit of 1954 the Georgian 3-penny stamp was modified, with a commemorative inscription and a portrait of the Queen substituted (5:35).

Monaco

The output of Monegasque stamps increased dramatically immediately after the war, and the principality was one of the first countries to exploit the possibilities of participating in international events. Thus stamps of 1947 and 1952–3 marked the international philatelic exhibition in New York and the Helsinki Olympics respectively, those of 1947 also exploiting the popularity of stamps portraying the late President Roosevelt (5:39, 40).

Definitive sets were changed at frequent intervals, with issues of 1946 portraying Prince Louis II and issues of 1950 portraying Prince Rainier III (5:37, 42). New values and colours appeared in the pictorial definitives originally introduced in 1939 (5:38), and small-format armorial sets appeared in 1951 and 1954 (5:43, 44).

Commemoratives relevant to Monaco were recess-printed in Paris and included a lengthy series honouring the sculptor Bosio in 1948, the National Postal Museum in 1952, and the golden jubilee of the discovery of anaphylaxis by Prince Albert I in 1953 (5:41, 45, 46). Two sets of 1954, designed by J. E. Lorenzi, adopted an unusual approach to portraiture in white lines against a coloured background (5:47).

Netherlands

Combat between the Dutch lion and the dragon of Fascism was the theme of C. A. Mechelse's stamp of July 1945 celebrating the liberation of the Netherlands (6:1). It is interesting to compare the Dutch treatment of this subject with its French counterpart (2:16). The comparatively large output of stamps in the first post-war decade – about two hundred and twenty, excluding postage-due labels – is explained partly by the frequent changes of portrait definitives and partly by the twice-yearly charity issues. Commemoratives in the true sense were relatively sparse. The series used by the government in exile was replaced in 1946 by a set, portraying Queen Wilhelmina, that was vaguely reminiscent of Britain's Penny Black of 1840. The lower values were printed in photogravure and the higher denominations were recess-printed (6:5, 6). The very low denominations consisted of a numeral design (6:4) that has remained current. A full-face portrait of Queen Juliana against a monogrammed background was used for the series of 1949–51 (6:9), but this was superseded two years later by a series of stark simplicity in which the queen's profile was given an oddly luminescent quality (6:16).

The first of the post-war Child Welfare sets had a uniform design by E. Fernhout, featuring the portrait of a refugee child (6:2). Subsequent issues struck a happier note. The series of 1946 portrayed the Princesses Irene, Margriet and Beatrix (6:3), and the sets from 1947 onwards concentrated on photographs of children (6:7) and aspects of children's play (6:11). The other annual semi-postal series, raising money for the Cultural and Social Relief Funds, featured scenery and landmarks in the earlier issues (6:12) but returned to the pre-war theme of famous Dutchmen in the series of 1954 (6:17).

Royal events and constitutional changes accounted for several commemoratives, including those for the golden jubilee of Queen Wilhelmina (6:8) and the coronation of Queen Juliana (6:10) – both of which took place in 1948. The ratification of the statute of the kingdom in 1954 was marked by a 10-cent stamp, the design of which was also used in the overseas territories (6:19). The 75th anniversary of the UPU in 1949 was marked by a pair featuring post-horns and the globe (6:13), and the centenary of Dutch stamps was celebrated three years later by the issue of stamps featuring aspects of the posts and telecommunications (6:15). Among other events commemorated, were the jubilee of the Limburg state coal-mines and the twelfth centenary of the martyrdom of St. Boniface (6:14, 18).

A distinctive series introduced in 1950 for use at the International Court of Justice in The Hague, featured a view of the Peace Palace or a profile of Queen Juliana (6:20, 1).

Norway

Independence was restored to Norway on 7th May 1945, and the stamps used by the government in exile were put into circulation. A 7-öre stamp showing a wartime convoy was added to the series

the following month (6:22). Otherwise, the lion rampant series of 1940 remained in use until 1950 when the öre values portraying King Haakon VII (6:32) were introduced. Large-format high values were released in 1946 (6:27). The post-horn and numeral series – which had made its début in 1872 – continued to supply the lowest denominations and, in fact, has now attained its centenary. In the first post-war decade new colours were introduced between 1950 and 1952 and a 20-öre surcharge was made on the obsolete 15-öre stamps (6:34).

With the exception of the King Haakon eightieth birthday series of 1952 (6:33) and isolated examples in the UPU and Winter Olympic issues, Norwegian commemoratives clung to the compact format used for the kroner definitives. In the immediate post-war years charity stamps marked the Norwegian Red Cross jubilee and raised money for the national relief fund, the latter issue portraying Crown Prince Olav in battledress (6:24, 26). The outstanding commemorative series of this period was the set of eleven issued in 1947 to celebrate the tercentenary of the Norwegian Post Office, the designs featuring historic personalities and transport (6:28). The remaining commemoratives were confined to pairs or sets of three (6:23, 25, 29, 30, 35–37). Two stamps of 1950, showing a child picking flowers, bore a small premium in aid of the infantile paralysis fund (6:31).

Poland

In June 1945 a government of national unity was formed, combining elements from the London government in exile and the provisional government established under Soviet aegis at Lublin in July 1944. The earliest post-war stamps reflected the problems of production during a period of shortage. A few stamps, such as the Grunwald memorial issue (6:38), were printed in Moscow but the majority were printed in Lodz or Cracow and were often released imperforate (6:39, 41). The early definitives ranged from 'before and after' views of devastated Warsaw (6:39) to portraits of cultural personalities of 1947–8 (6:42) and aspects of industry and agriculture (6:43). Airmail sets released in 1946, 1952 and 1954 depicted aircraft over Polish landmarks and scenery (6:40, 51, 53).

Commemoratives contained a fair proportion of issues alluding to historical anniversaries, including the uprising of 1848 (6:44), or current events such as the Music Festival of 1951 and the International Gliding Championship of 1954 (6:42, 54). Many stamps publicised post-war reconstruction and government six-year-plans (6:45, 49, 52). The revaluation of the currency (one new zloty of 100 groszy being equal to 100 old zloty) in 1950 was indicated by the hand-stamping of existing stamps with their equivalent value in groszy (6:46). The definitives portraying President Beirut were released in December 1950 with values in groszy instead of zloty (6:47).

A stamp of 1951 marked the 25th anniversary of the death of Dzerzhinsky, the Polish-born head of Stalin's secret police (6:50); but after the proclamation of the People's Republic in 1952, stamps tended to become less ideological in character.

Portugal

A curious feature of Portuguese stamps in the immediate post-war period was the wide range of printers and processes involved in their production. The Navigators series of 1945 (7:1) was recess-printed by Bradbury Wilkinson, and a set of 1947 commemorating the eighth centenary of the liberation of Lisbon from the Moors was produced by Waterlow and Sons – both English companies. Courvoisier of Switzerland printed photogravure or intaglio sets including the President Carmona definitives of 1945, the castles series of 1946, the regional costumes set of 1947 and the Aviz dynasty issue of 1949 (7:2–4, 6). The UPU set of 1949 was recess-printed by De La Rue (7:7), and Enschedé of Holland produced in photogravure the stamp centenary series of 1953 (7:14). Two points are notable regarding the latter stamps: the portrait of Queen Maria II, based on a painting, was inadvertently reversed, and gold metallic ink – employed increasingly in the 1960s – was used in the framework. Some other sets of this period were recess-printed by the Bank of Portugal, including the Holy Year series of 1950 (7:10); but the majority were lithographed, by Litografia Maia of Oporto or Litografia Nacional of Lisbon (7:8, 9, 11, 12, 15).

A high proportion of Portuguese stamps continued to hark back to the glories of the Middle Ages. This penchant for medieval subjects was shown in the definitives, the Caravel design of 1940–49 being superseded by the Knight series in 1953 (7:13).

Although many sets were printed abroad, all Portuguese stamps were designed by indigenous artists. The majority of designs were commonplace, but the work of Martins Barata (7:1, 5, 8, 10, 13) had the angularity and economy of line reminiscent of medieval woodcuts.

Romania

The paradox of Romania – a kingdom with a Communist government – was mirrored in the country's stamps. New definitive issues in 1945 and 1947 (7:16, 19) portrayed King Michael whereas the commemorative and charity stamps of the same period (7:17, 18) extolled agrarian reform, Labour Day, friendship with the Soviet Union and other subjects favoured by the Russian satellite states. Romania was declared a People's Republic on 30th December 1947, and stamps of the pictorial definitive series were overprinted 'R.P.R.' (Republica Populara Romana). This inscription appeared on all definitives and special issues up to 1954. Sets featuring the republican emblem were released in July 1948 and May 1950 (7:20, 21). From 1947 there had been several attempts to reform the currency in the face of rapidly mounting inflation and the 1948 republican definitives were surcharged in new bani currency in January 1952, prior to the release of a similar series in a rather larger format.

The commemorative and semi-postal issues of the People's Republic became more intensely ideological from 1948 onwards, abounding in stamps portraying Lenin, Stalin and even non-political Russians such as Pushkin and Pavlov. Numerous sets marked current events in the Communist calendar but tended towards allegory and the abstract (7:22). A stamp issued in 1952 to mark the quingentenary of Leonardo da Vinci was the prelude to the numerous sets of the late 1950s and 1960s honouring international celebrities.

Russia

Almost eight hundred stamps were produced by the Soviet Union in the period from 1945 to 1954 – twice the output of the previous decade and by far the most prolific of any country. The acceleration in Soviet issues began during the war, when stamps were used increasingly as morale boosters. Many of the lengthy sets of the post-war period consisted of stamps of the same denomination, usually prepaying internal letter rates. In effect, postage stamps were used extensively as an educative medium aimed directly at the Russian populace rather than to promote the Soviet image to the world at large.

In the immediate post-war period numerous sets featured the orders and medals of the Soviet Union, and this was also the theme of the Victory set (7:23). Other sets paid tribute to the various arms of the fighting services. The United States was content to use single stamps for this purpose, but Russia issued lengthy sets. Thus Aviation Day, 19th August 1945, was marked by a series of nine 1-rouble stamps depicting the fighters and bombers then in service (7:24). In the following March, the same designs were reissued in different denominations. Other sets of 1945–6 publicised artillery, armoured units and home-defence forces.

By 1947 the emphasis had switched from the recent war to reconstruction and Soviet achievements in many different fields (7:27). Here, again, this was promoted by means of long thematic issues, ranging from the Five-Year-Plan of Rolled-iron, Steel and Machine-building in 1948 to the frequent sets featuring state sanatoria (7:28). Specific achievements were celebrated generously with long sets of stamps, the size of which tended to increase correspondingly. The series of 1951 featuring newly-completed hydro-electric power plants is a typical example (7:38).

Shorter sets, and sometimes even single stamps, were used to commemorate anniversaries such as the golden jubilee of the Moscow Arts Theatre (7:26), the anniversaries of the Tadzhik and Turkmen republics (7:29, 30) and friendship with Mongolia (7:37). Photogravure was used almost exclusively in this period and the subjects usually derived from actual photographs in the interests of 'realism', the meaning of which would be readily apparent (7:31–33). Two- and three-colour combinations had been used from time to time since the late 1930s; but from 1950 onwards multicolour photogravure became more ambitious (7:34–36), culminating in the full-colour miniature posters of 1952–4 (7:39–42). The screen used was still relatively coarse compared to that employed by Courvoisier of Switzerland, but it cannot be denied that Russian stamps of this period were eye-catching.

By contrast, the definitive stamps continued to be in the distinctively small format devised in 1858. A new series featuring workers and servicemen was introduced in 1948. The first printings were in photogravure but subsequent printings were lithographed or typographed, and new denominations were added between 1950 and 1959 (7:25).

Saar

The general series of stamps issued throughout the French zone of Germany was also used in the Saar until 1947, when a distinctive series was adopted. The stamps, designed by Professor Jonynas, were printed in photogravure by Burda of Offenbach in the same formats as the sets for the three German provinces under French control (8:1, 2). In November 1947 they were surcharged in French currency, and they were soon replaced by new definitives recess-printed at the Paris Mint or in photogravure by Helio Vaugirard (8:3). A pictorial series featuring scenery and landmarks was released between 1952 and 1955. These stamps, designed and engraved by French artists, had a close affinity with the contemporary French definitive range (8:5).

Many of the commemoratives reflected the intense religious feelings of the Saarlanders, ranging from stamps portraying Adolf Kopling (the miners' padre) to an issue of 1951 depicting Calvin and Luther and celebrating the 375th anniversary of the Reformation. The majority of the religious issues were Catholic in content, sets of three stamps each being released in honour of the Holy and Marian Years (8:4, 7). An annual issue made for Day of the Postage Stamp proved extremely popular with philatelists all over the world. It featured various aspects of the postal services, old and new (8:6).

San Marino

Political events in the tiny mountain republic of San Marino paralleled those in Italy, by which it is entirely surrounded. The definitives of the Fascist era, overprinted in 1943 to obliterate the original inscriptions, were superseded in August 1945 by a new series featuring the coats of arms of the Sammarinese towns (8:8). New parcel-post and postage-due stamps were released at the same time (8:9). An airmail series appeared the following year, the designs by G. Zani being both simple and pleasing as well as ahead of their time with their striking combination of symbolism and stark silhouettes (8:10). A pictorial definitive series showing views of the republic in two-colour photogravure was released in 1949–50 (8:11). New colours and designs were added in 1955.

San Marino has been alive to the possibilities of the enormous revenue to be derived from philatelic sales ever since 1894. Consequently, it has issued large numbers of stamps on the slightest pretext, often referring to events and personalities outside the republic. A series honouring President Roosevelt (8:12) appeared in 1947 but was subsequently boycotted by many dealers and catalogue editors on the grounds that it was completely speculative. Long sets were issued in connection with philatelic exhibitions held not only in various parts of Italy (8:14) but also in the United States in 1947. Two of the outstanding series of this period paid tribute to Garibaldi and Columbus (8:13), the first being justified as marking the centenary of Garibaldi's retreat to San Marino in 1849; but the 460th anniversary of the first voyage of Columbus, in 1952, seems to have been little more than an excuse to depict American scenery and landmarks, no doubt with an eye on hard currency sales. This policy was taken to its logical conclusion in April 1953 by the issue of the world's first purely thematic series, connected with no specific event or anniversary. A sports series (8:15) was followed by a flower set (8:16) and a second sports series in 1954 (8:17), which established a pattern adopted by many other countries in the ensuing decades.

Spain

The post-war stamps of Spain stand out from those of other European countries in that there was no clear-cut division between pre-war issues, let alone wartime issues, and those of the late 1940s. Many of the definitives introduced during the Civil War continued to be used throughout the decade. But subtle changes in perforation, design details and colour, as well as the presence or absence of the printer's imprint in the margin, divide the issues of 1937–41 from those of 1945–50. Thus the 'El Cid' 15-centavo was reissued in 1950 with new perforations (8:27), the Franco 10-peseta appeared in 1945 with the abbreviation for pesetas changed from 'PTS' to 'PTAS' (8:18) and the Juan de la Cierva airmail stamps were redrawn, ending up with a much coarser appearance (8:19). New definitives portraying General Franco augmented the pre-war designs. A photogravure series appeared between 1948 and 1954 (8:21) and a lithographed series, portraying Franco beside La Mota Castle, was issued during the same period (8:22).

Anti-tuberculosis fund stamps, issued annually since 1937, continued throughout this period. Those released up to 1947 were lithographed with motifs in which the Cross of Lorraine was the predominant feature (8:20), but later issues were produced by photogravure with a more pictorial treatment in which the emblem was reduced to a subsidiary role (8:26, 29, 32, 35). The Cid definitive design was adapted in 1949 for a 5-centavo stamp in aid of war victims (8:25); but the inclusion of the date '1946' is puzzling since the victims presumably related to the Civil War period rather than the Second World War, in which Spain was only indirectly concerned.

The majority of commemorative issues in this period consisted of photogravure stamps in the standard definitive format (8:28–37, 39–41, 43). Intaglio, employed for the printing of many commemoratives up to 1948, lost ground to photogravure but was gradually revived in the late 1950s. Among the few intaglio sets of this period were the two sets of 1950 celebrating the centenary of Spanish stamps: the ordinary and airmail sets depicted the 6-cuarto and 6-real stamps of 1850 respectively (8:38, 42) and were released imperforate. A double-sized horizontal format was used for the UPU commemoratives of 1949 (8:24) and the recess-printed Stamp Day issues of 1951–2 portraying Isabella and Ferdinand the Catholic. Photogravure stamps commemorating the quingentenaries of Their Catholic Majesties were issued in the same period (8:31, 33). As a rule, the annual Stamp Day issues were linked to the commemoration of historic personages and events (8:41) such as the seventh centenary of Salamanca University (8:36). Secular subjects ranged from a series of 1950–53 portraying famous Spaniards (8:28) to a single of 1951 for the sixth conference of the Spanish–American Postal Union (8:30). Religious themes were well to the fore, with sets marking the International Eucharistic Congress in Barcelona, St. James of Compostella and Marian Year (8:34, 37, 43).

Sweden
The definitive series portraying King Gustav V, introduced in 1939, was augmented in 1948 by changes in colour as a result of increases in postal rates (9:11). Following the death of the king and the accession of Gustav VI Adolf in 1950, a new portrait series was introduced in June 1951 (9:17). The original version had a background of fine horizontal lines, but this was replaced in 1957 by a background pattern of cross-hatching. The higher denominations consisted of a series featuring the triple-crown emblem of Sweden. New values and changes of colour appeared between 1949 and 1969 (9:12). A 5-öre stamp in a numeral design by K. E. Forsberg (9:19) was introduced in 1951 and was subsequently used for other low values between 1957 and 1965. A series reproducing neolithic rock carvings was introduced in 1954 to cover the higher denominations (9:26).

This conservative approach to definitive stamps was matched by commemoratives and semi-postals that appeared at infrequent intervals. A striking feature of Swedish special issues was their use of the small format, which, in other countries was confined mainly to the definitive stamps. This had been Swedish practice with commemorative issues since 1920, and although a slightly larger format was used occasionally in the 1940s it did not become commonplace until the end of the immediate post-war decade. Intaglio was used exclusively and the commemoratives, like the definitives, tended to have a fairly solid background on which the principal motifs, inscriptions and emblems were carefully arranged. Occasionally, lettering and figures of value were superimposed on the vignette (9:5, 18); but as a rule, each element in the design appeared separately.

A distinctive feature of Swedish stamps was the fact that they were very seldom issued in normal sheet form. Usually, they were only in coils or booklets with the outer edges left imperforate. Booklet stamps can be found with one or more adjoining straight edges. Coils had straight edges on opposite sides. With the exception of the Red Cross stamp of 1945 (9:1), the majority of commemoratives of this period were released in pairs (9:2–4, 6–9, 15, 18, 20, 24, 25). Sets of three stamps marked the octingentenary of Lund Cathedral in 1946 (9:5), the 40th anniversary of King Gustav V's reign in 1947 (9:10), the centenary of Swedish pioneers in the United States in 1948 (9:13), the centenary of the birth of the playwright Strindberg in 1949 (9:14), the 7th anniversary of the UPU in 1949 (9:16), the jubilee of the Swedish Athletic Association in 1953 (9:21) and the centenary of Swedish telecommunications in 1953 (9:23). Charity stamps were confined to sets of three in 1948 and 1952, marking the ninetieth birthday of Gustav V and the seventieth birthday of Gustav VI Adolf respectively. The premiums were given to national youth and cultural funds.

Switzerland
Unlike Sweden, Switzerland made several references to the war in the stamps of this period, beginning with a pair and miniature sheet of 1945 with premiums in aid of a war relief fund (9:27). A set of thirteen stamps, from 5-centime to 10-franc, was released on 9th May 1945 to celebrate peace in Europe (9:29). The fact that this set was released so soon after VE-Day indicates that it had been prepared some time earlier in anticipation of the end of the war. As a result, neutral Switzerland had the honour of releasing some of the first Peace commemoratives anywhere in the world. Stamps were subsequently issued with a surcharge in aid of the Red Cross (9:28). The Latin inscription, meaning 'Peace to men of goodwill', circumvented the problem, in a country with four official languages, of giving offence to any by using captions that would be equally unintelligible to all. And to maintain this neutrality, even the name of the country was rendered in Latin – either 'Helvetia' or 'Confoederatio Helvetica' (Swiss Confederation).

The various 1936–41 definitive issues – landscapes, historical figures and parliamentary symbolic designs – continued to be used in the immediate post-war years, being partially superseded by a series in 1949–50 featuring technical aspects of the Swiss landscape (9:40) – including railways, snowploughs, power stations and reservoirs – designed and engraved by Karl Bickel, who had also been responsible for the pre-war series. Two versions of the 20-centime exist, the second having the cross-hatching above the numerals strengthened.

Charity stamps continued to appear annually, following the pattern established in the 1930s. These consisted of the Pro Patria and Pro Juventute issues of June and December respectively, with premiums in aid of various national and children's funds. The Pro Patria stamps, coinciding with the National Fête, pursued various themes continued serially from year to year – domestic architecture and cantonal occupations being predominant in this period (9:31, 41, 43). The Pro Juventute stamps also followed certain themes, each set portraying children or a famous Swiss (9:39, 46, 48) and featuring flowers or butterflies (9:32, 42).

In the early part of this period, separate issues were made to commemorate specific events such as the centenaries of the railways in 1947, the Confederation in 1948, post and telecommunications in 1952 (9:30, 34, 36, 38, 44) and important current events like the Winter Olympic Games of 1948 (9:35); but from 1954 onwards, such anniversaries and current events were grouped together in a single publicity issue (9:47). The 75th anniversary of the UPU in 1949 was celebrated by a commemorative set (9:37) that featured the Union monument in Berne as well as symbolic motifs. Alpine postal coaches in summer and winter landscapes were the subject of two stamps of 1953 (9:45) publicising the Mobile Post Office service.

The various international organisations with headquarters in Switzerland were provided with Swiss stamps suitably overprinted. Stamps for the use of the League of Nations were current from 1922 to 1944 and were superseded by a similar series in 1950, overprinted for the use of the European office of the United Nations. Contemporary Swiss stamps were also overprinted for the use of the International Labour Office, the International Education Office, the World Health Organisation and the International Refugees Organisation (9:49, 50).

Trieste

The district surrounding the city of Trieste, on the north-eastern coast of the Adriatic, was claimed by both Italy and Yugoslavia at the end of the Second World War. Administered jointly by the Anglo–American and Yugoslav military administrations, respec-Venezia Giulia (see below). The district was constituted a free territory in 1947 and was divided into two zones governed by the Anglo–American and Yugoslav military administrations, respectively. Italian stamps overprinted 'A.M.G. F.T.T.' (Allied Military Government Free Territory of Trieste) were used in Zone A (10:1–4), and stamps inscribed with the Serbo–Croat equivalent 'STT VUJA', 'S.O. TRSTA VUJA' or 'T.L. TRIESTE' were used in Zone B (10:5). The respective zones were handed over to Italy and Yugoslavia in 1954 and the ordinary stamps of these countries were subsequently introduced.

Turkey

Like Portugal, Turkey made use of local printers and overseas firms – hence the uneven quality of Turkish stamps and the variety of processes involved during this period. In 1946, when stocks of the definitive series produced at the Austrian State Printing Works ran out, a series portraying President Inönü was lithographed by the Damga Matbaasi Press (10:7). This was replaced two years later by an intaglio series by De La Rue (10:12). The letterpress series produced by Damga Matbaasi between 1931 and 1942, portraying the national hero Kemal Atatürk, was revived in 1950–55 (10:20). It was augmented in 1952 by a photogravure series from the Austrian State Printing Works that featured scenery and portraits of Atatürk (10:21, 23). Airmail stamps in two-colour photogravure were printed by Courvoisier in 1949–50 (10:15).

The same hodge-podge of printers and processes resulted in a diverse range of commemoratives. Lithography was favoured for sets produced locally, the quality varying from the striking series of 1946 by Guzel Sanatlar Matbaasi of Ankara, marking the visit of the U.S.S. *Missouri* (10:8), to the fuzzy vignettes of the Coastal Trading Rights set of 1951 by Klisecilik ve Matbaacilik of Istanbul (10:22). Fortunately, most of the special issues were entrusted to Courvoisier, who produced a number of excellent designs in photogravure between 1947 and 1949 (10:9–11, 14–17). Klisecilik ve Matbaacilik experimented with two-colour lithography (10:18, 19), but at that time it could not compete with the multicolour of which the Austrian State Press was capable (10:24).

The silver jubilee of the republic and the treaty of Lausanne (10:13, 14) were celebrated during this period, and several other sets referred to the birth of the modern republic. But Turkey also made numerous references to her past and many designs were inspired by classical antiquities (10:24) or mythology – as witness the flight of Icarus on a stamp of 1950 marking the International Civil Aviation Congress in Istanbul (10:18).

Vatican City

The inflation that overtook the Italian lira after the war, resulted in a spate of provisional surcharges on stamps originally issued in 1940 to celebrate the coronation of Pope Pius XII, but subsequently retained as a definitive series (10:26). A large-sized pictorial series, printed in photogravure by the Italian Government Printing Works, appeared in 1949 (10:28). Not surprisingly, even in secular matters the special issues of the Vatican adopted a religious tone – such as in the prisoners of war relief fund issues of 1942–5 (10:25), with their portrait of Christ in the background. The quatercentenary of the Council of Trent was celebrated in 1946 by a set of twelve ordinary stamps and two express-letter stamps portraying church dignitaries (10:27) among whom figured John Fisher, Bishop of Rochester, and Reginald Pole, Archbishop of Canterbury.

Papal portraits and views of St. Peter's Basilica formed the subjects of a lengthy thematic series of 1953 (10:30), and the inauguration and termination of Marian Year in 1954 were celebrated by sets portraying Pope Pius IX and Pope Pius XII and featuring the Madonna of Ostra Brama in Poland (10:31, 32).

The majority of Vatican stamps were produced in photogravure, but among the exceptions was a stamp and miniature sheet of 1952 marking the centenary of the first stamps of the Roman States (10:29).

Venezia Giulia

This district on the northern coast of the Adriatic was liberated by Yugoslav partisans at the end of the war, when various Italian stamps were overprinted for use in Istria (10:33), Trieste and Fiume. The territory was subsequently partitioned and administered by the Anglo–American and Yugoslav forces respectively. Italian stamps overprinted 'A.M.G. V.G.' (Allied Military Government Venezia Giulia) were employed by the Anglo–Americans, and distinctive stamps inscribed 'ISTRA' were used by the Yugoslavs (10:34, 35). These stamps were superseded in 1947 by the issues of Trieste.

Yugoslavia

The first stamps issued by Yugoslavia, reconstituted after the war, were the Monasteries series of the puppet state of Serbia, overprinted to signify the Democratic Federative Republic (10:36). They were replaced later in the year by a lithographed series portraying Marshal Tito (10:37), which was superseded by a typographed set in the same genre (10:39) that remained current until 1950. Industrial and agricultural occupations were the theme of the intaglio series of 1950–51, reissued between 1951 and 1955 in new colours and values (10:42). Airmail sets of 1947 and 1951–2 featured aircraft over Yugoslav scenery (10:40, 44).

A singular feature of Yugoslav philately, revived from pre-war days, was the annual Red Cross stamp (10:38, 41), the use of which was compulsory on all mail posted at certain times of the year. Special Red Cross postage-due labels were also provided to surcharge mail on which the obligatory stamps had not been used.

Apart from a spate of stamps in 1951–2 marking the 10th anniversaries of partisan battles, Yugoslav commemoratives in this period were remarkably free of political bias and thus reflected the independent policy followed by Tito in relation to the Soviet bloc. Instead, stamp designs were concentrated on the southern Slav cultural heritage and historical traditions (10:43).

Asia

Aden

A change of currency from the Indian system of annas and rupees to the East African shilling of 100 cents resulted in the Georgian series of 1939–48 being surcharged in 1951 (11:1). Nevertheless, Aden was one of the first British colonies to produce a distinctive Elizabethan series – a set of pictorials recess-printed by Waterlow and Sons in 1953 (11:2). The shilling stamp was re-engraved to mark the royal visit of 1954 (11:3); but otherwise, Aden confined its commemoratives to the colonial omnibus issues. The accession of Sultan Hussein meant a change of portrait on the stamps of the Kathiri State of Seiyun in 1954 (11:4). Seiyun and the neighbouring state of Shihr and Mukalla (11:5) overprinted their definitive issues in 1946 to celebrate victory, but the standard colonial designs were used on other commemorative occasions.

Afghanistan

The two extremes in design and production were evident in Afghan post-war stamps, the home-produced commemoratives (11:7) contrasting strangely with the technical perfection of the 1951 definitives (11:6) produced by Waterlow and Sons in a combination of photogravure, intaglio and lithography. Apart from frequent issues on behalf of the Red Crescent, Afghan commemoratives appeared annually to mark Independence Day and Pakhtunistan Day – the latter being part of a campaign for the cession of the Pathan districts by Pakistan.

Bahrain

The postal services in this sheikhdom were administered by India until April 1948, when control was transferred to the United Kingdom. Indian stamps overprinted 'BAHRAIN' were then superseded by British stamps with a similar overprint and surcharged in Indian currency (11:8, 9).

Brunei

The accession of a new ruler, Sultan Omar Ali Saifuddin, provided an opportunity to replace a definitive series that had been current for forty-five years. The series of 1952, recess-printed by De La Rue, portrayed the sultan on the low values (*11*:10) and featured a view of Brunei Town on the higher denominations. The latter design was adapted from one used for a set of three stamps celebrating the silver jubilee of the late Sultan Ahmed Taijudin in 1949. Brunei's only other special issue in this period was the colonial omnibus series marking the 75th anniversary of the UPU.

Burma

Burma had three definitive sets in rapid succession: in 1945 the pre-war series overprinted 'MILY ADMN' to denote the military administration, in 1946 the un-overprinted series in new colours to signify the return to civil government, and in 1947 the same set overprinted in Burmese to denote the interim Burmese government (*11*:11). The civil and interim government issues were also over-printed 'SERVICE' for use on official correspondence. The independent Union of Burma was proclaimed on 6th January 1948, a set of five stamps being released to mark the occasion (*11*:12). The first anniversary of the murder of Aung San and his government was marked by a lengthy set featuring the Martyrs' Memorial (*11*:13). The framework of this set was later adapted for the higher values of the definitive series of 1949, reissued four years later with denominations in the new currency of pyas and kyats (*11*:15). The only other special issues of this period commemorated the 75th anniversary of the UPU, the 5th anniversary of independence and the Sixth Buddhist Council (*11*:14).

Cambodia

The kingdom of Cambodia, as a member of the French Union, was established in 1951 and the stamps of Indo-China were superseded by a Cambodian series in November of that year (*11*:16). An airmail set and a second definitive issue appeared in 1953–4. All three sets were engraved and printed in Paris and had motifs deriving from Cambodian art and mythology. Four stamps of the first definitive set were surcharged in 1952 to raise money for a students-aid fund. Five of the Indian 1949 definitives were overprinted in December 1954 for the use of Indian personnel serving with the International Commission in Cambodia. Similar sets were provided for the Commission staffs in Laos and Vietnam.

Ceylon

The transition from crown colony to dominion status was anticipated in November 1947 by a set of four stamps recess-printed by Bradbury Wilkinson. Oddly enough, the stamps continued to show strong colonial influence, with their inset portraits of King George VI (*11*:18). Although Ceylon attained dominion status in February 1948, no stamps recorded the fact until a year later (*11*:19) and the Georgian colonial style definitives were only gradually replaced by the dominion series between 1951 and 1954 (*11*:20, 21, 25). The definitives, with principal inscriptions in English and subsidiary captions in Sinhala and Tamil, were produced by two printers – intaglio by Bradbury Wilkinson and photogravure by Courvoisier. These processes, involving other printers, were also used for the commemoratives. Harrison and Sons produced the Colombo Plan stamp of 1952 (*11*:22), and Bradbury Wilkinson and De La Rue recess-printed the coronation stamps and royal visit stamps of 1953 and 1954 respectively (*11*:23, 24). Ceylon was the only dominion created in the post-war years to issue stamps for these occasions.

China

The Japanese surrender in China on 14th August 1945 was immediately followed by a struggle for power between the Nationalists and the Communists. The philately of the ensuing period is exceedingly complex, illustrating the steady advance of the Communists and the rapid inflation that beset the Nationalist economy. Numerous stamps of local validity were issued in various districts controlled by the Communists, and after their decisive defeat of the Nationalists at Hwai-Hai in January 1949, the Communists swiftly completed their conquest of the remaining parts of mainland China and established a series of 'liberation areas', each with its own distinctive stamps. The regional issues of central, east, north, north-

west, south and south-west China in 1949–50 (*11*:26–32), with values in people's currency, were valid for postage in any part of mainland China. They were superseded by the issues of the People's Republic, introduced in October 1949 (*11*:39). A definitive series featuring the Gate of Heavenly Peace in Peking (*11*:40) was adapted from the design used in north China (*11*:32) and was introduced in 1950. An airmail set, recess-printed by the People's Printing Works, Shanghai, was released in 1951 (*11*:41). Prominent landmarks and various occupations were the subjects of a series issued in 1953 (*11*:43).

Relatively few commemorative stamps appeared in this period. Annual sets were made for the Peace campaign (*11*:44) and in honour of 'Glorious Mother Country' (*11*:46). From June 1953 the majority of stamps was produced at the People's Printing Works in Peking, the first such issue being a pair marking the seventh National Labour Union Conference and portraying Karl Marx (*11*:45). The educational uses to which stamps could be put were illustrated by a series of forty stamps, in ten blocks of four, showing sequences of gymnastic exercises described in a radio programme of 1952 (*11*:42).

Dr. Sun Yat-sen, founder of modern China, was the subject of the Nationalist definitives in the post-war period (*11*:33) – and the fact that no fewer than seven such sets appeared between 1945 and 1949 is an indication of the speed at which inflation outstripped successive issues. Each distinctive set was surcharged in a vain attempt to keep up with inflation; but even after the currency reform of August 1948, when the gold yuan replaced the paper dollar at the rate of three million to one, emergency stamps continued to be issued. Revenue stamps were surcharged in gold yuan in January 1949 (*11*:34), but within two months the gold yuan had collapsed. In May 1949, so-called 'unit' stamps were issued without denominations and were sold at the rate of the day (*11*:35).

After Taiwan (Formosa) was surrendered by the Japanese, stamps similar to those of mainland China were used, differing only in inscriptions and denominations. After the evacuation of Nationalist forces from the mainland in 1949, Taiwan became the Nationalist stronghold and was restyled the Republic of China. The first distinctive series of this régime, portraying the medieval Koxinga (*11*:36), appeared in 1950. This was replaced by a series of 1953 featuring Chiang Kai-shek (*11*:37). Several commemorative sets were recess-printed by the Bank of Taiwan (*11*:38), and they were invariably issued without gum.

Hong Kong

This colony had the distinction of departing from the colonial omnibus design for its victory stamps of 1946 (*11*:47), the phoenix motif having been designed by W. E. Jones while a captive of the Japanese. The pre-war Georgian series was resurrected in 1945, and new values and colours were added between 1946 and 1952 (*11*:48). The same design, with the profile of Queen Elizabeth, was typographed by De La Rue in 1954 (*11*:50). Otherwise, Hong Kong's stamps conformed to the colonial omnibus issues of 1949–53 (*11*:49).

India

The last stamps of the British Raj were the victory set of January 1946, with a symbolic motif and a profile of the King-Emperor in Durbar robes (*12*:1). The sub-continent was partitioned in 1947 to form the dominions of India and Pakistan. India celebrated independence with three stamps featuring national emblems (*12*:2), though the Georgian definitives were not replaced by the dominion pictorial series until 1949 (*12*:4). The design of the 1-anna stamp, showing a statue of Bodhisattva, was printed in reverse in 1950 (*12*:9) and a series showing an Asokan capital was released for official use in the same year (*12*:8).

With the exception of a set of four portraying the late Mahatma Gandhi (*12*:3), produced by Courvoisier in 1948, the post-war stamps of India were all printed at the Security Press in Nasik. Offset-lithography was used up to 1951 (*12*:5–7, 11), but photo-gravure was introduced in 1952 and used for the Saints and Poets series (*12*:10) and all subsequent commemoratives in this period (*12*:12–17). An independent republic within the British Commonwealth was proclaimed in January 1950, celebrated by four stamps with allegorical designs by D. J. Keymer (*12*:6).

The stamps of the princely states were gradually phased out after the war. Stamps of India overprinted for use in the so-called 'convention states' of Chamba, Gwalior, Jind, Nabha and Patiala were invalidated on 1st April 1950. The stamps of the few feudatory states still issuing them were replaced by the republican series on 1st April 1950 and invalidated a month later. In the post-war period, new issues were made by Bhopal (for official use only), Bundi, Cochin, Hyderabad, Jaipur and Travancore (*12*:18–20). In 1948 several Rajput states, including Bundi, Jaipur and Kishangarh, formed the union of Rajasthan. Stamps of these three principalities were overprinted the following year for use in the area (*12*:21). Other amalgamations of this period included the United State of Saurashtra – consisting of some two hundred and twenty-two principalities – and the United State of Travancore-Cochin, which continued to issue its own stamps until 1951 (*12*:22).

In a series of referenda, the French Indian Settlements voted for union with India. Chandernagore joined the republic in 1950, and the other settlements joined in 1954. Pictorial definitive and airmail sets featuring Indian deities and temples were produced by Vaugirard between 1949 and 1952 (*12*:23).

The Portuguese settlements in Goa, Damao and Diu resisted pressure from India, and their stamps of this period followed the pattern of the Portuguese colonies in general. However, distinctive lithographed sets bearing historic portraits appeared in 1946 and 1948 (*12*:24).

Indonesia
Dutch rule was restored to those parts of the East Indies liberated by American and Australian forces – Borneo, Celebes, West New Guinea, Timor and Sumba – but the surrender of the Japanese in Java, Sumatra and Madura allowed the independence movement of Dr. Sukarno to establish the republic of Indonesia. Stamps inscribed 'Nederlandsch–Indie' or an abbreviated form of it (*12*:25–27) were used in Dutch-controlled areas from 1945 to September 1948, when this territory was renamed Indonesia. The Wilhelmina definitives were released with an overprint to that effect later in the same year (*12*:28), pending the introduction of a pictorial series by Kolff of Batavia in 1949 (*12*:29).

Meanwhile, the republicans produced separate issues for Sumatra (*12*:30), Java and Madura. These continued until 1950, when the republican areas and the Dutch-controlled districts – with the exception of West New Guinea – formed the United States of Indonesia. Stamps inscribed 'Republik Indonesia Serikat' or overprinted 'RIS' were issued between January and August 1950 (*12*:31). As the former Dutch areas were absorbed into the republican administration, the status of the country was changed to a unitary republic and the stamps released from August 1950 onwards were merely inscribed 'Republik Indonesia' (*12*:32–34).

West New Guinea, excluded from the Dutch–Indonesian agreement of 1949, continued as a Dutch colony for the time being. Distinctive stamps in the standard Dutch designs were introduced in 1950 (*12*:35), and they were augmented in 1954 by a series featuring birds of paradise in two-colour photogravure (*12*:36).

Iran
In 1945, changes of colour and new values were added to the series of 1942 (*12*:37) and remained current until 1949, when a pictorial series with the Shah's portrait inset was lithographed by the Mejliss Press in Teheran (*12*:38). Various portraits of the Shah were used in sets of 1951 and 1954 (*12*:40), and a profile was incorporated in the scenic airmail series of 1953 (*12*:42). Among the special issues of this period were two obligatory tax stamps of 1950, which raised money for a hospitals fund (*12*:39). Although most stamps were printed locally, a notable exception was the series of semi-postals raising money for the restoration of Avicenna's tomb. These stamps, with various historical subjects, were recess-printed by Bradbury Wilkinson and were issued annually between 1948 and 1950 (*12*:41).

Iraq
Bradbury Wilkinson recess-printed definitive sets with progressively older portraits of King Faisal II in 1948 and 1954 (*12*:43, 46). In both instances, a larger format was used for the higher denominations. The same firm produced an intaglio airmail series, featuring aircraft over prominent landmarks (*12*:44), and two commemorative sets – one marking the 75th anniversary of the UPU (*12*:45) and

the other, in 1953, celebrating the coronation of King Faisal. The definitives were overprinted 'ON STATE SERVICE' with its Arabic equivalent for use on official mail, and several of these stamps were overprinted in 1949 to denote compulsory use as a levy on correspondence to finance the war against Israel.

Israel
No postage stamps were added after the war to the series issued under the British mandate in Palestine. A state of civil war existed between the Arab and Jewish communities from late 1945 onwards. The British mandate came to an end on 15th May 1948, but the British-controlled postal service had gradually broken down between 15th April and 5th May. During the interim period of April to May 1948, many local postal services were operated by the Jewish communities and numerous stamps were issued (*13*:1).

The state of Israel was proclaimed on 14th May 1948, and stamps were introduced two days later. They were inscribed in Hebrew and Arabic to signify 'Hebrew Post', and they featured coins dating from the period of the two Jewish revolts against Roman rule (*13*:2). Considerable variation exists in the perforations and types of paper used for these stamps. Similar designs, printed on yellow paper and overprinted in Hebrew, were used as postage-due labels.

The original Coins series was typographed at the Haaretz Press in Sarona. A second Coins series inscribed 'Israel' in Hebrew, English and Arabic appeared in December 1949 (*13*:6) in a slightly larger format. A third series with similar designs was released between 1951 and 1954, lithographed by Lewin-Epstein of Bat Yam, who also printed many of the commemorative issues in the same process. Other special issues were printed in photogravure by the Government printer at Hakirya. A distinctive feature of all Israeli stamps, except the postage-due issues, was the descriptive sheet margins, known as tabs, which have been continued to the present day.

The Israeli stamps of 1949–54 period were predominantly religious or historical in character; and even when the subject of the design was secular, the accompanying tab often bore a biblical text. Regular issues were made annually, from 1948, to celebrate the Jewish New Year and, from 1950, to mark the anniversaries of independence. The independence issues began with a pair featuring immigrants and immigrant ships; but in later years, various themes including views and flowers were utilised. A similar thematic approach was adopted for the New Year stamps, the subjects chosen usually being concerned with aspects of the Jewish faith (*13*:7, 8, 10, 12, 13, 16, 18).

Many of the commemoratives consisted of single stamps, such as those marking the adoption of a national flag in 1949 (*13*:3) and celebrating the silver jubilee of the Hebrew University in 1950 (*13*:4). Others, like the Constituent Assembly stamp of 1949 and the Elat post office commemorative of 1950, were subsequently retained as part of the definitive range. Airmail sets featured birds in 1950 and scenery in 1953, and a postage-due series depicting the stag emblem of the Israeli postal service appeared in 1952. A pair of stamps was issued in 1952 to mourn Chaim Weizmann, first president of the republic. Other historical figures honoured by stamps in this period included the founder of the World Zionist Movement, Theodor Herzl in 1951, the philosopher Maimonides in 1953 and financier Baron Edmond de Rothschild in 1954 (*13*:9, 11, 14, 15, 17, 19–21).

Japan
The unconditional surrender of Japan in August 1945 did not have the dramatic impact on philately that the collapse of Nazi Germany had had earlier in the year. Subjects of a bellicose nature were dropped from the definitive series and were replaced by less controversial designs in 1945. In the closing months of the war, however, the production of stamps had presented problems with which the Government Printing Works in Tokyo could not cope. No fewer than seven other printers in Tokyo and Osaka were involved in the printing of the 1945 definitives, and these had to be issued imperforate because of the breakdown of the machinery. Between August 1946 and August 1947 an entirely new series appeared, augmenting the denominations of the 1945–6 series by the higher values required because of inflation. These stamps were likewise 'farmed-out' to various subcontractors and were issued without perforation. Both sets varied considerably in the colour and quality of paper. The majority of stamps were issued ungummed, but certain printings of some values are known to have been gummed (*13*:22–28).

Between 1947 and 1952 the definitive series was reissued both gummed and perforated. In addition, the inscriptions had been redrawn so that the characters read from left to right instead of right to left. The chrysanthemum emblem of imperial power was omitted from all special issues from August 1947 onwards and from the definitives of 1948. An intaglio series was introduced in November 1948. Printings from 1951 onwards were made on paper without the ribbed vertical watermark introduced in 1937. Seven additional denominations appeared in 1950–51, produced variously in photogravure, intaglio and letterpress. Continuing inflation drove the sen from circulation, and the double noughts, indicating sen values, were accordingly omitted from the value inscriptions of stamps issued from 1952 (13:32–34, 43).

Between 1949 and 1952 a series of eighteen stamps portraying famous Japanese augmented the permanent range. Airmail sets consisted of the Pheasant series of 1950 and an issue of 1951–2 showing aircraft over the Horyuji Pagoda or over Mount Tate, reissued in 1952–3 with the noughts omitted from the value. Saburo Watanabe designed an airmail series, released in August 1953, depicting the Great Buddha of Kamakura (13:30, 39, 46).

Among the special issues were several perennial favourites. The pre-war practice of producing at regular intervals stamps featuring scenery in the national parks was revived in 1949. Stamps for national athletic meetings appeared annually from 1947 onwards. New Year greetings stamps were reintroduced in 1948. Philatelic Week, 'Know your Stamps' campaigns and philatelic exhibitions accounted for many of the immediate post-war period special issues, which were often produced in miniature sheets. Stamps commemorating important anniversaries or current events were usually released in singles or pairs, the exceptions included sets of four for the 75th anniversaries of the postal service and the UPU in 1947 and 1949 respectively (13:29, 31, 35–38, 40–42, 44, 45, 47, 48).

Seven stamps of the Australian definitive series were overprinted 'B.C.O.F. JAPAN 1946' for the use of the British Commonwealth Occupation Force. The three lowest values were released on 11th October 1946 but were withdrawn after two days, following protests from the Japanese authorities. They were eventually permitted, however, and were reintroduced with the remaining denominations in May 1947. All seven were finally withdrawn on 28th March 1949 (13:49).

Jordan

Rapid constitutional changes were reflected in the stamps of the late 1940s. The emirate of Transjordan was raised to the status of a kingdom in May 1946, and the event was celebrated by a set of nine stamps featuring a map of the country (14:2). A year later, a set covering the same denominations marked the inauguration of the first national parliament (14:3). In the Arab–Israeli conflict of 1948 the kingdom acquired territory on the west bank of the river Jordan and the name of the country became the Hashemite Kingdom of Jordan – an inscription first used on the UPU commemoratives of 1949 (14:4). Stamps of 1952 marking the unification of Jordan and Arab Palestine (14:5) were retained as a definitive series. Transjordanian stamps overprinted 'PALESTINE' were used in the occupied areas of the west bank between December 1948 and April 1950, being then superseded by ordinary Jordanian stamps (14:5).

Korea

Following the defeat of Japan in August 1945, Korea was divided into Russian and American zones of occupation. Ordinary Japanese stamps continued to be used in both areas until early 1946, when distinctive stamps were released by both authorities. The military administrations came to an end in 1948 with the establishment of the Republic of Korea in the south and the People's Democratic Republic of Korea in the north. Early stamps of North Korea were not dissimilar in character to those of the south, both using the national hibiscus emblem (14:11, 13). But North Korean stamps became more politically biased, especially during and after the period of the Korean War of 1950–52. South Korean stamps of this period were lithographed locally (14:9–12) on Japanese watermarked paper.

Twelve stamps of the 1949 Indian series were overprinted in 1953 for use by Indian custodian forces supervising the cease-fire in Korea (14:14).

Kuwait

Indian stamps were overprinted and used in the postal agency established in this Arab state (14:15); but responsibility for the agency passed from India to the United Kingdom in 1948, and thereafter British stamps were employed. The stamps used in the sheikhdom of Kuwait were inscribed with its name (14:16, 17) and surcharged with values in Indian currency.

Laos

Laos became an independent kingdom within the French Union on 19th July 1949 but did not issue its own stamps until November 1951 (14:18). The inscription 'Union Française' was incorporated in the design of Laotian stamps from then until 1953, when it was replaced by the monogram 'UF' which continued in use until Laos left the French Union in December 1956. Definitives and special issues were recess-printed in Paris; but it was the inclusion of traditional motifs that gave Laotian stamps their distinctive character.

Indian troops serving with the International Commission in Indo-China used contemporary Indian stamps with a distinctive overprint (14:19) from December 1954 onwards.

Lebanon

The famous cedars of Lebanon appeared in every definitive series from 1925 to 1964. During the first post-war decade there were no fewer than six different cedar designs (14:21, 23). The higher denominations depicted scenery and classical antiquities (14:22). The storks motif of 1946 (14:20) was used for one ordinary stamp and four airmail stamps.

The sameness of Lebanese stamps in this decade may be explained by the fact that they were all lithographed at the Catholic Press in Beirut, and the majority were designed by P. Koroleff.

Macao

The majority of stamps used in this Portuguese colony conformed in design and technique to those of the mother country and the other overseas territories. The sole concession to oriental atmosphere was provided by a set of 1950–51 with a dragon motif, lithographed by the Sin Chun Printing Company in the colony (14:24). Other stamps, though featuring local scenes, were lithographed in Portugal or produced in multicolour photogravure by Courvoisier.

Malaya

Following the Japanese surrender, stamps of the pre-war Straits Settlements series were overprinted 'BMA MALAYA' and circulated in the Malay states and Singapore, then under British military administration (14:25). From 1948 onwards, this general series was gradually replaced by sets provided for each of the twelve Malay states. A standard formula – a frame design of palm trees flanking the portrait of the particular ruler – was used for the stamps typographed by De La Rue for Johore, Kedah, Kelantan, Pahang, Perak, Perlis (14:1, 8, 37, 50, 51), Selangor and Trengganu (15:19, 35). The state emblem was used for Negri Sembilan (14:32) and for the lower values of Kedah (14:7). King George VI appeared on the stamps of Malacca, Penang and Singapore (14:26, 48; 15:20). A portrait of Queen Elizabeth was substituted on stamps of Malacca and Penang in 1954 (14:27, 49).

Maldive Islands

An intaglio series by Bradbury Wilkinson was issued in 1950 (14:28), with a palm tree and a boat replacing the Juma Mosque design that had been used since 1909. Bradbury Wilkinson produced 3-laree and 5-laree stamps in different designs two years later. The islands became a republic in January 1953 and reverted to a sultanate the following year, but neither of these changes was reflected in commemorative stamps.

Mongolia

All of the stamps issued in the immediate post-war years were photogravure-printed at the State Printing Works in Moscow. Few appeared in this period apart from lengthy sets celebrating the twenty-fifth and thirtieth anniversaries of independence, in 1946 and 1951 respectively, (14:29) and the first anniversary of the death of Marshal Choibalsan, in 1953. A set of five small-format definitives, featuring the national coat of arms, was lithographed in Peking and released in 1954.

Muscat
Apart from the contemporary Indian definitives overprinted in 1944 to mark the bicentenary of the Al-Busaid dynasty, the Indian postal agency in Muscat used ordinary Indian stamps. In 1948, the agency was transferred to the British Post Office and British stamps surcharged in Indian currency were then issued. Definitives and commemoratives of 1948–53 were surcharged in this way (14:30). The Elizabethan definitives with similar surcharges were released in 1952–4 (14:31).

Nepal
The Siva definitives, which had been current since 1907, were replaced in October 1949 by a pictorial series produced in offset-lithography by the Indian Security Press, Nasik (14:33). The adoption of the decimal rupee in 1954 necessitated a new series, portraying King Tribhuvana. A map series in the same denominations was issued simultaneously.

North Borneo
Rapid changes in the status of the territory after the war were marked by the stamps of the pre-war series being released in 1945 with a 'BMA' overprint, signifying the military administration, and in 1947 with an overprint obliterating 'THE STATE OF' and 'BRITISH PROTECTORATE' and substituting the royal cypher (14:34) to denote crown colony status. North Borneo was one of the first colonies to issue a post-war photogravure series, a set of fifteen being released in July 1950 (14:35). A similar set, with the portrait of Queen Elizabeth, appeared gradually between March 1954 (14:36) and February 1957.

Pakistan
Indian stamps were overprinted lithographically at Nasik for use in the dominion of Pakistan, and existing stocks all over the country were similarly overprinted by hand (14:38). Distinctive stamps did not appear until July 1948, when a set of four marked the first anniversary of independence (14:39). De La Rue recess-printed this set and all subsequent sets up to the postal centenary stamps of 1952 (14:40–44), and also early printings of the definitives of 1948 (14:40); but the 7th anniversary set of 1954 and the stamp celebrating the conquest of Mount Godwin-Austen (14:45, 46) were recess-printed by the Pakistan Security Printing Corporation. Saracenic leaf patterns, arabesques and other motifs derived from Islamic art, characterised the framework and ornament of early Pakistani stamps.

The princely state of Bahawalpur embarked on a short but highly prolific stamp programme in 1948. In the space of a year, some twenty-nine ordinary and thirty-one official stamps were released (14:47) before the independent postal service was suppressed. These stamps were all recess-printed by De La Rue and had only local validity.

Philippines
Stamps of the 1935 and 1937 series were reintroduced in January 1945, overprinted 'VICTORY' to celebrate liberation from the Japanese (15:1). Similar stamps with handstruck overprints had already been issued in Leyte in 1944. The attainment of full independence was marked by three stamps in July 1946 (15:2), followed by a pictorial series in 1947 (15:3). This issue was augmented by occasional stamps featuring presidential portraits (15:4, 8) and by a series of 1952–60 portraying famous Filipinos (15:11). Four sets of three, each depicting the arms of a Filipino city, were released in 1951 (15:7).

Intaglio was used for the majority of special issues (15:6, 7, 9, 10, 12–14); but two-colour letterpress was used in the production of stamps commemorating the Economic Commission in 1947 and the Boy Scouts in 1948, as well as the flower stamp of 1948 (15:5).

Ryukyu Islands
This group of islands south of Japan was under American military government from 1945 to 1952 and then under US civil administration. Locally overprinted Japanese stamps were replaced by distinctive stamps in 1948. The Japanese Government Printing Works typographed a series of pictorials in 1948, followed by photogravure sets in 1950 and 1952 (15:15).

Sarawak
In December 1945 the pre-war series was revived, overprinted 'BMA' to denote the British Military Administration. The centenary of the Brooke dynasty was to have been celebrated by stamps in 1941, but the Japanese invasion delayed their release until 1946 (15:16). With the resumption of civil government, Sarawak became a crown colony and its status was indicated by an overprint of the royal cypher on the definitive series. Bradbury Wilkinson, who had produced the definitives and the commemorative set, recess-printed a pictorial series in 1950 with portraits of King George VI inset (15:17). The original scaly ant-eater design of the 10-cent stamp was replaced by a map design in 1952.

Saudi Arabia
The 1934 definitive series – introduced on the revaluation of the guerche at the rate of 880 to the gold sovereign – remained current throughout the post-war decade, but an airmail set was introduced in 1949 (15:18). Apart from the medical-aid charity stamps of 1945–53, a railway series in 1952, and a set of 1950 celebrating the golden jubilee of the capture of Riyadh by King Abdul Aziz, Saudi commemoratives of this period consisted entirely of singles or pairs marking visits by foreign heads of state and Ibn Saud's meeting with King Farouk of Egypt.

Syria
Stamps of this period were printed by photogravure or offset-lithography in Cairo or were lithographed by the Catholic Press in Beirut. The resumption of constitutional government in 1945 was marked by a series portraying President Shukri Bey al-Quwatli, who appeared on subsequent airmail and definitive issues of 1946–7 (15:21, 23). The revolution of March 1949 brought Husni el Zaim briefly to power until further upheavals restored the former president, and these coups and counter-coups of 1949–55 were faithfully recorded in the stamps of the period (15:25, 26). The style of pictorial definitive stamps established under the French mandate, however, continued in this decade (15:22, 24, 27, 28) but gave way to a series in 1954 with allegorical designs symbolising labour, communications, industry and family life (15:29).

Apart from the political events, commemorative stamps concentrated on current events – ranging from the evacuation of Allied forces in 1946 to the various Arab conferences held in Damascus. Several of these issues were effected by overprinting definitive or airmail stamps with a commemorative inscription.

Thailand
Although the modern name Thailand had been used on stamps from 1940, it did not become standardised until 1950 with the release of the series celebrating the coronation of King Bhumibol (15:31). The definitives of 1947–9 (15:30) and the set of 1947–8 marking the king's majority continued to use the obsolescent name 'Siam'. A series with an up-to-date portrait of the king was introduced in 1951 (15:32). Like the 1947 series, it was recess-printed by Waterlow and Sons.

Apart from the royal events already mentioned, the only Thai commemoratives of this period were those marking the 60th anniversary of the Thai Red Cross in 1953 and United Nations Day from 1951 to 1954.

Timor
Pre-war stamps of this Portuguese colony were reissued in 1947 with an overprint to celebrate liberation from the Japanese. In 1948 a definitive series featuring native types and occupations was introduced – the first stamps to depart from the standard colonial designs (15:34). The few commemoratives of this period, however, continued to conform to Portuguese omnibus patterns (15:33).

Vietnam
Indo-Chinese stamps overprinted 'VIET-NAM DAN-CHU CONG-HOA' were issued in 1945 by the Nationalists, led by Ho Chi-minh, to signify the Vietnam Democratic Republic established by them at

the time of the Japanese surrender. France recognised this republic as a member of the Indo-Chinese Federation; but by the end of 1946 war had broken out between the French and the Viet-Minh forces, who withdrew to northern Tongking and central Annam, where the democratic republic – otherwise known as North Vietnam – continued to function. Very few stamps were released in the ensuing period (15:38), the most notable series being the set of 1954 celebrating the defeat of the French at Dien Bien Phu (15:39).

After the French broke off relations with Ho Chi-minh, they established a rival government under the Annamese emperor Bao Dai. Stamps inscribed 'VIET-NAM BUU-CHINH' were issued by the state of Vietnam – now South Vietnam – between 1949 and 1955, in photogravure by Vaugirard (15:40, 41) and intaglio by De La Rue (15:42, 43).

By the Declaration of Geneva, in July 1954, Vietnam was partitioned at the Seventeenth Parallel. Indian troops supervising the cease-fire and the subsequent demarcation line, used contemporary Indian stamps with a distinguishing overprint (15:44).

Yemen
Non-figurative designs with a crescent motif and lengthy Arabic inscriptions dominated Yemeni stamps from their inception in 1926 until 1947, when a pictorial series was recess-printed at the Institut de Gravure in Paris. Further pictorial sets, in photogravure by the Italian Government Printing Works, appeared in 1951 and 1953 (15:45, 46).

Several commemorative sets combining photogravure vignettes and intaglio frames were produced in this period by the Austrian State Printing Works. A number of sets was issued in 1948–50 with an eye to foreign philatelic sales. In particular, the series marking admission to the United Nations pandered to the then current fashion for Roosevelt commemoratives.

Africa

Africa
In the immediate post-war period, five major European powers produced stamps on behalf of more than forty colonies and protectorates. In many instances there were very few changes in the post-war stamps and each of the colonial powers pursued its own uniform policy in its respective sphere of influence. The independent and semi-independent countries are treated separately. Morocco, although under European control, is dealt with individually because of the multi-national nature of its postal services.

Belgian Congo and Ruanda–Urundi
Two definitive sets appeared in the Congo in the post-war period, both of them thematic. A series featuring native masks and idols, recess-printed by the Institut de Gravure in Paris, was released between 1947 and 1950 (16:14). It was followed in 1952–3 by a floral series in multicolour photogravure by Courvoisier (16:15). Similar sets were issued in the mandated territory of Ruanda–Urundi (17:34, 35).

The majority of the commemoratives of this period celebrated golden jubilees of colonial development, such as the series of 1947 marking the anniversary of the abolition of slavery (16:13), recess-printed by Enschedé of Haarlem.

British Colonies and Protectorates
The output of new stamps in the four countries of West Africa varied considerably. Sierra Leone produced no new definitives in this period. The Gold Coast, on the other hand, introduced a pictorial series in two-colour intaglio by Bradbury Wilkinson in July 1948 (16:41). The same designs, with a portrait of Queen Elizabeth substituted, were utilised for a series issued between December 1952 and March 1954 (16:42). Gambia and Nigeria adopted Elizabethan sets in 1953, entirely new pictorial designs being used in both cases. The Gambian series replaced the semi-heraldic elephant and palm-tree set of 1938–46 and was printed by De La Rue. Maurice Fievet broke away

from the British colonial tradition in his Nigerian designs, which were among the earliest to dispense with the ornate frames characteristic of the Georgian issues (17:20). None of these territories issued commemoratives other than the colonial omnibus sets (17:40).

The countries of central Africa were much more prolific. In 1945 Nyasaland abandoned its heraldic series in favour of an intaglio pictorial set (17:24). The original design of the 1-penny stamp was regarded as unsatisfactory, and its portrait of an askari of the King's African Rifles was replaced by a naturalistic treatment of the protectorate emblem. The Elizabethan series of 1953–4 retained the same designs as the Georgian series but with a change of profile (17:26). Northern Rhodesia's Elizabethan series of 1953 retained the wildlife motif hitherto used in the George V and George VI sets (17:21, 23). Although no changes were made in Southern Rhodesia's definitives until 1953 (18:18), the country – as befitted its self-governing status – produced its own victory set and coronation stamp (18:17). Both Northern and Southern Rhodesia celebrated the centenary of Cecil Rhodes with stamps (17:22; 18:16) and, together with Nyasaland released 6-penny stamps in 1953 for the Rhodes Centenary Exhibition (17:25). The distinctive issues of the three territories were superseded by a joint series (17:33) in July 1954, following the creation of the Central African Federation.

Of the three High Commission territories in southern Africa, Basutoland alone produced an Elizabethan series within this period, the pictorials of 1954 being recess-printed by De La Rue (16:10). All three countries – Basutoland, Bechuanaland and Swaziland – issued identical sets of four stamps in 1947 to mark the royal visit (16:11, 12; 18:27), and this was also the occasion for commemorative stamps in South Africa (18:2) and Southern Rhodesia (18:15). The High Commission territories participated in the colonial omnibus issues, but substituted for the victory set, an issue of the South African series suitably overprinted (18:28).

East Africa – Kenya, Uganda and Tanganyika – did not adopt an Elizabethan definitive series until June 1954. The entirely new designs for it were anticipated in April 1954, when a 30-cent stamp was released to mark the royal visit (16:45, 46, 47). Two years earlier, the same expedient of adding a commemorative inscription to the definitive design had been used for a pair of stamps honouring the royal visit of February 1952, cut short by the death of King George VI (16:45). In the Somaliland protectorate the introduction of the East African shilling of 100 cents brought about in 1951 the temporary surcharge on the Georgian series, which was replaced in September 1953 by a pictorial series with the Queen's portrait inset (17:43).

In the offshore islands there was relatively little philatelic activity. St. Helena replaced the Georgian heraldic series with a recess pictorial set by De La Rue in 1953 (17:36). The same firm printed new 1-penny, 1½- and 2-pence stamps (16:9) for the dependency of Ascension in 1949, but no Elizabethan series appeared until 1956. St. Helena's other dependency, Tristan da Cunha, made its philatelic début in January 1952 with the St. Helena Georgian series overprinted (18:31) and made up for lost time by releasing a two-colour pictorial set two years later (18:32).

In 1938 the Seychelles had had the distinction of being one of the first British colonies to issue a photogravure series. Fourteen years later, the designs were up-dated by the substitution of a more mature portrait of King George VI (17:38); and the same designs were used for the Elizabethan series of February 1954. All three sets were the work of Harrison and Sons, who also produced a photogravure series for Mauritius in July 1950 (17:4). Like that of the Seychelles, this series was adapted three years later for the Elizabethan definitives. In deference to the position of Mauritius as the first colony to issue stamps, a set appeared in 1948 – somewhat belatedly – to mark the centenary of the 'Post Office' stamps of 1847 (17:3). In 1946, Zanzibar, like the Aden states, overprinted two definitives to mark victory (18:36). An intaglio series, portraying Sultan Kalif or depicting the Seyyid Kalifa schools at Beit el-Ras (18:37), was produced by De La Rue in 1952. The 75th birthday of the sultan was the occasion of a set of five photogravure stamps in August 1954 (18:38).

British stamps with a 'BMA' overprint were used in the former Italian colonies of Eritrea, Somalia and Tripolitania from 1948 onwards, replacing the wartime 'MEF' overprints of the Middle East Forces (16:16–18). A distinctive series featuring an Arab horseman was recess-printed by Waterlow and Sons and issued in Cyrenaica in 1950 (*16*:23), prior to its incorporation in the kingdom of Libya. Somalia reverted to Italian rule in 1950 and subsequently issued stamps printed at the Government Printing Works in Rome (*17*:41, 42).

French Colonies and Protectorates

At the end of the war, contemporary French stamps with a distinguishing overprint were used in Algeria (*16*:1). They were superseded in 1947 by a letterpress series depicting the arms of Constantine, Oran and Algiers (*16*:2). Other arms designs were added to the series in 1956–8. An intaglio series featuring classical sculpture appeared in 1952, and a letterpress issue showing the courtyard of the Bardo Museum appeared in 1954 (*16*:3, 5). Intaglio airmail sets depicting aircraft and birds over Algerian scenery appeared in 1946 and 1949–53 (*16*:4). A high proportion of the post-war commemoratives and charity issues focused attention on the armed forces and the Foreign Legion. As in metropolitan France, annual issues marked the Day of the Stamp. Tunisian philately in this period was comparatively conservative – merely changes of colour and new values added to the 1926 series between 1945 and 1949 (*18*:34). Islamic and Punic antiquities provided the subject-matter of many of the special issues as well as the definitive series of 1950–53 (*18*:35) designed by M. Besson, who was also responsible for several of the commemoratives including the UPU series of 1949 (*18*:33).

The majority of French colonies in Africa ceased issuing their own stamps when the general series of French West Africa was introduced in 1944. This grouping of colonies followed the precedent established in French Equatorial Africa in 1937. The distinctive definitives of the eight colonies in this region were replaced in 1945 by a series lithographed by De La Rue (*16*:36). A monochrome intaglio series of 1947–51 featured pictorial subjects from each of the component territories (*16*:37, 38), and multicolour intaglio designs were added in 1953 (*16*:39). In this case, a recess-printed series was adopted in 1946 (*16*:34), with additional values in two- or three-colour intaglio following in 1955–7. The former German colonies administered by France – Cameroun and Togo – were excluded from this grouping and both issued new intaglio definitives, in 1946 and 1947 respectively (*16*:21; *18*:29, 30). A new series was adopted in the outlying territory of the French Somali Coast in 1947, printed in two-colour photogravure by Vaugirard (*16*:35); and in the same year, for the island of Réunion, the same company produced a similar series with a matching set of postage-due labels (*17*:30, 31). In 1949 Réunion became a French overseas *département* and since then it has used contemporary French stamps surcharged in CFA (Colonies Françaises Africaines) currency (*17*:32). Vaugirard of Paris produced photogravure stamps for Madagascar in 1946–7. These were replaced by an intaglio series in 1952–5 (*17*:1, 2). The Comoro Islands, previously administered by Madagascar, became a separate colony in 1950 and introduced a recess-printed series of pictorials that year (*16*:22). From 1943 to 1951, France administered the Fezzan region of Libya. Joint issues for Fezzan and Ghadames appeared in 1946 (*16*:33), but distinctive stamps for each territory were introduced the following year (*16*:43). These were withdrawn at the end of 1951, when both districts were transferred to the kingdom of Libya.

Portuguese Colonies

Although the five Portuguese African territories abandoned the Ceres keyplate series after the war, their stamps continued to reflect a uniformity of policy laid down in Lisbon. Between 1946 and 1948 they all introduced pictorial definitives. For Angola, Cape Verde Islands and St. Thomas and Prince Islands they were lithographed at Oporto; for Mozambique they were typographed locally; and for Portuguese Guinea they were photogravure-printed by Courvoisier. Scenery provided the subjects for the issues of all of them (*16*:6; *17*:15) except St. Thomas and Prince, whose stamps depicted various native fruits. A more frankly thematic approach was developed in the early 1950s, and multicolour offset-lithography was used for sets of definitives that changed every two or three years. In this period, Cape Verde featured famous explorers and historical maps (*16*:20), Angola featured birds and animals (*16*:7), Mozambique featured fish, butterflies and maps (*17*:16–18), Guinea featured insects (*17*:28) and St. Thomas and Prince featured historic navigators

(*17*:37). The few commemoratives that appeared usually conformed to colonial omnibus designs, such as the stamps of 1948 honouring Our Lady of Fatima (*17*:27). Both Angola and Mozambique, however, issued a few pairs or singles marking local events and anniversaries (*16*:8).

Spanish Colonies

Although a number of general issues was made for Spanish West Africa in 1949–51 (*18*:23), both Ifni and Spanish Sahara continued to produce their own stamps in this period. An even greater degree of uniformity was evident in the stamps of the Spanish territories than in their Portuguese counterparts. Up to 1950, the majority of issues were designed by M. Bertuchi and printed by Rieusset of Barcelona in two-colour lithography or photogravure. Thereafter, monochrome photogravure definitives with portraits of General Franco inset were produced by the Government Printing Works in Madrid (*18*:19, 23). Guinea, Ifni and Sahara released special sets at regular intervals, the great majority being for child welfare (*18*:22) and Colonial Stamp Day (*16*:44; *18*:20). Wildlife and native types provided the bulk of the subject matter in these sets. Curiously enough, there was no attempt to apply the concept of omnibus issues to the Spanish colonies – not even in cases where a subject could be regarded as relevant to them all. Thus Sahara alone issued stamps in 1953 to mark the 75th anniversary of the Royal Geographical Society of Spain (*18*:21).

The territory of Cape Juby was incorporated in Spanish Sahara in 1950 and discontinued its own stamps, which latterly had consisted of overprints on the issues of the Spanish zone of Morocco (*16*:19).

Egypt

Various denominations were added to the Farouk series of 1944, and the pictorial series of 1939–46 was updated by substituting a more mature portrait of the king. An airmail series with the king's portrait inset appeared in 1947 (*16*:26). The expansionist policy of King Farouk reached its height in 1952 when he proclaimed himself King of Egypt and the Sudan, and ordinary and airmail stamps were released in January 1952 with a two-line overprint in Arabic to signify his change of title (*16*:27). This new-found imperialism failed to assuage discontent at home, however, and Farouk was overthrown by a military coup in July of the same year. In June 1953 Egypt became a republic, and the Farouk definitives – with or without the Sudan overprint – were issued with parallel bars obliterating the royal features (*16*:28). Distinctive republican definitives featuring soldiers and workers were released in 1953–4 (*16*:29, 31).

The fact that King Farouk was a keen philatelist may have had some bearing on the high quality of Egyptian stamp production – definitives and commemoratives of this period being printed in photogravure by the Survey Department in Cairo (*16*:24, 25).

Ethiopia

A set of Red Cross stamps – printed in photogravure by Courvoisier and intended for release in 1936 but postponed because of the Italian invasion – was released in 1945 overprinted in Amharic and Roman lettering to signify victory. Thereafter, Ethiopian stamps were recess-printed in England by Bradbury Wilkinson (*16*:32) or De La Rue – a curious exception being a set of 1947 in memory of President Roosevelt produced by the Wright Bank Note Company of Philadelphia. For many years the status of this series (in intaglio combined with letterpress or photogravure) was questioned, since only limited quantities were put on sale in Ethiopia and the remainder was handled by an American philatelic agency.

Apart from its lengthy pictorial series of 1947–55, Ethiopia issued several commemorative sets marking anniversaries of liberation and federation with the former Italian colony of Eritrea.

Liberia

In 1945 the Wright Bank Note Company secured the contract to print Liberian stamps and, with very few exceptions, all the stamps of this country have been produced in Philadelphia ever since. Although the majority within the immediate post-war decade were recess-printed, Wright pioneered more colourful designs by combining intaglio frames with photogravure or lithographed vignettes; but from 1953 onwards, offset-lithography alone was increasingly employed. Two other American firms – H. L. Peckmore and Son and the Jaffe & D'Arcy Litho Company of New York – also printed stamps for Liberia on occasion. Not surprisingly, many stamps of this period had a pronounced American appearance. Even the definitives of 1948–60 were modelled on the contemporary American pattern, with portraits of successive presidents.

Libya

In 1951 the independent kingdom of Libya was reconstituted out of the British-occupied territories of Cyrenaica and Tripolitania and the French-held areas of Fezzan and Ghadames. Stamps of these territories were overprinted 'LIBYA' (*16*:49) pending the introduction of a series in April 1952 portraying King Idris (*16*:50). No commemoratives appeared in this period.

Morocco

Prior to 1956, Morocco was divided into two protectorates under French and Spanish control and stamps in the prevailing colonial patterns were issued in each zone. Thus the majority of stamps used in the French zone were recess-printed from dies engraved by French artists such as Gandon. In the early post-war period they were produced by Lugat of Casablanca (*17*:6), but the definitives of 1951–4 were printed in Paris (*17*:7). The rather monotonous appearance of the Spanish issues resulted from the fact that from 1928 onwards they had all been designed by M. Bertuchi and lithographed by Rieusset, usually with red frames and small rectangular vignettes (*17*:8, 9). An exception was made in the case of the Spanish post office in the international zone of Tangier (*17*:10), for which the stamps of 1948–51 were recess-printed in Madrid.

In the post-war period, British stamps were overprinted for use at British post offices. Three separate issues were made: those with the overprint 'MOROCCO AGENCIES' alone, primarily for use on parcels; those with an additional surcharge in Spanish currency, used in the Spanish zone; and those with an overprint for use in Tangier (*17*:11–14). Definitive and commemorative stamps were issued in this manner.

South Africa

In 1945 the pre-war pictorial definitives, temporarily replaced by the wartime 'bantam' series, were revived. The desire to save paper by reducing the size of the stamps – which had inspired the bantams – continued after the war with the appearance of a greatly reduced $1\frac{1}{2}$-pence in 1948 and a reduced version of the 2-pence in 1950 (*18*:3). Changes in postal rates in 1953 necessitated the release of three additional denominations, and these were in entirely new designs (*18*:12). This was the prelude to a series devoted to wildlife, issued in October 1954 (*18*:14).

In the immediate post-war period, stamps continued to appear in Afrikaans and English pairs (*18*:1–6); but from the bilingual Voortrekker series of 1949 onwards (*18*:7) Afrikaans and English appeared on each stamp. For the silver wedding stamps of 1948 (*18*:4), silver metallic ink was incorporated in the design – a novel feature at that time.

Very few commemoratives were issued in the early 1950s. A set of five in 1952 marked the tercentenary of the landing of Van Riebeeck (*18*:8). Two of these stamps were subsequently overprinted 'SATISE' or 'SADIPU', the initials of the South African Tercentenary International Stamp Exhibition in the two languages (*18*:9). The centenaries of the first stamps of the Cape of Good Hope in 1953 and the Orange Free State in 1954 were celebrated by pairs of stamps in each instance (*18*:11, 13).

South African stamps overprinted 'SWA' were used in South West Africa until 1954, when a distinctive definitive series was released. Printed in Pretoria, the stamps (*17*:46) had a marked affinity with the contemporary South African series. Overprinted stamps also served as commemoratives (*17*:44); but a distinctive set of five celebrated the coronation in 1953 (*17*:45).

Sudan

The 'camel postman' designs of 1898 to 1940 were revived in 1948 with a slightly different inscription. Such was the obsession with this long-lived design that it formed the basis for the three commemorative sets issued between 1948 and 1954 (*18*:25). An intaglio airmail series featuring scenery and landmarks appeared in 1950, followed by a letterpress definitive set the following year (*18*:24, 26). Different vignettes were used for each denomination, but the celebrated camel postman retained place of honour on the top value. Having lost the contract to the Indian Security Press during the war, De La Rue regained their monopoly of Sudanese stamps in 1948.

North America

Canada

A definitive series with the theme of reconversion to peace was issued in September 1946, replacing the 'war effort' series of 1942. The new series emphasised aspects of rural industry and scenery and included a 7-cent airmail stamp featuring Canada geese in flight (*19*:6). The lower values of the war effort series – depicting King George VI in various military uniforms – remained on sale until 1949, with semi-imperforate coil versions appearing in 1948. Civilian portraits of the king from photographs by Dorothy Wilding were used for a series of low values issued in November 1949. The colours of the 2-cent and 4-cent stamps were changed in 1951, but a series of stamps in the original colours was released in January 1950 with the inscription 'POSTES POSTAGE' omitted (*19*:13, 14). The Peace Reconversion series of pictorials was replaced piecemeal between March 1950 and November 1953, beginning with a 50-cent stamp showing oil wells (*19*:15). The 10-cent 'drying furs' stamp of October broke new ground with a design that dispensed with the customary ornate frame (*19*:16). In contrast, the 'fisherman' dollar stamp (*19*:17) of February 1951 had an elaborate framework of fishing nets and marine life. The 20-cent stamp of April 1952 and the 50-cent stamp of November 1953 developed the theme of products and industries and featured wood-pulp and textiles respectively (*19*:24, 35). A Canada goose was the motif of the airmail stamp of 1952 (*19*:26), and a dollar stamp in the now standard frameless style was introduced in February 1953 (*19*:29). The accession of Queen Elizabeth II led to the replacement of the low denominations in May 1953 by a series portraying the Queen – from a photograph by Karsh of Ottawa (*19*:33). The great outcry at the unflattering likeness on these stamps and on the coronation stamp issued a month later (*19*:34) led to the adoption in 1954 of a more satisfactory design for the definitives (*19*:36), based on a photograph by Dorothy Wilding.

Two types of occasional stamps, issued from time to time to augment the permanent range, were introduced in this period. In June 1951, stamps portraying Sir Robert Borden and William L. Mackenzie King (*19*:18, 19) formed the first part of a series devoted to former Prime Ministers. The second part, portraying Sir John Abbott and Alexander Mackenzie (*19*:27, 28), appeared in November 1952; and the third part, showing Sir John Thompson and Sir Mackenzie Bowell (*19*:40, 41), was issued in November 1954. National Wild Life Week, held annually in April, was marked by stamps featuring Canadian fauna – the first series, showing polar bear, moose and bighorn sheep, was released in 1953. It was followed by a set depicting walrus, beaver and gannet (*19*:30–32, 37–39).

Few commemoratives, in the strict sense, were issued in this decade. With the exception of a set of four marking the centenary of the first Canadian stamps (*19*:20–22), they were limited to single stamps. Two appeared in 1947 – one celebrating the centenary of the birth of Alexander Graham Bell and the other marking the 80th anniversary of the Confederation (*19*:7, 8). An allegorical approach was adopted for both – the anniversary stamp symbolising the advent of Canadian citizenship. Canada was one of the two Commonwealth countries that issued a stamp in honour of the wedding of Princess Elizabeth (*19*:11) in 1948. The centenary of responsible government was celebrated by a stamp of 1948 depicting the parliament building in Ottawa flanked by profiles of Queen Victoria and King George VI (*19*:9). A novel approach was adopted the following year by selecting a view of Cabot's ship *Matthew* for a stamp marking the entry of Newfoundland into the Confederation (*19*:10). A stamp of 1949 commemorated the bicentenary of Halifax, Nova Scotia, with the reproduction of a painting by C. W. Jeffries showing the foundation of the city (*19*:12). In 1951 Canada became the first country to portray the Duke of Edinburgh, on a stamp marking the royal visit of that year (*19*:23). The only other commemorative of this period was a 4-cent stamp of July 1952 marking the eighteenth International Red Cross Conference in Toronto – the first Canadian stamp printed in two-colour recess (*19*:25).

All Canadian stamps of this period were recess-printed by the Canadian Bank Note Company of Ottawa and incorporated the date of issue in minute figures concealed in the design.

Greenland

The unavailability of stamps of the 1939 series printed in Denmark during the war, resulted in a series in two-colour intaglio being produced by the American Bank Note Company and released in February 1945. The vignettes featured Arctic scenes and a portrait of King Christian X of Denmark (*19*:42). Later in the year, this series was overprinted to celebrate the liberation of Denmark from Nazi rule. A series featuring King Frederick IX on the low values and the Arctic vessel *Gustav Holm* on the high values (*19*:43), designed by Viggo Bang, was released between August 1950 and October 1959.

Newfoundland

The last of the colonies of British North America, Newfoundland continued to issue its own stamps until it joined the Canadian Confederation in April 1949. In the last remaining years of its philatelic career, Newfoundland produced three new stamps: a temporary 2-cent surcharge on the 30-cent value in 1946 and two commemoratives in 1947 – one marking Princess Elizabeth's twenty-first birthday and the other marking the 450th anniversary of Cabot's discovery of the island. Both commemoratives were recess-printed by Waterlow and Sons (*19*:44–6).

St. Pierre and Miquelon

The Free French issues of 1942–6 – photogravure-printed by Harrison and Sons – were superseded by a pictorial series, recess-printed at the Institut de Gravure in Paris (*19*:47), accompanied by a postage-due series featuring the coat of arms of the colony (*19*:48).

United Nations

For six years after its foundation, the United Nations Organisation's administrative offices in the United States used contemporary American stamps. The transfer of the Secretariat from Lake Success to New York City in 1951 was followed by the negotiation of a postal treaty with the United States providing for the operation of a UN post office in the new headquarters building. A series of distinctive stamps with designs prepared by an international team of artists was introduced in October 1951, recess-printed by De La Rue and Enschedé. The eight designs selected for the initial series of eleven ordinary and four airmail stamps (*22*:48–50) were carefully chosen to symbolise international co-operation, using motifs that would be readily significant to people all over the world. Considerable ingenuity was shown in cramming in inscriptions in the five principal languages – Chinese, English, Russian, French and Spanish. The first definitive series remained in use for more than a decade. Various printings were made of most denominations, resulting in shade variations and changes in the marginal inscriptions of the 10-cent value.

A pair of stamps was released on 10th December of each year to mark Human Rights Day; and in 1952 a pair appeared on 24th October, United Nations Day, to mark the 7th anniversary of the signing of the Charter. They featured the Veterans' War Memorial Building in San Francisco, venue of the first UN conference (*22*:51). United Nations Day was celebrated in 1954 by two stamps depicting the Palais des Nations, the UN headquarters in Geneva. Olav Mathiesen designed two stamps in April 1953 focusing attention on the international refugee problem and a further pair in October 1953 publicising technical assistance for undeveloped areas (*22*:52). Other stamps in this period paid tribute to various agencies of the United Nations, including the Universal Postal Union in 1953, the Food and Agricultural Organisation and the International Labour Organisation, both in 1954. With the exception of some definitives and the 7th anniversary pair of 1952, produced by the American Bank Note Company, the United Nations stamps of this period were recess-printed by De La Rue.

United States of America

The end of the Second World War brought no change in American philatelic policy. The presidential definitive series, introduced in 1938, remained in use throughout the immediate post-war decade and was only gradually superseded by a new series from 1954 onwards (*22*:22–48). The presidential element continued to be strong, with portraits of Washington, Jefferson, Lincoln, Monroe, Theodore Roosevelt, Wilson and Benjamin Harrison dominating the lower values. By a tradition dating back to the first American stamps in 1847, Benjamin Franklin was included in this series; but other famous Americans of the revolutionary period – John Jay, Paul Revere, John Marshall, Patrick Henry and Alexander Hamilton – appeared on the higher denominations. As concessions to the South and to 'women's lib', the 30-cent and 50-cent stamps portrayed the Confederate general, Robert E. Lee and the pioneer of women's rights, Susan B. Anthony. The Statue of Liberty appeared on three denominations. On the 3-cent stamp and in the original version of the 8-cent stamp the torch divided the inscription 'U.S. POSTAGE', but the 8-cent stamp was redrawn in 1958 (*22*:33) so that the torch appeared below the inscription. This amended version was used for the 11-cent value adopted in 1961 (*22*:37). Although strictly outside this period, the 8-cent stamp featuring General Pershing belongs to this series and is included here (*22*:34). Stylistically, it marked a departure from the heavy backgrounds associated with the series of 1938 and continued in the series of 1954 and foreshadowed the abandonment of both frame and background, which were features of many of the definitives of 1965–8.

Seven denominations of the 1954 series depicted famous buildings or monuments: the Palace of the Governors at Santa Fé, 1¼-cent; Mount Vernon, 1½-cent; the obelisk on Bunker Hill, 2½-cent; the Hermitage, 4½-cent; the Alamo, 9-cent; Independence Hall, 10-cent; and Jefferson's home, Monticello, 20-cent (*22*:22, 23, 25, 28, 35, 36, 40). Several values from 1-cent to 25-cent were issued in coil form, with vertical or horizontal imperforate sides (*22*:22, 25).

Very few commemorative stamps had appeared during the war – a notable exception being the lengthy series devoted to the flags of the oppressed nations – but at the beginning of 1945 a more liberal policy was adopted. An interesting precedent was established in April of that year, with a 5-cent stamp marking the United Nations Conference on International Organisation held in San Francisco (*20*:1). This was the first American commemorative to adopt a non-figurative design, using instead a quotation of three lines by Franklin D. Roosevelt, set in Gothic dark-face lettering. At the time of the stamp's production, Roosevelt was still alive. The inclusion of his name beneath the quotation would therefore have broken the ban on philatelic tribute to living Americans (the sole exception having been the Lindbergh airmail stamp of 1927). But Roosevelt died on 12th April 1945 – a fortnight before the stamp was released.

Following the tradition established after the death of Warren G. Harding in 1923, mourning stamps were released on various dates between 27th June 1945 and 30th January 1946. The lower denominations featured Roosevelt's residences: the family seat at Hyde Park (*20*:3), the 'Little White House' at Warm Springs, Georgia, where he had died (*20*:4) and the White House in Washington. The 5-cent stamp pre-paying the foreign-letter rate featured a terrestrial globe inscribed with the Four Freedoms – of speech and religion, from want and fear – with which Roosevelt had summed up America's war aims and which had become the initial principles of the United Nations Organisation.

As a tribute to the armed forces, five stamps – all of the 3-cent inland rate though printed in different colours – were released between July 1945 and January 1946. The first to appear honoured the Marines, and showed the raising of the Stars and Stripes on Mount Surabachi during the ferocious battle for Iwo Jima (*20*:2). The horizontal stamp commemorating the Army showed United States troops in procession past the Arc de Triomphe, in Paris, with an escort of six bombers overhead (*20*:5). By contrast, the Navy commemorative featured an informal group of sailors in summer uniform (*20*:6). The Coast Guard stamp bore the dates of the service, 1790–1945, and showed two landing-craft with a supply ship in the background (*20*:7). The Merchant Marine stamp depicted a Liberty ship unloading cargo, with the caption 'PEACE AND WAR' (*20*:11). To this group can be added the stamp of May 1948 honouring the four chaplains of the U.S.S. *Dorchester*, who went down with their ship.

A 5-cent internal airmail stamp depicting a DC-4 Skymaster was released in September 1946. The following year a smaller version of this stamp was produced – the original vignette being truncated and the inscriptions reduced (*20*:14, 17). When the rate was increased to 6 cents in 1949, the design was redrawn in this denomination. Higher denominations, for overseas airmail, appeared between 1947 and 1952 and featured aircraft over the Pan-American Union building, the Statue of Liberty, the San Francisco–Oakland Bay Suspension Bridge, and Diamond Head in Honolulu (*20*:26–28; *21*:37). Five of the commemorative issues within this period took the form of airmail stamps, including a set of three for the 75th anniversary of the UPU in 1949 and in the same year, a 6-cent stamp marking the 46th anniversary of the Wright Brothers' first flight (*21*:13, 14, 16).

By the end of 1954 the United States had brought out just over a hundred commemoratives and special issues. With the exception of the Roosevelt, Armed Forces and UPU sets already mentioned, there was only one multiple issue – a set of four stamps released between June and November 1950 to mark the 150th anniversary of the national capital (*21*:19, 22, 25, 27). Three of the stamps featured buildings associated with the executive, judicial and legislative branches of government. The fourth depicted the statue of Freedom on the Capitol Dome. All other issues consisted of single stamps, with the exception of a miniature sheet which honoured the Centenary International Philatelic Exhibition of 1947 by reproducing the first American stamps (*20*:21). Apart from the airmail issues, these commemoratives invariably prepaid the inland letter rate and were aimed at uniting and educating the people of the United States. Because of this didactic element – a characteristic of American stamps to this day – the obscure symbolism of British stamps of this period was carefully avoided. The message conveyed by American stamps was nothing if not explicit, though the results were not always satisfactory from the aesthetic point of view.

Eighteen stamps were directly concerned with the commemoration of celebrated men and women of the United States, and many other people appeared as subsidiary subjects. The stamp honouring politician Alfred E. Smith (*20*:8) used the small format of the definitive series, but the majority of such stamps adopted the larger size pioneered in the Famous Americans series of 1940. The stamps honouring Thomas A. Edison, William White, Joel Chandler Harris, Edgar Allan Poe and George Washington Carver actually perpetuated the symbolism incorporated in the framework of the original Famous Americans sets (*20*:15; *21*:7, 15). Analogously, the scales of justice appeared on the stamp commemorating Chief Justice Stone (*20*:35) and an olive branch was worked into the design of the stamp honouring labour leader Samuel Gompers (*21*:18). Although this format was retained for the stamp of 1954 honouring the inventor George Eastman (*22*:18), a plain background, devoid of ornament, was adopted – and this was to become a standard pattern for other commemoratives in the next decade.

Many of the stamps specifically honouring famous Americans, however, used the horizontal format associated with most commemorative stamps, the larger area permitting the inclusion of a quotation (*20*:18) or a symbolic motif connected with the person. The stamp of 1948 honouring Francis Scott Key, who wrote the words of 'The Star-Spangled Banner', had his portrait flanked by the original and modern American flags and, for good measure, minuscule pictures of his home and Fort McHenry, where the national anthem was composed (*20*:33). Subsequent issues of this type were not so ambitious. Clara Barton, Juliette Gordon Low and Moina Michael – founders of the American Red Cross, the Girl Scouts and the Memorial Poppy – were the subjects of individual stamps in 1948, and the appropriate emblem was depicted in each case (*20*:38; *21*:4, 5). The twin-flags motif was applied to a stamp of 1952 honouring Lafayette (*21*:40). In the George S. Patton stamp of 1953 (*22*:13) the general's portrait was integrated with a vignette featuring tanks, the dual purpose of this stamp – honouring Patton and the Armoured Forces – being explained in the twin captions. But one stamp in this category – the 3-cent stamp of January 1952 marking the bicentenary of the birth of Betsy Ross – did not conform at all with the portrait commemoratives. Instead, it featured the reproduction of a painting by C. H. Weisgerber of Betsy Ross

with the Flag Committee (George Washington, Robert Morris and George Ross) examining the first American flag, which she sewed at her Philadelphia home.

Within this decade no fewer than seventeen stamps celebrated anniversaries of statehood. Inevitably, the designs appear rather stereotyped. Variations on the theme of the state flag were used in the case of stamps honouring Texas and Iowa (*20*:9, 12); the state capitol or some other historic building was featured on the stamps commemorating Tennessee, Indiana, Wisconsin and Colorado (*21*:31); state seals and maps appeared on the stamps for Mississippi, Iowa, Wisconsin, Ohio, and Washington (*20*:25, 29; *21*:24; *22*:5, 6). But by far the most popular subject was the covered wagon, which graced the stamps of Utah, Oregon, Minnesota, California and Kansas (*20*:22, 36; *21*:8, 26; *22*:17). The penchant for covered wagons also extended to other commemoratives, including the Swedish Settlers, Fort Kearny and Gadsden Purchase stamps of 1948–53 (*20*:31, 40; *22*:15). The most original designs among the statehood commemoratives, however, were the log cabin motif for Nevada in 1951 and the statue of the sower for Nebraska in 1954 (*21*:29).

An important group of special issues centred on various sections of the community. In the aftermath of war it was understandable that stamps should honour Discharged Veterans, in 1946, and Gold Star Mothers, in 1948 – the latter being for those who had lost sons or daughters on active service (*20*:10; *21*:1); but the immediacy of many of the other stamps in this group was less apparent. Sir Luke Fildes' painting 'The Doctor' was reproduced on a stamp of 1947 honouring the medical profession (*20*:20). During 1948 the vogue of such stamps reached its peak, with issues honouring American Women, American Youth, the poultry industry, volunteer firemen and the American Turners' Society (*20*:34, 39; *21*:2).

Subsequent issues marked anniversaries of the Bankers' Association, the Chemical Society, and the Bar Association, and paid tribute to railroad engineers, the Boy Scouts, 4-H clubs and Future Farmers of America (*21*:17, 20, 23, 32, 34, 36; *22*:9, 11). No profession was too humble for philatelic recognition. The classic example of this genre was the newspaperboys issue of 1952, with its verbose caption that typified the spirit of the period: 'In recognition of the important service rendered their communities and their nation by America's newspaperboys.' Even the satchel depicted was emblazoned with a slogan – 'Busy Boys – Better Boys'; and the torch of free enterprise was included for good measure (*22*:2). The women's services and the National Guard were honoured by stamps of 1952–3, following in the tradition of the armed forces stamps of 1945.

Only six stamps and a miniature sheet, already mentioned, were issued for current events. In view of the many important occasions of the decade, the choice of subjects is rather surprising. The inauguration of the Everglades National Park in 1947, the dedication of Mount Palomar Observatory in 1948, the first gubernatorial election in Puerto Rico in 1949, and the opening of Theodore Roosevelt's home to the public in 1953 accounted for four of these stamps (*20*:30, 37; *21*:10; *22*:10). The other two marked the final encampment of the Grand Army of the Republic in 1949 and the last reunion of the United Confederate Veterans in 1951. Similar designs in different colours were used (*21*:12, 28).

The largest category of special issues concerned historic anniversaries and reflected a wide range of events and interests. Centenaries were naturally the commonest pretext, drawing on the rich material of the pioneer days. The Santa Fé expedition of Stephen Watts Kearny, the Swedish settlers of the Middle West, the discovery of gold in California and the five civilised tribes of Oklahoma (*20*:16, 24, 31) augmented the statehood issues. The stamp marking the centennial of Fort Bliss (*21*:6) had a guided missile as its central motif, but the triangular surround contained a microscopic cavalcade representing a century of history. The use of twin motifs to produce a 'then and now' subject was applied to a stamp of 1950 showing Kansas City in pioneer days and modern times (*21*:21), and the same device was used for the stamp of 1951 to commemorate the 250th anniversary of Cadillac's landing in Detroit (*21*:30). Other centennial stamps honoured the Smithsonian Institution, friendship with Canada (*20*:13, 32), American engineering, and Commodore Perry's visit to Japan (*22*:1, 8). The bicentenary of Washington and Lee University in 1949 and Columbia University in 1954 resulted in stamps (21:9; 22:16); and the 'then and now' device, with one motif superimposed on the other, was utilised in the stamp of 1953 celebrating the tercentenary of New York (22:14). A map design was used for the stamp marking the tercentenary of Annapolis (21:11).

Not all stamps were concerned with round centenaries. The 85th anniversary of Lincoln's Gettysburg Address in 1948, the 150th anniversaries of the frigate *Constitution* in 1947, the Louisiana Purchase in 1953 and the Lewis and Clark Expedition in 1954, the 125th anniversary of the Baltimore–Ohio Railroad in 1952 and the 175th anniversary of the Battle of Brooklyn in 1951 were appropriately commemorated (20:23; 21:33, 35; 22:7, 19). Golden jubilees included those of the New York City Council in 1948, the American Automobile Association in 1952, the Columbia Basin reclamation and American aviation in 1953 (21:36, 39). Lesser anniversaries included the silver jubilee of the Mount Rushmore National Park (21:41) and the third anniversary of NATO (21:38), both in 1952. Only two events of truly international importance were commemorated in this period – the quingentenary of Gutenberg's invention of printing (22:3) and the International Red Cross (22:4), both in 1952. All of these stamps were recess-printed at the US Bureau of Engraving and Printing, the last-named having the Red Cross emblem inserted lithographically.

Central America

Mexico
Having produced numerous lengthy commemorative issues before and during the war, Mexico settled down in the late 1940s and issued relatively few stamps in this period. The last of the long sets consisted of six ordinary and five airmail stamps honouring the United Nations in 1946 (23:1).

The practice of issuing ordinary and airmail stamps in commemorative sets continued throughout this decade, but the number of stamps in each set was drastically reduced and they appeared far less frequently than before. A set of 1947, marked the centenary of the first United States stamps and also contrived to honour Presidents Roosevelt and Washington, whose portraits were included in the designs (23:2). Historic anniversaries commemorated, included the quatercentenary of Zacatecas in 1946, centenaries of battles in the 1847 campaign in 1947, and the bicentenary of the birth of Hidalgo in 1953. Stamps of 1950–53 marked the opening of the Mexican section of the Pan-American Highway and the Mexico–Campêche railroad (23:3, 4), and three stamps of 1954 publicised the Central American and Caribbean Games.

The airmail and ordinary series of 1934 were reissued in 1947 with a new watermark 'GOBIERNO MEXICANO' in a multiple pattern – but entirely new sets of ordinary and airmail stamps appeared in 1950 (23:5, 6). From 1953, this series was reissued on paper with the 'MEX-MEX' watermark. Compulsory tax stamps (23:7) raised money for the literacy campaign.

British Honduras
No changes were made in the Georgian series apart from the release of the 2-cent stamp with a different gauge of perforation in 1947. An Elizabethan series, recess-printed by Waterlow and Sons, appeared in September 1953 (23:9). The same firm printed a set of six stamps in 1949 celebrating the 150th anniversary of the Battle of St. George's Cay (23:8). All the other commemoratives conformed to the colonial omnibus designs.

Canal Zone
A new definitive series, issued between 1946 and 1949, continued the tradition established in the series of 1928–40 of portraying Americans associated with the Panama Canal (23:10). An airmail series featuring a map of the Western Hemisphere was introduced in 1951 (23:11), various denominations being added in later years.

Only three commemorative issues were made in this period – singles marking the silver jubilee of the Canal Zone Biological Area in 1948 and paying tribute to the West Indian labourers on the Canal in 1951, and a 1949 set of four commemorating the centenary of the gold rush of 1849.

Costa Rica
The lengthy ordinary and airmail series, recess-printed by the American Bank Note Company and introduced in 1942, continued in use throughout the first post-war decade. Many denominations were added between 1945 and 1948, especially to the airmail series (23:13). A series devoted to national industries was introduced in 1954, produced by De La Rue, with photogravure vignettes and intaglio frames (23:15). The stamp of 1945 marking the diamond jubilee of the Costa Rican Red Cross portrayed two English nurses – Florence Nightingale and Edith Cavell (23:12). A set of thirteen stamps by the American Bank Note Company paid tribute to Franklin D. Roosevelt in 1947 (23:13).

Several lengthy sets were issued in 1948–50, including one marking the National Agricultural, Cattle and Industries Fair (23:14). The majority of these commemoratives were recess-printed by Waterlow and Sons (23:14, 15).

El Salvador
A definitive series portraying famous Salvadoreans was produced by the American Bank Note Company and released in 1947 (23:16). The stamps were revalued in 1952–3 by means of surcharges.

Three lengthy commemorative sets appeared in this period and provided a wider range of denominations than the definitive series. The most elaborate set, released in 1948 to mark the third anniversary of the death of Roosevelt, depicted portraits and scenes from his career (23:17). The revolution of 1948 and the new constitution of 1950 were celebrated by a lengthy set printed in two-colour photogravure by Courvoisier (23:18). Latterly, several sets were lithographed locally by L. Dreikorn, including the Marti centenary series and a set honouring the 132nd anniversary of independence, both in 1953 (23:19, 20).

Guatemala
The majority of the stamps up to 1950 were recess-printed at the National Printing Works, including the definitive series of 1945 portraying the writer Payo Enriquez de Rivera (23:21). These stamps were reissued in 1952 with a commemorative inscription added to the design. The map stamp of 1939 was reissued in 1948 with the date overprinted (23:23).

Among the commemoratives produced locally in this period were a 1945 pair celebrating the first anniversary of the 1944 revolution (23:22) and a set of five in 1949 honouring Bartolome de Las Casas, the Apostle of the Indians (23:24). Foreign printers were employed from 1950 onwards. The Austrian State Press produced a tourist propaganda series in 1950 and commemoratives honouring state schools, in 1951, and the national anthem, in 1953 (23:25, 27, 28); and the Wright Bank Note Company used two-colour intaglio for their production of the Central American Games issue of February 1950 (23:26).

Honduras
Among the relatively few stamps issued by Honduras in this decade were two miniature sheets, of October 1945, overprinted to celebrate victory. The pictorial definitives of 1946 included stamps portraying the late President Roosevelt and celebrating victory over Japan. A lengthy series of 1949 marked the inauguration of President Galves and featured scenery and portraits (23:29). Waterlow and Sons recess-printed a long set for the quingentenary of Isabella the Catholic in 1952. Many obsolete commemoratives were revalidated by means of an overprint 'HABILITADO' or were overprinted to commemorate some other event.

Nicaragua
At the end of the war, Nicaragua embarked on a policy of lengthy sets – both ordinary and airmail – released at frequent intervals. Several of these had intaglio frames and photogravure vignettes printed by the Wright Bank Note Company or Waterlow and Sons. Thirteen stamps of 1946 commemorated Roosevelt and featured scenes from his career (23:30). The most ambitious set consisted of twenty-four triangular pictorials released in 1947 (23:31). The tenth

World Amateur Baseball Championships in 1949 were marked by no fewer than twenty-six stamps plus a matching number of miniature sheets, each containing one denomination in a block of four. The designs showed sports that were irrelevant to the pretext for the issue (23:32). Lengthy sets marked the 75th anniversary of the UPU in 1950 and the quingentenary of Isabella the Catholic in 1952 (23:33, 34), both recess-printed by De La Rue. The same printer adopted the combined process of intaglio and photogravure for a series of 1953 portraying Nicaraguan presidents in hexagonal or octagonal frames (23:35). Other long sets of the early 1950s included those commemorating the United Nations and the Nicaraguan Air Force (23:36, 37).

Panama
Although a few stamps were lithographed locally at the office of the newspaper *La Estrella de Panama*, the majority of the prolific issues of this period were produced by Waterlow and Sons. Individual sets were also recess-printed by the American Bank Note Company, the Security Bank Note Company and De La Rue (23:38–40). The definitive series of 1942 was used throughout this period, and new values were added to the set up to 1957 (23:38). Apart from the virtually statutory sets marking Roosevelt in 1947 and Isabella the Catholic in 1952 (23:40), sets paid tribute to Cervantes in 1948 and the Cuban scientist, Carlos Finlay in 1950. Lengthy sets marked the 45th anniversary of independence in 1948, the golden jubilee of the Colon Fire Brigade in 1948, and the 50th anniversary of independence in 1953. Obsolete definitives were overprinted in 1949 in honour of the UPU anniversary (23:39).

South America

Argentina
The series of 1936–7, lithographed at the Mint in Buenos Aires, was reissued in 1945–7 on unwatermarked paper, but the 1-peso stamp (24:13) was redrawn in 1951 to include the sector of Antarctica to which Argentina laid claim. Preoccupation with the polar regions in the post-war period was reflected in the stamps from 1947 onwards. There was one marking the 43rd anniversary of the first Argentinian polar mail in 1947, and there were stamps commemorating the rescue of the polar ship *Antarctic* by the *Uruguay* in 1953 and the golden jubilee of the Argentinian post office in the South Orkneys in 1954 (24:5, 17, 18). This was but one aspect of a three-sided war between Argentina, Chile and Britain, largely fought out in the stamp album (25:1; 27:34). The expansionist policy in Antarctica was the corner-stone of the Peronist régime.

Stamps with allegorical motifs celebrated the anniversaries of the 1945 revolution that brought Colonel Juan Peron to power (24:3) and his installation as president, but none of them bore his portrait. By contrast, a lengthy definitive series introduced shortly after the death of Eva Peron in 1952 bore her profile or portrait (24:15, 16). The initial printings did not bear her name, but in November 1952 stamps were issued with her name inscribed above the country name. The design of the peso values was used as the basis of stamps released in 1954 to mark the second anniversary of her death (24:20).

The majority of commemorative issues in this period consisted of single stamps for which a symbolic interpretation was favoured (24:19), a more modern style being detected in the stamps from 1947 onwards (24:4, 6, 9–12). Pictorial stamps were issued to mark the centenary of the death of Rivadavia in 1945 (24:1), the jubilee of the frigate *Presidente Sarmiento* and the quatercentenary of Cervantes, both in 1947 (24:7, 10). A lengthy set of 1950 commemorated the centenary of the death of San Martin, whereas the death of Roosevelt had rated only a single stamp in 1946 (24:2). Allegory and realism were combined in the designs used for a series of 1951 marking the completion of the first Five-Year-Plan (24:14).

Bolivia
A higher proportion of Bolivian stamps than those of other Latin-American countries was produced locally. In 1951, however, the

Security Bank Note Company of the United States secured contracts to print two lengthy sets commemorating the quatercentenary of La Paz and the South American tennis championships. Both issues were recess-printed, the latter bearing various sports motifs other than tennis (24:23, 25). All the other stamps of this period were lithographed in La Paz, four different firms being involved. The Offset Company produced the series of 1946 for the centenary of the national anthem (24:21); the Don Bosco Printing Works printed the Pan-American Motor Race and Catholic Education Congress stamps of 1948; La Papelera S.A. produced the Lloyd-Aero Boliviano series of 1950 and the First National Agronomical Congress pair of 1954 (24:22, 26); and Lito-Unidas printed several sets including the four stamps for the quingentenary of Isabella the Catholic in 1952 (24:24).

Brazil
The small-format definitive series of 1941 – featuring allegories of commerce and industry on the low values and portraits on the higher denominations – continued until 1954, with a change of watermark in 1945–6 and inscriptions in the reformed currency of centavos and cruzeiros in 1947–54 (24:27, 28). Letterpress was used for the allegorical designs and intaglio for the 1941–54 portraits.

During the immediate post-war decade Brazil produced numerous special issues, ranging from singles to short sets of five or six (24:29, 35). A set of five with motifs symbolising glory, victory, co-operation, tranquillity and peace was prepared early in 1945 and actually released on 8th May – the first of the Allied victory stamps (24:30). Two months later, a series lithographed in multicolour celebrated the return of the Brazilian Expeditionary Force. The only other sets of this length were those commemorating the fifth Ibero–American Postal Union Congress in 1946, the inauguration of President Dutra in 1947, the 150th anniversary of the birth of the Duke of Caxias in 1953 and the quatercentenary of Sao Paulo in 1953 and 1954 (24:38, 39).

More than fifty stamps honouring individuals encompassed a wide range of subjects. Not surprisingly, the bulk of these were Brazilians; but a comparatively large number of them were only indirectly connected with Brazil. They ranged from Ludwig Zamenhof, on a stamp of 1945 marking the tenth Brazilian Esperanto Congress, to Dr. S. Hahnemann, on a stamp of 1954 for the first World Congress of Homoeopathy. Stamps of 1947 portraying the presidents of Chile and the United States, and commemorating their visits to Brazil, revived a practice that had begun in 1920 with the state visit of King Albert of the Belgians. In this period, seven foreign heads of state were thus honoured. Brazilian participation in the spate of Roosevelt commemoratives was to be expected (24:33) but in view of the traditional rivalry of Spain and Portugal in the Americas, the stamp of 1952 for the quingentenary of Isabella the Catholic was a less obvious choice. Other commemoratives marked the anniversaries of Brazilians, including two members of the erstwhile royal family – Princess Isabel in 1946 and Dom Pedro II in 1952.

A quasi-symbolic style was adopted for most of the stamps commemorating anniversaries and current events such as the Industry Exhibition of 1948 (24:32), the World Cup football championship of 1950 and the Grape Festival of 1954, but scenic motifs were applied to many of the stamps honouring conferences such as the Rotary Congress of 1948 (24:31), the Inter-American Catholic Congress of 1951 and the Fourth World Conference of Young Baptists in 1953 (24:37). Obligatory tax stamps for the Leprosy Research Fund were introduced in 1954 (24:40).

British Guiana
Several stamps of the George V pictorial series were current until 1954, and changes in the gauge of perforation added variety to the continuing George VI series of 1938. In 1945, however, 2-dollar and 3-dollar values were introduced (24:41) – and even these late-comers were subject to changes of perforation in 1948–50. The Elizabethan series was released in December 1954 with several vignettes adapted from the previous issue but with up-dated frame designs and the introduction of several new subjects (24:42). Apart from the colonial omnibus sets, British Guiana produced no distinctive commemoratives in this period.

Chile

The pre-war system of three separate definitive sets continued in the post-war period. Stamps inscribed 'CORREOS DE CHILE' were used on internal surface mail, those additionally inscribed 'LINEA AEREA NACIONAL' were used on internal airmail, and those inscribed 'CORREO AEREO CHILE' were intended for overseas airmail. Numerous changes of colour and new values were added to the 1941 inland airmail set up to 1950, and from then until 1955 similar stamps, in new designs, were used (25:8). The 'industries and landscapes' ordinary series of 1938 also continued in use, augmented by stamps of 1948–54 portraying Bernardo O'Higgins (25:3, 4). The external air series of 1934 continued without change into the next decade. Several commemoratives of this period, however, were inscribed for external airmail use (25:6, 7, 9, 10).

The majority of special issues consisted of pairs or singles. In most cases, pairs were issued with one denomination intended for ordinary postage and the other for airmail (25:2). Two stamps appeared in 1947 for no other purpose than to underline Chilean claims to part of Antarctica (25:1). The most ambitious series consisted of twenty-five stamps in each of three values – 60-centavo, 2.60-peso and 3-peso – featuring Chilean flora and fauna, issued in 1948 to mark the centenary of Claude Gay's book on the subject. The silver jubilee of the national airline was marked by a 3-peso stamp in 1954 (25:11).

Colombia

A curious feature of Colombian philately was the regular issue of tiny stamps as a levy on correspondence for the construction of a new post office in Bogota. Various artists' impressions of the proposed building were featured on these obligatory stamps, which were released each year from 1939 to 1952 (25:13, 18, 19, 25). At various times they were converted for ordinary or airmail use by means of overprints (25:16, 22). Conversely, many obsolete commemorative stamps were transformed into tax stamps by overprinting them 'SOBRETASA'.

A definitive series portraying General Sucre was introduced in 1946 and supplemented later that year by a stamp featuring a map of South America (25:15). Stamps depicting scenery and landmarks and inscribed 'SOBREPORTE AEREO' were issued in 1945 for internal airmail (25:14). A 5-centavo stamp of 1947, depicting a coffee plant, was produced by Waterlow and Sons with an intaglio frame and a multicolour offset vignette (25:16). The same pattern was used later in the year by the American Bank Note Company for a series depicting Colombian orchids. In 1948, the 1941 airmail series for external mail was reissued in new colours.

Orchids formed the subject of the monochrome recess-printed series of 1950 in honour of the UPU (25:20). The majority of the special issues of the early 1950s were recess-printed by Waterlow (25:12, 17, 24), but De La Rue won the contract to print the lengthy airmail series of 1954 (25:23) and then produced intaglio sets for the jubilee of the academy of history and the tercentenary of the Senior College of Our Lady of the Rosary (25:27). Courvoisier produced photogravure sets, publicising the countryside in 1950 and commemorating the centenary of Manizales in 1952 (25:21, 22). De La Rue emulated the multicolour effects of their rivals by printing the airmail stamps of 1954 with an intaglio frame and multicolour offset vignette (25:28).

Ecuador

The choice of printer for post-war stamps was remarkably wide-ranging. Apart from the American Bank Note Company, Waterlow and Sons and De La Rue – who dominated Latin-American philately – stamps were recess-printed at the Institut de Gravure in Paris (25:34) and the Italian Government Printing Works in Rome, and photogravure-printed by Heraclio Fournier of Vitoria, Spain (25:35, 36). Despite these excellent contacts overseas, Ecuador had frequent recourse to an age-old Latin-American expedient – the overprinting or surcharging of obsolete stamps to revalidate them, or issuing commemoratives without the expense of producing new designs. On various occasions revenue and consular fee stamps were converted to postal duty by means of overprints (25:29, 30). These makeshifts seemed to indicate a chronic shortage of stamps in spite of the excellent intaglio series of 1947 (25:31, 32) produced by the

American Bank Note Company. Three 30-centavo stamps in different colours were lithographed at the National Printing Works in 1947 for use on official mail (25:33).

French Guiana

This territory was the last to issue a Free French definitive series, a set lithographed by De La Rue being released in 1945 (25:37). In March 1946 French Guiana became a French *département*, but it continued to issue its own stamps until 1949. An intaglio pictorial series with a matching postage-due set was released in June 1947 (25:38). Ordinary French stamps superseded this series in 1949.

Paraguay

Waterlow and Sons recess-printed a series of ordinary and airmail stamps released between November 1944 and the end of 1945 (25:39). Most denominations were reissued in September 1946 in new colours. A series portraying Marshal Lopez was produced by De La Rue in the same year and remained current for several years. A 5-centimo stamp depicting the arms of Paraguay was lithographed in 1946 – an adaptation of a design which, with variations, had been current since 1913. The arms design was subsequently used for a series of 1954. The very few commemoratives that appeared in this period invariably consisted of lengthy sets. A stamp from the series of 1947 marking the jubilee of the Archbishopric of Paraguay was surcharged two years later in aid of victims of the earthquake in Ecuador (25:41). Issues of 1948–52 publicised the 'Barefeet' political movement, the Columbus memorial lighthouse in the Dominican Republic (25:42) and the Paraguayan merchant fleet. Other sets, released between 1950 and 1954, commemorated Roosevelt (25:40), Isabella the Catholic, the aviator Pettirossi and the centenary of San Roque church. A series of ordinary and airmail stamps devoted to national heroes was lithographed locally in 1954 (25:43).

Peru

The definitive series of 1938, produced originally by Waterlow and Sons, was reprinted during 1945–7 by the Columbian Bank Note Company – the new printings identifiable by the marginal imprint (26:1). The contract reverted to Waterlow in 1949, who held it until 1951 and the stamps were reissued with their imprint but in new colours (26:3). These designs were subsequently adapted for an intaglio series of 1951 printed by the Institut de Gravure in Paris (26:5). An entirely new series, lithographed by De La Rue, was released gradually between 1952 and 1960 (26:8, 9); and this, too, was printed by other companies: by Enschedé of Holland in 1960, by De La Rue in new colours in 1962 and by the Austrian State Press during 1966–7. The various printings can be identified by the marginal imprints.

Few commemoratives appeared in the immediate post-war decade. On two occasions, stamps prepared for a specific purpose but not issued at the time, were later overprinted to commemorate other events: in 1947 for the First National Tourist Congress and in 1951 in belated commemoration of the 75th anniversary of the UPU (26:2, 7). The Institut de Gravure recess-printed a series in 1951 to mark the Fifth Pan-American Highways Congress, and De La Rue produced sets commemorating the quatercentenary of San Marco University in 1951 and the quingentenary of Isabella the Catholic in 1953 (26:6).

Obligatory stamps were issued between 1950 and 1954 to raise money for state education, the unemployed and the National Marian Eucharistic Congress fund (26:4).

Surinam

A series recess-printed by the American Bank Note Company was issued in 1945. The denominations up to 6 cents were pictorials with a profile of Queen Wilhelmina inset, and the higher values portrayed the queen alone (26:10). Standard Dutch designs, printed by Enschedé, were adopted in 1948 (26:11) and were superseded in 1951 by the omnibus designs portraying Queen Juliana. Three stamps of the 1930 airmail series surcharged with new values were issued in 1945, and the following year a further two were surcharged in aid of the anti-tuberculosis fund. Other semi-postals in this period consisted of sets in aid of the anti-leprosy, anti-cancer, child welfare and sports week funds. Two stamps were overprinted and surcharged in 1953 to raise money for victims of the Netherlands floods. A 27½-cent stamp of 1949 celebrated the inaugural flight between Paramaribo and Amsterdam, and a 15-cent stamp of 1954 commemorated the silver jubilee of Surinam Airlines.

Eleven stamps issued in 1953 to publicise the Colonial Exhibition in Paramaribo depicted scenery, native types and wildlife. Omnibus designs were used between 1948 and 1954 to celebrate the jubilee of Queen Wilhelmina, the coronation of Queen Juliana and the statute of the kingdom.

Uruguay

The small-format definitive series begun in 1941 was released in phases during this decade. The stamps, portraying the national hero Artigas, were lithographed by the National Press, whose imprint appeared in the margin. On the majority of stamps released up to 1950 the imprint appeared in the right bottom corner (26:12), but from 1949 onwards it appeared in the bottom centre (26:13). This series was supplemented from time to time by stamps portraying other historic figures (26:14). Between 1943 and 1948, small postal-tax stamps with an armorial design were overprinted to denote postage or airmail (26:17, 20). A distinctive airmail series featuring a four-engined aircraft was introduced in 1947 (26:18). Two stamps depicting the Santa Lucia Bridge were issued in 1948 as part of the permanent range (26:21) and occasional pictorials augmented the airmail series (26:15). The Artigas definitives were temporarily displaced by a pictorial series produced by Waterlow and Sons in 1948, of which the floral designs were printed in multicolour photogravure (26:29) and the other designs were printed in two-colour intaglio (26:30, 31).

Relatively few commemorative issues appeared in this period. Two stamps of the Rio Negro Dam series of 1937 were overprinted in 1946 to mark the inauguration of the dam (26:16). Lengthy sets commemorated the writer J. E. Rodo in 1948 and the centenary of the death of Artigas in 1952. Short sets marked the centenary of Montevideo University in 1949, the 75th anniversary of the UPU in 1952 and the fifth Ibero–American Postal Congress in 1953 – the last-named combined with homage to Franklin D. Roosevelt (26:22–28).

Venezuela

Unquestionably the most prolific of all the American countries in the immediate post-war decade, Venezuela reissued the sets of 1938 and 1940–44 in new colours in 1947–8. In addition, various obsolete stamps were surcharged with new values in the same period (26:32). A series of 1948, ostensibly commemorating the first anniversary of the Greater Colombia merchant marine (26:33), was retained as a definitive series. Various denominations were added in 1949–50.

The philatelic world was astounded when, in 1951, Venezuela began issuing an armorial series of ordinary and airmail stamps for each of the country's twenty-four provinces. Mercifully, no province issued the full range of thirty denominations; but the entire project, carried out between 1951 and 1954, represented the largest single contract undertaken by Courvoisier (26:40). Despite this, a lengthy series featuring the General Post Office in Caracas was printed in photogravure by Waterlow and Sons in 1953 with the inscription 'EE. UU. DE VENEZUELA' (United States of Venezuela), the inscription being amended in 1954 to 'REPUBLICA DE VENEZUELA' (26:38).

Long sets were issued to mark the sesquicentennial of General Sucre in 1945; the 110th anniversary of Venezuela's first participation in the Bogota Postal Convention in 1949; the 450th anniversary of the discovery of the American mainland by Columbus in 1949; the UPU anniversary, the protection of flora, the census of the Americas and the 450th anniversary of Ojeda's discovery of Lake Maracaibo, all in 1950; the transfer of the Bolivar statue to Central Park in New York, the quingentenary of Isabella the Catholic and the third Bolivarian Games (26:34–37). Thereafter, the spate of issues abated. Three stamps of the same value but of different sizes were issued in 1952–3 to celebrate the tercentenary of the Apparition of Our Lady of Coromoto (26:39), and relatively short sets of 1954 marked the centenary of the death of Rodriguez and the 10th Pan-American Games.

American Offshore Islands

Falkland Islands and Dependencies

A new denomination and various colour changes were introduced to the Georgian series between 1946 and 1949 (27:31, 32), but an entirely new series with a more up-to-date portrait of the king was released in 1952. The stamps were recess-printed by Waterlow and Sons in the post-war style that dispensed with formal framework and the portrait cartouche (27:33). The only commemoratives of this period were the standard omnibus sets of the crown colonies.

The escalation of the quarrel with Argentina and Chile over Antarctica resulted in the issue, in 1946, of a general series for use in the four polar dependencies of the Falkland Islands. De La Rue produced the stamps with a recess frame and a lithographed map of British Antarctica. All four colonial omnibus sets of 1946–53 were issued in the Dependencies (27:35). In 1954 the map stamps were replaced by an Elizabethan series depicting ships connected with Antarctic expeditions from 1897 to 1952 (27:37). The stamps were recess-printed by Waterlow and Sons until 1961 and subsequently by De La Rue.

British West Indies

Twelve of the British colonies of the West Indies added new values to their pre-war definitive issues or changed the colours of existing denominations to meet the requirements of increased postal rates. Stamps were added to the lower values of the Bahamas (27:6), Barbados, the Cayman Islands (27:21), Jamaica (28:4, 5), St. Lucia (28:23) and the Turks and Caicos Islands (28:40). In most cases there were also changes of perforation and pronounced shade varieties, and these affected the stamps of Bermuda and Grenada. Hitherto, most of the West Indian territories had managed with a series limited to the five-shilling denomination; but higher parcel and airmail rates necessitated the release, in many instances, of ten-shilling and 1-pound stamps between 1947 and 1950. Antigua (27:1), Dominica (27:25), Jamaica, Montserrat (28:12, 13), St. Kitts-Nevis (28:16), St. Vincent (28:30) and the Virgin Islands (28:44) issued stamps up to the 1-pound value in this period. A temporary shortage of penny stamps in Barbados in 1947 was met by surcharging the 2-pence stamp at the office of *The Advocate* newspaper (27:9).

In 1949 the majority of West Indian islands left the Sterling area and adopted the British Caribbean dollar of 100 cents. This did not affect the Bahamas and Bermuda – not strictly part of the West Indies – or Jamaica and its dependency the Turks and Caicos Islands. Trinidad and Tobago already had decimal currency, so their stamps were not affected by the change to a decimal system. Stamps inscribed in dollars and cents were issued between 1949 and 1952 by nine colonies. In the case of St. Lucia and St. Vincent the existing designs were merely adapted (28:24, 31, 33), but entirely new pictorial sets – with the post-war portrait of King George VI by Dorothy Wilding – were provided for Barbados (27:11, 12), the Cayman Islands (27:22), Dominica (27:26, 27), Monserrat (28:14), the Turks and Caicos Islands (28:43) and the Virgin Islands (28:45, 46). The pictorial series of St. Kitts–Nevis now bore the full name of the colony and included the island of Anguilla for the first time (28:20). Grenada abandoned the pictorial concept and for the low values of 1951, went back to the Perkins Bacon design, used for the Queen Victoria series of 1861. The higher denominations featured the badge of the colony – a device also adopted by St. Lucia (28:25).

No attempt was made to decimalise the stamps of the general series provided in the Leeward Islands. Indeed, the colours of six low values were changed in 1949 despite the fact that the change to dollar currency was imminent. These stamps were used in Antigua, Montserrat, St. Kitts–Nevis and the Virgin Islands alongside the distinctive sets of these territories. A decimal series did not appear until February 1954, when the set portraying Queen Elizabeth was released (28:10, 11) – the last of the colonial keyplate issues to be typographed by De La Rue; a relic of the turn of the century, when almost all British colonies used these designs. The general series of the Leeward Islands was discontinued at the end of June 1956.

Definitive sets portraying Queen Elizabeth began to appear in 1953, but several territories continued to use Georgian stamps to the very end of the first post-war decade. In 1953–4 the existing pictorial designs were adapted, with a portrait of the Queen substituted, in Antigua (27:2, 3), Barbados (27:14, 15), the Cayman Islands (27:23, 24), Dominica (27:30, 31), Grenada (27:40), Montserrat (28:15), St. Christopher–Nevis–Anguilla (28:21, 22), St. Lucia (28:28) and Trinidad and Tobago (28:36, 38). In those cases where a royal cypher was shown – Grenada and St. Lucia (28:29) – the monogram was altered accordingly. Bermuda alone adopted an entirely new definitive series, recess-printed by Bradbury Wilkinson and released in November 1953 (27:17, 18). The Bahamas adapted the designs hitherto used for a lengthy commemorative series in 1948, marking the tercentenary of the settlement of Eleuthera (27:4, 5). The commemoratives were printed in monochrome intaglio by the Canadian Bank Note Company; but the definitives of 1954 were produced in two-colour combinations by Bradbury Wilkinson, with the commemorative inscription deleted and the Queen's portrait substituted (27:7, 8).

Apart from the Eleuthera series, few commemoratives were issued by the West Indian territories in this period. All of them, including the Leeward Islands, took part in the colonial omnibus issues (27:10); and the fourteen colonies actually in the West Indies, excluding the Bahamas and Bermuda, issued two stamps each in omnibus designs to mark the inauguration of the British West Indies University College in 1951. The stamps featured the college arms (28:6) and a portrait of Princess Alice, the university's chancellor (28:39). In 1951, four stamps of the definitive sets of Dominica, Grenada, St. Lucia and St. Vincent were overprinted to celebrate the grant of new constitutions that year (27:27, 38; (28:27, 34–35).

Of the distinctive commemorative sets, two celebrated the centenaries of the first stamps of the West Indies: Bermuda, in 1948, and Barbados, in 1952, issued sets of four stamps, reproducing the Perot 'postmaster' issue and the 'Britannia' stamps respectively (27:13, 16). Bermuda and Jamaica each issued a stamp in 1953 to commemorate the post-coronation royal visit of the Queen and the Duke of Edinburgh. In both cases definitive designs were adapted with an additional inscription, that used by Jamaica being adapted from the Georgian series (27:19; 28:9).

Jamaica's new constitution of 1944 was commemorated by a set of seven stamps released in August 1945. Four values appeared the following year with changes of perforation (28:1–3). In March 1952, in honour of the first Caribbean Scout Jamboree, Jamaica issued two stamps lithographed in multicolour by Bradbury Wilkinson – an unusual process for that company at that time (28:7, 8).

Apart from the New Constitution stamps, two commemorative issues were made by overprinting contemporary definitives: six values of the St. Kitts–Nevis series were overprinted in November 1950 to celebrate the tercentenary of the colonisation of Anguilla (28:17–19); and two of the Bermuda Elizabethan series were overprinted to mark the Three Power Talks held on the island in December 1953. Two settings of this overprint exist (27:20). St. Lucia issued a 12-cent stamp in June 1951 to publicise the rebuilding of the capital, Castries, after it had been devastated by fire. The stamp was produced by Bradbury Wilkinson in combined letterpress and intaglio (28:26), and it showed a phoenix rising above the burning buildings.

The centenary of the detachment of the Turks and Caicos Islands from the Bahamas was celebrated in December 1948 by a set of seven stamps recess-printed by Waterlow and Sons. Four designs were used for denominations ranging from the ½-penny to ten shillings, featuring the badge, flag and map of the colony as well as portraits of Queen Victoria and King George VI (28:41, 42).

The restoration of the legislative council to the Virgin Islands in 1951 was marked by a set of four stamps featuring a map of the colony, recess-printed by Waterlow (28:47).

Cuba

A distinctive feature of Cuban stamps, dating from the First World War, was the use of paper tinted in the same colour as the design. The majority of stamps in this period were recess-printed locally, but Waterlow and Sons produced sets between 1948 and 1952 for the jubilee of the war of independence, the centenary of General Maceo and the bicentenary of coffee production. The definitive series of 1918 was superseded in 1954 by a set with the same theme of famous Cubans (29:22). These stamps were originally perforated. Lengthy sets of the early 1950s were issued to raise money for the postal employees' retirement fund (29:10, 11, 14). Obligatory stamps were produced periodically to raise money for anti-tuberculosis funds (29:13, 19, 21, 24) and the rebuilding of the General Post Office (29:15, 16). From 1951 onwards, special stamps were issued for use on Christmas greetings cards (29:18), with suitable festive motifs in letterpress set in intaglio frames. Sets of 1948 and 1954 extolled the merits of the tobacco and sugar industries respectively (29:9, 23), the latter combining an aeroplane motif to denote airmail usage. Commemorative issues were generally confined to short sets of up to four stamps, occasionally including an airmail denomination (29:1–6, 8, 12, 17, 20, 25, 26). Several special delivery stamps were issued between 1945 and 1954 (29:7).

Curaçao (Netherlands Antilles)

The stamps of the Dutch West Indies continued to bear the name of the principal island, Curaçao, until 1949. Two issues of that year were additionally inscribed 'NEDERLANDSE ANTILLEN', and subsequent issues were thus inscribed with the name of Curaçao omitted.

In the 'Curaçao' period there were few distinctive stamps. Two sets of semi-postals in 1946 featured maps of Holland and the East Indies and bore premiums in aid of war victims and reconstruction. A lengthy airmail series (29:28) with stylised aircraft motifs appeared in 1947. Three pre-war stamps were surcharged in 1947 in aid of the Dutch East Indies social welfare fund, and a set of five depicting children was released in 1948 for the Child Welfare fund.

Definitives and commemoratives in this period conformed to the prevailing Dutch pattern (29:27, 29). Child Welfare issues were continued in the 1950s and featured children's activities or West Indian flowers. Other charity issues of this period bore premiums for the seamen's welfare fund and the Netherlands flood relief fund. The definitive series of 1950 (29:31, 32) and the commemoratives for the UPU (29:30) and the ratification of the statute of the kingdom, between 1949 and 1954, followed the standard Dutch designs. Distinctive sets marked the 450th anniversary of the discovery of Curaçao in 1949 and the third Caribbean Tourist Association Conference in 1954. Definitive stamps were surcharged in 1953 to raise funds for the victims of the Dutch flood disaster (29:33).

Dominican Republic

With the exception of a lengthy series in 1952 to commemorate the 460th anniversary of the discovery of Santo Domingo by Columbus, recess-printed by De La Rue, all stamps of the Dominican Republic in this decade were lithographed locally. Until 1952, the contract was held by A. Tabacolera of Santiago; but after the Columbus series it reverted to the Ferrua Company of Ciudad Trujillo, who had produced many of the earlier issues. The local printers vied with each other in producing bigger and gaudier stamps, using two- or three-colour lithography (29:34–38), culminating in the series of 1947 with multicoloured vignettes. The sets produced by both printers were intended as definitives. Relatively short definitive sets were produced at frequent intervals, later sets of this period featuring San Francisco church in 1949, hotels (1950–1) and the monument to Trujillo Peace (1954–7). Annual stamps were issued for the anti-tuberculosis and cancer relief funds (29:38).

With the exception of the Columbus series of 1952 commemoratives were confined to singles or short sets ranging from the centenary of the constitution in 1945 to the birth centenary of the Cuban patriot, Jose Marti, in 1954 (29:37, 39).

Haiti

Until 1954, the majority of Haitian stamps were recess-printed by the American Bank Note Company. In 1951, however, Waterlow and Sons photogravure-printed sets featuring natural products and commemorating Isabella the Catholic (29:44), and three years later they lithographed a series publicising the restoration of Christophe's citadel. The sesquicentennial of independence was celebrated in 1954 by two long sets produced in photogravure – one by Courvoisier and the other by Waterlow and Sons (29:45). These paved the way for many sets of the next decade by the Swiss printers.

The recess issues of the American Bank Note Company were in monochrome with the exception of a Red Cross set in 1945 and an anti-tuberculosis set in 1949 in which the relevant emblems were printed in red (29:40). An ordinary and airmail series of 1946 portrayed Capois-la-Mort (29:42), the hero of independence, and commemorative sets honoured President Roosevelt (29:41), Jean-Jacques Dessalines in 1947, the bicentenary of Port-au-Prince in 1949 and the Bicentenary Exhibition in 1950 (29:43).

French West Indies
The islands of Guadeloupe and Martinique became French overseas *départements* on 19th March 1946 and ceased issuing their own stamps in 1949. In the brief period of philatelic independence left to them after the war, however, they both contrived to issue two definitive sets and a series of postage-due labels. In 1945 De La Rue lithographed sets for both islands featuring the Free French emblem – the Cross of Lorraine. The series issued by Guadeloupe had a symbolic design, by Edmund Dulac, featuring dolphins (29:46). The Martinique series portrayed Victor Schoelcher, the slavery abolitionist (29:49). These sets were replaced in June 1947 by pictorial series, recess-printed at the French Government Printing Works in Paris (29:47, 50). The same formula was adopted in each case, native occupations and scenery providing the material for nine designs in each set. Uniform designs, featuring a coastal village in Guadeloupe and a map of Martinique, were used for the postage-due sets (29:48, 51).

Australasia

Australia
The 1938 definitive series, the subjects of which were a mixture of royal portraiture and wildlife, continued in use for much of the post-war decade. The three highest denominations were printed on a distinctive, thin, rough paper in 1948–9; and between 1948 and 1956 the majority of stamps up to the shilling value were printed on unwatermarked paper. None the less, entirely new designs were introduced piecemeal between 1948 and 1952. In practice, they constituted a separate definitive series. Four designs combining heraldry, allegory, aboriginal art and a purely pictorial motif appeared between 1948 and 1950 (30:10–13). More up-to-date portraits of King George VI and Queen Elizabeth II were introduced in 1950–51 (30:20, 21). Increases in postal rates led to the introduction of several denominations combining an odd halfpenny. An aborigine known as 'One Pound Jimmy' was portrayed on the 8½-penny stamp of 1950 (30:22) and a medallic profile of the king was used for five stamps of 1951–2 from the 3½-penny to the shilling-and-a-halfpenny (30:31, 32). Following the accession of Queen Elizabeth II, a standard portrait design was adopted in 1953 for five values from 1-penny to 6½-penny (30:33).

Australian stamps of this period were recess-printed at the printing establishment of the Commonwealth Bank of Australia in Melbourne, the sole exception being an issue of 1953 to boost food production. Two strips of three different designs, printed side by side, were typographed by the Melbourne press (30:38). Identical designs featuring butter, wheat and beef production were used for 3-penny and 3½-penny stamps. The practice of printing stamps *se-tenant* (different designs side by side) was adopted by Australia in 1950 for two stamps reproducing the first issues of New South Wales and Victoria (30:23, 24). It was used the following year for pairs of 3-penny stamps marking the jubilee of the Commonwealth of Australia, the centenary of gold-mining and the centenary of responsible government in Victoria (30:25, 27, 29, 30). Double-size horizontal designs showing the opening of the first federal

parliament and the parliament buildings in Canberra were also issued in 1951 (30:26, 28).

In the immediate post-war period, commemoratives were issued in sets of three. Uniform designs were used for sets marking the arrival of the Duke and Duchess of Gloucester in 1945 and the centenary of Sir Thomas Mitchell's expedition to central Queensland in 1946 (30:1, 5). Different symbolic motifs were employed in the victory series of 1946 (30:2–4) and pictorial designs featured in the set of 1947 marking the sesquicentennial of Newcastle N.S.W. (30:6–8); the stamp honouring Lieutenant John Shortland erroneously portrayed his father. Subsequent issues consisted mainly of single stamps commemorating the marriage of Princess Elizabeth in 1947, the 75th anniversary of UPU in 1949, and several prominent Australians, also in 1949 (30:9, 14, 15, 17–19). Stamps of 1948 and 1952 depicting a Boy Scout were issued in connection with the Pan-Pacific Scout Jamborees of those years (30:16).

Three stamps with a common design celebrated the coronation of 1953 (30:34), and two designs were used for the set of three issued in February 1954 to mark the post-coronation royal visit (30:41, 42). A *se-tenant* pair of 3½-penny stamps – one portraying early lieutenant-governors, and the other a pictorial design showing Sullivan's Cove – commemorated the 150th anniversary of the colonisation of Tasmania in 1953 (30:36, 37, 39). The remaining commemoratives of this period consisted of single stamps celebrating the centenaries of the first Tasmanian stamps in 1953 and the telegraph service, the railways and the first stamps of Western Australia in 1954 (30:40, 43, 45, 46), and honouring Young Farmers in 1953 and the Australian Red Cross and the national Antarctic research expeditions in 1954 (30:35, 44, 47). The release in 1954 of a 2-shilling stamp publicising the Melbourne Olympic Games two years ahead of the event was greeted with protests at the time, although such 'pre-publicity' issues have since become commonplace (30:48).

New Zealand
Higher denominations from 15-shilling up to £5, were added to the arms series between 1945 and 1958 (31:1). A larger version of the George VI portrait design, recess-printed in two colours, was introduced in 1947 – denominations from the 1-shilling to the 3-shilling produced by De La Rue, and the small-format low values from the 2-penny to the 9-penny printed by Bradbury Wilkinson (31:12). Temporary shortages of certain denominations were filled by surcharging undenominated arms stamps in 1950 and obsolete values of the George VI series in 1952–3 (31:18, 26). An Elizabethan series using three designs was released between December 1953 and March 1954. The two-colour middle values were printed by De La Rue and the monochrome low and high values were produced by Bradbury Wilkinson (31:35–7), who also recess-printed a series of official stamps in 1954 bearing a profile of the queen on an engine-turned background (31:38). Having used a stylised lighthouse motif for all its stamps since 1891, the Government Life Insurance Department introduced a pictorial intaglio series with the theme of lighthouses in 1947. Seven New Zealand lighthouses and the Eddystone Lighthouse, off the English coast, were featured (31:40–42).

Chief among the special issues were the annual Health stamps, with premiums in aid of children's health camps and sanatoria. The immediate post-war issues featured prominent London landmarks – the statue of Peter Pan in Kensington Gardens (31:2) and the statue of Eros in Piccadilly Circus (31:10) – and the issues of 1947–9 and 1953 featured aspects of New Zealand childhood (31:11, 16, 17, 31, 32). Photographs of the royal children were used in 1950 and 1952 (31:19, 23, 24), but a view of 'Takapuna' class yachts was depicted on the 1951 pair. The stamps of 1954 struck a particularly topical note by showing a young climber gazing up at Mount Aspiring, with the vision of Everest in the background – an allusion to the conquest of the world's highest mountain by the New Zealand climber Sir Edmund Hillary in the previous year (31:39).

New Zealand's peace issue of April 1946 was one of the longest and most ambitious sets produced for this purpose anywhere in the world. The eleven designs were the work of James Berry, but three different printers shared the contract – Harrison and Sons printing the 1½-penny and shilling stamps by photogravure, and Waterlow and Sons and Bradbury Wilkinson recess-printing the others (31:3–9). Four designs featured badges or the national arms flanked by vignettes of peace and war, two featured scenery appropriate to peace and tranquillity and two showed landmarks in Wellington. The figure of St. George on the 8-penny was taken from a memorial stained-glass window. The royal family were portrayed on the 2-penny, and a view of St. Paul's Cathedral with a quotation from a speech by Sir Winston Churchill appeared on the 1½-penny.

There were only three commemorative issues, in the strict sense, in this period. Four stamps of February 1948, recess-printed by Bradbury Wilkinson, marked the centenary of Otago province and featured scenery and landmarks (31:13–15). The same firm recess-printed a set of five stamps two years later in honour of the centenary of Canterbury province (31:20–22). Five stamps were released in May 1953 to celebrate the coronation of Queen Elizabeth, the series epitomising New Zealand philately in that three printers were involved in its production – De La Rue, Waterlow and Sons, and Harrison; and free rein was given to the New Zealand penchant for English themes, with views of Buckingham Palace and Westminster Abbey – their first appearance on stamps – and the coronation coach and regalia (31:27–30).

Australian Pacific Territories

Philatelically, there was little activity in the territories under Australian control. Nauru continued to use the definitive series of 1924 throughout this period, and did not adopt a new pictorial series until February 1954 (32:15, 16). Norfolk Island – which hitherto had used ordinary Australian stamps – received a distinctive series, featuring a view of Ball Bay, in 1947 (32:23). Increases in Australian postal rates in 1953 led to the issue of six new denominations, each depicting a different landmark on the island (32:24, 25). Papua and New Guinea, whose separate issues were withdrawn during the Second World War, used Australian stamps until a pictorial series was introduced in October 1952 (32:27–9). All stamps of the Australian Pacific territories were recess-printed by the Commonwealth Bank in Melbourne.

British Pacific Islands

There was less activity in the British Pacific territories – only one of which produced an Elizabethan definitive series within the period. Both the British Solomon Islands and the Gilbert and Ellice group retained their pre-war Georgian sets until 1956 and, apart from a few changes of perforation, made no alteration to them. Neither territory produced any distinctive commemorative stamps, although they took part in the various colonial omnibus issues (32:1, 2, 14). Pitcairn did not adopt an Elizabethan series until 1957 – more than five years after the queen's accession – and was, in fact, the last British colony to take note of the new reign. However, two new values featuring the *Bounty* Bible and the island school were added to the Georgian series in 1951 (32:30, 31). Pitcairn also took part in the various colonial omnibus issues (32:32).

The most prolific of the British colonies was Fiji, which added new values to its Georgian series up to 1955 (32:7) although it had begun to introduce a pictorial series adapting the designs of the Georgian set in February 1954 (32:10–12). In addition to the colonial omnibus issues of 1946–53 (32:6), Fiji released an 8-penny stamp in December 1953 to mark the royal visit. Like the majority of other issues for this event, the definitive design was modified by a commemorative inscription (32:9). Fiji emulated New Zealand by issuing health stamps in 1951 and 1954 with premiums in aid of the war memorial anti-tuberculosis campaign (32:7, 13). Both sets were recess-printed by Bradbury Wilkinson. Three designs, recess-printed by Waterlow and Sons, were used for a series issued by the Anglo–French Condominium of the New Hebrides in April 1953. In accordance with previous practice, sets were issued with inscriptions in either French or English (32:18, 19). The UPU and coronation stamps were issued in an English version, but a French version of the UPU set was also released.

French Pacific Islands

In addition to the joint issues of the New Hebrides, France provided stamps for use in three Pacific territories. A lengthy pictorial series, photogravure-printed by Vaugirard, was released in New Caledonia in 1948 (32:17). Four stamps of 1953 celebrated the centenary of French administration and portrayed historic colonial administrators. Otherwise, the various French colonial omnibus sets were issued.

The Free French issue of the Oceanic Settlements was surcharged with new values in 1945, but in 1948 it was superseded by a recess-printed series depicting scenery, wildlife and islanders (32:26). A numeral motif was used for the postage-due set released simultaneously. A 14-franc airmail stamp of 1953 commemorated the 50th anniversary of the death of Paul Gauguin and reproduced his painting 'Nafea'.

The Wallis and Futuna Islands continued to use their Free French series of 1944 throughout the immediate post-war decade. Various surcharges were introduced in 1945 as a result of increases in postal rates (32:43).

Both the Oceanic Settlements and the Wallis and Futuna Islands produced commemorative issues in the French colonial omnibus designs.

New Zealand Pacific Territories

The three Pacific territories under New Zealand control – the Cook Islands, Niue and Western Samoa – followed an identical pattern in their post-war stamp issues. In each case, the pre-war definitives were reissued with a change of watermark in the immediate post-war years, pending the introduction of entirely new pictorial sets between 1949 and 1952. They all issued New Zealand arms high values with an appropriate overprint, and in each case four values of the Peace set were similarly overprinted in 1946 (32:3, 20). James Berry designed the pictorial sets for the Cook Islands in 1949 and Niue in 1950, recess-printed by Waterlow and Sons and Bradbury Wilkinson respectively (32:4, 5, 21, 22). Bradbury Wilkinson also printed the series for Western Samoa in 1952 (32:33, 34). The Tokelau Islands, administered as part of Western Samoa before becoming a dependency of New Zealand in January 1949, began issuing their own stamps in 1948. Three denominations – ½-penny, 1-penny and 2-penny – were deemed sufficient, the designs featuring scenery and maps (32:36, 37). All four territories released stamps in the standard New Zealand designs to mark the coronation of 1953 (32:35, 38).

Tonga

In 1953 a pictorial series designed by James Berry was recess-printed by Bradbury Wilkinson to replace a definitive series that had first appeared in 1897.

Tonga issued UPU stamps in the British colonial omnibus designs in 1949 but produced distinctive commemoratives celebrating Queen Salote's fiftieth birthday in 1950 and the golden jubilee of the treaty with Great Britain in 1951 (32:39, 40). Both sets were produced by Waterlow and Sons, using photogravure and intaglio respectively.

1

2

3

4

5

6

7

8

9

10

11

12

13

14

15

16

17

18

19

20

21

22

23

24

25

26

27

28

29

30

31

32

33

34

35

36

37

38

39

40

41

42

43

44

45

46

47

1

2

3

4

5

6

7

9

10

11

12

13

14

16

17

18

19

20

21

23

24

25

26

27

28

30

31

32

33

34

36

37

38

39

41

42

43

44

1

2

3

4

5

7

8

9

10

11

1

13

14

15

16

18

19

20

21

2

24

25

26

27

28

29

30

31

32

33

3

35

36

37

3

1 — ADEN, 10 CENTS on 2

2 — ADEN, DHOW 35 CENTS

3 — ADEN, 1/- ROYAL VISIT 1954, SHIP BUILDING

4 — ADEN, 5¢ KATHIRI STATE OF SEIYUN

5 — ADEN, VICTORY ISSUE 8th JUNE 1946, QU'AITI STATE OF SHIHR AND MUKALLA

6 — AFGHANISTAN, 30 POUL, POSTES AFGHANISTAN

7 — POSTES AFGHANES, 10 P., JOURNÉE DU CROISSANT ROUGE 1952

8 — BAHRAIN, POSTAGE REVENUE, 6 ANNAS

9 — BAHRAIN, POSTAGE REVENUE, 6 ANNAS

10 — BRUNEI, 8c, EIGHT CENTS

11 — BURMA POSTAGE, 1R, SERVICE

12 — BURMA, 2A² POSTAGE

13 — UNION OF BURMA, 2As POSTAGE

14 — UNION OF BURMA, 6th BUDDHIST COUNCIL

15 — UNION OF BURMA, K1, POSTAGE

16 — ROYAUME DU CAMBODGE, 10c, POSTES, APSARA

17 — INDIA POSTAGE, GOLDEN TEMPLE AMRITSAR

18 — CEYLON, 10c, NEW CONSTITUTION 1947

19 — CEYLON, 25, INDEPENDENCE COMMEMORATION 4th FEBRUARY 1948

20 — CEYLON, 30 CENTS

21 — CEYLON, 3c, POSTAGE AND REVENUE

22 — CEYLON, 1931–1932, 15 CENTS

23 — CEYLON, 5

24 — CEYLON, ROYAL VISIT 1954, 10 CENTS

25 — CEYLON, 10, POSTAGE AND REVENUE

26 — ₹1

27 — $7,000

28 — 290, 1949

29 — 1.00

30 — 1

31 — 100.00

32 — 10000, 中国人民邮政

33 — 40000, 政邮国民中

34 — 1000

35 — 壹圆

36 — 1.00

37 — 2.00, REPUBLIC OF CHINA, 政邮国民中

38 — 500

39 — 100.00, 中国人民邮政

40 — 1000

41 — 3000圓, 中国人民邮政航空邮票

42 — 400, 中国人民邮政

43 — 200, TIENTSIN

44 — 250, 中国人民邮政

45 — KARL MARX 1818–1883, 400, 中国人民邮政

46 — 80, 中国人民邮政

47 — HONG KONG, $1

48 — HONGKONG, TWENTY CENTS

49 — HONG KONG, UNIVERSAL POSTAL UNION 1874–1949

50 — HONGKONG, FIVE DOLLARS

II

13

15

1

2

3

4

5

6

7

8

9

10

11

12

13

14

15

16

17

18

19

20

21

22

23

24

25

26

27

28

29

30

31

32

33

34

35

36

37

38

39

40

41

42

43

44

45

46
47
48
49
50

1

2

3

4

5

6

7

8

9

10

11

12

13

14

15

16

17

18

19

20

21

22

23

24

25

26

27

28

29

30

31

32

33

34

35

36

37

38

39

40

41

42

43

44

45

46

I

1

2

3

4

5

6

7

8

9

10

11

12

13

14

15

16

17

18

19

20

21

22

23

24

25

26

27

28

29

30

31

32

33

34

35

36

37

38

20

21

22

1

2

3

4

5

7

8

9

10

11

13

14

15

16

17

18

19

20

21

22

23

25

26

27

28

29

30

31

32

33

34

35

36

37

38

39

40

23

1

2

3

4

5

7

8

9

13

14

15

16

19

20

21

22

24

25

26

27

30

31

32

33

34

36

37

38

39

40

41

24

1

2

3

4

5

6

7

8

9

10

11

12

13

14

15

16

1

18

19

20

21

22

23

24

25

26

27

28

29

30

31

32

33

34

35

36

37

38

39

40

1

2

3

4

5

6

7

8

9

10

11

12

13

14

15

16

17

18

19

20

21

22

23

24

25

26

27

28

29

30

31

32

33

34

35

36

37

38

39

40

1

2

3

4

5

6

7

8

9

10

11

12

13

14

15

16

17

18

19

20

21

22

23

24

25

26

27

28

29

30

31

32

33

34

35

36

37

38

39

40

41

42

43

44

45

46

1   2   3   4   5

7   8   9   10   11   1

13   14   15   16   17   18   1

20   21   22   23   24   25   26

27   28   29   30   31   32   3

34   35   36   37   38   39

40   41   42   43   44   4

1

2

3

4

5

6

7

8

9

10

11

12

14

15

16

17

18

19

20

21

22

23

24

25

27

28

29

30

31

33

34

35

36

38

39

40

41

1

2

3

4

6

7

8

9

10

1

12

13

14

15

17

18

19

21

22

23

24

25

27

28

29

30

31

33

34

35

36

37

38

39

40

41

42

43

1945-1954
Captions to Plates 1-32

PLATE 1

ALBANIA:
1. 1945; Permet landscape, 1f.
2. 1946; People's Republic, 20q.
3. 1953; Film studio, 5l.

ANDORRA (Spanish):
4. 1948–51; Edelweiss, 2c.

AUSTRIA:
5. 1945; German 6pf., overprinted in Vienna.
6. 1945; German 40f., overprinted for use in Styria.
7. 1945; Posthorn, 6gr.
8. 1945; National arms, 6g.
9. 1945–7; Pictorial series, 4g.
10. 1948; Provincial costumes, 5s.
11. 1946; St. Stephen's Cathedral, 10g. + 40g.
12. 1947–9; Famous Austrians, 60g.
13. 1947; National art exhibition, 35g. + 15g.
14. 1947; Prisoners of war relief fund, 35g. + 15g.
15. 1947; Telegraph centenary, 40g.
16. 1948; Reconstruction, 10g. + 5g.
17. 1950; Josef Madersperger, 60g.
18. 1953; Christmas, 1s.
19. 1947; Vienna prize race, 60g. + 20g.
20. 1954; Newspaper, 1s.

BELGIUM:
21. 1945; Prisoners of war, 10c. + 15c.
22. 1946; 5f. King Leopold III, surcharged 10%.
23. 1946; Ostend–Dover mailboat, 1f.35.
24. 1947; Antarctic expedition, 2f.25.
25. 1947; Film festival, 3f.15.
26. 1948; Production and industry, 6f.
27. 1949; Stamp centenary, 1f.75.
28. 1951; Belgian lion, 1f.
29. 1952; UPU, 1f.75.
30. 1952; King Baudouin, 2f.
31. 1953; King Baudouin, 2f.

BULGARIA:
32. 1945; Official, 5l.
33. 1951; A. S. Popov, 4l.
34. 1951; Steamroller, 2l.
35. 1954; D. Blagoev, 44st.

CYPRUS:
36. 1946; Victory, 3p.

CZECHOSLOVAKIA:
37. 1945; Linden leaf, 120h.
38. 1945; War heroes, 3k.
39. 1945; War heroes, 10k.
40. 1945; President Beneš, 7k.
41. 1946; Air, 20k.
42. 1946; Independence Day, 3k.
43. 1948–53; President Gottwald, 3k.
44. 1949; Poets, 2k.
45. 1949; F. Chopin, 8k.
46. 1949; Zvolen Castle, 10k.
47. 1952; Agriculture, 3k.
48. 1952; Music festival, 1k.50.
49. 1953; President Zápotocký, 60h.

50. 1953; Labour Day, 1k.50.
51. 1954; Metal worker, 75h.
52. 1954; Poets, 30h.

PLATE 2

DENMARK:
1. 1945; King Christian, 40ö.
2. 1946; Tycho Brahe, 20ö.
3. 1946; Arms, 1k.
4. 1951; Naval officers' college, 25ö.
5. 1951; Stamp centenary, 15ö.
6. 1953; Netherlands flood relief, 30ö. + 10ö.
7. 1953–6; Danish history, 60ö.
8. 1954; Royal Academy of Fine Arts, 30ö.

FINLAND:
9. 1947; Definitive, 12m.
10. 1945; J. Sibelius, 5m.
11. 1946; Porvoo, 8m.
12. 1947; Anti-tuberculosis, 6m. + 1m.50.
13. 1954; Definitive, 10m.
14. 1949; Tuberculosis relief, 15m. + 5m.
15. 1949; Red Cross, 9m. + 3m.

FRANCE:
16. 1945; Liberation, 4f.
17. 1945; Shield and broken chains, 50c.
18. 1945–6; Marianne, 3f.
19. 1945; Devastated towns, 4f. + 4f.
20. 1946; Air, 200f.
21. 1946; Arms, 30c.
22. 1946; Scenery, series, 20f.
23. 1946; Peace, 10f.
24. 1946; UNESCO, 10f.
25. 1947; Boy Scouts, 5f.
26. 1949–50; Air, 1,000f.
27. 1949; Telephone and Telegraph Congress, 100f.
28. 1948; National relief fund, 20f. + 8f.
29. 1949; Franco–American amity, 25f.
30. 1950; Madame Récamier, 12f.
31. 1951; St. Jean-Baptiste De La Salle, 15f.
32. 1951; Art exhibition, 15f.
33. 1951; UN General Assembly, 30f.
34. 1951; Scenic, 40f.
35. 1951; M. Noguès, 12f.
36. 1952; Marshal de Lattre, 15f.
37. 1952; Chambord château, 20f.
38. 1952; R. Laënnec, 12f.
39. 1952; Versailles gateway, 18f.
40. 1953; General Leclerc, 8f.
41. 1953; Sports, 50f.
42. 1953; Arms, 2f.
43. 1953; Industries and literary figures, 12f.
44. 1954; Air, 200f.
45. 1954; Views, 10f.
46. 1954; Harvester, 4f.
47. 1954; Villandry château, 18f.
48. 1954; Romanesque Studies Conference, 30f.

PLATE 3

GERMANY:
1. 1945; Defaced Hitler head, 15pf.

GERMANY (Allied Occupation):
2. 1945; British and American Zones, 15pf.
3. 1946; American, British and Russian Zones, 8pf.
4. 1947; American, British and Russian Zones, 6pf.
5. 1947; American, British and Russian Zones, Dr. von Stephan, 75pf.
6. 1948; Russian Zone, district overprint, 60pf.
7. 1945; French Zone, 5pf.
8. 1949; French Zone (Baden), Goethe, 30pf. + 15pf.
9. 1947; French Zone (Rhineland–Palatinate), 45pf.
10. 1947; French Zone (Württemberg), 24pf.
11. 1945; Russian Zone (Thuringia), 12pf.
12. 1945; Russian Zone (Saxony–South East), 20pf.
13. 1945; Russian Zone (Mecklenburg–Vorpommern), 6pf.
14. 1946; Russian Zone (Saxony–North West), 20pf. + 10pf.
15. 1948; Russian Zone (General issue), 5pf.
16. 1948; Russian Zone (General issue), Portraits, 30pf.
17. 1949; Russian Zone (General issue), Leipzig Spring Fair, 50pf. + 25pf.
18. 1948; British and American Zones, 25pf.
19. 1948; British and American Zones, Cologne Cathedral, 12pf. + 8pf.
20. 1948; British and American Zones, Buildings, 50pf.
21. 1949; British and American Zones, Goethe, 10pf. + 5pf.

GERMANY (West Berlin):
22. 1948; Allied Occupation, 50pf. overprinted.
23. 1949–54; Berlin buildings, 20pf.

GERMANY (Anglo–American Zone):
24. 1948; Berlin Airlift, tax, 2pf.

GERMANY (French Zone):
25. 1949; Reconstruction fund, 2pf.

GERMANY (West Berlin):
26. 1949; 5pf. surcharge on 45pf.
27. 1950; Philarmonic Orchestra, 30pf. + 5pf.
28. 1954; Memorial Library, 40pf.
29. 1952; Beethoven, 30pf.
30. 1952; Famous Berliners, 4pf.
31. 1953; East German uprising, 20pf.
32. 1954; Richard Strauss, 40pf.

GERMANY (West Germany):
33. 1949; Parliament, 20pf.
34. 1951; Numeral and posthorn, 5pf.
35. 1951; Charity, 20pf. + 5pf.
36. 1951; Philatelic exhibition, 20pf. + 3pf.
37. 1951; Humanitarian relief fund, 30pf. + 10pf.
38. 1953; Science Museum, 10pf. + 5pf.
39. 1954; Prisoners of war, 10pf.
40. 1951; W. C. Röntgen, 30pf.
41. 1952; A. N. Otto, 30pf.
42. 1953; J. von Liebig, 30pf.
43. 1953; Transport exhibition, 20pf.

44. 1953; Humanitarian relief fund, 20pf. + 10pf.
45. 1954; President Heuss, 10pf.
46. 1954; P. Ehrlich and E. Behring, 10pf.

GERMANY (Democratic Republic):
47. 1949; Postal workers, 12pf.
48. 1949; UPU, 50pf.
49. 1951; Friendship with China, 24pf.
50. 1951; Winter sports, 24pf.
51. 1950; Wilhelm Pieck, 24pf.
52. 1950; Philatelic exhibition, 84pf. + 41pf.
53. 1950; Academy of Sciences, 1pf.
54. 1953; Five-Year-Plan, 35pf.
55. 1951; Youth festival, 12pf.
56. 1952; Handel festival, 6pf.
57. 1954; Official, 6pf.

PLATE 4

GIBRALTAR:
1. 1950; New Constitution, 6d.
2. 1953; Definitive, 2½d.

GREECE:
3. 1945; Resistance, 40d.
4. 1946–7; 10d. surcharged 100d.
5. 1946; Restoration of the monarchy, 50d. on 1d.
6. 1947; Dodecanese Islands, 1,600d.
7. 1948; Church restoration fund, 50d.
8. 1951; Reconstruction issue, 1,600d.
9. 1950; Battle of Crete, 1,000d.
10. 1954; Ancient Greek art, 1,000d.
11. 1954; NATO, 4,000d.

GREEK OCCUPATION OF THE DODECANESE ISLANDS:
12. 1947; 10d. surcharge on 2,000d.

GREAT BRITAIN:
13. 1946; Victory, 2½d.
14. 1948; Silver wedding, 2½d.
15. 1948; Liberation of the Channel Islands, 1d.
16. 1948; Olympic Games, 2½d.
17. 1950–51; King George VI definitive, 1½d.
18. 1949; UPU, 2½d.
19. 1951; Festival of Britain, 2½d.
20. 1951; HMS *Victory*, 2s. 6d.
21. 1952; Elizabethan series, 2½d.
22. 1953; Coronation, 4d.

HUNGARY:
23. 1945; Reconstruction, 120p.
24. 1945; Inflation provisional.
25. 1946; Currency reform, 1fo.40.
26. 1947; Liberty, 12fi.
27. 1948; Insurrection, 60fi.
28. 1950; Five-Year-Plan, 60fi.
29. 1950; Children's Day, 60fi.
30. 1951; May Day, 40fi.
31. 1954; Scientists, 1fo.
32. 1951–8; Rebuilding plan, 12fi.

ICELAND:
33. 1947; Air, 75a.
34. 1948; Mt. Hekla, 1k.
35. 1950; Pictorial series, 90a.
36. 1953; Manuscript, 1k.

IRELAND:
37. 1945; Thomas Davis, 2½d.
38. 1946; Parnell and Davitt, 2½d.
39. 1948–65; Air, 1d.
40. 1948; Insurrection anniversary, 2½d.
41. 1949; J. C. Mangan, 1d.
42. 1950; Holy Year, 2½d.
43. 1952; Thomas Moore, 2½d.
44. 1953; Ireland at Home, 1s. 4d.
45. 1953; Robert Emmet, 3d.
46. 1954; Marian Year, 3d.

PLATE 5

ITALY:
1. 1945; Romulus, Remus and wolf, 5l.
2. 1945; 25c. surcharged 2l.
3. 1945; Freedom, 80c.
4. 1945–7; Air, 50l.
5. 1945–8; Work, justice and family, 100l.
6. 1946; Medieval Italian Republics, 5l.
7. 1948; Air, 100l.
8. 1949; Giuseppe Mazzini, 20l.
9. 1950; Provincial occupations, 50l.
10. 1950; Milan Fair, 20l.
11. 1951; Levant Fair, Bari, 25l.
12. 1951; Montecassino Abbey, 20l.
13. 1952; Armed Forces Day, 60l.
14. 1952; Mission to Ethiopia, 25l.
15. 1951; Art exhibition, 20l.
16. 1951; Cycling, 25l.
17. 1953; Arcangelo Corelli, 25l.
18. 1954; INTERPOL, 60l.
19. 1954; Carlo Lorenzini, 25l.
20. 1953; Tourist series, 60l.
21. 1953; Coin of Syracuse, 80l.
22. 1954; Encouragement to tax-payers, 25l.

LIECHTENSTEIN:
23. 1948; Air, 25r.
24. 1954; Marian Year, 1f.
25. 1951; Pictorial series, 20r.

LUXEMBOURG:
26. 1946; Definitive, 20c.
27. 1946; Air, 10f.
28. 1948–58; Grand-Duchess Charlotte, 2f.50.
29. 1947; General Patton, 1f.50.
30. 1948–55; Tourist propaganda, 4f.
31. 1954; Fencing, 2f.

MALTA:
32. 1948; New Constitution, 6d.
33. 1950; Visit of Princess Elizabeth, 1d.
34. 1951; Seventh centenary of the Scapular, 1s.
35. 1954; Royal visit, 3d.
36. 1954; Dogma of the Immaculate Conception, 1½d.

MONACO:
37. 1946; Prince Louis II, 10f.
38. 1949–59; Palace gateway, 30f.
39. 1953; Olympic Games, 15f.
40. 1947; Philatelic exhibition, 50c.
41. 1948; F. J. Bosio, 50c.
42. 1950–51; Prince Rainier III, 6f.
43. 1951–5; Seal of Prince Rainier III, 30f.
44. 1954; Arms, 2f.
45. 1952; Monaco Postal Museum, 15f.
46. 1953; Anaphylaxis, 5f.
47. 1954; St. Jean-Baptiste De La Salle, 15f.

PLATE 6

NETHERLANDS:
1. 1945; Liberation, 7½c.
2. 1945; Child Welfare, 5c. + 5c.
3. 1946; Child Welfare, 12½c. + 7½c.
4. 1946; Numeral definitive, 1c.
5. 1947; Queen Wilhelmina, 5c.
6. 1947; Queen Wilhelmina, 45c.
7. 1947; Child Welfare, 2c. + 2c.
8. 1948; Golden Jubilee, 10c.
9. 1949; Queen Juliana, 50c.
10. 1948; Coronation, 10c.
11. 1948; Child Welfare, 10c. + 5c.
12. 1949; Child Welfare, 10c. + 5c.
13. 1949; UPU, 10c.
14. 1952; Miner, 10c.

15. 1952; Stamp exhibition, 2c.
16. 1953; Queen Juliana, 85c.
17. 1954; Cultural and social relief fund, 10c. + 5c.
18. 1954; St. Boniface, 10c.
19. 1954; Queen Juliana, 10c.
20. 1951; Hague Court, 4c.
21. 1951; Hague Court, 1g.

NORWAY:
22. 1945; Wartime convoy, 7ö.
23. 1935; Henrik Wergeland, 20ö.
24. 1945; Red Cross, 20ö. + 10ö.
25. 1945; Folklore Museum, 10ö.
26. 1946; Relief fund, 30ö. + 10ö.
27. 1946; King Haakon VII, 1½k.
28. 1947; Post Office tercentenary, 15ö.
29. 1947; Petter Dass, 25ö.
30. 1950; Oslo, 45ö.
31. 1950; Infantile paralysis, 45ö. + 5ö.
32. 1950–57; King Haakon VII, 30ö.
33. 1952; King Haakon VII, 55ö.
34. 1952; Posthorn, 15ö. surcharged 20ö.
35. 1953; Archbishopric of Nidaros, 30ö.
36. 1954; Railways, 55ö.
37. 1954; Telecommunications, 55ö.

POLAND:
38. 1945; 50g. surcharged 1z.
39. 1945; Warsaw, 1z.50.
40. 1946; Air, 15z.
41. 1946; Bedzin Castle, 5z.
42. 1947–8; Polish culture, 20z.
43. 1947; Occupations, 10z.
44. 1948; Revolution, 30z.
45. 1949; Populist, 10z.
46. 1949; UPU, 8oz.
47. 1950; President Bierut, 10g.
48. 1951; Music festival, 45g.
49. 1950; Reconstruction, 15g.
50. 1951; F. Dzerzhinski, 45g.
51. 1952; Air, 5z.
52. 1951–2; Reconstruction, 30g. + 15g.
53. 1954; Air, 1z.55.
54. 1954; Gliding, 1z.35.

PLATE 7

PORTUGAL:
1. 1945; Navigators, 50c.
2. 1945; President Carmona, 1E.75.
3. 1946; Castles, 2E.
4. 1947; Costumes, 2E.
5. 1948; St. João de Brito, 50c.
6. 1949; Aviz dynasty, 2E.
7. 1949; UPU, 2E.
8. 1951; Holy Year, 1E.
9. 1951; Fisherman, 1E.
10. 1950; Holy Year, 2E.
11. 1951; Revolution, 2E.30.
12. 1952; Public Works, 3E.50.
13. 1952; Medieval knight, 20c.
14. 1953; Stamp centenary, 1E.40.
15. 1954; Education, 1E.

ROMANIA:
16. 1945–7; King Michael, 600l.
17. 1945; Child Welfare, 40l.
18. 1946; Agrarian reform, 80l.
19. 1947; King Michael, 12l.
20. 1948; Republic emblem, 1l.
21. 1952; Republic emblem, 5b.
22. 1952; Students' Union, 10b.

RUSSIA:
23. 1946; Victory, 30k.
24. 1946; Air, 15k.

25. 1945; Miner, 15k.
26. 1948; Moscow Arts Theatre, 40k.
27. 1947; Five-Year-Plan, 30k.
28. 1946; Health resorts, 45k.
29. 1950; Carpet-making, 50k.
30. 1949; Tadzhikstan, 40k.
31. 1948; Chess championship, 50k.
32. 1949; Women's Day, 50k.
33. 1949; Malyi Theatre, 50k.
34. 1950; Moscow museums, 40k.
35. 1950; Aivazovsky, 1r.
36. 1951; State Theatre, 1r.
37. 1951; Friendship with Mongolia, 25k.
38. 1951; Power stations, 30k.
39. 1951; Vasnetsov, 1r.
40. 1954; Sports, 40k.
41. 1954; Lenin, 40k.
42. 1953; Volga–Don Canal, 40k.

PLATE 8

SAAR:

1. 1947; Coal miner, 6pf.
2. 1947; Loop of the Saar, 1m.
3. 1950; Colliery, 15f.
4. 1950; Holy Year, 25f.
5. 1952–5; GPO Saarbrücken, 30f.
6. 1953; Stamp Day, 15f.
7. 1954; Marian Year, 15f.

SAN MARINO:

8. 1945; Arms, 10c.
9. 1945; Postage due, 15c.
10. 1946; Air, 25c.
11. 1949; Definitive, 1l.
12. 1947; President Franklin D. Roosevelt, 1l.
13. 1952; Columbus, 5l.
14. 1952; Stamp Day, 2l.
15. 1953; Sports, 2l.
16. 1953; Flowers, 2l.
17. 1954; Sports, 2l.

SPAIN:

18. 1945; General Franco, 10p.
19. 1941–50; Air, 2p.
20. 1946; Anti-tuberculosis, 10c.
21. 1948; General Franco, 5c.
22. 1948; General Franco and Castillo de la Mota, 1p.
23. 1948; Railways, 5p.
24. 1949; UPU, 4p.
25. 1949; War victims relief, 5c.
26. 1949; Anti-tuberculosis, 10c.
27. 1949–50; El Cid, 15c.
28. 1950–53; Portraits, 5c.
29. 1950; Anti-tuberculosis, 10c.
30. 1951; Spanish–American Postal Union, 1p.
31. 1951; Birth of Isabella, 75c.
32. 1951; Anti-tuberculosis, 5c.
33. 1952; Ferdinand the Catholic, 50c.
34. 1952; Eucharistic Congress, 1p.
35. 1953; Anti-tuberculosis, 10c.
36. 1953; Stamp Day, 50c.
37. 1954; Holy Year, 3p.
38. 1950; Stamp centenary, 1p.
39. 1948; 7th Centenary of the Castilian Navy, 30c.
40. 1948; Ferdinand III of Castile, 25c.
41. 1954; Stamp Day, 80c.
42. 1950; Stamp centenary, 50c.
43. 1954; Marian Year, 50c.

PLATE 9

SWEDEN:

1. 1945; Red Cross, 20ö.
2. 1945; Press tercentenary, 5ö.

3. 1945; Viktor Rydberg, 20ö.
4. 1945; Savings banks, 40ö.
5. 1946; Lund Cathedral, 20ö.
6. 1946; Agricultural show, 5ö.
7. 1946; E. Tegner, 10ö.
8. 1946; A. Nobel, 30ö.
9. 1947; E. G. Geijer, 5ö.
10. 1947; King Gustav V, 10ö.
11. 1948; King Gustav V, 5ö.
12. 1948–69; Arms, 50ö.
13. 1948; Pioneers in USA, 15ö.
14. 1949; J. A. Strindberg, 20ö.
15. 1949; Lingiad, 15ö.
16. 1949; UPU, 20ö.
17. 1951–7; King Gustav VI Adolf, 10ö.
18. 1951; C. Polhem, 25ö.
19. 1951; Numeral, 5ö.
20. 1952; O. Petri, 25ö.
21. 1953; Athletics, 40ö.
22. 1953; Stockholm 7th centenary, 25ö.
23. 1953; Telecommunications, 25ö.
24. 1954; Ski championship, 10ö.
25. 1954; Anna Maria Lenngren, 20ö.
26. 1954; Rock-carvings, 50ö.

SWITZERLAND:

27. 1945; War relief, 10c. + 10c.
28. 1945; Red Cross, 5c. + 10c.
29. 1945; Peace, 20c.
30. 1946; J. H. Pestalozzi, 10c.
31. 1946; National Fête, 5c. + 5c.
32. 1946; Pro Juventute, 10c. + 10c.
33. 1947; 'Swissair', 2f.50.
34. 1947; Railways, 10c.
35. 1948; Olympic Games, 20c. + 10c.
36. 1948; Neuchâtel Castle, 10c.
37. 1949; UPU, 10c.
38. 1949; Federal post, 5c.
39. 1950; Pro Juventute, 5c. + 5c.
40. 1949; Grimsel Reservoir, 20c.
41. 1950; National Fête, 20c + 10c.
42. 1951; Pro Juventute, 40c. + 10c.
43. 1951; National Fête, 10c. + 10c.
44. 1952; Telecommunications, 10c.
45. 1953; Mobile post office, 10c.
46. 1953; Pro Juventute, 5c. + 5c.
47. 1954; Publicity, 40c.
48. 1954; Pro Juventute, 5c. + 5c.

WORLD HEALTH ORGANISATION:

49. 1948–50; Definitive, 40c.

INTERNATIONAL REFUGEES ORGANISATION:

50. 1950; Definitive, 1f.

PLATE 10

TRIESTE:

1. 1947; Air, 10l.
2. 1948; 1848 Revolution, series, 30l.
3. 1950; Weaver, 10l.
4. 1951; Third Trieste Fair, 20l.
5. 1949; Air, 20d. on 50l.
6. 1950; Animals series, 1d.

TURKEY:

7. 1946; President Inönü, set, 50k.
8. 1946; Battleship *Missouri*, 10k.
9. 1947; Smyrna Fair, 30k.
10. 1947; Battle of Dumlupinar, 20k.
11. 1947; Vintners' Congress, 60k.
12. 1948; President Inönü, series, 60k.
13. 1948; Treaty of Lausanne, 40k.
14. 1948; Proclamation of Republic, 1l.
15. 1949; Air, 1l.
16. 1949; Navy Day, 40k.

17. 1949; UPU, 40k.
18. 1950; Air, 20k.
19. 1950; General election, 30k.
20. 1950–55; Kemal Atatürk, 20k.
21. 1952; Views and portraits, set, 50k.
22. 1951; Coastal trading rights, 30k.
23. 1952; Views and portraits, series, 20k.
24. 1953; Ephesus, 15k.

VATICAN CITY:

25. 1945; Prisoners of war relief fund, 5l.
26. 1946; Pope Pius XII, 3l. surcharge on 1l.50.
27. 1946; Council of Trent, 1l.50c.
28. 1949; Basilicas, series, 25l.
29. 1952; Stamp centenary, 50l.
30. 1953; Popes, set, 10l.
31. 1954; Marian Year, 35l.
32. 1954; Termination of Marian Year, 35l.

VENEZIA GIULIA AND ISTRIA:

33. 1945; Italian definitive, 50c. surcharged 1l.
34. 1945; Air, 10l.
35. 1946; Postage due, 2l.

YUGOSLAVIA:

36. 1944–5; Monasteries, 4d. + 21d.
37. 1947; Marshal Tito, 6d.
38. 1948; Red Cross, 50p.
39. 1945; Marshal Tito, 2d.
40. 1947; Air, 10d.
41. 1947; Red Cross, 50p.
42. 1950; Occupations, series, 3d.
43. 1951; P. P. Njegos, 15d.
44. 1951; Air, 30d.

PLATE 11

ADEN:

1. 1951; 10c. on 2a. surcharge.
2. 1953; Elizabethan definitive, 35c.
3. 1955; Elizabethan definitive, 1s.

KATHIRI STATE OF SEIYUN:

4. 1954; Sultan Hussein, 5c.

QU'AITI STATE IN HADHRAMAUT:

5. 1946; Victory, 2½a.

AFGHANISTAN:

6. 1951; Definitive, 30p.
7. 1952; Red Crescent Day, 10p.

BAHRAIN:

8. 1948; King George VI, 6a.
9. 1952–4; Queen Elizabeth II, 6a.

BRUNEI:

10. 1952; Sultan Omar Ali Saifuddin, 8c.

BURMA:

11. 1947; Official, 1r.
12. 1948; Independence Day, 2a.
13. 1948; Martyrs' memorial, 2a.
14. 1954; Buddhist Council, 1k.
15. 1954; Royal throne, 1k.

CAMBODIA:

16. 1951; Apsara, 10c.

INTERNATIONAL COMMISSION IN INDO-CHINA:

17. 1954; Definitive, 12a.

CEYLON:

18. 1947; New constitution, 10c.
19. 1949; Independence, 25c.
20. 1950; Lion Rock, 30c.
21. 1951; Photogravure definitive, 3c.
22. 1952; Colombo Plan, 15c.
23. 1953; Coronation, 5c.
24. 1954; Royal visit, 10c.
25. 1954; Coconuts, 10c.

NORTH EAST CHINA:
26. 1949; Labour Day, $1,000.

CENTRAL CHINA:
27. 1949; Peasant, soldier and workman, $70.
28. 1949; Hankow, $290.

EAST CHINA:
29. 1949; Shanghai and Nanking, $1.

NORTH CHINA:
30. 1949; Industry, $6.

NORTH WEST CHINA:
31. 1949; Great Wall, $100.

PORT ARTHUR AND DAIREN:
32. 1950; Gate of Heavenly Peace, $100.

CHINA:
33. 1948; Dr. Sun Yat-sen (12th series), $40,000.
34. 1949; $10. surcharge on revenue stamp.
35. 1949; Undenominated stamp, surcharged 20c.

CHINA (Formosa):
36. 1950; Koxinga, $1.
37. 1953; President Chiang Kai-shek, $2.
38. 1954; Silo Bridge, $5.

CHINA (People's Republic):
39. 1949; Political conference, $100.
40. 1950; Gate of Heavenly Peace, $1,000.
41. 1951; Air, $3,000.
42. 1952; Gymnastics, $400.
43. 1953; Shepherdess, $200.
44. 1953; Peace, $250.
45. 1953; Karl Marx, $400.
46. 1953; Glorious Mother Country, $800.

HONG KONG:
47. 1946; Victory, $1.
48. 1938–52; King George VI, 20c.
49. 1949; UPU, 10c.
50. 1954; Elizabethan series, $5.

PLATE 12

INDIA:
1. 1946; Victory, 1½a.
2. 1947; Independence, 3½a.
3. 1948; Independence anniversary, 12a.
4. 1949; Red Fort, 2r.
5. 1949; UPU, 3½a.
6. 1950; Republic, 2a.
7. 1951; Asian Games, 12a.
8. 1950; Official, 2a.
9. 1950; Definitive, 1a.
10. 1952; Saints and poets, 12a.
11. 1951; Geological survey, 2a.
12. 1953; Railways, 2a.
13. 1953; Mount Everest, 14a.
14. 1953; Telegraph, 2a.
15. 1954; Stamp centenary, 1a.
16. 1954; UN Day, 2a.
17. 1954; Forestry Congress, 2a.

COCHIN:
18. 1946; Maharaja Sri Ravi Varma, 9p.

HYDERABAD:
19. 1947; Reformed legislature, 1a.

JAIPUR:
20. 1947; Silver Jubilee, 8a.

RAJASTHAN:
21. 1949; Kishangarh, 8a. handstamped.

TRAVANCORE-COCHIN:
22. 1950; Conch shell, 2p.

INDIAN SETTLEMENTS:
23. 1948; Apsara, 1c.

PORTUGUESE INDIA:
24. 1946; St. Francis Xavier, 1r.

NETHERLANDS INDIES:
25. 1945; Paddy field, 1c.
26. 1946; Tondano scene, 5c.
27. 1947; Queen Wilhelmina, 12½c.

INDONESIA:
28. 1948; Queen Wilhelmina, 15c.
29. 1949; Toradja House, 1r.
30. 1946; Oil well and factories, 40s.
31. 1950; Flag, 15s.
32. 1951; Olympic Games, 30s.
33. 1951; Definitive, 25s.
34. 1951–3; President Sukarno, 4r.

NETHERLANDS NEW GUINEA:
35. 1950; Numerals, 1c.
36. 1954; Bird of paradise, 5c.

IRAN:
37. 1945; Muhammed Riza Pahlavi, 1r.
38. 1949; Mosque, 1r. 50.
39. 1950; Hospital fund, undenominated.
40. 1954–6; Muhammed Riza Pahlavi, 25d.
41. 1949; National monuments, 50d. + 25d.
42. 1953; Air, 2r.

IRAQ:
43. 1948; King Faisal II, 8f.
44. 1949; Air, 50f.
45. 1949; UPU, 20f.
46. 1954; King Faisal II, 4f.

PLATE 13

ISRAEL:
1. 1948; Interim period local, 10m.
2. 1948; Coin, 20m.
3. 1949; Flag, 20pr.
4. 1949–52; Library, 100pr.
5. 1952; Postage due, 5pr.
6. 1949–52; Coin, 5pr.
7. 1951; Independence bonds, 80pr.
8. 1953; New Year, 20pr.
9. 1953; Air, 10pr.
10. 1948; New Year, 10m.
11. 1951; Zionist Congress, 80pr.
12. 1952; Independence, 30pr.
13. 1951; Third anniversary, 15pr.
14. 1949; Petah-Tikva, 40pr.
15. 1950; Air, 40pr.
16. 1954; New Year, 25pr.
17. 1951; National fund, 15pr.
18. 1951; New Year, 15pr.
19. 1951; National fund, 80pr.
20. 1954; Dr T. Z. Herzl, 160pr.
21. 1954; Baron de Rothschild, 300pr.

JAPAN:
22. 1945; Mt. Fuji, 10s.
23. 1946; Temple, 2y.
24. 1947; National art, 10y.
25. 1948; National art, 10y.
26. 1948; Farm girl, 2y.
27. 1949; Mt. Hodaka, 16y.
28. 1949; Afforestation, 5y.
29. 1949; National Park, 16y.
30. 1949–52; Portraits, 10y.
31. 1950; New Year, 2y.
32. 1950–51; Long-tailed cock, 5y.
33. 1950–51; Pictorial definitive, 10y.
34. 1950–51; Phoenix Temple, 24y.
35. 1951; Tourist issue, 24y.
36. 1951; New Year, 2y.
37. 1951; Tourist, 24y.

38. 1951; National Park, 14y.
39. 1952–63; Air, 25y.
40. 1951; Peace Treaty, 2y.
41. 1951; Athletics, 2y.
42. 1952; UPU, 5y.
43. 1952–64; Temple, 20y.
44. 1952; Athletics, 5y.
45. 1952; Investiture, 10y.
46. 1953; Air, 70y.
47. 1953; New Year, 5y.
48. 1954; Athletics, 5y.

BRITISH COMMONWEALTH OCCUPATION FORCE (Japan):
49. 1946–7; ½d. Australian definitive, overprinted.

PLATE 14

JOHORE:
1. 1949; Sultan Sir Ibrahim, 15c.

JORDAN:
2. 1946; Independence, 200m.
3. 1947; Parliament Building, 100m.
4. 1949; UPU, 4m.
5. 1954; Definitive series, 5f.

JORDANIAN OCCUPATION OF PALESTINE:
6. 1948; Jordanian stamp, overprinted, 200m.

KEDAH:
7. 1950; Sheaf of rice, 4c.

KELANTAN:
8. 1951; Sultan Tengku Ibrahim, 10c.

KOREA (South):
9. 1950; UPU post-horse warrant, 65wn.
10. 1954; Deer, 100h.
11. 1953; Hibiscus, 20h.
12. 1954; Air, 35h.

KOREA (North):
13. 1946; Hibiscus, 20ch.

INDIAN CUSTODIAN FORCES IN KOREA:
14. 1953; Indian stamp, overprinted for use in Korea, 1r.

KUWAIT:
15. 1945; Indian stamp overprinted, 3½a.
16. 1950; King George VI 1d. surcharged 1a.
17. 1952; Elizabethan 6d. surcharged 6a.

LAOS:
18. 1951; River Mekong, 30c.

INTERNATIONAL COMMISSION IN INDO-CHINA:
19. 1954; Indian stamp for use in Laos, 8a.

LEBANON:
20. 1946; Storks, 12p.50.
21. 1946–7; Cedar of Lebanon, 6p.
22. 1947; Air, 5p.
23. 1952; Cedar of Lebanon, 5p.

MACAO:
24. 1950–51; Arms and dragon, 1a.

MALAYA (British Military Administration):
25. 1945; King George VI, $2.

MALACCA:
26. 1949; King George VI, 3c.
27. 1954; Elizabethan series, 5c.

MALDIVE ISLANDS:
28. 1950; Definitive, 2l.

MONGOLIA:
29. 1951; 30th anniversary of Independence, 2t.

MUSCAT:
30. 1948; Olympic Games 1s. surcharged 1r.
31. 1952–4; Elizabethan 1s. 3d. surcharged 12a.

NEGRI SEMBILAN:
32. 1949–55; Arms, 5c.

NEPAL:
33. 1949; Pictorial definitive, 6p.

NORTH BORNEO:
34. 1947; Crown Colony, $2.
35. 1950; King George VI definitive, 2c.
36. 1954; Elizabethan series, 10c.

PAHANG:
37. 1950; Sultan Sir Abu Bakar, 25c.

PAKISTAN:
38. 1947; Indian stamp, overprinted, 12a.
39. 1948; Independence, 1r.
40. 1948; Pictorial series, 4a.
41. 1949; Anniversary of Mr. Jinnah's death, 10a.
42. 1949; Crescent moon, 1a.
43. 1951; Independence anniversary, 10a.
44. 1952; Stamp centenary, 12a.
45. 1954; Independence anniversary, 1r.
46. 1954; Conquest of K2, 2a.

BAHAWALPUR:
47. 1949; Silver Jubilee, 1a.

PENANG:
48. 1949; King George VI series, 10c.
49. 1954; Elizabethan definitive, 5c.

PERAK:
50. 1950; Sultan Yussuf 'Izzuddin Shah, 50c.

PERLIS:
51. 1951; Raja Syed Putra, 10c.

PLATE 15

PHILIPPINE ISLANDS:
1. 1945; Victory, 2c.
2. 1946; Independence, 6c.
3. 1947; Mayon volcano, 20c.
4. 1947; Manuel L. Quezon, 1c.
5. 1948; National flower, 3c.
6. 1949; UPU, 18c.
7. 1951; Arms, 18c.
8. 1948; President Roxas, 2c.
9. 1950; Baguio Conference, 18c.
10. 1950; Roosevelt, 4c.
11. 1952; Portrait series, 5c.
12. 1953; Manila Fair, 6c.
13. 1954; Marian Year, 6c.
14. 1954; Stamp centenary, 5c.

RYUKYU ISLANDS:
15. 1952; Pictorial series, 1y.

SARAWAK:
16. 1946; Centenary, $1.
17. 1950; King George VI pictorial series, $1.

SAUDI ARABIA:
18. 1949; Airmail, 3g.

SELANGOR:
19. 1949; Definitive, 4c.

SINGAPORE:
20. 1948; King George VI, $2.

SYRIA:
21. 1946; Presidential series, 12p.50.
22. 1946; Wheat ear definitive, 1p.
23. 1946; Shukri Bey, 25p.
24. 1948; Surcharged definitive, 25p.
25. 1949; Presidential Election, 50p.
26. 1950; Arms, 0p.50.
27. 1950; Latakia, 15p.
28. 1953; Pictorial series, 15p.
29. 1954; Industry, 25p.

THAILAND:
30. 1947; King Bhumibol, 50s.
31. 1950; Coronation, 20s.
32. 1951; King Bhumibol, 2b.

TIMOR:
33. 1952; St. Francis Xavier, 1a.
34. 1948; Definitive, 4a.

TRENGGANU:
35. 1949; Sultan Ismail, 10c.

VIETNAM DEMOCRATIC REPUBLIC:
36. 1945; Alexander of Rhodes, 15c.
37. 1945; Independence, 3c.

NORTH VIETNAM:
38. 1953; Production campaign, 100d.
39. 1954; Victory at Dien Bien Phu, 50d.

SOUTH VIETNAM:
40. 1951; Temple of Remembrance, 1p.
41. 1952; Airmail, 3p.30.
42. 1952; Day of Wandering Souls, 3p.70.
43. 1952; ITU membership, 1p.

INTERNATIONAL COMMISSION IN INDO-CHINA:
44. 1954; Indian stamp, overprinted for use in Vietnam, 1a.

YEMEN:
45. 1951; Yemeni flag, 5b.
46. 1951; Coffee plant, 8b.

PLATE 16

ALGERIA:
1. 1945; French 50c., overprinted.
2. 1947; Arms, 1f.50.
3. 1952; Isis of Cherchel, 12f.
4. 1949; Air, 50f.
5. 1954; Courtyard of Bardo Museum, 15f.

ANGOLA:
6. 1948; Restoration of Angola, 10c.
7. 1953; Animals series, 3a.
8. 1949; Founding of Mocámedes, 1a.

ASCENSION:
9. 1938–53; King George VI, 1d.

BASUTOLAND:
10. 1954; Elizabethan definitive, 1d.
11. 1947; Royal visit, 1d.

BECHUANALAND:
12. 1947; Royal visit, 1s.

BELGIAN CONGO:
13. 1947; Abolition of slavery, 10f.
14. 1947–50; Native art, 15c.
15. 1952; Flowers, 40c.

BRITISH MILITARY ADMINISTRATION (Eritrea):
16. 1948–9; King George VI, 65c.

BRITISH MILITARY ADMINISTRATION (Somalia):
17. 1948; King George VI, 25c.

BRITISH MILITARY ADMINISTRATION (Tripolitania):
18. 1948; King George VI, 12l.

CAPE JUBY:
19. 1948; Overprint, 2c.

CAPE VERDE ISLANDS:
20. 1952; Portuguese navigators, 5c.

CAMEROUN:
21. 1946; Bowman, 4f.

COMORO ISLANDS:
22. 1950; Anjouan Bay, 10c.

CYRENAICA:
23. 1950; Mounted warrior, 5m.

EGYPT:
24. 1945; King Farouk, 10m.
25. 1945; Khedive Ismail Pasha, 10m.
26. 1947; Air, 7m.
27. 1952; 2m. overprinted King of Egypt and the Sudan.
28. 1953; Republican, 4m.
29. 1953; Defence, 20m.
30. 1953; Agriculture, 4m.
31. 1954; Agriculture, 3m.

ETHIOPIA:
32. 1947; Pictorial series, 1c.

FEZZAN:
33. 1946; Fort of Sebha, 1f.

FRENCH EQUATORIAL AFRICA:
34. 1946; Bacongo girl, 20f.

FRENCH SOMALI COAST:
35. 1947; Danakil tent, 10c.

FRENCH WEST AFRICA:
36. 1945; Soldiers, 4f.
37. 1947; Dahomey labourer, 4f.
38. 1947; Girl and bridge, 30c.
39. 1953–8; Pictorial series, 25f.

GAMBIA:
40. 1953; Elizabethan definitive, 5s.

GOLD COAST:
41. 1948; King George VI series, 3d.
42. 1952–4; Elizabethan definitive, ½d.

GHADAMES:
43. 1949; Cross of Agadem, 100f.

IFNI:
44. 1951; Colonial Stamp Day, 5c. + 5c.

KENYA, UGANDA AND TANGANYIKA:
45. 1952; Royal visit, 1s.
46. 1954; Royal visit, 30c.
47. 1954; Elizabethan series, 10c.

LIBERIA:
48. 1952; United Nations, 1c.

LIBYA:
49. 1951; Cyrenaican stamp, surcharged 1 mal.
50. 1952; King Idris I, 25m.

PLATE 17

MADAGASCAR:
1. 1946; General Galliéni, 2f.
2. 1947; Postage due, 10c.

MAURITIUS:
3. 1948; Stamp centenary, 12c.
4. 1950; King George VI series, 2c.
5. 1953; Queen Elizabeth II definitive, 15c.

MOROCCO (French):
6. 1947; Marrakesh, 6f.
7. 1951–4; Oudayas Point, Rabat, 15f.

MOROCCO (Spanish):
8. 1948; Camel caravan, 50c.
9. 1954; Anti-tuberculosis fund, 10c.
10. 1948–51; Tangier palm tree, 5c.

MOROCCO (British):
11. 1952; Elizabethan 2½d., overprinted.
12. 1954; Elizabethan ½d., surcharged 5c.
13. 1946; Tangier overprint on Victory, 3d.
14. 1952–4; Tangier overprint on Elizabethan, ½d.

MOZAMBIQUE:
15. 1948–9; Lourenco Marques, 80c.
16. 1951; Fish, 30c.
17. 1953; Butterflies, 1E.
18. 1954; Map, 1E.

NIGERIA:
19. 1949; UPU, 1d.
20. 1953; Elizabethan definitive, 5s.

NORTHERN RHODESIA:
21. 1938–52; King George VI, 2d.
22. 1953; Cecil Rhodes, 2d.
23. 1953; Elizabethan series, 4½d.

NYASALAND:
24. 1945; King George VI definitive, 6d.
25. 1953; Rhodes centenary, 6d.
26. 1953; Elizabethan series, 9d.

PORTUGUESE GUINEA:
27. 1951; Termination of Holy Year, 1E.
28. 1953; Insects, 5c.

RÉUNION:
29. 1945; Free French issue surcharged, 4f.50.
30. 1947; Cascade, 1f.
31. 1947; Postage due, 10c.
32. 1949–59; French 40f., surcharged 8f.

RHODESIA AND NYASALAND:
33. 1954; Elizabethan series, 5s.

RUANDA–URUNDI:
34. 1948; Native art, 10c.
35. 1953; Flowers, 10c.

ST. HELENA:
36. 1953; Elizabethan definitive, 3d.

ST. THOMAS AND PRINCE ISLANDS:
37. 1952; Navigators, 10c.

SEYCHELLES:
38. 1952; King George VI series, 2c.
39. 1954; Elizabethan definitive, 45c.

SIERRA LEONE:
40. 1953; Coronation, 1½d.

SOMALIA:
41. 1950; Airmail, 1s.
42. 1950; Postage due, 2c.

SOMALILAND PROTECTORATE:
43. 1953; Elizabethan definitive, 35c.

SOUTH WEST AFRICA:
44. 1947; Royal visit, 2d.
45. 1953; Coronation, 4d.
46. 1954; Pictorial series, 4d.

PLATE 18

SOUTH AFRICA:
1. 1945; Victory, *se-tenant*, 3d.
2. 1947; Royal visit, *se-tenant*, 3d.
3. 1950; Union buildings, *se-tenant*, 2d.
4. 1948; Silver Wedding, *se-tenant*, 3d.
5. 1949; British settlers, *se-tenant*, 1½d.
6. 1949; UPU, *se-tenant*, 1½d.
7. 1949; Voortrekker monument, 1d.
8. 1952; Van Riebeeck, 2d.
9. 1952; Stamp exhibition, 1d.
10. 1953; Coronation, 2d.
11. 1953; Stamp centenary, 4d.
12. 1953; Aloes, 1s. 6d.
13. 1954; Orange Free State, 2d.
14. 1954; Springbok, 1s. 3d.

SOUTHERN RHODESIA:
15. 1947; Royal visit, 1d.
16. 1953; Cecil Rhodes, 1d.
17. 1953; Coronation, 2s. 6d.
18. 1953; Elizabethan definitive, 1s.

SPANISH GUINEA:
19. 1949; Pictorial series, 5c.
20. 1951; Colonial Stamp Day, 10c. + 5c.

SPANISH SAHARA:
21. 1953; Royal Geographical Society, 5c.
22. 1953; Child Welfare, 15c.

SPANISH WEST AFRICA:
23. 1950; Pictorial series, 2c.

SUDAN:
24. 1951; Cotton picking, 2p.
25. 1954; Self-government, 15m.
26. 1950; Air, 4p.

SWAZILAND:
27. 1947; Royal visit, 3d.
28. 1945; Victory, *se-tenant*, 2d.

TOGO:
29. 1947; Pictorial definitive, 10c.
30. 1947; Postage due, 10c.

TRISTAN DA CUNHA:
31. 1952; St. Helena 5s., overprinted.
32. 1954; Elizabethan series, 10s.

TUNISIA:
33. 1949; UPU, 5f.
34. 1945; Pictorial series, 20f.
35. 1950–53; Horse, 15f.

ZANZIBAR:
36. 1946; Victory, 10c.
37. 1952; Sultan Kalif bin Harub, series, 5s.
38. 1954; Sultan's 75th birthday, 1s.25.

PLATE 19

CANADA:
1. 1946; Peace, 8c.
2. 1946; Peace, 10c.
3. 1946; Peace, 14c.
4. 1946; Peace, 20c.
5. 1946; Peace, $1.
6. 1946; Air, 7c.
7. 1947; Alexander Graham Bell, 4c.
8. 1947; Citizenship, 4c.
9. 1948; Responsible government, 4c.
10. 1949; Cabot's ship, 4c.
11. 1948; Princess Elizabeth's wedding, 4c.
12. 1949; Halifax, 4c.
13. 1949; King George VI, 2c.
14. 1950; King George VI, 2c.
15. 1950; Oil wells, 50c.
16. 1950; Drying furs, 10c.
17. 1951; Fisherman, $1.
18. 1951; Prime Ministers (first series), 3c.
19. 1951; Prime Ministers (first series), 4c.
20. 1951; Stamp centenary, 4c.
21. 1951; Stamp centenary, 7c.
22. 1951; Stamp centenary, 15c.
23. 1951; Royal visit, 4c.
24. 1952; Forestry products, 20c.
25. 1952; Red Cross, 4c.
26. 1952; Canada goose, 7c.
27. 1952; Prime Ministers (second series), 3c.
28. 1952; Prime Ministers (second series), 4c.
29. 1953; Totem pole, $1.
30. 1953; Wild Life Week, 2c.
31. 1953; Wild Life Week, 3c.
32. 1953; Wild Life Week, 4c.

33. 1953; Elizabethan definitive, 4c.
34. 1953; Coronation, 4c.
35. 1953; Textile industry, 50c.
36. 1954; Queen Elizabeth, 6c.
37. 1954; Wild Life Week, 4c.
38. 1954; Wild Life Week, 5c.
39. 1954; Wild Life Week, 15c.
40. 1954; Prime Ministers (third series), 4c.
41. 1954; Prime Ministers (third series), 5c.

GREENLAND:
42. 1945; Dog team, 30ö.
43. 1950; Arctic Sea ship, 1k.

NEWFOUNDLAND:
44. 1946; 30c. stamp surcharged, 2c.
45. 1947; Princess Elizabeth's 21st birthday, 4c.
46. 1947; Cabot's discovery, 5c.

ST. PIERRE & MIQUELON:
47. 1947; Pictorial series, 10c.
48. 1947; Postage due, 10c.

PLATE 20

UNITED STATES OF AMERICA:
1. 1945; San Francisco Conference, 5c.
2. 1945; US Marines, 3c.
3. 1945; President Roosevelt, 1c.
4. 1945; President Roosevelt, 2c.
5. 1945; Army, 3c.
6. 1945; Navy, 3c.
7. 1945; Coast Guard, 3c.
8. 1945; Alfred E. Smith, 3c.
9. 1945; Texas, 3c.
10. 1946; War veterans, 3c.
11. 1946; Mercantile Marine, 3c.
12. 1946; Iowa, 3c.
13. 1946; Smithsonian Institution, 3c.
14. 1946; Air, 5c.
15. 1947; Thomas Edison, 3c.
16. 1946; Kearny Expedition, 3c.
17. 1947; Air, 5c.
18. 1947; Joseph Pulitzer, 3c.
19. 1947; Stamp centenary, 3c.
20. 1947; Medical profession, 3c.
21. 1947; Stamp centenary, miniature sheet.
22. 1947; Utah, 3c.
23. 1947; Frigate *Constitution*, 3c.
24. 1948; California, 3c.
25. 1948; Mississippi, 3c.
26. 1947; Air, 10c.
27. 1947; Air, 15c.
28. 1947; Air, 25c.
29. 1948; Wisconsin, 3c.
30. 1947; Everglades, 3c.
31. 1948; Swedish pioneers, 5c.
32. 1948; US–Canadian friendship, 3c.
33. 1948; F. S. Key, 3c.
34. 1948; Youth, 3c.
35. 1948; H. F. Stone, 3c.
36. 1948; Oregan Territory, 3c.
37. 1948; Mount Palomar Observatory, 3c.
38. 1948; Clara Barton, 3c.
39. 1948; American Poultry Industry, 3c.
40. 1948; Fort Kearny, 3c.

PLATE 21

UNITED STATES OF AMERICA:
1. 1948; Bereaved mothers, 3c.
2. 1948; Volunteer firemen, 3c.
3. 1948; Rough Riders, 3c.
4. 1948; J. G. Low, 3c.
5. 1948; Moina Michael, 3c.

6. 1948; Fort Bliss, 3c.
7. 1948; J. C. Harris, 3c.
8. 1949; Minnesota, 3c.
9. 1949; Washington and Lee University, 3c.
10. 1949; Gubernatorial election in Puerto Rico, 3c.
11. 1949; Annapolis, 3c.
12. 1949; Grand Army, 3c.
13. 1949; UPU, 10c.
14. 1949; UPU, 15c.
15. 1949; Edgar Allan Poe, 3c.
16. 1949; Wright brothers, 6c.
17. 1950; Bankers' Association, 3c.
18. 1950; Samuel Gompers, 3c.
19. 1950; National Capital sesquicentenary, 3c.
20. 1950; Railway engineers, 3c.
21. 1950; Kansas City, 3c.
22. 1950; National Capital sesquicentenary, 3c.
23. 1950; Boy Scouts, 3c.
24. 1950; Indiana, 3c.
25. 1950; National Capital sesquicentenary, 3c.
26. 1950; California, 3c.
27. 1950; National Capital sesquicentenary, 3c.
28. 1951; United Confederate veterans, 3c.
29. 1951; Nevada, 3c.
30. 1951; Landing of Cadillac, 3c.
31. 1951; Colorado, 3c.
32. 1951; Chemical Society, 3c.
33. 1951; Battle of Brooklyn, 3c.
34. 1952; 4-H Clubs, 3c.
35. 1952; Railway, 3c.
36. 1952; Automobile Association, 3c.
37. 1952; Air, 80c.
38. 1952; NATO, 3c.
39. 1952; Columbia Basin reclamation, 3c.
40. 1952; Lafayette, 3c.
41. 1952; Mt. Rushmore, 3c.

PLATE 22

UNITED STATES OF AMERICA:
1. 1952; Civil Engineers Society, 3c.
2. 1952; Newspaper boys, 3c.
3. 1952; Printing of first book from movable type, 3c.
4. 1952; Red Cross, 3c.
5. 1953; Ohio, 3c.
6. 1953; Washington Territory, 3c.
7. 1953; Louisiana Purchase, 3c.
8. 1953; Opening of Japan to foreign trade, 5c.
9. 1953; American Bar Association, 3c.
10. 1953; Theodore Roosevelt's home, 3c.
11. 1953; Future farmers of America, 3c.
12. 1953; Trucking industry, 3c.
13. 1953; General G. S. Patton, 3c.
14. 1953; New York City, 3c.
15. 1953; Gadsden Purchase, 3c.
16. 1954; Columbia University, 3c.
17. 1954; Kansas, 3c.
18. 1954; George Eastman, 3c.
19. 1954; Lewis and Clark Expedition, 3c.
20. 1954–65; Franklin, ½c.
21. 1954–65; Washington, 1c.
22. 1954–65; Palace of the Governors, Santa Fé, 1¼c.
23. 1954–65; Mount Vernon, 1½c.
24. 1954–65; Jefferson, 2c.
25. 1954–65; Bunker Hill monument, 2½c.
26. 1954–65; Statue of Liberty, 3c.
27. 1954–65; Lincoln, 4c.
28. 1954–65; The Hermitage, 4½c.
29. 1954–65; Monroe, 5c.
30. 1954–65; Theodore Roosevelt, 6c.
31. 1954–65; Woodrow Wilson, 7c.
32. 1954–65; Statue of Liberty, 8c.

33. 1954–65; Statue of Liberty, 8c.
34. 1954–65; General J. J. Pershing, 8c.
35. 1954–65; The Alamo, 9c.
36. 1954–65; Independence Hall, 10c.
37. 1954–65; Statue of Liberty, 11c.
38. 1954–65; Benjamin Harrison, 12c.
39. 1954–65; John Jay, 15c.
40. 1954–65; Monticello, 20c.
41. 1954–65; Paul Revere, 25c.
42. 1954–65; Robert E. Lee, 30c.
43. 1954–65; John Marshall, 40c.
44. 1954–65; Susan B. Anthony, 50c.
45. 1954–65; Patrick Henry, $1.
46. 1954–65; Alexander Hamilton, $5.
47. 1958; Airmail, 5c.

UNITED NATIONS:
48. 1951; Air, 15c.
49. 1951; Peoples of the world, 1c.
50. 1951; UN headquarters, 1½c.
51. 1952; Signing of Charter, 5c.
52. 1953; Technical assistance, 5c.

PLATE 23

MEXICO:
1. 1946; United Nations, 6c.
2. 1947; USA stamp centenary, 15c.
3. 1950; International Highway, 20c.
4. 1950; South-eastern railway, 20c.
5. 1950; Pictorial series, 5c.
6. 1950; Air, 80c.
7. 1946; Literacy campaign, 1c.

BRITISH HONDURAS:
8. 1949; Battle of St. George's Cay, 5c.
9. 1953; Elizabethan series, 10c.

CANAL ZONE:
10. 1946; Portraits, series, 5c.
11. 1951; Air, 21c.

COSTA RICA:
12. 1945; Red Cross, 1col.
13. 1947; Franklin D. Roosevelt, 15c.
14. 1950; Agricultural, Cattle and Industries Fair, 3c.
15. 1954; Industries, 80c.

EL SALVADOR:
16. 1947; Portraits, 3c.
17. 1948; F. D. Roosevelt, series, 14c.
18. 1952; Revolution and 1950 Constitution, 1col.
19. 1953; J. Marti, 10c.
20. 1953; Independence commemoration, 1col.

GUATEMALA:
21. 1945; Payo Enriquex de Rivera, 2c.
22. 1945; Anniversary of revolution, 5c.
23. 1948; Air, 5c.
24. 1949; Bartolomé de las Casas, 2c.
25. 1950; Tourist propaganda, 3c.
26. 1950; Central American and Caribbean Games, 4c.
27. 1951; State Schools, 1c.
28. 1953; National anthem commemoration, 3c.

HONDURAS:
29. 1949; Inauguration of President, 40c.

NICARAGUA:
30. 1946; President Roosevelt commemoration, 8c.
31. 1947; Triangular series, 3c.
32. 1949; Baseball championships, 2cor.
33. 1950; UPU, 20c.
34. 1952; Isabella the Catholic, 2cor.30.
35. 1953; Presidential series, 1cor.20.
36. 1954; United Nations, 3c.
37. 1954; Air Force, 1c.

PANAMA:
38. 1942–57; Pictorial series, 10c.
39. 1949; UPU, 1c.
40. 1952; Isabella the Catholic, 5c.

PLATE 24

ARGENTINE REPUBLIC:
1. 1945; B. Rivadavia, 20c.
2. 1946; President Roosevelt, 5c.
3. 1946; Argentina and populace, 15c.
4. 1946; Industrial exhibition, 5c.
5. 1947; Antarctic mail, 20c.
6. 1947; Week of the Wing, 15c.
7. 1947; Training ship, 5c.
8. 1947; Bridge, 5c.
9. 1947; Educational Crusade, 5c.
10. 1947; Cervantes, 5c.
11. 1949; Constitution Day, 1p.
12. 1948; Safety First campaign, 5c.
13. 1951; South America and Antarctic, 1p.
14. 1951; Five-Year-Plan, 5c.
15. 1952; Eva Peron, 25c.
16. 1952; Eva Peron, 1p.
17. 1953; Rescue ship Uruguay, 50c.
18. 1954; Argentine Post Office in South Orkneys, 1p.45.
19. 1954; Stock Exchange, 1p.
20. 1954; Eva Peron, 3p.

BOLIVIA:
21. 1946; National anthem, 15c.
22. 1950; Air, 20c.
23. 1951; La Paz, 10b.
24. 1952; Isabella the Catholic, 6b.30.
25. 1951; Sports series, 50c.
26. 1954; Agrarian reform, 5b.

BRAZIL:
27. 1947–54; Smelting works, 60c.
28. 1947–54; Count of Porto Alegre, 10cr.
29. 1945; Baron do Rio Branco, 40c.
30. 1945; Victory, 20c.
31. 1948; Rotary congress, 3cr.80.
32. 1948; Exhibition at Petropolis, 40c.
33. 1949; President Roosevelt, 3cr.80.
34. 1950; Football, 5cr.80.
35. 1951; Week of the Wing, 3cr.80.
36. 1952; Telegraph centenary, 5cr.
37. 1953; Young Baptists Conference, 3cr.80.
38. 1953; Duke of Caxias, 5cr.80.
39. 1954; Portraits, series, 50c.
40. 1954; Obligatory tax, 10c.

BRITISH GUIANA:
41. 1938–52; King George VI series, $3.
42. 1954; Elizabethan definitive, 4c.

PLATE 25

CHILE:
1. 1947; Antarctic Territory, 2p.50.
2. 1947; Miguel de Cervantes, 40c.
3. 1948; Portrait, series, 60c.
4. 1948–54; Portraits, 1p.
5. 1949; B. V. Mackenna, 60c.
6. 1949; School of Arts and Crafts, 10p.
7. 1950; UPU, 10p.
8. 1950–55; Air, 20c.
9. 1951; General San Martin, 5p.
10. 1952; Isabella the Catholic, 10p.
11. 1954; National airline, 3p.

COLOMBIA:
12. 1952; Doctors, 1c.
13. 1945–8; Obligatory tax, 1c.
14. 1945; Air, 20c.

15. 1946; Map, 15c.
16. 1947; Coffee, 5c.
17. 1947; J. C. Mutis and J. J. Triana, 25c.
18. 1948; Obligatory tax, 20c.
19. 1952; Proposed new post office, 5c.
20. 1950; UPU, 3c.
21. 1952; Manizales, 23c.
22. 1950; Farm, 5c.
23. 1954; Air, 50c.
24. 1953; Chorographical Commission, 23c.
25. 1948–50; Obligatory tax, 2c.
26. 1953; Air, 25c.
27. 1954; Senior College of Our Lady of the Rosary, 10c.
28. 1954; Air, 5c.

ECUADOR:
29. 1950; Consular service stamp, overprinted 'CORREOS', 10c.
30. 1952–3; Consular service stamp, surcharged, 30c.
31. 1947; Father J. de Velasco, 1s.
32. 1947; Jesuit Church, Quito, 30c.
33. 1947; Official, 30c.
34. 1952; Literacy Campaign, 1s.
35. 1954; Obligatory tax, 20c.
36. 1954; Obligatory tax, 10c.

FRENCH GUIANA:
37. 1945; Arms, 40c.
38. 1947; Hammock, 10c.

PARAGUAY:
39. 1944–5; Ytororo Heroes Monument, 1g.
40. 1950; Roosevelt, 1g.
41. 1949; Aid to earthquake victims, 5c. + 5c.
42. 1952; Columbus memorial lighthouse, 30c.
43. 1954; National heroes, 5c.

PLATE 26

PERU:
1. 1945; Airmail, 5c.
2. 1947; Tourist congress, 1s.
3. 1949; Pictorial series, 4c.
4. 1950; Education, 3c.
5. 1951; Pictorial series, 15c.
6. 1951; San Marcos University, 2s.
7. 1951; UPU, 20s.
8. 1952; Pictorial definitive, 25c.
9. 1952; Pictorial series, 1s.

SURINAM:
10. 1945; Pictorial definitive, 1c.
11. 1948; Queen Wilhelmina, 60c.

URUGUAY:
12. 1940–61; Artigas, 3c.
13. 1940–61; Artigas, 12c.
14. 1945; José Pedro Varela, 5c.
15. 1945; Air, 8c.
16. 1946; Rio Negro power dam, 20c.
17. 1946; Arms, 3c.
18. 1947–59; Air, 36c.
19. 1948; J. E. Rodo, 10c.
20. 1948; Air, 24c.
21. 1948; Santa Lucia Bridge, 10c.
22. 1949; Montevideo University, 36c.
23. 1950; Cordon, 3c.
24. 1952; General Artigas, 5m.
25. 1952; General Artigas, 5c.
26. 1952; UPU, 7c.
27. 1953; Postal Congress, 7c.
28. 1950; Parcel post, 1c.
29. 1954; Pictorial series, 3c.
30. 1954; Pictorial definitive, 7c.
31. 1954; Pictorial issue, 1p.

VENEZUELA:
32. 1947; Bolivar 20c. surcharged 10c.
33. 1948; Merchant Marine, 10c.
34. 1950; UPU, 90c.
35. 1950; Alonso de Ojeda, 10c.
36. 1950; Census of the Americas, 60c.
37. 1951; Bolivar statue, 40c.
38. 1953–4; General Post Office, Caracas, 5c.
39. 1952; Our Lady of Coromoto, 1b.
40. 1951; Provinces, series, 10c.

PLATE 27

ANTIGUA:
1. 1938–49; King George VI series, £1.
2. 1953; Elizabethan series, 6c.
3. 1953; Elizabethan series, 8c.

BAHAMAS:
4. 1948; Tercentenary, 8d.
5. 1948; Tercentenary, 1s.
6. 1938–52; King George VI, 10d.
7. 1954; Elizabethan series, 8d.
8. 1954; Elizabethan definitive, 2s. 6d.

BARBADOS:
9. 1947; Badge of the Colony surcharged, 1d.
10. 1949; UPU, 1s.
11. 1950; King George VI, 1c.
12. 1950; Pictorial series, 24c.
13. 1952; Stamp centenary, 12c.
14. 1953–7; Elizabethan series, 3c.
15. 1953–7; Elizabethan definitive, 5c.

BERMUDA:
16. 1949; Postmaster Perot's stamp, 2½d.
17. 1953; Elizabethan series, ½d.
18. 1953; Elizabethan definitive, 1½d.
19. 1953; Pictorial series, 6d.
20. 1953; Three Power Talks, 1s. 3d.

CAYMAN ISLANDS:
21. 1938–47; King George VI definitive, 2½d.
22. 1950; King George VI series, ¼d.
23. 1953–9; Elizabethan, 9d.
24. 1953; Elizabethan definitive, 4d.

DOMINICA:
25. 1938–47; King George VI series, 10s.
26. 1951; King George VI definitive, 48c.
27. 1951; King George VI series, $2.40.
28. 1951; New Constitution, 5c.
29. 1954; Queen Elizabeth, ½c.
30. 1954; Elizabethan definitive, 12c.
31. 1954; Elizabethan series, 24c.

FALKLAND ISLANDS:
32. 1938–49; King George VI series, 6d.
33. 1938–49; King George VI definitive, 1s. 3d.
34. 1952; King George VI series, 1d.

FALKLAND ISLANDS DEPENDENCIES:
35. 1946–9; King George VI definitive, 2½d.
36. 1948; Silver Wedding, 1s.
37. 1954; Elizabethan series, 2½d.

GRENADA:
38. 1951; King George VI, 1c.
39. 1951; New Constitution, 4c.
40. 1953; Elizabethan series, 6c.

PLATE 28

JAMAICA:
1. 1945; New Constitution, 3d.
2. 1945; New Constitution, 2s.
3. 1945; New Constitution, 4½d.
4. 1938–52; King George VI, ½d.

5. 1938–52; Bananas, 3d.
6. 1951; British West Indies University College, 2d.
7. 1952; Boy Scouts, 6d.
8. 1952; Boy Scouts, 2d.
9. 1953; Royal visit, 2d.

LEEWARD ISLANDS:
10. 1954; Elizabethan, 60c.
11. 1954; Queen Elizabeth II, $4.80.

MONTSERRAT:
12. 1938–48; Botanic Station, 10s.
13. 1938–48; Carr's Bay, £1.
14. 1951; Picking tomatoes, 24c.
15. 1953; Elizabethan series, 3c.

ST. KITTS–NEVIS:
16. 1938–48; King George VI, 10s.
17. 1950; Anguilla tercentenary, 2½d.
18. 1950; Anguilla tercentenary, 6d.
19. 1950; Anguilla tercentenary, 1s.

ST. CHRISTOPHER NEVIS AND ANGUILLA:
20. 1952; King George VI, 2c.
21. 1954; Elizabethan definitive, 4c.
22. 1954; Elizabethan series, 12c.

ST. LUCIA:
23. 1938–48; King George VI, 3½d.
24. 1949; King George VI, 12c.
25. 1949; Device of St. Lucia, 24c.
26. 1951; Reconstruction of Castries, 12c.
27. 1951; New Constitution, 2c.
28. 1953–4; Elizabethan definitive, 4c.
29. 1953–4; Device of St. Lucia, 50c.

ST. VINCENT:
30. 1938–47; King George VI series, 2s. 6d.
31. 1949; King George VI definitive, 2c.
32. 1949; King George VI series, 1c.
33. 1949; King George VI definitive, 10c.
34. 1951; New Constitution, 3c.
35. 1951; New Constitution, 5c.

TRINIDAD AND TOBAGO:
36. 1953; Elizabethan series, 1c.
37. 1953; Discovery of Lake Asphalt, 6c.
38. 1953; Government House, 24c.
39. 1951; British West Indies University College, 12c.

TURKS AND CAICOS ISLANDS:
40. 1938–45; King George VI series, 1s.
41. 1948; Centenary of separation from Bahamas, 5s.
42. 1948; Centenary of separation from Bahamas, ½d.
43. 1950; King George VI definitive, 1s.

VIRGIN ISLANDS:
44. 1938–47; King George VI series, £1.
45. 1952; Cattle industry, 5c.
46. 1952; Road Town, $2.40.
47. 1951; Restoration of Legislative Council, $1.20.

PLATE 29

CUBA:
1. 1946; M. M. Sterling, 2c.
2. 1947; F. D. Roosevelt, 2c.
3. 1947; National cattle show, 2c.
4. 1949; Manuel Sanguily, 5c.
5. 1949; Isle of Pines, 5c.
6. 1948; Marti, 50th death anniversary, 2c.
7. 1945; Special delivery, 10c.
8. 1948; Leprosy Congress, 2c.
9. 1948; Tobacco industry, 2c.
10. 1948; Postal employees' retirement fund, 5c.
11. 1949; Postal employees' retirement fund, 1c.

12. 1949; UPU 75th anniversary, 1c.
13. 1949; Obligatory tax for TB fund, 1c.
14. 1950; Postal employees' retirement fund, 1c.
15. 1951; Post office rebuilding fund, 1c.
16. 1952; Post office rebuilding fund, 1c.
17. 1952; Isabella the Catholic, 25c.
18. 1952; Christmas, 1c.
19. 1953; TB fund, 1c.
20. 1953; Marti centenary, 5c.
21. 1953; TB fund, 1c.
22. 1954; Definitive, 2c.
23. 1954; Sugar industry, 25c.
24. 1954; TB fund, 1c.
25. 1954; J. M. Rodriguez, 5c.
26. 1954; Boy Scouts, 4c.

CURAÇAO:
27. 1946; Definitive, 12½c.
28. 1947; Air, 30c.
29. 1948; Definitive, 25c.

NETHERLANDS ANTILLES:
30. 1949; UPU 75th anniversary, 25c.
31. 1950; Definitive, 25c.
32. 1950; Numeral, 5c.
33. 1953; Dutch flood relief, 22½c. + 7½c.

DOMINICAN REPUBLIC:
34. 1945; Communications emblem, 3c.
35. 1946; Law Courts, 3c.
36. 1946; Caribbean air routes, 10c.
37. 1949; UPU 75th anniversary, 2c.
38. 1947; TB fund, 1c.
39. 1949; Battle of Las Carreras, 10c.

HAITI:
40. 1945; Red Cross, 60c.
41. 1946; Roosevelt, 60c.
42. 1946; Capois-la-Mort, 50c.
43. 1950; Bicentenary of Port-au-Prince, 1g.
44. 1951; Isabella the Catholic, 30c.
45. 1954; Lamartine, 1g.50.

GUADELOUPE:
46. 1945; Free French definitive, 15f.
47. 1947; Woman and Basse Terre, 50c.
48. 1947; Postage due, 30c.

MARTINIQUE:
49. 1945; Victor Schoelcher, 10c.
50. 1947; Definitive, 10c.
51. 1947; Postage due, 10c.

PLATE 30

AUSTRALIA:
1. 1945; Duke and Duchess of Gloucester, 3½d.
2. 1946; Victory, 2½d.
3. 1946; Victory, 5½d.
4. 1946; Victory, 3½d.
5. 1946; Sir Thomas Mitchell, 1s.
6. 1947; Newcastle, 3½d.
7. 1947; Newcastle, 2½d.
8. 1947; Newcastle, 5½d.
9. 1947; Princess Elizabeth's marriage, 1d.
10. 1948; Hereford bull, 1s. 3d.
11. 1948–56; Hermes and globe, 1s. 6d.
12. 1948; Aboriginal art, 2s.
13. 1948–56; Coat of arms, 10s.
14. 1948; William J. Farrer, 2½d.
15. 1948; Sir Ferdinand von Mueller, 2½d.
16. 1948; Boy Scout, 2½d.
17. 1949; Henry Lawson, 2½d.
18. 1949; UPU, 3½d.
19. 1949; Lord Forrest of Bunbury, 2½d.
20. 1950–51; King George VI, 3d.
21. 1950–51; Queen Elizabeth II, 2d.

22. 1950; Aborigine, 8½d.
23. 1950; Stamp centenary, 2½d.
24. 1950; Stamp centenary, 2½d.
25. 1951; Commonwealth of Australia, 3d.
26. 1951; Commonwealth of Australia, 5½d.
27. 1951; Commonwealth of Australia, 3d.
28. 1951; Commonwealth of Australia, 1s. 6d.
29. 1951; E. H. Hargraves, 3d.
30. 1951; Victoria, 3d.
31. 1951–2; King George VI, 6½d.
32. 1952; King George VI, 1s. 0½d.
33. 1953; Elizabethan definitive, 3½d.
34. 1953; Coronation, 3½d.
35. 1953; Young Farmers, 3½d.
36. 1953; Tasmania, 3½d.
37. 1953; Tasmania, 3½d.
38. 1953; Food production, 3 × 3½d.
39. 1953; Tasmania, 2s.
40. 1953; Tasmanian stamp centenary, 3d.
41. 1953; Royal visit, 7½d.
42. 1954; Royal visit, 2s.
43. 1954; Telegraph, 3½d.
44. 1954; Red Cross, 3½d.
45. 1954; Western Australia stamp centenary, 3½d.
46. 1954; Railways, 3½d.
47. 1954; Antarctic, 3½d.
48. 1954; Olympic Games, 2s.

PLATE 31

NEW ZEALAND:
1. 1945; Arms, £1.
2. 1945; Health, 2d. + 1d.
3. 1946; Peace, ½d.
4. 1946; Peace, 1½d.
5. 1946; Peace, 3d.
6. 1946; Peace, 1s.
7. 1946; Peace, 4d.
8. 1946; Peace, 5d.
9. 1946; Peace, 9d.
10. 1947; Health, 2d. + 1d.
11. 1946; Health, 1d. + ½d.
12. 1947; King George VI, 3s.
13. 1948; Otago, 1d.
14. 1948; Otago, 3d.
15. 1948; Otago, 6d.
16. 1948; Health, 2d. + 1d.
17. 1949; Health, 1d. + ½d.
18. 1950; Undenominated arms stamp, surcharged 1½d.
19. 1950; Health, 2d. + 1d.
20. 1950; Canterbury, 2d.
21. 1950; Canterbury, 1d.
22. 1950; Canterbury, 6d.
23. 1952; Health, 1½d. + ½d.
24. 1952; Health, 2d. + 1d.
25. 1951; Health, 1½d. + ½d.
26. 1953; King George VI ½d., surcharged 1d.
27. 1953; Coronation, 2d.
28. 1953; Coronation, 4d.
29. 1953; Coronation, 8d.
30. 1953; Coronation, 1s. 6d.
31. 1953; Health, 1½d. + ½d.
32. 1953; Health, 2d. + 1d.
33. 1953; Royal visit, 3d.
34. 1953; Royal visit, 4d.
35. 1953–8; Elizabethan definitive, 6d.
36. 1953–8; Elizabethan series, 1s. 6d.
37. 1953–8; Elizabethan definitive, 10s.
38. 1954; Elizabethan, official, 9d.
39. 1954; Health, 2d. + 1d.
40. 1947; Life Insurance, ½d.
41. 1947; Life Insurance, 6d.
42. 1947; Life Insurance, 1s.

PLATE 32

BRITISH SOLOMON ISLANDS:
1. 1946; Victory, 1½d.
2. 1953; Coronation, 2d.

COOK ISLANDS:
3. 1946; Peace, 2d.
4. 1949; Pictorial series, 5d.
5. 1949; M.V. *Matua*, 3s.

FIJI:
6. 1948; Silver Wedding, 2½d.
7. 1951; Health, 2d. + 1d.
8. 1938–55; King George VI series, 1s. 6d.
9. 1953; Royal visit, 8d.
10. 1954; Elizabethan definitive, ½d.
11. 1954; Government offices, 2d.
12. 1954; Pictorial series, 2s. 6d.
13. 1954; Health, 1½d. + ½d.

GILBERT AND ELLICE ISLANDS:
14. 1949; UPU, 1d.

NAURU:
15. 1954; Pictorial series, 1d.
16. 1954; Meeting house, 9d.

NEW CALEDONIA:
17. 1948; Kagu, 30c.

NEW HEBRIDES:
18. 1953; Natives, 5f.
19. 1953; Native carving, 50c.

NIUE:
20. 1946; Peace, 6d.
21. 1950; Native hut, 3d.
22. 1950; Cave, 1s.

NORFOLK ISLAND:
23. 1947; Ball Bay, 1½d.
24. 1953; Bloody Bridge, 5s.
25. 1953; Barracks entrance, 8½d.

OCEANIC SETTLEMENTS:
26. 1948; Pictorial series, 10c.

PAPUA–NEW GUINEA:
27. 1952; Tree kangaroo, ½d.
28. 1952; Papuan head-dress, 3½d.
29. 1952; Pictorial series, 6½d.

PITCAIRN ISLANDS:
30. 1940–51; King George VI series, 4d.
31. 1940–51; School 1949, 8d.
32. 1949; UPU, 6d.

SAMOA:
33. 1952; Pictorial definitive, ½d.
34. 1952; Seal of Samoa, 2d.
35. 1953; Coronation, 6d.

TOKELAU ISLANDS:
36. 1948; Atafu village ½d.
37. 1948; Fakaofo village, 2d.
38. 1953; Coronation, 3d.

TONGA:
39. 1950; Queen Salote, 1s.
40. 1951; Treaty of Friendship, 1d.
41. 1953; Royal Palace, 1d.
42. 1953; Pictorial definitive, 2d.

WALLIS AND FUTUNA ISLANDS:
43. 1945; Surcharged definitive 3f. on 25c.

1955-1964
General Survey of the Decade

There was no single earth-shaking event such as the end of a world war to divide the first decade from the second. None the less, the years from 1955 to 1964 were markedly different – socially, economically and politically – from the immediate post-war years, and the changes were faithfully recorded in philately: not that postage stamps mirrored them dramatically or quickly. In the early 1950s, stamps were still widely regarded as mere receipts for the prepayment of postage. They were certainly not yet the accurate barometers of public opinion and attitudes that they have since become. Only in relatively isolated cases were they felt to be a valuable medium for the dissemination of official viewpoints, and in such instances, régimes were more concerned with promoting an image for the benefit of their own peoples than with making an impression on the world at large. Moreover, the postage stamp was still too hampered by security considerations to rank with the press, the poster or the motion picture, and too confined by the limitations of format and printing processes to be regarded as a publicity medium or as a distinct art form.

By the end of the decade, however, the postage stamp everywhere had been transformed from a mere label denoting a monetary value to a highly important advertising and propaganda medium – a miniature poster, in effect, the impact of which depended largely on the skilful blend of colour and the latest techniques in graphic design. The sweeping political changes of this period and a greater spirit of internationalism had tremendous effects on stamps and were, in turn, affected by them – more so than at any other period since the inception of the adhesive stamp in 1840.

The decline of Colonialism

The First World War had toppled the old empires of Central Europe, and the Second World War had severely shaken the self-sufficiency and seeming invincibility of the remaining colonial powers of Europe. All six of them – Belgium, Britain, France, Holland, Portugal and Spain – had felt the effects of the war to a greater or lesser extent, but only those that had suffered defeat at the hands of Japan had been forced to yield to the clamour for independence in their Asiatic colonies. In the second post-war decade, however, the decolonisation of what was coming to be known as the Third World increased in momentum and switched largely from the Far East to Africa.

The first inkling of sweeping changes came at the end of the first decade, although the effects did not become obvious until 1955. The Netherlands put its overseas territories on an equal footing with the mother country and thenceforward the standard definitive stamp designs used by the Netherlands Antilles, Netherlands New Guinea and Surinam were replaced by distinctive sets, each reflecting local interests. The British attitude towards decolonisation at first took the form of attempts to group colonies into larger administrative units that would be more viable economically and politically. Thus Northern and Southern Rhodesia were linked with Nyasaland

to form the Central African Federation in 1954; the federated and unfederated Malay states, with the former Straits Settlements, and latterly with Sarawak and North Borneo, amalgamated in 1957 to form the Federation of Malaya and then, in 1961, Malaysia; and the fourteen island colonies of the British West Indies were grouped together as the Caribbean Federation in 1958. The birth of the Central African Federation and of Malaysia resulted in unified definitives – each of the Malaysian states nevertheless reserving the right to issue its own stamps as well. The Caribbean Federation, on the other hand, is philatelically remembered by the commemoratives issued by each colony in 1958 and nothing else, since the federation was an ephemeral union that never resulted in integration of the postal services.

After years of agitation within the colony, the Gold Coast was granted independence in March 1957 and promptly changed its name to Ghana – resurrecting the title of a medieval African empire. From its inception, Ghana pursued a much more liberal philatelic policy than had been feasible under colonial rule. The restrained intaglio stamps, in the familiar combination of royal portraiture and pictorial vignette, were replaced by gaudy multi-coloured stamps that would not be regarded as out of the ordinary in the seventies but which had enormous impact at the time. In keeping with the exuberant temperament of the independent African, the stamps captured the imagination of the collector in Europe and America who might never have given British colonial stamps a second glance. But at the same time, the too-frequent issue of stamps – and such questionable practices as the sale of 'cancelled-to-order' remainders well below face value – detracted from the popularity of Ghanaian stamps in Britain. Consequently, in later years, the stamps of Ghana tended to reflect the tastes of the American rather than the British market, pandering to the fashions and crazes of the moment.

Philatelic developments in Ghana in the late 1950s and early 1960s were paralleled all over the African continent. At the beginning of this period there were only four completely independent African countries – Egypt, Ethiopia, Liberia and Libya; but by the end of the decade only the Portuguese and Spanish colonies remained firmly under European control. Fresh impetus was given to the decolonisation of Africa in 1958, when the French colonial empire was transformed into the French Community and most of its components gained the status of independent republics. At first, only the former mandated territories of Cameroons and Togo opted for total independence. Senegal and the French Sudan tried the British technique of federation, but the resulting Federal Republic of Mali split up soon afterwards to form the separate republics of Mali and Senegal. Several republics within the French Community left it within a year or two but continued to maintain links with France and with each other. These ties were evident not only in the fact that most of their stamps continued to be produced in France but also in their tendency to follow a roughly uniform policy on stamp issues and design.

Independence brought about the dissolution of the vast combinations of colonies formerly known as French West Africa and French Equatorial Africa. Although their components had issued their own stamps at various times, the general issues of these two great combines had been the only stamps in use since 1944. In the conservative atmosphere of the late 1950s, none of the former French colonies leaped at the opportunity of issuing distinctive stamps on attaining independence. As a rule, the first individual stamps to appear in countries like the Central African Republic (formerly Ubangi-Shari) and Congo-Brazzaville (formerly Middle Congo) were commemoratives on the first anniversary of independence. The definitives of West Africa and Equatorial Africa continued in use for several years and were only gradually replaced by distinctive pictorial sets in each country.

Attempts at federation had mixed success in the British section of Africa. Internal dissension led to the break-up of the Central African Federation in 1963, the three component countries resuming their own stamps. Within a year, all three had changed their identity. Names redolent of colonialism were abolished in Northern Rhodesia and Nyasaland, which became known as Zambia and Malawi respectively – the white minority government in Southern Rhodesia retaliating by dropping the word 'Southern' and merely perpetuating the memory of empire-builder Cecil Rhodes. Further north, the British colonies and protectorates of East Africa went their separate ways on attaining independence in 1962–3. Although they were often at variance politically, they nevertheless continued to act in concert on such matters as posts and communications. Thus commemorative stamps bearing the names of all three countries – Tanganyika, Kenya and Uganda – were issued by the East African Posts and Telecommunications Corporation even though each country issued its own definitives. The stamps of Tanganyika were valid in Kenya and Uganda – and vice versa – but not in Zanzibar; and Zanzibari stamps were not valid on the East African mainland. The only change of name in this group came in 1964 when the United Republic of Tanganyika and Zanzibar was formed, the more euphonious title of Tanzania being adopted in 1965.

The transition from colonial to independent status was accomplished with relatively little trouble in most parts of Africa. Subsequent internal upheavals – the resurgence of tribalism and the tendency towards military coups ousting the original civil administrations – had little effect on the stamps of the emergent nations. The only repercussions on philately occurred in the former Belgian Congo and the mandated territory of Ruanda-Urundi, which became independent in 1960. Ruanda-Urundi was divided and became the republic of Rwanda and the kingdom of Burundi. The violent civil war which rent the former Belgian Congo, however, was reflected in the stamps of that unhappy country. Two provinces – Katanga and South Kasai – seceded from the republic soon after independence and stamps were produced for them in Switzerland during their brief bid for freedom. The stamps of the central government were inscribed 'République du Congo', but stocks looted by rebel troops during the sack of Stanleyville in 1964 were overprinted 'République Populaire' – the title 'République Démocratique' being eventually adopted by the central government. In two instances, colonial powers handed over responsibility to a single independent authority. First, in 1960, British and Italian Somaliland combined to form the independent republic of Somalia whose stamps continued to be printed in Rome or London, often trilingually in Arabic, Italian and English. Then, in the same year, that part of the former German colony of Cameroons administered by France since 1915, became an independent state and a plebiscite was held in the portion administered by Britain as part of Nigeria. Eventually, the Southern Cameroons – which had its own stamps during 1960 – joined the former French area, renamed the Federal Republic of Cameroons in 1961, and the Northern Cameroons voted for inclusion in the Federation of Nigeria. Later, stamps of the Cameroons were often inscribed in English as well as French.

The collapse of the British Caribbean Federation led to dominion status being conferred on Jamaica and Trinidad in 1962, the other islands receiving varying degrees of autonomy. These political developments resulted in a spate of 'self-government' or 'new constitution' overprints on the stamps of the smaller islands as well as the disappearance of the general issues of the Leeward Islands, which ceased to exist as a separate colony in 1956. Jamaica overprinted its definitive series in 1962 to celebrate independence but no changes were made in the definitives used by Trinidad and Tobago. Both countries issued short commemorative sets to mark the event. Unlike the emergent countries of Africa, neither Jamaica nor Trinidad and Tobago embarked on a prolific stamp policy after independence. Although Jamaica issued more stamps in 1962–4 than in the previous period, this was in line with the general increase in output everywhere; but in Trinidad and Tobago the conservative policy of one commemorative set a year was maintained.

The few territories that were too small or too remote to achieve independence presented something of a problem to the colonial powers. France found a solution by transforming them into overseas départements, following the example of French Guiana, Guadeloupe and Martinique in the 1940s. Unlike the three American territories, the remaining French possessions scattered around the Indian Ocean and the Pacific Ocean continued to issue their own stamps – providing, thereby, some new names for the stamp album. The detachment of Adélie Land and the sub-Antarctic islands from Madagascar (when it became the Malagasy Republic) led to the establishment of the French Southern and Antarctic Territories, which began issuing stamps in 1955; and the French Settlements of Oceania adopted the neater title of French Polynesia in 1958.

The achievement of independence by former colonies caused some reorganisation of colonial responsibilities in other parts of the world. Christmas Island and the Cocos Islands in the Indian Ocean, formerly administered by Singapore, were transferred to Australian control between 1952 and 1955. Ordinary Australian stamps were used at first, but distinctive sets were introduced in Christmas Island in 1958 and in the Cocos Islands in 1963. The former German colony of Western Samoa progressed steadily towards independence under New Zealand tutelage, adopting the Samoan title 'Samoa i Sisifo' on stamps in 1958 prior to full independence four years later.

Only in the colonial empires of Portugal and Spain was there little apparent change in this decade. Both powers emulated France by transforming their colonies into overseas provinces in 1960. In each case, stamps continued to appear as before except that 'España' or 'Republica Portuguesa' appeared in addition to the colony's name. If anything, there was a greater degree of regimentation in the subjects and designs of the stamps issued in the Portuguese and Spanish territories. The only major change brought about by these political developments was the disappearance of Spanish Guinea and its replacement by the provinces of Rio Muni and Fernando Pó, both issuing their own stamps in the prevailing colonial style.

The European scene

The shedding of imperial commitments in the far corners of the globe transformed Belgium, the Netherlands and France from world powers into European nation-states. The same process was at work in Britain, but it was much longer and slower in coming to fruition. In the late 1950s there were trends towards supranationalism in Europe: the traditional bonds of Norden (the Scandinavian countries) and Benelux (the Low Countries), both of which found expression in omnibus issues of stamps from time to time. In 1956, however, the European Economic Community was formed by the Benelux countries, France, West Germany and Italy, and all six countries issued a pair of stamps in a uniform design that symbolised the building of a united Europe. The following year each country chose its own design for 'Europa' stamps, but in 1958 and 1959 standard designs were utilised.

The original Europa theme had been confined to the six Common Market countries, but its scope was greatly widened in 1960 when it was transferred to the nineteen countries participating in the Conférence Européen des Postes et Télécommunications (CEPT). In that year, stamps were issued by all CEPT members, including Britain – which had, hitherto, been conspicuous in its neglect of such philatelic events. Indeed, Britain dropped out of the annual Europa commemoration in 1961; but almost every other country in the Western bloc – from Iceland and Ireland to Turkey and Cyprus – issued stamps with the Europa theme each year. Several of the smaller countries such as Liechtenstein and Monaco at first preferred their own distinctive designs, but eventually all CEPT members opted for the standard design produced by a prominent European artist each year. Considerable ingenuity was shown in the design of motifs symbolising the nineteen member countries: Rahikainen's wheel with nineteen spokes (a geometric impossibility), Lex Weyer's tree with nineteen leaves, Georges Bétemps' flower with nineteen petals, and Theo Kurpershoek's dove composed of nineteen little doves.

Less popular as a philatelic theme was the North Atlantic Treaty Organisation, although quite a sizeable number of stamps was produced by various member countries on the fifth anniversary in 1955 and on the tenth anniversary in 1960. Significantly, this subject seemed to have a stronger appeal to the newer members such as Greece, Portugal and Turkey than to the original NATO signatories. It should be noted, however, that both of the non-European members – Canada and the United States – issued stamps in honour of NATO. Both CEPT and NATO stamps were naturally confined to the countries of the Western bloc, and there was no comparable example of group issues from the Communist bloc. The Communications Ministers' Conference – the Communist equivalent of the CEPT – attracted a few desultory stamps from various countries in eastern Europe, but no attempt at a uniform motif was made until 1965. The political, economic and military alliances of this bloc found remarkably little expression in stamps. Instead, participation in joint issues was limited to such events as the spartakiads (Communist sports) and various world-peace conferences and congresses.

The fluctuations in the European atmosphere – the partial thaw in the cold war following the death of Stalin, the unrest in Poland and East Germany and the Hungarian uprising of 1956 with its consequent tightening of the Soviet grip on the satellite states – found little expression in stamps of this period. Only the Hungarian tragedy had immediate effects in the form of contemporary definitives overprinted by the rebels at Sopron in western Hungary; and several countries issued stamps with premiums in aid of Hungarian refugees. East Germany countered this with a stamp surcharged in aid of 'Socialist Hungary' and produced a similar stamp overprinted 'HELFT AGYPTEN' (Help Egypt) – a reference to the Anglo–French Suez campaign. This, the last of the colonialist adventures by European powers acting in concert was otherwise ignored – although Egypt assiduously charted the events of that turbulent year with stamps commemorating the nationalisation of the canal, the invasion of Port Said and the subsequent ignominious evacuation.

America

The influence of the United States on the rest of the American continent remained considerable during this decade. Only in Cuba was the pattern of propping up dictatorial régimes with overt assistance and financial aid shattered – by the overthrow of Fulgencio Batista in 1959 and the emergence of the first Marxist state in the Western Hemisphere. America's Suez was the Bay of Pigs débâcle of 1961, jubilantly celebrated by Cuba in many subsequent issues of stamps but referred to only indirectly by the United States in – of all things – the stamp marking the centenary of the Red Cross in 1963.

The role of the United States as protector of the western democracies had been reluctantly accepted in the 1940s, but in the 1950s there was a new consciousness of America's destiny in world affairs. Whatever the reality may have been, the idealism of the American role was vividly expressed in many of the stamps from 1955 to 1964 – from the 'Atoms for Peace' stamp, with its pious hope 'To find the way by which the inventiveness of man shall be consecrated to his life', to the Kennedy memorial stamp with the quotation from one of his speeches '. . . and the glow from that fire can truly light the world'. In between, came stamps honouring Ramon Magsaysay of the Philippines and nine other 'Champions of Liberty', ranging from Bolivar and Kossuth to the Mayor of West Berlin and Mahatma Gandhi. The highpoint came in 1960–61 with a set of six stamps, known as the 'Credo' series, inscribed with moral precepts by leading figures in American history.

In Latin America the pattern of the previous decade continued. In many cases the stamps were consciously modelled on those of the American Bank Note Company or the Wright Bank Note Company if not actually printed by them, florid intaglio being enlivened by the use of lithography. Apart from Argentina, Brazil and Chile, which had their own competent if undistinguished presses, the Latin-American countries produced relatively few stamps themselves. They relied on an increasingly wide range of printers which, by the end of the decade, included the government printers in Austria, Germany and even Japan. Castro's revolution in Cuba brought to an end the intaglio stamps closely modelled on those of the United States – or, more accurately, the type of stamps that the United States used to produce for the Philippine Islands. In their place came a steady stream of gaudy lithographs for which poster techniques were used. The ability of lithography to reduce lettering to microscopic proportions inspired several stamps of 1961–64 reproducing extensive passages from Castro's *Declaration of Havana* – a technique previously used by Greece, in 1954, in a series of propaganda stamps on behalf of Enosis for Cyprus (union with Greece).

Although the decline in the influence of the United States was most marked in the case of Cuba, its effects could be seen in the stamps of other Latin-American countries – not only in their tendency to have stamps printed elsewhere but also in the fact that they were no longer so ready to issue stamps portraying Americans or honouring events in the United States. The reasons for this were two-fold. They no longer felt so subservient to the wishes and policies of the United States, and they were less dependent on the revenue from philatelic sales to collectors in North America. Fewer stamps were produced in tribute to John F. Kennedy than had honoured the memory of Franklin D. Roosevelt in the late 1940s, and the New York World's Fair attracted little attention – a far cry from the prolific issues that had greeted the Golden Gate International Exposition and the New York World's Fair of 1939.

The three-cornered fight over Antarctica became fiercer in this decade. In accordance with a Latin-American tradition originating in the 1890s, however, this was a war fought largely in the stamp album, with all three contenders – Argentina, Chile and Great Britain – issuing stamps featuring maps of the disputed territory. Britain went so far as to establish the British Antarctic Territory as a separate crown colony complete with its own stamps, producing similar stamps for South Georgia. Chile's interest in Antarctica seemed to wane, if stamp issues were any guide, but Argentina kept up a relentless philatelic campaign that culminated in a set of three stamps in 1964 depicting maps of the Malvinas (Falkland Islands) and the other disputed territories with Argentinian flags. Much of the heat was taken out of the issue in 1961 when all three countries were among the original signatories of the Antarctic Treaty.

Asia

Map stamps were used by India and Pakistan in support of their respective claims to Kashmir, and the same technique was employed by Jordan, Egypt and other Arab states in their protracted struggle with Israel. Arab stamps even went so far as to ignore the existence of Israel on maps of the area, and this rather crude form of propaganda was supported by stamps marking Palestine Day. Egypt's expansionist policy during this period was marked by changes in the inscriptions on the stamps issued in Syria, which became part of the original United Arab Republic in 1959. And Syria continued to use the title or its initials in its stamps after opting out of the union in 1961. Egypt conspired at the overthrow of the monarchies in Iraq and the Yemen, where royalist guerrillas continued to produce stamps on behalf of the so-called Free Mutawakelite Kingdom – though it is questionable to what extent these stamps were ever postally valid.

Generally, there was a lull in the ideological struggle between the divided countries of the Far East; but propaganda stamps were occasionally issued by both sides in Korea and Vietnam. Only towards the end of the decade did the steady escalation of the conflict in Vietnam achieve philatelic recognition. In the early 1960s the solidarity of the Communist countries with the 'independence fighters' in Vietnam and other trouble spots, became evident in stamps publicising their struggles. No comparable stamps were issued in the western camp on behalf of South Vietnam.

Indonesia's policy of confrontation against Malaysia, British Borneo, the Netherlands New Guinea and the Philippines in the early 1960s, resulted in a number of commemoratives and the overprinted stamps that signified the transfer of North Borneo (renamed Sabah) to Malaysia and Dutch New Guinea (renamed West Irian) to Indonesia. Both India and Pakistan overprinted stamps for the use of their troops serving with the International Control Commissions in Indo-China and the United Nations Emergency Forces in Gaza, the Congo and West Irian; but none of the other non-aligned countries contributing to the custodian forces policing the world's trouble spots followed suit.

The Space Age

The Soviet Union celebrated the fortieth anniversary of the October Revolution in 1957 by launching Sputnik I, the first artificial satellite. Two stamps showing the satellite in orbit were issued a month later, thereby launching a collecting theme that was eventually to form a separate branch of the hobby under the name 'astrophilately'. For the launching of the second Sputnik, in December 1957, Russia produced a set of four stamps depicting progress allegorically. Thereafter, stamps traced the development of Soviet space achievements; and satellites and rockets were also featured on stamps commemorating such events as the International Disarmament Conference in Stockholm and the 21st Communist Party Congress. From 1959 to 1964, each stage in the space race was documented philatelically: the Lunik moon rockets; the first manned space-craft, 'piloted' by the dogs Belka and Strelka; the Venus rockets; the later sputniks; the historic flights by Gagarin and Titov; and, from 1962 onwards, the anniversaries of these flights. Ultimately, there were lengthy sets with the theme of 'First in Space' and 'The Way to the Stars'. The stamps became increasingly ambitious, ranging from the jumbo-sized rouble stamp of 1961 printed on aluminium foil, to the set of six in 1964 making a composite picture of the solar system with the trajectories of the various Soviet space-craft. The anniversary of Gagarin's first flight was eventually designated Cosmonauts' Day, and sets of bigger and more colourful stamps extolled Soviet exploits in space.

The Communist countries participated in astrophilately with equal enthusiasm and, significantly, many of the emergent nations of the Third World also issued stamps featuring Russian rocketry. By contrast, the United States contributed no more than a single stamp in 1962 for Colonel Glenn's 'Project Mercury' flight and completely ignored the sub-orbital flight previously made by Commander Shepard – although Surinam and several other countries issued stamps to mark the occasion. In 1962 Hungary issued a miniature sheet portraying Gagarin, Titov and Glenn, later the same year producing a set of seven stamps portraying the four Russians and three Americans who had then made orbital space flights. Czechoslovakia likewise portrayed American astronauts in the space exploration series of 1964, and several other Soviet satellites showed remarkable impartiality in honouring the space achievements of the United States. No doubt the growing revenue, in hard currency, from philatelic sales in America and Western Europe had some influence on this policy. Nevertheless, no country in Western Europe or North America returned the compliment by issuing stamps portraying Soviet cosmonauts.

Western Europe's role in the space race was a minor one compared with that of Russia and the United States, and none of the experiments by Britain, France and Germany in the early 1960s merited philatelic recognition – although France and her dependent territories issued stamps in 1962 to mark the inauguration of Telstar, the first trans-Atlantic telecommunications satellite. From the very beginning, space exploration captured the imagination of people all over the globe. Space stamps literally rocketed to the top of the thematic league, surpassing the old favourites such as flora, fauna, art and religion. Saturation point had probably been reached before the end of this decade, however – by which time the market was being swamped with lengthy and colourful sets from every country whose stamps were controlled by external philatelic agencies.

Incidental Philately

This term was coined in 1955 to describe a phenomenon that had been established in the previous decade with the flood of victory stamps in 1945–6 and UPU stamps in 1949–50. At the time, however, these world-wide issues were regarded as isolated cases and no attempt was made to exploit the situation and make them a regular feature. In the same period there had been many stamps in honour of the late Franklin D. Roosevelt – but these could be regarded mainly as a spontaneous gesture by countries that had admired him and had cause to be grateful for his role in the Second World War. For the same reason, it was quite natural that Spain and the countries of Latin America should issue stamps in 1947 for the quatercentenary of Cervantes and in 1951 for the quingentenary of Isabella the Catholic. The common denominator in all of these issues was that the person or subject being commemorated had some direct relevance to the country concerned.

From 1955 onwards there was a significant change, and by the end of the decade many countries were issuing stamps in honour of people and events that had absolutely no connection with their part of the world.

The concept of incidental philately developed very slowly. In 1955 many countries in which the Rotary movement was established marked the golden jubilee of its foundation by issuing stamps, a number of which portrayed Paul P. Harris, the American founder. This gave stimulus to the United States hobby of collecting stamps with an American theme. Rotary stamps were largely confined to Latin America and the more philatelically conscious countries of Europe – although, curiously, San Marino neglected this opportunity – and apart from the United States, Australia was the only English-speaking country to issue a Rotary stamp in 1955. The tenth anniversary of the United Nations also produced a modest harvest of commemoratives, including many from the Third World and quite a few from the Communist bloc; but again, this event was largely ignored by the Western countries. The Communist countries had their own cause for celebration that year, many of them issuing stamps to mark the fiftieth anniversary of the Russian revolution of 1905.

The Olympic Games held in Melbourne in 1956 provided the opportunity for a spate of sports stamps from many parts of the world, but the participants were essentially those countries that were now becoming acutely aware of the lucrative revenue to be gained from stamps with a sporting theme. Two other Olympiads fell within this decade, and in each case the number of stamps and the number of countries issuing them increased dramatically. Commemoration of the Rome Olympics of 1960 was largely confined to the participating countries – who frequently used the revenue to finance their national teams – or those countries that had become notorious for issuing stamps on the slightest pretext. By the time of the Tokyo Games in 1964, however, the issuing of Olympic stamps had spread to 'respectable' countries – including a number in the British Commonwealth that had hitherto ignored the Olympic theme. At the same time, the practice of issuing pre-publicity stamps in advance of the Games – begun by Australia in 1954 – had developed to such an extent that Japan produced no fewer than seven sets between 1961 and the event itself.

One of Britain's few commemoratives of this period appeared in 1957 in honour of the Scout Jamboree at Sutton Coldfield that year. As the jamboree marked the jubilee of Scouting and the centenary of the birth of Lord Baden-Powell, founder of the movement, it proved an ideal occasion for stamps from all parts of the world – from South Korea, Formosa and the Philippines to Iran, Brazil, Belgium and Liechtenstein. Many of the stamps portrayed Baden-Powell, who became the first Englishman to receive this global accolade.

Of greater significance, however, was the designation of 1957 as International Geophysical Year by the United Nations – the consequence of which was a spate of stamps that can be divided into two major categories: those issued in connection with scientific expeditions to remote parts of the world, especially Antarctica, and those publicising aspects of the work being carried out in the course of the year. Australia, New Zealand and Great Britain issued stamps for use in Antarctica, and many other countries, from Canada to Yugoslavia, highlighted the work they were undertaking in this connection. But the event also provoked issues from countries that were not even remotely concerned with the scientific work, and whose only interest was the income from sales of their stamps in Europe and North America. This resulted in some curious anomalies and incongruities, the most startling of which was the series from Haiti depicting penguins on an ice-floe. One wonders what the average Haitian – who had never seen a penguin, let alone an ice-floe, in the Caribbean – made of these stamps. But increasingly a pattern began to emerge: stamps that were neither relevant to the country of issue nor, to a great extent, available in that country. In such cases, the bulk of the edition would be earmarked for distribution through the philatelic markets in western Europe and the United States. The subjects depicted on the stamps would therefore be immaterial in the countries for whom they were ostensibly produced.

Three World's Fairs were staged during this period and were the subject of world-wide stamps to a greater or lesser degree. Before the Second World War there had been a considerable number of stamps in honour of the Paris International Exhibition of 1937 and the New York World's Fair of 1939 and, as already mentioned, some philatelic participation by the Latin-American countries in the Golden Gate Exposition in San Francisco in 1939. The first World's Fair to be held after the Second World War was that staged in Brussels in 1958. Not surprisingly, it attracted philatelic attention from countries as far afield as Brazil and Russia. Two points of interest emerged here: the United Nations pavilion had a special issue of stamps that were valid only at the UN post office in the exhibition, and Portugal and her colonies issued an omnibus series in honour of the event. Hitherto, in the colonial countries, such omnibus issues had been confined to events directly relevant to the mother country. By contrast, very little attention was paid to the Century 21 World's Fair at Seattle in 1962. This exhibition was denied full World's Fair status by the international body governing such events on the grounds that one World's Fair in a decade was enough; but this disapproval would have been insufficient reason for the scanty philatelic recognition given at the time. Significantly, although the New York World's Fair two years later was granted official recognition it did not fare much better in terms of stamps. It is noteworthy, however, that Russia was one of the countries that released stamps on that occasion.

If World's Fairs somehow failed to attract the interest of the philatelic public in the early 1960s, the same cannot be said for events sponsored by the United Nations. A gratifying number of countries issued stamps in 1958 either in honour of the inauguration of the new UNESCO headquarters building or for the tenth anniversary of the *Declaration of Human Rights* – or for both – and these stamps were straws in the wind, indicating that despite its political shortcomings the United Nations was a firm favourite with philatelists. From 1960 onwards, the United Nations chose a problem of world-wide significance as the topic for each year and urged member countries to publicise it by means of stamps. The first of these events was World Refugee Year, heralded by two stamps issued by the United Nations post office in New York in December 1959. Designed by Olav Mathiesen, the stamps featured the WRY symbol – hands shielding a human silhouette – and this or an uprooted tree appeared on many of the stamps subsequently issued to mark the event. Ireland and the Vatican, however, chose a religious theme with representations of the Flight into Egypt. In 1961 the United Nations International Children's Emergency Fund celebrated its fifteenth anniversary and this prompted commemoratives, some with premiums in aid of UNICEF. But the main event of the year was the United Nations campaign organised by UNESCO for the preservation of the temples of Nubia, threatened with inundation by the rising waters of the Aswan Dam. The stamps on behalf of the Nubian temples were issued over a long period, in some cases as much as five years after the campaign was launched, and the colossal statues of Abu Simbel and the temples at Philae provided enormous scope for individual interpretation of the theme.

The United Nations sponsored a campaign for the eradication of malaria in 1962 and one for freedom from hunger in 1963. For each of these they produced an officially approved symbol – the World Health Organisation emblem surmounting, in 1962, a mosquito and in 1963, three ears of corn – and the world's stamp designers exercised their talents in producing variations on these themes. Relatively few countries made any attempt to interpret these somewhat abstract concepts in naturalistic terms. Several African countries featured tractors and crop-growing to publicise the Freedom from Hunger campaign, and Iceland reproduced a photograph of a trawler landing a catch of herring.

By the time the United Nations began sponsoring these annual events, the traditional approach – using either a pseudo-classical allegory or a purely naturalistic picture – had been almost totally eclipsed by modern symbolic or poster techniques.

Other fifteenth anniversaries connected with the United Nations precipitated a flurry of stamps in 1962–3. The anniversary of UNESCO was in many cases allied to the then current preoccupation with the Nubian temples; and the anniversary of the *Declaration of Human Rights* was linked to the memory of the late Eleanor Roosevelt, whose portrait appeared alongside the flame emblem on many of the stamps.

In addition to the United Nations, there was only one other international organisation that merited global commemoration in this period. In 1963, the International Red Cross celebrated its centenary, and stamps were issued in over ninety member countries. Designers had by now become so conditioned to a purely symbolic approach that the majority of the stamps showed no more than variations on the theme of the Red Cross or Red Crescent emblems, or the special centenary symbol. For that reason, the Red Cross series tended to be more monotonous than most of the other issues of this type. Comparatively few stamps portrayed the founder, Henri Dunant, or attempted to convey something of the work done by the Red Cross in peace and war.

The centenary of the Paris Postal Conference in 1963 was commemorated on a minor scale by the fifteen countries, or their modern counterparts, that had attended the original conference – the precursor of the Universal Postal Union. Fortunately, no centenary emblem was devised. Each country was therefore thrown back on its own resources, and the resulting stamps proved to be both varied and full of interest.

Incidental philately in this decade was largely preoccupied with events, but outstanding personalities were not entirely overlooked. There was a smattering of stamps in 1956, for example, in honour of St. Ignatius of Loyola; and in 1960 the tercentenary of St. Vincent de Paul received sporadic recognition. In 1959, however, the 150th anniversary of the birth of Abraham Lincoln proved an incentive for commemorative stamps from most of the emergent nations of Africa as well as from the Latin-American republics. Treatment of this subject varied from the lengthy series from Honduras, depicting scenes from the life of Lincoln, to the set of three and a miniature sheet from Ghana – that had Dr. Nkrumah posing self-consciously, like any tourist, in front of Lincoln's statue in Washington.

The death in 1961 of the UN Secretary-General Dag Hammarskjöld in an air-crash while flying to mediate in the Congolese civil war produced a flood of mourning stamps from the Third World but little response from anywhere else. The United Nations issued suitably symbolic stamps showing the flag at half-mast, and the United States issued a 4-cent stamp in two colours. When a sheet of the American stamps was discovered with the yellow background inverted, the US Post Office promptly printed 120,000,000 with the error to prevent the original sheet from fetching an inflated sum. This was the first American stamp with an error of this kind since the famous 'inverted Jenny' airmail stamp of 1918 – which now ranks among the major rarities of the world, attempts to suppress its sale having failed. Forty years later the postal authorities neatly prevented a repetition of this by giving every collector the opportunity to own a 'Hammarskjöld' misprint. Later in the year a sheet of Canal Zone stamps appeared with the central motif of the Thatcher Ferry Bridge missing, but on this occasion the owner of the sheet took legal action to stop the American authorities from reprinting the error.

The assassination of John F. Kennedy in November 1963 shook the world and prompted an immediate response in the form of memorial stamps. Colombia had the honour of being the first country to issue a Kennedy stamp barely three weeks after the tragic event – a tribute to the designing skill of Imre Mosdossy and the productivity of De La Rue of Bogota (59:37). Within a year, over fifty countries had issued such stamps. A comparison of these with the Roosevelt issues of the previous decade raises some interesting points. The portraits used in the late 1940s were astonishingly varied for the period, reflecting the fact that Roosevelt had been in the public eye of the world for a dozen years. Kennedy, on the other hand, had been in the limelight for scarcely a quarter of that time; yet the spirit of the New Frontier, the confrontation with Khruschev over the Cuban missile crisis, and his emotive 'Ich bin ein Berliner' speech – all brought into countless millions of homes by means of television – had made him a familiar figure all over the world as no previous holder of his office had been. Moreover, stamp designers in 1964 had the seemingly infinite resources of press photographs, motion-pictures and television newsreels to draw upon. In the case of Roosevelt, El Salvador alone had featured the funeral cortège on stamps; but a significant proportion of the Kennedy stamps drew on the funeral scene – the mourning relatives and heads of state, and the flame of remembrance – made familiar by television satellite. A single commemorative set invariably sufficed for Roosevelt; but such was the international demand for Kennedy stamps that many of the philatelically alert countries produced several sets, continuing the theme right through to 1967 when they could legitimately issue stamps to commemorate what would have been his fiftieth birthday.

One historical figure whose anniversary occurred in 1964 was almost overlooked in the Kennedy furore, the output of stamps for the quatercentenary of Shakespeare being comparatively small. Stamps were issued by only twelve British colonies – a single apiece – a handful of European countries (mainly in the Communist bloc), Britain and the United States. For Britain, however, the Shakespeare stamps represented a break with tradition on two counts: the commemoration of a historic anniversary rather than a current event, and the portrayal of a person other than a member of the royal family. The British Post Office explained away both facts by stating that it was the quatercentenary festival – a current event – that was being celebrated, not the quatercentenary itself; and as the Droeshout portrait of Shakespeare had been reversed and stylised it could not really be regarded as the portrayal of a person but was in accordance with previous design policy, which showed a marked preference for symbolism. Both arguments seemed specious at the time but were taken as precedents, which were to have major repercussions in the following decade.

Omnibus Issues and Hardy Annuals

In comparison with the first post-war decade, there were few omnibus issues in this period. The chief protagonists of the lengthy colonial series using standard designs were the Crown Agents, who controlled the production and distribution of stamps for the British colonies and protectorates. The number of stamp-issuing entities had fluctuated over the years: forty-five territories issued stamps in the colonial omnibus designs for the coronation of 1937 and for victory in 1946, but the number rose to a peak of sixty-four in 1949, with the individual Malay states participating in the UPU celebration; and in 1953 the number issuing the standard coronation stamps had dropped by only two. By 1963, however, half the former colonies had been granted varying degrees of independence, so the number participating in the 'Freedom from Hunger' omnibus issue was cut to thirty-seven; and later the same year there were only thirty-five countries using the colonial design for the Red Cross stamps. Apart from political changes, the general unpopularity and the monotony of omnibus issues were having serious effects on sales to collectors. When the 'colonial ensemble', as they were usually called, were given the choice of having Shakespeare stamps, only twelve of them decided to participate. In general, it was the smaller and poorer territories – more dependent on philatelic revenue than the others – that issued Shakespeare stamps; but Bermuda, with its obvious Shakespearean connection – the 'still-vex'd Bermoothes' of *The Tempest* – declined to take part.

Omnibus issues appeared at more frequent intervals in the other colonial empires. Possibly because fewer territories were involved, there was not the same sales resistance and, as a rule, such issues were confined to single stamps. Eleven or twelve countries took part in the French omnibus issues of this period, eight in the Portuguese colonial issues and four in those of the Netherlands, including the mother country.

In addition to the issues in which virtually every territory in a group participated, there was a steady growth in what became known as 'mini-omnibus' issues involving only a few territories. The first example from the British Commonwealth had been the British West Indies University pair of 1951. A similar issue of this decade was the set of three marking the inauguration of the British Caribbean Federation in 1958. The French community made much greater use of the limited omnibus issue, however, especially from 1960 onwards when the republics in the French sphere of Africa took advantage of it on several occasions. The number of African countries taking part in these issues varied from eleven to fifteen, with stamps for such events as the inauguration of the Technical Co-operation Commission for Africa south of the Sahara (CCTA) in 1960, the African and Malagasy Union in 1962 and the African and Malagasy Postal Union (UAMPT) in 1963.

Both French and Portuguese territories extended the omnibus idea beyond the commemorative stamp. In 1959 the French countries issued stamps depicting flowers of their particular region, and in 1962 the Portuguese territories each issued a set of five diamond-shaped sports stamps. The Portuguese colonies went so far as to have a rigidly uniform policy regarding the themes of their definitives, which were changed at regular intervals. The four Spanish colonies or overseas provinces in Africa had an even more regimented policy in regard to stamp issues. Although there were no omnibus issues in the strict sense, all stamps for definitive purposes and their special issues – confined to Child Welfare and Colonial Stamp Day – conformed to a set pattern even though different designs were used in each case.

As the omnibus issue in the traditional sense – uniform designs throughout – declined, the concept of joint issues by several countries gradually developed. The annual Europa stamps of western Europe were the best example of this, but there were numerous other cases of countries using identical designs to commemorate events of mutual interest. Thus the United States collaborated with Canada in 1959 for the St. Lawrence Seaway stamp and with Mexico in 1960 for the sesquicentennial of Mexican independence. Australia and New Zealand went a stage further by issuing stamps honouring Kingsford Smith in 1958 and the COMPAC cable in 1963, both issues being designed and printed in Australia. Although such joint issues were still sporadic by the end of the decade, they were a break with the hidebound tradition whereby the stamps of each country or colonial group should stand apart from those of all other countries. They were indeed an indication of the much closer ties being forged between countries, especially in the field of communications.

The increase in the number of annual issues in this decade reflected the growing feeling that stamps had a much wider application than the mere everyday franking of correspondence or the occasional commemoration of events. Semi-postal issues for Health, Child Welfare, social and cultural funds, anti-tuberculosis campaigns and other charities remained fairly constant in this period. There was, however, a steady growth in the number of countries issuing stamps for such non-events as Stamp Day; and with the attainment of independence by the African countries, annual issues for Independence Day or Republic Day became commonplace.

Austria had issued stamps for use on Christmas greetings intermittently, in 1937 and 1953–4, but the first country to issue Christmas stamps regularly was Cuba in 1951. Other countries were slow to imitate this charming custom. Spain introduced Christmas stamps in 1955, and the idea spread to Australia in 1957 and Costa Rica in 1958. In subsequent years similar stamps were issued by the Australian dependencies, and from 1960 onwards New Zealand followed suit. The United States introduced the idea in 1962, and Canada took it up two years later. Thus by the end of the decade, Christmas stamps had become an annual event in about a dozen countries, joining such seasonal issues as the Japanese, Chinese and Korean stamps marking the lunar New Year and the Israeli stamp marking the Jewish New Year. But Christmas alone had universal appeal, and the extension of such issues in the ensuing period was to be one of the dramatic phenomena of the late 1960s.

Thematics
The pattern of stamp-collecting changed in the late 1950s. Hitherto, most philatelists had collected stamps according to country of origin or some clearly defined political grouping. But with the growth in the number of independent countries and the increase in global stamp output, the traditional pattern of collecting all British colonial stamps or all French colonials or all Latin-American stamps disappeared since it was no longer possible for the average person to collect on a global basis. At one end of the spectrum, collecting became more selective as a growing number of philatelists confined their interest to the stamps of one country. At the other end, however, philatelists switched from a geographical to a thematic approach, collecting stamps according to the purpose of issue or the subjects depicted on them. Thematic or topical collecting became increasingly fashionable from 1955 onwards, and postal administrations pandered to this taste by issuing stamps in thematic sets. From the 1930s, the policy in the British 'colonial ensemble' had been to produce a definitive series covering a variety of subjects – scenery, flowers, wildlife, native occupations and so on – but by 1957 the concept of the single-theme series was well established. This was coupled with a change in the frequency of definitive sets. At one time, nothing short of the death of a monarch would have warranted a change in definitive sets; but by 1960 the idea of changing a definitive series every six years as a matter of course had been accepted. It was a policy that forced designers to think in terms of a single theme per series.

There was a parallel development in the French and Portuguese territories; and in Europe and Latin America, thematic sets at annual intervals, to augment the definitive range, became fashionable in the late 1950s. In some countries, such as San Marino and Poland, the traditional definitive series was entirely replaced by frequent thematic issues.

Philatelic Agencies
External philatelic agencies were no new phenomenon in this decade. Ever since stamp-collecting had graduated from a childish pursuit to a commercial enterprise in the 1860s there had been middlemen and entrepreneurs who were prepared to handle – and at times even manipulate – the stamps of a country, controlling philatelic sales and often arranging for design and production. The Crown Agents and other quasi-governmental bodies all over the world had conducted this type of business for many years and had built up reputations for integrity and fair-dealing. Alongside the reputable organisations, however, there had long existed less scrupulous private individuals – the notorious Nicholas Seebeck, whose activities affected the stamps of several Central American countries in the 1890s, being a prime example.

An unfortunate outcome of decolonisation in the early 1960s was the tendency of many of the emergent nations to place stamp design, production and distribution in the hands of external agents who did not always have the best interests

of the hobby in general or the country in particular at heart. The countries so affected were all in the Third World – the emergent nations of Africa, the sheikhdoms of the Arabian Gulf, and remote countries such as Afghanistan and Bhutan. Apart from the dubious practices of issuing far more stamps than the volume of mail justified and, the commemoration of events totally irrelevant to the country concerned, the more questionable agencies resorted to the issue of stamps in limited editions – either imperforate or in altered colours – the proliferation of miniature and souvenir sheets, and the sale of stamps cancelled to order at a fraction of face value. In many cases, no more than a token supply of stamps would be put on sale in the nation's capital. The bulk of the printing would be handled directly by the philatelic agency without ever going anywhere near the country allegedly issuing the stamps. Philatelic entrepreneurs naturally kept a close watch on political upheavals, ready to step in and offer their services to breakaway provinces in the Congo and to revolutionary governments.

To be fair, not all of the questionable practices of this decade emanated from countries manipulated by commercial philatelic agencies. The countries of the Communist bloc were particularly prone to such devices. From 1958, Bulgaria and Hungary frequently issued imperforate stamps in limited editions – a practice adopted by Albania in 1962. Most of the Communist countries, from Czechoslovakia to North Korea, sold stamps cancelled to order; and several of them, notably East Germany, created artificial shortages of certain stamps mainly to prevent speculation and smuggling.

Whether or not a country made use of an external philatelic agency, it was apparent by 1960 that postage stamps had become the kind of big business few countries could afford to ignore. No longer regarded as a nuisance, the philatelist was to be alternately wooed and exploited. And it is significant that from 1955 onwards every country became more ready to give the philatelic public what it wanted. The enormous development of incidental philately and thematics in this decade was the direct result of the new awareness of the lucrative revenue available from philatelic sales.

Technical Developments
The period from 1955 to 1964 was one of unparalleled development in stamp production. Every year witnessed some innovation that, often passing unnoticed at the time, was to have important repercussions in the future. At the beginning of the decade, the shape, composition and printing processes of postage stamps were all clearly defined and had remained fairly constant for many years, but by the end of the decade there had been revolutionary changes in all three.

Before 1955, every postage stamp had been printed on paper with a limited range of quality and substance. In that year, however, Hungary reissued a stamp on aluminium foil to commemorate the Light Metal Industries International Conference in Budapest. This novelty excited little comment and there was no rush to imitate it. Indeed, six years elapsed before the Soviet Union produced a space commemorative on aluminium foil. Both the Hungarian and Russian stamps were otherwise conventional in appearance – rectangular in format, perforated in the usual way and printed by intaglio or letterpress. In 1963, however, Tonga issued its first gold coins and commemorated this by producing a series of stamps that resembled the coins as closely as possible, circular in shape and embossed on metal foil. These stamps were the heaviest and most expensive stamps ever printed, and the higher denominations – with a diameter of 80 millimetres – were also among the largest. Tonga's coin stamps had a very mixed reception. Collectors of the old school, who liked their stamps to look like stamps, derisively dubbed them the 'beermats'; but countless others scrambled to purchase a set for the sheer novelty of it. Tonga produced another odd-shaped set embossed on metal foil the following year. Some of the stamps were heart-shaped, and others took their shape from the map of Tonga. Though Tonga was the only country in this decade to issue foil-embossed stamps, the idea spread to a number of other countries in later years.

In 1956, Italy celebrated the first anniversary of her admission to the United Nations by issuing two stamps depicting the globe. An anaglyphic technique was used whereby a slightly mis-aligned image of the globe was imposed upon another, giving a three-dimensional effect when viewed through red-and-green spectacles. This was the first attempt to create three-dimensional stamps; but as very few people appreciated the significance of what appeared to be faulty registration, the experiment was never repeated. The problem of producing satisfactory three-dimensional stamps remained unsolved until the late 1960s.

For more than a century, any printed image occurring on a stamp had been an integral part of the design; but in 1957 the advent of automation added an entirely new aspect to stamp production. The earliest experiments in automatic letter-facing, sorting and postmarking were conducted in Southampton, England, in November 1957, to which end certain low-value British stamps were issued in that district with vertical black lines on the back. The substance used, initially known as Naphthadag (deflocculated Atcheson's graphite) but later as graphite lines, activated electronic scanners in the facing and sorting equipment. Two years later, phosphor bands were applied to the face of the stamps and the graphite-lined stamps were phased out. These phosphor bands, visible to the naked eye, gave philatelists another technical facet to add to the minutiae of perforations and watermarks that distinguished seemingly identical stamps from each other.

Electronic sorting equipment gradually spread to other countries. In 1962 Sefacan (segregating, facing and cancelling) equipment was installed in Winnipeg, and Canadian stamps were issued with a phosphor 'tagging'. Paper coated with a special luminescent substance was adopted by West Germany in the same year and was introduced in the United States in 1963. In December 1963 Australia began using Helecon ink in the printing of stamps or as a coating on the surface of the paper. Helecon was later replaced by Derby Luminescence in electronic sorting experiments.

For many years the 'colonial ensemble' had used paper with watermarks featuring a crown and the initials of the Crown Agents. The Script CA watermark of the Georgian stamps was used on the Elizabethan stamps for much of this decade, but by 1963 a more up-to-date watermark – with the crown of St. Edward the Confessor and block capitals – was being used instead. In 1963–4 late printings of many colonial stamps appeared with the Block CA watermark, adding considerably to the interest of these issues. But as Commonwealth countries became independent, they dropped the CA watermark and adopted their own – Maltese crosses for Malta, pineapples for Jamaica and, in the cases of Malaysia and Nigeria appropriate monograms. Three different watermarks

were used on British stamps in this decade, but the need for such security devices no longer seemed so urgent as it had in the days when there were many competent engravers capable of forging stamps. As a result, there was a tendency in many parts of Europe, Asia and America to dispense with water-marks altogether.

The circular foil-embossed stamps of Tonga were produced by the Walsall Lithographic Company of England – new-comers to stamp production, who created an even greater furore in 1964 with the world's first free-form self-adhesive stamps. These were die-stamped, like Victorian scraps, printed in combined intaglio and lithography in the shape of the map of Sierra Leone, with superimposed designs and inscriptions in honour of the New York World's Fair and John F. Kennedy. The backing paper bore the butterfly trade-mark of Samuel Jones Ltd., who manufactured the special adhesive. Later issues of this kind used the backing paper for all kinds of commercial advertisements, thus helping to defray the costs of production.

In general, stamps became more colourful in this decade. Although Giori presses capable of multicolour intaglio had been available since 1939 they were used very infrequently in the early 1950s, usually only for two-colour combinations. From 1955 onwards, however, the countries that used intaglio to a large extent – France, the United States, Czechoslovakia – became more adventurous in the use of colour, and by 1960 multicoloured stamps had become a regular feature. The colour potential of photogravure was even greater, but developments with this process roughly paralleled those in intaglio with Courvoisier of Switzerland leading the way. Harrison of England and Enschedé of Holland attempted to rival the Swiss printers; but their early efforts in multicolour photogravure as exemplified by the Ceylon stamp centenary and the Melbourne Olympic series of 1956–7 were coarse compared with those of Courvoisier, with whom they shared these contracts. But by 1960 both companies had mastered the technique of multicolour photogravure, which thereafter became the rule rather than the exception.

The quest for colour without an increase in costs led other countries to experiment with lithography – a process used in the middle of the nineteenth century for stamp production but largely neglected in favour of letterpress or intaglio from 1900 onwards. Two British companies – Bradbury Wilkinson, who had specialised in intaglio, and De La Rue, who had specia-lised in letterpress – turned to lithography in the late 1950s to compete with the photogravure printers in the multi-colour market. From 1955, combinations of processes became more common with Austria, Czechoslovakia and, latterly, the United States seeking to inject more colour into design without losing the superior aesthetic qualities of intaglio.

The more colourful appearance of stamps was in line with the greater use of colour in everyday life – in book and magazine illustration, in motion pictures and eventually in television. And the application of colour revolutionised stamp design, the symbolism and allegory of the forties being replaced by techniques of lettering and presentation that had been developed in posters and other advertising media. The new colour processes enabled printers to repro-duce paintings in their full, natural colours and this triggered off the craze for art stamps from 1961 onwards.

1955-1964
Philatelic Survey by Country

Europe

Albania

Reliance on printers in other countries of eastern Europe came to an end in 1957, reflecting Albania's growing estrangement from the Soviet bloc and her realignment with the People's Republic of China. Among the last of the stamps to be printed by photogravure in Budapest was the set of four celebrating the 45th anniversary of independence in 1957 (33:1). Subsequent issues of this period were lithographed by Mihal Duri in Tirana. At first, monochrome lithography was used in the production of short sets of three or four stamps marking such anniversaries as liberation from Fascist rule, in 1959, Lenin's birthday, the Alphabet Study Association, and the jubilee of the Elbasan Normal School, all in 1960; and the death of the patriot Luarasi, in 1962 (33:2–6); but two- and three-colour combinations became increasingly common after late 1961 (33:7–9).

The traditional concept of a definitive series was abandoned in 1961, at a time when Albanian stamps were moving away from the politically-slanted designs of the early post-war years. In place of definitives, four short thematic sets featuring costumes, animals, birds and flowers were released between April and October 1961 (33:8). They were the prelude to longer sets with the same themes and others, such as insects, sports, fish and space exploration. Significantly, from 1962 onwards, many Albanian stamps were also released in miniature sheets, issued imperforate or produced in different colours, in limited printings designed especially for the international philatelic market. The political introversion of Albania in the 1960s was oddly at variance with a philatelic policy that countenanced issues for events ranging from the World Cup Football Championships in Chile to the Tokyo Olympic Games – issued two years ahead of the event in 1962 – and the 'Space Stamps' Exhibition in Riccione, Italy, in 1964.

Andorra

For the first time in ten years, the Spanish Post Office introduced new stamps in July 1963 (33:10). A larger format than that for the series of 1948–53 was adopted, and the appearance of the stamps was enlivened by the use of two-colour intaglio – both developments being parallel to design trends within Spain. The inscriptions were imposed on the vignettes instead of appearing in elaborate frames as in previous issues.

The French series of 1955–8 continued the tradition of monochrome intaglio that had been established in the 1944–51 series (33:11). The introduction of the new 'heavy franc' currency in 1961, however, heralded a definitive series in which up to four colours were subtly blended (33:12). As well as issuing stamps paralleling French commemoratives for Telstar (1962) and the Philatex Exhibition (1964), the French Post Office embarked on occasional issues devoted to aspects of Andorran history. The first of these sets appeared in 1963. The Virgin of Santa Coloma was featured on a charity stamp of July 1964, with a premium in aid of the Red Cross.

Austria

A 1-schilling stamp commemorating the 800th anniversary of Mariazell Basilica in 1957 signalled the end of the 'costumes' definitives, that had been current for almost twenty years. No commemorative inscription appeared on the Mariazell stamp, which was later used as a definitive and served as the model for a series – featuring prominent landmarks – that continued in use until 1974. The commemorative version of the Mariazell stamp was recess-printed, and it can be found with white or yellow gum. The definitive version was originally typographed in October 1957, but it was lithographed from January 1959 – the later stamp being readily identifiable by the omission of the engraver's name, G. Wimmer, from the imprint at the foot of the design (33:14). A much smaller version of the design was printed in photogravure by Harrison and Sons in 1960. During the long currency of this series there were considerable variations in paper and gum, the earlier printings being on greyish paper with yellow gum; but white paper and white gum were adopted in 1959. The majority of the series were lithographed; but three values were photogravure-printed by Harrison and Sons, and the two top values, 10- and 20-schilling, were recess-printed.

The majority of commemoratives were recess-printed and issued as singles. Experiments with more colourful designs, however, led to combinations of processes. The Town-planning Congress stamp of 1956 had a photogravure background in green with an overlay and inscriptions typographed in red and black (33:15), and a combination of intaglio and lithography was used to print the Choir Festival stamp of 1958 and the Red Cross stamp of 1963 (33:17, 25). A combination of intaglio and photogravure was employed in the production of the Winter Olympics series of 1963 (33:26), resulting in coloured backgrounds, black subjects and gold metallic inscriptions. Multicolour lithography was used by Rosenbaum Brothers to print a set of six stamps for the International Horticultural exhibition of 1964 (33:27), and this process was used increasingly thereafter.

Nevertheless, a high proportion of Australian stamps continued to be recess-printed in monochrome. The formal frames of the early period (33:13, 16) gave way, by 1958, to designs with white lettering on an intaglio ground without frame-lines (33:18, 19, 21) and, eventually, to a style in which lettering was arranged outside the confines of unframed vignettes (33:22–24, 26, 28).

Apart from the commemoratives, Austria issued a stamp each year for Stamp Day. The only issue of a purely thematic nature began as a sports pair in 1959 (33:20). Others in the same style were added between 1962 and 1970.

Belgium

Several denominations were added to the Baudouin photogravure series that had been introduced in 1953, and which provided the definitive range throughout this period. The stamps were produced at the Government Printing Works at Malines, which was also responsible for all the special issues. Photogravure and intaglio were used, with no special preference for either, and the stamps were printed in monochrome up to 1957. From then on, however, two- or three-colour intaglio became increasingly popular (33:35, 38). Combined recess-printing and photogravure – providing a more colourful effect without losing the quality appearance of line-engraving – was introduced in 1960 and was used for a number of commemorative issues in the latter part of the decade (33:39, 41). Multicolour photogravure (33:42) was used from 1964 onwards, its effect enhanced by the occasional use of gold metallic ink.

In addition to the annual series released in December to raise money for anti-tuberculosis and other health funds, Belgium issued a high proportion of stamps with charity premiums. Sets, usually of six or seven stamps, were issued at other times of the year on behalf of cultural, patriotic and philanthropic funds. Like the health fund stamps, these issues generally pursued a single theme, ranging from paintings and architecture (33:37) to birds and animals. In many instances, commemorative issues bore a premium on behalf of unspecified funds.

Two issues that were to become regular features – Europa and Stamp Day – were established in this decade. Belgium was one of the six original countries to issue stamps with the now familiar 'Europa' theme, a pair in the standard 'flag and scaffolding' design being released in September 1956 (*33*:31). And she remained faithful to the international motif each year – the stamps from 1961 onwards incorporating the initials CEPT (Conférence Européen des Postes et Télécommunications), indicating the expansion of the original Europa concept from the six Common Market countries to include the members of the Council of Europe participating in the postal and telecommunications conferences. In May 1957 a 2-franc stamp was issued to mark Stamp Day, but in subsequent years it was issued in March. Although Stamp Day was apparently a 'moveable feast', the theme of these issues was consistent and traced the history of the Belgian postal services from medieval times.

Stylistically, there were few developments in Belgian stamps in this period. White lettering on coloured vignettes continued to be a characteristic of photogravure (*33*:29, 30) and intaglio (*33*:33, 34) commemoratives, but from 1960 onwards there was an increasing tendency to use intaglio motifs and lettering on a plain white background, with either a thin frame-line or no frame at all (*33*:36).

Bulgaria

Out of a prodigious number of stamps – an average of fifty-seven issues a year throughout this decade – comparatively few illustrated the political complexion of the People's Republic of Bulgaria, and it is significant that most of those that did were released in the earlier years, including stamps honouring Friedrich Engels, Marx, Lenin and other immortals of the Communist pantheon. This was balanced by the introduction in 1955 of an annual series, devoted to cultural anniversaries, that provided an opportunity to pay tribute to famous men and women from many countries. The first series included Schiller, Cervantes and Walt Whitman, and the second included Benjamin Franklin, Mozart and George Bernard Shaw. Such catholicity was reflected in the other commemoratives that were not devoted to purely Bulgarian or Communist events. A series of six sports stamps appeared in 1956 in honour of the Olympic Games in Melbourne (*34*:2), and subsequent issues ranged from the Brussels Fair in 1958 to the World Cup Football Championships in Chile in 1962.

Definitive sets in the traditional pattern, with a common design for all denominations, were not issued in this period. The nearest equivalent was the series of 1959–61 devoted to the Five-Year-Plan (*34*:4) and sets of six stamps in 1962 and 1964 featuring landscapes (*34*:11). Instead, Bulgaria concentrated on frequent sets of a thematic nature including fruits in 1956; birds in 1959; Bulgarian roses and butterflies, both in 1962; forest animals, Black Sea coastal resorts, and Thracian tombs, all in 1963 (*34*:1, 3, 6–10).

As a rule, current events and anniversaries were commemorated by pairs or single stamps; but anniversaries of the liberation, youth conferences and sports meetings (*34*:5) tended to be marked by longer sets of five or six stamps.

The majority of stamps in this decade were printed in photogravure, although lithography was used occasionally from 1963 onwards (*34*:9, 10).

Cyprus

Three full-length definitive sets appeared during this decade. Bradbury Wilkinson recess-printed a set of fifteen stamps released in August 1955 (*34*:12). Very pronounced shade variations in later printings of the 15-mil denomination are of considerable rarity.

Cyprus became a republic within the British Commonwealth on 16th August 1960, and this was celebrated by a set of three stamps featuring a map of the island with Turkish and Greek inscriptions signifying 'Cyprus Republic'. The entire Elizabethan definitive series was similarly overprinted (*34*:13). Again a pronounced variation of shade occurred in the stamps of 15-mil value, making them – together with the double overprint errors of the 20- and 30-mil values – the rarest of modern Cypriot stamps.

Although an independent republic, Cyprus became increasingly aligned with Greece – and from 1962 onwards Cypriot stamps were produced by the Greek firm of Aspioti-Elka in place of the British

printers. A distinctive series, with trilingual inscriptions, appeared in September 1962 in two-colour lithography (*34*:14).

After independence, the output of stamps increased considerably. Cyprus took part in the annual Europa issues from 1962 and also issued several sets publicising the United Nations campaign for malaria eradication in 1962 and freedom from hunger in 1963, and the jubilee of the Scout movement and the centenary of the Red Cross, both in 1963 (*34*:15). Sets commemorating the Shakespeare quatercentenary and the Tokyo Olympics, in 1964, interpreted these subjects from the local angle, reproducing ancient theatres and a scene from *Othello*, set in Famagusta, and sporting scenes from classical friezes.

Czechoslovakia

The high standards of design and line-engraving – twin hallmarks of Czechoslovak stamps since pre-war times – were maintained throughout the late 1950s and early 1960s. If anything, there was a conscious attempt to imbue stamp design with a greater degree of artistry. Designers were concerned less with producing almost-photographic qualities in portraits and vignettes than with creating an impression – conveying movement or grace, as in the Olympic stamps of 1956 and 1964 and the Spartacist Games issues of 1960 (*34*:16, 19, 25), or epitomising the achievements of modern Russia in the stamps of 1962 marking the 40th anniversary of the Soviet Union (*34*:22). The artists were given free reign in their interpretation of subjects, as witness Karel Svolinsky's treatment of the theme of aid for farmers in underdeveloped countries in the stamp of 1963 publicising the UN Freedom from Hunger campaign (*34*:23). The irregularity of lettering in this stamp was a conceit deliberately cultivated by Czech artists in this period as a reaction against the formalised sculpted lettering invariably used on the stamps of other countries. Cursive script was also used on many occasions, when the flowing lines of the engraving demanded (*34*:18).

At the beginning of this decade, the desire for brighter stamps led to the introduction of photogravure to provide a coloured background to the intaglio engraving. It was applied with restraint – always as a foil to the engraving and never swamping it (*34*:16, 17, 19). By 1962, however, the photogravure element was becoming more closely integrated with the design and this led to a more liberal use of colour (*34*:22, 24, 25). At the very end of the period, in 1964, Czechoslovakia introduced offset-lithography for a multicoloured series featuring birds (*34*:26). Several sets in multicolour lithography have appeared since then, but the process was used sparingly and intaglio continued to be paramount.

A definitive series featuring Czechoslovak castles was released between 1960 and 1963 (*34*:20). Annual sets were released to mark sporting and cultural anniversaries (*34*:21), and short sets of commemoratives for individual events and personalities were also released from time to time.

Denmark

Intaglio continued to be used exclusively on Danish stamps of this period, and no attempt was made to inject colour into the designs other than the Red Cross emblem on occasional semi-postals in aid of the Red Cross (*34*:40). The numeral definitives of 1933 continued as the low-value definitives, with provisional surcharges in 1955–6 and several changes of colour and additional denominations in the 1960s. The original series portraying King Frederick IX was replaced in 1961, however, by a set reproducing a profile of the king that had previously appeared in a set of 1959 celebrating his sixtieth birthday (*34*:28, 33). Fluorescent paper, to facilitiate automatic letter-sorting, was introduced in November 1962.

There were relatively few special issues in this period. On three occasions definitive stamps were surcharged with premiums in aid of charity funds, continuing a practice established during the war. The majority of commemoratives consisted of single stamps, the few exceptions including the pair of 1960 celebrating the royal silver wedding and the pair of 1964 portraying the three Danish princesses (*34*:31, 40).

At the beginning of the period the tradition of realism in design was still in force (*34*:27, 29). A stamp of 1961 commemorating the jubilee of Dansk Fredning, the society for the preservation of natural amenities, paved the way for an annual issue publicising this organisation and featuring Danish beauty spots (*34*:35). But a more abstract approach was gradually adopted. Symbolic motifs were used to commemorate the first Danish Food Fair in 1960; the 10th anniversary of Scandinavian Air Lines in 1961; the sesquicentennial of Carstensen, founder of the Tivoli Gardens in 1962; the opening of the Bird-flight Line in 1963; and the conference on sea exploration in 1964 (*34*:30, 32, 36, 37, 41). A more impressionistic style was used in pictorial designs from 1962 onwards (*34*:34, 38). The stamp of 1964 marking the 150th anniversary of primary schools had a child's slate as the basis of the design (*34*:39).

Finland
The lion definitives – introduced in 1954 – were augmented with new values up to 1959, and higher denominations were provided by a series of intaglio pictorials released between 1956 and 1961. In 1963 the currency was reformed, 100 old markkaa being equal to 1 new markka of 100 pennia. Both lion and pictorial designs were issued in January 1963 with the values redrawn (*34*:45, 46).

There was no appreciable change in philatelic policy during this decade. Short thematic sets with charity premiums continued to appear regularly in aid of tuberculosis relief in May, and Red Cross funds in November each year. The majority of commemoratives consisted of single stamps, and monochrome intaglio was used throughout with the exception of typographed stamps of 1956 and 1960 reproducing the first stamps and marking their centenaries. Apart from the Red Cross and Cross of Lorraine emblems, typographed in red, no attempt was made to inject colour into the special issues. Portraits and motifs deriving from historic paintings accounted for a high proportion of Finnish commemorative designs. Architectural motifs featured in a number of stamps marking anniversaries of cities and institutions, but otherwise a distinctive style of quasi-symbolic design pioneered before the war by Hammarsten Jansson was pursued by her pupils – A. Karjalainen, Olavi Vepsäläinen and Pentti Rahikainen – who, between them, produced the majority of Finnish stamps in this decade.

France
Between February 1955 and January 1959 a series of six small-format stamps portraying Marianne, spirit of the republic, was typographed from dies engraved by J. Piel (*35*:1). Two existing versions of the 18-franc value differ in the appearance of the numerals. The previous symbolic designs – 'harvester' and 'Gallic cock' – were retained, new values and colour changes appearing in 1957–9. Sets depicting provincial coats of arms, typographed in full colour, also appeared at regular intervals and provided the lowest denominations as before. The higher values of the ordinary postage series likewise continued to feature scenery, and these stamps were changed at frequent intervals. Although two- and three-colour intaglio had been introduced previously, monochrome designs were still used occasionally (*35*:4), especially for the lower values of the pictorial issues. Thus the stamps of 1957 featuring Le Quesnoy (*35*:11) consisted of an 8-franc in green and a 15-franc in black and green. Care was taken to include scenery in the overseas *départements* from time to time (*35*:14). For the most part, these stamps were intended to boost tourism. They supplemented the 'flammes publicitaires' (local publicity postmarks), which became more visually attractive at this time (*35*:26, 34).

In October 1958 the inauguration of the Fifth Republic, under President De Gaulle, took place and without philatelic commemoration; but the effects of the régime were soon apparent in the stamps of France. Within eighteen months the currency had been reformed, necessitating changes in the definitive series – released in January 1961 with values redrawn in new centimes and francs – that coincided with a new issue of coins, which significantly reverted to the 'sower' design sculpted by Oscar Roty in the late nineteenth century. This emblem of stability and a return to traditional values was also featured in the design of 20- and 30-centime stamps (*35*:19). Similar designs had been used for the definitives of 1903 to 1931. The modern versions were typographed in two-colour combinations, reflecting the more colourful appearance of French stamps in general. Other small-format definitives issued in 1960–61 showed the figure of Marianne in the ship of state, or her profile. No less a figure than Jean Cocteau was commissioned to design the Marianne stamp of February 1961 (*35*:24). Multicolour intaglio versions of the 'Gallic cock' stamps were issued in 1962–5 – examples with numerals on the

back being from coils. During 1962–3 experiments in electronic sorting were conducted with the 25-centime stamp on fluorescent paper, which can be detected with a quartz lamp. Pre-cancelled stamps depicting an ancient Gallic coin were introduced in 1964 (*35*:35).

The only airmail stamps issued in this decade were the aircraft designs of 1954–9 with the values in new francs (*35*:20). Printings of the 2-franc stamp between November 1963 and November 1964 had the deep purple colour omitted, but this was restored in printings from June 1965 onwards. Apart from a 50-franc stamp of 1955 honouring the aviatrix Maryse Bastie, there were no airmail commemoratives; but several ordinary commemoratives had aviation subjects (*35*:29).

The annual charity sets on behalf of the National Relief fund in July, and the Red Cross, in December, continued to appear (*35*:6), pursuing the same themes as before – the fine arts and famous persons. From 1959, however, the midsummer series was also devoted to Red Cross funds, but this was not indicated in the inscriptions and the designs continued to portray historic figures. Other than these annual sets, there were very few semi-postal issues. A stamp was issued each March in honour of Stamp Day, and it invariably carried a small premium (*35*:21). The 25-franc 'Marianne in the ship of state' definitive was surcharged 5 francs in December 1959 in aid of the Fréjus disaster fund.

Although the previous policy of frequent issues commemorating famous people continued throughout this decade, there was a tendency to group such issues in the manner of the National Relief and Red Cross sets. Two sets appeared, in 1955 and 1957, portraying French inventors and their inventions (*35*:2, 12). Six stamps formed the first series and four stamps the second, but the project was then abandoned and the earlier practice of single commemoratives was resumed. Another short-lived scheme consisted of sets portraying famous men whose centenaries fell in the same year. For the first time, France went beyond her frontiers in selecting subjects for commemoration – following an example set by Romania and other countries of the Communist bloc. These sets, portraying Benjamin Franklin, Van Gogh, Chopin, Newton and Goethe among others (*35*:10), were released in 1956 and 1957 only; but in 1963 the same idea inspired a series of five stamps portraying celebrities from France's partners in the Common Market countries (*35*:33). Several individual stamps commemorated anniversaries of liberation and kept alive the memories of wartime concentration camps. A series of five stamps portraying heroes of the Resistance was issued in 1957. This became an annual issue until 1961 (*35*:25), and it was followed by regular issues featuring Resistance memorials.

Two sets with a sporting theme, following the pattern established in 1953, were released in 1956 and 1958 (*35*:9); but the theme was not developed in later years. Probably the most important innovation of this decade, however, was the regular issue of large-format stamps reproducing French works of art. It began in November 1961 with four paintings of the Impressionist school; but in later years every aspect of the fine and applied arts of France was explored, from stained glass (*35*:36) to tapestry and metalwork. The stamps, printed in multicolour intaglio, triggered off a world-wide craze for art stamps that attained epidemic proportions in the late 1960s.

The remaining special issues covered a very wide range of topics. Those honouring famous Frenchmen varied in style from a straightforward portrait (*35*:37) or profile (*35*:5) to a design in which subjects connected with the person formed the background of the stamp (*35*:3, 7, 30). Generally, personal commemoratives featured a portrait – the 1961 stamp marking the centenary of the sculptor Maillol (*35*:23) was exceptional in that it showed his allegory of the Mediterranean instead.

Apart from the annual Europa stamps from 1956 onwards, very few French stamps were concerned with international events. A stamp of 1958 publicised the Brussels Fair (*35*:15) and stamps acknowledged the United Nations Freedom from Hunger campaign in 1962 (*35*:32) and Anti-Malaria campaign in 1963. Other current events were essentially of French interest (*35*:17, 27, 31). Several stamps commemorated anniversaries of First World War battles (*35*:8, 38) and historic cathedrals (*35*:16), and others focused attention on public works or nature conservation (*35*:13, 18, 22).

Stamps provided by the French authorities for the use of international bodies made their début in this period. An overprinted stamp was released in January 1958 for use by the Council of Europe at Strasbourg (35:39), followed by a series featuring the Council's flag. Stamps featuring Buddha and Hermes, symbolising oriental and occidental cultures, were introduced in 1961 for use on mail sent from the UNESCO headquarters building in Paris (35:40).

Germany

West Berlin issued no fewer than six distinct definitive sets from the beginning of 1956 to the end of 1964. There was considerable overlapping, with new values and designs being added to some of the earlier issues after later sets had become obsolete. The first series continued the theme of Berlin buildings and monuments established by the series of 1949–54, the stamps now being inscribed 'DEUTSCHE BUNDESPOST BERLIN' instead of merely 'DEUTSCHE POST'. The much longer inscription was arranged neatly on two sides of the design, with the caption to the design across the top. Initially, letterpress was used for the low values and intaglio for the higher denominations (36:2, 3); but the original version of the 7-pfennig and a 3-pfennig issued in 1963 were lithographed. Ten large-format stamps portraying famous Berliners were released between June 1957 and May 1959. Again, this series emulated an earlier set with the same theme but was produced in two-colour intaglio (36:4). Between January and May 1959 letterpress or intaglio stamps portraying President Heuss were released. Similar stamps, without the word 'BERLIN' were issued in West Germany (36:5). A lengthy series portraying famous Germans was issued between June 1961 and April 1962, of which the low values up to 25-pfennig were typographed and the higher denominations were recess-printed (36:6). Between June 1962 and December 1963, a series of twelve stamps featuring views of Berlin taken from old prints was recess-printed in two-colour combinations (36:7). In December 1964 the first three denominations in a series devoted to twelve centuries of German architecture were released, but the set was not fully issued until the next decade.

The few commemoratives produced by West Berlin in this decade consisted mostly of single stamps honouring celebrities or historic events (36:1). Both intaglio and multicolour lithography were used in their production by the Federal Printing Works in Berlin.

The Federal Republic was far less ready than Berlin to change the definitives. The Heuss series of 1954 remained in use until the early 1960s, although the Heuss-numeral design was also adopted in 1959 with the word 'BERLIN' omitted. A 1-pfennig stamp, with an ornate numeral motif in grey letterpress (36:12) was released in December 1955. Stamps on white paper with a multiple DBP watermark were printed in sheets; those with a multiple BP watermark were issued only in booklets in 1958. The sheet version was reprinted on fluorescent cream paper in 1963. Following West Berlin, West Germany introduced the 'famous Germans' series in 1961, the designs being identical but for the inscription (36:30); and the series featuring German architecture was initiated in December 1964. There was no series comparable to the 'famous Berliners' issue, but the counterpart of the 'old Berlin' series was a set of twelve stamps released in 1964–5 featuring landmarks in the capitals of the Federal districts. This cannot be regarded as a definitive series in the strict sense since each stamp was of the same 20-pfennig denomination (36:35). The series was lithographed in multicolour – a process much favoured by the Federal Republic for its commemorative stamps.

Throughout this period the annual charity series, with premiums on behalf of humanitarian relief and welfare funds, continued to appear in September or October each year. The portraits of 'helpers of mankind', which was the theme of the earlier issues, were superseded in 1956 by more general subjects ranging from child care to agricultural occupations – although portraits of the obstetrician Semmelweis and the philanthropist Raiffeisen were included in the sets of 1956 and 1958. In 1959, however, the Grimm Brothers were portrayed on a stamp of a series devoted to scenes from their fairy tale *The Star Thaler*, and illustrations of other stories from Grimms' *Fairy Tales* were used in subsequent years (36:37).

From 1956 stamps were issued annually in the prevailing Europa design (36:29), those from 1960 incorporating the CEPT emblem. From 1962 a set was released annually, usually in April or May, inscribed 'Jugendmarken' (children's stamps) or 'Für die Jugend' (for the young). These stamps bore a charity premium and differed from the welfare fund stamps in their frankly thematic approach. In this period they featured butterflies (36:32), fish and birds, lithographed in their natural colours. The only other serial type of issue in this decade was devoted to scientific anniversaries, the first series of three stamps appearing in August 1964 and followed by a pair in 1966 and a set of three in 1968 (36:36). Symbolic motifs and chemical formulae were featured in the inaugural series.

The majority of West German commemoratives were issued as single stamps, but pairs were occasionally released – such as the issue of 1957 for Nature Protection Day (36:23). The only exceptions consisted of sets of four stamps commemorating the re-establishment of Lufthansa in 1955 and the Flora and Philately Exhibition in 1962 (36:8, 34).

Not surprisingly, a high proportion of the special issues commemorated famous Germans – but not all of them featured a portrait. The stamp of 1956 marking the 125th anniversary of the birth of Heinrich von Stephan merely reproduced his signature, and in the same year the bicentenary of Mozart was marked by a stamp depicting a spinet and the opening bars of a minuet (36:13). In 1955–6 most portrait stamps featured silhouette profiles (36:14, 15), but this gave way to a more naturalistic interpretation. A few of these stamps were recess-printed, but the majority were lithographed in a style that sometimes bordered on caricature (36:19, 21). From 1960 onwards, a formula was adopted in which portraits were delineated in black on coloured grounds.

This stylised approach was also extended to other commemoratives with a quasi-symbolic motif in black on a coloured ground (36:24, 25). The two- or three-colour poster style was a characteristic of many German stamps in this decade (36:8, 9, 17, 18, 27, 28). Even where intaglio was used, the poster treatment was predominant (36:16, 22). And also in the depiction of monuments and scenery, a stylised approach was often adopted (36:20, 26), one of the few exceptions being the Mainz bi-millenary stamp of 1962 in which a medieval woodcut was reproduced. This stamp, incidentally, was the first to be regularly issued on fluorescent paper (36:31). Human figures, too, conformed to this design policy (36:11, 33). The stamp of 1955 was reissued ten years later in grey instead of brown-lake, to mark the twentieth anniversary of the flight of refugees from East Germany (36:11).

Many of the lithographed stamps were produced by A. Bagel of Düsseldorf, and the intaglio stamps were the work of the Federal Printing Works in Berlin. Apart from the low-value definitives, the only letterpress stamp of this period was the 20-pfennig Transport commemorative of 1955 (36:9). In the same year, a stamp publicising cosmic research was printed in photogravure (36:10) – but a decade was to elapse before this process was revived.

The second decade after the war began with a drastic change in East German philatelic policy. To prevent speculation and illegal dealing in stamps – which were being smuggled out of the Democratic Republic in exchange for hard currency – a system of state-registration of collectors was introduced. Thereafter, only state-registered philatelists were permitted to purchase complete sets of stamps. One denomination in each commemorative set was limited to permit-holders, who were allowed to buy a few specimens only. These Sperrwerte (blocked values) were not available to the general public but were exported by the state philatelic bureau at a very much higher price than their face value indicated.

In 1957 the small-format definitives featuring workers and landmarks were given a new watermark that incorporated quatrefoils instead of post-horns. And in 1958 these stamps were reissued without the marginal imprint. The series continued until a new series of scenery and landmark designs was introduced in March 1961 (36:45); but this was superseded in August of the same year by a set portraying Walter Ulbricht (36:46) of which the low values were typographed and the deutschmark values were recess-printed. The majority of commemorative stamps were lithographed by the German Bank Note Printing Company or the Graphical Workshop, both of Leipzig (36:41–44, 47–49). A few stamps of the late 1950s, however, were produced in photogravure (36:38, 39). The historic buildings series of 1955 was originally photogravure-printed but a lithographic printing was made of the 20-pfennig value, surcharged in December 1956 in aid of victims of the Anglo–French Suez operation (36:39) and the Hungarian uprising.

Commemorative stamps of this period continued the styles of the previous decade, with regular issues for the Leipzig Fair (36:47) and Stamp Day (36:48).

Gibraltar

A photogravure definitive series incorporating a design technique not hitherto used for British colonial stamps was introduced in October 1960. Each element – the vignette, the Annigoni portrait of the queen, the symbolic ornament, the crown, the lettering and value – was arranged on a plain background without frame-lines (37:1). The series was produced by De La Rue, who also recess-printed a £1 denomination featuring a view of the Rock and the badge of the Gibraltar Regiment. Two of these definitives were overprinted in 1964 to mark the introduction of a new constitution, but the remaining commemoratives of this period were all in the colonial omnibus designs. The watermark on the definitives was upright, but a new printing of the 4-penny stamp in 1966 had the watermark sideways.

Greece

The revaluation of the currency at the end of 1954 (one new drachma being equal to a thousand old drachmae) led to the reissue of the 1954 definitives between 1955 and 1960 with values ranging from 10-lepta to 4-drachma. In addition to this series, lengthy thematic sets appeared at regular intervals – two of which were later repeated in new colours and new denominations. Thus a series of fourteen stamps portraying members of the royal family was released in May 1956 and reissued the following year in new colours (37:3). Although the stamps were designed by the Greek artist, A. Tassos, the dies were engraved either by the Austrian H. Woyty-Wimmer or by staff engravers of De La Rue. The series was recess-printed by Aspioti-Elka of Athens. With the exception of the various Europa stamps, Tassos was responsible for all the stamps issued in this decade. His versatility is demonstrated by the wide range of designs involved. Most of the stamps were produced by Aspioti-Elka, but notable exceptions were the coin stamps of 1959 and 1963 (37:4), which were lithographed by Perivolaraki-Lykogianni. Other lengthy thematic sets included those featuring Greek shipping through the ages in 1958, Greek theatres in 1959, Olympic sports in 1960, and Minoan art in 1961. An airmail series, issued in July 1958, took views of Greek seaports as its subject (37:2). A set of seventeen stamps featuring scenery and landmarks was recess-printed and released in February 1961 as tourist publicity (37:5).

Commemorative stamps ranged from singles and pairs commemorating historic anniversaries and current events (37:8) to longer sets of seven or eight (37:6, 7). In many cases, classical motifs were applied to modern events. Several issues marked royal events, such as the 2.50-drachma stamp of 1961 celebrating Crown Prince Constantine's gold medal in the Rome Olympics, a series of nine honouring the centenary of the dynasty in 1963 (37:7), a set of ten mourning stamps for King Paul I in 1964, and the series of three marking Constantine's wedding to Princess Anne-Marie of Denmark, also in 1964.

Great Britain

Prior to 1960, only three commemorative issues were made. Three stamps appeared in August 1957 in honour of the World Scout Jubilee Jamboree (37:10), the contemporary 4-penny definitive was issued the following month with an inscription added to the sides to mark the 46th Inter-Parliamentary Union Conference in London (37:11), and in 1958 a set of three publicised the Sixth British Empire and Commonwealth Games in Cardiff (37:12). Four years had elapsed, in fact, since the previous commemorative issues marking the coronation in 1953. This dearth of special issues was more than compensated by the complexity of the definitives.

The early printings of the low-value definitives were on paper with a watermark that showed the royal monogram and the Tudor crown. As this was heraldically incorrect, the stamps were reissued between 1955 and 1958 on paper with a watermark featuring the crown of St. Edward the Confessor. This paper was also used for early printings of the four high denomination stamps, which featured castles from each of the four countries of the United Kingdom (37:9), recess-printed by Waterlow and Sons in September 1955. The contract for the high values passed to De La Rue at the end of 1957 and they printed all four denominations from new plates, using the

original dies. Apart from marginal sheet markings, the De La Rue and Waterlow printings can be distinguished by their shades and the generally lighter and cleaner appearance of the De La Rue versions. Between 1958 and 1965 the royal monogram was phased out of the watermark used for both low- and high-value stamps and a watermark of multiple crowns took its place. Stamps with sideways watermarks were issued in coils, and those with inverted watermarks appeared in booklets.

Graphite lines were printed on the backs of some low-value stamps issued in the Southampton area in November 1957 in connection with the world's first electronic letter-facing and cancelling experiments. Two years later, stamps were issued with phosphor bands printed across the face in addition to the obsolescent graphite lines on the back. In June 1960, stamps with only the phosphor bands were introduced. Considerable variation exists in the positioning of these lines and bands, their printing process – photogravure or letterpress – and the colour emitted under an ultra-violet lamp. Eventually, phosphor banding was extended to all denominations of the definitive range printed by photogravure and to all photogravure commemoratives released from November 1962 onwards. Throughout this period, however, such phosphor stamps were issued only in Southampton, Glasgow and south-east London, where automatic letter-sorting experiments were in progress. Ordinary non-phosphor stamps were issued everywhere else.

The use of the Dorothy Wilding portrait of Queen Elizabeth II in lieu of the name of the country gave to British stamps of this period a distinctive, almost idiosyncratic, appearance. For the most part, the designs of the commemoratives were purely symbolic (37:15, 18–20, 23, 24). An attempt to introduce a pictorial element was made in 1960, however, when a seventeenth-century post-boy was featured on a 3-penny stamp marking the tercentenary of the General Letter Office (37:13) and in 1961, when architectural motifs from the Palace of Westminster were used on two stamps (37:17). At the same time, monochrome photogravure gave way to two- or three-colour combinations, beginning with the CEPT stamps of 1960–61 – Britain's only contribution to the Europa theme (37:14, 16). But by May 1963 a more pictorial approach was becoming fashionable – though sometimes with odd results – as designers grappled with the problem of combining the royal portrait with the pictorial elements (37:21, 22). Throughout this period, commemoratives were limited to current events such as conferences and congresses (37:16, 17, 22, 23, 26–28) – the sole exceptions being anniversaries of events connected with the postal services (37:13, 15, 20). The Shakespeare series of 1964 (37:25) theoretically marked the Quatercentenary Festival – a current event – but it established a precedent for stamps marking historical anniversaries. More importantly, the appearance of the Droeshout portrait of Shakespeare breached the traditional ban on the portraits of persons other than royalty on British stamps, and this ban was relaxed in the following year, when stamps were issued in memory of Robert Burns.

Of even more far-reaching consequence, however, was the decision in 1958 to make separate issues of stamps for the 'regions' of the United Kingdom – England alone being curiously exempt from this doubtful privilege. Thus in August 1958 regional stamps were released in Scotland, Northern Ireland, Wales, the Isle of Man, Guernsey and Jersey (37:29–34). In each case, the Dorothy Wilding portrait was the dominant feature with symbolism appropriate to the region incorporated in the framework. The first three areas had three stamps apiece – 3-penny, 6-penny and 1s 3d but the others had only 3-penny stamps. In 1964, however, 2½-penny stamps were issued in the Isle of Man and the Channel Islands for use on holiday postcards.

Hungary

The small-format definitives featuring buildings continued in use in the late 1950s, but from June to November 1955 a series of twenty stamps featuring occupations and professions was released (37:35). Nineteen of the 'buildings' set and two of the 'workers' series were overprinted at Sopron during the uprising of October 1956 (37:37), and although the issue was promptly suppressed by the counterrevolutionary forces seven of these stamps were made available later to state-registered philatelists. Early in 1960 a new series, depicting castles, was photogravure-printed on white paper with a multiplestar watermark (37:40). Tinted paper was used for a printing of some values in September 1960, and unwatermarked paper was used for three denominations printed in 1964. The first values of a series depicting forms of transport and aspects of the postal services were released in July 1963 and other denominations were added up to 1970 (37:41).

After 1956 very few special issues were ideological in character. Commemoratives concentrated on non-political events and anniversaries (37:38, 42, 43) and were interspersed at frequent intervals with lengthy thematic issues (37:36, 39). Triangles, diamonds and unusually elongated rectangles (37:42, 43), combined – with multi-colour photogravure – to heighten the visual impact of Hungarian stamps throughout this decade.

Iceland
Apart from two stamps of 1956 in the Scandinavian omnibus design marking Northern Countries Day, all the stamps in this decade were produced by either De La Rue or Courvoisier – a rivalry that extended to the definitives issued piecemeal between September 1958 and July 1963. The Icelandic salmon, pony and other fauna designs (38:4, 6) were recess-printed by De La Rue, but the buildings designs (38:9) were produced in monochrome photogravure by Courvoisier. De La Rue enjoyed a monopoly of the special issues until 1960, including the monochrome intaglio sets of 1955–7 featuring national sports (38:1), power plants and waterfalls, publicising the re-afforestation campaign of 1957 (38:2), and commemorating the 40th anniversary of Icelandic civil aviation in 1959 and World Refugee Year in 1960 (38:5, 7). Two stamps commemorating the national flag were lithographed in two-colour combinations, and the same process was used in 1958 for the first of an occasional series devoted to flowers (38:3). Courvoisier used multi-colour photogravure for the later floral sets (38:8) and applied the same process to the bulk of the commemoratives from 1962 onwards (38:10, 11).

Taking part in several of the United Nations issues, Iceland was never content to use the standard motifs but endeavoured to interpret the subjects from a local viewpoint – hence Jonsson's statue of 'The Outcast' for the World Refugee Year pair of 1960 (38:7) and herring trawlers on the Freedom from Hunger pair of 1963 (38:10).

Ireland
Most Irish stamps of this decade were recess-printed by De La Rue's Dublin subsidiary. In 1961 Bradbury Wilkinson recess-printed three stamps marking the 15th centenary of the death of St. Patrick (38:22), but all other commemoratives were issued in pairs. In 1957–8 there were six pairs honouring famous people. Departing from previous tradition, only one of them (38:14) was inscribed entirely in Gaelic – the others showed the name of the person in English. The small format of the definitive series was used for these portrait stamps, which ranged stylistically from the solid backgrounds of the Redmond and Wadding stamps (38:13, 16), through the toned background of the O'Crohan pair (38:14), to the light grounds of the Brown and Clarke sets (38:15, 17) and, finally, the unframed design of the stamps commemorating Mother Mary Aikenhead (38:18). The last-named set was recess-printed by Waterlow's Brussels subsidiary, Imprimerie Belge de Sécurité. The later issues favoured a double-sized format, but the Guinness pair of 1959 were in the medium size used for several portrait designs of the early 1950s (38:21). Portraits in circular cartouches against solid backgrounds were used for stamps honouring the Gaelic scholars O'Donovan and O'Curry in 1962 and the patriot Wolfe Tone in 1964 (38:23, 25).

Ireland participated in the annual Europa stamps from 1960 but also issued stamps for the World Refugee Year campaign in 1960 and Freedom from Hunger in 1963, giving both designs a particularly Irish slant (38:19, 24). A monochrome intaglio pair celebrated the silver jubilee of Aer Lingus in 1961 (38:20); but multicolour photogravure was introduced in 1963 for the Red Cross centenary pair and the New York World's Fair stamps of 1964 (38:26), both produced by Harrison and Sons.

Italy
Although the 'Siracusa' definitives continued throughout this decade, Italy departed from this subject on two occasions. High-value stamps on which were reproduced the bust of St. George by Donatello (38:29) were issued in 1957, and a set of nineteen stamps featuring details from Michelangelo frescoes in the Sistine Chapel (38:34) was released in 1961. Photogravure was used for the values up to 200-lira and intaglio for the higher denominations. The winged-wheel watermark, used on Italian stamps since 1945, was superseded by a multiple-star watermark in 1955 – not only for later printings of the 'Siracusa' definitives but also for seven values of the 1950 series featuring provincial occupations. There were no issues of airmail definitives, but one of the 1945–7 series was released in a new colour and overprinted to mark the visit of the Italian president to North America in 1956.

Both photogravure and intaglio were used for commemorative stamps, as in the previous period, with a tendency towards more colourful designs from 1957 onwards. The majority of stamps commemorated Italian events and personalities (38:27, 30, 35–39, 42). Of particular note were the issues publicising the winter and summer Olympics of 1956 (38:27, 33) and several pairs reproducing the stamps of the old Italian states on the occasion of their centenaries (38:31, 32). In 1956 the first anniversary of Italy's admission to membership of the United Nations was marked by two stamps lithographed in red and green with the images slightly out of alignment so that a three-dimensional effect was created with the aid of special tinted spectacles (38:28). Italy took part in the Europa issues from their inception and also released stamps for such international events as the anti-malaria campaign, in 1962, the Paris Postal Conference and the Red Cross centenary, both in 1963 (38:39–41).

Liechtenstein
With the exception of several portrait designs and the anti-malaria stamp of 1962, recess-printed by the Austrian State Press or the Swiss PTT Bureau, all the stamps produced between 1955 and 1964 were printed in photogravure by Courvoisier. Between 1959 and 1964 a new definitive series depicting scenery was released (38:43). Regular issues in the Europa theme were instituted in 1960, the designs of which invariably departed from the standard motif. From 1961 to 1963, sets with the medieval Minnesingers as their subject appeared annually in multicolour photogravure. From 1964 onwards, similar sets featured the arms of Liechtenstein's nobility (38:44). Apart from an annual set of three stamps for Christmas, begun in 1962, commemoratives consisted mainly of single stamps.

Luxembourg
New values were added to the definitive series introduced in 1948 and recess-printed by Courvoisier. The same firm recess-printed a new series with a more up-to-date portrait of the Grand-Duchess Charlotte, and this was released between 1960 and 1964 (38:48). In this decade the majority of stamps were produced by Enschedé or Courvoisier, the former preferring intaglio or lithography and the latter using multicolour photogravure (38:45, 47). These printers shared the contract for the series of 1963 celebrating the millenary of Luxembourg, in which each value related to a century of history. Monochrome intaglio was used by Enschedé (38:46). With the exception of the annual Europa pairs and the sets of six semi-postals for the National Welfare fund, the stamps of this period were mainly issued as singles.

Malta
An Elizabethan series, recess-printed by Bradbury Wilkinson and Waterlow and Sons, was released between January 1956 and January 1957 (39:1). The usual Script CA watermark was used for these stamps, but late printings of the 1- and 2-penny, in 1963–4, appeared on paper with the more modern Block CA watermark. Waterlow and Sons applied the technique of lithography combined with an intaglio frame, hitherto used for many of their Latin-American contracts, to a set of three stamps marking the Maltese stamp centenary (39:3), but the remaining commemoratives of this decade were printed in photogravure by Harrison and Sons. Several sets marked anniversaries of the award of the George Cross for gallantry during the war (39:2, 4). Apart from the various colonial omnibus issues, there were distinctive stamps commemorating the shipwreck of St. Paul (1960) and, in 1962, the Great Siege of 1565 (39:5). The majority of the special issues were designed by Chevalier E. V. Cremona, who was also responsible for the series of six in 1964 celebrating independence (39:6). Silver or gold metallic ink

was an increasingly common feature of Maltese stamps from 1957.

Monaco

A series portraying Prince Rainier III, designed and engraved by Henri Cheffer, was recess-printed at the French Government Printing Works in 1955. The series was reissued between 1960 and 1971 with values expressed in new francs and centimes (*39*:8). These definitives were supplemented at regular intervals by lengthy sets portraying Princess Grace and views of the principality. In 1960 Monaco adopted the practice, initiated by San Marino in the early 1950s, of issuing frequent thematic sets. The first of these depicted marine life (*39*:9), and later sets featured veteran cars, birds useful to agriculture, and underwater exploration. Pre-cancelled stamps depicting the Aquatic Stadium were introduced in 1964 (*39*:12). Like Liechtenstein, Monaco participated in the Europa issues but preferred to use its own designs (*39*:10). The commemoratives of this period ranged from single stamps, in 1963, commemorating the 50th anniversary of the first trans-Mediterranean flight (*39*:11) to long sets that were not directly relevant to Monaco. From 1955 an annual stamp publicised the Monte Carlo Car Rally, depicting scenery in the countries of the eight starting points. Five ordinary and three airmail stamps were issued in April 1956 to celebrate the wedding of Prince Rainier and the American actress Grace Kelly (*39*:7).

Netherlands

The numeral and Juliana definitives remained current throughout this period, but in 1962–3 three small-format stamps featuring Dutch scenery were added to the permanent range. The early printings of these stamps were on ordinary watermarked paper (*39*:19). All Dutch stamps were printed by Enschedé of Haarlem, and three different processes were used: photogravure (*39*:13, 14, 16, 18–23, 25, 26, 28–30), lithography (*39*:17, 24) and intaglio (*39*:15, 27).

Of the semi-postal issues, those on behalf of child welfare and the cultural and social funds continued to appear annually in November and April respectively (*39*:18, 24, 28). The 'summer stamps' featured a wide range of subjects from the fine and applied arts, and the children's stamps concentrated on children's portraits, nursery rhymes, and children's activities at various times during this period. Stamps with a charity premium appeared on other occasions, raising money for the Queen Wilhelmina anti-cancer fund (*39*:14) and the Dutch national team taking part in the Olympic Games.

The Netherlands was one of the earliest countries to issue Europa stamps. Standard designs were used by the participants every year from 1956 onwards (*39*:23) except for 1957, when each country produced its own designs (*39*:16). On two occasions the Netherlands took part in issues common to the other Benelux countries: the 10th anniversary of NATO in 1959 (*39*:17) and the 20th anniversary of Benelux in 1964. Similar 'mini-omnibus' issues were made, in common with the Dutch overseas territories, to celebrate the royal silver wedding in 1962 (*39*:20) and the 10th anniversary of the statute of the kingdom in 1964 (*39*:29).

Apart from the charity stamps that reproduced Old Master paintings, the majority of special issues adopted symbolic or stylised motifs (*39*:13, 21, 22, 27, 30). Even the stamps portraying historic personages tended to use a stylised treatment (*39*:15, 25) that departed from the more naturalistic portraiture of the previous decade.

Norway

The accession of King Olav V in September 1957 necessitated a change of definitives. The low-value 'numeral and post-horn' design continued in use, but in April 1958 a series of higher denominations appeared on which were reproduced photographs of the King by E. Rude (*39*:35). The 'post-horns', typographed from 1872 to 1937 and thereafter printed in photogravure, were issued in an intaglio version between 1962 and 1974. At the same time, the King Olav series was superseded by an intaglio series depicting traditional motifs including runic drawings, reef-knots and stave-churches (*39*:42). Between 1955 and 1974 a new series of official stamps was introduced, featuring the Norwegian national emblem and the abbreviated inscription 'OFF. SAK' (official matter) (*39*:33). These stamps, designed by J. Haukland, were printed in photogravure by

Emil Mostue of Oslo. Phosphorescent paper was introduced for the definitive and official stamps in 1969 in connection with electronic sorting experiments.

Fittingly, the first commemorative issue of this decade was a set of three stamps celebrating the centenary of Norwegian stamps in 1955. The designs reproduced the first stamp and two long-lived definitives – the 'lion' of 1922–37 and the 'post-horn' of 1872 onwards (*39*:31). On two occasions Norway released stamps in designs common to the other Scandinavian countries: a pair in 1956 for Northern Countries Day (*39*:34) and a single in 1961 for the 10th anniversary of the Scandinavian Airlines System (*39*:39). From 1960 onwards, with the exception of 1961, stamps in the prevailing Europa motif were issued each year. Norway was one of the few countries to issue stamps publicising International Geophysical Year in 1957, the three stamps featuring maps of Spitzbergen and Queen Maud Land and a view of Jan Mayen Island (*39*:32). The only other issue for an international event in this period was in 1963, when four stamps marked the UN Freedom from Hunger campaign (*39*:45). The treatment of subjects was generally more naturalistic than in Germany and the Netherlands in the equivalent period, although symbolic designs were often used (*39*:36–38) in issues marking the centenaries of important institutions. The nearest to an abstract design was that used in the series of 1963 celebrating the 150th anniversary of the textile industry – a herringbone pattern (*39*:46). As a rule, portrait stamps concentrated exclusively on the subjects portrayed (*39*:43, 44, 48), the only exception being the pair of 1961 – for the 50th anniversary of Amundsen's arrival at the South Pole – in which Amundsen was portrayed with his ship *Fram* and a dog-team in the background (*39*:40). Several stamps had a purely pictorial motif, however, showing shipping, vintage aircraft (*39*:41) and architectural subjects.

Poland

As in other countries of the Communist bloc, Poland dispensed with formal definitive stamps at the beginning of this decade. With the possible exception of a series of twenty stamps featuring Polish cities and coats of arms, issued in 1960–61 (*40*:10), no issues were current for any length of time. Instead, there were frequent releases of sets of a thematic nature. The first of these, issued in December 1954, was a modest set of four depicting forest animals. Between March and May 1955 it was followed by a series of eight stamps, featuring Warsaw monuments, recess-printed on toned paper – a feature that characterised several subsequent issues (*40*:12). The 40-groszy stamp of the monuments series (*40*:1) was one of the last to be engraved by Czeslaw Slania before he fled to Denmark. (Poland's loss was Scandinavia's gain, for many of the intaglio stamps of Denmark and Sweden were engraved by Slania in later years.)

At first the most popular themes were explored, a high proportion of such issues being linked to the tourist industry. Thus the Polish countryside and urban landmarks (*40*:4, 5) were recurring subjects at frequent intervals. Poland was one of the first countries to exploit topical philately for no other reason than to raise revenue from the hard-currency areas of the world, however, and from 1959 onwards the subjects became infinitely more varied. Mushrooms, insects and technical aspects of man's conquest of space (*40*:7, 11, 13) vied with cats, dogs, birds, reptiles and even prehistoric animals. Throughout this period photogravure was the principal medium for these issues, but lithography – occasionally combined with embossing – was used increasingly from 1960 onwards. Shipping was a popular subject, and sets ranged from modern merchant shipping to sailing ships throughout the ages (*40*:3, 12).

Relatively few stamps were issued purely for commemorative reasons. Several sets marked anniversaries of the People's Republic, but the series of three stamps of 1959 (*40*:6) was almost apologetic in its small format – unusual for Poland – and rather nondescript designs. Apart from a few stamps portraying famous people, commemoratives of this period were generally symbolic in design (*40*:2, 8) or depicted stylised figures in a poster treatment of the subject (*40*:9). For the World Youth Fencing Championships of 1957, two 60-groszy stamps, each depicting a fencer were printed side by side. Together, the stamps gave the impression of a duel, thereby constituting the world's first composite stamps – an idea developed later by many other countries.

Portugal

The 'medieval knight' definitive series of 1952 remained current, and new values were added until 1972. With an average of fourteen stamps a year Portugal ranked as one of the most conservative countries during this period, the first series of which was a set of nine stamps, in 1955, portraying historic kings. This thematic series – the only one of its kind in this decade – supplemented the definitives (40:14). The stamps were recess-printed by Bradbury Wilkinson and, apart from a series of 1957 produced by the Austrian State Press and a pair of 1961 printed by Enschedé, they were the only intaglio stamps released before 1968. Harrison and Sons produced sets of four in 1958 and 1963 (40:25) by photogravure, and the same process was used by Courvoisier in 1960 for a set of six marking the quingentenary of the death of Prince Henry the Navigator (40:19). All other commemoratives of this decade were lithographed locally. The technique of bleeding the design into the perforations, hitherto used in the definitives, was extended to the pair of 1958 marking the Brussels Fair (40:18). Stamps honouring historic celebrities usually showed their portrait on a flat lithographic background (40:16, 28), in contrast with the photogravure treatment by Courvoisier of a medieval painting and a bas-relief by Harrison and Sons (40:19, 25).

The majority of stamps commemorating anniversaries or current events adopted a purely symbolic approach, often showing elements juxtaposed on a flat lithographic ground (40:21, 27) or superimposed (40:17, 18, 23). A stylised treatment of human figures was used for stamps honouring the Republican Guard and the 10th International Paediatrics Congress in 1962 (40:22). A more pictorial approach was manifest, however, in such stamps as the centenary sets for the railways, Sameiro shrine and the Paris Postal Conference (40:15, 24, 26).

Portugal began issuing Europa stamps in 1960, usually diverging from the standard designs. The only other attempt at a regular issue in this period was the introduction of a Stamp Day series in 1962. In March of that year two stamps honoured the Archangel Gabriel, patron saint of communications (40:20), and three stamps in December portrayed St. Zenon the Courier. There were no further sets in this theme.

Romania

Second only to Russia in philatelic fecundity, Romania produced almost a thousand different stamps between 1955 and the end of 1964. From an average of thirty stamps a year in the early 1950s, output doubled in 1955 alone and increased rapidly thereafter. Small-format definitives featuring occupations and aspects of the Romanian way of life (40:37) were issued in 1955 and 1960 and were supplemented at very frequent intervals by lengthy thematic sets ranging from eight to twenty stamps and often including denominations intended for airmail. In keeping with this prolific output, Romania utilised every process in stamp production. Photogravure continued to be widely used, but a good percentage of designs was typographed (40:35) or lithographed (40:30). Typography occasionally combined with lithography, as in the United Nations series of 1961, and with embossing, as in the Olympic Medals series of 1964. After an absence of more than thirty years, intaglio was revived in 1963 and was employed sparingly from then onwards – but the quality of engraving was crude compared to that used in Czechoslovakia (40:39).

Special stamps for Stamp Day, consisting of a single stamp with an attached coupon denoting the charity premium, were introduced in 1959. Bipartite stamps of this sort were also used for postage-due, the left half usually being retained by the postman as a form of receipt. Postally-used examples of complete stamps were sold through the State Philatelic Bureau (40:33).

Purely thematic sets featuring flowers, birds, butterflies, fish and other popular subjects were issued from November 1955 onwards with ever-increasing frequency. In addition to the annual series honouring world-wide cultural celebrities, there were several sets between 1955 and 1962 devoted solely to Romanian personalities. Thereafter, these sets were combined so that half of the stamps were devoted to Romanians and half to foreign celebrities (40:38). A comparatively large number of stamps had a political slant (40:32, 34, 36) or were Soviet-oriented, but this trend decreased in the early 1960s and by 1964 Romania was issuing stamps honouring the space exploits of Soviet cosmonauts and American astronauts with equal impartiality. A poster style of design was used for many of the commemorative issues (40:29, 40). The formalised frame-lines characteristic of the earlier stamps disappeared, and in many cases the back-ground colour was bled into the perforations (40:31, 34, 35).

Russia

All the trends that had been initiated in the early 1950s continued in this decade. Stamps became bigger and more colourful, and the rigid conventions that had governed the naturalistic treatment of subjects and the traditional principles of graphic design were abandoned as Soviet artists groped their way towards more attractive presentations of hackneyed themes. This break with the past was most noticeable in stamps portraying famous people. The policy as regards portraiture was greatly liberalised, not only in the criteria applied to those worthy of portrayal but also in the treatment of portraits and their integration with pictorial backgrounds. An inset portrait in a pictorial design – a technique widely used in the 1930s and 1940s – was seen in a few stamps of 1955–7 (41:6), but thereafter, the portrait was generally integrated into the vignette (41:13) or was the dominant feature (40:24). Following the example of Romania, Russia widened the scope of her portrait commemoratives to include foreign celebrities. Although stamps portraying personalities from other countries of the Communist bloc had occasionally been issued before, the release of a stamp devoted to the German poet Schiller marked an important breakthrough in 1955. It was followed by occasional stamps devoted to men and women of many countries (41:5, 15), including British, French and American celebrities as well as those from the Third World and the Soviet bloc.

Multicolour lithography and letterpress (41:1) were used increasingly from the beginning of the period, but a few issues continued to appear in monochrome photogravure (41:2, 5, 7) until 1958. More significant was the use of two or more colours in occasional intaglio issues from 1956 onwards (41:3). A stamp portraying Robert Burns was originally printed in monochrome photogravure in 1956 and was reissued in two-colour intaglio a year later. Photographs continued to provide the basis for the vignettes in most commemorative stamps (41:1, 2, 4, 7, 9, 10, 13, 19, 21), often combined with a symbolic treatment of the frame. Inevitably, however, the trend towards poster designs – evident in the stamps of many other countries in the late 1950s – spread to Russia by 1958. It was applied to a series publicising civil aviation (41:8) and was subsequently developed in the numerous stamps commemorating Soviet space achievements (41:12, 22). It was even tentatively employed in designs where photographs of people would formerly have been used, such as in the Children's Day series of 1960 and the 'costumes' set of 1961 (41:14, 17). But the two sets of 1961–2 featuring scenes from Russian ballet returned to the traditional style reminiscent of the 1940s (41:20). Nevertheless, by 1962 the more liberal approach to stamp design had progressed to the abandonment of a formal rectangular lay-out, and stamps with irregular designs became increasingly common (41:23, 25). Many stamps from 1958 onwards were released imperforate or perforated, with little difference in their value (41:24).

Of the relatively few stamps depicting landmarks or scenery, a notable example was the 60-kopek stamp of 1959 featuring the Kremlin and the Capitol (41:11) in commemoration of Prime Minister Khruschev's visit to the United States. In 1958, stamps with a scenic motif marked the International Philatelic Exhibition in Moscow (41:7) and the 850th anniversary of the city of Vladimir (41:9). A long series of 1958 celebrated the centenary of the first Russian stamps by depicting scenes from Russian postal history (41:10), and the 40th anniversary of the first Soviet stamps was marked in 1961 by a set of four stamps reproducing previous issues arranged according to their themes (41:18).

Russian currency was reformed in 1961, one new rouble becoming equal to ten old roubles. This necessitated the release of a new definitive series in values from 1 kopek to 16 kopeks. The majority of the stamps were lithographed (41:16), but two were recess-printed and one was photogravure-printed. The same small format and the same subjects – workers, monuments and landmarks – were used as for previous Soviet definitives.

Saar

New designs were added to the intaglio pictorial series that had been introduced in 1952 – recess-printed at the French Government Printing Works, as before (41:26). Between 1955 and 1957 the philatelic policy of the Saar remained unchanged with commemoratives consisting mainly of single stamps interspersed by annual issues for Stamp Day and semi-postals on behalf of the national relief fund and the Red Cross (41:28).

As a result of the referendum in October 1955, the Saar's return to the German Federal Republic came into effect on New Year's Day 1957. The contemporary federal definitives portraying President Heuss were modified in design and inscription for use in the Saar (41:27), and the majority of commemorative stamps issued after that date were in designs similar to those used by West Germany (41:29). Distinctive stamps were withdrawn from use on 6th July 1959, when German currency was introduced, and thereafter the Saar used ordinary German stamps.

San Marino

The unashamedly philatelic nature of Sammarinese stamps, begun in the early 1950s, was more pronounced from 1955 onwards as purely thematic sets became longer and more colourful. The fact that the Winter Olympics of 1956 and the Summer Olympics of 1960 were both staged in Italy, gave San Marino the opportunity for a spate of Olympic stamps, beginning with a pair in June 1955 publicising the first international exhibition of Olympics stamps and continuing with ten stamps giving advance publicity to the Winter Games at Cortina (41:30). Advance publicity for the Summer Olympics – an idea pioneered by Australia – took the form of a set of seven stamps portraying members of the Olympics executive committee (41:33). Two sets of ten stamps appeared in 1963–4 in connection with the Tokyo Olympics (41:36, 37).

The rather stereotyped appearance of Sammarinese stamps during this decade is because most of them were designed by three artists – C. Mancioli, A. Vicini and R. Franzoni – who, between them, executed an impressive total of almost three hundred designs. Few of the commemorative stamps were directly concerned with events in the republic. Several sets celebrated the centenaries of the stamps of Sardinia (41:35) and the other old Italian states, and San Marino was assiduous in commemorating such events as the Milan Fair (41:31), the Brussels Fair in 1958 and the European Baseball Championships in Milan in 1964. Several issues had American themes, including sets marking the 150th anniversary of Abraham Lincoln (41:32), the jubilee of Lions International (41:34) and the first anniversary of the death of John F. Kennedy.

With the exception of two airmail high values, recess-printed in 1958, all Sammarinese stamps of this decade were produced in multicolour photogravure.

Spain

A photogravure series portraying General Franco was released between 1955 and 1960 (42:1). The marginal imprint of the normal series bore the initials of the state printing works – 'F.N.M.T.' (Fabrica Nacional de Moneda y Timbre), but 1- and 5-peso stamps with an additional letter 'B' were printed at the International Philatelic Exhibition in Barcelona in May 1960. A modern airliner and a medieval caravel were featured on a series of photogravure airmail stamps released between November 1955 and March 1956 (42:3).

The various regular issues of the previous period continued in this decade. Stamps appeared each October to mark Stamp Day, and they were generally linked to some important anniversary such as the quatercentenary of the death of St. Ignatius Loyola (42:2). At first, the number of stamps per set decreased each year; but in 1958 Stamp Day was switched to 24th March, and the number of stamps in a set increased from then onwards.

Spain took part in the annual Europa issues from 1960. After 1961, however, the standard designs were abandoned in favour of motifs with a particularly Spanish connotation: thus the pair issued in 1963 featured Santa Maria de Europa (42:12). Several other issues initiated in this period were produced at regular intervals thereafter. Vertical stamps depicting the arms of the provincial capitals were introduced in January 1962 (42:9) and continued to appear, one at a time, until September 1966. Beginning in December 1959, a stamp was released annually for use on Christmas mail. These stamps, inscribed 'NAVIDAD', reproduced paintings of a religious nature (42:17) – but no attempt was made to reproduce the natural colours of the paintings, monochrome photogravure being used until 1965.

Apart from the 'provincial arms' series, little attempt was made to exploit the colour potential of photogravure. The only notable exceptions were the annual sets portraying colonisers and explorers of America, inaugurated in 1961 (42:13). Up to 1962, monochrome photogravure – in the definitive format or the larger vertical or horizontal format – was used for the majority of commemorative stamps (42:4–6, 10, 11). The only concession to multicolour was a lengthy series of large square stamps issued in 1961 to celebrate the silver jubilee of the National State. By contrast, however, this larger format was used increasingly for two- or three-colour intaglio stamps, often of a purely thematic nature, issued from 1961 onwards (42:7, 8, 14–16).

Sweden

The definitive designs of 1951 – both the numeral and the Gustav VI Adolf profile – were redrawn in 1957, the former horizontal-lined background being replaced by quadrille lines or cross-hatching. Se-tenant pairs of these stamps appeared in stamp booklets (42:23). In addition to the changes in the background, the stamps now bore a marginal imprint giving the initials of the designers and engravers. With the exception of two stamps of June 1955 in honour of National Flag Day, all Swedish stamps of this decade were recess-printed at the stamp printing office of the Royal Swedish Postal Administration. The flag stamps were lithographed in three colours by Esselte Aktie-Bolag of Stockholm (42:19). The stamps portraying the king were again redrawn in 1961, with white instead of solid numerals and lettering.

The tempo of special issues increased noticeably from 1955 onwards. To mark the centenary of Swedish postage stamps in 1955, the first series – typographed originally by Count Sparre – was reissued with two lines through the bottom panel obliterating the archaic currency (skilling banco), the stamps serving as the equivalent öre denominations. These stamps were sold only at the centenary stamp exhibition and cost 2.45 kroner each, which included the price of the admission ticket. At the same time, two intaglio stamps with a similar design to the first series were put on general release (42:18).

Stylistically, there was little change from the previous period except that the slightly larger format was now standard for all commemoratives other than the stamp centenary issues. In 1964 an elongated vertical format was adopted for stamps marking the 800th anniversary of the archbishopric of Uppsala (42:32), and this was subsequently used more frequently. Although a few designs favoured a lighter or varied background (42:21, 22, 31), most of them had the lettering and motif in white on a quadrille background (42:20, 24–30). The 40-öre stamp of 1960 for World Refugee Year was appropriately engraved by the Polish emigré Czeslaw Slania. It was the first of many stamps he engraved for Sweden in the ensuing years (42:28) including the pair of 1962 for the centenary of the Swedish local mail delivery service, with the unusual motif of a postman's footprints (42:30).

In December 1961 Sweden issued the first stamps in what has since become an annual series, portraying winners of the Nobel Prize (42:29). Initially commemorating the diamond jubilee of the Nobel Prize, these stamps have since appeared annually portraying the winners of sixty years before.

Switzerland

No changes occurred in the 'technical landscape' definitives of 1950 until 1960. A new series was released on 10th May of that year, featuring aspects of Swiss postal history (42:40) on the low values and architectural monuments on the high values. The stamps were recess-printed by the Swiss PTT, initially on white paper. Several denominations, from 1.30- to 2.80-franc, were added to the series in 1963. They were printed on paper containing blue and red fibres. Four high-value stamps, from 3- to 20-franc, showing reproductions of medieval wood-carvings of the Four Evangelists (42:43) were introduced in September 1961.

Special issues presented a picture of orderliness and restraint that other countries might have done well to emulate. The majority of issues throughout this decade consisted of four annual sets.

Miscellaneous anniversaries and current events were grouped together into a publicity series issued every March (42:34, 38, 39, 41, 44, 45). In this way commemoratives were confined to single stamps for each occasion, in sets of from four to six stamps. Symbolic motifs were generally employed, but increasing use was made of French, German and Italian in the inscriptions in addition to the Latin name of the country (42:39, 44). In May or June came the set of five stamps inscribed 'PRO PATRIA' (for the fatherland), combining a symbolic motif on one stamp with four individual designs of a thematic nature on the others (42:36). In December came the 'PRO JUVENTUTE' (for youth) stamps, with a portrait on one denomination and thematic designs on the other four. The only divergence from this practice was in 1962, when stamps featuring children's activities marked the 50th anniversary of the Pro Juventute Foundation (42:42). Switzerland began issuing Europa stamps in July 1957, initially with original designs to symbolise United Europe (42:35) but using the standard motifs from 1960 onwards. Very few stamps were issued other than these perennials. One of these exceptions was a stamp of 1959 honouring the second United Nations Atomic Conference in Geneva (42:37).

In 1956–7 the Swiss PTT provided distinctive sets of stamps for the use of the International Labour Office (42:49), the Intërnational Education Office, the Universal Postal Union (42:46), the World Health Organisation, the World Meteorological Organisation (42:47) and the United Nations European Office in Geneva (42:48). Six denominations, using two designs with symbolic motifs, were provided in each case. In 1960 new values were added and there was a change of colour for the 20-centime stamp.

Turkey

Philatelic policy followed the pattern of the previous decade without change from 1955 to 1964. The majority of stamps were lithographed by a variety of printers in Istanbul or Ankara, and commemoratives were occasionally produced in photogravure by the Austrian State Press between 1955 and 1959, and by Courvoisier, between 1960 and 1963. In 1959, the Federal German Printing Works in Berlin lithographed a 500-kurus stamp with an embossed profile of Kemal Atatürk (43:11) and Harrison and Sons printed a photogravure series commemorating the 1960 revolution (43:12). Intended to augment the permanent range, the Atatürk stamp was also released in a different colour as a souvenir miniature sheet. Klisecilik ve Matbaacilik of Istanbul lithographed no fewer than four distinct definitive sets between March 1955 and January 1958, all portraying Atatürk (43:1–3). As if this were not sufficient, a mammoth series depicting scenery in sixty-seven Turkish towns and cities was produced in photogravure by Courvoisier between January 1958 and July 1960. The stamps were issued in pairs of 5- and 20-kurus denominations and appeared alphabetically, beginning with Adana and ending with Zonguldak (43:4, 5). This was followed in 1959–60 by a pictorial series featuring modern technical achievements (43:9), with the customary portrait of Atatürk reserved for the top value. Despite this proliferation of definitives, totalling 209 stamps in five years, a shortage of 20-kurus stamps in June 1959 had to be filled by surcharging various denominations of the 1936 postage-due series for ordinary postal duty (43:10). A new Atatürk portrait series appeared in 1961–2, followed in March 1963 by a pictorial series in which Atatürk was not portrayed – but his mausoleum and home accounted for two of the nine motifs used (43:16). The definitive series of 1964–5 featured his profile.

Not surprisingly, a high proportion of the commemoratives were also devoted to the founder of modern Turkey. A se-tenant pair of 1958 marked the 20th anniversary of his death (43:6), and one of the first sets to be photogravure-printed within Turkey marked the 25th anniversary in 1963 (43:17). His portrait, in many different guises, also cropped up in sets commemorating events or anniversaries not directly related to him, such as the 1960 Revolution series (43:12) and the issues marking the silver jubilee of the History and Geography Faculty (43:13) and the 50th anniversary of the Turkish Air Force.

Several commemorative sets bore premiums in aid of unspecified charities (43:15), and in 1962 a semi-postal series featuring flowers in multicolour lithography was issued as a purely thematic venture (43:14). Stamps honouring NATO anniversaries were assiduously produced, and from 1958 onwards stamps were issued in the Europa theme – the earliest, inscribed 'AVRUPA', being distinctive to Turkey (43:7).

The only airmail stamps in this period consisted of a set of eight depicting various birds, lithographed in two-colour combinations by Guzel Sanatlar Matbaasi of Ankara and released in 1959 (43:8). Two-colour lithography was widely used for commemorative stamps until 1963, when more colourful designs were adopted (43:18).

Vatican City

No definitive series was released in this period, but two high-denomination airmail stamps depicting the Annunciation, after F. Valle, were issued in March 1962. The intensely religious character of Vatican stamps was maintained even in the commemoration of secular subjects such as the Brussels Fair in 1958 and the malaria eradication campaign in 1962. Most issues, however, were devoted to anniversaries of saints (43:23), churches, shrines and other places of religious importance (43:19).

Reflecting the enormous popularity of Vatican stamps in the late 1950s and early 1960s, there was an upsurge of stamps of a purely philatelic nature. Lengthy thematic sets on the same lines as those of San Marino appeared frequently from February 1956 onwards, the first series being an airmail set depicting religious paintings in monochrome intaglio. In 1959 a similar series featured Roman obelisks. More colourful designs began to appear a year later, with a two-colour photogravure series devoted to Corporal Works of Mercy (43:20). Thereafter, two-colour photogravure was increasingly used for commemorative sets (43:22).

On two occasions, sets featuring the papal emblems were released – during the Vacant See caused by the deaths of Popes Pius XII (1958) and John XXIII (1963). Both sets were followed by commemoratives celebrating the coronation of John XXIII and Paul VI.

In 1959 an annual issue for Christmas greetings was introduced, for which reproductions of 'Old Masters' paintings were inevitably selected. The earliest issues were recess-printed in monochrome, but multicolour photogravure was used from 1960 onwards (43:21).

Yugoslavia

The 'occupations' definitives of 1950–55 were superseded in March 1958 by a series depicting aspects of the industrialisation of the country (43:29). Initially the printings were in letterpress, but from September 1958 onwards the stamps were recess-printed. New colours and new denominations were introduced between 1961 and 1965. The obligatory stamps for the Red Cross and Children's Week (43:37) continued to appear each year, but the special postage-due stamps issued in conjunction with them were discontinued in 1963. Thereafter, mail on which the obligatory stamps had not been used had them affixed at the nearest post office to the addressee and the recipient was charged postage-due.

Intaglio had been used for stamps with fairly solid designs, but from 1957 onwards a much lighter technique – emulating the styles favoured in Czechoslovakia – began to evolve. This style also influenced the definitives of 1958–9, but it came to fruition in the larger format of the commemoratives. Frame-lines were dispensed with, and the lettering and numerals of value were made as unobtrusive as possible. These stamps were often printed on toned paper, but the overall effect was much lighter than that achieved by Poland in about the same period (43:30, 36). Photogravure was used occasionally by the Belgrade Mint (43:24) without ever attaining the full colour qualities of which Courvoisier was capable. The Swiss firm was therefore given the contract to produce the various flowers, fish, butterflies and animals sets of the late 1950s (43:26, 34, 38). Courvoisier also produced sets in 1963–4 reproducing medieval Slavonic art, incorporating gold metallic ink to simulate the gilding of the originals.

The majority of the stamps actually produced in Yugoslavia were lithographed – at first in two-colour combinations (43:25) but in multicolour from September 1957, beginning with a series featuring Yugoslav costumes (43:27). Tourist publicity sets featuring poster treatment of landmarks and beauty spots were lithographed in 1959, 1961 and 1963 (43:32, 35). The same treatment was accorded to the design of stamps marking anniversaries and current events (43:28, 39); and the trend towards Post-Impressionism and Cubism in the depiction of the human body is clearly discernible in the various sports stamps (43:25, 31, 33, 40).

Asia

Abu Dhabi
A postal service operated by the British was established in this Arab sheikhdom in March 1963, the British stamps overprinted for use in Muscat being used initially. A distinctive series portraying the Sheikh of Abu Dhabi and depicting scenery and wildlife was introduced in March 1964. The naye paise (new paise) values were photogravure-printed by Harrison and Sons, and the rupee denominations were recess-printed by Bradbury Wilkinson (44:1).

Aden
In 1959, the low values of the Elizabethan series were reissued in new colours and the sepia vignettes of the shilling denominations were replaced by black (44:3). The stamps were recess-printed by Waterlow until 1961, when the contract passed to De La Rue. Two stamps were overprinted, one in English and the other in Arabic, in 1959 to celebrate the introduction of a revised constitution. In 1964–5, stamps up to the 2-shilling value were reprinted on paper with the Block CA watermark instead of the Script CA watermark of the original printings. The stamps of Aden were superseded in April 1965 by those of the South Arabian Federation.

Apart from three denominations added to the 1954 definitives, there were no changes in the stamps of the Kathiri State of Seiyun. In 1955, however, the Qu'aiti State of Shihr and Mukalla adopted the neater title of Qu'aiti State in Hadhramaut, and this appeared on a series of stamps featuring local trades and occupations that was recess-printed by De La Rue (44:4). The accession of Sultan Awadh bin Saleh el Qu'aiti in 1963 resulted in the issue of similar stamps with his portrait in place of the previous ruler (44:5).

Afghanistan
Except for a few sets printed in photogravure by Harrison and Sons and the Austrian State Press, Afghan stamps of this period were lithographed locally and appeared regularly in honour of Pakhtunistan Day, United Nations Day, the anniversary of independence and the Shah's birthday. Semi-postals in aid of the Red Crescent (44:8) were also released at frequent intervals. Between 1961 and 1964, however, numerous sets of a more sophisticated appearance were produced by an overseas philatelic agency acting under contract to the Afghan Government. Very few of these stamps were actually sold in the Kabul post office, the majority being handled direct by the foreign philatelic agency (44:6, 7).

Ajman
An independent postal administration was established in Ajman – one of the Trucial States – in June 1964. Pictorial stamps incorporating a portrait of Sheikh Rashid were produced in combined photogravure and lithography. Ajman was one of the first countries to jump on the Kennedy band-wagon by issuing a set of eight stamps and a miniature sheet in December 1964. The stamps, printed in two-colour photogravure by the Austrian State Press, reproduced various photographs of John F. Kennedy and his family (44:9).

Bahrain
Responsibility for the Bahrain Post Office continued in the hands of the British, whose stamps were used with a surcharge in local currency. In 1957, the Indian currency circulating in Bahrain was decimalised and British stamps surcharged in naye paise were released (44:10). Later that year, the Scout Jamboree stamps were similarly overprinted (44:11). A decimal version of the local stamps portraying Sheikh Sulman was recess-printed by De La Rue and released in October 1957. These stamps bore values in paise, the adjective 'naye' (new) being omitted (44:12). The overprinted British stamps, used on external mail, were superseded in July 1960 by a set portraying Sheikh Sulman. The low values were photogravure-printed by Harrison and the rupee values were recess-printed by De La Rue (44:13). The accession of Sheikh Isa bin Sulman led to a new series appearing in 1964.

Bhutan
This Himalayan kingdom, having managed without stamps for many years, soon made up for lost time with a spate of issues from May 1962 onwards, mostly in multicolour lithography or photogravure by Harrison or De La Rue. Apart from a pictorial definitive series featuring Bhutanese scenery and wildlife, sets of this period pandered to the current fashions, including World Refugee Year in 1962, the Innsbruck Winter Olympics and Kennedy commemoration in 1964 (44:14). Most of these stamps were handled through a philatelic agency based in Nassau, Bahamas.

Brunei
The 1952 definitives remained current in this decade, but from March 1964 they were gradually reprinted on paper with the new Block CA watermark. The only commemoratives of this period consisted of a set of three in 1958 celebrating the inauguration of the Brunei Mosque (44:15).

Brunei took part in the 'colonial omnibus' issue for the Freedom from Hunger campaign in 1963 but, in contrast to previous issues of this type, the portait of the Sultan was substituted for that of Queen Elizabeth.

Burma
Reversing the world-wide trend, fewer stamps were produced in this decade than in the previous period. A definitive series featuring birds was printed in photogravure at the Japanese Government Printing Works in Tokyo and released in 1964 (44:17).

Distinctive stamps appeared in honour of the Buddha Jayanti anniversary in 1956, the second South East Asia and Pacific Games (44:16), UNICEF in 1961 and Revolution Day in 1963, and overprints on definitive stamps marked the centenary of Mandalay, Freedom from Hunger and Labour Day in 1963.

Cambodia
Political and economic events that altered the country's philately took place in 1955. Cambodia left the French Union on 25th September and became an independent kingdom, and the currency was changed to the riel of 100 cents. The output of stamps in the ensuing decade was steadily increased, including a new definitive series and two lengthy sets celebrating the coronation of King Norodom Suramarit in 1955. The Indian map definitives were overprinted for the use of Indian personnel in Cambodia in April 1957 (44:20).

A high proportion of the stamps of this period referred to Buddhist festivals and religious anniversaries, but from 1961 onwards they reflected a growing awareness of the outside world – especially the UN campaigns. Short thematic sets were introduced in 1962. With the exception of a series featuring Cambodian resorts in 1963, produced in multicolour photogravure by Delrieu of Paris, all Cambodian stamps continued to be recess-printed at the French Government Printing Works (44:19).

Ceylon
The designs used in the definitive series of 1951–4 were retained in this period but, significantly, the inscriptions were redrawn in 1958–9 with Sinhalese in the most prominent position – English being relegated to the subsidiary position, on a par with Tamil (44:24). The stamps were recess-printed by Bradbury Wilkinson or produced in photogravure by Courvoisier as before.

Most commemoratives were confined to single stamps (44:21, 26), notable exceptions being the sets of four marking the centenary of Ceylonese stamps and Buddha Jayanti. Courvoisier printed the Buddha series in two-colour photogravure, but shared the contract with Enschedé for the stamp centenary set (44:22, 23). Several of the issues of this decade referred to Buddhist anniversaries and personalities (44:25, 27).

A photogravure definitive series, including several values in multicolour, was introduced in 1964 (44:28). The contract for it was shared by Courvoisier, Harrison and De La Rue.

China
Although there was an underlying ideological strain in the stamps of the People's Republic throughout this decade – exemplified in the stamps portraying Marx and Lenin and those publicising

five-year-plans, the collectivisation of agriculture, and the proletariat (*44*:30, 31) – it was significant that as the output of issues increased in the late 1950s non-political subjects became more common. Beginning in August 1955, sets portraying famous scientists of ancient China were issued at regular intervals. The earliest of these were recess-printed on toned paper, but later sets reproduced the portraits in multicolour photogravure (*44*:29, 33). Multicolour offset-lithography was widely exploited in the long sets – often all of the same denomination – from 1955 to 1960, and photogravure was used thereafter. An enormous range of subjects was depicted, from children's games to ancient ritual vessels (*44*:34, 35). Small-format definitives of this period consisted of the 'occupations' issue of 1955–7, flowers in 1959 and scenery in 1961–2 (*44*:32). The scenery stamps were originally recess-printed, but in 1962 they appeared in a slightly reduced format printed by lithography.

The stamps produced by the Nationalist régime in Formosa (Taiwan) were usually recess-printed at the China Engraving and Printing Works in Taipeh (*44*:36–38), but definitives were invariably lithographed. Many of the commemorative sets continued to imply an interest in the mainland but were never so blatant as the definitives of 1957, which featured a map of mainland China with the 'bright star' of Taiwan offshore (*44*:40). Harrison and Sons photogravure-printed a series in 1956 marking President Chiang's seventieth birthday (*44*:39); but from 1958 onwards, stamps in multicolour photogravure were printed at the Japanese Government Printing Works in Tokyo (*44*:41). From 1959 the numerous definitive sets consisted of variations of the Chü Kwang Tower on the island of Quemoy, bastion of the Nationalist defences off the coast of the People's Republic (*44*:42).

Dubai

Overprinted British stamps were superseded by distinctive stamps in June 1963, when control of the Dubai Post Office passed to the local authorities. Other Trucial States followed suit in 1964, and it is significant that in every instance, definitive stamps appeared in great profusion – printed in Spain or Lebanon and handled by philatelic agencies in the United States and the Middle East.

Dubai quickly exploited current fashions by issuing long sets in 1963 to mark the Red Cross centenary (*45*:1), Freedom from Hunger and Malaria Eradication. The New York World's Fair, Kennedy, space exploration and the Innsbruck Winter Olympics were some of the subjects commemorated in 1964 alone.

Fujeira

Three other Trucial States began issuing stamps in 1964, all commencing with eighteen definitives and nine official stamps in multicolour photogravure and lithography (*45*:2). All three – Fujeira, Ajman and Umm al Qiwain – produced stamps for the Tokyo Olympics before the end of the year and followed this with numerous other issues of little or no relevance to the Arab world.

Hong Kong

Within months of celebrating the centenary of the first stamps – appropriately using a statue of Queen Victoria as the motif for the commemoratives (*45*:3) – Hong Kong abandoned the simple letterpress design that had been used since 1862 and replaced it by a photogravure series by Harrison and Sons. The Annigoni portrait of Queen Elizabeth II was reproduced in monochrome on the lower values and in full colour on the higher denominations (*45*:4). The Block CA watermark was used for this series – upright on the earlier printings, and sideways on those from 1966 onwards. Glazed paper was introduced in 1971–2 for certain denominations, recognisable by their pronounced shade variations.

Apart from the stamp centenary set and a stamp of 1961 marking the golden jubilee of the university, commemoratives were confined to the colonial omnibus sets publicising the Freedom from Hunger campaign and celebrating the centenary of the Red Cross in 1963.

India

The five-year-plan, inaugurated in 1955, was the theme of a pictorial definitive series produced – as were all the Indian stamps of this decade – in photogravure by the Security Press at Nasik (*45*:6). It was superseded, two years later – the decimal rupee of 100 naye paise having been adopted – by a series featuring a map

of the country. Both definitive and commemorative stamps had the value denoted in 'n.p.' from 1957 to March 1964, after which the abbreviation for 'new' was omitted. The map definitives (*45*:7) were printed on paper with a multiple-star watermark until 1958, when a watermark featuring the Asokan capital was introduced. Some denominations with this watermark have serial numbers on the reverse. They were originally intended for use in coils, but as the necessary vending machines were never purchased the numbered stamps were sold over the counter in the usual way.

Most commemorative stamps of this decade were issued as singles. Although a high proportion of them honoured Indian celebrities (*45*:8, 12, 16, 22, 23), some international figures such as Henri Dunant, in 1957 and 1963, and Eleanor Roosevelt (*45*:10, 21) were accorded similar recognition. The majority of the portrait commemoratives had a plain background, the exceptions being stamps honouring the Rani of Jhansi in 1957 (*45*:9) and Subhas Chandra Bose in 1964. The double-sized format used in the early 1950s was occasionally employed for stamps commemorating events such as the silver jubilee of the Indian Air Force (*45*:13) and the 40th anniversary of the International Labour Office (*45*:15), and it was also used for publicising the defence campaign against Communist China in 1963 (*45*:19). A slightly larger format was introduced in 1956 and used for the two stamps celebrating the Buddha Jayanti anniversary (*45*:5). It was subsequently used for several of the portrait stamps (*45*:8, 10, 20, 21, 23) and general commemorative issues.

Very little use was made of colour in this decade. A few isolated examples were produced in two-colour combinations (*45*:10, 17, 18), but no attempt was made to develop this technique. Stamps were issued annually on Nehru's birthday to mark Children's Day – 14th November – and they usually took the theme of child care or education (*45*:11, 14). A stamp was issued in October 1962 to mark Wild Life Week (*45*:18), followed a year later by a thematic series featuring Indian animals.

In the last years of the Portuguese colony in India, lengthy thematic sets appeared at almost annual intervals. In 1959, the escudo of 100 centavos replaced the tanga as the unit of currency and numerous stamps of obsolete sets were surcharged with new values (*45*:24). The Portuguese settlements of Goa, Diu and Damao were absorbed into India in 1962.

Indonesia

A small-format definitive series featuring wildlife was photogravure-printed by Pertjetakan Kebajoran of Jakarta and released between 1956 and 1958 (*45*:26). Although G. Kolff & Company of Jakarta continued to produce occasional stamps (*45*:25), the bulk of Indonesian stamps was printed in photogravure by Pertjetakan Kebajoran (*45*:27). Agricultural products was the subject of the pictorial series of 1960 (*45*:28), but the permanent range was frequently supplemented by very long thematic or commemorative sets. Twenty-four stamps depicting various sports marked the fourth Asian Games, held at Jakarta in 1962 (*45*:29).

Because the currency in the Riau archipelago was tied to the Singapore dollar, Indonesian stamps were overprinted 'RIAU' for use in these islands between 1954 and 1960 (*45*:30). Pakistani troops superintending the transfer of Netherlands New Guinea (West Irian) to Indonesia used a 13-paisa stamp overprinted 'U.N. FORCE W. IRIAN' in 1963 (*45*:31), and the stamps of the Dutch territory were overprinted 'UNTEA' (United Nations Trustee Emergency Administration) pending the transfer to Indonesia (*45*:32). Subsequently, Indonesian stamps overprinted or inscribed 'Irian Barat' were used.

Iran

No fewer than six definitive sets – all of them portraying the Shah – were released between 1955 and 1964, continuing the tradition that has characterised most Iranian definitives since 1876. More immediately, however, it continued the trend, established in the post-war period, of changing the colours of stamps at almost annual intervals and up-dating the portraits every other year (*45*:33–35, 37).

The most significant feature of the commemoratives of this decade was that they seemed to be issued in honour of every head of state to visit the country. In this respect Iran emulated Brazil, with the notable difference that the Shah's portrait was usually included with that of the visiting dignitary. Between 1957 and the end of 1964, stamps of this type were produced on twelve occasions. Only those issued in 1963 in honour of De Gaulle, Brezhnev, and President Lubke of West Germany portrayed the distinguished visitors alone (45:36, 38).

Iran participated in all the international events of the period, issuing stamps with symbolic designs (45:39).

Iraq
A more mature portrait of King Faisal II was used for a definitive series recess-printed by Bradbury Wilkinson and released in 1958. Shortly afterwards, the monarchy was overthrown in one of the bloodiest coups of modern times, and the stamps of the 1948, 1954 and 1958 definitive sets were overprinted with a two-line inscription in Arabic to signify 'Iraqi Republic' (45:40). Courvoisier produced a multicolour photogravure series in July 1959, partly celebrating the first anniversary of the revolution and partly intended as a definitive set (45:41). A pictorial series, recess-printed in Prague, was issued in February 1963 (45:42).

Between 1958 and 1963, the majority of the commemoratives portrayed the revolutionary leader General Kassem and quoted extensively from his speeches. But he, in turn, was overthrown by the Fourteenth Ramadhan Revolution in 1963 – a fact commemorated by two stamps and a miniature sheet produced by Courvoisier (45:43).

Israel
A definitive series featuring the emblems of the Twelve Tribes of Israel was printed in photogravure and introduced in November 1955. Early printings were made on paper with a watermark showing the stag symbol of the Israeli Post Office, but unwatermarked paper was used from September 1957 onwards (46:2). Following the reform of the currency in 1960 and the division of the Israeli pound into 100 agora, an undenominated coin design printed in various colours was surcharged with values expressed as decimal fractions of the pound (46:7). A series featuring the signs of the zodiac was introduced in February 1961. The low values, depicting individual signs (46:8), were produced in photogravure; but the pound denomination, showing all twelve signs, was lithographed. Two airmail sets were issued during this period. The first, depicting scenery in a poster treatment, appeared in 1960–61 and the second, featuring birds, was released in February 1963 (46:12).

There were two regular commemorative issues each year – to mark the anniversary of Independence in April and the Jewish New Year in August/September. For the first of these, the purely symbolic designs favoured in the years immediately after Independence were continued until 1958 – the motif often being based on the numeral of the anniversary (46:3); but a more thematic approach was introduced in 1959 with the issue of three stamps featuring flowers. Although the floral theme was repeated in later years (46:11), Vauteur fighter-bombers were depicted in 1962 (46:9) and aspects of Israeli technical achievements were shown in 1964. For the New Year stamps, issued in sets of four, biblical subjects were chosen. Biblical musical instruments were featured in 1955 and 1956 and ancient Hebrew seals in 1957 (46:4). Agricultural produce was the theme of the 1958 and 1959 sets, but the accompanying tabs had appropriate biblical texts. In 1960 the subject was biblical kings – Saul, David and Solomon – followed by Jewish heroes in 1961. There was a slight change of direction from 1962, each set illustrating texts from a particular book of the Bible – Isaiah in 1962 and Jonah in 1963 (46:10). Then, in 1964, ancient glass vessels from the Haaretz Museum were depicted.

Purely thematic issues – not linked to either of these anniversaries – began in 1962 with a set of four stamps, in multicolour lithography, devoted to Red Sea fish. A second series with the same subject appeared the following year, but no thematic issue was made in 1964.

General commemorative sets were confined to three or four stamps, the only exception being the series of six in May 1955 to mark the 20th anniversary of the youth immigration scheme (46:1). Sets of four honoured the Israeli Merchant Marine in 1958, the 10th anniversary of the postal service in 1959 and the Tokyo Olympic Games in 1964. In most cases, however, two stamps sufficed, with different designs for each denomination. A stylised treatment of the subject was invariably used – such as the symbolic leaf, seedling and tree on the Afforestation stamps of 1961 (46:6). Some very dramatic effects were achieved in this poster interpretation of subjects, one of the best examples being the immigrant-ship motif on the stamp designed by the Shamir brothers to mark 'Year of the Blockade-runners' in 1964 (46:14).

Israel was very sparing in the commemoration of famous persons, single stamps being issued in honour of nine in this decade. A vertical format was used by the Shamir brothers and Z. Narkiss for stamps honouring the writer Sholom Aleichem, the poet Bialik, the linguist Ben-Yehuda and the Zionist leader Herzl. Semi-stylised portraits with background motifs were used for stamps commemorating the physicist Einstein, the children's writer Korczak and the youth immigration pioneer Henrietta Szold (46:5), but photographs served as the basis of the stamps issued in memory of President Ben-Zvi (46:13) and Eleanor Roosevelt.

Throughout this period the stamps of Israel were produced, as before, either in photogravure by the government printer at Hakirya – and, later, Jerusalem – or in multicolour lithography by Lewin-Epstein of Bat-Yam.

Japan
Between 1955 and 1959 various designs were added to the definitive series of 1952, printed either in recess or photogravure (46:15). The 5-yen 'mandarin ducks' design was issued in sheets, booklets and coils, and these versions can be distinguished by their perforations or the *se-tenant* combinations with other denominations. A new series, in values from 4- to 120-yen, was released between April 1961 and December 1965. Continuing the style of the previous series, it was standardised both in format and in the use of photogravure or intaglio (46:33, 34, 36, 37).

The perennial issues of the previous decade were all retained in this period. Single stamps prepaying the inland rate on greetings cards were released in December of each year for the New Year celebrations. These stamps, in multicolour photogravure, featured toys and dolls – usually with some symbolic meaning and often related to the Japanese zodiacal calendar. Thus the toy dog Inu-hariko was featured on a stamp of December 1957 to herald the Year of the Dog (46:23). The New Year stamps were issued in normal sheet form, but at a later date – usually in early January – they were also released in miniature sheets of four in a presentation folder (46:18, 23, 28). A few of the numerous stamps publicising the national and quasi-national parks were recess-printed, but the majority were produced in photogravure. Monochrome was used from 1955 to 1957 and multicolour was used thereafter (46:16, 31). These stamps, ranging from singles to sets of four, appeared at irregular intervals. As the captions to the designs are entirely in Japanese, their identification presents considerable problems for those unacquainted with the language. Fortunately, however, most Japanese commemoratives include the date in their design and this enables one to locate them in stamp catalogues with relative ease.

Two other regular issues made their début in this period. Although Hiroshige's 'Moon and Geese' was reproduced on a large stamp to mark Postal Week in 1949, no further stamps with this theme appeared until the idea was revived in 1955 for Philatelic Week. Thenceforth, a large-format stamp on which was reproduced prints by the Bijin-gwa and Ukiyo-e artists of the seventeenth and eighteenth centuries was issued in November of each year (46:20). Portraits of actors and courtesans and 'scenes of the floating world' were chosen for the Philatelic Week stamps; but other classical prints were reproduced on stamps released each October in honour of International Letter-writing Week. This series, introduced in 1958, contained the only Japanese stamps to be regularly inscribed in English. From 1958 to 1962 the stamps depicted stages of the Tokaido Road (46:29) taken from the series of fifty-three woodcuts by Hiroshige; from 1963 onwards the subject was views of Fujiyama from Hokusai's series of thirty-six woodcuts, which continued until 1969. From 1958 onwards, the issue of the Philatelic Week stamp was transferred to April to avoid clashing with the Letter-writing Week issue.

The annual national athletic meeting – the subject of regular issues since the war – was marked by a pair of stamps each October, the two designs being printed alternately throughout the sheet. Unlike the other regular issues, the athletic sets were always printed in monochrome intaglio (46:24, 32, 41).

Purely thematic issues began with a long series in 1961 devoted to Japanese flowers. Several sets in later years featured national festivals (46:35, 39), and stamps depicting birds appeared in 1963–4 (46:40). These sets were invariably printed in multicolour photogravure.

Curiously, very few Japanese stamps of this period portrayed people. A set of four depicted Crown Prince Akihito and Princess Michiko on the occasion of their wedding in 1959, and the first postmaster-general Baron Maeshima was featured in the definitive series. The only other portrait stamps were singles honouring the educationists Yoshida and Fukuzawa (46:25), Yukio Ozaki and the Antarctic explorer Shirase (46:30). Scenery was depicted on several commemoratives (46:38), but symbolic motifs – arranged with an economy of line and a deceptive simplicity that was typically Japanese – formed the basis of most designs (46:17, 19, 21, 22, 26, 27, 42–44).

Jordan
In June 1955 De La Rue recess-printed a definitive series portraying King Hussein (47:3) in black with coloured frames. This set continued in use until 1956, and some denominations remained current long after that date. In 1962 several sets were produced by Bradbury Wilkinson in intaglio or lithography (47:4) or a combination of these processes. Some other issues were photogravure-printed by Harrison and Sons, but the majority were lithographed in the Lebanon (47:5–7). From 1962 onwards, many sets were released imperforate in new colours as special limited printings for collectors. This policy coincided with an increase in the output of stamps and the release of lengthy thematic sets at frequent intervals.

Korea
The 1953 definitive series remained in use in South Korea until 1961, when a series in a slightly larger format was adopted. This was accompanied by an airmail series (47:15) featuring scenery. A change of currency in 1962 resulted in these stamps being issued with the values redrawn (47:16). Three different types of paper were used for the series between 1962 and 1964. Printings of 1962 and early 1963 were on plain unwatermarked paper; from May 1963 to May 1964 they were on granite paper, with fine coloured fibres and a watermark showing the Ministry of Communications symbol; and from September 1964 they were on unwatermarked granite paper.

The commemorative stamps of this period – mostly in singles, pairs or short sets – were lithographed in one to three colours, usually in symbolic designs (47:12, 14). Apart from occasional issues showing President Synghman Rhee and President Pak Chonghui, the only portrait stamps of this period depicted President Eisenhower (47:13) in 1960 and Eleanor Roosevelt in 1963 – reflecting the close ties between South Korea and the United States.

In the People's Republic of North Korea, frequent thematic sets replaced the conventional definitive series and most of these in the earlier part of the decade were geared to the various government development projects, industrial mechanisation and production targets, known as 'great perspectives' (47:17). Later issues were less politically oriented and featured views of the capital (47:18), famous Koreans and temples (47:21). But between 1962 and 1964 there appeared sets of small-format stamps featuring aspects of industry and transport (47:19).

Monochrome lithography gave way to multicolour offset in 1960, and this was used increasingly for sets showing scenery, animals, birds and butterflies (47:20). Intaglio was introduced in 1962 and was employed occasionally in monochrome pictorials (47:21).

Kuwait
British stamps surcharged in naye paise were issued in June 1957 (47:22), but in 1959 they were replaced by a distinctive pictorial series recess-printed by De La Rue (47:23). The currency was changed again two years later, when the Arab dinar of 1,000 fils was adopted, and the pictorial definitives were reissued with new values and additional designs (47:24). This series remained in use after Kuwait became a completely independent state in June 1961. A series in multicolour photogravure by Harrison and Sons, portraying Sheikh Abdullah was introduced in 1964. After Independence, the output of Kuwaiti stamps increased sharply with frequent sets

marking National Day (47:25), Mothers' Day, Education Day and other annual events.

Laos
Although Laos left the French Union on 7th December 1956, stamps continued to be recess-printed at the French Government Printing Works in Paris. No definitives as such appeared in this decade, but short thematic sets featuring the art, architecture, customs and traditions of the country (47:26) were released at frequent intervals. Two sets of 1961–2, mourning King Sisavang Vong (47:27) were issued in the very large format that was characteristic of Laotian stamps from 1957 onwards. Indian map definitives were overprinted in 1957 for the use of troops serving with the International Commission in Indo-China (47:28).

Lebanon
The never-ending cedars continued to provide the motif for the definitive low values, no fewer than seven issues being released between March 1955 and March 1964 (47:29, 30, 33, 38). However, the monotony of the cedar designs was relieved by frequent issues of a thematic nature from October 1955 onwards. Sets featuring fruits were lithographed in multicolour in 1955 and 1962 (47:35), and a series of ordinary and airmail stamps depicting flowers was released in 1964 (47:36). The majority of Lebanese stamps were lithographed locally until 1964, but the flower series was produced by De La Rue. Higher values of the definitive sets invariably included airmail stamps in pictorial designs (47:37). Symbolic motifs were used for the higher denominations of the 1957–60 series (47:32) and for most commemorative issues of this period (47:31, 34).

Macao
As a result of the policy introduced in 1953, thematic sets served in lieu of definitives in this decade. Multicolour lithographed sets featured maps and sports, and an airmail series of 1960 depicted scenery (47:40). The stamps were lithographed in Portugal or by Enschedé, but the charity tax stamps issued annually were lithographed in the colony from plates manufactured in Hong Kong (47:39).

Malaysia
The letterpress small-format stamps issued in the component states of Malaya were in most cases superseded in 1957 by a pictorial series recess-printed by De La Rue. The exception was Johore, where the letterpress series continued in use until 1960 when the accession of Sultan Sir Ismail made a new issue necessary (47:2). The same designs were used for corresponding values of the series, with the portrait of the ruler and the name of the state providing distinguishing features. A change of ruler necessitated new sets of similar design in Kedah (47:8, 10), Perak (48:31) and Selangor (49:4, 5). In Malacca and Penang the profile of Queen Elizabeth II was used initially, but after the creation of the Malayan Federation in 1957 the status of these territories was changed and the royal portrait was replaced by state emblems in 1960 (47:41; 48:29, 30). Other states using this series without change were Kelantan (47:11), Pahang (48:15), Perak (48:31), Perlis (48:32) and Trengganu (49:28). No portrait was used in Negri Sembilan ('nine states'), the federal emblem being used instead (48:10).

A few commemoratives were released by individual states. An intaglio stamp celebrated the diamond jubilee of the Sultan of Johore in 1955 (47:1), and multicolour photogravure stamps marked the installation of new rulers in Johore and Kedah in 1959 and 1960 (47:9).

General issues for use throughout Malaya were introduced in 1957 but did not supersede the individual state issues. These stamps were inscribed in English in 1957–8 (48:1), in English and Malay in 1958–9 (48:2) and in Malay alone from then onwards (48:3). The name of the country was changed to Malaysia when it became fully independent in September 1963, and stamps issued after that date were thus inscribed (48:4, 5). The stamps issued in 1963–4 were printed in multicolour photogravure by Harrison and Sons (48:4) and Enschedé (48:5).

Briefly a member of the Federation of Malaysia, Singapore was a self-governing territory for most of this period and is therefore treated separately.

Maldive Islands

A pictorial definitive series was recess-printed by Bradbury Wilkinson and issued in February 1956 (47:42). Similar stamps, by the same printer – but with more elaborate frames – were released four years later. Having managed with very few stamps since 1906, the Maldives embarked on a prolific philatelic policy in 1960 and issued lengthy sets for World Refugee Year, Malaria Eradication and the other fashionable causes of the early 1960s. These stamps were handled by a philatelic agency in the United States of America.

Mongolia

The production of stamps in this decade sheds an interesting light on the country's political alignment. A series depicting the state arms was lithographed in Peking in 1954, but in 1955 and 1956 reliance was placed on the State Printing Works in Moscow. In 1958 and 1959, however, several sets were lithographed locally; but subsequent issues were produced by the Hungarian State Printing Works in Budapest.

Mongolia swiftly became the San Marino of Central Asia, with a spate of large and gaudy pictorial stamps ranging in theme from animals and flowers to space exploration (48:6, 8). The 40th anniversary of independence was celebrated by no fewer than six lengthy sets in 1961, each depicting a different aspect of Mongolian life such as modernisation, the postal services, animal husbandry, sports and culture (48:7).

Muscat

The last of the Arab states to have a British-run postal service, Muscat continued to issue British stamps surcharged in Indian currency throughout this period (48:9). Responsibility for the postal service was not transferred to the state government until 29th April 1966.

Nepal

Between 1956 and the end of 1964 ninety-six stamps were issued – exactly the same number that had been produced between their inception in 1881 and 1956. This sudden prolificity was brought about by the issue of three long definitive sets in 1957, 1959–60 and 1962 (48:11) and a host of commemoratives ranging from international events to the annual issues for the King's birthday (48:12). Many of these stamps were produced by the Gurkha Press in Katmandu, but others were printed by Courvoisier, De La Rue and the security presses of India and Pakistan.

North Borneo (Sabah)

Waterlow and Sons, who had recess-printed most of the pictorials of this territory since 1894, regained the contract from Harrison and Sons in 1961 and replaced the photogravure definitives with an intaglio series featuring scenery and wildlife in the best tradition of their earlier work (48:14). Similar vignettes had been used in 1956 as the basis of a series of four stamps celebrating the 75th anniversary of the British North Borneo Company (48:13). Production of the stamps passed to De La Rue in 1962, but the later printings can be distinguished only by marginal specimens bearing the printer's name on the sheet selvedge. Waterlow printings of some denominations, as well as De La Rue printings of all values, were overprinted 'SABAH' in July 1964 when the territory adopted this name on joining the Federation of Malaysia (49:1).

Pakistan

Apart from a few issues printed in lithography or photogravure by De La Rue, Harrison or Courvoisier (48:18, 21–23), the stamps of Pakistan were recess-printed by the State Security Printing Corporation until the end of 1964. In addition to the definitive series of 1948, the various sets issued to mark each anniversary of independence (48:16, 19, 20, 22) were kept in circulation to supplement the permanent range – which accounts for the diversity of denominations. Map stamps were used to emphasise the unity of West and East Pakistan in 1955–6 (48:17). Pakistan became a republic in 1956, after which stamps were released on each anniversary and kept in circulation (48:20). A set of four stamps appeared on Republic Day 1960 as propaganda for Pakistan's claims to Kashmir (48:25), and the 21st anniversary of independence in 1968 was celebrated by a set of four stamps featuring sports equipment

(48:27) – but neither set was specifically inscribed for the occasion.

Relatively few commemoratives other than the independence and republic anniversary sets were released between 1955 and 1964, and most of these consisted of singles or pairs (48:21, 23, 24, 28). The introduction of the rupee of 100 paisa in 1961 led to the temporary surcharge of existing definitives, followed by a pictorial series released in stages up to January 1963. In the original version of the pictorial definitives, the Bengali inscription in the upper-right corner had each letter engraved separately. The design was redrawn in 1962 to show the inscription in a single line (48:26). Various denominations in this redrawn design were added to the series up to 1970.

Philippines

New designs were added to the 1952 portrait definitives up to 1960. The same format but with a new style of framework and lettering was used for stamps portraying José Rizal (48:34) and President Quezon from 1959 to 1962, when they were superseded by a taller portrait series. This series (48:36) and all subsequent issues were inscribed 'PILIPINAS'. Intaglio by the American Bank Note Company, De La Rue and Bradbury Wilkinson was used in the manufacture of most Philippines stamps up to 1962 (48:33, 38), but multicolour photogravure by Harrison, Courvoisier and the Japanese Government Printing Works (48:35, 37) became increasingly common thereafter.

Qatar

Surcharged and overprinted British stamps were used until September 1961 when a series – recess-printed by De La Rue and photogravure-printed by Harrison and Sons – was released (48:39). The postal department of the sheikhdom took over the responsibility for the service from the British in May 1963. Unlike other states in this area, however, Qatar was slow to exploit the situation philatelically. Two overprints appeared in 1964 – one marking the Tokyo Olympics and the other in memory of John F. Kennedy.

Ras al Khaima

A postal service was established in this Trucial State in December 1964, and photogravure stamps by Harrison and Sons were introduced. The definitives portraying Sheikh Saqr bin Mohammed were surcharged in Arabian Gulf currency two years later (48:40).

Ryukyu Islands

A single stamp commemorating the 350th anniversary of the introduction of the sweet-potato plant appeared in 1955, but thereafter the tempo of stamp production increased dramatically. Stamps were issued regularly for the New Year (48:41), Press Week, Afforestation Week and other annual events. The introduction of United States currency in 1958 resulted in a new definitive series with a stylised dollar sign superimposed on the yen symbol. Thematic sets depicting fish, butterflies, dances and flowers in multicolour photogravure augmented the definitive range from 1959 onwards.

Sarawak

Although a 30-cent stamp portraying Queen Elizabeth II was introduced in June 1955 (49:2), the rest of the Elizabethan pictorial series was not released until October 1957. The set was recess-printed by Bradbury Wilkinson, but the coat of arms incorporated in the framework of the 6- and 12-cent values was printed by letterpress. The Script CA watermark was used for early printings, but the Block CA watermark was adopted in 1964–5.

Saudi Arabia

Very few commemoratives were issued in this decade, but there was ample compensation in the plethora of definitives. In 1960 an enormous series was produced in combined lithography and photogravure at the Survey Department in Cairo. Three designs were employed (49:3) and each one was printed in fifteen or sixteen denominations, making a total of forty-seven stamps. The original printings were on unwatermarked paper, but a crossed-swords and palm-tree watermark was introduced in 1963. By this time Saudi Arabia and Egypt had severed diplomatic and trade relations and these later printings were made at the government press in Mecca.

Similar stamps, with the inscriptions slightly redrawn, were lithographed by De La Rue from 1964 onwards.

Sharjah
The Trucial State of Sharjah established an independent postal service in July 1963 and swiftly embarked on a policy of frequent and lengthy issues, all printed in photogravure by Harrison and Sons. These stamps of 1963–4 covered a wide range of topics, from the Red Cross and Human Rights (49:6) to space research and John F. Kennedy – to whom two sets were devoted.

Singapore
A crown colony until the end of 1957, like the other former Straits Settlements, Singapore enjoyed a measure of individuality not shared by Malacca and Penang. This was reflected in the stamps, which diverged from the standard designs of Malaya. A pictorial series was introduced in September 1955, the photogravure low values featuring shipping and the intaglio high values featuring the arms, scenery and monuments of Singapore (49:8). In March 1962 a multicolour photogravure series depicting birds, fish and orchids was issued, the contract being shared by Harrison and De La Rue (49:9).

Few commemoratives were released. There was a series celebrating the new constitution (49:7) by which Singapore became a self-governing state, and there were annual sets for National Day (49:10). These commemoratives were produced by Harrison, Enschedé and Courvoisier.

Singapore joined the Malaysian Federation in 1963 but became an independent republic two years later.

South Arabia
Aden and most of the sheikhdoms and sultanates of the Western Aden Protectorate plus one from the Eastern Aden Protectorate formed the Federation of South Arabia in 1963, but no changes took place in the stamps until the next decade. The only stamps bearing the name of the country and issued in this period were two marking the centenary of the Red Cross in the colonial omnibus design but with the federal arms substituted for the royal portrait (49:11).

Syria
The dramatic political changes that took place between 1958 and 1961 had their impact on Syrian stamps. On 1st February 1958 Syria and Egypt amalgamated to form the United Arab Republic, each continuing to issue its own stamps but often using identical designs that can only be distinguished by the currency – milliemes (in Egypt) and piastres (in Syria). During this phase, the French inscriptions – a relic from the days of the French mandate – were replaced by English, used by Egypt since the Suez crisis of 1956 (49:12, 13). Syria's relations with Egypt deteriorated rapidly, however, and the United Arab Republic split up in November 1961, whereupon the title Syrian Arab Republic was adopted and appeared on subsequent stamps (49:14, 15, 17–20).

All Syrian stamps, other than those in the Egyptian designs, were produced by offset-lithography at the Government Printing Works in Damascus. The style and quality of production remained unchanged throughout this decade, but multicolour lithography was used occasionally from 1963 onwards (49:15).

Thailand
Waterlow and Sons recess-printed definitive and commemorative stamps until 1961 (49:21, 22) when their contracts passed to De La Rue, who produced an intaglio definitive series with a profile of King Bhumibol (49:24). Since 1957, however, an increasing number of Thai stamps had been and was still being produced in photogravure by the Japanese Government Printing Works.

Stamps were issued annually for United Nations Day and International Letter-writing Week, the approach to those for the latter event being purely symbolic (49:26). Several sets marked Buddhist anniversaries (49:23), but the stamps featuring a view of Bangkok (49:25) actually commemorated the Century 21 World's Fair in Seattle.

Timor
The thematic definitives of this period conformed to the policy throughout the Portuguese territories and featured maps, uniforms, sports and indigenous arts. The same policy applied to the commemoratives, mostly single stamps in the standard colonial designs but occasionally adapted to suit local requirements (49:27).

Trucial States
Stamps thus inscribed were produced in 1961 (49:29), ostensibly for use in the seven trucial sheikhdoms of the Arabian Gulf area but in fact confined to Dubai – which was the only state with a postal service at that time. These stamps were withdrawn on 14th June 1963, when the British postal agency was closed and the independent postal administration was established.

Umm al Qiwain
Stamps of this Trucial State came into use in June 1964 and were similar in design and production to those issued by Ajman and Fujeira (49:30). An Olympic Games series, printed in multicolour photogravure by the Austrian State Press, was released in November 1964.

Vietnam
By the Geneva Declaration of 21st July 1954, Vietnam was partitioned near the Seventeenth Parallel. South Vietnam became an independent state within the French Union, under Emperor Bao Dai, but was transformed into a republic in October 1955, severing the French connection. A definitive series portraying President Ngo Dinh-diem was recess-printed and released in July 1956 (49:31). In the late 1950s a wide variety of printers was used, including the Japanese Government Printing Works for photogravure, Giesecke and Devrient of Leipzig for lithography, and De La Rue and the American Bank Note Company for intaglio; but from 1959 onwards the majority of stamps were recess-printed by the French Government Printing Works, as in the colonial period (49:32, 34).

The advent of a period of comparative peace was reflected in the stamps of North Vietnam, which appeared more frequently and were better produced from 1955. Apart from a few stamps of 1958 in monochrome letterpress, the stamps of this period were lithographed – mostly in two colours (49:35). Multicolour stamps began to appear in 1959, coinciding with a change of policy that included frequent short thematic sets (49:36). Very few stamps of the early 1960s were politically motivated other than those portraying Lenin or Marx (49:37); but the resumption of fighting between North and South and the gradual escalation of the war resulted in several stamps of 1963–4 depicting guerrilla fighters.

Indian map definitives were overprinted for use by Indian troops and officials serving with the International Commission supervising the terms of the Geneva Declaration (49:33).

Yemen
Hardly any stamps were issued prior to 1959 (49:38), when the appointment of an overseas philatelic agency to handle Yemeni stamps led to a vast increase in output. After the overthrow of the Imam and the establishment of the Yemen Arab Republic in September 1962, purely philatelic issues continued to proliferate (49:39). Stamps were overprinted 'Free Yemen fights for God, Imam and Country' by the royalist guerrillas, but subsequent issues of the 'Mutawakelite Kingdom of Yemen' were also handled by external philatelic agents and proliferated as rapidly as the republican stamps.

Africa

Algeria
Distinctive stamps in the style of the previous decade were issued under the French administration up to 22nd July 1958 (50:1). Ordinary French stamps were introduced thereafter and remained current until July 1962, when Algeria became an independent republic. Contemporary French stamps were overprinted 'EA' (État Algérienne), and the French scenic stamps featuring views of Algeria were redesigned with the inscription 'République Algéri-

enne'. A small-format definitive series, typographed by the Central Bank of Algiers, was introduced in 1964 (50:2).

Angola
Like the other Portuguese colonies, Angola issued lengthy thematic definitive sets with increasing frequency. They featured maps (50:3); native types, in 1957 and 1961; sports in 1962; civic arms and churches, both in 1963. The majority of commemoratives were single stamps in the pattern of the other colonies but using distinctive designs. With the exception of the native series of 1957, in photogravure by Courvoisier, these issues were all lithographed in multicolour in Portugal.

Ascension
Apart from the colonial omnibus issues for the Red Cross centenary and Freedom from Hunger, all the stamps issued by Ascension were definitives. A two-colour intaglio series by Bradbury Wilkinson appeared in 1956 (50:4), depicting assorted scenery, wildlife and the island map in the prevailing colonial style. By 1963, however, such designs and the multi-subject concept were regarded as old-fashioned, and they were replaced by a multicolour photogravure series with the single theme of birds of the South Atlantic (50:5).

Basutoland
The pictorial definitives of 1954 were surcharged in South African decimal currency in 1961 and subsequently reissued with the values redrawn. Block CA watermarks superseded the Script CA type in 1964. The inauguration of the National Council in 1959 was marked by three stamps in which the name 'Lesotho' appeared for the first time (50:6).

Bechuanaland
An Elizabethan series, recess-printed by Waterlow and introduced in 1955, merely perpetuated the design with the portrait of the reigning monarch (50:7) that had been used for all definitives since 1932. This set was surcharged in rands and cents in 1961 but was replaced later that year by a multicolour photogravure series by Harrison and Sons (50:8).

Belgian Congo
An intaglio pictorial series, with a portrait of King Baudouin inset, appeared in 1955 (50:9); but the Congo reverted to multicolour photogravure by Courvoisier in the 'animals' series of 1959 (50:10). Few commemoratives appeared in the last years of Belgian rule, but it should be noted that in 1959 the Congo was the first country in Africa to issue Christmas stamps.

Burundi
The Belgian-administered territory of Ruanda–Urundi became independent in 1962 and was divided into the kingdom of Burundi and the republic of Rwanda. Obsolete stamps of the Belgian administration were suitably overprinted and were followed the same year by a distinctive series portraying King Mwambutsa (50:11), photogravure-printed by the Israeli government printer. A lengthy series of ordinary and airmail stamps depicting animals was lithographed in multicolour and issued in 1964 (50:12). A curious feature of these and many other Burundian stamps of this period was the edging of gold metallic ink.

Cameroons
The intaglio series of 1948–53 was augmented in 1955 by stamps recess-printed in multicolour (50:13). The Cameroons became an autonomous member of the French Community in 1958 and a republic in 1959, withdrawing from the French Community in 1960. These rapid political changes had little effect on the stamps, which continued to be recess-printed in Paris. In 1961 the former British-controlled territory of the Southern Cameroons was joined to the republic, which then became a federal state. Stamps issued from 1962 onwards were so inscribed (50:14).

Central African Republic
The former French colony of Ubangi-Shari – hitherto part of Equatorial Africa – became the Central African Republic in December 1958 but continued to use the stamps of French Equatorial Africa until 1960, when a distinctive pictorial series was released. Triangular postage-due stamps (50:16) appeared two years later. The stamps of the republic were all printed in multicolour intaglio by the French Government Printing Works in Paris.

Chad
The stamps of French Equatorial Africa remained current until 1961–2, when a recess-printed series was issued. Animal motifs were integrated into the scenic designs with an unusual silhouette treatment (50:17). Although the definitives and many of the commemoratives of the early 1960s were produced by the French government printers, several commemoratives were printed in multicolour photogravure by Delrieu and the Société Générale d'Imprimerie, both of Paris.

Comoro Islands
A multicolour photogravure series featuring sea-shells of the Indian Ocean was produced by Hélio-Comoy of Paris in 1962 (50:18). The few commemoratives, however, conformed to the French colonial pattern and were recess-printed at the Government Printing Works in Paris.

Congo (Brazzaville)
Formerly the French colony of Middle Congo, this republic was established in 1958 but did not issue a distinctive definitive series until 1961, when a set featuring tropical fish was released (50:19). From 1959 onwards, however, commemoratives – usually singles or pairs – were issued at frequent intervals, including thematic sets featuring flowers and native artefacts.

Congo (Kinshasa)
Stamps of the Belgian Congo were overprinted 'CONGO' when the country attained independence in 1960. A series by Courvoisier, featuring the national map, was released at the same time (50:20). Later definitives portraying President Kasavubu, featuring protected birds, and showing the national palace (50:21) were also produced in photogravure by Courvoisier. The commemorative issues of 1961–4, including many overprinted sets, referred to the political upheavals in the wake of the Belgian departure.

Indian stamps of the map series were overprinted in English for the use of troops serving with the UN peace-keeping force in the Congo (50:22).

Dahomey
In 1960 – two years after independence was granted – Dahomey issued stamps with a republican inscription; but a definitive series, featuring artisans, did not appear until 1961. A series devoted to tribes of Dahomey (50:23) was released in 1963. In addition to short sets marking anniversaries of the republic and participation in international events, intaglio sets featuring native dances and sports were issued.

East Africa
Following the unification of their postal services in 1935, stamps inscribed 'KENYA, UGANDA AND TANGANYIKA' were issued in these countries until 1964. The last of the joint definitives appeared in 1960 (51:7). It portrayed Queen Elizabeth II, with the symbols of the three countries in the corners and various examples of East African flora and fauna. Waterlow and Sons recess-printed a pair of stamps in 1958 celebrating the centenary of the Burton–Speke expedition (51:6), and distinctive sets were photogravure-printed by Harrison in 1963 to mark Freedom from Hunger, the inauguration of the East African University and the centenary of the Red Cross (51:8).

The postage stamps inscribed 'KENYA, UGANDA AND TANGANYIKA' were withdrawn on 11th December 1963, when each country adopted its own separate definitive issue. But joint issues of commemorative stamps continued to be produced by the East African Posts and Telecommunications Corporation after that date. The only issue made in 1964 was additionally inscribed 'ZANZIBAR', referring to the union of Tanganyika and the former sultanate – but these stamps did not, in fact, circulate in Zanzibar (50:24).

Egypt

The use of French in Egyptian stamp inscriptions ended in 1957, following the Suez campaign, and English was then substituted. The reason given for this was that it was a protest against French involvement in the invasion and that American – rather than English – would be used instead. Following the amalgamation with Syria in February 1958 and the establishment of the United Arab Republic, the definitives were redrawn to include the initials 'UAR' (50:26) and were reissued a year later with the word 'EGYPT' omitted. The practice of bleeding the background tint into the perforations – begun tentatively in 1937 and used intermittently in the post-war decade – now became standard, and very few stamps failed to conform to this pattern (50:28). The majority of commemorative issues were printed in monochrome photogravure (50:25–29), but two-colour combinations were occasionally used.

Egyptian stamps overprinted 'PALESTINE' were used in the Gaza area until 1967 (50:30). Egyptian stamps additionally inscribed 'PALESTINE' and sometimes in different colours were issued from 1960.

Ethiopia

All stamps were recess-printed by Bradbury Wilkinson, De La Rue or the Czech state printers until 1962, but many sets were printed in multicolour photogravure by Courvoisier or Harrison thereafter (50:31). Long sets devoted to Ethiopian emperors, empresses and spiritual leaders at least provided a welcome change from the more hackneyed subjects that dominated the thematic stamps of other countries.

French Somali Coast

In 1958 a series featuring animals, fish and birds in multicolour intaglio replaced the photogravure pictorial series of 1947 (50:33), and it was partially superseded in 1962 by a set depicting Somali flora and fauna, and sea-shells. Shorter sets depicting flowers, in photogravure, and boats, in intaglio, appeared in 1963. The few commemoratives issued between 1956 and 1964 consisted of singles, mainly conforming to the French colonial omnibus patterns.

French Southern and Antarctic Territories

Following the independence of Madagascar in 1955, the various islands in the southern Indian Ocean and the Antarctic region known as Adélie Land – formerly administered by Madagascar – were formed into a separate colony. Distinctive stamps of the Southern and Antarctic Territories, introduced in April 1958, depicted scenery and wildlife of the polar regions (50:34). Additional ordinary and airmail denominations were released in 1959–60 and 1963.

Apart from a set of three stamps publicising International Geophysical Year in 1957 and a pair for International Year of the Quiet Sun in 1963, commemoratives consisted of single stamps honouring the explorers Kerguelen in 1960 and Charcot in 1962.

Gabon

A multicolour intaglio definitive series featuring birds and flowers replaced the stamps of French Equatorial Africa between 1961 and 1964 (50:36). Short thematic sets featuring sports, the evolution of air transport, animals and flowers supplemented the definitives between 1962 and 1964.

Commemoratives of this period honoured Dr. Schweitzer and John F. Kennedy as well as Gabonese personalities.

Gambia

Four recess-printed stamps featuring the Annigoni portrait of Queen Elizabeth II, marked the royal visit of 1961. A multicolour photogravure series with the theme of birds replaced the two-colour intaglio definitives in November 1963 (50:35). Four of the 'birds' series were subsequently overprinted to celebrate the attainment of self-government in the same month.

Ghana

The Gold Coast achieved independence within the British Commonwealth in March 1957, and the pictorial definitives of 1952 were overprinted to mark the occasion and signify the change of name (50:37). A multicolour pictorial series was printed in photogravure by Harrison in 1959, and the numerous commemoratives of the post-independence period were also produced by this firm (50:38).

Guinea

Stamps of French West Africa were overprinted for use in Guinea in January 1959, following the emergence of this territory as a fully independent republic. Complete separation from the French Community was reflected in the subsequent stamps of Guinea, many of which were printed by De La Rue (50:39), Courvoisier or the Wright Bank Note Company in preference to the French Government Printing Works as had been the tradition. The pictorial series of 1959 (50:39) was followed by long thematic sets, released at frequent intervals, depicting animals, musicians, wild game, African heroes and martyrs, birds (50:40), sports, and butterflies in multicolour photogravure. Many sets released from mid-1963 onwards were also available in limited, imperforate editions for sale to collectors.

Ivory Coast

Animals and scenery formed the subject of the definitive series adopted when the French colony of Ivory Coast was granted independence in 1959, but this was superseded a year later by a thematic set featuring native masks (51:2). Flowers, tourism and hunting scenes were the subjects of subsequent issues.

Katanga

Stamps of the former Belgian Congo were overprinted 'KATANGA' in this breakaway Congolese province in 1960–61, pending the production by Courvoisier of a distinctive series in photogravure (51:3). Katanga was re-absorbed by the Congo in 1963.

Several commemorative issues, all in multicolour photogravure by Courvoisier, were released during the brief life of this secessionist state.

Kenya

Independence was marked in 1963 by the issue of a definitive series inscribed 'KENYA UHURU' (independence). The stamps, designed by Victor Whiteley and photogravure-printed by Harrison, depicted scenery, wildlife and occupations (51:4). The inauguration of the republic in December 1964 was celebrated by five stamps, in multicolour photogravure by Enschedé, portraying President Kenyatta and featuring symbols of independence (51:5).

Liberia

The great majority of stamps in this decade continued to be produced by the Wright Bank Note Company as before – the only difference being that whereas most of the stamps in the earlier period were recess-printed, those from 1955 onwards were mainly lithographed. One of the few exceptions was a series in 1958 produced by H. L. Peckmore and Sons in intaglio, with flags of European countries lithographed in natural colours (51:9). The American bias of Liberian stamps continued, but now many issues referring to the United Nations and other fashionable philatelic themes were included.

Libya

Bradbury Wilkinson produced an 'arms' definitive series in 1955, with intaglio vignettes and lithographed frames for the £1 value and the whole design recess-printed for lower denominations (51:10). The early printings were mainly on white paper, but tinted paper was used for later printings.

The many commemoratives of this period were produced by Courvoisier, the Italian Government Printing Works, the Survey Department in Cairo and even the Czech State Printing Works – reflecting Libya's 'non-aligned' position in the Third World.

Madagascar

Stamps followed the pattern of French colonial designs and printing techniques up to 1958. The last series prior to independence was a short set with the theme of food plants (51:11). Stamps were inscribed 'RÉPUBLIQUE MALGACHE' from February 1959 until December 1961, when the native term 'REPOBLIKA MALAGASY' was substituted. Subsidiary inscriptions, however, continued to be in French. All stamps were recess-printed at the French Government Printing Works until 1962, after which many of them – especially the thematic sets – were printed in multicolour photogravure by Delrieu or Société Générale d'Imprimerie (51:12).

Mali
The former French Sudan and Senegal formed the Federation of Mali on gaining independence in 1959. A year later, Senegal seceded from the federation and began issuing stamps under its own name; but the name Mali was retained in the Sudan. Obsolete stamps of the federation were overprinted 'République du Mali' in 1960–61. Small-format sets of official and postage-due stamps, typographed in 1961, were superseded by photogravure sets in 1964 in square and triangular formats respectively (51:14).

Mauritania
The Islamic Republic of Mauritania was inaugurated in January 1960. An intaglio series featuring wildlife and occupations was printed in Paris and released in 1960–61 (51:15), followed by a series featuring animals in 1963 (51:16). Subsequent sets included airmail stamps with the themes of space telecommunications, birds, and the preservation of the temples of Nubia, and a set of four featuring fish, for ordinary postage.

Mauritius
The 1953 definitive series was used throughout this decade, the only change being the adoption of the Block CA watermark for three denominations issued in 1963–4. Apart from the colonial omnibus issues of 1963, the only commemoratives were four stamps marking the sesquicentennial of British rule in 1961. This was the first series for a British colony to be lithographed by Enschedé (51:17).

Morocco
The sovereign independence of Morocco was recognised by France and Spain in March 1956, and the colonial issues of these countries were replaced by stamps portraying King Mohamed V. Spanish and French currency continued to circulate until the end of 1957 in the respective zones formerly controlled by the European powers and stamps were accordingly inscribed in Spanish (51:21) or French with values in centimos and pesetas or centimes and francs, remaining in use until August 1956. They included a lengthy pictorial series, issued in the French zone in August 1955 (51:20). The $\frac{1}{2}$- and 4-penny stamps, on paper with the St. Edward's Crown watermark, were surcharged in Spanish currency in June and August 1956 (51:18). British post offices in Morocco were closed at the end of December 1956 but for the one in Tangier, which was allowed to remain open until 30th April 1957. Stamps overprinted 'TANGIER', which remained in use until the end of May 1957, were additionally overprinted with dates to mark the centenary of the post office on 1st April 1957 (51:19).

Moroccan currency of 100 francs to the dirham was adopted in 1959, and a definitive series with values from 1 franc to 80 francs and bearing the portrait of King Hassan II was issued between 1962 and 1965 (51:22). This series was printed in Paris, but many of the commemorative issues were lithographed or recess-printed in Belgrade.

Niger
The philately of the Republic of Niger, formerly part of French West Africa, followed the familiar pattern of the other emergent countries of the French group: intaglio definitives from 1959 to 1962, followed by increasingly frequent commemoratives – many of them printed in multicolour photogravure by Delrieu or Société Générale d'Imprimerie in competition with the French Government Printing Works.

All the events and personalities of the period, from the temples of Nubia and the Tokyo Olympics to John F. Kennedy (51:25), were faithfully commemorated.

Nigeria
In the closing years of the colonial period only three commemoratives were produced – the 2-penny definitive, overprinted to mark the royal visit of 1956, and two pairs in uniform designs celebrating the centenary of Victoria and the attainment of self-government in the northern region in 1959 (51:27, 28). Four stamps in two-colour photogravure by Waterlow marked independence in 1960 (51:29). A pictorial definitive series featuring occupations, wildlife and landmarks was released in 1961 (51:26). This series and all subsequent commemoratives of the decade were printed in photogravure by Harrison and Sons.

Northern Rhodesia (Zambia)
The disintegration of the Central African Federation of Rhodesia and Nyasaland in 1963 resulted in the resumption of stamp issues by the individual territories. An arms series in multicolour photogravure was produced in December 1963 for use in Northern Rhodesia (51:30). On the attainment of independence, in October 1964, these stamps were superseded by definitives bearing the new name of the country (53:38). At the same time, a set of three stamps celebrated independence (53:37). Both issues were designed by Gabrielle Ellison and printed by Harrison.

Nyasaland (Malawi)
Intaglio revenue stamps overprinted 'POSTAGE' were introduced in November 1963, when Nyasaland resumed its own stamp issues (51:31). A pictorial series in multicolour photogravure by Harrison appeared two months later (51:32). On the attainment of independence under the name of Malawi, in June 1964, the series was reissued with the new name (51:13).

Portuguese African Colonies
Each of the five African territories – Angola (50:3), Cape Verde Islands (50:15), Mozambique (51:23, 24), Portuguese Guinea (51:33), and St. Thomas and Prince Islands (52:4, 5) – produced frequent changes of definitive sets that conformed to certain themes: maps, native types, sports and coats of arms. The same element of standardisation dominated the commemoratives, which were either in omnibus issues of uniform designs or with distinctive motifs but related themes for each territory. The stamps were lithographed in multicolour in Portugal.

Réunion
No distinctive stamps were issued in this period. Instead, French stamps were surcharged with CFA currency (51:34). French postage-due stamp, suitably surcharged, were introduced in 1964.

Rhodesia and Nyasaland
The 1954–6 portrait series was replaced in August 1959 by a pictorial definitive set recess-printed by Bradbury Wilkinson and Waterlow and Sons. Leter printings of the Waterlow stamps were produced by De La Rue (51:35).

Several commemorative issues, all in photogravure by Harrison or De La Rue, were produced between 1960 and 1964, when the federation was dissolved (51:36, 37). The stamps of Rhodesia and Nyasaland were withdrawn on 19th February 1964.

Ruanda-Urundi
The animal definitives designed by Jean van Noten and printed in multicolour photogravure by Courvoisier were released in 1959 (51:39). They were similar to the series issued in the Congo but had distinctive inscriptions. Apart from a series of semi-postals in 1961 raising funds for Usumbura Cathedral (51:40), all special issues – up to the time of independence in July 1962 – were identical with those of the Belgian Congo. The stamps of the joint territory were superseded by the separate issues of Burundi and Rwanda.

Rwanda
Stamps of Ruanda-Urundi were overprinted 'RÉPUBLIQUE RWANDAISE' from January to March 1963, although an independence series portraying President Kayibanda and the map of Rwanda had appeared in July 1962. With the exception of a set for the Freedom from Hunger campaign, printed by Enschedé, all commemoratives up to the end of 1964 were printed in photogravure by Courvoisier (51:41).

Saint Helena
The intaglio definitives of 1953 were superseded by a multicolour photogravure series in 1961 (52:3).

Two commemorative sets appeared in this period, celebrating the centenary of the first stamps in 1956 and the tercentenary of the colony in 1959. These sets were recess-printed by De La Rue and Waterlow respectively (52:1, 2). Four stamps of the Tristan da Cunha definitives – a stock of which was held in St. Helena – were surcharged in October 1961 to raise money for the Tristanians following the evacuation of their island, but the stamps were suppressed after a week and very few sets were sold.

Senegal
Stamps of French West Africa were used until 1959 and those of the Mali Federation were used until November 1960, when Senegal seceded and became a republic within the French Community. The first distinctive stamps consisted of ordinary postage denominations featuring scenes in the Niokolo–Koba national park and airmail stamps depicting birds. These sets were recess-printed by the French Government Printing Works or were produced in multicolour photogravure by Hélio-Comoy. Thematic sets showing sports (52:6) and butterflies were issued in 1961–3.

The commemoratives of 1960–64 were mainly issued as singles or short sets and were either recess-printed at the Paris Mint or photogravure-printed by Delrieu (52:7–9).

Seychelles
The monochrome photogravure series remained in use until 1962. Several new values were added to it in 1956–7, and a shortage of 5-cent stamps in 1957 was met by surcharging a quantity of 45-cent stamps (52:10). A multicolour photogravure series with the Annigoni portrait of Queen Elizabeth II inset was introduced in February 1962 – one of the first of the full-colour sets produced by Harrison (52:12).

Two stamps in the definitive photogravure pattern were issued in 1956 for the bicentenary of La Pierre de Possession, but a combination of letterpress and intaglio was used for the postal centenary series of 1961 (52:11).

Sierra Leone
An Elizabethan series was recess-printed by Waterlow and Sons and released in 1956 (52:13). Following the grant of independence in 1961, a pictorial intaglio series was produced with the state emblem replacing the royal profile (52:14). Two years later, a multicolour photogravure series with the theme of flowers was released (52:15). This series was surcharged in 1964, converting it to decimal currency: the numerals were the largest ever used for this purpose (52:17).

In 1963 obsolete definitives were overprinted to mark the second year of independence and the 110th anniversary of the postal service, but the following year Sierra Leone made philatelic history with the world's first free-form self-adhesive stamps, in honour of the New York World's Fair and John F. Kennedy (52:16). The stamps, die-stamped and shaped like the map of the country, were issued with peelable backing paper.

Somalia
The progress of the British protectorate towards independence was charted by overprints on the definitives, in 1957 and 1960, concerning the legislative council (52:20). On 25th June 1960 it was ceded to the independent republic of Somalia – formerly Italian Somaliland – and stamps of Italian Somaliland were overprinted in English for use in the former British protectorate (52:18). The currency was changed in 1961, the somalo of 100 centesimi being replaced by the Somali shilling of 100 cents. Stamps issued after that date were inscribed in the new currency (52:19). Throughout this period, Somali stamps were printed in photogravure by the Italian Government Printing Works in Rome.

South Africa
The animals' definitive series that had been introduced in 1954 remained current until 1961, the watermark being changed from multiple springboks to the Union coat of arms in 1959. A stamp portraying Andreas Pretorius (52:22) was issued in Afrikaans and English language pairs in 1955, but the other commemoratives of this period (52:23–28) had the inscriptions in both languages on each

stamp. In February 1961 the currency was decimalised and the animals designs were issued with denominations in cents and rands (52:32). Several of the designs used for the Union Jubilee and Union Day stamps of 1960 were reissued with decimal values (52:29). On 31st May 1961, South Africa became a republic and left the British Commonwealth. No stamps commemorated the event but a new definitive series in multicolour photogravure was released on that date (52:33), printed on unsurfaced paper with the Union watermark. Unwatermarked paper was used from late-1961 to 1963, and chalk-surfaced paper with a watermark showing the initials 'RSA' (Republic of South Africa) was adopted in 1963. Beginning in 1964, the designs of the stamps were redrawn – the main difference being larger and bolder inscriptions (52:38).

The commemoratives of the early republican period were issued as singles (52:31, 34, 35, 39, 41) or pairs (52:30, 36, 37, 40) in two- or three-colour photogravure by the Government Printer, Pretoria.

South Kasai
Congolese stamps were overprinted for use in the breakaway province of South Kasai in 1961, followed by a symbolic series in photogravure by Courvoisier (53:1). The secessionist régime of Albert Kalonji was suppressed by the central government in 1961 and ordinary Congolese stamps have been in use ever since. Doubts have been expressed concerning the validity of the stamps of South Kasai.

South West Africa
The 1954 pictorial series, several denominations of which were issued on the Union watermarked paper of South Africa in 1960, remained in use until 1961. The introduction of rands and cents in 1961 resulted in an entirely new pictorial series in two-colour photogravure (53:2) on Union watermarked paper. Between 1962 and 1966, however, several values were reissued on unwatermarked paper.

The only commemoratives in this decade consisted of sets in 1963 and 1964 for the inauguration of the Hardap Dam, the opening of the legislative assembly and anniversaries of the Red Cross and the Protestant reformer John Calvin.

Southern Cameroons
Nigerian stamps overprinted 'CAMEROONS U.K.T.T.' (United Kingdom Trust Territory) were issued in the Southern Cameroons in October 1960, pending the transfer of this region to the Federal Republic of Cameroons the following year (53:3). These stamps were also valid in Northern Cameroons before that district voted for union with Nigeria.

Southern Rhodesia
The federal series of Rhodesia and Nyasaland was replaced by a photogravure pictorial definitive set in February 1964 (53:4). When Northern Rhodesia changed its name to Zambia in October of that year, Southern Rhodesia dropped the 'Southern' from its name – but stamps inscribed 'Rhodesia' did not appear until 1965.

Spanish African Colonies
Like the Portuguese territories, the Spanish colonies adopted a uniform policy on stamp issues. Spanish Guinea was divided into two administrative regions, each ranking as an overseas province of Spain, and separate issues for Fernando Poo (50:32) and Rio Muni (51:38) were introduced in 1960. In format, design and photogravure process, the stamps conformed to those issued by Ifni (51:1) and Spanish Sahara (53:5) in the same period. Few stamps were produced in these territories other than the annual sets for Colonial Stamp Day and Child Welfare.

Sudan
Three stamps with a winged-map motif were issued in September 1956 to celebrate the attainment of independence (53:6). A pictorial definitive series was released in October 1962, the low values lithographed (53:8) and the £1 value recess-printed. With the exception of two Arab League commemoratives of 1960 and 1962, photogravure-printed in Egyptian omnibus designs in Cairo, all stamps in

this decade were lithographed or recess-printed by De La Rue and designed by the Sudanese artist S. Baghdadi (53:7, 9).

Swaziland
One of the last territories to adopt an Elizabethan pictorial series, in 1956, Swaziland made up for this by surcharging the entire series in rands and cents in February 1961 and issuing the set later the same year with the value tablets re-engraved. All three sets were recess-printed by Bradbury Wilkinson in two-colour combinations. Note the arrangement of the Queen's profile, the crown, the assegais and shield motif, and value – on the map of the country – in each corner (53:10). A multicolour photogravure series by Enschedé was released within months of the decimal intaglio series (53:11).

Apart from the colonial omnibus issues of 1963, the only distinctive commemorative set was that marking the opening of the Swaziland Railway in November 1964 (53:12).

Tanganyika
A definitive series, photogravure-printed by Harrison in December 1961, also served to commemorate independence (53:13). The designs, by Victor Whiteley, were a blend of scenery, symbolism and aspects of life in Tanganyika. Four stamps were issued in July 1964 to mark the inauguration of the United Republic of Tanganyika and Zanzibar (53:14), subsequently renamed Tanzania.

Togo
This former German colony, mandated to France, progressed from being an autonomous republic within the French Union in 1957 to complete independence three years later. These political changes were reflected in the stamps of the period. At first they were recess-printed in Paris, as before; but in 1960 Togo turned to De La Rue, who produced multicolour commemoratives in lithography or photogravure (53:15–17). In 1962, the series marking the second anniversary of independence was printed by Aspioti-Elka of Athens. From 1963, however, the stamps of Togo were produced in Israel.

Tristan da Cunha
The 1954 pictorials were replaced in February 1960 by an intaglio series depicting fish. Fourteen months later, this set was superseded by one with similar designs but with the values in South African decimal currency. Both sets were recess-printed by Waterlow and Sons (53:19). Five postage-due stamps, typographed by De La Rue, were issued in February 1957 (53:18). The island's long-dormant volcano erupted at the beginning of October 1961 and the Tristanians were evacuated. Existing stocks of stamps were dumped into the ocean at the time of the evacuation, but some of the stamps held in reserve at St. Helena were subsequently surcharged on behalf of the islanders. The island was reoccupied in April 1963, and the contemporary stamps of St. Helena were released with an overprint 'TRISTAN DA CUNHA RESETTLEMENT 1963' (53:20).

Tunisia
An independent kingdom was proclaimed on 20th March 1956. In anticipation of this, the definitive series featuring views and portraying the Bey of Tunis was reissued on 1st March with the 'RF' monogram omitted (53:21). On 25th July 1957 Tunisia became a republic under Habib Bourguiba, whose portrait appeared on various definitives issued between 1960 and 1964 (53:27, 30). The introduction of the dinar of 1,000 milliemes resulted in a pictorial definitive series, issued between 1959 and 1961 (53:23).

Many of the commemoratives of this decade continued to be recess-printed in France (53:22, 24–27, 31), but some were produced in photogravure in Rome (53:29) or were recess-printed by Enschedé (53:32). Tunisian stamps of this period had distinctive designs by Hatem Elmekki (53:24, 26, 28, 31), ranging from the whimsical to the surrealist.

Uganda
The definitives of Kenya, Uganda and Tanganyika were replaced by an independence series in October 1962 (53:33), a set of four stamps commemorating the centenary of Speke's discovery of the source of

the Nile having appeared some months earlier. During this period, however, Uganda continued to issue the commemoratives produced by the East African Posts and Telecommunications Corporation.

Upper Volta
Although independent since 1958, Upper Volta did not issue its own definitives until April 1960 when a series featuring animal masks was released (53:34). The restrained intaglio designs, with their two- or three-colour combinations, gave way to a multicolour photogravure series two years later. This set, depicting flowers, was printed by So. Ge. Im., as the Société Générale d'Imprimerie is usually known (53:35). Diamond-shaped stamps with an elephant motif were photogravure-printed by Delrieu and issued in 1963 for use on official mail (53:36).

Zanzibar
Bradbury Wilkinson recess-printed a pictorial definitive series released in August 1957 (53:39). In 1961 the series was reissued with the portrait of Sultan Seyyid replacing that of Sultan Kalif (53:40). Zanzibar participated in the colonial omnibus series marking Freedom from Hunger but portrayed the Sultan instead of Queen Elizabeth II (53:42). No stamps marked the accession of Sultan Jamshid, but his portrait appeared on a set of four issued to celebrate independence in December 1963. A month later, however, the Sultan was overthrown and Zanzibar was declared a republic (Jamhuri). Stocks of definitives and the recent commemoratives were overprinted locally by hand or by machine in London pending the introduction of a republican series printed in East Germany (53:41).

North America

Canada
The Canadian Bank Note Company of Ottawa recess-printed all the Canadian stamps issued in this decade. The designers who had been predominant in the immediate post-war years – E. Hahn, A. L. Pollock and L. Hyde – continued to work on postage stamps, other artists only gradually coming to the fore. Thus the styles formulated in the late 1940s continued throughout the 1950s. Pollock, in particular, was largely responsible for the stamps designed up to 1963 (54:15, 16, 23, 34, 37), collaborating with G. Trottier and a three-man team of American artists on the design of the St. Lawrence Seaway stamp of 1959 – a similar stamp being released in the United States (54:27). Trottier designed a number of stamps from 1958 onwards (54:18–21). Philip Weiss made his début with the NATO commemorative of 1959 (54:24) and went on to produce several of the issues in the early 1960s (54:28, 40, 41). Helen Fitzgerald also began in 1959 – with a 5-cent stamp honouring Associated Country Women of the World (54:25) – and went on to produce the Girl Guides commemoratives of 1960 (54:29) and the Education stamp of 1962.

The most significant development was the introduction of two-colour intaglio in 1955, starting with the Scout Jamboree stamp (54:5). But monochrome intaglio remained the principal process, the use of contrasting colours being confined to fairly modest touches – with a symbol picked out in a contrasting colour (54:8, 23, 34); contrasting lettering (54:27, 29); or the background in a colour contrasting with that of the principal subject (54:19, 30–32, 35, 38), especially in stamps portraying historic personalities. The first attempt to use colour more adventurously came in June 1964, when a series depicting provincial flowers and heraldry was launched (54:39). In this instance, the frame and lettering were recess-printed and the flowers and arms were lithographed.

For most of this decade the low-value definitives of 1954 were in use, but a series bearing a profile of Queen Elizabeth II was introduced in 1962. Each design incorporated in the corner a tiny motif symbolising some aspect of Canadian industry (54:36). The higher values were replaced from time to time, beginning with the Eskimo hunter design of 1955 (54:1), continuing with the paper and chemical industries pair of 1956 (54:7) and culminating in the export dollar stamp of 1963 (54:37).

The last of the Prime Minister series of stamps appeared in 1955, but in 1961 a larger stamp portrayed the politician Arthur Meighen (54:33). The Wild Life series continued until 1957 (54:2, 9) when, having decreased to a single stamp, it was then phased out. Christmas stamps were first issued in October 1964 and have since become an annual feature (54:42). The issue of 1964 can be found with or without phosphor bands. Several issues were not tied to any specific event. In this category came singles honouring ice-hockey, the mining industry, the Canadian press and national health (54:6, 13, 15, 20) and a set of four stamps, produced as a *se-tenant* block, featuring outdoor recreations (54:10). Royal visits accounted for several stamps in this period (54:14, 26), the design of 1959 being adapted from the portrait of the Queen by Pietro Annigoni.

Provincial anniversaries (54:4, 17) and events in the political development of Canada (54:21, 40, 41), together with anniversaries of aviation (54:3, 22) and postal services (54:38), accounted for the bulk of the commemoratives. Among the few current events honoured by single stamps were Fire-prevention Week in 1956, the 14th UPU Congress in Ottawa and International Geophysical Year (54:8, 12, 16).

Greenland

Several denominations were added to the 1950 definitive series in 1959 and 1960 but an entirely new series was introduced in 1963–4, with three designs by Viggo Bang featuring the Northern Lights, King Frederick IX and a polar bear (54:43). Two stamps – one in 1957 and one in 1961 – featured Greenland legends, and three stamps portrayed men associated with the island. The Niels Bohr commemorative of Denmark was adapted for use in Greenland in 1963 (54:44).

St. Pierre and Miquelon

A pictorial series, recess-printed in Paris in two- and three-colour combinations, was issued between 1955 and 1959 (54:45). Short thematic sets featuring flowers, animals and birds appeared between 1962 and 1964 (54:46). Apart from the various French colonial omnibus issues of 1959–64, single stamps were issued to commemorate the referendum of 1958, the anniversary of adherence to the Free French in 1962, and the anniversary of the appointment of the first governor in 1963.

United States of America

The Liberty series inaugurated in 1954 remained current throughout this decade, various denominations being added up to 1961. In addition to the stamps issued in sheets, rotary press coil stamps for use in automatic vending machines and dispensers were produced without perforations on either vertical or horizontal sides. The coil stamps were released at various times up to February 1965. A new 5-cent stamp portraying Washington, after the bust by Houdon, was issued in November 1962 (57:7). Four months later, the Washington 1-cent was replaced by a stamp portraying Andrew Jackson (57:6). Both denominations were subsequently released imperforate horizontally in coils. Examples with no perforations on adjoining sides are from stamp booklets. From August 1963, these and many of the airmail and commemorative stamps were issued with a coating of luminescent phosphor, invisible to the naked eye but distinguishable with the aid of an ultra-violet lamp. These luminescent stamps were used in connection with electronic sorting experiments.

Increases in the domestic airmail rates in 1958 led to the introduction of a 7-cent blue stamp with the silhouette of a jet airliner (55:31). The colour was changed to red in 1960. Double-sized stamps, printed in two colours, were used for the higher denominations and were issued between 1959 and 1961. Two versions of the 15-cent Statue of Liberty design exist. In the original version, both parts of the design were enclosed in a thin yellow-orange frame that joined them together (56:17); but the design was redrawn in 1961 without the overall frame-line, leaving the two components separate as in the design of the Liberty Bell 10- and 13-cent stamps and the Lincoln 25-cent stamp. Small-format 8-cent stamps featuring the Capitol in Washington and 6-cent stamps featuring the American

Bald Eagle were issued in 1962 and 1963 respectively (57:8, 9). The 8-cent Capitol was also issued in booklets and coils.

Excluding definitives, about one hundred and fifty stamps were produced in this period. Of these, eight were airmail stamps (55:24; 56:4, 10, 14; 57:11) and the rest were for ordinary postage. Compared to the previous decade, there were very few stamps commemorating anniversaries of statehood. No stamps in this theme appeared until 1957, when Oklahoma's golden jubilee was celebrated by a stamp featuring the state map and motifs symbolising 'from arrows to atoms' (55:23). Maps were a recurring subject in several of the later issues – notably for West Virginia (57:12), which included the state Capitol for good measure and came closest to the 1940s style. Maps and suitable motifs of each territory were featured on the airmail stamps of 1959 celebrating the attainment of statehood by Alaska and Hawaii (56:10, 14) and the Nevada centennial issue of 1964 (57:25), but other issues steered clear of hackneyed themes. To be sure, the state map appeared as a shadowy background in the New Jersey tercentenary stamp of 1964 (57:32), but it was subsidiary to the reproduction of a painting showing Philip Carteret at Elizabethtown. Inevitably, the Oregon centennial stamp showed a covered wagon; but the other issues ranged from scenery for Minnesota and New Mexico and flowers for Kansas and Arizona to a picture of a Mississippi riverboat for Louisiana and the state charter for Carolina (55:28; 56:32, 35, 41; 57:10).

Stamps issued specifically in honour of people formed the largest category. In comparison with the previous decade, women fared rather badly with only two stamps – one for Eleanor Roosevelt and one for Amelia Earhart (57:17). But there was now a much greater awareness of the famous men of other countries. The Marquis de Lafayette, who had been portrayed on a stamp of 1952 to mark the 175th anniversary of his landing in America, was the first foreigner to be honoured twice. A stamp reproducing his portrait at Versailles was issued in 1957 to celebrate the bicentenary of his birth (55:38). A large three-coloured 8-cent stamp of 1957, prepaying the letter rate to the Philippines, paid tribute to the late Ramon Magsaysay and bore the caption 'CHAMPION OF LIBERTY'. This inspired nine subsequent issues in this theme, each consisting of two stamps prepaying the domestic and foreign letter-rates. The lower denomination was printed in monochrome and the higher value was in three-colour intaglio. These stamps covered a wide range of international figures, beginning with Simon Bolivar (55:30), Lajos Kossuth (55:33) and San Martin (56:9) in 1958, continuing with Ernst Reuter in 1959, and ending with Jan Masaryk, Ignace Paderewski, Gustav Mannerheim, Giuseppe Garibaldi and Mahatma Gandhi in 1960–61 (56:21, 25–27). Distinctive stamps of 1961 and 1964 honoured Sun Yat-sen and Shakespeare respectively (57:34).

The large square format pioneered in the Famous Americans series of 1940, but with the plain background and frame initiated in the Eastman stamp of 1954, was used occasionally up to 1960. Portrait stamps of this type honoured Andrew Mellon in 1955 and Noah Webster in 1958 and were issued in commemoration of five men – Robert Taft, Walter George, Andrew Carnegie, John Foster Dulles and Horace Greeley (55:7, 35; 56:23, 28) – in 1960–61 but were subsequently dropped in favour of the double-sized stamps, which gave more scope for background detail relevant to the life and career of the person portrayed. On one occasion the transverse of this format was used, with a more ornamental frame, on a stamp honouring James Monroe (55:27). Prior to 1961, the larger format was used in certain exceptional cases. Thus the 250th anniversary of the birth of Benjamin Franklin was marked by a stamp reproducing Benjamin West's celebrated portrait (55:16) and the bicentenary stamp of Alexander Hamilton featured his portrait and Federal Hall, New York (55:13). Four stamps were released in 1958–9 to mark the 150th anniversary of the birth of Abraham Lincoln. Three of them bore reproductions of painting and sculpture, and the fourth featured a contemporary print of the Lincoln–Douglas Debates (55:32). In general, however, greater use was made of the larger format from 1961 onwards. At first the portrait and simple symbolic or scenic motifs were juxtaposed, as in the Norris and McMahon commemoratives (56:30, 40), and then the portrait and background were integrated by the judicious use of two or three colours (57:2, 11, 26, 31, 35). Monochrome designs could still make an impact as was demonstrated by the Kennedy memorial issue of 1964 (57:24) and the stamps of that year honouring Cordell Hull and the Mayo brothers (57:28, 37).

Some stamps issued in honour of persons, carried no portrait. That for Booker T. Washington showed a log cabin (55:8), and the one for J. A. Naismith featured a basketball. Conversely, a stamp portraying Harvey Wiley (55:17) commemorated the 50th anniversary of the Pure Food and Drug Laws, and one portraying Dr. Ephraim McDowell (56:15) commemorated the 150th anniversary of the first successful abdominal operation. Similarly, the sesquicentennial of the Pennsylvania Academy of Fine Arts was marked by a stamp reproducing Rembrandt Peale's self-portrait (55:14). A stamp of 1961 commemorating the centenary of the artist Frederic Remington depicted his painting 'The Smoke Signal' and was the first American stamp to be recess-printed in full colour by the modern Giori presses (56:37). The same approach was adopted in 1964 when a stamp marking the centenary of Charles Russell bore a reproduction of his Western painting 'Jerked Down' (57:20). The advent of multicolour intaglio facilitated accurate reproduction of works of art, and the Remington stamp was followed by stamps featuring Winslow Homer's 'Breezing Up' and J. J. Audubon's 'Columbia Blue Jays' (57:5, 30). Finally, an abstract lithograph was commissioned from Samuel Davis specifically for a stamp dedicated to the fine arts. The appearance of these multicoloured art stamps coincided with the world-wide craze for the reproduction of paintings in this medium, and since then, the United States has issued art stamps at regular intervals.

Stamps commemorating historic events and anniversaries ranged from the 10th anniversary of NATO (56:11) to the tercentenary of the Flushing Remonstrance (55:40). The common factor linking so many disparate subjects was their essentially American interest, with the possible exception of a stamp of 1960 celebrating the 150th anniversary of Mexican independence. In general, there was no change of policy concerning the criteria applied to commemoratives in this decade. The practice of honouring the trades and professions was continued, but it now tended to be restricted to important anniversaries – usually centenaries. No stamps in this category appeared in 1955 and 1956, but in 1957 there was a spate of them honouring architects, the coast survey, teachers and the steel and ship-building industries (55:18, 21, 22, 25). In 1959, a stamp for the centenary of the Dental Association was linked to publicity for better dental hygiene among children. Education was a prominent theme, with stamps for the centenary of the Land Grant colleges (55:1), the sesquicentennial of the Pennsylvania Academy (55:14) and the centenary of the National Academy of Sciences (57:18) – providing a tremendous contrast in the treatment of the subjects, from the rather stereotyped allegory popular in the early 1950s to the more symbolic approach of the 1960s. Two stamps celebrated centenaries of the discovery of important natural resources: silver in Nevada and oil at Titusville, Ohio in 1959 (56:3).

Historic buildings and national parks were the subjects for several commemoratives. Stamps marked the bicentenaries of Fort Ticonderoga in 1955 (55:6) and Fort Duquesne in 1958 (56:8), both vignettes being based on contemporary prints. The stamp marking the bicentenary of Nassau Hall was unusual at that time, being printed in black on coloured paper (55:12). Other stamps in this group commemorated 'Wheatlands' (the home of James Buchanan), and Gunston Hall (55:11). Two stamps publicised national monuments – in 1955, featuring the Old Man of the Mountains for its sesquicentennial, and in 1956 featuring the Devil's Tower for its golden jubilee (55:15, 19), but this theme was not developed until many years later.

Anniversaries of important legislation provided fresh scope for commemoratives, beginning with the 50th anniversary of the Pure Food and Drug Laws in 1956 (55:17). Two stamps of 1962 commemorated the centenary of the Homestead Act and the 25th anniversary of the National Apprentices Act, furnishing a contrast in interpretation from the realistic to the symbolic (56:36; 57:1). Other symbolic stamps of the period 1961–3 marked the 50th anniversary of Workmen's Compensation in 1961 and the centenary of Emancipation in 1963 (57:15).

Transport and communications were the subject of several stamps, including those for the centenary of the Soo Locks in 1955 (55:4), the centenary of the transatlantic cable and that of the overland mail, both in 1958, and the first mail-carrying balloon *Jupiter* in 1959 (55:34). Other stamps marked the centenary of the Pony Express in 1960 and that of city mail delivery in 1963 (57:29). Important institutions received philatelic honour on their golden jubilees, those singled out including Rotary International (55:2), the Camp Fire Girls (56:7), the Boy Scouts (56:18) and the Girl Scouts (56:39). The subject matter of these stamps was very obvious, but a much more subtle approach was adopted for the stamp honouring the centenary of the International Red Cross in 1963. The principal motif was the Red Cross flag over silhouetted figures (57:19) – seemingly innocuous if not quite obscure. But in fact it depicted a scene on board the ship *Morning Light*, which had repatriated Americans who had taken part in the abortive Bay of Pigs invasion of Cuba. Two stamps referred to American exploration and expansion: one for the 50th anniversary of Arctic exploration in 1959 (56:12) and the other for the centenary of the treaty with Japan in 1960.

The most important centenary to occur in this decade was that of the American Civil War, but philatelic commemoration was restricted to a single stamp annually over the five-year period 1961 to 1965. Each stamp highlighted an aspect of a battle in each of the five years of the war, and the variations in the treatment of the subject provide a commentary on the trends in American stamp design in the early 1960s. The first stamp, commemorating the siege of Fort Sumter (56:29), belonged to the traditional school of American monochrome intaglio; but the Shiloh commemorative of 1962 broke new ground, being without frame-lines and reproducing a contemporary line-drawing on a pink background (56:34). Poster treatment and semi-stylised silhouettes were used for the Gettysburg stamp of 1963 and the Wilderness stamp of 1964 (57:13, 22) – both in two-colour intaglio, which was becoming more fashionable by that time.

Current events accounted for nineteen stamps and a miniature sheet. The sheet, reproducing the 3- and 8-cent Liberty definitives in a larger format, was issued with a 3-cent commemorative (55:9) to mark the Fifth International Philatelic Exhibition (FIPEX) in New York. Several stamps marked exhibitions and fairs: the Jamestown Festival, the Brussels World Fair, Century 21 at Seattle, and the New York World's Fair (55:26; 56:42; 57:21). Only the Seattle stamp broke away from the conventional treatment of such subjects, with a design that might not be out of place in the twenty-first century. Stamps were issued in connection with two international sporting events – the Pan-American Games in 1959 and the Winter Olympics of 1960 (56:4, 5), the red, white and blue motif of the former suggesting the airmail-stickers of that period. Indeed, the stamp was intended for airmail postage.

The inauguration of important public works provided four stamps, featuring the Mackinac bridge, the Verrazano Narrows bridge (55:42), the St. Lawrence Seaway – in a design similar to that used by Canada – and the first fully-automatic post office. And the launching of the first manned spacecraft was celebrated by a Project Mercury stamp in 1962 (56:33).

International events and campaigns sponsored by the United Nations produced five stamps, marking International Geophysical Year (55:29), World Refugee Year, the South-east Asia Treaty Organisation (56:19), malaria eradication, and Freedom from Hunger (57:27). The usual blend of symbolism and poster effects was used for all of these stamps save the one for International Geophysical Year. This reproduced a detail from Michelangelo's 'Creation of Adam', and was one of the most original designs to be used to mark the event. The only other stamps for current events marked the 5th World Forestry Congress in 1960 (56:6) and Labor Day in 1956 (55:18).

Although there were fewer stamps of a miscellaneous nature in this decade than in the previous one, nevertheless they accounted for a considerable number of special issues. Stamps depicting the American flag were issued on five occasions, one being linked to the 'Register and Vote' campaign of 1964 (57:33). The others were primarily designed to acquaint the public with the appearance of the national flag as the number of stars was increased with the inclusion of Hawaii and Alaska (56:13). The 'flag' stamp of 1963 (57:14) is of particular interest as the only American stamp not showing the name of the country of issue, despite the Universal Postal Union regulations which restrict this privilege to the United

Kingdom. It was felt that the Stars and Stripes above a view of the White House would be sufficient identification.

Six 4-cent stamps of 1960–61 formed the American Credo series, quoting maxims by Washington, Franklin, Lincoln and other historic personalities that summed up the aims and ideals of the United States (56:16). This series marked the high tide of the ideological stamps that appeared intermittently in America throughout this period. To the same genre belong such stamps as the 'Atoms for Peace' of 1955, 'Freedom of the Press' of 1958, 'World Peace through World Trade' of 1959, 'Communications for Peace' and 'Wheels of Freedom', both of 1960, and 'Alliance for Progress', which was the theme of many stamps in other American countries in 1963 (55:5; 56:1, 24; 57:16).

Several stamps honoured sections of the community without being linked to a particular anniversary. In this group came the stamps focusing attention on friendship with children, help for polio victims (55:20), gardening and horticulture (55:41), American womanhood (56:22), the handicapped, the nursing profession (56:38), higher education (57:4), American music, homemakers (57:36) and radio 'hams' (57:38). This type of stamp tended to inspire allegorical treatment, but the theme of the American womanhood stamp was ten years out of date in its concept. In contrast, the music stamp and the homemakers stamp made full use of the latest developments in printing, the latter being produced in combined intaglio and lithography to simulate the appearance and texture of a nineteenth-century sampler.

Concern for the protection of wildlife and the conservation of natural resources was a recurring theme in this decade, beginning with a series of three stamps devoted to wildlife in 1956 (55:10) and continuing with a single in 1957 featuring whooping cranes (55:39). Subsequent issues, in three-colour intaglio, dealt with forest, soil, water, and range-conservation (56:2, 20).

In contrast with the immediate post-war decade, very few stamps were devoted to the armed forces. The only non-commemorative issue in this theme paid tribute in 1955 to the armed forces reserves (55:3) and was merely a hangover from the occasional issues of 1952 and 1953. Stamps were issued in 1957 and 1961 to mark the golden jubilees of the United States Air Force and of naval aviation (55:24; 56:31).

Christmas stamps were introduced in 1962 with a single 4-cent stamp featuring candles and a wreath (57:3). A similarly non-religious motif was used for the 1963 stamp (57:23), and flowers associated with Christmas were the subject of a block of four se-tenant stamps in 1964. Nevertheless, the issue of Christmas stamps provoked considerable protest from Jewish and other non-Christian organisations on the grounds that the non-political, non-sectarian code of American philately had been violated. Despite these initial protests, however, Christmas stamps became an established feature and in subsequent years a more overt religious approach was adopted.

United Nations (New York)

The 1951 definitive series was gradually replaced between 1962 and 1964 by new designs printed in multicolour photogravure by Harrison, De La Rue and Courvoisier. Various symbolic motifs were designed by a galaxy of international artists, including Kurt Plowitz of the United States, Hatem Elmekki of Tunisia, and George Hamori of Israel (57:44). Increases in American postal rates led to the introduction of a 30-cent denomination in June 1961, the design, of which – symbolising the unity of the nations – was produced by H. Sanborn and printed in multicolour photogravure by Courvoisier (57:43).

Special issues, usually produced in pairs, continued to publicise the work of the UN specialised agencies including the UN Emergency Force and the World Meteorological Organisation (57:40, 41). An occasional series, instituted in 1958, featured buildings in which the UN General Assembly had met in various parts of the world (57:42). Stamps were released each December from 1952 to 1956 inclusive, to mark Human Rights Day (57:39), but this practice ceased after 1959 and attention thereafter was focused on other programmes and campaigns. Monochrome intaglio was used for the majority of the special issues up to 1960. After that date two- or three-colour combinations became more common, giving way to multicolour photogravure in 1961.

Central America

British Honduras

The pictorial definitive series of 1953 remained current until 1962. In addition to pronounced shade variations in the 3- and 50-cent denominations, there were changes of perforation in the 2-, 3- and 5-cent stamps in September 1957. Four stamps of the definitive series were overprinted on two occasions: to mark the new constitution in 1960 (58:1), and to raise money after the colony was devastated by Hurricane Hattie in 1962. A multicolour photogravure series, with reproductions of bird paintings by Don Eckelberry, was released in April 1962 (58:3). Five stamps of this series were subsequently overprinted to celebrate self-government in 1964.

Three intaglio stamps were issued in 1960 to commemorate the centenary of the postal service (58:2), and there were the colonial omnibus issues of 1963 marking Freedom from Hunger and the Red Cross centenary.

Canal Zone

No new definitives appeared in this decade; but several stamps of the 1934 and 1946 issues appeared between 1960 and 1962 in coil form, without perforations on opposite sides.

Several commemoratives were released, culminating in a series of six airmail stamps to mark the 50th anniversary of the Panama Canal. Although no stamps were issued in the United States for the event, a 4-cent stamp of 1958 celebrated the birth centenary of Theodore Roosevelt – during whose presidency the construction of the canal was taken over by the United States (58:4).

Costa Rica

The airmail series of 1954, featuring aspects of industry, was used until 1963 – various designs and denominations having been added until 1959. A curious feature in this decade was the fact that the majority of stamps were intended for airmail postage. Indeed, the only exceptions were two issues of 1963 – marking the centenary of the Anglo-Costa Rican Bank and that of the first stamps (58:8) – both issues being printed in photogravure by the Japanese Government Printing Bureau.

A new airmail definitive series with the theme of archaeological discoveries, printed in multicolour by the Austrian State Press, was issued in 1963–4 (58:9, 10). Lengthy sets celebrated the centenary of the war of independence (58:5) and the 1960 Olympic Games, and shorter sets publicised the Pan-American Games and the tercentenary of the death of St. Vincent de Paul, both in 1960 (58:6).

Stamps for compulsory use on all correspondence during the Christmas period were introduced in 1958, the money thus raised being given to the juvenile-delinquents' fund for Ciudad de los Ninos (children's city – modelled on Boys' Town, Nebraska). Subsequent issues featured reproductions of religious paintings and sculpture (58:7).

El Salvador

Courvoisier, who produced the 1954 photogravure definitives, were responsible for most of the stamps issued in this decade. A new series, featuring animals on the ordinary stamps and birds on the airmail values (58:12), was introduced in 1963.

Relatively few commemoratives appeared, but they consisted of lengthy sets with both ordinary and airmail values. Waterlow lithographed an allegorical series in 1956 to mark the centenary of the province of Chalatenango (58:11), and Courvoisier produced multicolour sets publicising hotels and other building projects of 1958–60 as well as the sets marking the presidential visit to the United States in 1959 and the sesquicentennial of the national revolution in 1961 (58:13, 15). Comparatively simple designs were used for the Kennedy memorial stamps of November 1964, issued on the first anniversary of the president's assassination (58:14).

Honduras

Several sets issued in this period consisted of overprints or surcharges on obsolete sets (58:18) – a practice that became more prevalent in later years. Waterlow printed all the stamps up to 1961, using intaglio, lithography (58:17) or a combination of the two (58:16). Thereafter, Honduras turned to De La Rue – who had taken over many of the Waterlow contracts – and, later, to Heraclio Fournier of Spain, who lithographed the Olympics series of 1964 (58:19). In July 1958, as a security measure after stocks of stamps had been looted from government stores, the stamps already in the post offices were overprinted with facsimile signatures, no fewer than eighteen different names being recorded.

Mexico

The definitive series instituted in 1950 was current throughout this period, but new colours and denominations were introduced and the watermark was changed in 1956 – the 'GOBIERNO MEXI-CANO' watermark being replaced by a multiple 'MEX-MEX' motif. The designs were later redrawn with a lighter almost white background. Like its predecessors, the original version of this series was recess-printed, but from 1962 onwards the stamps were produced in photogravure. A single 'MEX' watermark was adopted in 1963. New express-letter stamps, with symbolic designs, were introduced between 1956 and 1962 (58:24).

Of the relatively few commemoratives produced in this decade, several adopted the same style of lay-out for lettering and vignettes as the higher denominations of the definitive series (58:20). The most important events were the sesquicentennial of independence and the golden jubilee of the 1910 revolution, both celebrated by lengthy sets in 1960. Several stamps portrayed visiting heads of state – Mexico being the first country to issue a stamp portraying John F. Kennedy, in connection with his visit in 1962 (58:23). Other sets of this period marked the centenary of the first stamps (58:21, 22) and the quatercentenary of friendship with the Philippines in 1964.

Nicaragua

The great majority of the stamps issued in this period consisted of very long sets incorporating both ordinary and airmail denominations. These issues took the place of conventional definitives. Obligatory tax stamps were issued at annual intervals to raise money for various welfare funds. In the earlier years they adopted the small format pioneered by Colombia (58:36), but a set of ten stamps – each of 5-centavo denomination and all featuring various orchids – was issued for this purpose in 1962 and used a much larger size (58:32). A number of different printers produced the stamps, and various processes were used.

In 1957 the Wright Bank Note Company recess-printed a series marking the centenary of the war of 1856 (58:26), but many of the subsequent sets were produced in two- or three-colour photogravure or lithography in Vienna (58:26, 35). Heraclio Fournier of Vitoria, Spain, used multicolour photogravure for sets in 1957–8 (58:27, 28), and the Eureka Speciality Printing Company of Scranton, Pennsylvania, lithographed a series honouring Cardinal Spellman in 1959 (58:29). Enschedé lithographed sets in 1961 devoted to the Nicaraguan Military Academy and the Junior Chamber of Commerce (58:30, 31), but several issues of 1963–4 were lithographed in Japan by the Dai Nippon Printing Company (58:33) and the Toppan Company of Tokyo (58:34). De La Rue also produced sets in intaglio or multicolour lithography between 1960 and 1964.

Panama

Although a few sets were lithographed by De La Rue or recess-printed by the American Bank Note Company in 1963–4, the majority of stamps in this decade were lithographed locally by Editora Panama (58:38, 40) and Estrella de Panama (58:37, 39). Short sets, including pairs or singles, marked mainly local events (58:38–40); but lengthy sets including airmail values were issued to celebrate international events – fashionable rather than directly relevant – such as the Brussels Fair of 1958 (58:37), or those having a pronounced thematic appeal to philatelists in other parts of the world. The latter group included a set of twenty-four portraying the presidents of all the American republics, in 1956, and a set of twenty featuring churches of different sects with the theme of freedom of worship, in 1962.

South America

Argentina

The falling value of the peso made the pictorial definitives of 1954 impracticable and, although new denominations were added to the series up to 1964, an entirely new series was launched in 1959 and was augmented periodically up to 1968 (59:2). All four major processes – typography, intaglio, lithography and photogravure – were used in its production, and in some instances the same stamps were produced by two of these processes at different times. These pictorials were periodically supplemented by single photogravure stamps portraying Argentinian personalities (59:1), culminating in a series released between 1962 and 1967 (59:8). A lithographed airmail series with an abstract motif symbolising flight was introduced in April 1963 (59:6).

During this period Argentina began issuing semi-postal stamps in aid of Child Welfare (59:4, 5) and extended the practice of a charity premium to other occasions, with commemoratives for the Pan-American Games in 1959, United Nations Day in 1960 and the International Thematic Stamp Exhibition, 'Temex-61', in 1961 (59:3). Most commemorative issues, other than the semi-postals, were released as single stamps (59:7).

Bolivia

Inflation overtook the economy in 1957, and during the following six years obsolete stamps were surcharged to compensate the falling value of the boliviano. An unissued series of 1960 commemorating the Tiahuanacu archaeological excavations was similarly surcharged, the stamps being unusual in that they were lithographed on gold metallic backgrounds (59:9). Surcharges were also applied to unsold remainders of commemorative stamps (59:11). In this welter of provisional surcharges there was little opportunity for the issuing of distinctive stamps, the pair of 1962 marking the Eucharistic Congress in Santa Cruz (59:10) being an exception. Even after the currency was stabilised by adoption of the Bolivian peso or escudo of 100 centavos in 1963, no definitives and relatively few commemoratives (59:12) appeared in this period. All the stamps of this decade were lithographed locally by La Papelera (the paperworks) of La Paz.

Brazil

Although intaglio was still used occasionally (59:13), most of the stamps from 1953 onwards were printed in monochrome photogravure of a quality that varied considerably both in the coarseness of the screen used and in the suitability of design for this process. The rather fussy framework of the Itutinga commemorative of 1955 (59:15) resulted in a much less satisfactory stamp than the comparable design for the San Francisco commemorative of the same year (59:14). And the 1960 stamp portraying President Lopez Mateos of Mexico (59:18) would have been more pleasing if it had been recess-printed – clearly the process originally intended. Obscure symbolism was a feature of too many stamps of this period (59:17, 19), but a few designs managed to achieve the desired effect with simple motifs (59:20). Comparatively few stamps had realistic motifs – notable exceptions among them being the annual Spring Games issues (59:16). The others mainly combined stylised figures and allegory. Continuing previous practice, a high proportion of the portrait stamps honoured visiting heads of state (59:18, 21, 22); but curiously, one of 1957 and one of 1964 portrayed Allan Kardec and claimed to celebrate the centenary of the spiritualism code.

The definitive series of 1954 remained current throughout this decade, new values being added up to 1960. The original watermark, 'BRASIL CORREIO' was superseded by one inscribed 'CASA DA MOEDA DO BRASIL' in printings of certain values made in August 1961.

British Guiana

The 1954 Elizabethan pictorial series was recess-printed by Waterlow and Sons until 1961, when the contract passed to De La Rue.

Apart from the different printer's imprint on the sheet margins, most of the stamps showed little change. De La Rue printings of the 4-, 48-, and 72-cent and 5-dollar stamps in 1961 can, however, be identified by a single wide-toothed perforation on each side at the bottom of the stamps, whereas this peculiarity occurs at the top of the stamps printed by Waterlow. Between 1963 and 1965 several denominations were reprinted on Block CA paper instead of the original Script CA paper.

In addition to the colonial omnibus issues, two commemorative sets were produced in this period, publicising History and Culture Week in 1961 (59:23) and the Tokyo Olympic Games in 1964.

Chile

Although inscribed '1954', three stamps honouring the centenary of President Prieto were belatedly issued between October 1955 and January 1956 (59:24). The continuing argument about Antarctica between Chile, Argentina and Britain was manifest in a set of four stamps in 1958 on which were reproduced a map of 1588 and an ancient document wherein Chile sought to prove that the disputed territory was hers by right of succession from the original Spanish claim (59:25). New external airmail stamps appeared between 1955 and 1960 (59:26) but were rendered invalid as a result of the reform of the currency in 1960 and the introduction of the escudo of 100 centesimos or 1,000 milesimos. Similar designs inscribed in the new currency were provided for ordinary, inland and external airmail postage (59:27, 28).

A few commemoratives had the same format as the airmail stamps (59:32), but the majority were in the excessively large format introduced in the 1940s and were either lithographed in monochrome (59:29) or recess-printed in two-colour combinations (59:31). As a rule, all stamps were produced at the Chilean Mint – an exception were the four semi-postals of 1961, photogravure-printed in Madrid and presented to Chile by Spain to raise money for the victims of the earthquake of 1959 (59:30).

Colombia

Stamps of this period, like those of Chile since the war, fell into three categories. Those inscribed 'Correos' were intended for ordinary postage; those inscribed 'Aereo' were intended for both inland and external airmail; and those inscribed 'Extra Rapido' were used from 1953 to 1964 (59:34) to prepay additional charges on inland airmail handled by the national postal service. At the beginning of this decade a high proportion of the stamps were produced by De La Rue, often in intaglio combined with photogravure or lithography (59:33), but stamps were occasionally photogravure-printed by the Austrian State Press (59:34, 38). Two sets, of 1958 and 1959, were printed by Enschedé in monochrome photogravure (59:35, 36); but the same firm used multicolour, sometimes combined with gold or silver ink, for the tourist series of 1961 (59:39). Several 1961 sets were produced by the Japanese government printer (59:37).

Up to November 1961, all De La Rue stamps were printed in London. Thereafter, they were produced by the subsidiary company in Bogota, which not only produced the bulk of Colombian stamps but also printed stamps for many other countries in Latin America (59:40, 41). Nearly all of the stamps of this period were designed by Imre Mosdossy, whose early work displays a penchant for bold motifs on frameless and often colourless backgrounds (59:35–37, 40).

Ecuador

A wide range of local and foreign printers produced occasional stamps during this period, but the majority were printed by De La Rue – in London until 1961 (60:1–3) and in Bogota thereafter (60:5, 7). The lengthy pictorial definitive series of 1955–9 was produced in monochrome photogravure, but De La Rue preferred intaglio for the stamps in the first half of this decade (60:1, 2, 6) and lithography from then onwards (60:3–5, 7), gradually introducing more colour into the designs.

A set of six pictorial stamps photogravure-printed by the Austrian State Press was released in the Galapagos Islands – Ecuador's Pacific dependency – in July 1957. The only other issue made for this sparsely inhabited archipelago was the United Nations commemorative of 1959, similar to that used by Ecuador but with the inscription altered (60:6).

Paraguay

The small-format 'arms' definitives of 1954, themselves a modification of a design dating from the First World War, were reissued in 1957 on paper with a multiple-star watermark. New values were added to the series up to 1959. Otherwise, lengthy commemorative sets with both ordinary and airmail denominations served as quasi-definitives – often being retained for much longer periods than was usual for commemoratives. Typical of this practice, which dated from the 1930s, was the 1959 series celebrating the sacerdotal jubilee of Monseñor Rodriguez (60:9).

Like many other Latin-American countries of this period, Paraguay was eclectic in her choice of printers – who ranged from the Chilean and Argentinian Mints (60:8), the latter producing a series of 1955 in combined lithography and photogravure, to the local Art Press for the lithographed Scouts series of 1962 (60:11). There was a marked preference for stamps of French origin, however, with the Institut de Gravure producing intaglio and Delrieu producing photogravure (60:9, 10). As elsewhere, production policy was rationalised from 1962 onwards. The bulk of the contracts went to De La Rue of Colombia whose industrious designer was Professor Mosdossy (60:12, 13).

From the end of 1962 to December 1964 there was a spate of issues of a speculative nature, covering such unlikely themes as Europa, space exploration and the historic venues of the Winter Olympics. Most of these sets were subsequently boycotted by dealers and catalogue editors.

Peru

Comparatively few stamps were issued in this decade. There were none at all in 1955 and only one – to mark the visit of the Venezuelan president, General Pérez Jiménez – in 1956. An exhibition of French products in September 1957 was the occasion for a set of stamps recess-printed by the French Government Printing Works in its characteristic three-colour style (60:14), and several later issues were printed in Paris. The 1952 definitives lithographed by De La Rue continued, with various colour changes and additional denominations, until 1960. The contract then passed to Enschedé, whose imprint appeared at the foot of the stamps produced between February of that year and 1962 (60:15), when the contract reverted to De La Rue. Similar designs were employed, but the colours were changed and watermarked paper was used (60:16).

Surinam

The measure of independence gained at the end of 1954 was reflected in the more liberal stamp policy pursued during this decade. The standard definitive designs were replaced by colourful thematic sets, changed at frequent intervals (60:17); and a new awareness of the international philatelic market and its tastes was evident in the pair of space stamps issued in 1961. With these, Surinam became the first country to honour American space flights, one of the stamps bearing a portrait of Commander Shepard (60:18) – although it must be pointed out that the companion stamp impartially honoured the Soviet cosmonaut Yuri Gagarin.

Uruguay

The intaglio and photogravure definitives produced by Waterlow in 1954 remained current throughout this decade, but two airmail sets – both featuring a statue of Icarus – were lithographed locally in 1959 and 1960–61.

With the exception of two sets in 1956, photogravure-printed at the Mint in Buenos Aires, all commemoratives of this period were lithographed variously by the National Printing Works in Montevideo and by two local companies – Impresora Uruguaya and Colombino Brothers.

A lengthy series of ordinary and airmail stamps featuring birds was issued in 1962–3 (60:21). The device of a coloured surround bled into the perforations in lieu of a frame, was subsequently extended into an over-all background for the commemoratives of 1963–4 (60:24, 25). It was combined with a crude but vigorous poster technique that was an improvement on the rather insipid symbolism of the Americas Day and Human Rights issues of the late 1950s (60:20, 22).

Straightforward portrait designs were used to commemorate

historic personalities, only the Larrañaga pair of 1963 combining symbolic elements in the framework (60:23).

Venezuela
Although the marathon series of 1951–4 was not repeated, very long sets continued to be released at regular intervals. What distinguished them from the prolific issues of other Latin-American countries was the use of only one design for an entire series. In 1957–8, De La Rue recess-printed a set of twenty-six ordinary and airmail stamps depicting the Tamanaco Hotel in Caracas (60:26). This was followed between 1958 and 1962 by an equally lengthy set featuring the General Post Office, lithographed by the Federal Printing Works in West Berlin (60:28). De La Rue produced a series of double-sized coil stamps in 1958, also depicting the General Post Office (60:30). Thereafter, Venezuela succumbed to the temptation of a lucrative revenue from thematic sets and produced flowers, birds and wildlife in quick succession – all three sets being lithographed in multicolour by the Berlin printers (60:35–37).

Commemoratives were generally released in long sets of ordinary and airmail stamps, and many printers were involved in their production. Courvoisier photogravure-printed a series honouring the first American Book Festival in 1956 (60:27), and the State Printing Works in Berlin printed sets marking the quatercentenary of Santiago de Merida in 1958 and that of Trujillo in 1959, using photogravure and lithography respectively (60:29, 31). The Pan-American Press in Caracas lithographed a set in 1959 publicising the eighth Central American Games (60:32); but most of the later contracts went to Berlin, for intaglio (60:33) and lithography (60:34, 38).

American Offshore Islands

Bahamas
The intaglio pictorial definitives of 1954 remained current during this period. Stamps of this series were overprinted to mark the Bahamas Talks of 1962 and the Tokyo Olympics of 1964 (61:4), and in October 1964 the 2-penny value was reprinted on paper with the Block CA watermark instead of the Script CA watermark. The entire series was overprinted in 1964 to celebrate self-government.

In addition to the colonial omnibus issues, two commemorative sets were issued. The first of these was a series of 1959 marking the centenary of the first stamps for which the original Victorian design was adapted. The other consisted of an outsize pair in 1962 in honour of the centenary of Nassau – among the first colonial stamps to be printed by Enschedé (61:3).

Bermuda
The Elizabethan series of 1953 remained in use until 1962. Two definitives were overprinted in 1956 to mark the jubilee of the United States–Bermuda Yacht Race (61:7). Distinct shades appeared in various later printings of the series and a new design, featuring the original Perot post office, was introduced in 1959 (61:8). A combination of intaglio and lithography was used by De La Rue for the armorial set of 1959 celebrating the 350th anniversary of the colony (61:9). Two-colour intaglio gave way to multicolour photogravure in October 1962, when a definitive series with the theme of historic buildings was released (61:10).

British West Indies
The high-point of this decade was the inauguration of the British Caribbean Federation in April 1958, celebrated by an omnibus issue of three stamps apiece in ten of the territories concerned (61:33). The stamps, recess-printed by Bradbury Wilkinson in a common design, were issued by Jamaica, Trinidad and the Windward and Leeward groups but not by the Cayman, Virgin or Turks and Caicos Islands. Dissension between the most powerful members of the federation – Jamaica and Trinidad – led to its dissolution in 1960. In its place, each territory was granted a new constitution involving ministerial government. Few territories recorded this political change in their stamps, but Antigua had an overprint and the Cayman Islands and the Turks and Caicos group each issued a pair of stamps to celebrate their new constitution (61:12; 62:39). Both Jamaica and Trinidad received full independent status in 1962, celebrated by the overprinting of the definitive series in Jamaica and the issuing of distinctive stamps in Trinidad (62:14, 15). The British West Indies issued colonial omnibus stamps marking the Freedom from Hunger campaign and the Red Cross centenary in 1963 (62:30) and several islands participated in the more limited commemoration of Shakespeare in 1964 (61:2).

Between 1955 and 1957 the last of the territories to change over to an Elizabethan series issued new definitives (61:13; 62:8, 13, 21, 38). Grenada retained the armorial design of the previous series but with the royal cypher changed from GR to EIIR (62:8), and St. Vincent went back to the finely-engraved designs of the Victorian period – the Waterlow version of 1955 being rather coarser than the Perkins Bacon originals of 1861 (62:34). The Virgin Islands introduced a series in 1956, substituting the profile of Queen Elizabeth II for the portrait of King George VI. The series was surcharged in United States currency in 1962 (62:40) pending the production of an entirely new pictorial series by De La Rue in November 1964 (62:41).

By 1960, the territories that had been the first to adopt Elizabethan stamps were beginning to change their definitives. Thenceforth, the two-colour intaglio that had been paramount since the 1930s was gradually superseded by multicolour photogravure. Harrison and Sons produced sets for Trinidad in 1960, for Dominica and St. Lucia in 1963 and for Jamaica and St. Christopher–Nevis–Anguilla in 1964. With the exception of the Dominican series, most of these stamps were designed by Victor Whiteley (61:34; 62:19, 33, 36).

Very few commemoratives were issued in this decade. The territories that celebrated their stamp centenaries issued intaglio stamps reproducing the first issues (62:32). Antigua combined this theme with a scenic vignette and the Annigoni portrait of Queen Elizabeth II (61:1). This portrait became very fashionable in the early 1960s and was used on a number of commemoratives, as well as on definitives, at that time (61:3, 5, 6, 13). The golden jubilee of the Scouts and Guides movements in the West Indies provided scope for some commemoratives with widely varying interpretations of the theme (61:6; 62:35, 37).

Jamaica was the most prolific in the issue of commemoratives. Prior to independence in 1962, there were two sets – marking the tercentenary of British occupation and the centenary of the first stamps – recess-printed by De La Rue and Waterlow respectively (62:12). After independence, however, Jamaica opted for multicolour photogravure by Harrison (62:16, 20) and De La Rue (62:14, 17). De La Rue used offset-lithography for the Freedom from Hunger pair of 1963 – their first use of this process for Commonwealth stamps (62:18).

St. Christopher–Nevis–Anguilla issued a two-colour intaglio stamp in 1957 to mark the bicentenary of the birth of the American patriot Alexander Hamilton. Like the American stamp for the same event, this stamp combined portraiture with scenery (62:29). For the St. Kitts Arts Festival in 1964, however, this country reverted to the time-honoured expedient of overprinting two stamps of the definitive series (62:31).

Cuba
Various designs and denominations were added to the 1954 portrait series early in 1956. In 1962 further changes included the re-engraving of the inscription on the 2-centavo Gomez stamp, replacing the original date of birth – 1833 – by a question-mark. The colours of the 3- and 13-centavo stamps were changed in 1964 and rouletting was substituted for perforation (61:32). The annual obligatory tax stamps on behalf of the anti-tuberculosis campaign appeared until 1958 but were then discontinued (61:18). Christmas stamps were issued each December – except in 1959, the year in which the Batista régime was overthrown. But the custom was revived in 1960 and was greatly expanded. Instead of being issued in pairs, as in

earlier years, these stamps were now released in sheets of twenty-five subjects with *se-tenant* stamp-sized labels forming a central cross between blocks of four, forming composite pictures, and as singles with related themes. A different topic was selected each year, including flowers, reptiles and birds (*61*:27). Stamps for the postal employees' retirement fund were issued each year up to 1957 (*61*:15, 19).

The Castro revolution had little immediate effect on Cuban stamps, though it was the watershed between the restrained intaglio designs of the earlier period and the more flamboyant lithographed stamps of later years. Combined intaglio and lithography was used for the Stamp Day issue of 1957 (*61*:14); but other stamps of this period were entirely recess-printed, often in monochrome (*61*: 16, 17). Coloured or toned paper with motifs and lettering in one or two contrasting colours became popular in 1962 (*61*:20, 21), but the background colour was not always bled into the perforations (*61*:28). As stamps became larger and more colourful, designs tended to become more stylised (*61*:25, 26). The numerous sports issues, however, usually used naturalistic motifs (*61*:29, 30). A certain number of stamps showed a pronounced political bias, confined in this period to anniversaries of the revolution (*61*:24) and battles in the protracted guerrilla war that had preceded the overthrow of Batista, and the defeat of the Cuban exiles in the Bay of Pigs expedition of 1961. But, in general, less controversial subjects were chosen – such as the anniversary of the anthropological museum in 1963 (*61*:22) and scenes from the novels of Ernest Hemingway.

A set of six denominations appeared in 1962 to commemorate the national sports institute. Each denomination was printed in five different designs, repeated five times in the sheet of twenty-five stamps. The diamond-shaped stamps were lithographed in two colours on cream-toned paper (*61*:21).

Purely thematic issues began in 1963 with a series featuring Cuban fruits (*61*:23) and continued the following year with a set of twenty stamps depicting animals in Havana Zoo (*61*:31).

Dominican Republic
No definitives were released in this period, but short thematic sets lithographed in multicolour began appearing at regular intervals from October 1957 (*62*:1). In addition to the numerous sets extolling the merits of members of the Trujillo family – then nearing the end of their thirty years of dictatorship – lengthy sets from 1957 to 1960 featured past Olympic gold medallists. These sets were later often overprinted for other events, such as the jubilee of Scouting and International Geophysical Year. From 1962 onwards, however, the pace of new issues abated – although there was a keen awareness of the international events that were currently fashionable with stamp collectors, including the Malaria Eradication campaign of 1962 and the UNESCO campaign in 1964 for the preservation of the temples of Nubia (*62*:2, 3).

Falkland Islands and Dependencies
Between 1955 and 1957 various stamps of the Georgian series were reissued with a portrait of Queen Elizabeth II substituted (*62*:4), but a complete series with the theme of birds of the South Atlantic was released in February 1960 (*62*:5). The stamps were recess-printed by Waterlow with black vignettes and coloured frames. The upright Block CA watermark was used, but a reprint of the half-penny in 1966 had a sideways watermark.

Four values of the 'ships' series of the Falkland Islands Dependencies were overprinted and issued in January 1956 in connection with the trans-Antarctic expedition led by Sir Edmund Hillary and Sir Vivien Fuchs as the British contribution to International Geophysical Year (*62*:7).

In 1963 Graham Land, the South Orkneys and the South Shetlands were transferred from the administration of the Falkland Islands and established as a separate crown colony under the title of the British Antarctic Territory. A distinctive series of pictorial stamps, with the Annigoni portrait of Queen Elizabeth II inset, was recess-printed by Bradbury Wilkinson and released in February 1963 (*61*:11). The Falklands Dependencies series remained current in South Georgia and the South Sandwich Islands until the following July, when a series inscribed 'South Georgia' was issued. This set, featuring wildlife of the sub-Antarctic islands, was recess-printed by De La Rue (*62*:6).

Haiti
Relatively few distinctive stamps were produced from 1955 to 1964, but this in no way diminished the output. The majority of the stamps issued from 1959 onwards consisted of overprints or surcharges on remaindered stocks of previous issues (*62*:9, 10). In many cases, these reissues bore premiums in aid of such worthy causes as the Haitian Red Cross, the literacy campaign and the building of Duvalierville.

The stamps of this period were mainly photogravure-printed by Courvoisier or the Austrian State Press, each company producing stamps that were characteristic of their work in the late 1950s (*62*:11).

Netherlands Antilles
The standard Dutch definitive designs were superseded in July 1958 by a pictorial series, lithographed by Enschedé, with stylised motifs on solid backgrounds (*62*:23). This unusual technique was also used for a number of commemoratives – in particular, for the tourist publicity series of 1957 and the various singles marking the opening of new hotels (*62*:25). Child Welfare sets were issued annually, usually featuring aspects of childhood (*62*:26). The series of 1964 broke new ground, however, in reproducing paintings by schoolchildren (*62*:24). The popularity of the Antilles as a conference venue is reflected in the high proportion of stamps issued in honour of such events (*62*:22, 27).

Historical events commemorated by stamps included the 185th anniversary of the first salute to the United States flag, celebrated by a 20-cent stamp in 1961, and the 35th anniversary of the first flight between the United States and Curaçao, for which a pair was issued in 1964 (*62*:28).

Australasia

Australia and Dependencies
New definitives with a sculpted profile of Queen Elizabeth II replaced the middle denominations, which had previously portrayed King George VI (*63*:2). This design served as the basis for the first stamps issued by Christmas Island in 1958 (*63*:38). Entirely new small-format low values were recess-printed between 1959 and 1962 with a variety of photographs of the Queen by Baron Studios (*63*:12). Higher denominations featured animals, flowers and the Northern Territory cattle industry (*63*:15). The design used for one of the royal-visit stamps of 1963 was subsequently adapted for 5-penny stamps issued in between 1963 and 1965. Examples of the green version with no perforations between adjoining stamps or with very wide margins at the left are from uncut booklet panes that were subsequently sold as complete sheets over the post-office counter (*63*:30). The middle denominations consisted of stamps featuring Australian birds in multicolour photogravure, issued in March 1964 (*63*:33), and the high values were recess-printed and portrayed explorers (*63*:31). Toned paper was used initially in the production of the 10-shilling and £1 stamps, but later printings were on white paper – as for the other denominations.

Australia was the first British Commonwealth country to issue Christmas stamps, two with a reproduction of 'The Spirit of Christmas' by Sir Joshua Reynolds being issued in November 1957 (*63*:10). The following year came a pair of stamps showing a Nativity scene, but thereafter a single stamp sufficed. The stamp of 1960, featuring an open Bible, also commemorated the 350th anniversary of the Authorised Version of the Bible (*63*:21).

The majority of commemoratives up to 1962 also consisted of single stamps, exceptions being the pair honouring the Cobb mailcoach service in 1955 (*63*:4) and the pair for the Melbourne Olympic Games of 1956 (*63*:9). The Olympic series was technically unusual in that three printers were involved – the two lowest denominations being recess-printed at the Government Printing Works in Melbourne and the pictorial shilling values being printed in multicolour photogravure by Harrison and Courvoisier respectively. The quality of the Courvoisier 2-shilling stamp (63:9) was far superior to that of the Harrison 1-shilling stamp; but within five years Harrison and Sons had made enormous progress in multicolour photogravure, and in the early 1960s they could equal anything produced in Switzerland.

Only one *se-tenant* pair was issued in this period – two 5½-penny stamps being produced in 1958 for the dedication of the Canberra Hall of Memory (63:13). The stamps had identical vignettes but the figures of servicemen in the side panels varied. Monochrome intaglio was used for all commemoratives actually produced in Australia (63:1, 3, 4, 6–8, 11, 13, 14, 16–23) except the YMCA stamp of 1955, in which the triangular emblem was typographed (63:5). Two-colour intaglio was used for a stamp of 1959 marking the centenary of self-government in Queensland, but there were no further developments in this process. Instead, Australia turned to photogravure with a stamp for the jubilee of the Australian Inland Mission (63:24) in September 1962. Two months later, a pair in multicolour photogravure was issued for the Commonwealth Games (63:25). Although intaglio lingered on until as late as April 1965 (63:26, 28, 29, 34), photogravure was well-established by the end of 1964 (63:27, 32, 35). That the process had its teething troubles is evident in the number of commemoratives of 1962 to 1964 recorded with missing colours. Oddly enough, the photogravure definitives of the same period were comparatively free from such errors.

As a result of renewed Australian interest in Antarctica during International Geophysical Year, distinctive stamps for use in that region were introduced in March 1957 (63:36). The original 2-shilling stamp was followed by a set of four in December 1959. The original version of the 5-penny was printed in brown, with the value typographed in black to obliterate a denomination rendered obsolete by increases in postal rates. The stamp was reissued in blue in 1961 with the value redrawn (63:37). A stamp of October 1961 honoured the 50th anniversary of Mawson's expedition of 1910–11.

Two Australian dependencies in the Indian Ocean – Christmas Island and the Cocos Islands – formerly administered by Singapore, began issuing their own stamps in this decade. Christmas Island used ordinary Australian stamps from 1952 to 1958, when the large definitive design was adapted for use in the island. The Malaysian currency values and the name were typographed in black, and the basic design was recess-printed in various colours (63:38). A pictorial intaglio series followed in August 1963 (63:39). The Cocos (Keeling) Islands were transferred to Australia in 1955 and used Australian stamps until June 1963, when a series of six pictorial stamps was released (63:40). Both of these sets were produced by the Note Printing Branch of the Reserve Bank of Australia in Melbourne.

Nauru issued a pictorial series between 1963 and 1965, two values in intaglio and the rest in multicolour photogravure (63:41). Norfolk Island released an intaglio definitive series with the theme of flowers and birds between May 1960 and April 1962. The Annigoni portrait of the Queen was incorporated in the design of the 9-penny value (63:44). From 1962 onwards, however, most of the stamps were printed in multicolour photogravure by Harrison, including new definitives featuring fish in 1962–3 and scenery in 1964 (63:45).

In addition to Christmas stamps – similar to the Australian issues but with a different inscription – Norfolk Island issued two stamps in 1956 to mark the centenary of the colonisation by the Pitcairn islanders (63:42) and a stamp in 1960 to celebrate the introduction of local government. Between July 1958 and September 1960 various definitives were surcharged with new values as a result of increases in postal rates (63:43).

Papua, New Guinea, surcharged two stamps of the 1952 definitive series in 1957 (63:46) pending the introduction of seven additional denominations in new designs the following year (63:47). Thereafter, other values were added piecemeal as required. Four stamps of 1963 were photogravure-printed by Harrison and Courvoisier, but in 1964 the definitives reverted to intaglio for a pair featuring shipping and aircraft (63:48). Harrison, Courvoisier and the Reserve Bank of Australia produced several commemoratives between 1961 and 1964. In 1964 two short sets with the themes of native artifacts and the health services were released.

British Pacific Islands

An Elizabethan definitive series was introduced in March 1956, and various values were added until 1960. In some cases the existing designs were merely modified, the Queen's profile replacing that of King George VI (64:20), but in others, entirely new designs were used. The series was recess-printed by the three British printers using this process – Bradbury Wilkinson, Waterlow and De La Rue. De La Rue took over the Waterlow portion of the contract in 1961. The Script CA watermark was originally employed but the Block CA watermark was used in printings of 1963–4.

Various denominations were added to the definitive series initiated by Fiji in 1954 including low-value stamps featuring the Annigoni portrait, which were introduced in 1956 (64:22). Between 1959 and 1963 a new pictorial series was released. The Annigoni portrait was retained for the low values, but the inscription was redrawn. Most of this series was recess-printed as before, but two values were produced in multicolour photogravure by Harrison (64:23). This led to a third series, between 1962 and 1966, in which the proportion of photogravure stamps was greatly increased (64:24), although Bradbury Wilkinson continued to print the majority of the series in intaglio. Definitive stamps were overprinted on two occasions for commemorative purposes, but four distinctive sets were released in 1963–4, all photogravure-printed by Harrison (64:25).

The Gilbert and Ellice Islands introduced an Elizabethan series in August 1956, merely adapting the designs of the Georgian definitives (64:29). Two stamps were reissued in 1964–5 with the Block CA watermark instead of the original Script CA watermark. Commemoratives, in photogravure by De La Rue and Enschedé, marked the diamond jubilee of phosphate mining in 1960 and the inauguration of the air service in 1964.

Pitcairn's Elizabethan series did not appear until July 1957; but entirely new designs were used, with uniform styles of lettering and a more up-to-date lay-out replacing the jumble of styles and elaborate frames of the Georgian series (64:34). This series, recess-printed by De La Rue in two-colour combinations, was superseded in August 1964 by a multicolour photogravure series with the theme of island boats and birds (64:35). Apart from the usual colonial omnibus issues, Pitcairn issued three stamps in 1961 marking the centenary of the return of the islanders from Norfolk Island.

French Pacific Islands

The Oceanic Settlements were renamed French Polynesia in 1958 and a definitive series thus inscribed appeared between November of that year and December 1960. The stamps featured island scenery and occupations and were recess-printed in multicolour (64:26). Additional denominations in the same genre were issued in May 1964 (64:27). Short sets featuring flowers, fish and landscapes in multicolour intaglio or photogravure were released at annual intervals from 1962 to 1964 (64:28). The same formula, combining pictorial definitives with short thematic sets, was followed by the other colonies – New Caledonia and the Wallis and Futuna Islands (64:42).

In addition to the French colonial omnibus issues of this period (64:31), each territory produced a number of commemoratives – usually in singles – marking both local and international events (64:30).

New Hebrides Condominium

The Anglo-French condominium of the New Hebrides continued the practice of issuing sets simultaneously in English and French versions. Both versions bore the British and French cyphers – their positions generally being reversed on the respective issues. A set of four stamps appeared in 1956 to celebrate the golden jubilee of joint rule, both versions of which were printed in photogravure by Harrison (64:32). Monochrome intaglio pictorials appeared in 1957, with three designs by the French artists Cheffer and Gandon but printed by Waterlow. Conversely, this series was superseded in 1963 by a series by British designers but recess-printed in Paris (64:33). For the Freedom from Hunger and Red Cross commemoratives of 1963, the appropriate colonial omnibus designs were used in each case.

New Zealand and Dependencies

Between 1955 and 1959 several denominations of the low-value Elizabethan series were redrawn, omitting the Southern Cross constellation in the lower right corner and increasing the size of the numerals of value (64:3). A much whiter, more opaque paper was introduced in 1958 and can readily be distinguished from the thinner, slightly toned and transparent paper of the earlier printings. A pictorial series, photogravure-printed by De La Rue and Harrison, was introduced in July 1960 (64:13).

Health stamps were issued in September or October of each year as before, but sets of three, featuring children, were issued in 1955 and 1956 (64:2), and from 1957 onwards two stamps were issued in miniature sheets of six. Beach scenes and youth movements were the subjects in 1957 and 1958; and in subsequent years native birds were featured, either in photogravure (64:11) or intaglio (64:14). The pair issued in 1963, however, portrayed Prince Andrew – resuming the practice of earlier years when other royal children had been featured.

In 1960 New Zealand followed Australia's example by issuing Christmas stamps. A single stamp was produced each year, usually featuring the reproduction of a religious painting (64:15). An exception was made in 1964 when the stamp featured an artist's impression of the first Christmas service held in New Zealand, on the occasion of its 150th anniversary (64:19).

Intaglio remained the principal medium for commemoratives, which usually consisted of single stamps, up to 1959 (64:1, 4, 5, 8, 10); but monochrome photogravure by Harrison and Sons was used occasionally from 1957 (64:6, 9, 12). The Kingsford-Smith commemorative of 1958 was designed and recess-printed by the Commonwealth Bank of Australia, an identical stamp of 8-penny denomination being released in Australia at the same time (64:7). After 1960, however, multicolour photogravure by Harrison and De La Rue was used exclusively for the few commemoratives issued in this period (64:16–18), coinciding with a break from the purely pictorial style of the 1940s and 1950s and the adoption of poster techniques.

There was remarkably little philatelic activity in the New Zealand dependencies in this decade, Tokelau issuing a surcharged shilling stamp in 1956 and Niue producing no stamps at all after 1953. Like Australia, however, New Zealand began issuing stamps for its Antarctic territory – Ross Dependency – in 1957, a set of four pictorials being recess-printed by De La Rue (64:36, 39). In the Cook Islands a temporary surcharge was made on the 5-penny definitive in 1960 and a pictorial series was issued in June 1963, lithographed in multicolour by Bradbury Wilkinson (64:21).

Samoa

A New Zealand dependency until 1962, the only issue in the remaining years of the mandate was a set of three stamps in 1958 to mark the inauguration of the parliament. Bradbury Wilkinson produced a pictorial series in July 1962, lithographed in multicolour, to celebrate independence but subsequently retained as a definitive set (64:38).

The only commemoratives issued after 1962 marked the first anniversary of independence (64:37) and the second anniversary of the treaty of friendship with New Zealand. Both sets were photogravure-printed, the first by Harrison and the second by Enschedé.

Tonga

No stamps were issued between 1953 and 1961, when five stamps in monochrome photogravure by Harrison celebrated the 75th anniversary of the postal service (64:40). A taste of things to come, however, was the overprinting of the definitives in 1962 to produce a set of eight ordinary stamps and six official stamps for the centenary of emancipation (64:41).

In addition to colonial omnibus stamps for Freedom from Hunger, and the Red Cross, with the portrait of Queen Salote substituted, Tonga embarked on a prolific policy of issues that quickly became notorious for their gimmickry. Considerable furore was created in 1963 on the release of a series of circular stamps embossed on gold foil to simulate gold coins. The top values of this series had a diameter of $3\frac{1}{8}$ inches (79 millimetres), and they were promptly nicknamed the 'Tonga beermats'. The majority of Tongan stamps since then have been free-form and self-adhesive, die-stamped or embossed by the Walsall Lithographic Company.

1

2

3

4

5

6

7

8

9

10

11

12

13

14

15

16

17

18

19

20

21

22

23

24

25

26

27

28

29

30

31

32

33

34

35

36

37

38

39

40

41

42

43

44

45

46

47

36

1

2

3

4

5

6

7

8

9

10

11

12

13

14

15

16

17

18

19

20

21

22

23

24

25

26

27

28

29

30

31

32

33

34

35

36

37

38

39

40

41

42

43

44

45

46

47

48

39

1

2

3

4

5

6

7

8

9

10

1

12

13

14

15

16

17

18

19

20

21

22

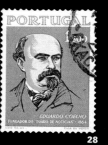

24

25

26

27

28

30

31

32

33

34

35

36

37

38

39

40

1

2

3

4

5

7

8

9

10

11

12

13

14

15

16

17

18

19

20

21

22

23

24

25

26

27

28

29

30

31

32

33

34

35

36

4

1

2

3

4

5

6

7

8

9

10

11

12

13

14

15

16

17

18

19

20

21

22

23

24

25

26

27

28

29

30

31

32

33

34

35

36

37

38

39

40

41

42

43

44

45

46

47

48

42

1

2

3

4

5

6

7

8

9

10

11

12

13

14

15

16

17

18

19

20

21

22

23

24

25

26

27

28

29

30

31

32

33

34

35

36

37

38

39

40

43

44

1

2

3

4

5

6

7

8

9

10

11

12

13

14

15

16

17

18

19

20

21

22

23

24

25

26

27

28

29

30

31

32

33

34

35

36

37

38

39

40

41

42

43

45

46

1 2 3 4

6 7 8 9 10 1

12 13 14 15 1

17 18 19 20 2

22 23 24 25 26 2

28 29 30 31 32 33 3

35 36

1

2

3

4

5

6

7

8

9

10

11

12

13

14

15

16

17

18

19

20

21

22

23

24

25

26

27

28

29

30

31

32

33

34

35

36

37

38

39

40

1

2

3

4

5

6

7

8

9

10

11

12

13

14

15

16

17

18

19

20

21

22

23

24

25

26

27

28

29

30

31

32
33

34

35

36

37

38

39

40

41

51

1

2

3

4

5

6

7

8

9

10

11

12

13

14

15

16

17

18

19

20

21

22

23

24

25

26

27

28

29

30

31

32

33

34

35

36

37

38

39

40

41

1

2

3

4

5

7

8

9

10

11

12

13

14

15

16

17

18

19

20

21

22

23

24

25

26

27

28

29

30

31

32

33

34

35

36

37

38

39

40

41

53

1   2   3   4   5

6   7   8   9   10   11

12   13   14   15   16   17

18   19   20   21   22

23   24   25   26   27   28

29   30   31   32   33   34   35

36   37   38   39   40

41   42   43   44   45

1

2

3

5

6

7

8

10

11

12

14

15

16

17

18

19

21

22

23

25

26

27

28

30

31

32

33

34

FREEDOM OF THE PRESS
U.S. POSTAGE 4¢

CONSERVATION
FOREST
4¢ U.S. POSTAGE

U.S. POSTAGE
1859–1959
PETROLEUM INDUSTRY
4¢

PAN AMERICAN GAMES
CHICAGO 1959
10¢ U.S. AIR MAIL

VIII OLYMPIC WINTER GAMES
CALIFORNIA 1960
4¢ UNITED STATES POSTAGE

FIFTH WORLD FORESTRY CONGRESS
4¢ U.S. POSTAGE

1910 1960
CAMP FIRE GIRLS
UNITED STATES POSTAGE 4¢

1

FORT DUQUESNE
1758 1958
U.S. POSTAGE 4¢

CHAMPION OF LIBERTY
JOSE DE SAN MARTIN 1778–1850 HERO OF THE ANDES
UNITED STATES POSTAGE 4¢

U.S. AIR MAIL 7¢
ALASKA STATEHOOD 1959

UNITED FOR FREEDOM
NATO 1949–1959
4¢ UNITED STATES POSTAGE

ARCTIC EXPLORATIONS 1909
RED BANK JUL 6 3 PM 1959
U.S. POSTAGE 4¢

2 ... 8 ... 9 ... 10 ... 11 ... 1

JULY 4, 1959 4¢
UNITED STATES POSTAGE

HAWAII STATEHOOD 1959
U.S. AIR MAIL

UNITED STATES POSTAGE
EPHRAIM McDOWELL 4¢

4¢ The UNITED STATES
I have sworn... Hostility against every form of TYRANNY over the mind of man
Credo OF AMERICA

LIBERTY FOR ALL
U.S. AIR MAIL 15¢

13 ... 14 ... 15 ... 16 ... 1

BOY SCOUTS OF AMERICA
1910–1960
U.S. POSTAGE 4¢

SEATO
UNITY PEACE PROGRESS
4¢ U.S. POSTAGE

WATER CONSERVATION
UNITED STATES POSTAGE 4¢

CHAMPION OF LIBERTY
IGNACY JAN PADEREWSKI STATESMAN
UNITED STATES POSTAGE 4¢

THE AMERICAN WOMAN
U.S. POSTAGE 4¢

18 ... 19 ... 20 ... 21 ... 2

UNITED STATES POSTAGE
ROBERT LA FOLLETTE 4¢

WHEELS OF FREEDOM
UNITED STATES POSTAGE 4¢

CHAMPION OF LIBERTY
BARON VON MANNERHEIM
UNITED STATES POSTAGE 4¢

CHAMPION OF LIBERTY
ITALIAN UNIFICATION GARIBALDI
UNITED STATES POSTAGE 4¢

CHAMPION OF LIBERTY
MAHATMA GANDHI APOSTLE OF NONVIOLENCE
UNITED STATES POSTAGE 8¢

UNITED STATES POSTAGE
WALTER F. GEORGE 4¢

23 ... 24 ... 25 ... 26 ... 27 ... 2

CIVIL WAR CENTENNIAL
FORT SUMTER 1861
UNITED STATES POSTAGE 4¢

4¢ UNITED STATES POSTAGE
GENTLE KNIGHT OF PROGRESSIVE IDEALS GEORGE W. NORRIS

1911 · NAVAL AVIATION · 1961 4¢
UNITED STATES POSTAGE

4¢
NEW MEXICO STATEHOOD
1912 U.S. POSTAGE 1962

29 ... 30 ... 31 ... 3

4¢ U.S. MAN IN SPACE
PROJECT MERCURY

CIVIL WAR CENTENNIAL
SHILOH
1862 1962
UNITED STATES POSTAGE 4¢

4¢
1812 1962
LOUISIANA

4¢
THE HOMESTEAD ACT
U.S. POSTAGE 1862 1962

33 ... 34 ... 35 ... 36

FREDERIC REMINGTON ARTIST OF THE WEST 1861 1961
1¢

U.S. POSTAGE 4¢

4¢ U.S. POSTAGE
GIRL SCOUTS · U.S.A.

ATOMIC ENERGY ACT
PEACEFUL USES
4¢ U.S. POSTAGE BRIEN McMAHON

1912 ARIZONA 1962

SEATTLE WORLD'S FAIR 1962
UNITED STATES POSTAGE 4¢

39 ... 40

NATIONAL APPRENTIGESHIP PROGRAM — UNITED STATES 4¢
1

DAG HAMMARSKJOLD — UNITED STATES POSTAGE 4¢
2

Christmas 1962 4¢
3

HIGHER EDUCATION — UNITED STATES POSTAGE 4¢
4

U.S. POSTAGE — WINSLOW HOMER 4¢
5

ANDREW JACKSON 1¢ U.S. POSTAGE
6

WASHINGTON 5¢ U.S. POSTAGE
7

8¢ U.S. AIR MAIL
8

U.S. AIR MAIL 6¢
9

Carolina Charter 1663-1963 5 cents U.S. postage
10

1ST INTERNATIONAL POSTAL CONFERENCE — 100th ANNIVERSARY — MONTGOMERY BLAIR U.S. AIR MAIL 15¢
11

WEST VIRGINIA 1863-1963 5¢
12

CIVIL WAR CENTENNIAL GETTYSBURG 1863-1963 UNITED STATES POSTAGE 5¢
13

14

1863-1963 UNITED STATES 5 CENTS — EMANCIPATION PROCLAMATION
15

ALLIANCE FOR PROGRESS 5¢ U.S. POSTAGE
16

ELEANOR ROOSEVELT 5¢ U.S. POSTAGE
17

U.S. POSTAGE — THE SCIENCES 5¢
18

1863 INTERNATIONAL RED CROSS 1963 5¢ UNITED STATES POSTAGE
19

5¢ U.S. POSTAGE — C.M. RUSSELL AMERICAN ARTIST
20

NEW YORK WORLD'S FAIR 1964-1965 5¢ POSTAGE
21

CIVIL WAR CENTENNIAL 1864-1964 THE WILDERNESS 5¢ UNITED STATES POSTAGE
22

CHRISTMAS 1963 UNITED STATES 5¢
23

...AND THE GLOW FROM THAT FIRE CAN TRULY LIGHT THE WORLD 5¢ 1917 JOHN FITZGERALD KENNEDY 1963
24

U.S. POSTAGE NEVADA STATEHOOD 1864-1964 5¢
25

4¢ U.S. POSTAGE — SAM RAYBURN
26

FOOD FOR PEACE 5¢ UNITED STATES — FREEDOM FROM HUNGER
27

5¢ UNITED STATES POSTAGE — CORDELL HULL
28

CITY MAIL DELIVERY 1863-1963 5¢ UNITED STATES
29

Audubon American Artist 5¢ U.S. Postage
30

JOHN MUIR CONSERVATIONIST 5¢ UNITED STATES POSTAGE
31

NEW JERSEY TERCENTENARY 1664-1964 5¢ UNITED STATES POSTAGE
32

REGISTER VOTE 5¢ POSTAGE
33

UNITED STATES — SHAKESPEARE 1564-1964 5¢
34

ROBERT H. GODDARD 8¢ U.S. AIR MAIL
35

U.S. 5¢ HOMEMAKERS
36

U.S. POSTAGE 5¢ — DOCTORS MAYO
37

AMATEUR RADIO 5¢ U.S. POSTAGE
38

UNITED NATIONS — HUMAN RIGHTS · DROITS DE L'HOMME — NATIONS UNIES — ОБЪЕДИНЕННЫЕ НАЦИИ 8¢
39

UNITED NATIONS — UN EMERGENCY FORCE — NACIONES UNIDAS — ОБЪЕДИНЕННЫЕ НАЦИИ 9¢
40

UNITED NATIONS — ОБЪЕДИНЕННЫЕ НАЦИИ — NACIONES UNIDAS — World Meteorological Organization — NATIONS UNIES 3¢
41

NATIONS UNIES — CENTRAL HALL · LONDRES — ASSEMBLEE GENERALE 1946 — NACIONES UNIDAS 8¢
42

NATIONS UNIES — To unite our strength — NACIONES UNIDAS — UNITED NATIONS — ОБЪЕДИНЕННЫЕ НАЦИИ 30¢
43

UNITED NATIONS 10¢
44

57

1

2

3

4

5

7

8

9

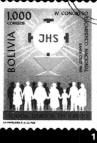

10

11

12

14

15

16

18

19

20

21

22

23

25

26

27

28

29

31

32

33

34

36

37

38

39

40

1

2

3

4

5

6

7

8

9

10

11

12

13

14

15

16

17

18

19

20

21

22

23

24

25

26

27

28

29

30

31

1

2

3

5

6

7

8

10

11

12

15

16

17

18

19

20

22

23

24

25

28

29

30

31

1955-1964
Captions to Plates 33-64

PLATE 33

ALBANIA:
1. 1957; Independence anniversary, 8l.
2. 1959; Liberation anniversary, 2l.50.
3. 1960; Lenin, 11l.
4. 1960; Alphabet Study Association, 1l.
5. 1960; Normal School, Elbasan, 6l.50.
6. 1962; P. N. Luarasi, 8l.50.
7. 1963; Red Cross, 6l.
8. 1962; Medicinal plants, 11l. 50.
9. 1962; Independence anniversary, 3l.

ANDORRA (Spanish):
10. 1963–4; Pictorial definitive, 6p.

ANDORRA (French):
11. 1955; Pictorial series, 3f.
12. 1961; Pictorial definitive, 30c.

AUSTRIA:
13. 1955; Anniversary of Republic, 1s.50.
14. 1957; Buildings series, 1s.
15. 1956; Town planning, 1s.45.
16. 1958; Alpine ski championships, 1s.50.
17. 1958; Choir festival, 1s.50.
18. 1959; United Europe, 2s.40.
19. 1959; Hunting Congress, 1s.
20. 1959; Sports, 1s.50.
21. 1961; Sonnblick Meteorological Observatory, 1s.80.
22. 1961; Nationalised industries, 1s.
23. 1961; World Bank Congress, 3s.
24. 1962; Electric power nationalisation, 6s.40.
25. 1963; Red Cross, 3s.
26. 1963; Winter Olympic Games, 3s.
27. 1964; Horticultural exhibition, 1s.80.
28. 1964; UPU Congress, 6s.40.

BELGIUM:
29. 1955; Ghent flower show, 4f.
30. 1955; Liège exhibition, 20c.
31. 1956; Europa, 2f.
32. 1957–8; Brussels exhibition, 2f.50.
33. 1957; Boy Scouts, 80c.
34. 1957; Nursing schools, 30c.
35. 1961; Interparliamentary Union, 6f.
36. 1962; Canon P. J. Triest, 3f.
37. 1962; Cultural and patriotic funds, 90c. + 10c.
38. 1963; Paris Postal Conference, 6f.
39. 1963; 350th Anniversary, Guild of St. Michel, 6f.
40. 1963; Union of Towns Congress, 6f.
41. 1964; Celebrities, 50c.
42. 1964; Millenary of Ostend, 3f.

PLATE 34

BULGARIA:
1. 1956; Fruit, 28st.
2. 1956; Olympic Games, 16st.
3. 1959; Birds, 2st.
4. 1959; Five-Year-Plan, 5st.
5. 1961; Games, 5st.
6. 1962; Roses, 1st.
7. 1962; Butterflies, 4st.
8. 1963; Black Sea resorts, 3st.
9. 1963; Woodland animals, 2st.
10. 1963; Thracian tombs, 20st.
11. 1964; Landscapes, 6st.

CYPRUS:
12. 1955; Elizabethan series, 50m.
13. 1960; Republican series, 10m.
14. 1962; Pictorial series, 5m.
15. 1963; Boy Scouts, 3m.

CZECHOSLOVAKIA:
16. 1956; Sports events, 75h.
17. 1958; Postal Congress, 45h.
18. 1959; Cultural anniversaries, 15h.
19. 1960; Spartacist Games, 1k.
20. 1960; Castles, 1k.
21. 1962; Cultural celebration, 10h.
22. 1962; USSR anniversary, 30h.
23. 1963; Freedom from Hunger, 1k.60.
24. 1964; Trade Union hotels, 60h.
25. 1964; Olympic Games, 1k.60.
26. 1964; Birds, 1k.60.

DENMARK:
27. 1956; Ellehammer's aircraft, 30ö.
28. 1959; King Frederick IX, 35ö.
29. 1962; Danish ballet, 60ö.
30. 1960; Food Fair, 30ö.
31. 1960; Royal silver wedding, 60ö.
32. 1961; Scandinavian airlines system, 60ö.
33. 1961; King Frederick IX, 40ö.
34. 1962; M.S. *Selandia*, 60ö.
35. 1962; Dansk Fredning, 20ö.
36. 1962; Tivoli, 35ö.
37. 1963; Denmark–Germany railway, 15ö.
38. 1963; Paris Postal Conference, 60ö.
39. 1964; Primary schools, 35ö.
40. 1964; Red Cross, 60ö. + 10ö.
41. 1964; Exploration of the sea, 60ö.

FINLAND:
42. 1959; Missionary Society, 30m.
43. 1960; Geodesy and geophysics, 30m.
44. 1963; Air, 45p.
45. 1963; Definitive, 5p.
46. 1963; Pictorial definitive, 40p.
47. 1963; Europa, 40p.

PLATE 35

FRANCE:
1. 1955–9; 'France', 20f.
2. 1955; Inventors, 10f.
3. 1955; Cinema industry, 30f.
4. 1955; Nice, 10f.
5. 1955; G. de Nerval, 12f.
6. 1955; Red Cross, 15f. + 5f.
7. 1956; Marshal Franchet d'Esperey, 30f.
8. 1956; Battle of Verdun, 30f.
9. 1956; Sports, 30f.
10. 1956; Famous men, 18f.
11. 1957; Le Quesnoy, 15f.
12. 1957; Inventors (second series), 8f.
13. 1957; Public works, 30f.
14. 1957; Tourist publicity, 8f.
15. 1958; Brussels exhibition, 35f.
16. 1958; Senlis Cathedral, 15f.
17. 1958; Paris–Rome Friendship, 35f.
18. 1959; Tancarville Bridge, 30f.
19. 1960; Sower, 20c.
20. 1960; Air, 5f.
21. 1960; Stamp Day, 20c. + 5c.
22. 1960; Nature Protection, 30c.
23. 1961; Maillol centenary, 20c.
24. 1961; Marianne, 20c.
25. 1961; Heroes of the Resistance (fifth series), 30c.
26. 1961–2; Tourist publicity, 1f.
27. 1962; World ski championships, 50c.
28. 1962; Gallic cock, 25c.
29. 1962; Civil and sports aviation, 20c.
30. 1962; Pascal, 50c.
31. 1962; Satellite link, 50c.
32. 1963; Freedom from Hunger, 50c.
33. 1963; Celebrities of EEC countries, 30c.
34. 1963; Tourist publicity, 50c.
35. 1964; Gallic coin, 10c.
36. 1963; French art, 1f.
37. 1964; G. Mandel, 30c.
38. 1964; Victory of the Marne, 30c.

COUNCIL OF EUROPE:
39. 1958; Tourist series, 35f. overprinted.

UNESCO:
40. 1961; Buddha and Hermes, 25c.

PLATE 36

GERMANY (West Berlin):
1. 1955; W. Furtwängler, 40pf.
2. 1956; Buildings and monuments, 25pf.
3. 1956; Buildings and monuments, 50pf.
4. 1957; Portraits, 30pf.
5. 1959; President Heuss, 10pf.
6. 1961; Famous Germans, 10pf.
7. 1962; 'Old Berlin' series, 10pf.

GERMANY (West Germany):
8. 1955; Lufthansa, 15pf.
9. 1955; Postal motor transport, 20pf.
10. 1955; Cosmic research, 20pf.
11. 1955; Refugees, 20pf.
12. 1955; Numeral, 1pf.
13. 1956; Mozart, 10pf.
14. 1956; Heinrich Heine, 10pf.
15. 1956; Robert Schumann, 10pf.

16. 1956; Evangelical Church Convention, 10pf.
17. 1956; Maria Laach Abbey, 20pf.
18. 1957; Saar, 10pf.
19. 1957; Heinrich Hertz, 10pf.
20. 1957; Justus Liebig University, 10pf.
21. 1957; Albert Ballin, 20pf.
22. 1957; Television, 10pf.
23. 1957; Nature Protection, 20pf.
24. 1958; Forest fires prevention, 20pf.
25. 1958; Frankfurt-am-Main Zoo, 10pf.
26. 1958; Munich, 20pf.
27. 1958; Currency reform, 20pf.
28. 1959; Evangelical Church, 10pf.
29. 1960; Europa, 40pf.
30. 1961; Famous Germans, 40pf.
31. 1962; Mainz, 20pf.
32. 1962; Child Welfare, 7pf. + 3pf.
33. 1963; CRALOG and CARE, 20pf.
34. 1963; Flora and philately, 40pf.
35. 1964; Capitals of the Federal Lands, 20pf.
36. 1964; Scientific anniversaries, 10pf.
37. 1964; Humanitarian relief, 40pf. + 20pf.

GERMANY (East Germany):
38. 1956; Robert Schumann, 20pf.
39. 1956; Egyptian relief fund, 20pf. + 10pf.
40. 1956; Berlin Zoo, 30pf.
41. 1957; Friedrich Froebel, 20pf.
42. 1957; Scientists' anniversaries, 10pf.
43. 1959; Handel, 20pf.
44. 1959; Gymnastics, 10pf. + 5pf.
45. 1961; Landscapes and buildings, 25pf.
46. 1961; Walter Ulbricht, 50pf.
47. 1961; Leipzig Autumn Fair, 25pf.
48. 1963; Stamp Day, 20pf.
49. 1964; Youth meeting, 10pf.

PLATE 37

GIBRALTAR:
1. 1960; Elizabethan series, ½d.

GREECE:
2. 1958; Greek ports, 10d.
3. 1957; Royal family, 2d.
4. 1959; Ancient Greek coins, 2d.50.
5. 1961; Tourist publicity, 1d.
6. 1963; Scouting, 3d.
7. 1963; Greek royal dynasty, 50l.
8. 1963; Freedom from Hunger, 4d.50.

GREAT BRITAIN:
9. 1955; Castles definitives, 2s. 6d.
10. 1957; Scouting, 2½d.
11. 1957; 46th Inter-Parliamentary Union, 4d.
12. 1958; Commonwealth Games, 6d.
13. 1960; General Letter Office, 3d.
14. 1960; European Postal and Telecommunications Conference, 1s. 6d.
15. 1961; Post Office Savings Bank, 1s. 6d.
16. 1961; CEPT, 2d.
17. 1961; Commonwealth Parliamentary Conference, 6d.
18. 1962; National Productivity Year, 2½d.
19. 1963; Freedom from Hunger, 2½d.
20. 1963; Paris Postal Conference, 6d.
21. 1963; Nature Week, 4½d.
22. 1963; Lifeboat Conference, 1s. 6d.
23. 1963; Red Cross, 3d.
24. 1963; COMPAC, 1s. 6d.
25. 1964; Shakespeare, 1s.6d.
26. 1964; Geographical Congress, 4d.

27. 1964; Botanical Congress, 6d.
28. 1964; Forth Road Bridge, 3d.

SCOTLAND:
29. 1958; Queen Elizabeth, 1s. 3d.

NORTHERN IRELAND:
30. 1958; Elizabethan series, 1s. 6d.

WALES AND MONMOUTHSHIRE:
31. 1958; Queen Elizabeth, 3d.

ISLE OF MAN:
32. 1958; Elizabethan series, 3d.

GUERNSEY:
33. 1958; Queen Elizabeth, 3d.

JERSEY:
34. 1958; Elizabethan definitive, 4d.

HUNGARY:
35. 1955; Workers, 2fo.60.
36. 1955; Transport, 60fi.
37. 1956; Sopron. 60fi.
38. 1959; Geophysical Year, 20fi.
39. 1962; Air, 2fo.
40. 1960–62; Hungarian castles, 80fi.
41. 1963; Transport, 70fi.
42. 1963; Siófok resort, 40fi.
43. 1964; Bridges, 1fo.50.

PLATE 38

ICELAND:
1. 1955–7; National sports, 1k.75.
2. 1957; Re-afforestation campaign, 35a.
3. 1958; Flowers, 1k.
4. 1958; Icelandic pony, 10a.
5. 1959; Air, 3k.50.
6. 1959; Salmon, 25a.
7. 1960; World Refugee Year, 4k.50.
8. 1960; Wild flowers, 2k.50.
9. 1962; Icelandic buildings, 2k.50.
10. 1963; Freedom from Hunger, 5k.
11. 1964; Icelandic Boy Scouts, 4k.50.

IRELAND:
12. 1956; John Barry, 3d.
13. 1957; John Redmond, 3d.
14. 1957; Thomas O'Crohan, 5d.
15. 1957; Admiral William Brown, 3d.
16. 1957; Father Luke Wadding, 3d.
17. 1958; Thomas J. Clarke, 3d.
18. 1958; Mother Mary Aikenhead, 3d.
19. 1960; World Refugee Year, 3d.
20. 1961; Aer Lingus, 6d.
21. 1959; Guinness brewery, 3d.
22. 1961; St. Patrick, 3d.
23. 1962; J. O'Donovan and E. O'Curry, 3d.
24. 1963; Freedom from Hunger, 4d.
25. 1964; Wolfe Tone, 4d.
26. 1964; New York World's Fair, 5d.

ITALY:
27. 1956; Seventh Winter Olympics, 12l.
28. 1956; UNO, 60l.
29. 1957; St. George definitive, 500l.
30. 1957; Antonio Canova, 25l.
31. 1958; Naples stamp centenary, 25l.
32. 1959; Sicily stamp centenary, 60l.
33. 1959; Olympic Games, 60l.
34. 1961; Michelangelo definitive, 70l.

35. 1961; Unification and independence, 70l.
36. 1962; Pacinotti's dynamo, 70l.
37. 1962; World cycling, 70l.
38. 1962; Balzan medal, 70l.
39. 1963; Paris Postal Conference, 70l.
40. 1963; Red Cross, 70l.
41. 1962; Malaria eradication, 30l.
42. 1964; Carabinieri, 30l.

LIECHTENSTEIN:
43. 1959; Views, definitive, 10r.
44. 1964; Arms, 20r.

LUXEMBOURG:
45. 1956; Rose, 4f.
46. 1963; Millenary of Luxembourg, 11f.
47. 1961; Animal protection, 3f.
48. 1960–64; Grand-Duchess Charlotte, 6f.

PLATE 39

MALTA:
1. 1956; Elizabethan series, 1½d.
2. 1959; George Cross, 1¼d.
3. 1960; Stamp centenary, 1½d.
4. 1961; George Cross, 3d.
5. 1962; Great Siege, 2d.
6. 1964; Independence, 3d.

MONACO:
7. 1956; Royal wedding, 3f.
8. 1960; Prince Rainier, series, 50c.
9. 1960; Marine life, 20c.
10. 1962; Europa, 2f.
11. 1963; Air, 2f.
12. 1964–7; Pre-cancelled, 15c.

NETHERLANDS:
13. 1955; Liberation, 10c.
14. 1955; Anti-cancer fund, 25c. + 8c.
15. 1957; Admiral M. A. de Ruyter, 10c.
16. 1957; Europa, 30c.
17. 1959; NATO, 12c.
18. 1962; Cultural, health and social welfare funds, 8c. + 4c.
19. 1962; 'Polder' landscape, 6c.
20. 1962; Silver wedding, 12c.
21. 1962; Automatic telephone, 30c.
22. 1963; Freedom from Hunger, 30c.
23. 1963; Europa, 30c.
24. 1963; Child Welfare, 6c. + 4c.
25. 1963; Kingdom, 30c.
26. 1964; States-General Meeting, 12c.
27. 1964; Groningen University, 30c.
28. 1964; Child Welfare, 40c. + 15c.
29. 1964; Statute of the Kingdom, 15c.
30. 1964; Bible Society, 15c.

NORWAY:
31. 1955; Stamp centenary, 20ö.
32. 1957; Geophysical Year, 35ö.
33. 1955; Official, 5ö.
34. 1956; Northern Countries' Day, 65ö.
35. 1958–62; King Olav V series, 90ö.
36. 1959; Royal Norwegian Agricultural Society, 45ö.
37. 1959; Royal College of Agriculture, 90ö.
38. 1961; Norwegian sport, 90ö.
39. 1961; Scandinavian airlines, 90ö.
40. 1961; Amundsen's arrival at South Pole, 45ö.
41. 1962; Norwegian aviation, 1k.50.
42. 1962–9; Definitive, 65ö.
43. 1963; Ivar Aasen, 90ö.

44. 1963; Camilla Collett, 50ö.
45. 1963; Freedom from Hunger, 25ö.
46. 1963; Textile industry, 50ö.
47. 1964; Oslo Workers' Society, 50ö.
48. 1964; Law of mass action, 35ö.

PLATE 40

POLAND:

1. 1955; Warsaw monuments, 40g.
2. 1956; Winter sports, 20g.
3. 1956; Merchant Navy, 5g.
4. 1956; Tourist propaganda, 1z.15.
5. 1956; Warsaw monuments (second series), 30gr.
6. 1959; Crane, 60gr.
7. 1959; Mushrooms, 1z.
8. 1959; World Peace, 60gr.
9. 1959; Red Cross, 60gr.
10. 1960; Old Polish towns, 1z.
11. 1961; Insects, 2z.50.
12. 1963; Sailing ships, 5gr.
13. 1963; Space, 30gr.

PORTUGAL:

14. 1955; Portuguese kings, 1E.
15. 1956; Railways, 2E.50.
16. 1957; Cesario Verde, 3E.50.
17. 1960; Philatelic exhibition, 1E.
18. 1958; Brussels exhibition, 3E.30.
19. 1960; Prince Henry, 3E.50.
20. 1962; St. Gabriel, 3E.50.
21. 1962; Scout Conference, 6E.50.
22. 1962; Paediatrics Congress, 50c.
23. 1963; Benfica, 1E.
24. 1963; Mailcoach, 5E.
25. 1963; St. Vincent de Paul, 20c.
26. 1964; Sameiro Shrine, 5E.
27. 1964; Olympic Games, 20c.
28. 1964; Newspaper centenary, 1E.

ROMANIA:

29. 1957; Women's gymnastics, 20b.
30. 1957; Flowers, 10b.
31. 1957; Athletics, 20b.
32. 1957; Russian revolution, 10b.
33. 1957; Postage due, 20b.
34. 1958; Republic flag, 1l.
35. 1959; Birds, 10b.
36. 1961; Sculpture, 20b.
37. 1960; Grand piano, 40b.
38. 1964; Cultural anniversaries, 35b.
39. 1964; Mountain resorts, 1l.75.
40. 1964; Anniversaries, 20b.

PLATE 41

RUSSIA:

1. 1955; North Pole, 60k.
2. 1956; Builders' Day, 60k.
3. 1956; Marshal Suvorov, 40k.
4. 1957; Factory plant, 40k.
5. 1957; P. Béranger, 40k.
6. 1958; Tchaikovsky, 1r.
7. 1957; Philatelic exhibition, 40k.
8. 1958–9; Civil aviation, 2r.
9. 1958; Vladimir, 60k.
10. 1958; Stamp centenary, 60k.
11. 1959; Prime Minister's visit to USA, 60k.
12. 1959; Space, 40k.
13. 1960; A. P. Chekhov, 20k.
14. 1960; Children's Day, 25k.
15. 1960; Mark Twain, 40k.
16. 1961–5; Workers' statue, 10k.

17. 1961; Provincial costumes, 6k.
18. 1961; Stamp anniversary, 6k.
19. 1961; Irkutsk, Siberia, 4k.
20. 1961; Russian ballet, 6k.
21. 1962; Lenin's family, 4k.
22. 1962; Titov's space flight, 10k.
23. 1962; Botanic gardens, 3k.
24. 1963; V. Tereshkova, 10k.
25. 1964; Moscow Zoo, 1k.

SAAR:

26. 1955; Colliery shafthead, 15f.
27. 1957; President Heuss, 6f.
28. 1956; Red Cross, 15f. + 5f.
29. 1958; Europa, 30f.

SAN MARINO:

30. 1955; Winter Olympics, 3l.
31. 1958; Milan Fair, 125l.
32. 1959; Abraham Lincoln, 15l.
33. 1959; Olympic Games, 60l.
34. 1960; Lions International, 115l.
35. 1961; Italian independence, 70l.
36. 1963; Olympic Games, 5l.
37. 1964; Olympic Games, 5l.

PLATE 42

SPAIN:

1. 1955; General Franco, 80c.
2. 1955; Stamp Day, 25c.
3. 1955–6; Air, 3p.
4. 1956; Civil War, 3p.
5. 1956; Floating exhibition, 3p.
6. 1960; St. Vincent de Paul, 1p.
7. 1960; Samos monastery, 1p.
8. 1961; Escorial, 5p.
9. 1962; Arms, 5p.
10. 1961; Stamp Day, 1p.50.
11. 1962; Teresian Reformation, 1p.
12. 1963; Europa, 1p.
13. 1963; Explorers (third series), 5p.
14. 1964; Tourist series, 1p.
15. 1963; Order of Mercy, 3p.
16. 1964; Spanish Navy, 70c.
17. 1964; Christmas, 1p.

SWEDEN:

18. 1955; Stamp centenary, 25ö.
19. 1955; Flag Day, 10ö.
20. 1955; P.D.A. Atterbom, 20ö.
21. 1956; Olympic Games, 20ö.
22. 1956; Railways, 40ö.
23. 1957; 15ö. and 5ö., *se-tenant*.
24. 1958; Postal services, 15ö.
25. 1958; Football, 15ö.
26. 1958; Selma Lagerlöf, 80ö.
27. 1959; Power Board, 30ö.
28. 1960; Refugee Year, 40ö.
29. 1961; Nobel prize, 40ö.
30. 1962; Local mail, 30ö.
31. 1962; Swedish monuments, 50ö.
32. 1964; Archbishopric of Uppsala, 60ö.

SWITZERLAND:

33. 1955; Pro Juventute, 20c. + 10c.
34. 1955; Publicity issue, 10c.
35. 1957; Europa, 40c.
36. 1958; Pro Patria, 5c. + 5c.
37. 1958; Atomic symbol, 40c.
38. 1959; Publicity, 50c.
39. 1960; Publicity, 10c.
40. 1960; Postal history definitive, 10c.
41. 1961; Publicity, 10c.

42. 1962; Pro Juventute, 30c. + 10c.
43. 1961; St. Matthew, 3f.
44. 1963; Publicity, 30c.
45. 1964; Publicity, 20c.

UNIVERSAL POSTAL UNION:

46. 1957; Monument, 5c.

WORLD METEOROLOGICAL ORGANISATION:

47. 1956; Elements, 10c.

UNITED NATIONS:

48. 1959; Definitive, 20c.

INTERNATIONAL LABOUR OFFICE:

49. 1960; Miners, 50c.

PLATE 43

TURKEY:

1. 1955; Kemal Atatürk, 50k.
2. 1955; Kemal Atatürk, 20k.
3. 1956; Kemal Atatürk, 1k.
4. 1958–60; Turkish towns, 5k.
5. 1958–60; Turkish towns, 20k.
6. 1958; Kemel Atatürk, 75k. and 25k., *se-tenant*.
7. 1958; Europa, 40k.
8. 1959; Air, 85k.
9. 1959; Oil refinery, 30k.
10. 1959; Postage due, surcharged, 20k.
11. 1959; Kemal Atatürk, 500k.
12. 1960; Revolution, 30k.
13. 1960; Kemal Atatürk's statue, 60k.
14. 1961; Flowers, 30k. + 10k.
15. 1961; Kandilli Observatory, 30k. + 5k.
16. 1963; Landmarks series, 30k.
17. 1963; Kemal Atatürk, 50k.
18. 1964; Reformation, 60k.

VATICAN CITY:

19. 1957; Mariazell Basilica, 15l.
20. 1960; 'Works of Mercy', 10l.
21. 1960; Christmas, 15l.
22. 1961; Vatican newspaper, 40l.
23. 1962; Paulina M. Jaricot, 10l.

YUGOLSAVIA:

24. 1956; Art, 35d.
25. 1956; Olympic Games, 20d.
26. 1957; Flowers, 30d.
27. 1957; Costumes, 30d.
28. 1958; Human Rights, 30d.
29. 1958; Pictorial definitive, 10d.
30. 1962; UNESCO, 50d.
31. 1959; Physical culture, 20d.
32. 1959; Tourist publicity, 15d.
33. 1962; Athletics, 25d.
34. 1963; Medicinal plants, 65d.
35. 1963; Tourist publicity, 15d.
36. 1963; Sculptures, 50d.
37. 1964; Red Cross, 5d.
38. 1964; Butterflies, 25d.
39. 1964; Fireman, 25d.
40. 1964; Olympic Games, 30d.

PLATE 44

ABU DHABI:

1. 1964; Ruler's palace, 1r.

ADEN:

2. 1959; Revised constitution, 1s.25.
3. 1953–9; Elizabethan series, 1s.

QU'AITI STATE IN HADHRAMAUT:
4. 1955; Pictorial series, 1s.
5. 1963; Pictorial definitive, 10s.

AFGHANISTAN:
6. 1964; Boy Scouts and Girl Guides, 2a.50.
7. 1963; Red Cross, 4a.
8. 1964; Red Crescent Day, 1a. + 50p.

AJMAN:
9. 1964; President Kennedy, 1r.

BAHRAIN:
10. 1957; Elizabethan 6d. surcharged, 40 n.p.
11. 1957; Boy Scout 4d. surcharged, 25 n.p.
12. 1957; Local stamp, 6p.
13. 1960; Definitive, 50 n.p.

BHUTAN:
14. 1964; President Kennedy commemoration, 3n.

BRUNEI:
15. 1958; Brunei mosque, 35c.

BURMA:
16. 1961; SEAP Games, 25p.
17. 1964; Birds series, 3p.
18. 1956; Buddha Jayanti, 40p.

CAMBODIA:
19. 1961; Foreign aid programme, 5r.

INTERNATIONAL COMMISSION IN INDO-CHINA:
20. 1957; Indian 6 n.p. for use in Cambodia.

CEYLON:
21. 1956; Prime Minister's twenty-five years of service, 10c.
22. 1956; Buddha Jayanti, 15c.
23. 1957; Stamp centenary, 35c.
24. 1958; Pictorial series, 2r.
25. 1959; Pirivena University, 10c.
26. 1962; Boy Scouts, 35c.
27. 1964; Anagarika Dharmapala, 25c.
28. 1964; Pictorial definitive, 20c.

CHINA (People's Republic):
29. 1955; Scientists, 8f.
30. 1957; Co-operative agriculture, 8f.
31. 1959; Labour Day, 22f.
32. 1958; Flowers, 5f.
33. 1962; Scientists, 8f.
34. 1963; Children, 4f.
35. 1964; Bronze vessels, 10f.

CHINA (Taiwan):
36. 1954–5; Afforestation campaign, $20.
37. 1956; Children's Day, 40c.
38. 1956; Railways, $2.
39. 1956; President Chiang Kai-shek, 40c.
40. 1957; Map of China, 40c.
41. 1959; Air, $8.
42. 1960; Chü Kwang Tower, Quemoy, 40c.

PLATE 45

DUBAI:
1. 1963; Red Cross, 3 n.p.

FUJEIRA:
2. 1964; Definitive, 30 n.p.

HONG KONG:
3. 1962; Stamp centenary, 50c.
4. 1962; Queen Elizabeth, $5.

INDIA:
5. 1956; Buddha Jayanti, 14a.
6. 1955; Five-Year-Plan, 2a.
7. 1957; Map of India, 2 n.p.
8. 1956; Lokmanya Bal Gangadhar Tilak, 2a.
9. 1957; Mutiny centenary, 15 n.p.
10. 1957; Red Cross, 15 n.p.
11. 1957; Children's Day, 15 n.p.
12. 1958; Dr D. K. Karve, 15 n.p.
13. 1958; Indian Air Force, 90 n.p.
14. 1958; Children's Day, 15 n.p.
15. 1959; ILO, 15 n.p.
16. 1960; Thiruvalluvar, 15 n.p.
17. 1961; Industries Fair, 15 n.p.
18. 1962; Wild Life Week, 15 n.p.
19. 1963; Defence campaign, 15 n.p.
20. 1964; Orientalists Congress, 15 n.p.
21. 1963; Human Rights, 15 n.p.
22. 1962; Rambai Ranade, 15 n.p.
23. 1964; Jawaharlal Nehru, 15 n.p.

PORTUGUESE INDIA:
24. 1959; 1½t. of 1948 surcharged, 40c.

INDONESIA:
25. 1955; Independence anniversary, 15s.
26. 1956; Animal series, 50s.
27. 1957; Telegraph centenary, 75s.
28. 1960; Agricultural products, 50s.
29. 1962; Asian Games, 10r.

RIAU-LINGGA:
30. 1958–64; Indonesian animals stamp, overprinted, 20s.

UNITED NATIONS FORCE IN WEST IRIAN:
31. 1963; Pakistan 13p. stamp, overprinted.

WEST NEW GUINEA:
32. 1962; Netherlands New Guinea stamp, overprinted UNTEA, 17c.

IRAN:
33. 1956; Muhammed Riza Pahlavi, 1r.
34. 1958–64; Muhammed Riza Pahlavi, 20r.
35. 1962; Muhammed Riza Pahlavi, 2r.
36. 1960; Visit of King Hussein, 6r.
37. 1962; Shah and Palace, 10r.
38. 1963; Visit of French President, 14r.
39. 1963; Human Rights, 6r.

IRAQ:
40. 1958; Republican, 30f.
41. 1959; Republican emblem, 40f.
42. 1963; Pictorial series, 1f.
43. 1964; Revolution anniversary, 30f.

PLATE 46

ISRAEL:
1. 1955; Youth immigration, 30pr.
2. 1955; Twelve Tribes, 100pr.
3. 1956; Independence, 150pr.
4. 1957; New Year, 50pr.
5. 1960; Henrietta Szold, 25a.
6. 1961; Afforestation, 30a.
7. 1960; Coin, 1a.
8. 1961; Signs of the Zodiac, 12a.
9. 1962; Independence, 30a.
10. 1962; New Year, 8a.
11. 1963; Independence, 30a.
12. 1963; Air, 20a.
13. 1964; National insurance, 12a.
14. 1964; Year of the blockade-runners, 25a.

JAPAN:
15. 1952–64; Mandarin ducks, definitive, 5y.
16. 1955; National Park, 10y.
17. 1956; Judo, 10y.
18. 1955; New Year, 5y.
19. 1957; Iron industry, 10y.
20. 1958; Philatelic Week, 10y.
21. 1957; UNO, 10y.
22. 1957; Geophysical Year, 10y.
23. 1957; New Year, 5y.
24. 1958; Athletic meeting, 5y.
25. 1958; Keio University, 10y.
26. 1958; Human Rights, 10y.
27. 1958; Kan-Mon Undersea tunnel, 10y.
28. 1958; New Year, 5y.
29. 1959; Correspondence Week, 30y.
30. 1960; Antarctic expedition, 10y.
31. 1961; National Park, 10y.
32. 1961; Athletic meeting, 5y.
33. 1961; Cherry blossom definitive, 10y.
34. 1961–5; Temple definitive, 30y.
35. 1962; National festivals, 10y.
36. 1961–5; Shell definitive, 4y.
37. 1961–5; Japanese cranes, 100y.
38. 1964; Himeji Castle, 10y.
39. 1964; Regional festivals, 10y.
40. 1964; Birds series, 10y.
41. 1964; Athletics, 5y.
42. 1964; International Monetary Fund, 10y.
43. 1964; Olympic Games, 5y.
44. 1964; Reclamation of Hachirogata Lagoon, 10y.

PLATE 47

JOHORE:
1. 1955; Diamond jubilee of Sultan, 10c.
2. 1960; Sultan Ismail, 5c.

JORDAN:
3. 1959; King Hussein, 25f.
4. 1962; Aqaba port, 35f.
5. 1963; East Ghor Canal, 10f.
6. 1963; Freedom from Hunger, 15f.
7. 1964; Pope Paul's visit, 15f.

KEDAH:
8. 1957; Sultan Tengku Badlishah, 10c.
9. 1959; Installation of the Sultan, 10c.
10. 1959; Sultan Tengku Abdul, 4c.

KELANTAN:
11. 1961; Sultan Yahya Petra, 10c.

KOREA (South):
12. 1957; Boy Scout, 40h.
13. 1960; President Eisenhower, 40h.
14. 1960; Assembly, 40h.
15. 1961; Air, 50h.
16. 1962; King Sejong definitive, 3w.

KOREA (North):
17. 1961; Vinalon factory, 10ch.
18. 1960; Views of Pyongyang, 70ch.
19. 1962–3; Trolley bus definitive, 40ch.
20. 1963; Mount Myohyang, 10ch.
21. 1964; Ancient buildings (second series), 10ch.

KUWAIT:
22. 1957; Elizabethan definitive surcharged, 75 n.p.
23. 1959; Sheikh Abdulla as-Salim as-Sabah, 20 n.p.
24. 1961; Definitive, 75f.
25. 1963; National Day, 50f.

LAOS:
26. 1957; Air, 18k.
27. 1962; King Savang Vatthana, 10k.

INTERNATIONAL COMMISSION IN INDO-CHINA:
28. 1957; Indian 13 n.p. for use in Laos.

LEBANON:
29. 1955; Cedar of Lebanon, 5p.
30. 1955; Cedar of Lebanon, 2p.50.
31. 1955; Definitive, 25p.
32. 1957; Miners definitive, 12½p.
33. 1957; Cedar of Lebanon, 50p.
34. 1962; Malaria eradication, 30p.
35. 1962; Fruits, 10p.
36. 1964; Flowers, 70p.
37. 1958; Air, 35p.
38. 1958; Cedar of Lebanon, 2p.50.

MACAO:
39. 1958; Charity tax, 2a.
40. 1956; Map, 1a.

MALACCA:
41. 1960; Definitive, 10c.

MALDIVE ISLANDS:
42. 1956; Malé harbour, 25l.

PLATE 48

MALAYAN FEDERATION:
1. 1957; Tin dredger, 25c.
2. 1958; Human Rights, 10c.
3. 1963; Hydro-electric scheme, 30c.

MALAYSIA:
4. 1964; Eleanor Roosevelt commemoration, 30c.
5. 1963; Orchids, 25c.

MONGOLIA:
6. 1960; Flowers, 10m.
7. 1961; Postal service, 5m.
8. 1963; Space flights, 5m.

MUSCAT:
9. 1957; Scout jamboree, 75 n.p.

NEGRI SEMBILAN:
10. 1957; Mosque, 5c.

NEPAL:
11. 1962; King Mahendra, 1p.
12. 1964; East–West Highway, 50p.

NORTH BORNEO:
13. 1956; British North Borneo Company, 35c.
14. 1961; Wild bull, 12c.

PAHANG:
15. 1957; Copra, 1c.

PAKISTAN:
16. 1955; Independence anniversary, 12a.
17. 1955; West Pakistan unity, 12a.
18. 1956; Republic Day, 2a.
19. 1956; Independence anniversary, 2a.
20. 1957; Anniversary of Republic, 10r.
21. 1957; Indian Mutiny, 12a.
22. 1957; Independence anniversary, 12a.
23. 1958; Muhammad Iqbal, 14a.
24. 1960; Armed Forces Day, 14a.
25. 1960; Map, 8a.

26. 1961; Khyber Pass, 5p.
27. 1962; Sports, 25p.
28. 1964; West Pakistan University, 15p.

PENANG:
29. 1957; Elizabethan definitive, 4c.
30. 1960; Mosque, 5c.

PERAK:
31. 1957; Tiger, 10c.

PERLIS:
32. 1957; Copra, 1c.

PHILIPPINE ISLANDS:
33. 1955; Air force heroes, 70c.
34. 1959; Dr. José Rizal, 6c.
35. 1961; Dr. José Rizal, 20c.
36. 1962–9; Portraits series, 1p.
37. 1962; Compulsory tax stamp, 6c. + 5c.
38. 1962; Special delivery, 20c.

QATAR:
39. 1961; Sheikh, 20 n.p.

RAS AL KHAIMA:
40. 1964; 15 n.p. later surcharged, 15d.

RYUKYU ISLANDS:
41. 1958; New Year, 1½c.

PLATE 49

SABAH:
1. 1964; North Borneo, $10 overprinted.

SARAWAK:
2. 1955–7; Queen Elizabeth, 50c.

SAUDI ARABIA:
3. 1960–61; Wadi Hanifa waterfront, 9p.

SELANGOR:
4. 1957; Government offices, $1.
5. 1961–2; Fishing craft, 20c.

SHARJAH:
6. 1964; Human Rights, 50 n.p.

SINGAPORE:
7. 1959; New Constitution, 50c.
8. 1955; Raffles statue, $1.
9. 1962–6; Orchids and birds, $1.
10. 1962; National Day, 10c.

SOUTH ARABIAN FEDERATION:
11. 1963; Red Cross, 1s.25.

SYRIA:
12. 1958; Human Rights, 35p.
13. 1959; School, Damascus, 12½p.
14. 1961; Antiquities, 100p.
15. 1963; Regional costumes, 55p.
16. 1959; Ornamental scrollwork, 2½p.
17. 1962; Jupiter Temple gate, 5p.
18. 1963; Zenobia, 10p.
19. 1963; Damascus buildings, 17½p.
20. 1964; Mosaic, 60p.

THAILAND:
21. 1955; Processional elephant, 80s.
22. 1955; Tao Suranari, 10s.

23. 1957; Buddhism, 25s.
24. 1961–8; King Bhumibol, 50s.
25. 1962; 'Centenary 21' exhibition, 2b.
26. 1964; Correspondence Week, 3b.

TIMOR:
27. 1958; Brussels Exhibition, 40a.

TRENGGANU:
28. 1957; Copra, 1c.

TRUCIAL STATES:
29. 1961; Palms, 40 n.p.

UMM AL QIWAIN:
30. 1964; Sheikh and palace, 15 n.p.

VIETNAM (South):
31. 1956; President Ngo Dinh-diem, 20p.
32. 1960; Air, 10p.

INTERNATIONAL COMMISSION IN INDO-CHINA:
33. 1957; Indian 75 n.p. stamp used in Vietnam.

VIETNAM (South):
34. 1964; Views, 1p.50.

VIETNAM (North):
35. 1957; Cotton mill, 300d.
36. 1961; Women musicians, 50x.
37. 1963; Karl Marx, 3x.

MUTAWAKELITE KINGDOM OF YEMEN:
38. 1962; Maternity and child centre, 4b.

YEMEN ARAB REPUBLIC:
39. 1963; President Kennedy, ½b.

PLATE 50

ALGERIA:
1. 1956; Marshal Franchet d'Esperey, 15f.
2. 1964; Apprentices, 10c.

ANGOLA:
3. 1955; Map of Angola, 5c.

ASCENSION:
4. 1956; Elizabethan series, 1d.
5. 1963; Birds series, 5s.

BASUTOLAND:
6. 1959; Inauguration of National Council, 1s. 3d.

BECHUANALAND:
7. 1955; Queen Elizabeth, 2d.
8. 1961; Photogravure definitive, 2½c.

BELGIAN CONGO:
9. 1955; King Baudouin and river, 4f.50.
10. 1959; Wild animals, 1f.50.

BURUNDI:
11. 1962; Independence, 50c.
12. 1964; Animals, 50f.

CAMEROUN:
13. 1954–5; Air, 50f.
14. 1963; Television satellite link, 3f.

CAPE VERDE ISLANDS:
15. 1958; Brussels Exhibition, 2E.

CENTRAL AFRICAN REPUBLIC:
16. 1962; Postage due, 50c.

CHAD:
17. 1961–2; Logone and elephant, 1f.

COMORO ISLANDS:
18. 1962; Seashells, 1f.

CONGO (Brazzaville):
19. 1961; Fish, 2f.

CONGO (Kinshasa):
20. 1960; Independence, 3f.50.
21. 1964; National palace, 3f.

INDIAN UNITED NATIONS FORCE IN CONGO:
22. 1962; Indian stamp overprinted, 13 n.p.

DAHOMEY:
23. 1963; Dahomey tribes, 5f.

EAST AFRICA:
24. 1964; Olympic Games, 2s.50.

EGYPT:
25. 1958; Economic Conference, 10m.
26. 1958; Rameses II, 10m.
27. 1959; Youth Conference, 10m.
28. 1961; Five-Year-Plan, 10m.
29. 1963; Air, 30m.

EGYPTIAN OCCUPATION OF PALESTINE:
30. 1958; Egyptian stamp of 1957, overprinted, 1m.

ETHIOPIA:
31. 1962; Federation of Ethiopia and Eritrea, 60c.

FERNANDO POO:
32. 1960; Woman at prayer, 50c.

FRENCH SOMALI COAST:
33. 1958; Animals, fish and birds series, 40c.

FRENCH SOUTHERN AND ANTARCTIC TERRITORIES:
34. 1963–72; Adélie penguins, 50f.

GAMBIA:
35. 1963; Birds series, 1½d.

GABON:
36. 1961; Flowers, 1f.

GHANA:
37. 1957; Independence, 2s.
38. 1961; Royal visit, 3d.

GUINEA:
39. 1959; Elephant, 25f.
40. 1962; Birds, 200f.

PLATE 51

IFNI:
1. 1958; Child Welfare, 70c.

IVORY COAST:
2. 1960; Masks, 50c.

KATANGA:
3. 1961; Katanga art, 3f.50.

KENYA:
4. 1963; Independence, 10c.
5. 1964; Inauguration of Republic, 30c.

KENYA, UGANDA AND TANGANYIKA:
6. 1958; Discovery of lakes by Burton and Speke, 1s.30.
7. 1960; Elizabethan series, 15c.
8. 1963; Red Cross, 50c.

LIBERIA:
9. 1958; President Tubman's European tour, 5c.

LIBYA:
10. 1955; Definitive series, 50m.

MADAGASCAR:
11. 1957; Plants, 2f.

MALAGASY REPUBLIC:
12. 1963; Birds and orchids, 1f.

MALAWI:
13. 1964; Photogravure series, 3d.

MALI:
14. 1964; Official, 3f.

MAURITANIA:
15. 1960; Pastoral well, 50c.
16. 1963; Animals, 1f.

MAURITIUS:
17. 1961; Post Office, 1r.

MOROCCO AGENCIES:
18. 1956; British 4d. surcharged in Spanish currency, 40c.
19. 1957; Centenary of British Post Office in Tangier, ½d.

MOROCCO (French):
20. 1955; Mahakma Casablanca, 20f.

MOROCCO (Spanish):
21. 1957; King Mohamed V, 3p.
22. 1962; King Hassan II, 50f.

MOZAMBIQUE:
23. 1961; Arms, 1E.
24. 1963; Sailing ships, 2E.

NIGER:
25. 1964; President Kennedy, 100f.

NIGERIA:
26. 1961; Pictorial series, 2d.
27. 1956; Royal visit, 2d.
28. 1959; Self-government, 1s.
29. 1960; Independence, 3d.

NORTHERN RHODESIA:
30. 1963; Arms, 2s.

NYASALAND:
31. 1963; Revenue stamp, overprinted, 3d.
32. 1964; Photogravure series, 6d.

PORTUGUESE GUINEA:
33. 1963; Snakes, 20E.

RÉUNION:
34. 1963; Saint-Flour, 30f.CFA.

RHODESIA AND NYASALAND:
35. 1959; Elizabethan series, 1s. 3d.
36. 1960; Hydro-electric scheme, 3d.
37. 1962; London–Rhodesia airmail, 1s. 3d.

RIO MUNI:
38. 1960; Colonial Stamp Day, 50c. + 20c.

RUANDA-URUNDI:
39. 1959; Wild animals, 10c.
40. 1961; Usumbura Cathedral, 3f.50. + 1f.50.

RWANDA REPUBLIC:
41. 1963; Admission to UPU, 20f.

PLATE 52

ST. HELENA:
1. 1956; Stamp centenary, 6d.
2. 1959; Tercentenary, 1s.
3. 1961; Photogravure definitive, 2s. 6d.

ST. THOMAS AND PRINCE ISLANDS:
4. 1958; Brussels Exhibition, 2E.50.
5. 1962; Sports, 1E.

SENEGAL:
6. 1961; Sports, 1f.
7. 1963; UPU, 15f.
8. 1963; Professor G. Berger, 25f.
9. 1963; Red Cross, 25f.

SEYCHELLES:
10. 1957; Elizabethan 45c. surcharged 5c.
11. 1961; Post Office centenary, 2r.25.
12. 1962; Map, 2r.25.

SIERRA LEONE:
13. 1956; Elizabethan series, 6d.
14. 1961; Independence, 1s. 3d.
15. 1963; Flowers, series, 6d.
16. 1964; World's Fair, 5s.
17. 1964; Decimal currency 3d. surcharged 3c.

SOMALIA:
18. 1960; Independence, 50c.
19. 1963; Freedom from Hunger, 75c.

SOMALILAND:
20. 1957; Legislative Council, 1s.

SOUTH AFRICA:
21. 1955; Pretoria, 3d.
22. 1955; Voortrekker, 2d.
23. 1958; German settlers, 2d.
24. 1959; Academy, 3d.
25. 1956; SANE, 3d.
26. 1960; Union, 6d.
27. 1960; Railways, 1s. 3d.
28. 1960; Union Day, 3d.
29. 1961; Currency change, 10c.
30. 1962; British settlers, 2½c.
31. 1963; Botanic gardens, 2½c.
32. 1961; Leopard, 1½c.
33. 1961; Republic definitive, 12½c.
34. 1961; Aerial post, 3c.
35. 1962; Folk-dancing, 2½c.
36. 1964; Nursing, 12½c.
37. 1963; Red Cross, 2½c.
38. 1964; Definitive redrawn, 12½c.
39. 1963; Transkei, 2½c.
40. 1964; Rugby, 2½c.
41. 1964; Calvin, 2½c.

PLATE 53

SOUTH KASAI:
1. 1960; Animals, 8f.

SOUTH WEST AFRICA:
2. 1961; Pictorial series, 12½c.

SOUTHERN CAMEROONS:
3. 1960; ½d. Nigerian stamp, overprinted.

SOUTHERN RHODESIA:
4. 1964; Photogravure series, 4d.

SPANISH SAHARA:
5. 1957; Stamp Day, 10c. + 5c.

SUDAN:
6. 1956; Independence, 15m.
7. 1962; Malaria eradication, 15m.
8. 1962; Date palms, 8p.
9. 1963; Red Cross, 55m.

SWAZILAND:
10. 1956; Elizabethan series, 1d.
11. 1962; Photogravure definitive, 1c.
12. 1964; Railways, 25c.

TANGANYIKA:
13. 1961; Independence, 20c.
14. 1964; United Republic of Tanganyika and Zanzibar, 30c.

TOGO:
15. 1961; United Nations, 25f.
16. 1962; Presidential visit to USA, 5f.
17. 1963; Independence, 50c.

TRISTAN DA CUNHA:
18. 1957; Postage due, 5d.
19. 1960; Fish series, 9d.
20. 1963; Resettlement, 5s.

TUNISIA:
21. 1955; Bey of Tunis, 15f.
22. 1955; International Fair, 12f.
23. 1959; Pictorial definitive, 100m.
24. 1962; Africa Day, 100m.
25. 1958; Brussels Exhibition, 30f.
26. 1959; Central Bank, 50m.
27. 1960; President Bourguiba, 30m.
28. 1962; Malaria eradication, 40m.
29. 1961; United Nations Day, 40m.
30. 1962; President Bourguiba, 40m.
31. 1964; World Meteorological Day, 40m.
32. 1964; National Day, 30m.

UGANDA:
33. 1962; Independence, 20c.

UPPER VOLTA:
34. 1960; Animal masks, 4f.
35. 1963; Flowers, 1f.
36. 1963; Postage due, 1f.

ZAMBIA:
37. 1964; Independence, 6d.
38. 1964; Pictorial series, 3d.

ZANZIBAR:
39. 1957; Sultan Kalif bin Harub series, 5s.
40. 1961; Sultan Seyyid Sir Abdulla series, 2s.
41. 1963; Independence, 1s.30.
42. 1963; Freedom from Hunger, 1s.30.

PLATE 54

CANADA:
1. 1955; Eskimo hunter, 10c.
2. 1955; Wild life, 5c.
3. 1955; Civil aviation, 5c.
4. 1955; Alberta and Saskatchewan, 5c.
5. 1955; Boy Scouts, 5c.
6. 1956; Ice hockey, 5c.
7. 1956; Pulp and paper industry, 20c.
8. 1956; Fire prevention, 5c.
9. 1957; Wild life, 5c.
10. 1957; Sports, 5c.
11. 1957; David Thompson, 5c.
12. 1957; UPU, 15c.
13. 1957; Mining, 5c.
14. 1957; Royal visit, 5c.
15. 1958; Canadian press, 5c.
16. 1958; Geophysical Year, 5c.
17. 1958; British Columbia, 5c.
18. 1958; La Verendrye, 5c.
19. 1958; Quebec, 5c.
20. 1958; National Health, 5c.
21. 1958; Assembly, 5c.
22. 1959; 'Silver Dart', 5c.
23. 1958; Oil industry, 5c.
24. 1959; NATO, 5c.
25. 1959; Country women, 5c.
26. 1959; Royal visit, 5c.
27. 1959; St. Lawrence Seaway, 5c.
28. 1959; Plains of Abraham, 5c.
29. 1960; Girl Guides, 5c.
30. 1960; Long Sault, 5c.
31. 1961; Northern development, 5c.
32. 1961; E. Pauline Johnson, 5c.
33. 1961; Arthur Meighen, 5c.
34. 1961; Natural resources, 5c.
35. 1961; Colombo Plan, 5c.
36. 1962–4; Queen Elizabeth II, 4c.
37. 1963; Export trade, $1.
38. 1963; Postal service, $1.
39. 1964; Provincial emblems, 5c.
40. 1964; Charlottetown, 5c.
41. 1964; Quebec, 5c.
42. 1964; Christmas, 5c.

GREENLAND:
43. 1963; Polar bear, 5k.
44. 1963; N. Bohr, 60ö.

ST. PIERRE AND MIQUELON:
45. 1955–9; Pictorial series, 40c.
46. 1963; Birds, 1f.

PLATE 55

UNITED STATES OF AMERICA:
1. 1955; Land Grant Colleges, 3c.
2. 1955; Rotary International, 8c.
3. 1955; Armed Forces, 3c.
4. 1955; Soo Locks, 3c.
5. 1955; 'Atoms for peace', 3c.
6. 1955; Fort Ticonderoga, 3c.
7. 1955; A. W. Mellon, 3c.
8. 1956; Booker T. Washington, 3c.
9. 1956; Philatelic exhibition, 3c.
10. 1956; Wildlife conservation, 3c.
11. 1956; James Buchanan, 3c.
12. 1956; Nassau Hall, 3c.
13. 1957; Alexander Hamilton, 3c.
14. 1955; Pennsylvania Academy, 3c.
15. 1955; The Old Man of the Mountains, 3c.
16. 1956; Benjamin Franklin, 3c.

17. 1956; H. W. Wiley, 3c.
18. 1956; Labour Day, 3c.
19. 1956; Devil's Tower, 3c.
20. 1957; Infantile paralysis, 3c.
21. 1957; Survey, 3c.
22. 1957; Institute of Architects, 3c.
23. 1957; Oklahoma, 3c.
24. 1957; Air, 6c.
25. 1957; Shipbuilding, 3c.
26. 1958; Brussels Exhibition, 3c.
27. 1958; President Monroe, 3c.
28. 1958; Minnesota, 3c.
29. 1958; Geophysical Year, 3c.
30. 1958; Simon Bolivar, 8c.
31. 1960; Air, 7c.
32. 1958; Abraham Lincoln, 4c.
33. 1958; Lajos Kossuth, 4c.
34. 1958; Overland mail, 4c.
35. 1958; Noah Webster, 4c.
36. 1957; Steel industry, 3c.
37. 1957; President Magsaysay, 8c.
38. 1957; Marquis de Lafayette, 3c.
39. 1957; Wildlife, 3c.
40. 1957; Flushing Remonstrance, 3c.
41. 1958; Gardening, 3c.
42. 1958; Mackinac Bridge, 3c.

PLATE 56

UNITED STATES OF AMERICA:
1. 1958; Freedom of the press, 4c.
2. 1958; Forest conservation, 4c.
3. 1959; Petroleum, 4c.
4. 1959; Air, 10c.
5. 1960; Winter Olympics, 4c.
6. 1960; Forestry, 4c.
7. 1960; Camp Fire Girls, 4c.
8. 1958; Fort Duquesne, 4c.
9. 1959; San Martin, 4c.
10. 1959; Alaska Statehood, 7c.
11. 1959; NATO, 4c.
12. 1959; Arctic, 4c.
13. 1959; New flag, 4c.
14. 1959; Hawaiian statehood, 7c.
15. 1959; Dr E. McDowell, 4c.
16. 1960; American Credo, 4c.
17. 1959; Airmail, 15c.
18. 1960; Boy Scouts, 4c.
19. 1960; SEATO, 4c.
20. 1960; Water conservation, 4c.
21. 1960; Jan Paderewski, 4c.
22. 1960; American womanhood, 4c.
23. 1960; Robert A. Taft, 4c.
24. 1960; Motor industry, 4c.
25. 1960; Marshal Mannerheim, 4c.
26. 1960; Garibaldi, 4c.
27. 1961; Mahatma Gandhi, 8c.
28. 1960; Walter F. George, 4c.
29. 1961; Civil War, 4c.
30. 1961; Senator G. W. Norris, 4c.
31. 1961; Naval aviation, 4c.
32. 1962; New Mexico, 4c.
33. 1962; Project Mercury, 4c.
34. 1962; Civil War, 4c.
35. 1962; Louisiana, 4c.
36. 1962; Homestead Act, 4c.
37. 1961; Frederic Remington, 4c.
38. 1961; Nursing, 4c.
39. 1962; Girl Scouts, 4c.
40. 1962; Senator McMahon, 4c.
41. 1962; Arizona statehood, 4c.
42. 1962; Seattle exhibition, 4c.

PLATE 57

UNITED STATES OF AMERICA:
1. 1962; Apprenticeship, 4c.
2. 1962; Dag Hammarskjöld, 4c.
3. 1962; Christmas, 4c.
4. 1962; Higher Education, 4c.
5. 1962; Winslow Homer, 4c.
6. 1962–3; Andrew Jackson, 1c.
7. 1962; George Washington, 5c.
8. 1962; Airmail, 8c.
9. 1963; Airmail, 6c.
10. 1963; Carolina Charter, 5c.
11. 1963; Air, 15c.
12. 1963; West Virginia, 5c.
13. 1963; Civil War, 5c.
14. 1963; Flag, 5c.
15. 1963; Emancipation, 5c.
16. 1963; Alliance For Progress, 5c.
17. 1963; Eleanor Roosevelt, 5c.
18. 1963; National Academy, 5c.
19. 1963; Red Cross, 5c.
20. 1964; C. M. Russell, 5c.
21. 1964; World's Fair, 5c.
22. 1964; Civil War, 5c.
23. 1963; Christmas, 5c.
24. 1964; President Kennedy, 5c.
25. 1964; Nevada, 5c.
26. 1962; Sam Rayburn, 4c.
27. 1963; Freedom from Hunger, 5c.
28. 1963; Cordell Hull, 5c.
29. 1963; City Mail delivery, 5c.
30. 1963; John James Audubon, 5c.
31. 1964; John Muir, 5c.
32. 1964; New Jersey, 5c.
33. 1964; Register and Vote, 5c.
34. 1964; William Shakespeare, 5c.
35. 1964; Air, 8c.
36. 1964; Homemakers, 5c.
37. 1964; Mayo brothers, 5c.
38. 1964; Amateur Radio, 5c.

UNITED NATIONS:
39. 1956; Human Rights, 8c.
40. 1957; U.N. Emergency Force, 8c.
41. 1957; World Meteorological Organisation, 3c.
42. 1958; Central Hall, Westminster, 8c.
43. 1961; Flags, 30c.
44. 1964; Races united, 10c.

PLATE 58

BRITISH HONDURAS:
1. 1961; New Constitution, 15c.
2. 1960; Post Office centenary, 10c.
3. 1962; Birds definitive, 50c.

CANAL ZONE:
4. 1958; Theodore Roosevelt, 4c.

COSTA RICA:
5. 1957; War of 1856–7, 40c.
6. 1960; St. Vincent de Paul, 50c.
7. 1960; Obligatory tax, 5c.
8. 1963; Stamp centenary, 3col.
9. 1963; Archaeological discoveries, 25c.
10. 1963; Archaeological discoveries, 10c.

EL SALVADOR:
11. 1956; Chalatenango Province, 2c.
12. 1963; Birds, 40c.
13. 1959; President Lemus' visit to USA, 15c.
14. 1964; President Kennedy, 20c.
15. 1961; 150th anniversary of revolution, 30c.

HONDURAS:
16. 1959; Abraham Lincoln, 12c.
17. 1957; Revolutionary flag, 1c.
18. 1964; 1b. surcharged 30c.
19. 1964; Homage to sport, 5c.

MEXICO:
20. 1956; Portraits series, 1p.20.
21. 1956; Stamp centenary, 1p.20.
22. 1956; Centenary philatelic exhibition, 30c.
23. 1962; President Kennedy's visit, 80c.
24. 1956–72; Express letter, 1p.20.

NICARAGUA:
25. 1956; War of 1856, 30c.
26. 1957; Churches and priests, 2cor.
27. 1957; Merchant Marine, 30c.
28. 1958; Arms of La Salle, 30c.
29. 1959; Cardinal Spellman, 2cor.
30. 1961; Military Academy, 1cor.5.
31. 1961; Junior Chamber of Commerce, 4c.
32. 1962; Obligatory tax, 5c.
33. 1963; Independence anniversary, 30c.
34. 1964; Alliance for progress, 30c.
35. 1963; 'Blessing', 1cor.
36. 1959; Obligatory tax, 5c.

PANAMA:
37. 1958; Brussels Exhibition, 1b.
38. 1959; Obligatory tax, 1c.
39. 1959; National Institute, 21c.
40. 1962; Social Security Hospital, 3c.

PLATE 59

ARGENTINE REPUBLIC:
1. 1956–7; Portraits, 2p.40.
2. 1961; Pictorial definitive, 100p.
3. 1960; Stamp exhibition, 50c. + 50c.
4. 1961; Child Welfare, 1p.80. + 90c.
5. 1961; Child Welfare, 2p. + 1p.
6. 1963; Air, 18p.
7. 1962; Postal Union of Americas and Spain, 5p.60.
8. 1962; Portraits series, 2p.

BOLIVIA:
9. 1960; Unissued stamp surcharged, 800b.
10. 1962; Eucharistic Congress, 1,000b.
11. 1962; World Refugee Year stamp surcharged, 2,800b.
12. 1963; Alliance for Progress, 1p.20.

BRAZIL:
13. 1959; Brazilian–Portuguese Study Conference, 6cr.50.
14. 1955; Hydro-electric station, 60c.
15. 1955; Hydro-electric station, 40c.
16. 1955; Children's games, 60c.
17. 1960; Plan of Brasilia, 11cr.50.
18. 1960; Visit of Mexican President, 6cr.50.
19. 1961; Coffee Convention, 20cr.
20. 1963; Pan-American Games, 10cr.
21. 1964; Visit of West German President, 100cr.
22. 1964; Pope John XXIII, 20cr.

BRITISH GUIANA:
23. 1961; History and Culture Week, 30c.

CHILE:
24. 1955; President Prieto's death centenary, 3p.
25. 1958; Antarctic issue, 500p.
26. 1956; Air, 2p.
27. 1960–67; Pictorial series, 2c.

28. 1960; Air, 4m.
29. 1960; World Refugee Year, 10c.
30. 1961; Earthquake relief fund, 10c. + 10c.
31. 1960–65; 150th anniversary of first national government, 20c.
32. 1963; Fire Brigade centenary, 3c.

COLOMBIA:
33. 1955; Postal Union Congress, 23c.
34. 1956–8; Columbus memorial lighthouse, 3c.
35. 1958; Father Almanza, 10c.
36. 1959; Mons. R. M. Carrasquilla, 25c.
37. 1963; Alliance for Progress, 10c.
38. 1960; A. von Humboldt, 10c.
39. 1961; Atlántico tourist issue, 20c.
40. 1962–4; Women's Franchise, 45c.
41. 1963; Tennis championships, 55c.

PLATE 60

ECUADOR:
1. 1955; Rotary, 90c.
2. 1956; Printing, 1s.70.
3. 1960; Five-Year-Plan, 10c.
4. 1962; Duke of Edinburgh's visit, 2s.
5. 1964; Bananas, 4s.20.

GALAPAGOS ISLANDS:
6. 1959; United Nations, 2s.

ECUADOR:
7. 1964; President Kennedy, 10s.

PARAGUAY:
8. 1955; President Peron's visit, 5c.
9. 1955; Monseñor Rodriguez, 2g.
10. 1957; Chaco heroes, 1g.
11. 1962; Boy Scouts, 10c.
12. 1962; Malaria eradication, 30c.
13. 1962; Football, 25c.

PERU:
14. 1957; Air, 40c.
15. 1960; Pictorial series, 3s.80.
16. 1962; Pictorial series, 1s.80.

SURINAM:
17. 1961; Buildings, 15c.
18. 1961; Space, 20c.

URUGUAY:
19. 1956; President Batlle y Ordoñez, 31c.
20. 1958; Day of the Americas, 34c.
21. 1962–3; Birds, 3p.
22. 1958; Human Rights, 23c.
23. 1963; D. A. Larrañaga, 40c.
24. 1963; Alferez Campora, 10c.
25. 1964; Red Cross, 20c.

VENEZUELA:
26. 1957; Tamanaço Hotel, Caracas, 45c.
27. 1956–7; Book Festival, 20c.
28. 1958; GPO, Caracas, 65c.
29. 1958; Arms, 5c.
30. 1958; GPO, Caracas, 15c.
31. 1959; Trujillo, 20c.
32. 1959; Games, 50c.
33. 1959; Stamp centenary, 50c.
34. 1960; Pantheon, Caracas, 65c.
35. 1962; Orchids, 20c.
36. 1962; Birds, 5c.
37. 1963; Wildlife, 5c.
38. 1964; Pedro Gual, 1b.

PLATE 61

ANTIGUA:
1. 1962; Stamp centenary, 3c.
2. 1964; Shakespeare, 12c.

BAHAMAS:
3. 1962; Nassau centenary, 8d.
4. 1964; Olympic Games, 8d.

BARBADOS:
5. 1956; Elizabethan series, 24c.
6. 1962; Boy Scouts, 12c.

BERMUDA:
7. 1956; Yacht race, 1s. 3d.
8. 1959; Perot's post office, 6d.
9. 1959; Settlement, 1s. 3d.
10. 1962; Buildings definitive, 3d.

BRITISH ANTARCTIC TERRITORY:
11. 1964; Elizabethan series, 4d.

CAYMAN ISLANDS:
12. 1959; New Constitution, 1s.
13. 1962; Queen Elizabeth, £1.

CUBA:
14. 1957; Stamp Day, 4c.
15. 1957; Postal employees, 4c.
16. 1957; National Library, 4c.
17. 1957; J. J. Heredia, 8c.
18. 1957; TB, 1c.
19. 1956; Postal employees, 10c.
20. 1962; Labour Day, 3c.
21. 1962; Sports, 9c.
22. 1963; Museum, 9c.
23. 1963; Fruit, 1c.
24. 1964; Revolution, 13c.
25. 1964; Labour Day, 13c.
26. 1962; Cuban women, 9c.
27. 1961; Christmas, 5 × 2c.
28. 1962; Caribbean Games, 13c.
29. 1962; University Games, 1c.
30. 1963; Pan-American Games, 13c.
31. 1964; Zoo animals, 8c.
32. 1964; Carlos J. Finlay, 13c.

DOMINICA:
33. 1958; Caribbean Federation, 12c.
34. 1963; Pictorial definitive, 6c.

PLATE 62

DOMINICAN REPUBLIC:
1. 1957; Mahogany flower, 2c.
2. 1962; Malaria eradication, 13c.
3. 1964; Nubian monuments, 10c.

FALKLAND ISLANDS:
4. 1960; Elizabethan series, 1s.
5. 1960; Elizabethan definitive, 2s.

SOUTH GEORGIA:
6. 1963; Queen Elizabeth definitive, £1.

FALKLAND ISLANDS DEPENDENCIES:
7. 1956; Trans-Antarctic expedition, 6d.

GRENADA:
8. 1953–9; Elizabethan definitive, 25c.

HAITI:
9. 1959; Red Cross fund, 25c. + 25c.
10. 1961; President Duvalier, 25c.
11. 1959; Pope Pius XII, 2g.50.

JAMAICA:
12. 1955; Tercentenary, 2d.
13. 1956; Elizabethan series, 8d.
14. 1962; Independence, 2d.
15. 1962; Independence overprint, 1s.
16. 1962; Caribbean Games, 6d.
17. 1964; Miss World 1963, 1s.
18. 1963; Freedom from Hunger, 1d.
19. 1964; Stadium, 1s.
20. 1964; Human Rights, 1s.

MONTSERRAT:
21. 1953–8; Elizabethan set, 6c.

NETHERLANDS ANTILLES:
22. 1955; Caribbean Commission, 25c.
23. 1958; Church tower, 1g.
24. 1963; Child Welfare, 5c. + 2c.
25. 1963; Hotel Bonaire, 20c.
26. 1961; Child Welfare, 25c. + 8c.
27. 1963; Mental Health, 25c.
28. 1964; US–Curaçao flight, 25c.

ST. CHRISTOPHER, NEVIS AND ANGUILLA:
29. 1957; Alexander Hamilton, 24c.
30. 1963; Red Cross, 12c.
31. 1964; Arts festival, 25c.

ST. LUCIA:
32. 1960; Stamp centenary, 16c.
33. 1964; Pigeon Island, 15c.

ST. VINCENT:
34. 1955; Queen Elizabeth, 20c.
35. 1964; Boy Scouts, 1c.

TRINIDAD AND TOBAGO:
36. 1960; Pitch lake, 35c.
37. 1964; Girl Guides, 25c.

TURKS AND CAICOS ISLANDS:
38. 1957; Elizabethan series, 1s.
39. 1959; New Constitution, 8d.

VIRGIN ISLANDS:
40. 1962; US currency surcharge, 70c.
41. 1964; Road Harbour, 5c.

PLATE 63

AUSTRALIA:
1. 1955; Rotary, 3½d.
2. 1955; Elizabethan series, 1s. 0½d.
3. 1955; Australian–American friendship, 3½d.
4. 1955; Mail coach, 2s.
5. 1955; YMCA, 3½d.
6. 1955; Florence Nightingale, 3½d.
7. 1955; South Australian stamp centenary, 3½d.
8. 1956; Responsible government, 3½d.
9. 1956; Olympic Games, 2s.
10. 1957; Christmas, 3½d.
11. 1957; South Australia, 4d.
12. 1959; Queen Elizabeth, 1d.
13. 1958; Hall of Memory, 5½d.
14. 1958; Broken Hill, 4d.
15. 1954–61; Stockman, definitive, 5s.
16. 1959; Post office, 4d.
17. 1960; Girl Guides, 5d.

18. 1960; Northern Territory, 5d.
19. 1960; Melbourne Cup, 5d.
20. 1960; Queensland stamp centenary, 5d.
21. 1960; Christmas, 5d.
22. 1961; Dame Nellie Melba, 5d.
23. 1962; J. M. Stuart, 5d.
24. 1962; Inland Mission, 5d.
25. 1962; Commonwealth Games, 5d.
26. 1963; Canberra, 5d.
27. 1963; Red Cross, 5d.
28. 1963; Blue Mountains, 5d.
29. 1963; Export, 5d.
30. 1963; Elizabethan, 5d.
31. 1963–5; Explorers, 10s.
32. 1963; COMPAC, 2s. 3d.
33. 1964; Birds, 1s. 6d.
34. 1964; Airmail, 5d.
35. 1964; Christmas, 5d.

AUSTRALIAN ANTARCTIC TERRITORY:
36. 1957; Expedition, 2s.
37. 1961; Shackleton expedition, 5d.

CHRISTMAS ISLAND:
38. 1958; Queen Elizabeth, $1.
39. 1963; Pictorial series, $1.

COCOS (KEELING) ISLANDS:
40. 1963; Copra industry, 3d.

NAURU:
41. 1963; Pictorial definitive, 5d.

NORFOLK ISLAND:
42. 1956; Pitcairn islanders, 2s.
43. 1958; 7d. surcharge.
44. 1960; Queen Elizabeth II, 9d.
45. 1964; Slaughter Bay, 10d.

PAPUA–NEW GUINEA:
46. 1957; 4d. surcharge.
47. 1958–60; Cacao plant, 5d.
48. 1963; Port Moresby, 8d.

PLATE 64

NEW ZEALAND:
1. 1955; Stamp centenary, 2d.
2. 1955; Health, 1½d. + ½d.
3. 1955–9; Elizabethan series, 8d.
4. 1956; Southland, 8d.
5. 1957; Plunket Society, 3d.
6. 1957; Lamb export, 4d.
7. 1958; First Tasman flight, 6d.
8. 1958; Nelson, 3d.
9. 1958; Hawkes Bay, 2d.
10. 1959; Boy Scouts, 3d.
11. 1959; Health, 3d. + 1d.
12. 1960; Westland, 8d.
13. 1960; Pictorial definitive, 10s.
14. 1960; Health, 3d. + 1d.
15. 1960; Christmas, 2d.
16. 1962; Telegraph, 8d.
17. 1963; Railways, 3d.
18. 1964; Road Safety, 3d.
19. 1964; Christmas, 2½d.

BRITISH SOLOMON ISLANDS:
20. 1956; Elizabethan series, 1½d.

COOK ISLANDS:
21. 1963; Hibiscus, 6d.

FIJI:
22. 1954–6; Queen Elizabeth II, 1d.
23. 1959–63; Hibiscus, 8d.
24. 1962; Queen Elizabeth II, 3d.
25. 1963; South Pacific Games, 2s. 6d.

FRENCH POLYNESIA:
26. 1958; Girl on beach, 10f.
27. 1964; Dancer, 3f.
28. 1964; Landscapes, 20f.

GILBERT AND ELLICE ISLANDS:
29. 1956; Queen Elizabeth II series, 2s.

NEW CALEDONIA:
30. 1964; Olympic Games, 10f.
31. 1963; Red Cross, 37f.

NEW HEBRIDES:
32. 1956; Condominium, 50c.
33. 1963; Pictorial series, 2f.

PITCAIRN ISLANDS:
34. 1957; Elizabethan series, $2\frac{1}{2}$d.
35. 1964; Photogravure series, 2d.

ROSS DEPENDENCY:
36. 1957; Shackleton and Scott, 4d.

SAMOA:
37. 1963; Independence anniversary, 2s.
38. 1962; Independence, 1s.

ROSS DEPENDENCY:
39. 1957; Map, 8d.

TONGA:
40. 1961; Postal service, 1s.
41. 1962; Emancipation, 8d.

WALLIS AND FUTUNA ISLANDS:
42. 1962; Marine fauna, 25c.

1965-1975
General Survey of the Decade

After the dramatic changes in stamp design and production that took place in the middle period there were very few radical developments in the most recent decade. Consolidation was the keynote of this period and the novelties and gimmicks of the early 1960s were either accepted and became relatively commonplace, or were rejected out of hand. The transformation of the once humble postage stamp from a mere label denoting the prepayment of postage, into an extremely potent medium for advertising or promoting the national image, was completed in this period and those countries which hitherto had been slow to appreciate its potential, now made full use of stamps for this purpose. A superficial, snap judgment of the stamps of this decade would be that they had become much bigger, and there were many more of them. Both impressions, however, require to be qualified to some extent. It is true to say that in many countries the size of stamps increased particularly in the Communist bloc and the Third World, but also notably in the United States, France, Belgium, Canada and Brazil. Even in such countries as Sweden, that had previously had a long tradition of small-format stamps, the size of stamps increased significantly in the late 1960s and early 1970s. But it is important to note that the pendulum swung the other way in the 1970s. Japan in particular had mastered the art of reducing pictorial designs to a much smaller format than hitherto had been the case; and several countries, while embarking on jumbo-sized pictorial definitives, were forced to issue small-format stamps for use in automatic vending machines and stamp booklets.

The most significant feature of all, however, was the marked fluctuation in the numbers of different stamps issued throughout the world at different times in this decade. In 1965 the average global output of new issues had been steady for several years at about 3,000 stamps annually. Thereafter, it rose sharply and reached its peak in 1970 when approximately 7,000 stamps are thought to have been released. Since then the number has dropped considerably and in 1974–5 was estimated at about 5,000 stamps. The fluctuation in the output of stamps can be attributed to several factors. During the first half of this decade there was a sharp increase in the number of stamp-issuing countries, particularly in the Middle East where the various sheikhdoms and sultanates of the Arabian Gulf established independent postal administrations whose philatelic policies were largely in the hands of foreign philatelic agencies. In the period between 1965 and 1968, when the political situation in the Yemen and other parts of Southern Arabia was decidedly obscure, entrepreneurs from Spain, Lebanon and America seized the opportunity to manipulate stamp issues to their own advantage, but to the long-term detriment of the countries concerned. The majority of these stamps had absolutely no relevance to the sheikhdom concerned, but one must cite the example of Umm al Qiwain which celebrated the establishment of a 16 millimetre film theatre in 1969 by issuing a set of twelve stamps featuring clips from famous Hollywood epics; and, in the same year, a set of forty-eight stamps featuring vintage motor cars.

On an average, these Arab states, none of which had more than a few thousand inhabitants, each issued over a hundred stamps annually between 1965 and 1971 and thereby accounted for a fifth of the total world output. Distinctive stamps were superseded by a single issue on behalf of the United Arab Emirates from 1972 onwards, and these stamps were strictly controlled by the Crown Agents in whose capable hands the philatelic policy of the states now rests.

The late 1960s will probably be regarded in years to come as the hey-day of the commercial philatelic agencies who prospected the remote corners of the globe for any territory as yet unblessed by the doubtful benefits of its own stamps. As the supply of remote Himalayan kingdoms or Arab sultanates dried up, there was a tendency for certain countries to issue stamps for their 'dependencies'. This phenomenon may be blamed on the British Post Office which began issuing regional stamps as long ago as 1958, but these stamps were never regarded as more than a sop to the incipient nationalism of the Scots, Irish and Welsh, and as recognition of the anomalous position of the Crown dependencies of the Channel Islands and the Isle of Man that was a relic from feudal times. In 1966 the sheikhdoms of Ajman and Sharjah began producing separate issues ostensibly for use in their dependencies of Manama and Khor Fakkan, but as very few of the countless hundreds of stamps overprinted or inscribed for these two villages were actually used postally, the majority of international catalogue editors either listed them briefly in appendices or ignored them.

In 1968 the West Indian island of Barbuda suddenly began issuing its own stamps though it continued to form part of the postal administration of Antigua. The exact circumstances in which Barbuda came to issue its own stamps are obscure, but at least there were historic precedents for the issue, since Barbuda had had an overprinted series in the 1920s under the administration of the Leeward Islands. In contrast with the Arab states, Barbuda showed remarkable restraint, apart from a marathon series of thirty-seven 35-cent stamps portraying every English monarch from William the Conqueror to the present day. Antiguan stamps continued to be valid in Barbuda and vice versa, so the main purpose of these stamps seems to have been to raise revenue for Barbuda and its philatelic agent. In August 1971 the Antiguan authorities cancelled the contract with their philatelic agent and distinctive stamps were then discontinued, though the island issued an overprinted pair in 1973 in the royal wedding omnibus series and thereafter resumed its own distinctive issues.

The proliferation of stamp-issuing entities is a trend which, for one reason or another, is likely to continue. The reasons are partly political and partly philatelic. In the former category may be cited the territories that seceded from larger political units during this period. In this respect, some were more successful than others. Following the conferment of Associated Statehood status on the West Indian territory known as St. Christopher-Nevis-Anguilla, the last-named island seceded from the union and declared itself independent. At first, stamps inscribed 'St. Christopher-Nevis-Anguilla' were overprinted 'Independent Anguilla' but subsequently, distinctive Anguillan stamps were designed and produced under the auspices of a London stamp dealer who has acted as agent for the island ever since. After two years of 'cold war' which fortunately never degenerated into an actual outbreak of hostilities, St. Christopher and Nevis accepted the situation and recognised the stamps of Anguilla as valid on international mail, but continued to issue stamps bearing the names of all three islands. The British government rescinded the autonomy of Anguilla in 1971 and since then the island has been administered by a British Commissioner – a fact to which the inscription on Anguillan stamps since November 1971 has referred.

While Anguilla has survived its bid for independence, the eastern region of Nigeria failed in this respect. Fully a year elapsed after the eastern region declared itself independent as the Republic of Biafra, before its government issued stamps, and ordinary Nigerian stamps remained in circulation for some time. In this instance, it seems that the international entrepreneurs were slow off the mark. Eventually, however, Biafra came under the aegis of philatelic agencies, first in Portugal and latterly in France, who continued to produce stamps for some time after the last pocket of resistance had been wiped out by Federal Nigerian forces.

The appearance of new stamp-issuing countries is not, of course, synonymous with prolific output. In 1969 the British Post Office ceased to be a government department and was transformed into a nationalised corporation. At this time the Crown dependencies of the Channel Islands and the Isle of Man were given the option of continuing to use the facilities of the British Post Office, or establishing their own postal administrations. Both bailiwicks of Guernsey and Jersey chose the latter course and began issuing their own distinctive stamps in October 1969; but the Isle of Man continued to operate within the British postal administration until July 1973. All three islands have issued a large number of stamps since becoming postally independent but it cannot be said that they have overdone either the numbers or the face value of their stamps. Ecuador, which had issued a few stamps for the Galapagos Islands in the late 1950s, never developed this idea, and the continuance of separate issues in the Riau-Lingga archipelago and West Irian by the Indonesian authorities may be largely attributed to the fact that different currency systems are in force in these areas. Political motives undoubtedly explain the decision by Denmark to provide the Faeroe Islands with their own stamps in 1975. Here again, there have been several precedents for this, since the Faeroes have had to make do with locally produced surcharges and other make-shifts at various times between 1919 and 1941.

Although proliferation of stamp-issuing entities, on the scale of the Arab sheikhdoms in the late 1960s is, one hopes, a thing of the past, there has been a resurgence of this phenomenon in very recent years. In 1972–3 two islands of the Cook Islands group began issuing their own stamps with little apparent justification, although both of them, Aitutaki and Penrhyn, had their own stamps between 1902 and 1932 under New Zealand auspices. No such precedent exists in the case of the Grenadines, a string of islands in the West Indies, some of which are governed by Grenada and some, by St. Vincent. Both groups of Grenadines sprang to life, philatelically, in 1973 with stamps of their respective parent island overprinted in honour of the wedding of Princess Anne. Both groups have subsequently pursued a comparatively prolific policy.

Despite the fragmentation of postal administrations into smaller units, the number of stamp-issuing countries has remained remarkably stable in recent years. The emergence of Bangladesh in 1971 is balanced by the demise of the Mutawakelite Kingdom of the Yemen which disappeared in a final blaze of philatelic notoriety in 1970. The shrinking Spanish colonial empire was further diminished by the amalgamation of Fernando Pó and Rio Muni to form Equatorial Guinea in 1968 and by the transfer of Ifni to Morocco. Zanzibar ceased issuing stamps in 1968 when its postal service was fully integrated with mainland Tanzania, but this was balanced by the emergence of the British Indian Ocean Territory (carved from former dependencies of Mauritius and the Seychelles) with its own stamps in the same year. The number of countries, therefore, has tended to remain the same, even though the output of issues has not.

The commercial philatelic agencies not only created a need for distinctive stamps, but they also managed to win substantial contracts in a number of countries that had always managed their own affairs tolerably well in the past. It is important to realise that there are as many kinds of agency as there are agents and they ranged in this decade from the highly respectable and prestigious Crown Agents in London, who handled stamps for many Commonwealth countries, the United Nations, Egypt and even Russia during this period, to the ephemeral 'one-man' organisations who might handle only a single issue of a country before their less than scrupulous activities were unmasked. While highly responsible organisations such as the Crown Agents continually exerted a moderating influence on the philatelic policies of the countries for whom they acted, it is evident that in many other instances the increase in output was directly related to the degree of freedom given by a country to its external agency. In its most extreme form, this resulted in hundreds of unnecessary and irrelevant issues being marketed in London, Paris or New York for a country that might be totally oblivious of the fact that such stamps were being produced in its name – and with none of the resulting revenue finding its way back to the country concerned.

The activities of the less scrupulous agencies reached their peak in the late 1960s, but as the philatelic public became aware of their excesses, sales fell dramatically. Countries which hitherto had enjoyed a wide measure of popularity with collectors, found there was no longer any demand for their stamps. Unsold stocks of commemoratives were often over-printed for other occasions – a time-honoured device that has never met with favour among collectors – and the popularity of the countries concerned slipped even further. In the end, many of these countries became aware of the damage which was being done and revoked the contracts with their agencies. One could cite examples of former British colonies which, on gaining independence, had transferred their agencies from the Crown Agents to commercial organizations and then, after a period of years, had called in the Crown Agents to salvage the wreck of their reputations and sadly depleted sales.

The law of diminishing returns, however, operated on a global scale. With more and more countries competing for a diminishing slice of the philatelic cake, it no longer sufficed to outdo rivals by producing bigger and brighter stamps. The collecting public was becoming satiated with space and art stamps, and as world-wide output rose, most collectors concentrated their attention and their money on a more limited range of countries. Realising that collectors were being mulcted beyond endurance, many countries applied the brakes to their new-issue programmes and it is significant that since 1970 there has been a drastic cut-back of output in many

European countries and, in the territories handled by the Crown Agents. In others, such as Russia, where output has always been very high, the rate of increase has slowed down dramatically or even fallen back slightly.

The Fédération Internationale de Philatélie took the lead in black-listing unnecessary or speculative issues and imposed a ban on the display of these stamps at national or international exhibitions held under its aegis. The world's most influential catalogue publishers, Stanley Gibbons, at first refused to list these stamps at all, but eventually gave them the briefest of listings in appendices to their catalogues, and other publishers listed them in full, but indicated their disapproval by a system of black blots. Various attempts were made by trade organisations to boycott certain issues, but as there were always dealers and collectors prepared to break such embargoes, these policies were not very successful. At the highest level, the Universal Postal Union tried to discourage its members from issuing too many stamps, but such exhortation fell largely on deaf ears. The solution to the problem rested almost entirely in the hands of philatelists themselves. So long as they were prepared to go on paying good money for what was derisively dubbed 'wall-paper', the spate of new stamps would continue unchecked. Only when collectors became more discriminating in the quest for material to illustrate and complete their thematic collections did the situation improve. At the same time, dealers were forced by rising costs to restrict their new-issue business to a relatively few popular countries and, from about 1971 onwards, the sales of stamps of many of the more philatelically conscious countries started to fall dramatically. Vast quantities of unsold stamps from many of the philatelic agencies were dumped on the market and flooded the juvenile packet trade in Europe and America. The unedifying spectacle of rival agencies bickering in public, and each claiming to be the legitimate agent for the stamps of certain Arab states, tended to undermine public confidence in these stamps.

The philatelic market has matured and hardened considerably in very recent years. Rising costs of postal services have led to rapid increases in postal rates and, consequently, the outlay required to purchase the new stamps of most countries; since commemoratives, thematic sets and other special issues tend to reflect the most used denominations. This in itself has been an important factor in persuading many postal administrations to cut down on the number of new stamps issued each year. Moreover, during the past decade there have been tremendous developments all over the world in the mechanization of the posts. In particular the use of postage meters and permit mailing systems has been enormously expanded, thereby largely eliminating adhesive postage stamps from business correspondence. Nevertheless, the value of the adhesive stamp as an advertising medium and as a source of revenue will ensure its survival.

The End of Colonialism

If the process of decolonisation was accelerated in the previous decade, it was virtually completed in the present one. The pattern changed in the late 1960s and early 1970s. So far as Belgium, France and the Netherlands were concerned the process had been completed in the early 1960s; and only Britain, Portugal and Spain retained any sizeable overseas possessions. Spain granted independence to its two provinces in what has since become the republic of Equatorial Guinea and handed over Ifni to Morocco, leaving only the relatively unimportant and sparsely populated province of Spanish Sahara. Britain had already granted independence to the larger and more economically viable colonies and it was necessary now to ensure that the remaining territories were able to support themselves economically and politically. Several of the West Indian islands were granted a form of independence known as Associated Statehood – autonomy in free association with the United Kingdom – while the level of ministerial or responsible government in the other islands was raised as far as possible.

As the old British Empire was gradually dissolved, other countries looked on its fragments with covetous eyes. The independence accorded in 1965 to Guyana – formerly British Guiana – led to a revival of neighbouring Venezuela's claims to the western districts, and this manifested itself in several 'map' issues of the late 1960s and 1970s. Guatemala stepped up its claim to British Honduras, which became independent under the name of Belize in 1973, and Argentina continued to agitate for the cession of the Falkland Islands and its dependencies. There were even rumours that the British government was seeking some form of accommodation with Argentina over the Falklands but this did not materialise.

Speculation over the future of Gibraltar led to the revival of the Spanish claim, countered by vociferous resistance from the people of Gibraltar who voted decisively in a referendum against incorporation with Spain. No reference was made to this in Gibraltar's stamps, but Spain issued two stamps showing views of Gibraltar, ostensibly to raise funds for Spanish workers deprived of their jobs in Gibraltar, after the Spanish government applied economic sanctions to the British colony.

In Africa the process of decolonisation ran into difficulties over Rhodesia which had enjoyed the anomalous status of a self-governing colony since 1924. Although independent for all practical purposes, it was still under a measure of control from London, and the clash between the British and Rhodesian governments in 1965 over the principle of majority rule by the predominantly black population, resulted in the unilateral declaration of independence in November of that year. As part of the economic sanctions imposed by Britain on Rhodesia, there was a ban on the import of Rhodesian stamps and this continues to this day. At first, letters from Rhodesia to Britain were treated as unpaid if they bore the 'independence' stamps and accordingly were surcharged at double rates. This measure hit at the friends and relatives of Rhodesians and was regarded as an unnecessarily petty measure. It was rescinded by the Conservative government when it came to power in 1970 and has not been re-imposed by the Labour government since its return to power in 1974. At first, magazines and catalogues were not even allowed to illustrate Rhodesian stamps, but this ban has been relaxed in recent years, though trading in the stamps is still strictly forbidden.

The three British High Commission territories in southern Africa – Basutoland, Bechuanaland and Swaziland – all became independent in this period, the first two changing their names to Lesotho and Botswana respectively. By the end of the decade British colonial administration was confined to a sprinkling of islands in the South Atlantic, too small ever to become viable as independent countries, and too remote to be integrated with Britain or to be directly represented in the United Kingdom parliament.

The reaction against colonialism elsewhere in Africa led to the long and bitter war by various liberation movements against Portuguese rule in Angola, Mozambique and Guinea. This war of attrition finally brought down the right-wing dictatorship that had ruled Portugal itself for more than forty years and one of the first acts of the new left-wing government was to promise independence for the major Portuguese colonies. As 1974 drew to a close, Angola and Mozambique were decolonised, though not without serious internal troubles, and doubts for the future of the 'white' African countries of Rhodesia and South Africa.

The problem of granting independence to the remote Cape Verde Islands was solved by uniting the colony with Guinea-Bissau. Decolonisation in Africa had repercussions in other directions. The Afro-Shirazi Party rose in revolt against Arab rule in Zanzibar which was subsequently linked to Tanganyika to form the republic of Tanzania. Separatist movements in the southern Sudan and Eritrea have been struggling for independence against the Sudan and Ethiopia respectively, and pressure has been brought to bear by the United Nations on South Africa to remove its control from South West Africa, or Namibia as it is known in other parts of the continent. Stamps focusing world attention on Namibia have been issued in recent years by the United Nations and several other countries, though this name has not, as yet, appeared on the stamps of that country.

There were a few minor changes in those territories which remained under colonial administration. The French Somali Coast changed its name in 1967 to the French Territory of the Afars and Issas – the principal tribes of the area – to avoid any confusion with the neighbouring republic of Somalia with whom relations were increasingly strained. The granting of increasing measures of independence to the Seychelles and Mauritius led Britain to detach small remote groups of islands of some strategic importance from them both and these formed a separate crown colony known as the British Indian Ocean Territory.

In the Pacific, Australia and New Zealand had taken over the role of colonial powers from Britain, but as the decade progressed they relinquished most of their powers. The former German colonies of Nauru and Samoa, administered respectively by Australia and New Zealand under mandate from the League of Nations and, subsequently, from the United Nations, became Trust Territories as a prelude to independence granted in the 1960s. Nauru, subsequently, was admitted to membership of the British Commonwealth of Nations and Samoa maintains close links with New Zealand. Papua and New Guinea, formerly colonies of Britain and Germany respectively, had been administered by Australia for many years, but in the 1970s progressed towards independence.

At the beginning of this decade New Zealand granted internal self-government to the Cook Islands, but retained control over the island of Niue; by 1974 independence was conferred on Niue which has since continued in 'free association' with New Zealand. Fiji became independent in 1970 but has continued to maintain very close links with Britain, and is the headquarters of the Western Pacific High Commission which administers the scattered British colonies of Pitcairn, the Gilbert and Ellice Islands and the British Solomon Islands Protectorate. The various constitutional changes in the Pacific islands have been meticulously recorded in stamps.

Colonialism came to an end in every part of the world and was replaced by the free association of sovereign states in various economic, customs, postal and defence unions. These gave rise to a number of omnibus issues that have not, as yet, approached the 'Europa' or 'Norden' themes in uniformity of design. In this category come the stamps of the West Indies honouring Carifta (the Caribbean Free Trade Association), the stamps of Latin America honouring the Alliance for Progress and the OAS (Organisation of American States), the stamps of the Australian, British, French and independent Pacific islands publicising the South Pacific Commission, and the stamps of the African countries for such bodies as the Organisation of African Unity and the African Development Bank. At the purely postal level there was an increase in the number and importance of local postal unions. At one extreme came the example of Kenya, Tanzania and Uganda who combined their postal services in the East African Posts and Telecommunications Corporation, issuing joint commemorative and special issues, while the definitives of each country were valid in the other two. At the other extreme were the more loosely defined postal unions of the Arab states, the Latin-American countries and their former mother country, Spain (UPAE), and the postal union of the former French colonies in Africa and Madagascar.

European Unity

Politically, the keynotes of this decade in Europe were the various attempts to integrate the countries of western Europe more closely in the economic and political spheres. Philatelically, these were reflected in the stamps issued by the Council of Europe at Strasbourg, in the growth of the annual Europa issues by the countries adhering to the CEPT (Conférence Européen des Postes et Télécommunications) and in the omnibus issues of 1967, marking the European Free Trade Area and 1973, for the enlargement of the European Economic Community. On the other side of the Iron Curtain there was a corresponding growth of philatelic interest in Comecon, the Council for Mutual Aid, particularly in 1974 when its 25th anniversary was celebrated by stamps from the member countries.

The most significant development in Europe, however, was the gradual breakdown in the power blocs that had polarised during the Cold War. In 1969 Yugoslavia became the first Communist country to take part in the annual 'Europa' issues. More important was the enlargement of the Europa concept in 1972 when it was applied to stamps issued in several countries to mark the first European Security and Co-operation Conference, held in Helsinki, Finland. Subsequent conferences, involving countries of both eastern and western Europe as well as the North American members of NATO (Canada and the United States), have been marked by stamps of several of the participating countries with designs symbolising the peaceful unity of Europe.

Détente and Peaceful Co-existence

In the field of international relations, especially between the super-powers, the previous decade was highlighted by the 'brinkmanship' of John Foster Dulles and the epic confrontation of the United States and the Soviet Union during the Cuban missile crisis. The following decade, by contrast, inaugurated the era of the 'hot line', of *détente* between East and West, of West German Chancellor Brandt's *Ostpolitik* and of peaceful co-existence between Communism and the new political forces of the Third World. When posterity writes its epitaph on the ill-starred Nixon administration it may well regard President Nixon's role in diminishing the fears and hostilities of the great power blocs as his lasting achievement.

The international recognition of the People's Republic of China and its admission to the United Nations in 1971 was an important step towards stability in the Far East. The logical outcome of this was the unseating of the Nationalist Chinese representative from the UN Security Council and the allocation of the vacancy to the People's Republic. As relations between Communist China and the free world gradually became normal in the 1970s, Taiwan became increasingly isolated. The swing from Nationalist to Communist China in world affairs was reflected in the stamps issued by both countries, culminating in Taiwan's 'dignity with self-reliance' definitives of 1972.

Closer co-operation with the Communist world led to a relaxation of the American ban on philatelic trading with Communist China and other countries whose stamps were subsequently given full catalogue status in American publications. There was a significant lessening of the anti-American bias in the propaganda stamps issued by the Communist countries of Asia after the withdrawal of American forces from Vietnam. Moves towards reconciliation between the two régimes in Korea, however, were not reflected in the stamps of North or South Korea, both of whom continued to use philately as a medium for attacking each other's ideological stance. The widening rift between the Soviet Union and Communist China was ignored in Soviet stamps and Mongolia, which was closely embroiled in the power struggle in Central Asia, tactfully avoided taking sides and largely confined her stamps to non-controversial topics. Communist China, on the other hand, issued several sets from 1969 onwards, referring to the heroic defence of the Ussuri River area and marking subsequent anniversaries of this border conflict. Significantly China was the only Communist country not to issue stamps in honour of the birth centenary of Lenin in 1970, and even more significantly the only non-Chinese to be portrayed on stamps of that country after the Lenin ninety-fifth birthday stamps of 1965 was Enver Hoxha, the Albanian leader and China's only ally among the Communist countries of Europe.

The stamps of the People's Republic of China in this decade mirrored the introspective nature of the political scene. The great majority of the stamps issued between 1966 – when the Cultural Revolution broke out – and 1969, quoted extensively from the works of Chairman Mao or bore his portrait, often in a symbolic context, such as the series of 1967 which showed his image radiating like the sun above an admiring crowd.

In Europe, however, the conflict of ideologies was played down, at least so far as stamps were concerned. There was a much greater readiness, for example, for the Communist countries to honour American space achievements, especially the Apollo moon-landings and the subsequent Skylab mission. At a more humble level, events in the Western world, especially those concerning sport, were more frequently commemorated by stamps from Eastern Europe than before. This tendency was not matched by any reciprocal commemoration of Soviet events and personalities, in the West, but significantly there was an increase in the number of stamps issued by the emergent countries of the Third World, culminating in the numerous Lenin commemoratives of 1970. In West Germany, where Brandt's *Ostpolitik* did much to restore relations with the German Democratic Republic, Poland and Russia, it might even be said that stamps tended to negate the government's official policy. The Federal postal administration appears to have been incredibly tactless in issuing stamps devoted to 'twelve centuries of German architecture', showing buildings in towns or cities that now form part of East Germany, Poland or Russia. The appearance of these stamps, and the Brandenburg Gate definitives of 1966–8, seemed to imply that German *revanchismus* was not dead. To be sure, West Germany issued a stamp in honour of Karl Marx, on the occasion of the 150th anniversary of his birth in 1968, despite the fact that the ideology which he had founded was officially banned in the Federal Republic.

The Upheavals of War

Although the decade ended on a hopeful note, with the end of the war in Vietnam and curbs on American commitments in other parts of South-East Asia, the spectre of war had haunted much of the world throughout this period. The Vietnam War, at its height, had involved the total populations of both North and South Vietnam as well as the armed forces of the United States, Australia, New Zealand, Korea and China to a greater or lesser extent, and world opinion on the conduct of the war was evenly divided along ideological lines. Thus, while many countries in the Communist bloc and the Third World issued stamps showing sympathy for the struggles of the Vietnamese against American imperialism, only those countries directly involved issued stamps proposing the opposite point of view.

Apart from South Vietnam, whose morale-boosting stamps were legion, South Korea alone issued stamps expressing solidarity with the South Vietnamese. Australia ignored the war, New Zealand referred to it only obliquely in the Armed Services series of 1968, and the United States likewise made only passing and indirect reference to it, in a stamp of 1966 marking the 25th anniversary of the Savings Bank. The design featured the Stars and Stripes and the Statue of Liberty, with the caption 'We Appreciate our Servicemen'. Philatelically the most interesting aspect of the Vietnam war was the appearance of stamps purporting to be issued by the National Liberation Front, and latterly by the South Vietnam Provisional Revolutionary Government. These stamps, many of which had virulently anti-American themes, were distributed by the philatelic bureau in Hanoi, but doubts have been expressed as to their postal validity.

The other major trouble spot in this period, as in the previous decades, was the Middle East, where the hostility between Israel and her Arab neighbours flared up into open war on two occasions. Israel's pre-emptive strike against Egypt and Syria in June 1967 resulted in the shortest of blitzkriegs which left Israel in possession of the controversial Gaza strip, the west bank of the Jordan, the entire Sinai peninsula, the Golan Heights and even the left bank of the Suez Canal which henceforward was closed to all shipping. The balance was redressed to some extent by the Yom Kippur war of 1973 when Egypt regained the east bank of the canal, but the larger issues, of Arab recognition of the Jewish national state, or of the creation of a separate Arab state for the displaced Palestinians, were left unresolved. Philatelically, the period between 1965 and 1973 was marked by the disappearance of the Palestinian issues produced by Egypt for the Gaza district, by the issue of Indian stamps overprinted UNEF (for the use of Indian troops serving with the United Nations Emergency Force which policed the Gaza strip shortly before the June War), and by the use of Israeli stamps in areas that formerly had been part of Egypt, Jordan and Syria. There was an increase in the number of stamps issued all over the Arab world to mark Palestine Day, and Israel produced numerous stamps commemorating the re-unification of Jerusalem and other aspects of the wars.

Tension in the Middle East was not confined to the Arab-Israeli conflict. The deterioration in relations between India and Pakistan was charted by stamps issued on both sides, and the Indo–Pakistani War of 1971 resulted in the establishment of the independent republic of Bangladesh. The struggles of the Kurds against Iraq and the Nagas against India gave rise to various issues of labels purporting to be stamps of the liberation movements, but none of these is regarded as authentic. India referred to the Nagaland troubles in a propaganda stamp of 1967. The protracted struggle between the royalist guerrillas and the republican government in the Yemen continued for much of this decade. Even after the guerrillas ended their struggle, stamps allegedly issued on behalf of the Mutawakelite Kingdom of the Yemen mysteriously appeared on the philatelic market, but they were roundly condemned as bogus and were the subject of a lengthy fraud trial in London in 1974.

The withdrawal of the British from southern Arabia between 1967 and 1971 had important repercussions on the philately of the area. The South Arabian Federation, formerly Aden, became fully independent in 1967 after a long guerrilla campaign, and the National Liberation Front subsequently suppressed the multitude of semi-independent sheikhdoms and sultanates which constituted the former Aden protectorates. The victory of the guerrillas effectively frustrated various attempts to provide these tiny states with a super-abundance of stamps. In the closing months of 1967, for example, the remote state of Upper Yafa is alleged to have produced almost a hundred different stamps, though officials of the NLF have stated that none of these stamps was ever issued in that area. The Federation of South Arabia changed its name to the People's Democratic Republic of Southern Yemen (1968) and then to the Yemen People's Democratic Republic (1971). The withdrawal of the British presence from the Gulf area had a fortuitous effect on the philately of this region. The political unification of the various states, to form the United Arab Emirates, put an end to the torrent of unnecessary stamps that had made these diminutive countries the laughing-stock of the stamp world. The long drawn-out struggle between the British-backed Sultan of Muscat and Oman and the guerrilla movement led by the Imam of Oman, led to the issue of stamps purporting to come from the 'Imamate of Oman'. These stamps were undoubtedly 'masterminded' by an external philatelic agency and were roundly condemned by the Crown Agents (who acted for the Sultan). There seems to have been little use of or justification for the Imamate stamps, which so far, have been ignored in stamp catalogues. The turbulent political situation however, was reflected in the country's change of name, from the Sultanate of Muscat and Oman, to the Sultanate of Oman, in 1971.

The attempt to overthrow the government of Archbishop Makarios of Cyprus in 1974 led to a brief civil war and the intervention of Turkey, which now controls the north-eastern part of the island. Distinctive stamps have been issued that are used on mail carried in the Turkish sector and they have gradually received international recognition since the beginning of 1975. The other outcome of the Cypriot war was the downfall of the military régime in Greece which had backed the coup to oust Makarios. The return to democratic government in Greece had no visible effect on Greek stamps, and Portugal's stamps were unaffected when her right-wing government was toppled earlier in the same year. In South America, the overthrow of the Allende government, the first freely elected Marxist government in the Western Hemisphere, had little effect on the stamps of Chile, but several countries in Latin America, Eastern Europe and the 'non-aligned' parts of the Third World, have subsequently issued stamps in memory of Allende and his colleagues who were killed during the military coup.

Omnibus Issues
There was a marked increase in the number of events and personalities honoured by issues of stamps on a global basis. Omnibus issues continued to be a popular feature of the philately of the countries of the French group, but they had a mixed reception in the British Commonwealth. The reason for this is not far to seek. The Crown Agents undoubtedly overdid the omnibus issues in the early part of this decade.

From only two colonial omnibus issues throughout the 'colonial ensemble' between 1955 and 1964, the number rose rapidly in the period from mid-1965 to the end of 1966. Between twenty and thirty-three colonies, protectorates and dependencies issued stamps on six occasions, honouring the centenary of the International Telecommunications Union, International Co-operation Year (1965), Sir Winston Churchill, the World Cup football championship, the World Health Organisation and UNESCO (1966). The monotony of the symbolic designs and their dreary uniformity, made most of these issues unpopular. Six years elapsed before the Crown Agents returned to the omnibus issue as a convenient way of handling commemorative stamps for a number of countries simultaneously. For the royal silver wedding of 1972, however, they took care to produce distinctive motifs for each territory, even though the portraits of the Queen and the Duke of Edinburgh were uniform throughout. This issue was an unrivalled success and probably encouraged the authorities concerned to revert to purely uniform designs for the stamps issued a year later, to celebrate the wedding of Princess Anne and Captain Mark Phillips. Significantly, the number of territories issuing these stamps rose slightly above those of 1965–6, thirty-nine in both instances. For the centenary of the birth of Sir Winston Churchill, however, individual designs were produced for each of the participating countries and an enormous variety of portraiture was employed.

The principle of the omnibus issue even spread behind the Iron Curtain in 1965, when stamps featuring a red flag and profiles of Marx and Lenin were issued by those countries represented at the conference of postal ministers in Peking. Several omnibus issues were made by the Netherlands and its overseas associates, the Netherlands Antilles and Surinam, and on two occasions, the Nordic countries (Denmark, Finland, Iceland, Norway and Sweden) issued stamps in uniform designs – to mark the jubilee of the Northern Countries Union (1969) and Nordic postal co-operation (1973). Belgium and Luxembourg issued stamps in common designs in 1972 to mark the jubilee of their economic union, and, with the Netherlands, they issued stamps in an identical design in 1969 to celebrate the 25th anniversary of the Benelux Customs Union.

Apart from these, the 'Europa' stamps each year remained the only regular omnibus issue and even here the monotony of the designs began to tell. Up to 1974, a single symbolic motif was chosen as the basis of each year's stamps and the only variation lay in the different styles of lettering, format and printing processes employed. Whether it was the monotony of these symbolic designs or the exhaustion of suitable motifs cannot be ascertained, but by 1974 the CEPT members, though not wishing to jeopardise the solidarity of the organisation, nevertheless felt that a change was necessary. As a result it was decided to issue stamps showing the CEPT badge and the 'Europa' inscription and using a set theme, but it was left to individual countries to decide how the theme should be interpreted. For 1974, therefore, the theme of sculpture was selected and a wide range of statuary, from classical and baroque to abstract and modern, resulted. In 1975 the theme was paintings and here again the range of subjects was exceedingly varied.

Incidental Philately
The increase in the number of omnibus issues produced by the British and French colonial groups resulted partly from the increasing number of occasions felt to be worthy of commemoration on a world-wide basis. Very few of these issues commemorated historic anniversaries and it is interesting to note the events that were universally regarded as important.

The centenaries of the International Telecommunications Union (1965) and the Universal Postal Union (1974) were fairly obvious choices, but the jubilee of Interpol (1973) seems somewhat esoteric. Curiously enough, slightly fewer stamps were issued to mark the UPU centenary than had been issued in 1949–50 for the 75th anniversary of that body.

Those countries with an interest in the polar regions issued stamps in 1971 to mark the 10th anniversary of the Antarctic Treaty, and many countries in the tropical zone, issued stamps in 1973 to commemorate the centenary of the discovery of the leprosy bacillus by Dr. Armauer Hansen, whose portrait was featured on many of these stamps. Several countries – mainly in Asia, but including Belgium – commemorated the 2500th anniversary of the Persian Empire in 1971. The remaining anniversary issues were concerned with the United Nations or its specialized agencies and consisted of the golden jubilee of the International Labour Organisation (1969), the silver jubilee of the United Nations Charter (1970), the centenary of the International Meteorological Office (now the World Meteorological Office) in 1973 and the 20th and 25th anniversaries of UNESCO and UNICEF (1966 and 1971).

Many stamps were issued in 1966, in honour of the inauguration of the new headquarters of the World Health Organisation in Geneva and included a British colonial omnibus issue. Subsequently, similar issues throughout the world, commemorated the opening of new headquarters buildings for the Universal Postal Union (1971) and the International Labour Organisation (1973). The United Nations deliberately fostered incidental philately, to promote its aims or focus world attention on important social and economic problems. In some cases, these occasions were linked to anniversaries, such as International Co-operation Year (1965) which marked the 20th anniversary of the United Nations, or Human Rights Year (1968), honouring the 20th anniversary of the *Declaration of Human Rights*. This idea was then developed on an annual basis and countries were urged to issue stamps in honour of International Education Year and Nature Conservation Year (both 1970), Racial Equality Year (1971), International Book Year (1972), International Tree-planting Year (1973), International Population Year (1974) and International Women's Year (1975). Similarly, World Health Day in 1972 focused attention on heart disease and stamps with this theme were produced in many countries. In 1975 the concept was applied on a more limited geographical basis and resulted in stamps being issued to mark European Architectural Heritage Year.

The various American space flights, from the Apollo moon shots to the Skylab mission, precipitated a large number of stamps from many countries, but these stamps appeared haphazardly and without any co-ordination. The maiden flight of the Anglo–French Concorde was celebrated in 1969, not only by the countries involved, but also by the French colonial group – though the British colonial ensemble overlooked the occasion. World's Fairs produced a fine crop of stamps on both occasions: Canada's Expo '67 and Japan's Osaka '70 – but America's Hemisfair '68 was ignored outside the United States. Scouting, which hitherto had been one of the most popular themes, suffered a decline. The Idaho Jamboree of 1967, which coincided with the diamond jubilee of the movement, resulted in fewer stamps throughout the world than the golden jubilee jamboree ten years previously. Sporting events, however, were well to the fore with a marked increase in both current and pre-publicity issues connected with both the Mexico City and Munich Olympic Games (1968 and 1972) and the corresponding Winter Games at Grenoble and Sapporo. Three World Cup football championships fell within this decade and in each case the number of countries participating in stamp issues rose steadily.

There was a slight increase in the number of people honoured by stamps, though the selection of subjects is interesting. The decade began with world-wide commemoration of the 700th anniversary of the birth of Dante, and a number of countries, mainly among the African emergent nations, issued stamps to mark the centenary of the death of Abraham Lincoln. Interest in John F. Kennedy remained strong throughout the late 1960s and several countries returned to this subject almost at annual intervals. There was a fresh crop of Kennedy commemoratives on what would have been his fiftieth birthday in 1967 and, following the assassination of his brother Robert, a number of stamps linked the two men. Sir Winston Churchill died in January 1965 and was subsequently mourned during the next two years by a colonial omnibus issue and a spate of stamps from a wide range of countries, principally the 'agency' countries of the French group, Latin America and the Arabian Gulf. By 1968 it was becoming fashionable for many countries to issue mourning stamps, even if the person in question had never been concerned with them. The issue of stamps honouring Dr. Martin Luther King, by the West Indian countries, was understandable, as were the issues of the African states, but the many countries of the Third World that commemorated Germany's chancellor Adenauer and France's President De Gaulle were mainly taking advantage of the topicality of their deaths.

Many countries, including Britain, issued stamps in 1969 to mark the centenary of the birth of Mahatma Gandhi. The following year, Charles Dickens, Beethoven, Lenin and Franklin D. Roosevelt were commemorated. In 1971 a prominent French personality was commemorated, mainly as one would have expected, in France and the countries associated with the French Community. These stamps marked the 150th anniversary of the death of Napoléon. It is worth noting that two British Commonwealth territories honoured Napoléon – St. Lucia (birthplace of his wife, Josephine Beauharnais) and St. Helena (where he died). In 1972 another French personality was honoured by stamps all over the world, mainly in the French Community, though several Arab sheikhdoms profited from the topicality of the event. These stamps paid tribute to the late President De Gaulle and provided a pretext for a certain amount of nostalgic reflection on the wartime exploits of the Free French, rather than on more recent events. Another statesman who died that year, President Nasser, was honoured by stamps that were confined to the Arab countries and the emergent nations of Africa. The countries of southern, central and eastern Africa issued stamps in 1973 to mark the centenary of the death of David Livingstone; Britain issued two stamps portraying Livingstone and Sir Henry Stanley *se-tenant* against maps of the Dark Continent. The major celebrity of 1973, however, was the Polish philosopher and astronomer, Copernicus, whose quingentenary was celebrated all over the world and whose portraits dominated Polish stamps over a period of eighteen months. The only subject of world-wide philatelic commemoration twice in the same decade, was Sir Winston Churchill, the centenary of whose birth was celebrated in November 1974. Several countries that had omitted to issue mourning stamps in 1965–6 compensated by honouring his centenary, but the main commemoration came from Britain and the Commonwealth countries.

Global commemoration of outstanding historic anniversaries has now become almost axiomatic and it would be quite easy to predict what events and personalities will be the subjects of world-wide philatelic coverage in years to come. The bicentenary of American independence in 1976 has been accorded pre-publicity by the United States in numerous issues from 1971 onwards and is already attracting the attention of other countries.

Short-term Definitives and Thematic Sets

The practice of supplementing the permanent series by occasional sets devoted to specific subjects was well-established in the previous decade, but in the period from 1965 to 1975 it became virtually universal. The more conservative countries, such as Britain and the Netherlands, justified the release of these sets on the grounds that they obviated the necessity for issuing pictorial definitives; but many countries whose definitive stamps were large and colourful also resorted to frequent thematic issues for good measure. The principal motive for issuing these stamps was the lucrative revenue resulting from their sale. In some cases they were used prudently, to catch up on the backlog of famous men and women or national achievements whose commemoration had been neglected as a result of a previously conservative policy, but in most cases they had no justification other than to supply the demand from collectors. In many cases these stamps took the place of definitives in the traditional sense and were of full definitive length. They were often issued annually or at more frequent intervals (though rarely more often than every three months) and were often described in official announcements as 'short-term definitives'. This expression was also used by Australia which continued to issue definitive sets, but augmented them periodically by thematic sets which remained on sale for a comparatively long period.

In other countries, however, these thematic sets consisted of three or four stamps only, and were on sale for short periods of one or two months at most. Such sets were either of different denominations, covering the postal rates most frequently used, or all of one denomination, usually the prevailing inland letter rate. Britain adopted both types from time to time; the birds, flowers and cathedrals sets of 1966–9 were wholly or mainly of one denomination, but later sets tended to have varied denominations. The United States rarely issued thematic sets, and they were invariably of the letter rate value and issued in *se-tenant* strips or blocks. New Zealand's thematic sets concentrated mainly on tourism and included denominations that were intended for use on overseas mail. East Africa's sets of four stamps took care to represent each of the component countries in the subjects chosen. By the end of the decade, the concept of the stamp aimed primarily at the collector and designed to raise revenue rather than perform a specific function (definitives) or publicise historic or current events (commemoratives) was so firmly entrenched, that not to have issued these thematic sets would have seemed quite extraordinary.

Stamp Design

The increasingly competitive nature of the world philatelic market has forced most postal administrations and philatelic agencies to take a closer, harder look at the product they are selling. As a result, there was marked improvement in the production aspects of stamps in this decade, with greater emphasis on the use of colour. While there was also evidence of greater ingenuity in the choice of subject matter, especially if more than one theme could be depicted simultaneously, the quality of stamp design in general remained uneven as before. Few countries were in the happy position of satisfying all their

customers all of the time. Czechoslovakia alone, maintained consistently high standards in design and execution and showed the greatest originality in concept without descending to banality or gimmickry. Sweden had, perhaps, less pretensions to achieving artistry in her stamps but none the less regularly produced designs which were easily understood and pleasing to the eye. Much of the success of Czech and Swedish stamps may be attributed to the fact that the oldest stamp process of them all – intaglio – was still the predominant method employed. It has to be conceded that recess-printing and line-engraving impart aesthetic qualities that cannot be attained by offset lithography and photogravure. Therefore, no matter how artistic or well-balanced a design may be, it has an innate disadvantage if interpreted through the medium of these modern processes, compared to intaglio. Lithography and photogravure are superior to intaglio only from the point of view of photographic reproduction of subject matter in full colour, but this is not necessarily a virtue in itself. In fact, the technical versatility of lithography and photogravure have robbed the designer of the initiative and the need to conceive designs in terms of balanced motifs and well-cut lettering.

Consequently the majority of recent stamps can, regrettably, be dismissed on aesthetic grounds, as 'pretty-pretties' whose qualities are trite and superficial. The worst offenders in many instances, are those stamps which merely seek to reproduce works of art conceived in other media, principally oil-painting and sculpture. Nevertheless, the obsession with 'art' stamps in the 1960s had the beneficial result of making postal administrations and the public more aware of stamps as an art form in their own right, and subsequently there were a number of attempts to produce designs that could be regarded as works of art. Here again, however, the best examples tended to come from countries that continued to use the intaglio process – the Scandinavian group, Austria, Yugoslavia, Czechoslovakia and Switzerland. They ranged from the floral motifs of the Czech postage-due stamps, to the abstract, non-figurative 60-öre stamp issued by Denmark in 1969.

In an attempt to break with existing conventions, designers turned increasingly to the decorative qualities of lettering and numerals and consequently there was a significant increase in the number of stamps whose designs relied entirely on such seemingly unpromising material. In this category may be cited Denmark's Refugee '66 set (1966), Saudi Arabia's OPEC stamp (1971), Singapore's '100,000 Homes' stamps (1969) and, above all, the United States' 'Love' stamp (1973). The Netherlands conducted a number of experiments in this decade with stamps whose designs were made up entirely of lettering and numerals: the Inter-governmental Committee for European Migration (1966), the Red Cross centenary stamps, in which the dates were arranged in the form of a cross (1967), the national anthem quatercentenary issue (1968), the ILO jubilee pair (1969), the V-motif of the liberation commemorative (1970), the Census stamp (1971) and the flag issue (1972). A stamp honouring the statesman J. R. Thorbeke in 1972 departed from customary practice by reproducing a quotation in copperplate lettering, instead of a portrait.

The previous tendency to adapt contemporary poster techniques to the more limiting medium of the postage stamp continued unabated. Countries that hitherto had preferred a naturalistic pictorial treatment of a subject, succumbed to poster styles, with mixed results. Geometric motifs found increasing favour with stamp designers; the Scandinavian countries and the Netherlands being the outstanding exponents of such designs. The Netherlands even went so far as to produce a set of five stamps in 1970 that had been designed by a computer. The resulting designs, officially described as 'spirals, concentric circles in transition, parallel planes in cube and overlapping scales' were recess-printed against a lithographed background and created an optical illusion of three-dimensionalism. This series, of course, bordered on gimmickry and was not repeated by the Netherlands, or any other country for that matter, though several subsequent Dutch stamps explored the possibilities of three-dimensional effects in geometric motifs.

Apart from geometry, two other techniques were applied to postage stamps with considerable success. Significantly, both of them were pioneered by Czechoslovakia. The 20th anniversary of UNESCO was celebrated in 1966 by a set of seven stamps portraying contemporary cultural celebrities in caricature. This was an exceedingly adventurous – not to say foolhardy – approach, but it says much for the quality of the designs and production that the series was a success. The risks involved in the use of caricature have obviously deterred other countries from exploiting this to any extent. Australia used cartoon figures most effectively in a series publicising the conversion to the metric system (1973) and the United States has used modern cartoon techniques in stamps promoting the use of zip codes and urging the preservation of the environment (1974). Elsewhere, cartoons and caricatures have been reproduced on very few occasions: Britain's cricket series of 1973 and San Marino's Walt Disney series of 1970 were noteworthy examples, but Belgium alone has used a caricature of living royalty – Queen Fabiola – on a stamp. A satirical medium is unlikely to find a wide application in stamps honouring actual persons, yet Belgium's example proves that it can be done.

The variety of form, subject, style and treatment in the production of postage stamps is almost infinite and is limited only by the materials and dimensions employed. Every subject imaginable has been depicted on a postage stamp. Every kind of printing process has been used to produce stamps in every colour of the spectrum. Styles of lettering and artistic interpretation are enormously varied, from the naturalistic and realistic motifs based on photographs, to the whimsical, surrealist and abstract. There was only one common factor in every stamp from the Penny Black of 1840 onwards: they were designed and executed by craftsmen and artists of mature years. The design of a stamp, the balance of the subject, the lettering, portraiture and ornament, the restrictions of size and the limitations of the various printing processes – all were problems that could only be solved by highly trained artists after years of experience in graphics. Admittedly the more naïve and primitive stamps from the remoter and more backward countries often lacked the sophistication and polish found elsewhere, but in the most recent decade stamp design and production attained a peak of technical excellence everywhere. Increasingly over the years, a stamp came to represent the sum total of the creative efforts and talents of many people, and less the work of a single creative mind. In the search for perfection of design, a certain freshness and originality had to be sacrificed.

Throughout the period covered by this book, greater attention was given to the conception of a design that would embody the spirit of the subject it commemorated. One of the few areas in which it was possible to capture the mood of the subject, was in those designs having children's themes. Many of the stamps issued since the 1950s, devoted to child welfare, were rendered in a deliberately artless style, that seemed to imply that the stamps were not only for children, but had also been produced by children. It was only a matter of time,

therefore, before such stamps were actually designed by children. Surprisingly enough, the occasion was not one specifically associated with children. In 1958 Czechoslovakia issued a set of stamps in honour of UNESCO and Jiri Svengsbir adapted three drawings by young children. This unusual approach excited little comment or interest at the time and five years elapsed before the experiment was repeated by Monaco, who reproduced children's drawings on a series of stamps commemorating the United Nations Children's Charter. Later that year (1963) the Netherlands Antilles used children's paintings as the basis for the Child Welfare series, and Yugoslavia used a child's drawing for the annual Children's Week stamp.

The idea of using children's designs for stamps was born in the previous decade, but it was not until the late 1960s that it became widespread. From 1966 to 1970 they were still confined mainly to children's themes – Child Welfare charity stamps, UNICEF commemoratives and Christmas issues – but since then they have spread into other fields, showing a fresh approach to many a stereotyped subject. The vigorous colouring and flagrant disregard for perspective have brought an original spirit to a subject in which the quest for novelty has become all-important.

Technical Developments

Despite the enormous advances in multicolour photogravure and offset lithography achieved in the early 1960s, intaglio continued to hold its own throughout the most recent decade. Although comparatively expensive, it produced stamps of a quality that no other process could approach, let alone surpass. Increasingly, however, intaglio was combined with photogravure or lithography to achieve the best of both worlds – quality and aesthetic sensitivity combined with a full colour range. Finely engraved motifs against a lithographed background, in fact exploited the flatness of lithography (hitherto regarded as an aesthetic disadvantage) and heightened the effect of the intaglio, helping to create that elusive three-dimensional effect which stamp designers and printers sought like some kind of philosopher's stone.

Mention has already been made of the use of geometric motifs in quest of that same three-dimensional quality, but there were more mechanical approaches to this problem. No country repeated Italy's experiment of the 1950s using anaglyphic images, but Canada conducted several experiments in 1974–5 using a latent image technique in which a secondary motif was revealed when the stamps were tilted to the light at eye level. Embossing, die-stamping and thermography were all used sporadically in this period to create three-dimensional effects, but to the remote Himalayan kingdom of Bhutan must go the credit for producing the world's first truly three-dimensional stamps, using laminated, prismatic-ribbed plastic surfacing. These have appeared at various times since 1967 with themes devoted to space exploration, fish and even Old Master paintings (the last-named surely being the ultimate in philatelic *kitsch*).

There was a considerable increase in the circular gold foil type of stamp in the late 1960s, as coin stamps emulating those of Tonga were issued by Sierra Leone, Jordan, Bhutan and several of the Arab sheikhdoms. Sierra Leone and Tonga alone persevered with die-stamped, free-form stamps, though the principle of pressure-sensitive backing was taken up by Gibraltar and the United States in 1974, for UPU and Christmas stamps respectively. It seems probable that this convenient form of adhesive, now widely used in stationery, will become more commonplace in the stamps of the future.

Bhutan alone, through the efforts of its erstwhile agents in the Bahamas, explored every method of producing stamps in materials other than paper. In this decade stamps were successively printed on silk, thin steel plates, paper impregnated with scent, plastics simulating the surface of oil paintings and bas-reliefs, and finally, in 1973, in the form of phonograph records that played the Bhutanese national anthem or provided a commentary on Bhutanese history.

Bearing in mind the comparatively huge cost of producing stamps that smell or talk, it is hardly surprising that there has been no rush by other countries to imitate these curiosities. Instead, the use of novelty and gimmickry has been largely confined to the design of the stamps. *Se-tenant* stamps and composite designs became increasingly common in this decade. Composite stamps lent themselves admirably to the reproduction of religious triptychs (used on Christmas and Easter stamps), or in strips ranging from Britain's Bayeux Tapestry series of 1966 to Taiwan's numerous issues featuring traditional scroll paintings. In the majority of cases the components of these strips or blocks were individually perforated, but in several notable instances other forms of separation were utilised. Gibraltar's Christmas stamps of 1969, featuring three different interpretations of the Madonna and Child theme by Old Masters, were printed in strips of six, perforated horizontally between rows and separated vertically between units by rouletting. Rouletting was also used by Papua New Guinea in 1969 for composite pairs featuring the art of the Elema region. Each pair was perforated in the usual manner, but rouletting across the centre enabled each half to be detached and used as a separate stamp.

Technical improvements in perforating machinery enabled stamp designers to adopt unusual layouts, such as the staggered triptych formation of St. Lucia's 1970 Easter series, or the several issues of Malta and Malaysia which involved the use of isosceles triangles, rhomboids, diamonds, and trapezoids. Although perforators were capable of patterns other than straight lines, this potential was not exploited beyond three sets of stamps issued by the Bahamas, Malaysia and Gibraltar. In these instances, the basic designs were respectively kidney-shaped, circular and like the silhouette of the Rock of Gibraltar, and the perforations followed the outline of the stamps. In the case of Gibraltar conventional perforations at right angles were thoughtfully provided to make separation easier, but the other sets relied entirely on the perforations round the designs. Consequently, scissors were often required to separate these stamps, thereby undermining the object of the exercise. Gimmicks of this kind may well be of momentary interest to philatelists, but they are roundly cursed by the general public, or the long-suffering counter staff who have the unenviable task of selling them. Thus it is unlikely that free-form perforation will be a popular device in years to come.

The rapid expansion of electronic sorting and cancelling equipment since 1965 has meant that more and more countries each year are having to issue stamps incorporating substances which react to the electronic scanners. Britain, France and Canada have all used phosphor bands across the face of stamps to indicate 'fast' and 'slow' mail, or first and second class mail, but other countries have often been content merely to indicate to the equipment the position of the stamp on the envelope or card, so that the item can be sorted and 'faced' (put in the correct position, with the stamp in the upper right hand corner) to facilitate cancellation. The use of electronics in postal mechanisation has led to the use of paper impregnated with fluorescent or phosphorescent material, to the use of

printing ink containing such substances (Australia) or to the use of phosphor bands, applied horizontally and vertically over the perforations to form a frame round the design of the stamps (Taiwan and South Africa). The phosphor bands used in Britain, Canada and France are clearly visible to the naked eye; the fluorescence, phosphorescence and luminescence used elsewhere can often be detected only by means of ultra-violet light. In many cases, stamps have been issued with or without this form of treatment, and the composition of the phosphor materials has varied considerably in colour and wavelength. Moreover, the phosphor bands or coating may be applied by letterpress or photogravure, and these technical minutiae have tended to make advanced philately a much more complex science in recent years.

The traditional features by which seemingly identical stamps were differentiated, were the watermark and the perforations; but in an era of frequent change in definitives, these factors tended to become less important. Countries such as Britain, West Germany and New Zealand, which had traditionally used watermarked paper, gave up the practice in this decade. This security device survived in a number of the newly independent countries, which adopted distinctive watermarks almost as a symbol of sovereignty. Thus Samoa introduced the kava bowl emblem, Lesotho, the Basotho hat device and Jamaica revived the pineapple watermark which had not been used on Jamaican stamps since 1870. The paper used by the Crown Agents, underwent several important changes in this period, and as this affected the stamps of some forty countries (about a fifth of the world total) it is worth noting the following points. The so-called Script CA watermark was used for the earlier Elizabethan definitives, many of which survived into the late 1960s. In 1957, however, a new watermark bearing the crown of St. Edward the Confessor and block capitals was adopted, and was used on all new definitives and commemoratives, but also applied to late printings of previous definitives. At first this watermark appeared upright, but from 1966 onwards it was positioned sideways, and this also applied to later printings of definitives which had originally been produced with an upright watermark. The advent of multicolour photogravure led to the introduction of a chalk-surfaced paper, but this was replaced in 1970 by a general purpose paper which could be employed in intaglio and lithography as well as photogravure. This paper has a distinctively glazed surface but gives a negative reaction to the silver pencil test for chalky paper. With several of the Churchill commemoratives late in 1974, the Crown Agents introduced a new watermark which they have designated the Spiral CA (as opposed to the Block CA). In this watermark, the crown over CA motif is arranged in a staggered formation along the dandy roll (over which the paper pulp is spread during the manufacturing process). Stocks of the Block CA upright and sideways papers were exhausted by mid-1975 and all stamps printed since then, including reprints of existing definitives, had the new Spiral CA watermark.

Before 1968, the stamps used in Britain and the Crown Agents' countries had a gum arabic adhesive, but in that year, stamps printed by Harrison and Bradbury Wilkinson were produced on paper with a matt, almost invisible adhesive known as PVA gum (polyvinyl alcohol). This adhesive had the advantage of eliminating paper curl and the tendency of sheets to stick together in damp or tropical climates. There has subsequently been the added complication of distinguishing unused stamps coated with gum arabic or PVA gum. Such subtleties are of great interest to the specialist but are ignored by most stamp catalogues.

1965-1975
Philatelic Survey by Country

Europe

Albania

The political isolation of Albania, aligned with the people's Republic of China against the Soviet bloc, was reflected in many of the stamps of the late 1960s. Albania alone bothered to celebrate the ninetieth birthday of Stalin, with stamps in 1969, and several issues portrayed Mao Tse-tung. More than any other Communist country, Albania continued to use stamps to promote the totalitarian atmosphere of the country, even to the extent of celebrating the 30th anniversary of the State Security Police in 1973 with a stamp showing a prisoner under escort. All stamps of this period were printed in multicolour lithography and a high proportion of them were designed by N. Prizreni or S. Toptani. There were no definitives as such, but long thematic sets changed at monthly intervals (65:1, 4). There was, however, a more cosmopolitan air about the commemoratives, many of which celebrated Russian space achievements (65:2) or current events in the Western world, not excluding Italy (65:3) Albania's former fascist enemy.

Andorra

Neither French nor Spanish Post Offices issued new definitives in this period, but both resorted to short thematic sets, with Pyrenean flowers (1966) and customs (1972) from the Spanish administration, and winter sports (1966) and flowers (1973) from the French. The latter also issued two sets featuring sixteenth-century frescoes and four sets devoted to aspects of the altar screen in the church of St. Jean de Caselles. Both offices began issuing Europa stamps, the French in 1967 and the Spanish in 1972 (65:6). The French Post Office produced several stamps to publicise nature protection and important events in France, but indigenous commemoratives were confined to anniversaries of social legislation and visits of the co-princes (65:5).

Austria

The 1957 definitives continued in use throughout this period, various denominations being added between 1965 and 1970 (65:10). In 1973–4 a new series depicting scenery was introduced, the stamps being printed in combined photogravure and intaglio (65:35). The definitives were supplemented from 1966 onwards by short thematic sets, featuring flowers, fruits, baroque frescoes, antique clocks, Viennese operettas and art treasures (65:23, 24, 26).

Austria was one of the few countries to issue stamps regularly using the intaglio process alone (65:7, 11–14, 17, 18, 26, 29, 33), but this process was also combined with photogravure on many occasions, to inject more colour into a design (65:19, 25, 27, 28, 30, 32, 36, 38). Occasionally fine line-engraving was used on a background tint provided by photogravure (65:22–24), but intaglio was never used by itself to produce combinations of two or more colours. Photogravure alone, was used increasingly from 1966; at first applied to designs in which the colours were kept separate (65:9), then employed in designs in which the basic motif was printed on a background tint of a second colour (65:15, 16). Only latterly was photogravure utilised in multicolour designs (65:28, 31, 37). The International Labour Organisation commemorative of 1969 (65:21) was exceptional, being printed in monochrome photogravure, where one might have expected intaglio to have been used instead.

Lithography, which had been used occasionally in the previous decade, was seldom employed. The Alpine flora set of 1966 was printed in multicolour lithography, but the National Library series of the same year was printed in combined intaglio and lithography (65:8), but photogravure replaced lithography from 1967 onwards.

The majority of commemorative stamps were issued as singles. Longer sets, of three to eight stamps, marked the WIPA stamp exhibition (1965), the golden jubilee of the republic (65:19) and the bicentenary of the Albertine art collection (65:22). On two occasions miniature sheets consisting of six or eight stamps were issued, to commemorate the centenary of the State Opera in Vienna (65:20) and the quatercentenary of the Spanish Riding School. On both occasions deep purple-brown, red and gold were printed in intaglio and photogravure.

Of the hardy annuals, semi-postals in honour of Stamp Day continued to appear early in December each year, invariably taking historical aspects of the postal services as their theme. Christmas stamps (which Austria had pioneered in 1937) were made a regular feature from 1967 onwards, reproductions of the Nativity or the Madonna and Child from Austrian churches being selected. On the other hand, Austria dropped out of the annual Europa issues after 1964 except for a single stamp in 1969. Occasional stamps for Mother's Day (another pre-war innovation) appeared in 1967–8. From the beginning of 1969 all Austrian special issues bore the date in the bottom margin, in addition to the names of the designer and engraver.

Belgium

The Baudouin definitives of 1953 remained current to the end of this period, and underwent a number of important changes in the second decade. Phosphorescent paper was introduced in 1966 and subsequent printings of many denominations may be distinguished from those on ordinary paper by their lighter colours. The phosphorescence itself can only be detected by means of ultra-violet rays. New printings of this series continued until 1973 and were produced at the State Printing Works in Malines. In 1969, however, Enschedé was commissioned to print certain denominations for use in stamp booklets and these can easily be distinguished from the Malines printings because they are much smaller and always have one or two adjacent sides imperforate (66:38). Coil versions of the 1.50-, 2.50- and 3.50-franc stamps were released in 1970; every fifth stamp in the rolls of 500 and 1,000 was numbered on the reverse. Two years later the 2- and 4.50-franc stamps were also issued in coil form. In 1971, the designs of the 2.50- and 7-franc were redrawn, with larger figures of value. An intaglio 3.50-franc stamp was issued in September 1970 to celebrate the king's fortieth birthday. The same design, with the commemorative dates omitted, was used for a new definitive series introduced gradually from May 1971 onwards (66:24). Two denominations were issued in coils with reverse numbering. Enschedé likewise produced a smaller photogravure version of those denominations issued in booklets. The booklet panes consist of four stamps and two labels, each pair of stamps being arranged tête-bêche vertically. Thus, stamps upside down in relation to each other are common, and not of any particular value. Postage-due stamps, with a lion and T (Taxe) motif, were released between 1966 and 1970.

Pairs of stamps were released at half-yearly intervals, to supplement the definitives and provide publicity for tourist resorts and landmarks. These sets were introduced in November 1965 and have continued ever since (66:4, 32). In addition to the tourist publicity series, stamps were issued from time to time with such themes as 'national interest' (66:8) or 'historic towns' (66:17, 25). Annual issues for Stamp Day continued to feature historic aspects of the postal services (66:34). In addition to the Stamp Day issues, however, a stamp was issued each year from 1965 onwards with the theme of philately for the young. The first stamp depicted Sir Rowland Hill the postal reformer with young stamp collectors, but in several subsequent years, motifs designed by children were used (66:14). Charity stamps with premiums in aid of a wide range of good causes, from anti-tuberculosis and Child Welfare to the relief of disaster victims and former prisoners of war, were issued each December, different themes being selected each year. Stamps with a premium were also issued at other times and Belgium continued to make greater use of such semi-postal issues than any other country in this period. Europa stamps were released each year, using the standard designs. In common with the other CEPT countries, however, Belgium abandoned omnibus designs in 1974, choosing instead, variations on a common theme, the first subject being sculpture and statuary. Christmas stamps were introduced in 1967, a single stamp being released each November (66:9).

The printing processes used in previous years continued unchanged, though there was now a much greater utilisation of intaglio and photogravure in combination, the principal motif and lettering being recess-printed on a photogravure background (66:5, 8, 10, 11, 15, 17, 18, 29, 34, 39). Few attempts were made to integrate the two processes, but outstanding examples occurred in the period 1965–7 (66:1, 3, 9). Intaglio alone, was still employed in a number of cases, especially in relatively simple designs, such as buildings or portraits (66:21, 24, 26), the quality of engraving generally being very fine. By using thin, double-lined lettering and delicately engraved motifs with fine frame-lines, there was a tendency in the mid-1970s for Belgian stamps to become less substantial, more ethereal in quality (66:39). An exception was the stamp for the 50th anniversary of national war invalids' work in 1969, where a bold, vigorous but rather coarse style of engraving was used to emphasise the stark nature of the subject (66:13). In the Belgian painters series of 1965 intaglio was used for the sepia portraits, but the inscriptions were added in various colours by photogravure, though there was neither necessity for this purpose, nor the opportunity to exploit its tonal qualities (66:2).

Photogravure alone was used increasingly, but was seldom applied to fully integrated multicolour designs (66:6, 20, 22, 23, 25). In most instances, two or three colours were used in bold, contrasting combinations (66:7, 14, 16, 19, 27, 28, 30, 31, 33, 35–37) that were well-suited to the poster techniques introduced in the late 1960s. Very few stamps were produced in monochrome photogravure, a striking example being the stamp of 1969 celebrating the first moon landing (66:12). In common with many other countries in this period, Belgium tended to increase the size of stamps from 1967 onwards, though this has so far been confined to a relatively few issues (66:12, 21, 23). As an aid to electronic sorting phosphorescent paper was adopted for all stamps, both definitive and commemorative, from September 1967 onwards, the very lowest values (1- and 1.50-franc) being excepted. Since the end of 1972, denominations up to 3-francs have been printed on ordinary paper and all higher values printed on phosphorescent paper.

Bulgaria

The dividing line between definitives and thematic sets of a less permanent nature is very shadowy in the recent issues of Bulgaria, though the former may be defined as those issues in small formats and monochrome photogravure (67:1, 3, 10, 12), whereas the purely thematic sets are those in larger sizes and with more colourful designs (67:2, 6, 11). Both definitive and thematic sets were usually issued in the seven or eight most commonly used denominations up to 20-stotinki and few higher values were issued. An isolated example was the 1-lev airmail stamp of 1968, featuring the copper rolling mill at Medet (67:7).

The political nature of commemorative issues diminished considerably in this period and greater emphasis was laid on events outside the recent history of the country. Numerous sets commemorated anniversaries in the struggle for independence from the Turks (67:4), and both thematic and commemorative sets frequently recalled the Byzantine and Orthodox cultural heritage (67:5, 11). A more stylised approach supplanted the type of design preferred in the earlier periods, a favourite device being the grouping of quasi-symbolic elements and lettering, sometimes overlapping, on a plain white background with a border of solid colour (67:2, 8, 9). Photogravure continued to predominate, combined very occasionally with intaglio (67:6) or lithography.

Cyprus

Two definitive sets were issued in this decade, both lithographed by Aspioti-Elka of Athens and, like the series of 1962, drawing heavily on the classical art and artifacts of the island (67:13, 15). These sets were released in November 1966 and February 1971 respectively. Stamps of the latter series were overprinted in English, Greek and Turkish and surcharged to raise money for the refugee fund after the 1974 civil war. The intercommunal clashes, which had been a major political problem since independence, erupted into full-scale war between the Turks and Greeks in 1974 and culminated in the Turkish invasion and partition of the island. North and east of the Attila Line, Cyprus was ruled by the Autonomous Turkish Cypriot Administration which introduced its own stamps. A set of seven stamps celebrating the golden jubilee of the Turkish Republic had been used on local mail within the Turkish community in 1973. From July 1974 onwards these stamps were given full international status and adopted as an interim definitive series (67:17). Separate issues of stamps were made by the Turkish community and allegedly used postally in the areas under Turkish control but the validity and status of these stamps has been questioned.

Throughout the decade Cyprus continued to issue Europa stamps each year, and annual sets of Christmas stamps were introduced in 1969. The 1970 series included a se-tenant strip of three 25-mil stamps reproducing a religious triptych (67:14). This set was photogravure-printed by Harrison and, with a stamp produced by the French Government Printing Works in 1967, were the only stamps not lithographed by Aspioti-Elka in this decade. From 1969 onwards, short thematic sets were issued at annual intervals and featured birds, flowers, tourism (67:16), ancient coins and traditional architecture. Commemoratives consisted of pairs or sets of three, but from 1973 onwards current events were grouped together in annual anniversary sets, based on the Swiss and British models.

Czechoslovakia

Although the previous practice, of portraying presidents in intaglio definitives, was used intermittently in this period (67:31), Czechoslovakia succumbed to the general fashion for thematics and produced a series in 1965–6 devoted to landmarks in Czechoslovak towns (67:21). This series was superseded in 1971–2 by a set with the same theme, but using a larger format and a greater variety of colour (67:34). These definitives were supplemented by frequent sets covering a wide range of subjects. Several sets featured architecture and art treasures of Prague Castle (67:22), and such obvious subjects as flora, fauna and scenery (67:23, 25, 30) provided material for a number of sets, especially in the late 1960s. In more recent years, however, Czechoslovakia has systematically explored aspects of the applied and decorative arts, with sets devoted to such subjects as musical instruments (67:35), antique pistols, decorative shooting targets and maiolica drug jars. Thematic sets in the same genre were often used as commemoratives. Thus the series of 1966 marking the centenary of Naprstek's ethnographic museum in Prague, depicted North American Indians (67:24) and aspects of Czechoslovak folk art formed the theme of the series of 1971 celebrating the 25th anniversary of UNICEF (67:37). Several long sets from 1968 onwards featured the coats of arms of the regional capitals; most of these stamps were released in the same denomination (67:36).

Apart from a few sets in 1965–6, lithographed at the Cartographic Institute in Bratislava (67:25) all Czechoslovak stamps were produced by the intaglio method and in most cases this was combined with photogravure (67:18–21, 24, 26, 28–30, 32–43). Intaglio alone was still used occasionally (67:22, 23, 27). The treatment of subjects varied considerably, from the naturalistic approach of most of the purely thematic issues to the impressionism of the commemoratives especially in the 1970s (67:29, 32, 40). Czechoslovakia experimented with unusual techniques, from abstract to caricature (67:18, 28). As in the previous period, Czech designers and engravers continued to demonstrate their versatility in lettering and their fascination by the artistic potential of this medium (67:18, 19, 23, 42), though the red, white and blue treatment of the lettering forming the motif of the federal anniversary stamp of 1974 is clearly modelled on the United States airmails of 1968 (100:15). Czechoslovakia was one of the many countries that participated in International Women's Year (1975), issuing a 30h stamp bearing a woman's stylised head (67:43).

Denmark

Various denominations were added to the King Frederick IX definitive series between 1965 and 1967 and the set continued in use until 1974 when it was gradually superseded by a small-format series portraying Queen Margrethe. The death of the king in 1972 was followed by a memorial stamp (68:19). The use of fluorescent paper, introduced in the definitives in 1962, was extended to the commemorative stamps from June 1967 onwards. Technically there was no change in Danish stamps during this period, all issues being recess-printed as before. Combined intaglio and photogravure was used for one of the two Red Cross stamps issued in 1966, but this means of adding colour to a design, widely utilised elsewhere, was not subsequently employed by Denmark. The first three-coloured stamp appeared in 1969 (68:8), but even after that date the majority of commemoratives were printed in monochrome and two- or three-colour combinations were used sparingly (68:11, 12, 16, 18, 21–23, 26, 30, 31).

The conservative attitude to design remained steadfast in those stamps commemorating people, finely engraved portraits being used in each case (68:5, 13, 15, 19, 27, 29), though a slightly more impressionistic approach was evident in those stamps designed by Jane Muus (68:9, 17). The only exception was the 50-öre stamp of 1967, celebrating the wedding of Princess Margrethe and Prince Henri de Monpezat, in which colourless silhouettes were used on a solid background (68:4).

In non-portrait designs, however, the stamps of this period were freed from all convention. Comparatively few of them bore naturalistic interpretations of a subject, and these were largely confined to scenic or architectural motifs (68:1, 6, 21, 23, 24, 26, 32). Floral designs were used for stamps of 1972–3 commemorating the centenaries of the fund for homes for the disabled (68:22) and the Jutland Horticultural Society (68:30). An indication of a more colourful policy in years to come was the stamp of 1973, reproducing an illuminated manuscript in full colour – the first photogravure stamp issued by Denmark (printed by Harrison and Sons). A subsequent series devoted to church frescoes, was recess-printed in three-colour combinations on cream-tinted paper (68:31). Abstract designs were employed in a number of cases where a symbolic treatment might have been expected (68:2, 18, 28), but this policy was extended to subjects which would have been less obscure had a more naturalistic treatment been used. Stylised motifs were selected for the Copenhagen 800th anniversary series of 1967 (68:3) and sets of 1968 and 1972 publicising Danish construction projects and industries (68:7, 25), while the sports series of 1971 was totally abstract in concept (68:16). Lettering alone, provided the motif for the Giro stamp of 1970 (68:12) and varying degrees of stylisation marked the Slesvig, Refugees and railways commemoratives of 1970–72 (68:11, 14, 20). One of the most unusual stamps ever issued, however, was the non-figurative stamp of 1969 with its cubist motif by R. Mortensen (68:10). Separate issues of stamps were introduced in the Faeroe Islands in 1975, reflecting the autonomy of this Danish dependency.

Finland

Although intaglio was retained for the definitives that had been introduced in 1963 and augmented periodically up to 1973 (68:49), it lost ground as the principal medium for commemorative stamps. After 1965 it was used in combination with lithography (68:34, 37, 40, 45) or with photogravure (68:38, 41). The stamp of 1968 publicising the Finnish wood-processing industry actually combined three processes – intaglio, lithography and embossing (68:39). From 1966 onwards, however, multicolour lithography (68:33, 42, 44, 47, 50–51) or photogravure (68:43, 46) were used increasingly. The multicoloured stamp of 1973 celebrating the birth centenary of President Kallio (68:48) was produced in lithography and photogravure, a combination which is, so far, peculiar to Finnish stamps. During

1975, increase in postal charges resulted in several multicolour pictorial stamps being added to the definitive series (68:51).

Although the lion definitives remained current, a new die was adopted for many denominations in 1968, differing fundamentally from the original version in having virtually no white circle round the figures of value. In 1972 phosphorescent paper was introduced for several definitive stamps and was subsequently extended to commemorative issues. In the same year, a lithographic version of the 5-, 15- and 25-penniä definitive was released in stamp booklets and the same process was later used for several of the higher value pictorial designs.

Most commemoratives were released as singles. In addition to the annual semi-postals with premiums in aid of the Red Cross or the anti-tuberculosis fund (68:33) Finland introduced Christmas stamps in 1973. A set of ten stamps with the theme of ancient and national costumes was released in two instalments in 1972 and 1973 (68:47). The stamps were printed in se-tenant strips, five of 50- or 60-penniä denominations, in sheet form, though the 50-penniä stamps were also issued in booklets.

France

The previous policy, of armorial small-format low denominations and scenic double-sized higher values, changing at frequent intervals, continued throughout this decade. A significant change was the introduction of photogravure in place of letterpress for the arms stamps produced from December 1966 onwards. This process was not extended to commemoratives, with the sole exception of the 1967 stamp publicising the Grenoble Winter Olympic Games (69:11). New Marianne designs were adopted for low value definitives in 1967 and 1970 (69:20, 23). The first of these, designed by Henri Cheffer, was originally recess-printed, but in July 1969 a letterpress version of the 30-centime value was released. These stamps were issued in normal sheet form and also in coils, the latter having serial numbers on the back of every tenth stamp. Various stamps of the arms and Marianne designs were issued with phosphor bands in May 1970 in Clermont-Ferrand where trials with electronic sorting equipment subsequently took place. Four stamps were used in these experiments, the three lower values having an odd number of bands and the 40-centime two bands. The electronic scanner separated 'fast' mail (with an even number of bands) from 'slow' mail (with an odd number). The later Marianne design, by Bequet, was introduced in 1971 for 45-centime stamps in letterpress and 50-centime stamps in intaglio. The latter was also released with three phosphor bands. Both stamps were also issued in coils, serially numbered as before. In June 1970 the French Government Printing Works was transferred from Paris to Perigeux and the occasion was marked by a special printing of the 40-centime Marianne stamp with a descriptive label se-tenant. Special plates were prepared for this stamp but it was virtually indistinguishable from the normal definitive version.

French stamps of this period may be grouped into certain clearly defined categories. The semi-postals consisted of three issues as before: a single stamp for Stamp Day, a pair for the Red Cross each December, usually reproducing works of art in monochrome and inscribed with the Red Cross emblem, and a series of varying length, featuring historic celebrities, with premiums in aid of the Red Cross though not specifically inscribed for that purpose. The celebrities stamps were generally released in two or three instalments throughout the year. For much of this period the sets consisted of six or seven stamps, but in 1975 the number was reduced to four.

Thematic sets played an increasingly important role in the late 1960s and early 1970s. Of these, the most popular was the series reproducing works of art in full colour, using the multicolour Giori intaglio process. Normally, four stamps in this theme were released in the course of the year, originally in a single set but latterly one at a time. Stamps of 1974–5 had a narrow label se-tenant advertising 'Arphila', the philatelic exhibition devoted to Art stamps (69:30). France continued to issue Europa stamps each year, but, tiring of the monotony of the standard designs, injected some individuality into the series from 1971 onwards. One stamp conformed to the omnibus pattern, but the other featured a prominent building (69:25). In 1974, when the concept of a single standard design was replaced by stamps in a similar theme, France featured sculpture (1974) and paintings by Picasso and Van Dongen (1975).

The série touristique d'usage courant, the tourist publicity stamps which provided the higher denominations of the definitive series, were rotated at the rate of three or four designs annually (69:4). By contrast, there were no new arms stamps after 1966, though changes of perforation and the addition of phosphor bands in 1969 and 1970 respectively, provided some variety in these issues. Between 1966 and 1973 eight series devoted to periods in French history were issued, using a larger format than usual. The first series featured Clovis and Charlemagne (69:9) and continued, through the Middle Ages and the reigns of Louis XIV and Louis XV to the Revolution, the Directory and finally the Napoléonic period. The sense of the historic and renewed national pride which marked the era of De Gaulle also found expression in the annual sets devoted to *grandes réalisations*. This evolved out of the commemoratives marking French space achievements in 1965-7 (69:7, 13) and isolated singles celebrating the inauguration of public works and technical achievements (69:21), before becoming a regular series in 1973. Since then two or three stamps have appeared annually to publicise the latest technical, scientific and engineering developments in France (69:33). Although occasional stamps had appeared in the early 1960s with the theme of nature conservation this did not become a regular feature until 1969 (69:26); since then a stamp has been issued annually featuring wildlife.

The remaining stamps consist of singles commemorating historic anniversaries or current events, in roughly equal proportions. Generally speaking the stamps honouring anniversaries of institutions, cities and historic events have had a naturalistic treatment (69:1, 3, 5, 6, 18, 19, 32, 34), while those publicising current events have tended to use a poster style of design (69:2, 8, 10, 11, 14, 22, 24, 27, 28). Symbolic designs were also used to mark the jubilee of Lions International and the bicentenary of the Masonic Grand Orient Lodge (69:16, 29). In the early part of this period, stamps devoted to historic personalities followed the traditional patterns of portraits alone (69:17) or a combination of portraiture and pictorial background related to the persons commemorated (69:12, 13, 15). In 1973, however, Jacques Combet produced a distinctive design, using a close-up detail of the portrait of the radio pioneer, Eugène Ducretet, merging into a line diagram (69:31) and he used the same technique in the Red Cross fund celebrities issues of 1974 and other commemoratives.

No change was made in the flag series of stamps provided for the use of the Council of Europe offices in Strasbourg, but the UNESCO headquarters in Paris issued three stamps in 1966 featuring a stylised book and globe (69:35). Between 1969 and 1971 four stamps honouring the *Declaration of Human Rights* were released.

Germany (Federal Republic)

The definitive series devoted to twelve centuries of German architecture, introduced in December 1964, was in use for six years. Letterpress on slightly greyish paper was used for the original version of the series, but from 1966 onwards, intaglio on cream paper was adopted for new designs, in which the buildings were shown in white on coloured backgrounds (70:3). This series was beset with troubles of a political nature. The 50-pfennig of the letterpress series, showing Ellwangen Castle had an unfortunate arrangement of foliage in the tree shown in the background, which, by a considerable stretch of the imagination, was held to resemble the portrait of Adolf Hitler. More serious, however, was the objection raised by the Democratic Republic to the inclusion of three East German motifs – not to mention two in areas now forming part of Poland, and one in erstwhile East Prussia which now forms part of the Soviet Union. This definitive series was denounced by the East German authorities as yet another manifestation of West German revanchism. The Federal postal administration ignored these protests and when a series of five letterpress definitives was required to augment this set in 1966-8, chose the Brandenburg Gate (technically in East Berlin) as the subject (70:2).

West Germany reverted to the traditional practice of portraying the federal head of state, with a series depicting President Heinemann that was released in 1970-73 (70:28). This set was recess-printed, a process that was now mainly used for definitives. In 1971-3 a parallel series of small-format definitives was typographed for distribution in coils and booklets. This series of eleven stamps used the theme of accident prevention, each design focusing attention on a potential hazard in everyday life (70:30).

The Humanitarian Relief Fund sets continued to appear each October, with small premiums. The theme of the issues up to 1967 was fairy-tales, as in the previous decade, but later issues featured dolls and puppets (70:22), and musical instruments were introduced in 1973 (70:45). In 1969, it became customary to issue a single stamp in a similar motif but with the additional inscription *Weinachtsmarke* (Christmas stamp) at the beginning of December. Child Welfare semi-postals also appeared annually, usually in February or April. Various themes were used, ranging from animals and characters from the Minnesingers to children's drawings. Occasional double-sized stamps featuring landmarks and scenery were introduced in 1969 for tourist publicity (70:25, 44). These stamps had an intaglio vignette and a lithographed border bled into the perforations. Europa stamps in the standard designs were released each year as before (70:6, 10, 41). No fewer than seven sets were issued as advance publicity for the Munich Olympic Games of 1972, with premiums in aid of the promotion fund. The only other semi-postals of this period consisted of two stamps and a miniature sheet in 1973 for the Munich International Philatelic Exhibition (70:37). Occasional sets were released with the theme of nature conservation (70:16) and latterly the protection of the environment (70:42).

The majority of commemorative stamps were issued as singles. Those portraying historic personalities continued the previous practice of an intaglio motif on a lithographed background (70:12, 21, 38). Intaglio alone, was used for the Siemens commemorative of 1966 (70:5), but was combined with photogravure for the Schumacher commemorative of 1972 (70:34). Other stamps used lithography alone (70:9, 11). A curious feature of these stamps was the inclusion of Sir Winston Churchill (70:9) – in a series honouring European statesmen, and Karl Marx (70:12) the ideological creator of Communism – though the Communist party is banned in West Germany.

The same combination of printing processes was used for other commemoratives, with the addition of embossing, on a stamp of 1969 honouring the German Philatelic Congress (70:19). The traditional small format, either upright or transverse, adopted during the Third Reich, continued for most commemoratives issued in this period. In most cases, stylised or symbolic motifs appeared on solid backgrounds without frame-lines (70:1, 4, 7, 8, 13, 17, 18, 24, 26, 27, 29, 32, 33, 35, 36, 40, 43). The style adopted for the nature protection series of 1969, with a horizontal vignette and lettering on uncoloured bands above and below (70:16) was subsequently adapted to other stamps of 1969-70, with or without colour behind the lettering (70:20, 23). The Interpol stamp of 1973 was one of the few stamps whose design, in three colours, was lithographed on an uncoloured background (70:39). Apart from the accident prevention theme of the coil stamps, philately was used for propaganda purposes. Two sets of 1971 highlighted aspects of the new road traffic regulations, using poster designs (70:31).

Apart from the tourist publicity stamps, there were several issues using the larger, double-sized format. Combined intaglio and lithography was used for the stamp of 1968 marking the centenary of the first performance of Wagner's Die Meistersinger von Nürnberg (70:14), but lithography alone was used for subsequent issues, including the airmail jubilee pair of 1969 and the World Cup football stamps of 1974 (70:15). Stamps were released in 1975 to publicise the World Ice Hockey Championship to which West Germany was host (70:46).

Germany (West Berlin)

The majority of the stamps issued from 1965 onwards were identical with those of the Federal Republic, with the addition of the word BERLIN in the inscriptions. This applied particularly to the definitives, both the architectural series and the Heinemann issue (71:1). The Child Welfare and Humanitarian Relief Fund sets were similar in theme, though using different subjects in each case (71:6, 7). The majority of stamps issued by West Berlin in 1975 were similar to those of the Federal Republic, but with modified inscriptions. Among the few exceptions were stamps commemorating notable Berliners (71:10).

The principal differences between the stamps of West Berlin and the Federal Republic were the lengthy thematic sets released annually, and devoted to such subjects as new Berlin, Berlin art treasures and contemporaneous portraits of nineteenth-century

Berliners (71:2). A solitary stamp was issued for Stamp Day in 1972, but this was not repeated in subsequent years (71:7). Although lithography, sometimes combined with intaglio, was used for commemoratives in the same manner as in the Federal Republic (71:3, 9), West Berlin also used multicolour photography, for portrait commemoratives and stamps reproducing works of art (71:4, 5, 8) and extended the use of this process to a wider range of commemoratives in 1974.

Germany (Democratic Republic)

East Germany was one of the few countries of the Communist bloc to issue a proper definitive series and was quite exceptional in retaining the same series for a considerable number of years. The Ulbricht series, introduced in 1961, remained current throughout this period and various denominations were added up to 1971. At the beginning of 1965 the currency of the Democratic Republic was reformed, the mark being superseded by the Mark der Deutschen Notenbank. This had little effect on the definitive stamps themselves, except for the two mark values whose inscription was redrawn with values expressed in MDN instead of DM (Deutschemarks). It also affected the marginal inscriptions in the selvedge of the stamp sheets of the pfennig denominations, which now had the values of each row expressed in MDN instead of DM. A further change occurred in 1969 when the notation was altered from MDN to M. Finally a new version of the 1-mark stamp, in letterpress instead of intaglio, appeared in 1970. This stamp was released only in coils, with black serial numbers on the reverse of every fifth stamp. An intaglio 20-pfennig stamp of the same size as the mark definitives and printed in black, was released in August 1973 in mourning for Walter Ulbricht. A new definitive series, featuring prominent buildings and monuments in the Democratic Republic, was recess-printed and introduced in April 1973. Smaller versions of four denominations were produced as coil stamps (71:33).

The definitives were interspersed by frequent thematic sets, usually printed in multicolour lithography (71:18–21, 25, 30). Many sets featured reproductions of paintings, including several issues devoted to works in the Dresden Gallery (71:16, 24), but other branches of the decorative arts were also explored, and ranged from playing-cards (71:17) to porcelain (71:29). From 1969 onwards a larger, square format was often used for these thematic issues (71:26, 29).

Occasional stamps continued to appear with the theme of memorials in Germany or other countries, honouring victims of Nazi oppression (71:11, 31), while annual sets were devoted to cultural anniversaries and portrayed historic celebrities (71:34) of many countries. From 1966 onwards, sets of six stamps were issued in a miniature sheet, illustrating some well-known fairy-tale (71:32).

Numerous commemorative sets were released, ranging from singles and pairs to six or eight stamps per set. Those portraying famous people were generally confined to the portrait alone (71:23) and only occasionally incorporated some symbolic motif (71:22). East Germany was one of several countries to issue stamps in mourning for Salvador Allende and Luis Corvalan, the Chilean Marxist leaders killed in the counter-revolution of 1973. Like Belgium, East Germany experimented with stamps in which the principal motif was lightly sketched against a flat coloured background. A good example of this was provided by the Children's Spartakiad pair of 1975 (71:35). Other stamps of a political nature included semi-postals on behalf of the guerrilla movement in Vietnam, and issues commemorating the Socialist Youth Movement (71:13, 27), the International Brigade in Spain (71:12) and the annual Party Day of the Socialist Unity Party (71:14), but the political tone of East German stamps steadily decreased from 1967 onwards.

Gibraltar

The output of stamps since 1965 has increased enormously, Gibraltar having issued as many stamps in the last ten years, as in the period from 1886 – when distinctive stamps were introduced – up to the end of 1964. Before 1966, all commemoratives had consisted of the colonial omnibus issues or of overprints on the definitives, but numerous sets of distinctive designs were issued from August 1966 onwards. Two new definitive sets were introduced in this period, a

series in 1967–9 featuring ships associated with the Rock (71:37) and an ambitious series of 1971, each denomination being released in se-tenant pairs featuring old and modern views of Gibraltar (71:38). Christmas stamps were introduced in 1967 and several of the subsequent issues adopted unusual formats or composite designs (71:36). Annual sets from 1969 featured uniforms of regiments that had served on the Rock. Small-format stamps portraying Queen Elizabeth II were issued in 1971 for use in automatic vending machines. The watermark on the 1971 definitives was originally sideways, but in 1973–4 an upright watermark was used.

Great Britain

The liberalisation of British stamp policy, begun in 1964, was completed in the following year when the former taboos on the commemoration of historic events and personalities were swept away. The British Post Office stepped up its output of special issues considerably, so that the number released in this decade was about half of the total issued since the Penny Black in 1840 up to the time of its 125th anniversary. Not only was the tempo of special issues increased, but technical and economic factors had tremendous impact on the definitive issues.

The inveterate series featuring the Dorothy Wilding portrait of Queen Elizabeth II continued in use until 1968 and provided constant variety. The colour of the 4-pence stamp was deepened in 1965, following an increase in the letter rate, necessitating enormous quantities of this denomination. Increases in postal rates in the late 1960s affected the position of the phosphor bands on the 2-, 2½- and 3-pence denominations, all of which had represented the printed-matter rate at some time in this period. The expansion of the use of vending machines for stamp booklets resulted in various sideways watermark stamps and also in se-tenant combinations. Chalky paper was used for printings of the Castles half-crown stamp in 1968, but the entire series was reprinted by Bradbury Wilkinson on whiter, unwatermarked paper in 1967–8.

After a life of sixteen years the Wilding definitives were gradually replaced by a series depicting a profile of the queen by Arnold Machin (72:20), in a design of classic simplicity which at last did full justice to the tonal qualities of photogravure. This series was printed by Harrison on chalky paper with two vertical phosphor bands, except the denomination currently covering the postcard and printed paper rates. For the first time, British stamps were issued without a watermark, and this omission was extended to the commemoratives. At first, gum arabic was used but from 1968 an almost invisible adhesive composed of polyvinyl alcohol was used. Se-tenant combinations were available in coil strips and also in booklet panes. The number and position of the phosphor bands varied from time to time as postal rates increased, especially after the introduction of the two-tier postal system in September 1968. Stamps with one band prepaid the second class rate, while those with two, covered the first class rate. The 1s/6-penny stamp was released in 1969 with an over-all coating of phosphor as an experimental measure. Intaglio versions of this design were used for the larger-format high values released in 1969.

The change to decimal currency in February 1971 was reflected in the definitives which were reissued with the values redrawn, and 'P' substituted for 'D' (an abbreviation of the Latin word denarius – penny). Stamps up to 9-pence were photogravure-printed as before, the highest denomination being produced in two colours. The half-crown, five- and ten-shilling stamps were replaced by similar intaglio stamps in denominations of 10-, 20- and 50-pence (72:29), issued in June 1970, some seven months before decimalisation. The 1-pound stamp was not affected by decimalisation, but a new version of this stamp, with a Roman numeral instead of a seriffed Arabic numeral, was introduced in December 1972. Apart from numerous variations in phosphor bands, reflecting the rapid increase in postal rates, the original chalky cream paper was superseded in 1972 by fluorescent white paper. Gum arabic was re-introduced for certain denominations issued in se-tenant coil strips, and in 1973 dextrin was added to the polyvinyl alcohol adhesive, giving it a rather mottled appearance. The original 10-pence intaglio stamp was replaced in August 1971 by a photogravure version in the small format of the other low-value stamps.

Similar technical changes took place in the regional stamps used in Scotland, Northern Ireland, Wales, Guernsey, Jersey and the Isle of

Man, new values being added to the Wilding portrait series between 1966 and 1969. In the latter year Guernsey and Jersey established independent postal administrations and replaced regional and unified stamps by their own distinctive issues (73:27–32). Decimal regional stamps, using the Machin profile of the Queen, with appropriate emblems, were adopted in Scotland, Northern Ireland, Wales and the Isle of Man in 1971 (73:24–26, 33). Regional stamps were discontinued in the Isle of Man from July 1973 onwards, and distinctive stamps of the independent Manx administration were adopted (73:34). Initially, there were four denominations in each regional series, but increased rates in 1974 resulted in five new values, and a change in the phosphor band of the 3- and 3½-pence values. A 7-pence denomination was added to the unified and definitive set in 1975.

The change to decimal currency also provided the opportunity to replace the postage-due series, whose designs had remained unchanged since their inception in 1914, by a set ranging from a halfpenny to five pounds, printed in photogravure by Harrison and inscribed simply 'TO PAY'. These stamps were introduced ahead of decimalisation, in 1970, and other values were added up to 1975 (72:41).

The Dorothy Wilding three-quarter portrait of the queen was incorporated in the design of all commemorative stamps up to February 1966 (72:1–11); thereafter, a silhouette based on the coinage profile by Mrs. Mary Gillick was used in every issue, except the pair celebrating the royal silver wedding in 1972 (73:9). At times the silhouette was printed in gold ink, and in several issues it was die-stamped from metal foil (72:15) or embossed (72:25). In some cases the head was reduced to almost insignificant proportions and tipped into the design almost as an afterthought (72:22), but it was always less obtrusive than a 'proper' portrait had been and presented fewer practical problems for the designers.

With the exception of a half-crown stamp marking the 900th anniversary of Westminster Abbey (recess-printed by Bradbury Wilkinson) and a series of 1969 featuring Post Office technology (lithographed by De La Rue) all British special issues up to 1972 were photogravure-printed by Harrison and Sons. In 1973, however, Bradbury Wilkinson produced two sets, using combined lithography and letterpress for the Inigo Jones issue (73:17) and combined intaglio and letterpress for the Commonwealth Parliamentary Conference pair (73:15). Nevertheless, Harrison continued to have a virtual monopoly of British stamp contracts after that brief interlude.

A precedent was established in July 1965 by the issue of two stamps in memory of Sir Winston Churchill, who had died in January of that year (72:1). Subsequent issues commemorated Joseph Lister, though his portrait appeared on the higher value only – the 4-pence stamp showed a carbolic spray (72:4) and belated recognition was given to Robert Burns, whose devotees had been denied a commemorative issue on the occasion of his bicentenary (72:10). The only non-Briton to be honoured in this way was Mahatma Gandhi in 1969 (72:31). Having neglected to commemorate famous persons for so long, Britain began to make amends by releasing thematic sets, featuring explorers in 1972 and 1973 (73:3, 12). In a similar fashion, having lagged behind every other country in the commemoration of historic events, Britain issued a pair in 1965 honouring the seventh centenary of the parliament of Simon de Montfort (72:2) and a lengthy series in tribute to the Battle of Britain (72:6). In this series, six 4-pence stamps were printed in se-tenant combinations of different designs – a practice that was extended the following year to a series marking the 900th anniversary of the Battle of Hastings. In this series six 4-pence stamps were printed in a continuous strip forming a composite picture adapted from the Bayeux tapestry, and similar motifs appeared on 6-pence and 1-shilling 3-pence stamps (72:15).

Purely thematic stamps were introduced in 1966, the first series consisting of four stamps depicting British landscapes (72:12). Subsequent sets, featuring birds and flowers, included blocks of low values with different motifs se-tenant (72:17). In 1967 Britain succumbed to the Art craze then sweeping the world's post offices and philatelic bureaux (72:18). Having issued special Christmas aerogrammes since 1963, Britain introduced adhesive stamps for this purpose in 1966, using children's drawings initially, but reproducing Old Master paintings in 1967 (72:22), striking a more secular note

in 1968 (72:25) and returning to the religious theme in subsequent years (72:33, 38; 73:4, 7, 18). During 1975 sets of four stamps marked the bicentenaries of the birth of the painter J. M. W. Turner and the novelist Jane Austen. European Architectural Heritage Year and the 150th anniversary of the first public railway system were the occasion of sets of four stamps featuring prominent buildings (73:23) and locomotives respectively. The strongly thematic character of British special issues was reinforced by a quartet in July devoted to leisure sailing craft. Later thematic sets illustrated British technical achievements, bridges, ships, cathedrals, domestic architecture, modern university buildings, churches, trees and medieval heroes (72:14, 21, 23, 26, 30, 36; 73:2, 6, 11).

At the beginning of this decade, commemorative sets were issued in honour of individual events and personalities. As the number of sets increased, there was a tendency to decrease the number of stamps per set by way of compensation. With the exception of the Battle of Britain and Hastings sets already noted, the commemoratives from 1965 to 1968 consisted of pairs (72:1–5, 7–11, 16), one set of three for the World Cup football championship (72:13), the 4-pence stamp subsequently re-engraved with the inscription 'England Winners' and a single in honour of Sir Francis Chichester's yacht Gipsy Moth IV (72:19). The last-named was the nearest approach to a stamp commemorating a living person other than a member of the royal family, though Sir Francis himself was not portrayed. In 1968 a new policy was introduced; henceforth, anniversaries were grouped together in a single series, each stamp being devoted to an event in that year. These sets, known as the British Anniversaries series, continued until 1972 and ranged from three to five stamps in each case (72:24, 28, 34; 73:1, 5).

The Anniversaries series did not preclude the commemoration of events by individual sets. Since the Anniversaries sets consisted of different denominations, only one of which (the inland letter rate) was widely seen in the country itself, the clamour for individual sets for worthy causes tended to diminish the popularity of the general series. Thus, in 1969 a separate set of five stamps was issued to commemorate the investiture of the Prince of Wales, and a single stamp for Gandhi. The following year a separate series devoted to literary anniversaries was instituted, a block of four honouring Dickens and a single for Wordsworth. Subsequent sets honoured Keats, Gray and Scott (1971), and Jane Austen (1975) – the first woman to be commemorated in this way.

Although art thematic sets were discontinued in 1968 Britain never lost sight of the popularity of this subject and produced several issues in the same genre, but strictly as commemoratives. Paintings from the 'Ulster 71' exhibition were reproduced on stamps marking the golden jubilee of Northern Ireland (72:39), while sets of four stamps reproducing paintings were issued in 1973 and 1975 to mark anniversaries of Reynolds, Raeburn and Turner (73:14). Caricatures of Dr. Grace by Harry Furniss provided an unusual medium for a set marking the centenary of county cricket in 1973 (73:13). Apart from the four architectural thematic sets, there were two commemorative issues highlighting this subject; the four stamps of 1973, issued in se-tenant pairs in honour of Inigo Jones (73:17) and the set of five stamps in April 1975 in honour of European Architectural Heritage Year.

A thematic approach was also adopted in the case of sets, generally of four stamps, commemorating the anniversary of important technological achievements. Sets in this category began in 1972, with four stamps devoted to anniversaries of radio and broadcasting (73:8) and continued with a series of historic fire engines, for the bicentenary of the Fire Service legislation (73:19) and the set of historic locomotives for the sesquicentennial of the first public steam railway in August 1975.

Relatively few individual issues were made to commemorate current events. Sets were issued in honour of the Commonwealth Games in Edinburgh (72:35), the 'Philympia' international philatelic exhibition (72:37), Britain's entry into the European Economic Community in 1973 (73:10) and three royal events, the Prince of Wales' investiture (1969), the royal silver wedding (1972) and the wedding of Princess Anne (1973) (73:9, 16). In 1974 four stamps commemorated the centenary of the Universal Postal Union (73:20) and four stamps, portraying Sir Winston Churchill at different stages of his long career, were released in honour of his birth centenary – the first Briton to be commemorated by stamps on more than one occasion (73:21).

A decade that had witnessed changes in every aspect of British stamp policy ended with the release of Britain's first semi-postal issue, in January 1975. The stamp, featuring a figure in a wheelchair, bore a premium in aid of Health and Handicap charities and was issued on an experimental basis. Curiously enough, although Britain pioneered the use of the postal service for charitable purposes, with a semi-postal card and envelope in 1890, this was the first time that adhesive charity stamps were released (73:22).

When the British Post Office became a public corporation in October 1969, and ceased to be a Civil Service department, the Crown Dependencies were given the option of establishing their own postal administrations. Both Guernsey and Jersey chose to do so, but the Isle of Man continued to use the facilities of the British Post Office until July 1973. The Channel Islands introduced distinctive pictorial definitives in 1969, the Guernsey series incorporating motifs from coins portraying kings and queens associated with the bailiwick (73:27), while Jersey's assorted vignettes were framed by a montage of elements symbolising island life (73:30). Both bailiwicks reissued their definitives in 1971 with decimal denominations, and Guernsey introduced a new series in 1974 with the theme of uniforms of the Guernsey Militia (73:29). Both islands have issued a number of commemoratives, the majority in both cases being printed in multicolour photogravure by Courvoisier (73:28, 31). Four stamps illustrating aspects of farming in the nineteenth century were released in February 1975 (73:32). A similar policy was adopted by the Isle of Man in July 1973, a pictorial definitive series by Courvoisier being followed by numerous commemorative sets, mainly of local interest (73:34) or applying a Manx touch to events of British or international interest.

Greece
Remarkably few stamps took note of the turbulent situation in Greece for much of this decade. Apart from short sets in 1967 and 1972, celebrating the Colonels' coup and the 5th anniversary of the military junta, no stamps referred to the overthrow of democracy, the abortive counter-coup of King Constantine, his subsequent flight into exile, or the establishment of a republic in June 1973. Both in policy and design, Greek stamps continued much as they had done in the previous decade. There were no definitive sets as such, but lengthy thematic issues changed at regular intervals. These sets featured Greek popular art, 1966 (74:2), the Labours of Hercules, 1970 (74:6), regional costumes, 1972–3 (74:11), monasteries and churches, 1972 (74:12), archaeological discoveries, 1973 (74:13) and Greek mythology, 1972–3 (74:14). The majority of the stamps in this decade looked back, either to the struggles of the wars of independence in the early nineteenth century (74:9), the sesqui-centennial of whose battles fell in this period, or to the glories of classical Greece. Apart from the thematic issues which focused attention on the past, motifs from the art of the ancient world were frequently used to commemorate current events or recent anniversaries. Thus, ancient coins and friezes provided the subjects for stamps in 1969 marking the jubilee of the International Labour Organisation and the 20th anniversary of NATO (74:4), and, not surprisingly, the series of 1968 honouring the Olympic Games in Mexico (74:5) incorporated classical motifs. This continual harking-back to the ancient greatness of Greece was deliberately cultivated by the régime and attained its zenith in a lengthy series of 1968, coinciding with the first anniversary of the coup. Paintings, sculpture, bronzes and friezes were reproduced on stamps whose theme was 'the Hellenic fight for Civilization' (74:3).

Greece continued to participate in the annual Europa issues, using standard designs until 1974 (74:10) and featuring sculptures in that year (74:15). Two of these stamps featured ancient works of art, but the third chose a modern piece. Among the few commemoratives that broke away from the obsession with the past, were the series honouring the painter, El Greco, in 1965 (74:1), the pair marking the inauguration of the Satellite Earth telecommunications station at Thermopylae (74:7) and the set of four in honour of Nature Conservation Year, 1970 (74:8). Nearly all of the stamps issued in this decade were the work of three designers, A. Tassos, P. Gravalos and George Velissarides, though V. Constantinea began designing stamps regularly in 1973. Multicolour lithography,

by the Aspioti-Elka Graphic Arts Company of Athens, was used throughout. Since 1966 all Greek stamps have been inscribed HELLAS in the Roman alphabet as well as in Greek script.

Hungary
Between 1965 and the end of 1974 Hungary issued over 900 stamps, a fifty per cent increase in output over the previous decade which made her one of the world's most prolific countries. Multicolour photogravure or lithography were used for the great majority of special issues, the 1972 monuments protection stamp, in blackish green, being a rare exception to this rule (74:27). Although unusual shapes, such as triangles and diamonds, were confined to a handful of sports issues in this period – compared to the large number in the previous decade, stamps in general tended to become much larger (74:24, 26) and an elongated format became very fashionable (74:16, 17).

The small-format transport definitives of 1963 remained current throughout this period, with various new values and changes of colour up to 1970. The same small format was adopted for a new series, released in 1972–4, featuring landmarks in the main cities. A series of postage-due stamps in this style, featuring aspects of postal mechanisation, was introduced in December 1973. Airmail stamps, depicting cities all over the world, to which the state airline MALEV operated routes, were issued in 1966–7 (74:20). A 2.60-forint stamp in a similar design, featuring St. Stephen's Cathedral in Vienna, was issued in July 1968 to mark the 50th anniversary of the Budapest–Vienna airmail service.

Stamps commemorating historic and current events were usually issued in short sets or singles (74:23, 25). Children's prize-winning drawings were used in a set of three stamps of 1968 marking the 50th anniversary of the Hungarian Communist Party (74:22). Long thematic sets, however, constituted the bulk of Hungarian output, with variations on such popular subjects as flora, fauna and space exploration (74:16, 19, 21, 24). Among the more unusual themes were medals and decorations (74:18) and vintage motor cars (74:26). Few Hungarian stamps succumbed to the prevailing fashion for poster designs; an essentially naturalistic treatment being retained throughout this period.

Iceland
Courvoisier had a virtual monopoly of Icelandic stamp production throughout this period, occasional stamps being lithographed by De La Rue (1972–3) or printed in intaglio or lithography by the State Bank Note Printing Works in Helsinki. The latter printed the pair of 1973 in the omnibus design used by all the Nordic countries to publicise their postal co-operation (74:34). There were no definitives as such, but short thematic sets were issued frequently in a wide range of denominations for this purpose. Themes ranged from scenery and manuscripts to hot-house plant cultivation, birds and flowers (74:30, 32). Semi-postal stamps with premiums in aid of local charities, were introduced in 1967 and issued annually in November. Stamps in the prevailing Europa designs were issued each year (74:29). Among the more unusual stamps of this period were the set of three in 1965 celebrating the birth of the island of Surtsey, created as a result of submarine volcanic eruption (74:28). Most commemorative stamps were released as singles (74:33) or pairs (74:31), but seven stamps were issued in 1974 to celebrate the eleventh centenary of settlement in Iceland.

Ireland
Photogravure equipment was installed at the Stamping Branch of the Revenue Commissioners in Dublin in 1965 and thenceforward the majority of Irish stamps were printed by this process. The last of the commemoratives to be produced by Harrison was the pair of May 1965 marking the centenary of the International Telecommunications Union (75:1). In 1966–7, 3- and 5-pence values of the definitive series were reprinted in photogravure instead of letterpress. The photogravure versions were slightly smaller than the original designs. The 5-pence was initially released in stamp booklets but subsequently appeared in normal sheet form in a rather brighter shade of violet and with more regular lines of shading. The definitives, which had remained unchanged in design since the birth of the Irish Free State in 1922, were replaced in 1968–70 by a series

by Heinrich Gerl reproducing classical Irish art (75:8). Like all Irish stamps since 1922 these had the value denoted by a 'p' (*pingin*), whereas other countries using sterling currency favoured the abbreviation 'd' (*denarius*). When Irish currency was decimalised in 1971, in line with British currency, the notation 'p' would have been confusing, as this denoted 'new pence' in everyday commercial transactions; consequently the stamps were reissued with the abbreviation omitted altogether (75:10). This problem affected all commemoratives and special issues from May 1971 onwards.

Many of the commemoratives in this period celebrated 50th anniversaries of the struggle for independence, from the Easter Rising of 1916 (75:2) to the establishment of the Dail (75:6) and the deaths of Irish patriots in the 'Troubles' (75:9). Other stamps marked the centenaries of the Fenian movement (75:3) and the births of James Connolly and Countess Markievicz (75:5). In those stamps commemorating people, photographs were used as the basis of the designs, but the stamps commemorating events often chose a more abstract style (75:2). The more international outlook of Ireland in recent years was reflected in stamps celebrating the centenary of Canadian confederation and Mahatma Gandhi (75:4) or referring to international events, such as European Conservation Year, World Health Day, Racial Equality Year and International Women's Year (75:11).

Although Irish stamps made little use of the full-colour potential of photogravure, multicoloured stamps reproducing contemporary works of art were introduced in 1969, beginning with an outsize stamp – featuring a stained glass window in Eton College chapel – by Evie Hone. Monamy's painting of sailing boats was reproduced on a stamp of 1970 in honour of the 250th anniversary of the Royal Cork Yacht Club (75:7), but subsequent issues in the contemporary art series tended towards the abstract (75:12). Paintings were reproduced on a stamp of 1974 honouring the Royal National Lifeboat Institution and the Christmas issues which became an annual feature from 1971 onwards (75:13). For the 1975 Europa commemoration, Ireland chose a detail from the painting 'Castletown Hunt' by Robert Healy (75:15). The abstract nature of most commemoratives became absolute from 1970, a situation, the obscurity of which, was not helped by the continuance of Gaelic as the sole medium for inscriptions (75:11, 14).

Italy

The 'Siracusa' definitive series, introduced in 1953, remained current throughout this period, with various denominations being added to the original series up to 1966. In 1968, fluorescent paper was adopted and the series was redrawn in a reduced size. Denominations up to 180-lira were photogravure-printed, while the 200- and 300-lira were recess-printed with the coin and inscriptions on a colourless background (75:30). Between 1968 and 1974 several values were printed in two-colour combinations (75:35). From 1968 onwards, the majority of the special issues were also printed on fluorescent paper.

The majority of Italian commemoratives were printed in photogravure, but intaglio combined with photogravure (75:36) was used occasionally from 1971, and intaglio combined with lithography (75:40), or lithography alone, used from 1973 onwards. Several short thematic sets augmented the permanent range from 1966 and included trees (75:19), national parks (75:24), paintings of Venice and Italian fountains (75:39). Fewer countries celebrated Holy Year in 1975 with special stamps than had done in 1950. Among the few which continued to adhere to this jubilee was Italy whose set of four depicted famous religious statues (75:40). The Venetian paintings also served to publicise the national campaign for the conservation of Venice. The small upright format, used for portrait commemoratives, remained popular (75:29, 34), though greater variety was introduced in the colouring and by the inclusion of background material. The old commemorative format (double the size of the definitive stamps) lingered on until as late as 1968 (75:26) but a larger format, of the same length but of greater width, became standard for the majority of special issues from 1965 onwards (75:16–25, 27, 28, 31–33, 36–38, 40). Monochrome was used occasionally (75:21, 27) but a peculiarly Italian blend of soft, muted shades was more common (75:25, 38, 39). Formal designs with restrained use of colour remained the keynote of Italian stamps to the end of the decade (75:16, 18, 33), though the influence of modern

poster design was evident in many of the stamps from 1968 onwards (74:28, 31, 32, 37).

Liechtenstein

Landscapes formed the subject of an intaglio definitive series released in 1972–3 replacing the photogravure series of 1959–64. Apart from the annual Europa and Christmas stamps, Liechtenstein produced a moderate number of short thematic sets, often continuing a single theme over several years. Thus, several sets were devoted to coats of arms, followed by 'patrons of the churches' (76:1) and latterly, *their* coats of arms. Other recurring themes were Liechtenstein sagas, flowers and art treasures in the prince's collection. Appropriately, for a country that had once relied heavily on philatelic revenue, occasional sets were devoted to pioneers of philately (76:2). Apart from a few stamps lithographed in Berlin or recess-printed in Vienna, all stamps of this period were produced in Switzerland, either in photogravure by Courvoisier or intaglio by the Swiss PTT in Berne.

Luxembourg

The Grand-Duchess Charlotte abdicated in November 1964 and a definitive series portraying her successor, Grand-Duke Jean, appeared the following April (76:3). The series was recess-printed by the Swiss PTT Bureau in Berne and various denominations were added up to 1971. The series was supplemented from time to time by tourist publicity stamps on the French model, and these were recess-printed at the French Government Printing Works (76:9). The French connection even extended to the release of large-sized stamps reproducing paintings in multicolour intaglio, following the pattern of French art stamps, with lettering by the French designer, P. Bequet (76:7). Generally, however, Luxembourg continued to make use of the leading Swiss and Dutch printers as before. Enschedé used lithography for several issues between 1965 and 1971 (76:4) and photogravure thereafter. Most of the photogravure issues were produced by Courvoisier (76:5, 6, 8), though Harrison produced three sets between 1968 and 1971. There was no dramatic change in Luxembourg stamp policy in this decade. The semi-postals for the National Welfare fund continued to appear each December, illustrating a wide range of subjects and Europa stamps were released each May (76:8), but only a moderate number of commemoratives and special issues was produced and Luxembourg ranked as one of the more stable and conservative countries.

Malta

The rather staid intaglio series was replaced in January 1965 by a lengthy series with the same theme – the history of Malta – but produced by Harrison in multicolour photogravure (76:10). This series was technically one of the most complex ever produced by that firm, involving the use of two plates for the gold or silver framework and lettering on the higher denominations. The series was originally issued with gum arabic, but polyvinyl alcohol adhesive was introduced in 1969. New values were added in 1970 as a result of increased letter rates. Decimal currency was adopted in May 1972 and a set of eight stamps was issued to familiarise the public with the new coins (76:25). Several values of the definitive series were surcharged in the new currency, pending the release of a distinctive series in March 1973 (76:27).

Chevalier Cremona designed all the stamps up to 1970, when J. Casha produced the motif for a set of three stamps commemorating the 25th anniversary of the United Nations (76:24), but although several other artists had a hand in the production of Maltese stamps thereafter, Cremona continued to be responsible for the majority of the designs and left his indelible mark on them, particularly in his penchant for unusual formats (76:15, 17–19, 21, 23, 26) and the rich contrast of sombre colours and gold metallic ink (76:20, 22, 27, 28).

Malta took part in the annual Europa commemoration, but whereas other countries were content with singles or pairs, Malta tended to issue the standard designs in sets of three or four stamps. Local sculptures were used for the 1974 series (76:29). The Christmas stamps, introduced in 1964, were released annually, and one may detect the development in Cremona's style, from the somewhat ascetic figures of the 1965, 1966 and 1968 sets (76:13, 14, 21) to the stylised angels of 1967 and 1972 (76:17, 26). The characteristics of Cremona's art transcended the wide range of printers and processes used for the interpretation of his designs, ranging from Harrison (76:12) and the Italian Government Printing Works (76:11) to Enschedé (76:13, 16), De La Rue (76:14, 17) and the Israeli Government Printer. From 1969 onwards, lithography was used with increasing frequency, and stamps were produced in this process by Harrison, De La Rue and Format (76:25), but from 1972 onwards, all Maltese stamps have been lithographed in the island by Printex Limited.

Monaco

With more than 300 stamps in this period, Monaco continued to reflect or amplify the philatelic policy of her larger neighbour, often commemorating French anniversaries at greater length than France, or issuing stamps for occasions and individuals overlooked by France. This was particularly true in the late 1960s, with sets portraying Chateaubriand, Berlioz and Daudet and copiously illustrated with scenes and characters from their works. From 1970 onwards, however, Monaco drastically cut back the number of stamps per set, and latterly was content with single stamps, or even with several celebrities grouped together in a single anniversaries set. The long thematic sets, that were a notorious feature of the 1950s and early 1960s, were much less evident in this decade and were usually tied to a particular event or anniversary. Thus the series featuring vintage racing cars (76:31) commemorated the silver jubilee of the Monaco Grand Prix. The centenary of Monte Carlo was the pretext for a long set devoted to buildings and monuments in the city (76:30). The distinctive style of design, with motifs on a stippled background hedged by thin frame-lines, continued sporadically until 1970 (76:33), but increasingly, more solid designs, with white lettering, and no frame-lines, were adopted (76:32, 34–36). The first stamps devoted to the hobby of flower arranging, were produced by Monaco in 1975 to publicise an international competition held in the Principality (76:37). Christmas stamps were issued in 1972 (76:34), but the following year, a series was issued to mark the 50th anniversary of the National Committee for Monegasque Traditions and unseasonably featured the procession of Christ on the Cross on Good Friday. All Monegasque stamps were invariably designed and engraved by French artists and recess-printed at the French Government Printing Works.

Netherlands

Although all Dutch stamps of this period were produced by Enschedé as before, they presented a versatile range of printing processes and design styles. A new definitive series, with a more up-to-date profile of Queen Juliana, was introduced in 1969 and completed, by instalments, in February 1972 (77:20). Stamps perforated on three sides only were available from stamp booklets. The series was photogravure-printed, two sizes being used respectively for the cents and gulden denominations in accordance with previous practice. The majority of the special issues were printed in photogravure, ranging from monochrome (77:18) to multicolour (77:31), but as a rule, vigorous combinations of two or three primary colours were preferred for the adventurous experiments with lettering and layout. Dutch designers were pre-occupied with *trompe l'oeil* and other optical effects, to create a three-dimensional impression (77:1, 11, 15–17), especially between 1969 and 1972. In 1970 the cultural, social and health series was actually designed by a computer and the welter of concentric circles and parallel planes in cubes was printed in combined intaglio and lithography.

Intaglio alone was used for relatively few stamps (77:3) and was combined with yellow-green paper for the Erasmus issue of 1969 (77:12). Several issues were entirely freed from the traditional frame-lines to the extent of having the motif bleed into the perforations (77:21, 24, 27) and in many others the background colour was bled off in a similar manner (77:1, 13, 23, 25, 29, 30). Compared to the philatelic tributes paid to such international figures as Winston Churchill, John F. Kennedy and Charles de Gaulle, the homage to Dr. Albert Schweitzer was disappointing. The Netherlands was one of the few countries that commemorated in 1975 the centenary of his birth (77:31). Designers were often pre-occupied with the ornamental qualities of lettering for its own sake (77:8, 22), and the annual Child Welfare sets were often used as an excuse to experiment with esoteric subjects (77:19) or unusual approaches to a familiar theme (77:5, 26). For the 1972 Child Welfare stamps,

photographs of the royal children were used (77:26), but the 1974 series used photographs from a late nineteenth-century family potrait album; at the time of the issue the children depicted were all still alive, though now in their eighties.

Europa stamps were issued every year in the standard designs (77:4) or the uniform themes from 1974 onwards. Mini-omnibus issues appeared in 1969, in conjunction with the overseas territories of the Antilles and Surinam, to mark the 25th anniversary of the Statute of the Kingdom (77:10) and in conjunction with Belgium and Luxembourg for the silver jubilee of Benelux (77:11). During most of this period, commemoratives, in singles or pairs, were issued piecemeal (77:2, 3, 6–9, 12–16, 18, 21–24, 27), but in 1973 a number of events and anniversaries were grouped together into a single set of four stamps, following the Swiss pattern (77:28). There was a tendency also to relate the subjects of the cultural, health and social welfare stamps to anniversaries. Thus music, theatre and ballet were the theme of the 1974 series and two stamps portrayed the playwright Herman Heijermans and a character from one of his plays. Apart from the two annual charity sets, there were two issues on behalf of the Dutch Red Cross, in 1967 and 1972 respectively. The latter series bore premiums in the usual manner (77:25) but included a 5-cent stamp without premium, to cover the additional postage necessitated by increased postal charges.

Norway

The definitive series introduced in 1962 remained current throughout this decade, and new values and colour changes were adopted between 1965 and 1974. Phosphorescent paper was introduced in 1968 and all definitives and commemoratives from the beginning of that year were printed on this paper as an aid to electronic sorting. New kroner definitives were recess-printed in 1969–70 portraying King Olav V (77:37). The adoption of intaglio for the definitives in 1962 was extended to the commemoratives from 1965 onwards. Most Norwegian stamps since 1937 had been printed in photogravure, but in this decade a sizeable number of commemoratives were recess-printed at the Norwegian Bank printing works (77:33, 35–38, 40, 44, 45, 47, 49) or the Finnish Bank printing works in Helsinki (77:43). Emil Mostue of Oslo produced all the other commemoratives in photogravure up to 1973 (77:34, 39, 41, 42, 46) when multicolour lithography was adopted for sets featuring Norwegian flowers and paintings (77:48).

There was little change in Norwegian stamps in this period, either in frequency or design policy. Europa stamps were the only regular annual issue (77:32), though occasional thematic sets, in pairs or groups of three, were issued from 1968 onwards (77:42, 46, 48).

Poland

No definitives in the true sense were released in this period, though long thematic sets appeared at frequent intervals and covered the range of denominations in most common use. The more popular themes were repeated time and time again, but some attempt was made to explore the more esoteric aspects of each subject. Thus, sets devoted merely to flowers were superseded by more sophisticated issues illustrating flowers of the meadow, orchids or protected plants (78:6); fauna was sub-divided into forest animals (78:2), prehistoric animals and pedigree dogs (78:9), or combined with the art craze, as in the series reproducing hunting scenes by well-known artists (78:8). Apart from numerous sets reproducing paintings and other forms of fine art, purely as thematic issues, this medium was used for commemorative stamps, such as the UNICEF series of 1971 which utilised children's paintings (78:14). The use of stamps for advance publicity had already been established for such events as Olympic Games, but Poland was the first country to issue stamps in advance of a historic anniversary. Such anticipatory commemoratives appeared up to four years ahead of the Copernicus quingentenary.

Between 1969 and the actual anniversary in 1973 seven sets were released, including a Stamp Day semi-postal and two coil stamps; the majority of these stamps reproduced portraits of Copernicus by various artists, as well as aspects of his work, and buildings and views associated with his life (78:16).

Other forms of art were the subject of long sets, and ranged from stained-glass windows to cut-paper work (78:11). Several sets devoted to tourism were issued between 1966 and 1970 (78:4), as well as lengthy series featuring various aspects of Polish life, from castles and medieval artifacts to shipping (78:13, 17). Sporting events provided the source of numerous issues from national and European games (78:3) to the Olympic Games (78:10, 15). Few of the commemoratives bore any reference to politics, though several sets commemorated anniversaries connected with the Second World War, and included several sets, released at annual intervals, devoted to the Polish struggle against Nazi Germany (78:5). Individual commemoratives in the same theme featured war memorials (78:12) and paintings of battle scenes.

A set of eight stamps and a miniature sheet appeared in 1965 to celebrate the 700th anniversary of Warsaw, the stamps being recess-printed while the sheet was produced in combined intaglio and photogravure (78:1). Although this series was essentially commemorative, two denominations (40- and 60-groszy) were surcharged with various new values in 1972 to create a quasi-definitive series (78:7).

Portugal

All the stamps released in this decade were printed in Portugal, mainly by lithography at the Lisbon Mint, or by three commercial firms – Litografia de Portugal (Lisbon) or Litografia Maia and Litografia Nacional (Oporto). Intaglio was used on a very few occasions between 1969 and 1971 (78:25, 33) and combined with lithography twice, in 1970 and 1973. The medieval knight definitives, introduced in 1953, remained in use throughout this period, new colours being added in 1972. Thinner paper and whiter gum were adopted in 1967. Portugal's first definitive series to depart from the single, uniform design concept began appearing in March 1972. The stamps were in the same small, horizontal format as before, but featured a wide range of buildings, monuments and scenery in multicolour lithography, from designs by the Post Office art department (78:35). An unusual feature of this series was the continuous inscription, consisting of the initials CTT and the date in microscopic lettering, covering the backs of the stamps.

The Europa series continued to be the only regular issue; three stamps in the prevailing design or theme being released each year (78:38). Commemoratives were issued in short sets of two, three or four stamps, this number being exceeded on very few occasions. Seven stamps with the theme of 'Madeira – Pearl of the Atlantic' were issued in 1966 in honour of the Lubrapex Stamp Exhibition (78:25) and a set of six honoured the Munich Olympic Games in 1972. Two thematic sets of 1971, featuring windmills and sculptors respectively, each consisted of six stamps (78:32), but other thematic issues of this period, such as the port wine series of 1970 (78:31) were limited to four stamps. Very few of the special issues adopted a pictorial approach and those that did, usually employed a stylised treatment of the subject (78:20, 27, 30). In most cases, however, a purely symbolic style was employed, continuing the policy of the previous decade (78:18–23, 29, 34, 37, 39). Tombstones were depicted on stamps of 1967 celebrating the centenary of the abolition of the death penalty (78:24), and the series honouring the Osaka World's Fair in 1970 had designs symbolising the spread of European culture and the Christian religion to Japan by the Portuguese in the sixteenth century (78:28). Fortunately many of these issues had an explanatory text, in Portuguese, French and English, on the reverse. Even portraiture was often stylised; D. Costa's treatment of the portraits of Camoëns in the series of 1972 being a typical example (78:36).

Romania

Like Hungary, Romania continued to issue definitive sets throughout this decade. After a gap of seven years, this policy was revived in 1967 with a series whose theme was transport and communications (79:6). Various denominations were added up to 1969, two sizes being used. New designs were introduced in 1971 and the size of all stamps reduced to the standard format of the 1960 series and the postage-due set. The following year a similar series, featuring buildings and monuments was released and after little more than a year it was replaced by a small-format series, featuring landmarks and modern ships (79:14). New postage-due stamps, in bipartite pairs, were released in 1974 (79:16).

The annual series of cultural anniversaries stamps continued to be the only regular issue (79:5), though occasionally, separate sets were released in honour of individuals ranging from Marx, Engels and Lenin to heroes of the struggle for independence from the Turks and medieval princes (79:10). Long thematic sets, however, provided the bulk of Romania's prolific output, exploring every aspect of the more popular themes. American and Soviet space achievements provided a steady source of material for several sets in 1965–6 (79:1, 4), but the number of stamps diminished after that and significantly, it was mainly the American Apollo spacecraft which were commemorated in subsequent years. Flora and fauna, the principal stock in trade of thematic philately, resulted in numerous sets of a fairly abstruse nature, ranging from exotics of the Cluj Botanic Gardens (79:2) to crustaceans and molluscs, prehistoric monsters and their skeletons, hunting trophies and birds of the nature reserves (79:8).

Several sets from 1966 onwards were devoted to paintings in the Bucharest National Gallery, and paintings were also reproduced on stamps to commemorate anniversaries and current events. Between 1969 and 1971, three sets were devoted to frescoes from the monasteries of Northern Moldavia (79:9). Later sets were issued with the theme of paintings showing workers, marine paintings and Impressionist works. In 1973 two sets featured fourth-century treasures of Pietroasa (79:12) and Romanian ceramics (79:13). The centenary of the Romanian monetary system was the subject of two stamps in 1967 depicting old and new coins, and this was the theme of a lengthy series three years later, featuring historic coins from classical to medieval times (79:11).

Apart from sporting events, most commemoratives were released in singles or pairs. The Olympic Games and World Cup football championships of this period were all well documented, though not to the same extent as in the early 1960s (79:3). By contrast, such events as the World Population Conference, held in Bucharest in 1974, merited one stamp only (79:15).

The inauguration of the Derdap hydro-electric scheme in 1965, a joint Romanian–Yugoslav project, was marked by two stamps and a miniature sheet inscribed with the names and currencies of both countries and issued simultaneously in Romania and Yugoslavia. This was the first time that such a multi-national issue had been made, taking the omnibus idea to its logical conclusion, but none of the other mini-omnibus issues of this decade repeated this interesting experiment.

Russia

Russia maintained her position as the world's most prolific issuer of stamps, though there was no significant increase in output between 1965 and 1974, compared to the previous period (from 1,200 stamps in the middle period to 1,300 in the later years). The 1961 definitives remained in use until 1966, a 4-kopek stamp in a new colour being released in 1965. The same distinctive format was used for a similar series introduced in October 1966 and covering the denominations from 1- to 16-kopek (79:17), printed by lithography. A larger format, with the same layout of motifs and lettering, was used for the higher denominations, printed by photogravure. The 4-kopek stamp (covering the inland letter rate) was reissued in April 1969 on fluorescent paper. In June 1968 similar designs (also dated 1966) were recess-printed and new colours and values introduced. This series remained current throughout the rest of the decade.

Soviet stamps differed from those of the other Communist countries principally in purpose and content rather than in style of design. There were, proportionately, far fewer thematic sets and their treatment was often more impressionistic than was usually adopted for this purpose (79:22). Many of the recurring themes were peculiar to Russian philately – architecture of the Kremlin (79:21) and warships (79:26) were the subject of several sets over a period of years. Soviet war heroes, a theme introduced in 1963, were portrayed on many stamps of this decade, the stamps having a uniform layout featuring a portrait, the Order of Hero of the Soviet Union and a battle scene in the background (79:27). Inevitably Russia succumbed to the global craze for Art stamps, but produced relatively few in this theme (79:20), though occasionally using reproductions of paintings as the medium for commemorating events and personalities (79:25).

Stamps were issued each year to celebrate Lenin's birthday and a wide variety of portraits of the founder of the Soviet state were also used for stamps commemorating Russian organisations and institutions. On the occasion of his centenary, a stamp and miniature sheet were issued in connection with the Lenin Centenary All-Union Philatelic Exhibition in Moscow, while ten stamps and a miniature sheet celebrated the actual birthday. The stamps, each bearing a different portrait from various stages of his life, were issued in sheets of eight with sixteen marginal labels depicting scenes and symbolic motifs relating to his career. The other great event which occurred in this decade was the 50th anniversary of the October Revolution. A series of sixteen stamps appeared in August 1967 showing the emblems of each of the Soviet Republics, with a view of the respective capital (79:23). Subsequent issues took the themes of 'fifty glorious years' and 'fifty years of Communist development'. The diamond jubilee of the abortive 1905 revolution was commemorated by a modest series of four stamps (79:18).

Numerous stamps were issued to commemorate individuals, and in most cases a standard format and frame were used (79:24); these issues included stamps honouring the Communist leaders of many countries from the United States to Finland. Current events were usually publicised by single stamps, especially in more recent years (79:31) and the same policy was extended to issues marking historic anniversaries (79:28-30, 32). The miniaturised poster technique, begun in the early 1960s, continued in this period (79:19), but degenerated in the early 1970s into a stereotyped formula: a dominant symbolic motif, with a jumble of smaller elements, often overlapping, in the background (79:23, 28-30, 32).

San Marino

The policy of frequent thematic sets continued as before, but there were some significant changes in Sammarinese stamp production. Beginning with a series in honour of Dante in 1965, San Marino adopted the intaglio process, which had seldom been employed since the 1930s. This process was particularly effective in the large format of the Dante and many subsequent sets. The change from photogravure paralleled developments in Italy and after 1969 the two processes were often combined. The large intaglio stamps of 1965-9 included a series on tinted paper, devoted to Gothic cathedrals of Europe (80:4). Lithography was used for a series of 1968 featuring coats of arms, but photogravure remained the principal medium for multicolour stamps (80:1-3). All the more popular themes were repeated to the point of exhaustion, with flowers, animals, fish, sports and paintings accounting for the majority of the thematic issues. Paintings were also reproduced on stamps commemorating stamp exhibitions and the Save Venice campaign, as well as honouring important anniversaries of such artists as Uccello and Botticelli (80:6). By contrast, characters from well-known animated cartoons were the subject of ten stamps of 1970 in honour of Walt Disney; the stamps were designed by Walt Disney Studios (80:5).

Spain

The 1955 definitive series portraying General Franco remained current in this period, but no attempt was made to introduce new denominations to take account of the gradual depreciation of the peseta, and for all practical purposes definitive stamps were superseded by long sets devoted to various themes. These issues fell into two categories. The majority of sets had a wide range of denominations and were released as an entity, but the practice of issuing a large number of stamps of the same denomination in a single theme over a long period was continued in this decade. The arms series, instituted in 1962, continued until September 1966 and included the overseas provinces (80:7). The following year, stamps featuring provincial costumes were introduced and these continued at regular intervals, covering the prevailing letter rate, until May 1971 (80:15). Thereafter, Spain reverted to the original policy of multi-value sets released en bloc. Most of these themes recurred at annual intervals, over a period of several years. The most prolific of these sets was devoted to famous Spaniards and consisted either of vertical portrait stamps (80:24) or horizontal designs in which the portrait was linked to a background scene (80:12, 33). Up to 1970, intaglio was invariably used for the celebrity series, but thereafter, photogravure was used increasingly and different formats were used from time to time (80:17).

The format of the definitive series, widely employed in the previous period for both commemorative and thematic sets, was used only once in this decade, for two stamps of 1969 ostensibly in aid of

Spanish workers deprived of their employment by the embargo placed on Gibraltar, but actually intended as propaganda for the Spanish claim to the Rock (80:13). Both stamps depicted views of Gibraltar and were printed in monochrome photogravure. A much larger size in the same style was adopted for many thematic sets, particularly those featuring castles and scenery, but the previous policy of two- or three-colour intaglio remained active throughout this period (80:8, 30, 37). Another significant change was the increase by a third in the double-sized format. The original format remained in use – again for thematic sets devoted to castles, monasteries and monuments (80:19, 23, 38) – but the larger format was used from 1967 onwards, mainly for commemoratives. The characteristic two-colour intaglio process was used occasionally (80:31), but this format was more often allied to multicolour photogravure. Greater use of colour was made in the commemoratives in 1965 and they attained the full colour range two years later. Although white lettering on fairly solid backgrounds was preferred for most Spanish stamps (80:8, 13, 22-25, 28-31, 37-39), the white backgrounds of the arms and costumes issues encouraged a style of design which favoured coloured inscriptions and motifs on white, with thin frame-lines (80:17) and eventually even the frame-lines were eliminated (80:18, 20, 35).

The regular issues, established in the previous period, continued unchanged. Classical Spanish stamps and their postmarks provided the recurring theme of the Stamp Day issues of this decade (80:9, 35). Christmas stamps reproduced religious paintings and sculpture and gradually became more colourful (80:22, 32, 39). Although Spain took part in the annual Europa issues, she gradually moved away from the standard designs. Luigi Gasbarra's stylised colonnade motif of 1969 was given an entirely naturalistic interpretation by G. Belli. In later years Spain used her own designs, abandoning even the Europa inscription, though retaining the initials CEPT (80:34).

The majority of commemorative stamps were released as singles. A very large format was used for several issues in 1967 (80:11) but was later abandoned. Stamps printed in photogravure against a toned, frameless background, were issued to commemorate explorers and colonisers of America; each of these annual sets was devoted to a different country of Latin America (80:14). Both photogravure and intaglio were used for commemoratives, ranging from two-colour recess to multicolour gravure (80:10, 21, 25, 28, 29, 36).

Sweden

The Gustav VI Adolf definitives, with white lettering on a quadrille ground, introduced in 1961, remained in use for most of this decade and new values and colour changes were issued between 1966 and 1971. Fluorescent paper was adopted in June 1967 for the definitives, and was also used for all commemoratives from September of that year. Following the death of King Gustav VI Adolf, in September 1973 two stamps were issued in mourning (81:40). Two stamps of a new small-format definitive series had been issued in 1972-3 showing a more up-to-date portrait of the king, but after his death, the series was not developed. Stamps in the same two denominations – 75-öre and 1-krona – but portraying King Carl XVI Gustav, were released in April 1974 (81:44). Both of these definitive issues were engraved by Czeslaw Slania from photographs by L. Nilsson.

A new policy for definitive stamps was adopted in 1965, the portrait series being supplemented in that year by a 20-öre stamp with a recurring post-horn motif (81:1). The following year, higher denominations were supplied by stamps featuring Swedish landmarks and scenery (81:6) and thenceforward, stamps analogous to the French tourist publicity issues, were added to the permanent range from time to time (81:17, 34, 36). Between 1967 and 1970 other pictorial subjects were used, ranging from historic ships and postmen to painted ceilings and wildlife (81:8). Short thematic sets were introduced in 1968, commencing with a set of five 45-öre stamps featuring wild flowers (81:10). These stamps were issued in se-tenant strips containing two of each design. Subsequent sets were devoted to a wide range of subjects, including relics salvaged from the sunken ship Vasa (81:13), the seals of medieval rulers (81:14), Arctic Sweden (81:15), mailcoaches and mailplanes (81:21), art and artifacts (81:20, 22, 29, 35), the glass industry (81:39), historic buildings and aspects of tourism in different regions (81:42).

The annual issues honouring past Nobel prize-winners continued each December, though the early style of conjoined profiles (*81*:4) gave way to separate portraits in 1969 (*81*:18) and eventually to separate stamps for each person (*81*:32). Christmas stamps were introduced in 1972. Children's drawings were used in 1972, paintings in 1973 and folk embroideries in 1974 (*81*:31, 41); a curious feature of these stamps was that they were printed in multicolour photogravure by Harrison, whereas the majority of Swedish stamps were recess-printed at the Swedish Stamp Printing Office. Antiquities (*81*:45) and wildlife continued to provide the subjects for the higher denominations of the Swedish definitive range, with changes at relatively frequent intervals. De La Rue lithographed an Art series in 1969 – the first Swedish multicoloured stamps, and two stamps celebrating the 25th anniversary of the United Nations were produced in three-colour intaglio by the Bank of Finland in 1970 (*81*:16). Harrison also photogravure-printed the stamp of 1972 for the death centenary of L. J. Hierta (*81*:27).

Europa stamps were issued each year in the uniform designs and on two occasions Sweden participated in Nordic omnibus issues, marking the golden jubilee of Norden (1969) and the Nordic Countries postal co-operation (1973). The pattern of general commemorative issues remained unchanged until 1969, the designs being engraved in monochrome with relatively solid backgrounds (*81*:2–5, 7, 9, 11, 12). Although designs became more varied after that date, the old tradition lingered on (*81*:24), but lighter styles characteristic of the thematic sets, influenced the commemoratives of the 1970s (*81*:19, 37). Motifs were engraved on toned paper without formal frames or surrounds (*81*:25, 28), or less frequently, were printed on white paper without the restriction of a frame or solid background (*81*:23, 31). Inevitably, stamps tended to become larger in the 1970s, though monochrome intaglio remained the favourite medium for commemoratives (*81*:33, 43). Occasionally, two-colour combinations were used, but the use of colour was always restrained (*81*:38). The majority of designs were naturalistic, and even fairly abstract concepts to which a symbolic approach might have been expected, tended to be illustrated by simple motifs inspired by nature (*81*:19), such as the flight of birds on the stamps marking Nordic Help for Refugees.

On only two occasions did Sweden depart from this tradition, and experiment with non-figurative designs. The advent of the European Free Trade Association in 1967 was celebrated by a 70-öre stamp in which the designer, Per Olofsson made a play on the initials of the association and the digits of the date on which it was to come into effect (*81*:7). The bicentenary of the Swedish Royal Academy of Music was celebrated in 1971 by two stamps with a diagrammatic motif, representing a circular musical score, which could be played by starting at any point in the circle (*81*:26): the score was specially composed by I. Lidholm in honour of the occasion.

All Swedish stamps of this period were issued in coil or booklet form, with opposing sides imperforate. An increasing tendency to issue stamps in *se-tenant* combinations (*81*:10, 20, 22) often resulted in stamps with only one imperforate side.

Switzerland

The second series with the theme of architectural monuments, introduced in 1964, remained in circulation until 1973; new values were added between 1966 and 1968, and *tête-bêche* combinations from stamp booklets were introduced between 1970 and 1973. A smaller format was used for three coil stamps released in September 1970 (*82*:18). These stamps could also be obtained in sheets of fifty from the philatelic sales counters. All stamps from such sheets, and every fifth stamp in coils, bore serial numbers on the reverse. A new definitive series, depicting scenery typifying the various cantons, came into circulation between February and August 1973. The series was printed in two colours, using combined intaglio and photogravure (*82*:33) for the centime denominations, and monochrome intaglio for the franc values. Phosphorescent paper, hitherto used experimentally, was used for all Swiss stamps printed from September 1965 onwards.

The orderly pattern of Swiss stamps continued in this period. The year began with the annual Publicity series, ranging from three to five stamps publicising current events and historical anniversaries. These stamps, released each February or March, were invariably printed in multicolour photogravure by Courvoisier (*82*:8, 10, 12,

15, 16, 19, 25, 30, 34, 37). The Publicity series of 1975 marked the centenary of the Metric Convention, and spotlighted an aviation exhibition in Lucerne, International Women's Year (*82*:41) and the Geneva conference on Human Rights. From 1967 onwards, the Publicity issues were split into two sets, released in January–March and August–September respectively. A further change in these sets was the introduction of a recurring theme. In 1966 a 10-centime stamp featuring the Finsteraarhorn (*82*:3) was released and in subsequent years similar stamps, depicting views of the Swiss Alps, formed part of the Publicity sets issued in September (*82*:22). Occasionally, a single Europa stamp was issued as part of the Publicity series, but from 1967 onwards this became a separate issue and the number of stamps was increased from 1969 onwards (*82*:11, 20, 26, 31). The uniform designs were used until 1974 when the sculpture theme was adopted (*74*:36).

The Pro Patria charity stamps appeared in May–June each year and consisted of four or five semi-postals as before. Ceiling paintings from St. Martin's Church in Zillis, Grisons, formed the subjects of the sets issued in 1965–7 (*82*:2, 5), stained-glass windows were used in 1968–71 (*82*:7, 13, 21) and, in subsequent years, archaeological discoveries (*82*:27, 32, 40). The Pro Juventute children's charity stamps had a strong thematic character and featured animals in 1965–7 (*82*:1, 4, 6), birds in 1968–71 (*82*:9, 17, 24), flowers in 1972 (*82*:29) and fruits of the forest (*82*:35). The practice of issuing one stamp in each of the Pro Patria and Pro Juventute sets, bearing the portrait of a celebrated Swiss, or of a child, ceased in 1967. After the portrait stamps were dropped from the charity sets, Swiss celebrities became the subject of a separate series of five stamps, issued in September 1969 (*82*:14). The distinctive style of portraiture by G. Humair, produced in monochrome intaglio, was also used for a series of 1971, portraying famous physicians of various nationalities (*82*:23). Combined intaglio and photogravure, however, were employed in the Swiss celebrities series of 1972 (*82*:28) and the same technique was used in 1974 for the UPU centenary series, portraying the men who had founded the Union (*82*:39). The centenary coincided with the seventeenth UPU Congress, held in Lausanne, and this provided one of the rare occasions when a pair of stamps was released outside the annual Publicity series (*82*:38). Throughout this period, all intaglio stamps were produced by the PTT in Berne, while Courvoisier continued to print the photogravure stamps.

No new definitives were issued by the various international organizations whose headquarters were in Switzerland, though single commemoratives were issued by the International Labour Office in 1969 and 1974 and by the International Telecommunications Union in 1973. The stamps provided by the Swiss PTT for the use of the European headquarters of the United Nations in Geneva were withdrawn in October 1969 as a result of a postal treaty between the United Nations and the Swiss postal administration. Henceforward, stamps, mainly in designs similar to those issued by the United Nations in New York, were issued at the Geneva headquarters but with the values in Swiss currency. A definitive series ranging from 5-centimes to 10-francs was released at various times between October 1969 and January 1972 (*82*:42, 45). Eleven international artists designed the stamps and printers in West Germany, Austria, Switzerland and Finland produced them in various processes involving photogravure, lithography, intaglio and embossing. The special issues have followed the pattern of the United Nations New York stamps, with singles or pairs of stamps commemorating UN anniversaries or focusing attention on current world problems (*82*:44, 46). United Nations Art stamps were released in 1972 and 1974 (*82*:43).

Turkey

The output of Turkish stamps actually dropped in this decade – from about 550 in 1955–64 to just over 400 from 1965 to the end of 1974 – though Turkey still ranked among the more prolific countries. As in the previous period, the definitive stamps continued to portray the founder of modern Turkey, Kemal Atatürk, and were lithographed by various companies. A series with a left-facing profile was issued early in 1965, produced by Kiral Matbaasi of Istanbul (*83*:1), but a new design, with a right-facing profile and Kemal's signature, was produced in two-colour combinations, by Ofset Basimevi in September to December of the same year. The contract reverted to Kiral Matbaasi in 1966 and their imprint appeared in the margin of the stamps (*83*:3). A reduced version of the 10- and 50-kurus stamps was produced in June 1967 by Ajans-Türk of Ankara; these stamps were printed in *se-tenant* panes in booklets sold from automatic vending machines (*83*:6). An unusual moustached portrait was used for the series, by Kiral Matbaasi, in 1968 (*83*:9). A new version of the profile and signature design was lithographed by Türk Tarih Kurumu Basevi of Ankara in March 1970, but the following month saw the release of a series using a portrait of Kemal Atatürk wearing evening dress. This set was lithographed by Güzel Sanatlar of Ankara (*83*:13), who reprinted the 50-kurus value in 1971 with different perforations and a slightly narrower format. Türk Tarih and Güzel Sanatlar shared the contract for a series issued between February and May 1971 (*83*:17), but this was followed by a new profile series, lithographed by the same firms, in October 1972 (*83*:18). This series was comparatively long-lived and survived to the end of the decade. The equestrian statue of Kemal Atatürk was the subject of small-format stamps issued each December from 1966 onwards, for use on greetings cards celebrating Christmas and the New Year. Various printers were involved in their production and the stamps differ in imprint, inscriptions and the general layout of the designs (*83*:7, 8). Short airmail sets, with the theme of aircraft and birds, were released in January and August 1967 respectively (*83*:4, 5).

Turkey issued Europa stamps each year, but also produced a number of stamps in omnibus designs, in conjunction with Iran and Pakistan to mark the anniversaries of the Regional Co-operation for Development (RCD) pact. Each issue consisted of three stamps devoted to some aspect of the three countries, a different theme, such as scenery or art, being used each year (*83*:16). Annual sets featuring Turkish celebrities were issued between 1965 and 1967 (*83*:2). Of the commemorative sets, a high proportion marked anniversaries in the life and career of Kemal Atatürk, and no opportunity was lost of portraying him in sets devoted to other events and institutions (*83*:15). A few purely thematic sets were issued from 1966 onwards and ranged from pottery and miniatures to folk dances (*83*:12), game animals and export products. A propaganda series, focusing attention on aspects of the Turkish economy, was issued between April and August 1969 using symbolic motifs (*83*:11). Several commemoratives were issued with premiums in aid of the Red Crescent (*83*:10) or other charitable institutions and ranged from the Second International Tobacco Congress of 1965 to European Conservation Year in 1970 (*83*:14).

Vatican City
The increasingly cosmopolitan outlook of the pontificate under Pope Paul VI was reflected in the stamps of this period. A significant number of sets commemorated events of international importance, ranging from the Osaka 70 World's Fair to Racial Equality Year (*83*:24), and various issues between 1965 and 1970 publicised the Pope's visits to the United Nations, Uganda, Colombia and Oceania (*83*:22). Otherwise, the stamps of the Vatican followed the same policy as before, honouring current events in the Catholic calendar (*83*:21) and the anniversaries of saints and personalities connected with the Holy See (*83*:23, 25). The only regular issue consisted of the annual Christmas stamps, which continued to reproduce religious paintings (*83*:20). All stamps of the Vatican up to 1971 were produced at the Italian Government Printing Works in Rome, either in photogravure (*83*:20, 22, 24) or in a combination of intaglio and photogravure (*83*:19, 23, 25). Thereafter, occasional sets were printed by the Austrian State Press, in either intaglio or photogravure.

Yugoslavia
The revaluation of the currency in 1966, with one new dinar of 100 paras equal to 100 old dinars, resulted in the reissue of the intaglio definitives with the values redrawn and the colours changed (*83*:26). In May 1967 a set of ten stamps, issued in sheets of fifteen with dates and olive branch motifs in the sheet margins, celebrated the seventy-fifth birthday of President Tito. The same design, in new colours and different denominations, was used for a definitive series released between 1967 and 1972. The ordinary stamps were recess-printed and had perforations on all four sides (*83*:32). Coil versions of certain denominations were issued in 1968–9 and were photogravure-printed with vertical sides imperforate. Phosphor bands,

similar to those used in Britain, were introduced in October 1971 to facilitate electronic sorting. Between June 1971 and 1974, a series of scenic pictorials in a small format were designed by A. Milenkovic and recess-printed (*83*:42). The entire series was issued with or without phosphor bands. A much whiter paper, that had a pronounced effect on the shade of the stamp, was introduced in 1972 and used in the production of several values. A lithographed series portraying President Tito was adopted in March 1974 (*83*:44). Three coil stamps with a post-horn motif were photogravure-printed by Harrison and Sons in 1973–4.

Stamps for Christmas and New Year greetings were introduced in 1967 and featured good-luck symbols (*83*:34). The same designs were used the following year, but the colours and dates were changed (*83*:38). The issue of such stamps was then abandoned, but in December 1969, Yugoslavia released two stamps in the Europa 'colonnade' motif of that year, and since then, Europa stamps have been issued each year – the only such issue to come from a country in the Communist bloc, reflecting Yugoslavia's unique position with a foot in both political camps. Regular sets, in the characteristic format and style of engraving favoured by Yugoslavia, appeared each year in honour of famous Yugoslavs (*83*:37). The annual Children's Week stamps were based on drawings and paintings by children (*83*:27). Relatively few thematic sets were issued in this period and, as before, they were mainly printed in multicolour photogravure by Courvoisier (*83*:29, 30, 41). The Austrian State Press, however, produced several sets reproducing medieval icons, paintings and mosaics between 1968 and 1974 (*83*:35, 40).

Obligatory tax stamps continued to be issued on behalf of the Red Cross and, in addition, similar stamps raised money for the national Olympics team (*83*:36). A set of six stamps commemorated the Munich Olympic Games in 1972 (*83*:43). Various processes were used by the State Printing Works in Belgrade for commemorative stamps, ranging from monochrome lithography (*83*:28) to two-colour intaglio (*83*:33). Courvoisier produced multicoloured photogravure stamps featuring American and Soviet spacecraft in honour of the Montreal World's Fair 'Expo 67' (*83*:31).

Asia

Abu Dhabi
Responsibility for the postal administration was transferred from the British authorities to the government of Sheikh Zaid on 1st January 1967. Two definitive sets, both produced by De La Rue, were issued in this period. Stamps portraying Sheikh Zaid and featuring local scenery, were recess-printed or lithographed in 1967–9, and a series with a more up-to-date portrait was lithographed in multicolour in 1970–71 (*84*:1). The majority of commemoratives marked the anniversary of the sheikh's accession (*84*:2). Following the withdrawal of the British garrison from the Gulf area and the termination of the British treaty with the Trucial States in 1971, Abu Dhabi, with six other sheikhdoms (Ajman, Dubai, Fujeira, Ras al Khaima, Sharjah and Umm al Qiwain) formed the United Arab Emirates whose stamps have been used since 1972.

Aden States
Stamps were issued by three states in South Arabia, formerly the Eastern and Western Aden Protectorates, until they were suppressed by the National Liberation Front in October 1967. In addition to the Kathiri State of Seiyun and the Qu'aiti State in Hadhramaut, which had issued stamps since 1942, the Mahra Sultanate of Qishn and Socotra began issuing stamps in March 1967 (*84*:5). The flag series was lithographed by Harrison and Sons. The latter stamps of the other states were printed in multicolour photogravure by the Austrian State Press (*84*:3, 4). Stamps purporting to come from the state of Upper Yafa also appeared in 1967 but there is no evidence to suggest that they actually performed any postal service.

Afghanistan

The contract with an external philatelic agency was cancelled in 1964 and the stamps of this decade settled down to a more orthodox policy as regards frequency and subject matter. The majority of stamps from 1965 onwards were photogravure-printed by the Austrian State Press. The stamps were released in singles or pairs, mainly commemorating regular anniversaries and such events as the Shah's birthday, Pakhtunistan Day, Red Crescent Day and Independence Day (84:7). From 1966 onwards, short sets each year publicised tourism and invariably included a stamp with a map design (84:6). These issues were interspersed by stamps commemorating current international events (84:8). Thematic sets, usually of three stamps, featured wildlife or native handicrafts, and were issued from 1969 onwards. Stamps were issued annually to mark Independence Day (84:9).

Ajman

Comparatively few of the many hundreds of stamps allegedly issued by Ajman in the period from 1965 to 1972 have received full catalogue status, because after June 1967, Ajman's philatelic policy was entirely in the hands of a succession of external agencies, often operating simultaneously. Apart from the 1967 definitive series, with the theme of transport (84:10) all stamps of this period related to personalities and events outside the sheikhdom (84:11).

Bahrain

An independent postal administration was established in 1966 and a pictorial series photogravure-printed by Harrison was released in January of that year (84:12). The relatively few commemoratives since then, have all been printed by Harrison or De La Rue using multicolour photogravure or lithography (84:13).

Bangladesh

The civil war between the predominantly Hindu populace of East Pakistan and the Moslem government in West Pakistan, became a struggle for independence. Following the intervention of Indian forces, Pakistan was defeated and East Bengal was liberated, under the name of Bangladesh. Pakistani stamps were overprinted, mainly by hand, and issued pending the production of distinctive stamps (84:14). A propaganda series appeared in July 1971 and was superseded by a pictorial series, lithographed by Bradbury Wilkinson, in April 1973 (84:17). This series was later overprinted for official correspondence (84:16). The few commemoratives since independence were mostly lithographed by the Indian Security Printing Press at Nasik (84:15), to mark anniversaries of independence and in tribute to the martyrs of the recent war.

Bhutan

A few stamps of orthodox design and format were produced at Nasik in 1966–8 (84:18), but the majority of Bhutanese stamps in this decade were masterminded by a philatelic agency in Nassau, Bahamas and speedily acquired immense notoriety because of their unusual appearance. Stamps were printed with laminated prismatic-ribbed plastic surfaces which produced a three-dimensional effect; others were manufactured in moulded plastic to simulate the texture of bas-reliefs, and several sets were embossed on circular gold foil like the Tonga 'beermats'. The world's first 'smelling' stamps appeared in 1973 when Bhutan issued a series of stamps depicting roses and impregnated with scent (84:19). Later the same year, the world's first 'talking' stamps appeared, resembling miniature gramophone records that played the Bhutanese national anthem.

Brunei

Having pursued a very conservative policy until 1965, Brunei suddenly began to issue stamps at frequent intervals and increased the size of the stamps correspondingly. Nevertheless, the definitive series of 1952 remained in use until 1974, undergoing changes of watermark in 1964–71 and 1972–3. Brunei participated in the various omnibus issues from 1965 to 1973 (84:21), but from 1967 onwards also produced numerous indigenous commemoratives, usually in sets of three (84:20).

Burma

A new definitive series was released in July 1968. Like the 1964 series it featured birds (84:22), but was photogravure-printed by the German Bank Note Printing Company of Leipzig in different sizes and styles from those used in the series produced in Japan. The very few commemoratives that appeared in this period were produced by a wide variety of printers, including Harrison, Bradbury Wilkinson and the Pakistan Security Corporation as well as the East German and Japanese Government Printers.

Ceylon (Sri Lanka)

The 1964 series remained current throughout this decade, with new values and designs being added up to 1969. Provisional surcharges were made on certain denominations in 1971 during temporary shortages of 5-, 15- and 25-cent values. Even after the country changed from dominion status to a republic and adopted the name of Sri Lanka in 1972 the series inscribed 'Ceylon' remained current. The problem of tri-lingual inscriptions (in Sinhala, English and Tamil) was solved in many cases by grouping them on two sides of a small rectangular vignette (84:24, 25, 27, 30). Although relatively few commemoratives were issued, a wide range of printers was employed. Courvoisier, which had previously printed many stamps for Ceylon, produced only two issues in this period, both in 1965 (84:23) and thereafter many contracts were awarded to Rosenbaum Brothers of Vienna who used multicolour lithography (84:24, 29–31). The Poya Holiday stamps of 1967 were photogravure-printed by the Austrian State Press (84:25), and subsequent issues were produced by Harrison (84:27, 28), De La Rue (84:26, 32, 33) or Bradbury Wilkinson (84:34) using multicolour photogravure or lithography.

The inauguration of the republic of Sri Lanka was celebrated by a 15-cent stamp in May 1972 (90:12). Since then, there have been short thematic sets – fish and rock paintings – and single commemoratives, produced by De La Rue (90:13), Rosenbaum Brothers or the Pakistan Security Corporation.

China (People's Republic)

In the late 1960s and early 1970s, China was the only country in the world with an uncompromisingly political approach to philately. Even the frequent thematic sets usually had some political message, as, for example, the scenic series of 1965 featuring the Chinkiang Mountains – 'cradle of the Chinese Revolution' (85:1). At the time of the Cultural Revolution most stamps consisted entirely of quotations from Chairman Mao; one of the few exceptions in this period, from 1966 to 1968, was the set devoted to the third Five-Year-Plan (85:3). Commemoratives have largely been confined to anniversaries of the revolutionary struggle or to demonstrations of solidarity with Albania and Vietnam. The national games series of 1965 was the last series in the purely thematic style of the early 1960s (85:2).

China (Taiwan)

The stamps issued by the Nationalists in Taiwan (Formosa) continue to bear the inscription 'Republic of China'. An intaglio series depicting double carp was introduced in 1965 (85:4) and redrawn in 1969. Intaglio was also used for a series of 1966–72 featuring flying geese, and for occasional stamps portraying famous Chinese. Multicolour photogravure, by Courvoisier or the Japanese Government Printer, was used for the majority of commemorative issues (85:5, 6), though some stamps were lithographed locally (85:7). From 1968 onwards, many of the classical scroll paintings of China were reproduced in se-tenant strips, often issued in serial form over a period of several months (85:6).

Dubai

The output of stamps increased ominously during 1965–9, a period in which Dubai's philatelic affairs were in the hands of an external agency. Thereafter, they came under the aegis of the Crown Agents in London and a more moderate policy ensued. The majority of the stamps of this decade were produced by British printers. Bradbury Wilkinson used combined intaglio and lithography for the series of 1966 marking the installation of the automatic telephone exchange (85:8), and De La Rue used lithography for the definitive series of the same year and the oil exploration series (85:9). The

1966 definitives were surcharged in the following year, with values in dirhams and riyals in place of naye paise and rupees (85:10). Separate stamps were discontinued in 1973 when Dubai joined the United Arab Emirates.

Fujeira

Few of the prolific issues of this Arab state are listed in the catalogues, though they performed some postal service, albeit a purely token one. Apart from a series of eighteen ordinary and nine airmail stamps, featuring butterflies, issued in 1967 (85:11) and a thematic definitive issue of 1971 devoted to fish, Fujeira issued long commemorative sets in connection with every event and personality of any importance between 1965 and 1971 (85:12) when the stamps of the United Arab Emirates were adopted.

Hong Kong

The Annigoni Portrait series of 1962 remained in use until 1973, undergoing changes of gum and paper in 1971–2 and changing from a sideways to an upright watermark between 1966 and 1972. Floral and armorial designs were added in 1968 (85:13). A series featuring the coinage profile of Queen Elizabeth II was introduced in 1973 (85:14); the stamps were printed in photogravure by Harrison, the 10- and 20-dollar denominations having the profile embossed. Stamps celebrating the lunar New Year were introduced in 1967, each issue featuring an animal in the Chinese zodiacal cycle (85:15). The few other commemoratives, ranging from singles to sets of three stamps, marked local events and were produced variously in multi-colour photogravure or lithography by De La Rue, Harrison and Bradbury Wilkinson (85:16).

India

A series of eighteen stamps was introduced between August 1965 and October 1968. Scenery, wildlife, aspects of industry and agriculture and medieval sculpture formed the subjects of these stamps. A significant exception was the 5-paise denomination – the one most commonly used – which drew the public's attention to the need for family planning (85:17). This was the first time that a definitive stamp had been used for a didactic purpose. The stamp was overprinted 'Refugee Relief' in 1971, to pre-pay an obligatory tax on correspondence for the relief of victims of the war in Bangladesh. Subsequently, a distinctive stamp for this purpose was produced (85:24). There was no significant change in India's policy towards commemoratives. The majority of those released from 1965 onwards, paid tribute to Indian celebrities, though Maxim Gorky, Lenin, Bertrand Russell (85:25) and Marie Curie were non-Indians singled out for commemoration. Portrait stamps followed the pattern of the previous decade, though greater use was made of colour (85:19, 22). Naturalistic subjects were used for most of the commemorative singles (85:18, 23), though poster techniques were used occasionally, especially from 1968 onwards (85:20, 26). Only one thematic series, devoted to birds, was issued in this decade (85:21).

Indonesia

The revaluation of the currency in December 1965 resulted in surcharges being applied to obsolete definitives, pending the release of a series, portraying Dr. Sukarno, between 1965 and 1967. Thereafter, long thematic sets were used instead. A series featuring musical instruments was issued in 1967 (85:28), followed by a series publicising the Five-Year Development Plan in 1969 (85:32). Separate sets inscribed 'Irian Barat' were used in West Irian (formerly Netherlands New Guinea) throughout this period (85:33). Short thematic sets, generally of two to four stamps, featured paintings, fruits, wildlife and aspects of tourism (85:29). Express letter stamps, inscribed 'Poskilat' were issued between 1967 and 1969, the date being changed each year (85:31). Several sets commemorated the Thomas Cup badminton championships (85:27) and all of the international events sponsored by the United Nations were faithfully commemorated (85:30).

Iran

The frequency of new definitive sets portraying the Shah decelerated in this decade. A series was introduced in 1966 and remained in use until 1971 (85:34) when it was superseded by stamps bearing a more mature portrait of the Shah (85:36). The latter series was reissued a year later, with frames and inscriptions in yellow-bistre, whereas the original version had the entire design in monochrome. The volume of commemoratives rose in this period, as a result of a number of factors, of which, the prolonged celebrations marking the 2,500th anniversary of the Persian Empire was the most prominent. Numerous stamps publicised the Shah's White Revolution and several sets conformed to the RCD omnibus designs, issued in co-operation with Pakistan and Turkey. Semi-stylised motifs were used for a number of stamps, mostly depicting buildings (85:35) and symbolic or abstract designs were employed for current events (85:37). The passion for stamps portraying visiting heads of state continued unabated.

Iraq

The 1963 definitives were superseded in November 1967 by a series, lithographed by De La Rue, showing native costumes (86:2). This series was, in turn, replaced in June 1973 by a locally lithographed set of three pictorial designs in a small format (86:10). In the same year, various stamps of the Faisal definitives were reissued, with the late king's portrait obliterated and with an Arabic overprint to signify use on official mail. Regular issues of this period consisted mainly of stamps celebrating anniversaries of the 14th July Revolution, which had overthrown the monarchy, and latterly also, anniversaries of the 17th July Revolution which had overthrown General Kassem. Early revolts were also the subject of several commemoratives (86:1) and a high proportion of stamps continued to extol the armed forces (86:9). Although a wide range of printers was used, the stamps were designed by indigenous artists and showed a marked preference for triangles (86:8) and diamond shapes, often incorporating a circular motif which became virtually mandatory from 1969 onwards. A number of thematic sets, featuring birds, fish and flowers, was released between 1968 and 1970 (86:7). The majority of the commemorative sets consisted of two or three stamps, lithographed in multicolour (86:4–6), though five ordinary and five airmail stamps were issued to publicise International Tourist Year in 1967 (86:3).

Israel

All stamps issued in this period continued to have marginal tabs with inscriptions. Although Israeli designers still favoured a blend of realism and abstract, there was a tendency now to use many different formats, of which the most striking was the elongated vertical (86:13, 16, 28, 36). Two definitive sets appeared in this period, both featuring civic coats of arms. The first series appeared between March 1965 and February 1967 (86:11, 12) and the second between July 1969 and 1973 (86:22). Both sets were designed by the Shamir Brothers and printed in photogravure by the Israeli Government Printer in Jerusalem. Several denominations in both sets exist in tête-bêche pairs or in semi-tête-bêche pairs separated by a stamp-sized label with an ornamental pattern. The 10-agorot value of the 1965–7 series and the 15-agorot value of the 1969–73 series, in se-tenant combinations, were issued in 1973.

Between February and December 1968, a series of ten airmail stamps was released, with the theme of Israeli export industries (86:15). Several thematic issues supplemented the definitives and featured butterflies, museum exhibits, seaports, nature reserves, landscapes, Jewish Theatre and aspects of Jewish art (86:20, 24, 29, 30, 32). A 3-pound stamp reproducing Chagall's painting of King David was issued in September 1969 (86:23) and a series of twelve 1-pound stamps was produced in 1973, reproducing stained-glass windows by Chagall, depicting the twelve tribes of Israel (86:34).

The annual sets of the previous decades continued in this period. The Jewish New Year stamps of 1965 featured abstracts by A. Kalderon symbolising the Creation, but more naturalistic motifs were employed in subsequent years. The issues of 1966 and 1967 featured religious ceremonial objects and scrolls of the Torah respectively (86:13), and the series of 1968 depicted scenes in the old and new cities of Jerusalem (86:17). Stylised interpretations of the story of Noah and the Flood were shown on the stamps of 1969 (86:21). Synagogues in Europe, America and North Africa were the subject of the 1970 series, multicoloured on gold backgrounds (86:26). Illuminated verses from the Bible, in the manner of medieval rabbinical manuscripts, were featured on two sets of 1971, the first (in May) celebrating Shavuot or the Feast of Weeks, and the second (in August) marking the New Year (86:27). Holy Arks, from synagogues in Italy, were depicted on the 1972 series, and the 1973 set portrayed prophets of Israel (86:36). Rebuilt synagogues in the old city of Jerusalem – captured from Jordan in the 1967 war – were shown on the three stamps of 1974. In 1972, sets were also issued to celebrate Pesach (Passover) and Hanukka (the Feast of Lights) (86:33) but these never developed into annual sets.

Stamps were released each year in April or May, respectively, celebrating Independence Day (86:16, 35) and Memorial Day (86:14). Memorials or symbolic motifs signifying remembrance, were featured on the Memorial Day stamps, issued as singles each year, whereas the Independence Day stamps often appeared in short sets of three, featuring such thematic subjects as flowers and architecture. Occasionally, however, single stamps were released instead, and depicted emblems or subjects directly connected with independence. The 1-pound stamp of 1973 was also issued in miniature sheet form (86:35).

As in previous years, relatively few stamps commemorated individuals. The only non-Jew thus honoured was Lord Balfour, the British statesman whose declaration of 1917 established the principle of the Jewish national state. Most of the personal commemoratives reproduced photographs without any ornament, but a more decorative treatment was adopted for a stamp portraying Charles Netter, founder of the Miqwe Yisrael Agricultural College, one of a pair marking the centenary of the college in 1970 (86:25). Emblematic designs were used for various stamps publicising the Maccabiah Games (86:18), but actual athletic motifs were employed in the set of three stamps honouring the Hapoel Games in 1971 (86:28). The majority of commemoratives had poster designs ranging from stylised figures to ornamental treatment of lettering (86:31). A. Prath's aircraft design with a textile pattern symbolised Operation 'Magic Carpet' – the evacuation of Yemeni Jews to Israel in 1950 (86:19). As usual, there was an appropriate biblical text which was inscribed on the tab.

Japan

From January 1966 onwards, all Japanese stamps have been inscribed NIPPON, the name of the country rendered in the Roman alphabet. The definitives of 1952–61 and 1961–5 were reissued between June 1966 and September 1969 with this additional inscription (87:8). Phosphor bands were introduced experimentally on certain denominations in 1966 and were applied in horizontal and vertical bands which formed a frame round the designs of the stamps. Although some earlier designs, in new colours and with the 'NIPPON' inscription, were reissued in 1971–3, entirely new designs were employed for the major part of a definitive series introduced in March 1971 (87:33). The small upright format of the definitives was also adopted for a number of commemorative and propaganda issues from 1967 onwards, and in several instances these stamps were also released in booklets or coils. These small-format stamps consisted of the road safety and savings campaign stamps (87:13, 22, 24), the afforestation campaign stamps from 1971 onwards (87:35) and the postal codes campaign stamps issued every July from 1968 (87:18, 25, 30, 38) recognisable from the inclusion of a cartoon character clearly modelled on America's Mr. Zip. This small format was also extended to the New Year greetings stamps from 1971 onwards.

The New Year stamps before 1971 consisted of a single stamp at the inland letter rate, issued in normal sheet form and also in a miniature sheet of four stamps. As in previous years, these stamps featured the animals or birds associated with the twelve-year cycle of the Oriental calendar, through the medium of traditional toys, carvings, pottery or Yamagata cut-paper work (87:11, 14, 21, 27, 32).

Single stamps in honour of Philatelic Week and International Correspondence Week continued to reproduce traditional works of art, woodcut prints and even comparatively modern paintings (87:12, 20, 44). Various aspects of Japanese art were also featured in regular thematic issues, focusing attention on national treasures of different periods (87:16, 23). Short thematic sets from 1970 onwards, highlighted features of the Japanese Gagaku, Kabuki and Noh Theatre and the Bunraku puppet theatre (87:34, 40). Occasional issues, usually in pairs, publicised the seemingly inexhaustible scenic beauties of the national and quasi-national parks. A few of

these were printed in monochrome (87:3, 19, 29), but the majority were produced in multicolour photogravure (87:15, 26, 42, 45, 48).

The same style of design – using a photograph of buildings or scenery – made popular by the national park stamps, was adopted for many of the commemorative singles of this period and is typified by the stamps marking the completion of the Fuji meteorological station (87:1), the inauguration of the postal museum (87:2), and the completion of the Amakusa bridges (87:9). Not only current events, but also historic anniversaries, were treated in this way. The centenary of the Japanese rail system was celebrated by two issues. The stamp released in March 1972, reproduced a photograph of a high-speed train on the Sanyo line (87:43), whereas one of the two stamps released in the following October, reproduced a woodcut by Hiroshige showing the inauguration of the service in 1872 (87:47). Throughout this decade, however, the occidental poster style of design gradually gained ground (87:4–7, 17, 31, 39, 41, 46). The influence of traditional art remained strong, as witness Shimizu's penguins design for the stamp commemorating the Antarctic Treaty in 1971 (87:37). Photographs were occasionally used as the basis of designs featuring inanimate objects. Two semi-postal stamps marking the ninth International Cancer Congress in Tokyo featured a rotary cobalt radiator and X-ray equipment, based on photographs (87:10). Even the quasi-symbolic designs of the Osaka World's Fair series had a distinctly photographic quality (87:28).

Jordan

The 1959 definitive series, recess-printed with profiles of King Hussein in black, remained in use for much of this period, although a large-format photogravure series by Harrison was introduced in January 1966 (88:2). In 1974, the De La Rue series was reissued bearing a more mature portrait of the king (88:8). The influence of an external philatelic agency can be discerned in the unduly prolific issues of 1965–7 which included imperforate versions, diamond-shaped space stamps and gold-foil embossed 'coin' stamps, Thereafter, the spate of issues diminished considerably. Jordan was the only Arab country to issue Christmas stamps, introduced in 1966 and occasional stamps were issued for Mothers' Day, Children's Day and even Fathers' Day (1973). Short thematic sets appeared at frequent intervals and ranged from wildlife, aspects of life in the desert and paintings (88:5) to the Stations of the Cross and space achievements. Most of the commemoratives had symbolic motifs photogravure-printed in bold, primary colours (88:3, 4). The dove of peace was a recurring theme, treated in various ways (88:3, 6). Jordan issued stamps in 1973 to commemorate – belatedly – the 2,500th anniversary of the Persian Empire – some three years after the event (88:7). Several stamps, printed in Cairo, marked anniversaries of the Arab League (88:9) or spotlighted alleged Israeli atrocities against the Palestinian Arabs, but apart from these, there was little reference to the political situation in the Middle East.

Khmer (Cambodia)

In the late 1960s, the government of Prince Sihanouk became increasingly left-wing and this led to his overthrow by a military coup in 1970. Sihanouk escaped to the People's Republic of China, while a right-wing junta proclaimed Cambodia a republic and changed its name to Khmer. The name 'Cambodge' continued to appear on stamps until March 1971, but since then, stamps have been inscribed 'République Khmere' (88:13). A small-format definitive series, featuring an Apsara or dancing nymph, was released in 1972. These stamps, and the majority of the commemoratives were recess-printed in Paris. In 1975 the right-wing republic was overthrown and Sihanouk restored but these political changes had no immediate effect on stamps.

Korea

The definitives of 1964 remained in use in South Korea until 1969, various denominations being added, up to 1966. Forgeries of certain denominations, intended to defraud the postal authorities, led to the replacement of these stamps in 1967 by new designs, which also incorporated the inscription in English 'Republic of Korea'. Several designs of the 1964–6 series were redrawn in 1969–70 to include this inscription. A small-format 7-won stamp featuring the national flag, was issued in 1968 (88:14), but was replaced subsequently by a similar design in monochrome, with the value notation omitting the noughts (88:17). Similar small-format pictorials were issued in 1973–4. Stylised designs were used for the majority of the commemoratives, released in pairs or singles (88:15), apart from the numerous sports issues and occasional thematic sets (88:16).

Few stamps of South Korea could be described as having a political slant; but the opposite continued to be the case with the issues of the People's Democratic Republic of North Korea which frequently referred to the struggle against American imperialism, even to the extent of caricaturing President Nixon at the height of the Vietnam War. Numerous sets commemorated anniversaries of the Korean War and the earlier struggles against the Japanese, or illustrated the life and career of Marshal Kim Il-sung (88:19). The 'cult of the personality', however, never became so obsessive as it did in China. North Korea also produced a substantial number of thematic issues (88:18, 20, 21), in multicolour lithography or monochrome intaglio.

Kuwait
The majority of stamps in recent years have consisted of sets in honour of annual events, ranging from Family Day and Palestine Day (88:22) to International Literacy Day and Arab Cause Week. The stamps have mainly been lithographed in multicolour by a wide range of printers, from De La Rue and Bradbury Wilkinson to Enschedé and the State Printers of Hungary, East Germany and Pakistan.

Laos
There was no change in Laotian stamps during this decade and the majority of them were recess-printed in colour combinations, drawing heavily on traditional art forms as in previous years (88:24, 25). The sole exception was a pair of stamps marking the birth centenary of Lenin, lithographed in Moscow and presented to the Laotian postal administration by the Soviet authorities in 1970. Indian stamps, overprinted ICC, were issued from 1965 onwards for use by personnel of the International Control Commission in Laos and Vietnam (88:23).

Lebanon
The sempiternal 'cedar' designs, that had endured since 1925 in no fewer than twenty-one different guises, were superseded in 1965 by a pictorial series with the themes of birds and butterflies (88:26). The series was mainly recess-printed in Paris, though the top value was produced in combined intaglio and lithography by the Austrian State Press. The 'cedars of friendship' formed the subject of a multicoloured airmail stamp released in October 1965 (88:28), and the small-format stylised cedar motif was resurrected in 1967, for a series of postage-due stamps. Subsequently, lengthy thematic sets were issued, either for ordinary or for airmail postage (88:27, 29). These stamps were printed in multicolour photogravure at the State Printing Office in Budapest from the end of 1965 onwards.

Macao
The few stamps issued by Macao in this period, all conformed to the Portuguese colonial pattern. A definitive series featuring Portuguese military uniforms was issued in 1966 and the majority of the commemoratives clung to the themes of the Portuguese overseas provinces (88:30). The only concessions to local individuality were a pair in 1971, with the theme of Chinese masks, and a single in 1972, marking the centenary of the Pedro V Theatre in Macao.

Malaysia
Each of the component states of the Federation of Malaysia issued two short definitive sets – each of seven stamps – during this period. Standard designs were used in each case and featured orchids (1965) and butterflies (1971). These stamps provided the low denominations, the general series of Malaysia providing the higher values (88:34). The orchids series was photogravure-printed by Harrison, and the butterflies series was lithographed by Bradbury Wilkinson. An innovation with the orchids series was the rationalisation of the spelling of the names of the states, changes being made in several cases to conform to modern Malay orthography. Thus, Johore became Johor (88:1), Malacca became Melaka (88:31), Penang became Pulau Pinang (89:19, 20) and Negri Sembilan changed to Negeri Sembilan (89:5, 6). The names of the other states remained unchanged: Kedah (88:10, 11), Kelantan (88:12), Pahang (89:10, 11), Perak (89:21, 22), Perlis (89:23), Selangor (90:1, 2) and Tregganu (90:24, 25). Both Sabah and Sarawak issued definitives to accord with these series (89:37, 38) and discontinued their distinctive designs.

Apart from the general definitive issues of the Federation, featuring birds and butterflies respectively, a moderate number of commemorative sets was released in this decade. Several of these continued the Malaysian penchant for unusual shapes, including a circular series of 1971 with circular perforations. These commemoratives, in sets of three to five stamps, were produced by the Japanese Government Printing Works (88:35), Bradbury Wilkinson and Harrison (88:32, 33, 36–38), mainly in multicolour lithography.

Maldive Islands
The British protectorate came to an end in 1965 when the Maldive Islands became an independent sultanate. A definitive series featuring seashells was printed in photogravure by the Austrian State Press in 1966. The same printers produced a number of commemoratives, none of which was in any sense relevant to the islands (88:39). Later issues were produced by the Israeli Government Printer and Harrison and Sons. Many of the thematic sets from 1966 onwards were later overprinted for various current events, ranging from the Idaho Scout Jamboree (88:41) to the Philympia stamp exhibition in London. Most issues from March 1967 onwards were also released imperforate in limited editions. The Maldives became a republic in November 1968 and subsequent stamps were suitably inscribed (88:40). In the 1970s, the many thematic and 'bandwagon' issues were produced by the Austrian, Hungarian and Israeli Government Printers as well as by Rosenbaum Brothers, Harrison and Format International of London.

Mongolia
The output of stamps increased after 1966, as thematic sets appeared more and more frequently. These issues often lent to their subjects a peculiarly Mongolian slant, such as the sets featuring the local fur industry or Mongolian berries. At the same time, however, Mongolia was not slow to follow the current crazes, and emulated San Marino and Poland by issuing stamps featuring prehistoric monsters (89:2). A very few commemoratives referred to current events in the country, but the majority were concerned with a wide range of sporting events in other parts of the world (89:1, 3).

Muscat and Oman (Oman)
An independent postal administration was established in April 1966 and British stamps surcharged in Indian currency were then superseded by a distinctive series (89:4) in local currency (64 baizas to the rupee). The series was reissued in 1970 with the currency revalued at 1,000 baizas to the Rial Saidi; this entailed changes of colour in many denominations. In 1970, Sultan Qabus bin Said succeeded his father and announced that the country would henceforward be known simply as Oman. Consequently the definitive series of 1970 was overprinted by the National Press of Dubai in January 1971 (89:9), pending the release of an entirely new series based on paintings by Major R. Temple.

Nepal
Shorter sets, at more frequent intervals, became the policy in 1965 and thereafter most stamps were released as singles covering a wide range of local and international events, from the Nepali Red Cross (89:7) to Asian Productivity Year (89:8). From 1969 onwards, sets of three or four stamps were issued with such themes as flowers, images, costumes and mountain scenery. Although a few stamps were lithographed by De La Rue and the Security Press in Pakistan, the majority of stamps were printed in photogravure by the Indian Security Press at Nasik.

Pakistan
Up to the end of 1964, stamps were either recess-printed locally or photogravure-printed by De La Rue. From the beginning of 1965 onwards, however, all stamps were lithographed by the Pakistan Security Printing Corporation, with the exception of the intaglio definitives introduced in 1962. These remained in use throughout

this period, new values being added up to 1970 and a watermark of multiple stars and crescents being introduced between 1963 and 1968. From July 1965 onwards, stamps were released at regular intervals to publicise the Regional Development Co-operation pact with Turkey and Iran (89:16). Multicolour lithography was increasingly allied to poster styles of design, and even naturalistic themes, such as buildings and scenery, tended to become more stylised (89:17, 18), while outright poster designs were used for stamps publicising current events or anniversaries (89:13, 14). Portrait stamps were similar in treatment to those of India, but generally, a much larger format was employed (89:12) and in the 1970s there was greater use of colour (89:15).

Philippines
The portrait definitive series introduced in 1962 continued in this decade, with various denominations added between 1969 and 1973 (89:30). These stamps were all recess-printed by Bradbury Wilkinson, but a somewhat larger design, produced lithographically, was introduced in 1973 (89:31). Occasional issues of stamps portraying former presidents and giving quotations in Tagalog and English continued throughout this decade (89:24) and were clearly modelled on the American Credo series. The only other regular issue consisted of obligatory tax stamps, with premiums in aid of the government anti-tuberculosis fund; these stamps appeared annually and depicted such subjects as fruits, flowers and birds (89:28). Stamps celebrating the anniversaries of the defence of Corregidor and the Leyte landing featured General Douglas MacArthur in an unusual silhouette treatment (89:25). Very few of the stamps issued from 1965 onwards bore inscriptions in English, a curious exception being the 1971 Philatelic Week overprint (89:29). Multicolour lithography by De La Rue and photogravure by Courvoisier and Harrison were used for most of the stamps issued in this period (89:26-29, 32).

Qatar
In 1966 the currency was changed to the Arab riyal of 100 dirhems and various obsolete stamps were surcharged, pending the supply of a pictorial series, photogravure-printed by the Austrian State Press. From September 1967 onwards, all stamps of Qatar were produced by Bradbury Wilkinson, who printed a new definitive series in 1968, using lithography for the lower values and combined intaglio and lithography for the higher denominations (89:33).

Ras al Khaima
This small sheikhdom applied the policy of the external philatelic agencies with a vengeance – the smaller the country, the more numerous its stamps. The output of stamps for every conceivable event reached such a peak of irrelevance that the catalogues tired of listing them after 1967. Between 1968 and 1972, when the stamps of the United Arab Emirates were introduced, Ras al Khaima produced over forty sets, totalling almost five hundred stamps, mainly concerned with events of American interest (89:34).

Ryukyu Islands
Although remaining autonomous under an American civil administration for much of this decade, the Ryukyus were wholly Japanese in character, and this was evident in the stamps, which were designed and printed in Japan and differed stylistically only in the inclusion of the name and occasional inscriptions in English (89:35). New Year stamps were issued in much the same way as in Japan (89:36). Short thematic sets in multicolour photogravure were issued from 1965 onwards. The Ryukyu Islands reverted to Japan in 1972 and since then, ordinary Japanese stamps have been used.

Saudi Arabia
Between 1964 and 1968, the pictorial definitives were reissued with the inscriptions closer to the top frame. Between 1966 and 1968, the series was redrawn yet again, with the oval cartouche of King Faisal replacing that of King Saud inset (89:39). Paper with a large watermark covering four stamps, was introduced in 1967 and used for later printings of the definitives. From 1967 onwards, all stamps were lithographed by the Government Printer in Riyadh. Comparatively few stamps have been produced in recent years, an exception being a lengthy series of 1968, devoted to tourism (89:40). Since 1970, commemoratives, usually in singles or pairs, have been issued for a number of current events, mainly of Arab interest.

Sharjah
Sheikh Saqr was deposed during his absence from the country in 1965 and stamps bearing his portrait were reissued with parallel bars obliterating the portrait (90:4). The adoption of the Gulf currency of 100 dirhams to the riyal in 1967 led to a further spate of provisional surcharges. The definitives were interspersed by frequent thematic sets, ranging from birds (90:3) to science, transport and communications, flowers and butterflies. The influence of external philatelic agents was manifest from 1966 onwards in the production of expensive and wildly irrelevant issues, including overprints or separate sets for the coastal village of Khor Fakkan. The stamps of Sharjah were superseded by the issues of the United Arab Emirates in 1972.

Singapore
The orchid and bird definitives were reissued in 1966-7 on paper with the sideways Block CA watermark, but an entirely new series appeared in 1968 and various designs and denominations were added, up to 1973. The theme of this series was music and dancing (90:6) and it was produced in multicolour photogravure by De La Rue and the Japanese Government Printing Bureau in Tokyo. A series featuring flowers and fruits was printed in photogravure by Heraclio Fournier of Spain and was introduced in 1973 (90:8). Regular issues continued to mark National Day every August (90:5) and emphasised national unity or aspects of Singapore's recent development. Thematic sets, devoted to Singapore festivals, art, shipping and landmarks, were introduced in 1971. A moderate number of sets commemorated anniversaries and current events; though designed by local artists, such as W. Lee and Eng Siak Loy, they were produced by a wide range of printers, in Britain, Finland, Hungary, Spain and Japan (90:7, 9).

South Arabia
A definitive series featuring the national flag was printed in photogravure by Harrison and introduced in April 1965 (90:10). The only other stamps issued by the short-lived Federation of South Arabia consisted of the various colonial omnibus sets, modified with the Federation emblem in place of the queen's portrait. The country attained independence in 1967 and changed its name to The People's Republic of Southern Yemen (90:11), and in 1971 changed yet again, to become The People's Democratic Republic of Yemen (90:39). The latter adopted a definitive series in 1971, featuring the map of the country or the Dam-al-Akhawain tree.

Syria
The definitive series of 1967 and the airmail stamps of 1966 (90:14) drew inspiration from the classical and medieval antiquities of Syria, as in previous issues, and the long history of the country also provided much of the subject matter for the commemorative and thematic sets. The first break with this tradition came in 1968 when a short definitive series featured an oil derrick, symbolising modern industry. A similar motif, featuring a graph and symbols of industry (90:15), was used for the ordinary postage denominations of the 1970 series, though the airmails reverted to the subject of Syrian antiquities. In the 1970s, an increasing proportion of the stamps devoted to current events, chose a modern poster treatment in preference to the classical themes of the earlier period (90:16).

Thailand
The 1963 definitives portraying King Bhumibol remained in use until 1972 when they were superseded by an intaglio series with a more up-to-date portrait (90:20). A photogravure series with a new portrait appeared the following year (90:21). The majority of Thai stamps from 1965 onwards were produced by the Japanese Government Printing Bureau, using a variety of processes. Photo-lithography was employed in the late 1960s (90:17) but subsequently, intaglio (90:18), photogravure (90:19) or a combination of the two (90:22) were used. Lengthy sets, with such themes as birds, fish, architecture, dances, national heroes and costumes, were issued from 1967 onwards.

Timor
In common with the other Portuguese overseas provinces, Timor issued a definitive series in 1967 with the theme of military uniforms.

The majority of the commemorative stamps consisted of singles in the prevailing subjects of the Portuguese territories, though the designs were occasionally modified to suit local requirements. The only indigenous commemoratives marked the bicentenary of the capital (1969) and the jubilee of Ross Smith's England–Australia flight (1970).

Umm al Qiwain

Like many of the other sheikhdoms of the Arabian Gulf area, Umm al Qiwain succumbed to the temptation of the lucrative income from philatelic sales and produced an average of over a hundred stamps annually, in the period from 1965 to 1972, when its issues were superseded by those of the United Arab Emirates. The change to the Arab Gulf currency in 1967 provided the opportunity to surcharge unsold remainders of many earlier sets, with the new dirhams and riyal denominations. Obsolete stamps were often overprinted for subsequent events, the 1964 Tokyo Olympic Games series being thus overprinted for the Mexico Olympic Games of 1968 (90:27). Umm al Qiwain was in the forefront of the Art stamp craze of the late 1960s, and used reproductions of paintings on the series honouring Expo 67 in Montreal (90:26). Many of the sets issued between 1968 and 1972 were boycotted by most dealers and catalogue editors.

United Arab Emirates

An independent union of the sheikhdoms and sultanates of the Arabian Gulf was formed in December 1971, replacing the former Trucial States under British protection. The United Arab Emirates consisted initially of Abu Dhabi, Ajman, Dubai, Fujeira, Sharjah and Umm al Qiwain, but Ras al Khaima acceded to the union three months later. The component states continued to issue their own stamps until the end of 1972, when a definitive series was introduced, the subjects referring to landmarks in the various states (90:28). Subsequently, several short commemorative sets have been released, but the philatelic policy of the UAE has been very conservative, in marked contrast to the prolific outpourings of the previous decade.

Vietnam (North)

Multicolour lithography was used for short thematic sets, usually consisting of stamps of the same denomination, as in the previous decade (90:35), but from 1965 onwards, an increasing number of stamps was devoted to aspects of the war. Eventually the war overtook all normal considerations, and commemoratives were largely concerned with victories against the army of the South or the number of American aircraft shot down. This policy even extended to the thematic sets, which tended to cover such subjects as anti-aircraft defences and national liberation. Even the stamps in the fashionable theme of Art, concentrated largely on paintings of 'South Vietnam, Land and People' or 'Production and Fighting', including the inevitable artistic rendering of a crashed American plane (90:36). From 1972, however, martial themes were gradually displaced by the more commercial subjects.

Vietnam (South)

There was little change in South Vietnam's philatelic policy in this period. No definitive stamps were issued, though short thematic sets appeared at regular intervals, and a small-format 1-piastre stamp, featuring a pagoda, was issued in coil form in 1970. The thematic sets were released in pairs or sets of three stamps (90:34). The same policy was applied to frequent sets of a propaganda nature from 1967 onwards, with such themes as edification and democracy, revolutionary development, farmers as property owners (90:30), the reconstruction of Hue and Tet after devastation by the Viet Cong (90:33), the 'Open Arms' campaign for the rehabilitation of refugees from the North and aspects of national development. The most important change in the stamps of South Vietnam was in their production. Although stamps continued to be recess-printed in Paris as before (90:29, 33, 34), several issues from 1967 onwards were recess-printed in Rome by the De La Rue subsidiary, Staderini Carte Valori, or produced in multicolour photogravure by the Japanese Government Printing Bureau (90:30–32).

Yemen

Throughout this decade, stamps purporting to come from the Yemen were issued on behalf of both the republican and royalist factions, though largely handled by a variety of external philatelic agents. The stamps were respectively inscribed for use in the Yemen Arab Republic and the Mutawakelite Kingdom of Yemen and the situation became further confused after the South Arabian Federation (formerly Aden) adopted the name of Yemen in 1967. Both republican and royalist stamps mainly featured subjects that were totally irrelevant to either faction, and designed specifically to raise revenue in the philatelic markets of Europe and America. Occasionally, however, both sides issued stamps that were germane to the struggle – marking anniversaries of the revolution (90:37) on the one hand, or honouring guerrilla leaders on the other (90:38) – even if the latter should subsequently become more marketable by overprinting them in honour of Sir Winston Churchill. This type of commemoration may have been expedient at the time, but has since tended to be regarded as an insult to the memory of both men involved.

Africa

Algeria

Two stamps in multicolour photogravure were issued in 1966, to celebrate the return to Algeria of the remains of the Emir Abd el Kader and bore his portrait. The same design was used later, for a definitive series printed in monochrome photogravure by Courvoisier, and between 1968 and 1971 was produced in a lithographic version by the Central Bank press (91:2). Apart from these stamps, Algeria used thematic sets, issued at regular intervals, to provide the permanent range. Apart from flora and fauna, many of these sets concentrated on ancient and modern arts of the country, in many different media, from rock-paintings to tapestries and carpets (91:3). Although indigenous artists designed all Algerian stamps in this decade, a high proportion of them were produced in Paris as before, either typographed, recess-printed or photogravure-printed at the French Government Printing Works, or produced in photogravure by Delrieu (91:1). From 1969 onwards, however, the Central Bank printed many of the stamps in photogravure, lithography (91:4) or letterpress.

Ascension

Apart from the various colonial omnibus issues, Ascension began producing distinctive commemoratives in 1966, with sets marking the opening of the Apollo communications satellite station and the BBC relay station (91:9). Subsequently, a number of short thematic sets was introduced, devoted mainly to fish or the crests of ships associated with the island (91:10). A definitive series, released in 1971 in connection with the adoption of British decimal currency, took as its theme, the history of rocketry and space research.

Biafra

The eastern region of Nigeria seceded from the Federation in 1967 and issued its own stamps, under the title of Biafra, until the rebellion was suppressed by federal forces in January 1970. Distinctive stamps were lithographed at the Lisbon Mint and philatelic sales were originally handled through Portugal and, latterly, France. The majority of stamps had a strong propaganda bias (91:11) and were often surcharged with charity premiums. Several sets were in the hands of the French agency at the time Biafra was overrun by federal troops and it is doubtful whether these were ever postally used in the country.

Botswana

Bechuanaland attained independence in September 1966 under the name of Botswana. Four stamps in multicolour photogravure by Harrison celebrated independence (91:12) and the Bechuanaland definitives were overprinted with the new name. A republican series featuring birds was released in 1967 (91:13). The postage-due stamps were similarly overprinted, prior to the issue of a series featuring elephants that was lithographed by Bradbury Wilkinson. The few commemorative issues since independence have included annual Christmas stamps – introduced in 1969 – and several short thematic sets.

Burundi

The monarchy was overthrown in November 1966, during the absence of King Ntare V from the country, and a republic was proclaimed. The birds and flowers definitive sets of 1965 and 1966 were reissued with a republican overprint, but these were followed in quick succession by lengthy sets with the themes of fish and African art (91:14). Thereafter, Burundi continued to change its definitives at annual intervals, featuring butterflies, animals (91:17), beetles, birds and orchids, and took part in issues for most of the fashionable international events of the period (91:15, 16, 18).

Cameroun

The French influence remained particularly strong in the federal republic of Cameroun, not only in the design of stamps, which were predominantly inscribed in French, but also in their production, which continued in the hands of the French printers (91:19). From the end of 1968 onwards, however, the majority of stamps were inscribed bilingually, with at least the name of the country in English and French. There was also a greater tendency to commemorate subjects of interest to the people of West Cameroun – formerly the Southern Cameroons – in line with the language and culture inherited from the British during the period of the British mandate. In June 1972, the country changed its name to the United Republic of Cameroun, following a plebiscite which opted for a unitary instead of a federal form of government. Stamps issued since that date have been thus inscribed in both languages (91:20).

Central African Republic

The French monopoly of stamp design and production continued until 1970 when De La Rue lithographed a number of sets. Nevertheless, the Central African Republic has remained fairly constant to the connection with the former mother country and its stamps in this decade have not differed materially from those of the other African countries of the French Community. Multicolour intaglio is still the principal medium, and lends itself admirably to the numerous thematic sets, which have ranged from plant protection to native coiffures (91:22–24). Commemoratives, mainly publicising current events of world importance, have generally been confined to single stamps.

Chad

The same remarks can be applied to the stamps of Chad, at least up to 1969, and the sets featuring musical instruments, fish, butterflies and rock-paintings (91:26, 27) have the unmistakable quality associated with the products of the French Government Printing Works. Thereafter, however, Chad embarked on a more liberal policy, varying restrained intaglio with gaudy lithography and achieving a much higher output of stamps, that were issued under all kinds of pretexts and marked all kinds of events. Stamps for official use, featuring the map and national flag, were typographed in multicolour in Paris between 1966 and 1971 (91:25) – an unusually colourful application of the letterpress process which is seldom employed today.

Comoro Islands

With the exception of three stamps of 1970 featuring the Friday Mosque in Moroni, all stamps of the Comoro Islands in recent years, have been released in short thematic sets of relatively brief duration. The usual themes of flowers (91:28), seashells and birds, were enlivened by such purely local subjects as prayer-mats, indigenous costumes and landscapes.

Congo (Brazzaville)

The use of French language and currency by both the Congolese republics, made the stamps of the 1960s difficult to identify, though the marginal imprint was invariably a clue in the case of those issued by Congo–Brazzaville (91:31) and the characteristic appearance of stamps that were recess-printed by the French Government Printing Works or photogravure-printed by So. Ge. Im. or Delrieu. Following the introduction of a Marxist–Leninist constitution in January

1970, the country became a people's republic and inscriptions henceforth included the adjective *Populaire* (91:32).

Congo–Kinshasa (Zaire)

The confusion of names, between the two Congolese republics, was resolved in 1971 when Congo (Kinshasa) changed its name to the Republic of Zaire. From 1965 onwards, however, the name 'République Démocratique du Congo' was inscribed on all stamps of the former Belgian territory (91:29, 30) which is an aid to identification. A small-format arms definitive series was released in 1969 (91:29) with a portrait of President Mobutu on the higher values. Inflation led to the reissue of a number of obsolete sets in 1970, surcharged with new values, but thematic sets were also issued at frequent intervals (91:30). The arms and Mobutu definitives were reissued in 1972 with the title changed to Zaire (96:31).

Dahomey

With the exception of three arms definitives of 1969, lithographed in Berlin, the stamps of Dahomey continued to be produced in France as before and there was no attempt to formulate a national philatelic identity, in common with the other former French colonies. Indeed, the floral series of 1967 might well have been issued by Congo–Brazzaville. The similarity of the sets (91:34) arises from the fact that P. Lambert designed both of them, and Delrieu's multicolour photogravure was used in both instances. A more distinctive series, was the same designer's set featuring Bariba horsemen (91:35) – a departure from the solid backgrounds that distinguish so much of his work. Most of Dahomey's commemoratives were released in single or pairs, in honour of current international events (91:33).

East Africa

Since April 1965, stamps have been issued by the East African Posts and Telecommunications Corporation, for use in Kenya, Uganda and Tanzania – excluding Zanzibar, where only the definitives of Tanzania are valid for postage. These general issues bear the names of the three countries and care has been taken to vary the order in which the names appear. The issues fall into two categories, commemorative and thematic sets. With very few exceptions the sets consist of four stamps. One, or at most, two designs were employed in the earlier commemoratives and these were usually symbolic in nature (92:2, 7), though the visit of the Pope to Uganda in 1969 was celebrated by stamps featuring his portrait (92:5). Subsequently, different designs in related themes were used for the stamps marking anniversaries and current events. Thus, the series commemorating the 21st anniversary of East African Airways, depicted aicraft from different periods and the sets honouring the Commonwealth and Olympic Games had different subjects on each denomination (92:3). Related topics with a common theme, were depicted on stamps issued in connection with international anniversaries (92:12, 14, 15) or to publicise such important campaigns as the conversion to the metric system (92:8) and the rinderpest eradication project (92:10).

Before 1971, all of the commemorative issues dealt with events that were common to all three countries, but since then, several sets have been released to commemorate events in one or other of the countries, though the commemoration continues to be shared by all three. In this group, come the sets marking the 10th anniversaries of independence in Tanzania (92:11) and Kenya (92:16) and the 10th anniversary of the Zanzibari revolution (92:17). Four stamps of 1973 publicised the twenty-fourth World Scout Conference held in Nairobi, and included vignettes portraying Lord Baden-Powell and showing his grave in Kenya (92:13).

Thematic sets were introduced in April 1966, the first series being devoted to tourism (92:1). Subsequent sets featured archaeological relics, water transport (92:4), musical instruments and, railway transport (92:9) but this policy was discontinued in 1971. Harrison photogravure-printed all East African stamps up to the Papal visit series of 1969, but thereafter, other British firms – Questa, De La Rue, John Waddington, Bradbury Wilkinson and Walsall Security Printers – lithographed stamps, and the Kenya independence commemoratives of 1973 were lithographed by Enschedé.

Egypt

The definitive series introduced in 1964, remained in use until 1969 and various denominations were added to it up to 1967. The 4-millieme stamp, in different colours and with the date '1964', was issued in February of that year, for use on Ramadan greetings cards. Ramadan stamps were issued each year from then onwards (92:21). The 20- and 55-millieme stamps were redrawn in a rather larger size in 1969 (92:18) but recess-printed as before. Other denominations and designs in the same format, were printed in combined intaglio and photogravure or photogravure alone, and issued in 1970–71. Apart from the Ramadan stamps, a set was released annually to mark Post Day and several other annual events, such as Peasant Day, Police Day and the anniversary of the revolution, were marked by stamps from time to time. The most ambitious series of the late 1960s was a set of forty-one stamps for African Tourist Year (1969), each stamp depicting a view in one of the African countries from Algeria to Zambia – but excluding the 'white' countries and their colonies.

As the result of negotiations between Egypt, Syria and Libya in 1971, the Confederation of Arab Republics was inaugurated on New Year's Day 1972. Hitherto, Egyptian stamps had merely been inscribed UAR (United Arab Republic) – a reference to the ephemeral union with Syria in 1958–61 – but as a result of the new Confederation, Egypt reverted to its former name, prefixed by the letters AR (Arab Republic) and this has appeared on all stamps issued since January 1972 (92:19–22). The first anniversary of Nasser's death was marked by a set of four stamps (92:19) and many subsequent stamps have borne his portrait. The definitive series was reissued in 1972–4 with the inscription changed to AR EGYPT and several new colours or denominations were introduced in the same period. Little reference was made in the stamps of this decade to the two wars fought against Israel (1967 and 1973), though the attack on a Libyan airliner by Israeli fighters over the Sinai Desert a few months before the Yom Kippur War, prompted Egypt to issue a memorial stamp (92:22). Indian forces, policing the Gaza strip before the June War of 1967, used the Nehru commemorative stamp overprinted UNEF (United Nations Emergency Force) (92:23).

Equatorial Guinea

The Spanish provinces of Fernando Póo and Rio Muni combined in October 1968 to form the independent republic of Equatorial Guinea, a set of three stamps being issued to mark the occasion. No further stamps appeared until 1970, when a definitive series portraying President Nguema was released (92:24). After this tardy beginning, Equatorial Guinea entrusted its philatelic affairs to an external agency and as a result, a spate of irrelevant and unnecessary issues has flooded the world stamp market.

Ethiopia

A multicolour definitive series by Courvoisier was released in July 1965, concentrating on the modern development of the country (92:26); portraits of Emperor Haile Selassie were incorporated in each design. The series remained current for the rest of the decade, supplemented from time to time by short thematic sets, ranging from butterflies and animals to river craft and provincial architecture. Ethiopian stamps of this period were remarkably eclectic in their choice of printers and processes, and included De La Rue (92:25), Harrison and Bradbury Wilkinson of Britain, the Israeli Government Printer, the Austrian State Press, the State Printing Works, Berlin, the State Bank Note Printing Works in Helsinki, Fournier of Spain, Boccard of Geneva, Aspioti-Elka of Athens, Ercolano of Naples and the 'Light and Peace' Press in Addis Ababa.

French Southern and Antarctic Territories

The output of stamps for this remote French colony increased considerably from 1968 onwards. Large-sized commemoratives were issued as singles (92:27), but sets of six or eight stamps with such themes as maps, fish, insects, plants and polar ships were released twice-yearly from 1969 onwards.

French Territory of the Afars and Issas

The French Somali Coast changed its name in 1967, to avoid confusion with the independent republic of Somalia, and adopted the names of the principal tribes. A definitive series featuring native fauna was issued in 1967 (92:28) and was followed by similar sets devoted to landmarks, sports, marine fauna, birds and archaeological discoveries. Occasional commemoratives have been mainly concerned with current international events.

Gabon

Frequent thematic sets took the place of definitive stamps from 1965 onwards. These were mainly large-sized pictorials, although several small-format sets, featuring civic arms, were issued from November 1969. The commemoratives have mostly been in connection with international events, but, in common with other countries of the French Community, a number of sets have been issued in omnibus form and relate to anniversaries of French interest (92:29).

The Gambia

This former British colony attained independence in February 1965 and celebrated the occasion by issuing a set of four stamps, as well as overprinting the entire definitive series. In 1966, the country adopted the prefix 'the' (in reference to the river from which its name derives) and all stamps issued since then have been thus inscribed. A multicolour photogravure series, featuring birds, was released in February 1966 (92:30) and remained current until 1971, when the currency was decimalised and a series featuring fish was lithographed by Format International and issued with values in bututs and dalasys (92:31). A comparatively conservative policy has been pursued with regard to commemoratives (92:32) and occasional thematic sets, consisting of two or three stamps.

Ghana

Sterling currency was replaced by a decimal system based on the cedi of 100 pesewas in 1965 and the existing definitive series was surcharged accordingly (92:33). Economic crises during the next two years, however, led to a currency reform in February 1967 and the introduction of the new cedi equal to 1.2 old cedis. Stamps issued between that date and February 1972 were inscribed in n.p. (new pesewas) and included the definitive series of June–September 1967 (92:34). In 1972, the currency was reformed again, the cedi being now worth eight-tenths of a 'new' cedi. The prefix 'new' was dropped from currency notations on stamps so as to distinguish the new cedi from the old new cedi, and stamps from April 1972 have merely been inscribed 'p' or 'c' (92:35, 36). No new definitive series was introduced as a result of this change, though the lengthy commemorative sets cover a wide range of values from 1-pesewa to 1-cedi.

Guinea

The output of stamps in this period was almost entirely thematic, ranging from native masks, dances, costumes and village scenes (93:1, 5) to flowers and head-dress (93:2). Many of these sets ranged far beyond the confines of Africa, let alone Guinea, from Martyrs of Liberty (including the Kennedy brothers and Dr. Martin Luther King) to the ultimate in thematics – a series of 1972 devoted to 'imaginary creatures of outer space'. Commemorative stamps marked the leading international events (93:3) and reflected Guinea's political bias, with sets honouring African independence and solidarity, as well as Marxist–Leninist events and personalities. Guinea was one of the first countries to turn to children's drawings and paintings, for a series in honour of UNICEF (93:4) released in 1966.

Ivory Coast

Although it left the French Community in 1960, the republic of Ivory Coast has maintained its links with the former mother country, as well as with the other French-speaking republics of Africa. This is reflected in the issue of stamps which are still designed and printed in France (93:7) and in the release of commemoratives that refer to events of common interest to France and the French African republics.

Kenya

Mrs. Rena Fennessy designed both of the definitive sets issued in this decade. The first featured animals and was released in December 1966 (93:8). Chalk-surfaced paper was used for the original printings, but glazed, ordinary paper was substituted for certain denominations printed in 1971. In December of that year, a series depicting seashells was issued. Spelling errors occurred in the Latin names inscribed on the 50- and 70-cent values and these were rectified in January 1974 (93:9). Both sets were printed by Harrison in multicolour photogravure.

Lesotho
Basutoland became an independent kingdom in 1966 and adopted the name of Lesotho, which was overprinted on the Basutoland definitives, before the introduction of a photogravure pictorial series in April 1967. This series bore inset portraits of King Moshoeshoe II. The early printings were made on unwatermarked paper, but a watermark featuring the Basuto hat emblem, was introduced in 1968. Moshoeshoe II was deposed by the Prime Minister, Chief Jonathan in 1970 and the definitive series was reissued the following year, with the designs redrawn to omit the portrait of the king (93:11). Thematic sets, featuring rock-paintings, prehistoric reptiles and their footprints, birds and butterflies were issued between 1968 and 1974, in addition to a few commemoratives, mainly of local interest.

Liberia
A definitive series in a small upright format, portrayed Liberian presidents and was released between 1966 and 1969. Like all other Liberian stamps up to 1970, this set was lithographed by the Wright Bank Note Company of Philadelphia which had enjoyed a virtual monopoly of Liberian stamps since the Second World War. The Wright issues had a distinctive quality, characterised by their two-colour combinations and sculpted lettering (93:12). From 1970 onwards, however, the majority of stamps were produced in multicolour lithography by Format International and also tended to become very much larger in size (93:13, 14).

Libya
Before September 1969, when the monarchy was overthrown, the stamps of Libya were inscribed 'Libya' or 'Kingdom of Libya' in English, though occasionally all or part of the inscription would be rendered in French (93:15). After the revolution, existing stocks of stamps had the word 'Kingdom' obliterated or overprinted with a republican inscription (93:18). Subsequent stamps have been inscribed entirely in Arabic, though those from May 1970 onwards also incorporated the initials L.A.R. (Libyan Arab Republic) (93:16, 17). Even this clue to the identity of the stamps has disappeared from the issues made since July 1973.

Malagasy Republic
Thematic sets of short duration replaced the traditional definitive issues in 1965 and successively featured civic arms, postal transport, insects (93:19), religious buildings (93:20), paintings and seashells. All Malagasy stamps were printed in France as before, though increasingly, designs by indigenous artists were employed.

Malawi
The 1964–5 definitives were superseded by a series in 1966–7 featuring butterflies and this was replaced in 1968 by a birds series, both issues being designed by Victor Whiteley and photogravure-printed by Harrison (93:21). As a result of the adoption of decimal currency in 1971, a series featuring antelope was released. This series was designed and lithographed by John Waddington Ltd. (93:22). Stamps issued from 1973 onwards, had a circumflex accent over the W of MALAWI to denote the pronunciation (Malavi). Malawi was one of the first British Commonwealth countries to issue short thematic sets (93:23, 24), a wide range of subjects has been covered since 1966. Generally, these sets were accompanied by miniature sheets containing one of each denomination. The 1974 series, featuring game fish, also commemorated the 35th anniversary of the Malawi Angling Society (93:27). After Ruanda–Urundi, Malawi was the next country in Africa to issue Christmas stamps, sets of four or five having appeared each year since 1966 (93:26). Relatively few commemorative sets have been released and in most cases they have consisted of sets of four stamps in common designs, together with a matching miniature sheet (93:25).

Mali
Although all of its stamps have been produced in France, as before, Mali has shown extremely catholic tastes in the subjects commemorated, particularly with regard to the celebrities honoured. Among recent issues, have been stamps honouring Franklin D. Roosevelt, Sir Winston Churchill, Charles De Gaulle and Lenin – as well as Nat King Cole, Picasso and Marylin Monroe! The same panoramic view of the world is to be found in the stamps commemorating historic and current events of all kinds. Purely thematic sets, apart from those devoted to paintings or space achievements, tend to concentrate on subjects of indigenous interest, especially flora and fauna (93:28, 29, 31, 32), though two sets (in 1968 and 1969) featured ancient and modern French motor cars (93:30).

Mauritania
Like Mali, Mauritania has maintained a neutral policy with regard to commemorative stamps, honouring American and Soviet astronauts impartially. Other world-personalities ranged from Lincoln to Lenin, Adenauer, De Gaulle, Churchill and Dr. Martin Luther King (93:33). The same formula of thematic sets, recess- or photogravure-printed by the French presses, characterises the stamps of Mauritania.

Mauritius
Bird paintings by D. M. Reid-Henry were the subject of the photogravure definitives issued in March 1965 (93:34). Similar designs were used for a set commemorating self-government in 1967, while the entire definitive series was appropriately overprinted. The 1969–73 definitives featured fish and marine life, with the Annigoni portrait of the queen, inset (93:35). Both issues were produced by Harrison and Sons. The sideways watermark originally used for the fish series was superseded by the upright Block CA watermark in 1972–3. Since 1970, thematic sets have publicised tourism and aspects of the island's history and culture. Commemoratives have generally consisted of singles or pairs, a notable exception being the six stamps and matching miniature sheet of 1969, celebrating the birth centenary of Mahatma Gandhi who spent some time in Mauritius at the turn of the century (93:36).

Morocco
Between March 1968 and 1974, a definitive series portraying King Hassan was produced by De La Rue in multicolour lithography (94:1); a larger format was used for the five highest denominations. Although a 75-franc value was added to the series in 1974, a new series had been introduced the previous year. This portrayed the king in European dress, with the national arms in the background, and was printed in multicolour photogravure by the East German Bank Note Printing Company of Leipzig (94:2). The relatively few commemorative stamps of this period have been produced by many different printers, in Britain, France, Switzerland, Spain and Hungary.

Niger Republic
Although independent of the French Community, the old ties with the mother country are maintained to this day. All of Niger's stamps have been produced in France and many of the subjects, from the paintings of Delacroix to the portraits of Pompidou, De Gaulle and Napoléon, are obviously aimed at the French philatelic market. Frequent short thematic sets have taken the place of definitives, in the same pattern as the other former French African territories (94:8).

Nigeria
A definitive series, featuring wild animals and their footprints, was designed by Maurice Fievet and printed in multicolour photogravure by Harrison and Delrieu between November 1965 and October 1966 (94:9). Printings of this series between 1969 and 1972 were made by the Nigerian Security Printing and Minting Company whose initials appeared in the margin of the designs. In 1970–71, the 2- and 4-pence values were reprinted by Enschedé and can be identified by the omission of the printer's imprint, and by the designer's name appearing on the right instead of the left of the margin. In 1973, Nigeria adopted a decimal currency of 100 kobo to 1 naira and this necessitated a new definitive series, depicting

industries and occupations (94:12). Initially, the series was printed by photogravure, but subsequently, lithography was used. Apart from subtle variations in the designs, these two versions may be distinguished by the length of the marginal imprint – $5\frac{1}{4}$ mm in the case of the photogravure series and 6 mm in the case of the lithographed series.

Apart from a solitary set of three stamps in 1971, featuring Nigerian antiquities, no thematic sets have been released; and the great majority of the commemorative sets have been confined to two or three stamps in each case. Most of these issues have been concerned primarily with Nigerian events and anniversaries (94:11, 13, 14). A propaganda series, with the theme of 'one people, one destiny' celebrated the re-unification of the country after the tragic Biafran war (94:10). A semi-postal stamp of 1973 commemorated the centenary of the discovery of the leprosy bacillus by Dr. Hansen, whose portrait was depicted (94:15).

Portuguese African Provinces

Until the overthrow of the right-wing dictatorship in Portugal, in 1974, the African 'provinces' presented a superficially uniform picture of Portuguese rule, that was reflected in the stereotyped pattern of stamp design. Their definitive sets all followed the same theme, though changed at regular intervals. Thus, military uniforms (94:3) were succeeded by medals and decorations (91:6) and historic ships (91:7; 94:5, 38), different designs being used in each case in an endeavour to relate the subjects to the territory concerned. The same policy was applied to the commemorative issues which tended to be issued in omnibus fashion, while using distinctive designs in each case. The various portraits used in the Carmona centenary stamps illustrate this policy vividly (91:8, 22; 94:4). In certain cases, uniform designs were used by each province (94:16), whereas the stamps celebrating the 40th anniversary of the national revolution, featured different colonial buildings (91:5). As befitted the largest and most important of the provinces, Mozambique alone had any scope for individual issues, with a diamond-shaped series devoted to rocks, minerals and fossils in 1971 (94:6) and three obligatory tax stamps in 1965 raising money for local telecommunication improvements (94:7).

Réunion

Throughout this period, Réunion continued to use contemporary French stamps, surcharged in local currency (94:17). The only distinctive stamp was a 25-franc of 1971 marking nature protection and featuring a Réunion chameleon.

Rhodesia

The adjective 'Southern' was dropped from the name of the country in 1965, when Northern Rhodesia became Zambia, but the definitives inscribed 'Southern Rhodesia' remained in use. Commemoratives bearing the amended name, appeared in May 1965. Following the breakdown of negotiations with the British government over the future of Rhodesia, the Rhodesian government made a unilateral declaration of independence in November 1965. A stamp was lithographed locally to celebrate the occasion, and the definitive series was overprinted and released in January 1966. Both issues were banned in Britain and mail bearing these stamps was treated as unpaid and surcharged accordingly (94:18). Harrison and Sons produced a redrawn version of the definitives, omitting the word 'Southern' and these stamps were released in February 1966 (94:19). When sanctions were imposed in 1966, in an attempt to break down Rhodesian resistance, later printings of the definitives were lithographed by Mardon of Salisbury, who also produced all commemorative and thematic sets from 1966 onwards. In 1967–8, several denominations of the definitive series were reissued with values expressed in both sterling and decimal currency, but an entirely new series, minus the queen's portrait, was introduced in 1970 after Rhodesia had adopted a republican constitution (94:22).

Stamps reproducing paintings of famous Rhodesians were introduced in 1967 and have been issued annually since then (94:21, 24). Short sets, with such themes as works of art, nature conservation, bridges and birds (94:23) have been issued over the same period. Christmas stamps were introduced in 1972 (94:26). Relatively few commemorative sets have been produced and these usually consist of four stamps with different motifs for each denomination (94:20, 25, 27, 28).

Rwanda

Instead of definitive sets current for a reasonable period of years, Rwanda issued lengthy sets with the full range of definitive values, at the rate of two or three sets a year and devoted to specific subjects, such as butterflies, flowers and birds (94:31). Long, multi-value sets were also issued to commemorate a wide range of historic events and these stamps featured different aspects of a chosen theme. Thus, the history of malaria treatment and prevention was the subject of a series marking the centenary of the discovery of quinine (94:30) and the centenary of the first Vatican Council provided the opportunity for a series portraying all the popes since 1870 (94:29).

St. Helena

Four of the 1961 definitives were overprinted in January 1965 to mark the inauguration of the first local postal service on the island. Although St. Helena took part in the various colonial omnibus issues from 1965 to 1966, a more liberal policy ensued, with two or three distinctive sets being issued annually. In 1969, short thematic sets were introduced and these featured aspects of mail communications, military uniforms and badges (94:35). The commemoratives of 1967–8 honoured local events (94:32) but, with the exception of two stamps of 1971 marking the sesquicentenary of Napoléon's death, all of the later commemoratives were concerned with British events and personalities (94:34, 36, 37). A new definitive series, lithographed by Perkins Bacon, was introduced in 1968 (94:33) and reissued three years later with the values rendered in decimal currency.

Senegal

Unlike the other African countries formerly under French administration, Senegal did not employ French designers and printers to the same extent. Both Courvoisier (95:1, 3) and Enschedé (95:4) vied with the French companies in the production of Senegalese stamps. A more cosmopolitan atmosphere also prevailed in the choice of subjects, especially portrait stamps honouring a wide variety of people, ranging from Pushkin, Adenauer and Alfred Nobel to Mahatma Gandhi and President Nasser. Significantly, a high proportion of these portrait stamps featured Negro celebrities, such as Booker Washington and Louis Armstrong, and even Amilcar Cabral, leader of the guerrilla movement in the Portuguese African provinces. Apart from short thematic sets, single stamps were issued occasionally to provide definitive denominations (95:2), though there was no permanent definitive series.

Seychelles

The 1962 definitives remained in use for seven years, and were replaced by a historical series in 1969. The set, designed by Mrs. M. Hayward and lithographed by Enschedé, traced the development of the islands – once the haunt of pirates and now a satellite tracking station (95:6). Apart from the various omnibus issues of 1965–6 (95:5), the Seychelles has produced a few commemorative sets since 1967 and introduced short thematic issues in 1970.

The islands of Aldabra, Farquhar and Desroches were detached from the Seychelles in November 1965 and joined the Chagos archipelago (formerly administered by Mauritius) to form a separate Crown Colony to be known as the British Indian Ocean Territory. Seychelles stamps remained in use until January 1968, when the Seychelles definitives were overprinted B.I.O.T. for use in this territory. Between October 1968 and December 1970, a pictorial series, lithographed by De La Rue, was released (95:7). Upright instead of sideways watermarks were used from October 1973 onwards. Since 1969, the British Indian Ocean Territory has issued several short thematic sets but very few commemoratives.

Sierra Leone

The adoption of decimal currency in 1964, resulted in no fewer than four lengthy sets of surcharged provisionals made on obsolete issues, during a period of two years. Subsequently, some of these surcharged stamps were additionally overprinted to commemorate Sir Milton Margai and Sir Winston Churchill. From then until 1972, all stamps of Sierra Leone were die-stamped or embossed on metal foil with self-adhesive backing and free-form shapes (95:8). The return to orthodoxy was marked in 1972 by a definitive series, lithographed by De La Rue and portraying President Siaka Stevens (95:9).

Somalia
Short thematic sets at annual intervals, have provided the permanent range of Somali stamps since 1965 and these have included several sets devoted to antelope (95:11). Other subjects have ranged from flowers and fish to paintings in the Caresa Museum (95:10). Comparatively few commemorative issues have been directly relevant to Somalia; the majority have been concerned with international events and personalities.

South Africa
The 1964 're-drawn' definitives remained in use throughout this decade and various denominations were added between 1965 and 1972. A less distinct watermark was introduced in 1967 and polyvinyl gum was used instead of gum arabic from that date. Between 1969 and 1971, the stamps were released with phosphor bands, printed horizontally and vertically between the stamp designs and covering the perforations in order to produce a phosphorescent frame. New $\frac{1}{2}$- and 1-cent stamps were introduced in 1969, with the much neater inscription RSA solving the problem of bilingual inscriptions in English and Afrikaans (95:19). Larger designs, featuring a sheep and a lamb (95:30) were added in 1972. A new type of phosphorised, glossy paper without watermark, was used for the definitives issued since November 1972 (95:41).

The full name of the country in English and Afrikaans appeared on bilingual commemoratives issued up to 1966 (95:12, 14, 17), and a set of four stamps, marking the 5th anniversary of the republic (95:13) was issued in pairs, alternately inscribed in each language. Thereafter, stamps were inscribed in both languages, but the abbreviated form RSA was used exclusively, and considerable ingenuity was shown in letting the portraits or pictorial motifs speak for themselves, without any caption other than dates (95:15, 16, 18, 24, 25, 27, 29, 33, 34, 36, 39, 40), or confining the inscription to words that were the same in both languages (95:21, 22, 31). Where bilingual captions became absolutely unavoidable, initials were used as far as possible (95:28, 32), or the words were grouped in such a way that repetition of common words or initials was minimised (95:20, 23, 26, 37). On only two occasions was it felt necessary to incorporate lengthier captions in both languages (95:35, 38).

South West Africa
The technical changes in the definitives used in this period paralleled those in South Africa, where the stamps were produced. Thus, chalk-surfaced paper with the RSA watermark was used between 1966 and 1972 and unwatermarked phosphorescent paper was introduced in 1973. Between 1970 and 1973, several designs were redrawn, omitting the 'postage/revenue' inscription and increasing the size of the figures of value. A multicoloured series featuring plant life, was issued on unwatermarked paper in 1973. As in South Africa, the commemoratives were issued with bilingual inscriptions kept to a minimum, and the country name was replaced by the initials common to both Afrikaans and English (96:2). A curious exception, however, was the series honouring President Swart in 1968, issued in trilingual strips, with captions in English, Afrikaans and German (96:1).

Spanish African Provinces
The provinces of Fernando Póo and Rio Muni combined in 1968 to form the independent republic of Equatorial Guinea; before that date they had issued a few stamps in the standard Spanish colonial designs. The same pattern applied to the stamps issued by Ifni (93:6) and Spanish Sahara, both of which issued stamps each year for Colonial Stamp Day and Child Welfare. At the end of June 1969, Ifni was ceded by Spain to Morocco whose stamps are now used. Thereafter, Spanish Sahara was the only part of Africa still in Spanish hands. Apart from a lengthy series of 1972, featuring nomadic tribes, the only issues of Spanish Sahara consisted of the two annual pairs for Stamp Day and Child Welfare, as before. Since

1970, these stamps have been multicoloured where previously they had been printed in monochrome (96:3).

Sudan
Although the output of new issues accelerated in 1965, Sudan remains one of the more conservative countries, with a total of just over a hundred stamps in the past decade. The 1962 definitive series has remained in use, and no thematic sets have ever been produced. Commemorative sets generally consist of three or four stamps, relating to national events and personalities or international events with which the Sudan is concerned (96:4).

Swaziland
The former High Commission territory graduated to full independence in the late 1960s, becoming a protected state in 1967 and an independent kingdom in 1968. The 1962 definitives were overprinted on the latter occasion, pending the release of a pictorial series portraying King Sobhuza II in 1969 (96:5). Originally the series was inscribed with values in South African cents and rands, but it was reissued in 1975 with values expressed in the new local currency, based on the lilangeni (plural emalangeni) (96:6). Thematic sets, featuring flowers and aspects of tourism and natural resources, have been issued since 1971, but commemoratives have so far been confined to United Nations anniversaries and the 5th anniversary of independence (1973).

Tanzania
The United Republic of Tanganyika and Zanzibar was renamed Tanzania in 1965 and a pictorial definitive series, thus inscribed, was released in December of that year (96:7). This series was valid in Kenya and Uganda as well as in the mainland portion of Tanzania, but, paradoxically, it was not valid in Zanzibar. A series, depicting fish, was released in December 1969; originally printed on chalk-surfaced paper, it was reprinted on ordinary glazed paper in 1971–3. Both of these sets were printed in photogravure by Harrison and were issued with overprints for use on official mail (96:8). The latter series was extended to Zanzibar in 1968, when distinctive stamps of that island were withdrawn. Harrison photogravure-printed a butterflies definitive series released in December 1973 (96:9). No commemorative stamps were issued by Tanzania; instead, the joint issues of the East African postal service were used.

Togo
A striking exception to the usual pattern of the former French African countries was provided by Togo, all of whose stamps in this period were designed by M. Shamir or O. Adler and printed in Israel, either by the Government Printer in Jerusalem (photogravure), or by Lewin-Epstein of Bat-Yam (lithography). The 'non-aligned' position of Togo was reflected in stamps honouring achievements of both great powers, Russia and the United States, especially in the space race (96:10, 12). The choice of subjects for stamps was far-reaching and often resulted in some surprising combinations, such as the UNESCO commemoratives which portrayed Bach and Duke Ellington. The majority of commemorative stamps adopted a pictorial approach (96:11). Frequent thematic sets featured the wildlife, flora, industry and culture of the country. The nearest thing to the French style of definitives, was the series combining civic arms with tourist scenery (96:13).

Tristan da Cunha
The makeshift 'resettlement' series was replaced in February 1965 by a set recess-printed by Bradbury Wilkinson and featuring ships connected with the island's history (96:14). A change in postal rates led to the introduction of a 4-pence denomination in 1967 and this was met by surcharging the obsolete 4½-pence stamps (96:15) pending the supply of a stamp of this value. The entire series was surcharged in decimal currency in February 1971, but was superseded by an entirely new series the following year. The two highest denominations were produced by Bradbury Wilkinson in combined intaglio and lithography, but the rest of the series was lithographed by Alden and Mowbray of Oxford (96:16). Thematic sets of four values each, were introduced in 1968, and occasional commemoratives of indigenous interest have also been released, in addition to the various omnibus sets from 1965 onwards.

Tunisia

Although the French Government Printing Works has continued to produce intaglio stamps for Tunisia up to the present time (96:17, 20) an increasing number of sets has been produced elsewhere. Courvoisier concentrated on multicolour photogravure sets devoted to various themes (96:21, 22), Rosenbaum Brothers lithographed occasional issues, featuring aspects of Tunisian history (96:18), and Enschedé produced a number of commemorative sets, especially in the late 1960s (96:19). Hatem Elmekki continued to design many of the commemoratives in his distinctive style (96:17, 19, 20, 23, 24, 26) and Ben Abdallah produced the art work for many of the thematic sets (96:21, 22). Poster treatment of subjects was used for the majority of commemorative stamps and also for issues having a propaganda motif, such as the Road Safety Campaign issue (96:25).

Uganda

Two definitives were issued in this decade, both of which were designed by Rena Fennessy and photogravure-printed by Harrison. A series featuring birds was released in October 1965 (96:27); several denominations were produced using polyvinyl alcohol gum instead of gum arabic. A floral series was issued in October 1969 on chalk-surfaced paper, but ordinary glazed paper was used from 1971 onwards (96:29). The thirteenth Commonwealth Parliamentary Association Conference was held in Entebbe in 1967 and was the subject of a set of four stamps produced by the same designer and printer (96:28). Apart from this, Uganda has used the special issues of the East African Posts and Telecommunications Corporation.

Upper Volta

One of the more prolific countries in the French African group, Upper Volta produced about three hundred stamps in this decade alone, in frequent thematic sets (96:30) or in sets commemorating an enormous variety of events and personalities, from the Paris Motor Show to the Apollo moon project, from Winston Churchill to Lenin, Nasser and Roosevelt. All stamps of Upper Volta were produced in France as before.

Zambia

The 1964 definitives remained in use until 1968 when a series in the new decimal currency (100 ngwee to 1 kwacha) was released. An interesting feature of this series was the use of copper metallic ink as a background to the inscription (96:33). Up to 1970, all stamps were designed by Gabrielle Ellison and printed by Harrison, usually in multicolour photogravure (96:32), but since then, other firms have produced Zambian stamps by multicolour lithography, including Bradbury Wilkinson, Questa (96:34) and Format International (96:35). Christmas stamps were introduced in 1972 and short thematic sets in 1970.

Zanzibar

The East German Bank Note Printing Company printed several commemoratives in 1965 and lithographed a pictorial series in 1966. Zanzibar ceased to issue its own stamps at the end of 1967 – the last stamps were lithographed by De La Rue (96:36) – and since then, only the stamps of Tanzania have been used.

North America

Canada

A pictorial definitive series was released in February 1967, the small-format low values incorporating a portrait of Queen Elizabeth II (97:14). The larger, high values, reproduced paintings of Canadian landmarks and scenery in monochrome (97:15). Most denominations up to 25 cents were also issued with phosphor bands in connection with electronic sorting experiments in the Winnipeg and Ottawa areas. Stamps, imperforate either horizontally or vertically, were issued in coils, and se-tenant combinations of stamps were issued in booklets. Originally, the series was recess-printed by the Canadian Bank Note Company, but printings from 1968 onwards were made by the British American Bank Note Company, mainly for distribution in booklets and dollar packs. The printers used different gauges of perforation and this enables the stamps to be easily identified.

In 1972-3, a series featuring scenery (high values) and portraying prime ministers or Queen Elizabeth II (low values) was introduced (98:16, 17). Three printers were involved in the production of this series. The Canadian Bank Note Company recess-printed the lowest denominations (1- to 6-cent) and the American Bank Note Company recess-printed the 8-cent. Combined intaglio and photogravure was used by the British American Bank Note Company for the values from 10- to 50-cents and a version of the 1-dollar, issued in 1973. The original 1-dollar and the 2-dollar stamps were produced in a combination of intaglio by the British American Bank Note Company and multicolour lithography by Ashton Potter. These two stamps were issued without fluorescent bands, whereas the others – including the later 1-dollar stamp – had two fluorescent bands.

At the beginning of this decade, Canadian commemoratives were still being produced predominantly in monochrome intaglio (97:1, 2, 5-8, 10-13, 20-23) and the only two-coloured stamps, until mid-1967, were those featuring the national flag or publicising the Montreal World's Fair (97:3, 16, 19). The Churchill commemorative of 1965 (97:4) was printed by the duotone offset-lithography process, but no attempt was made to exploit the colour potential of this method and two years elapsed before lithography was employed again. In the meantime, the Highway Safety stamp of 1966 was recess-printed in three colours, though the design was uninspired (97:9). Two-colour lithography was used for the Women's Suffrage stamp of 1967 (97:17) and two-colour intaglio for the royal visit and Toronto centenary issues of the same year (97:18), but it was not until 1968 that the breakthrough was achieved and multicoloured stamps were released. The first stamps in multicolour lithography were the Wild Life and Meteorological bicentenary stamps of February and March 1968 (97:24, 25), printed by the Canadian and British American companies respectively.

Subsequently, both companies produced stamps with much more emphasis on colour. The British American Bank Note Company preferred lithography for the Narwhal and Hydrological Decade stamps of 1968 (97:26, 28), but used a combination of intaglio and photogravure for the Nonsuch tercentenary stamp and other issues of 1968 (97:29, 30, 33). Monochrome intaglio was used for the stamp of 1969 marking the 50th anniversary of the International Labour Organisation with its unique reversible design (97:36), but all later stamps produced by this company have been produced in colour using combined processes. For the 15-cent stamp of 1969, celebrating the jubilee of the first non-stop trans-Atlantic flight (97:34), the British American Bank Note Company used intaglio combined with lithography, but reverted to photogravure and intaglio for stamps portraying Leacock, Kelsey and Mowat in 1970 and Papineau in 1971 (97:38, 43, 46; 98:6). Combined intaglio and photogravure was also used by this firm for several non-portrait commemoratives of 1970-73 (97:11, 21, 27).

Having originally used multicolour lithography alone, the Canadian Bank Note Company experimented with combined intaglio and lithography in 1968 (97:27) and used this process for the Massey, Canadian Games and Brock issues of 1969 (97:35, 39, 40). Like its competitors, this company occasionally used intaglio alone (97:41, 98:1, 14). The majority of the stamps printed by the Canadian Bank Note Company, however, were lithographed in multicolour (97:31, 37, 42, 45; 98:3, 8, 12, 13, 15). The British American Bank Note Company then turned to lithography in 1971, printing the Insulin and Rutherford commemoratives by this method (98:4, 10). For the memorial stamp honouring Pierre Laporte they recess-printed the portrait and inscriptions on a pale buff background produced lithographically (98:7).

Ashton Potter began printing Canadian stamps in 1970, beginning with the 'Group of Seven' stamp and the thematic series featuring the maple leaf in four seasons (98:2, 5). Since then they have lithographed many other stamps, including the 1972 and 1973 Christmas stamps (98:22, 32) and the stamps portraying Jeanne Mance, Joseph Howe and Nellie McClung (98:26, 30, 31). An unusual treatment of the portrait, using silver or bright vermilion against dark backgrounds, may be found in several stamps produced by this company (98:24, 25). More orthodox multicolour designs were used for the stamps of 1973, honouring the artists Cornelius Krieghoff and J. E. H. MacDonald, and the bicentenary of the Scottish settlers in Nova Scotia (98:23, 28).

Since 1972, Canada has embarked on a much more adventurous stamp policy, beginning with a series devoted to the life and art of the Canadian Indians (98:19). These stamps are being released in pairs at half-yearly intervals and it is intended to release twenty stamps in this theme by 1976. Non-figurative motifs were used for the Cartographic stamps of 1974 (98:20) to simulate a three-dimensional effect. Advance publicity for the 1976 Montreal Olympic Games began in 1973, with large multicoloured stamps in stylised designs. Having patented the designs, the postal authorities subsequently produced the stamps in precious-metal replicas. More orthodox designs appeared in 1975 (98:29).

Greenland
Although it became an overseas province of the Danish realm in 1963, Greenland has continued to issue its own stamps. The definitive series of 1963 remained in use throughout this decade, several denominations being added between 1965 and 1968. Several commemoratives were issued in designs similar to those in Denmark, while periodical issues featured themes from Greenlandish legends (98:33, 34). The Greenlandish name of the country 'Kalatdlit Nunat' appeared on a stamp of 1964 honouring the lexicographer, Samuel Kleinschmidt, but bilingual inscriptions did not become standard until the issue of the definitive high values of 1969 (98:35). Large-format low values portraying Queen Margrethe were issued in 1973-4.

St. Pierre and Miquelon
As in the other French overseas territories which still produce their own stamps, output increased considerably from 1966 onwards. The revaluation of the local currency in 1973 led to the issue of a pictorial definitive series, the first for many years. Previously, short thematic sets had supplied a semi-permanent range of denominations. Although commemoratives were issued occasionally, to honour French events, an increasing number was devoted to local anniversaries and current events in neighbouring Canada (98:36).

United Nations (New York)
Progressive increases in United States postal rates led to the issue of new definitives in 1965-6 and 1969-72 (98:45). These stamps were printed in multicolour photogravure or lithography by various international companies as before. The majority of the special issues up to 1968 consisted of pairs of stamps publicising the specialised agencies of the United Nations (98:41, 43), but having virtually exhausted this field, the United Nations postal administration turned to aspects of international co-operation and focused attention on such global problems as aid for the underdeveloped nations (98:39) and disarmament (98:40, 44). Several sets marked current events, such as the inauguration of the World Health Organisation's new headquarters (98:37) or anniversaries of international agreements (98:38) and the United Nations itself (98:42). The earlier obsession for multi-lingual inscriptions gradually diminished and by 1972 stamps were being inscribed in English alone (98:44, 46). Short thematic sets, devoted to United Nations art, were introduced in 1967 and since then these have been issued annually. Five stamps, with values in Canadian currency, were issued in 1967 for use at the UN pavilion at the Montreal World's Fair 'Expo '67'. The United Nations took over responsibility for the operation of the postal service from its European headquarters in Geneva in 1969; the stamps of the European office are discussed after Switzerland and illustrated on Plate 82.

United States of America
A definitive series, known as the 'Prominent Americans' issue, was released in stages between November 1965 and October 1968. Apart from the fact that the stamps were all recess-printed in the traditional small format, there was no attempt at standardisation, either of portraits or lettering and frames. In many cases, frames were omitted (99:16). Several denominations were released in coil form with opposite sides imperforate. Two versions were issued of the 5-cent George Washington design, in the second of which the president's false teeth featured less obtrusively. The Prominent Americans series was supplemented from time to time by other small-format stamps. Having established the precedent for a flag stamp in the current letter rate, stamps featuring the Stars and Stripes above the White House were released in 1968 (99:42). When the rate was increased to 8 cents in 1971 the flag stamp was redrawn in this denomination. A 10-cent stamp showing crossed flags was issued in 1973 (101:33). Three stamps at the prevailing inland letter rate were also issued in 1971-4 featuring the US Post Office emblem (101:1), the Jefferson Memorial building (101:32) and publicity for the use of the Zip code (101:37). The design and lettering of the Zip code stamp can only be described as psychedelic and was in the same vein as a stamp issued in connection with Expo '74 with an exhortation to 'preserve the environment' (101:36).

Parallel with the ordinary postage definitives there were important changes in the airmail and special delivery stamps. The inland airmail stamps continued to be printed in red with contrasting white motifs. The 10-cent stamp of 1968 featured the fifty stars of the Union and was superseded by 9- and 11-cent stamps three years later, with silhouettes of delta-wing and jet aircraft (100:32). When the rate was raised to 13 cents in 1973, a stamp with a winged letter motif was issued. Increases in the foreign airmail rates in the corresponding period resulted in 20- and 21-cent stamps, whose designs featured a decorative treatment of the letters USA (100:15). A 17-cent airmail stamp, issued in 1971, showed a close-up of the head of the Statue of Liberty. When the rate was increased to 18 cents in 1974, the Statue of Liberty was again used for a stamp with a predominantly red, white and blue background (101:38) and a 26-cent stamp, featuring the Mount Rushmore national memorial in the same style, was issued simultaneously. A stylised arrows design was introduced for a 45-cent special delivery stamp in 1969 and the same motif was subsequently used for a 60-cent denomination. A 1-dollar stamp inscribed 'Airlift' was issued in 1968, for the prepayment of parcels sent to servicemen stationed in Alaska, Hawaii and Puerto Rico. The most unusual of all the American special issues, however, was an 8-cent stamp, produced in 1973 for use on Valentines and birthday greetings cards. Described at the time, as 'a special stamp for someone special', its motif consisted simply of the arrangement of the letters LOVE (101:21). The stamp remained on sale for a year and was then withdrawn. This interesting experiment has not been repeated.

Although the majority of special issues, and all of the definitives, were printed by the intaglio process as before, there were several major developments in stamp production in this period. The monochrome Cottrell and multicolour Giori presses were used in intaglio production, but increasing use was made of offset-lithography to increase the colour content, or to provide a flat background, especially in stamps with a poster-style design (99:20, 28, 35). The first United States stamp to be printed by photogravure, appeared in 1967 in the annual art series and was produced by the Photogravure and Color Company of Moonachie, New Jersey (99:39). The result cannot be regarded as entirely successful and subsequent multicoloured art stamps were produced in combined intaglio and lithography. The next photogravure stamp was that released in 1968, in memory of Walt Disney (100:6), printed by the Achrovure Division of Union-Camp Corporation, Englewood, New Jersey. Examples of this stamp have been recorded, where the ochre coloured 'Walt Disney' inscription has been omitted.

Again, this proved to have been merely an experiment, and combined intaglio and lithography continued to be used for multicoloured stamps (100:5, 8, 10, 12-14, 16). Photogravure, using Andreotti presses, finally became established in 1972 and has since been used increasingly (101:16, 20, 24, 27, 28, 30, 34, 36, 37). Traditional adhesives were used on all American stamps until 1974, when one of the three Christmas stamps, featuring a dove of peace, was issued with pressure-sensitive backing. It is likely that self-adhesive stamps will be issued more frequently in future.

Apart from technical developments, there was a radical change in issue policy. Before 1968, commemorative, and other special issues, were invariably issued as single stamps, but in that year, a set of ten stamps was issued with the theme of historical flags (99:44). This was the first occasion on which, more than one stamp had been issued for the same purpose at the same time, and the first example in the United States of an issue of *se-tenant* strips. Although this development was revolutionary, it was not speedily exploited. In fact, multiples of this number did not appear again until 1973, when a set of ten 8-cent stamps publicised the work of the postal services (*101*:25). The postal services series not only appeared in a *se-tenant* strip, but had the designs overlapping through the perforations, and an explanatory text was printed on the reverse. *Se-tenant* blocks of four different designs were revived in 1969, with a set encouraging the beautification of America (*100*:16); hitherto, this device had been used on one occasion only, for the 1964 Christmas stamps. Thereafter, bowing to demand from collectors, the United States Post Office began issuing stamps in sets of four, instead of singles, and used the *se-tenant* block as a means of producing four different designs in a related subject. The 'beautification' set was followed by stamps marking the centenary of the Natural History Museum, and by thematic sets devoted to wildlife and historic preservation (*100*:37; *101*:7, 14).

A further development was the release of stamps in pairs or blocks making up a composite design. The first of the composite stamps consisted of two 5-cent stamps of 1967, honouring American space achievements (*99*:38). Each component had a distinct motif, featuring the Gemini-4 spacecraft and an astronaut walking in space, but together they formed a single picture. This idea was extended to a block of four 2-cent stamps, issued in 1972 as part of a series commemorating the centenary of the National Parks. Subsequently, this idea was used for four stamps illustrating the Boston Tea Party (*101*:27).

Fewer stamps honouring individuals appeared in this decade, and, although the 'champions of liberty' style was not revived, a significant proportion of them portrayed famous men of other countries, including Churchill (*99*:4), Dante (*99*:7), Leif Erikson (*100*:7) and Copernicus (*101*:22). All of the portrait stamps up to 1969 were in the double-sized format. In the majority of cases a portrait alone was used (*99*:11, 34; *100*:19, 38; *101*:4, 8) but occasionally a more pictorial treatment was employed (*99*:9, 14). A very much larger format was introduced in 1969 and used for stamps honouring late presidents – Eisenhower (*100*:24), Truman and Johnson (*101*:26, 34). In 1973, multicolour photogravure was used for large horizontal stamps featuring artists, poets and composers, their profiles overlapping a montage of subjects associated with their work (*101*:24, 28, 30), and this style of design has been used for subsequent issues in this theme.

There were far fewer stamps in honour of state anniversaries in this decade than in the previous periods, only twelve such issues appearing between 1965 and 1974. The Florida quatercentenary stamp of 1965, designed by B. Temple, was issued in conjunction with Spain, whose version of the design was printed in photogravure. The old style of monochrome intaglio stamps, with their well-worn themes of covered wagons, maps, flags and state capitols gave way to a more colourful approach, the use of art forms, flowers and scenery, often presented in an unusual manner as in the Alaska Purchase centenary airmail stamp (*99*:30). Floral designs were used on stamps honouring Mississippi (*99*:40) and Alabama (*100*:22) and multicolour scenic motifs on the stamps of Illinois and Maine (*100*:1, 29). One of the few map designs was that marking the Indiana sesquicentennial in 1966 (*99*:19).

Very few stamps, compared to earlier decades, were devoted to the professions or to sections of the community, unless they commemorated an important anniversary. Between 1966 and 1972, there were only three such stamps, honouring the American circus, blood donors and the Peace Corps (*101*:9), and two stamps of 1975 were devoted to Banking and Commerce. Centenaries and jubilees of many institutions, however, provided the opportunity for a large number of stamps, whose style of design varied from the strictly literal Salvation Army (*99*:5) and Parents Teachers Association (*101*:13) stamps, to the elaborately pictorial Mail Order and Pharmacy stamps of 1972, with designs reminiscent of the *Saturday Evening Post* (*101*:16, 19). In between, came a variety of poster styles, on stamps honouring Women's Clubs, the Sokol Sports Movement, the Marine Corps Reserves, the Voice of America, the National Park Service, the National Grange (*99*:2, 20, 23, 24, 31, 35), the American Legion, professional baseball, intercollegiate football (*100*:17, 25), Osteopaths and the Veterans of Foreign Wars (*101*:15, 39).

A diverse range of historical events was commemorated by single stamps. The United States issued stamps honouring the 150th anniversary of Friendship with Britain and the 750th anniversary of Magna Carta, though both events were philatelically ignored by Britain (*99*:1, 6). The 'Friendship' stamp took a curiously negative line in featuring a scene from the Battle of New Orleans which brought the War of 1812 to a close. Although Britain neglected this anniversary, it is interesting to note that Belgium issued a stamp for the occasion, depicting the signing of the Treaty of Ghent which brought an end to hostilities. Britain, however, issued a stamp in 1970 to mark the 350th anniversary of the Pilgrim Fathers, the subject also of an American stamp with an off-beat treatment of the Pilgrims' landing (*100*:36).

Several stamps were issued to honour events connected with other countries, ranging from the millennium of Poland to the centenary of Canada and the jubilee of Finland (*99*:22, 32). An 11-cent stamp marked the centenary of the International Telecommunications Union (*99*:13) and a set of eight, reproducing paintings with the theme of the mails, marked the centenary of the Universal Postal Union in 1974. A poster-style stamp celebrated the silver jubilee of the United Nations in 1970 (*100*:35) and a stamp, in the same unframed pattern, marked the 10th anniversary of the Antarctic Treaty, in the following year (*100*:39).

Other commemoratives were largely concerned with purely domestic anniversaries. Although the actual anniversary was outside this period, the bicentenary of the American Revolution was the most important event to be commemorated by stamps in this decade. In 1971, five years ahead of the event, a stamp with a symbolic motif, marked the beginning of the 'bicentennial era', and this was but the prelude to a large number of stamps devoted to various aspects of the Revolutionary period. These stamps were issued in thematic sets of four, usually – though not always – produced in *se-tenant* blocks of four related designs. These sets featured craftsmen (*101*:11), the 'spreading of the word' (*101*:23), uniforms of the War of Independence and portraits of people who had helped the cause (1974–5). In addition, sets marked the bicentenaries of the Boston Tea Party (*101*:27), the Continental Congress (1974), the battles of Lexington, Concord and Bunker Hill and the establishment of the United States Post Office (all in 1975) (*101*:41).

Transport and communications anniversaries, resulted in stamps honouring the Erie Canal (*99*:33) and Arkansas River navigation (*100*:9) and the jubilee of the airmail service (*99*:43). Anniversaries of explorers and their expeditions contributed few stamps in this period, Father Marquette and John Wesley Powell alone being thus honoured (*100*:4, 20). Historic settlements were commemorated by several stamps, including Fort Snelling (*100*:31) and San Juan, Puerto Rico (*101*:5). The centenaries of the colonisation of the Cherokee Strip and the introduction of Angus cattle were the subjects of stamps in 1968 (*100*:11) and 1973 (*101*:31).

Current events provided the pretext for only nine issues in this period. Three of these were important space achievements connected with the Apollo 8 (*100*:21), first moon landing (*100*:26) and the Skylab mission of 1974. Pairs of stamps in 1967 and 1971 commemorated space achievement in general (*99*:38; *101*:3) and two multicoloured stamps were released in 1975 in connection with the Pioneer and Mariner space probes. Two issues were connected with international events, a single marking International Co-operation Year (*99*:8) and a set of four honouring the 1972 Olympic Games at Sapporo and Munich (*101*:12). Four stamps in a *se-tenant* block publicised the eleventh Botanical Congress held in Seattle (*100*:23) and a single stamp honoured the Hemisfair '68 exhibition (*100*:2). The customary single and miniature sheet marked the sixth international philatelic exhibition (SIPEX) held in Washington in 1966 (*99*:18). The only public work to be commemorated in this period was the Great River Road, inaugurated in 1966 (*99*:26).

Inevitably the world-wide interest in thematics or topical collecting had some effect on American stamps. The annual Art stamp continued fitfully in this period from 1965 to 1971 (*99*:12, 29, 39; *100*:10, 18, 28; *101*:2) and the colossal statuary at Stone Mountain, Georgia, was the subject of a stamp in 1970 (*100*:30), but this issue as a regular theme was then dropped, although several stamps since then, have made use of paintings as the basis of their designs. Stamps highlighting aspects of American folklore were also introduced in this period, beginning with a stamp honouring Johnny

Appleseed, in 1966. Subsequently, stamps featured Davy Crockett (99:37), Daniel Boone (100:8), Tom Sawyer (101:17) and the Legend of Sleepy Hollow (1974). A single stamp was issued for Christmas each year up to 1969 and reproduced religious works of art (99:15, 28; 100:13, 27). Five stamps appeared in 1970, combining traditional toys (100:34) with religious paintings. Two stamps were issued each season from 1971 to 1973, one showing a religious motif and the other adopting a more secular subject (101:18, 35).

Most of the stamps in the category of miscellaneous issues, had a strong didactic element, publicising government campaigns against cancer (99:3) or on behalf of road safety (99:10). A number of stamps had political overtones echoing the sentiments of the 1960s. Thus, the stamp celebrating the 175th anniversary of the Bill of Rights, symbolised Freedom opposing Tyranny (99:21). A stamp marking the 25th anniversary of the National Savings Movement was issued in 1966, at a time when the Vietnam commitment was rapidly escalating, and was used as the pretext for some philatelic flag-waving and bore the caption 'We appreciate our servicemen' (99:27). Two stamps were issued in connection with projects sponsored by charitable organisations: the Lions International essay competition on the theme of 'the search for peace' (99:36) and the Elks 'Support our Youth' programme (99:41). The year 1968 marked the high-tide of didactic stamps, typified by the 'Law and Order' and 'Register and Vote' stamps (100:3, 5).

The twin themes of 'conservation of natural resources' and 'the fight against pollution of the environment' recurred in the stamps of this period. Conservation of waterfowl and wildlife (100:12, 37; 101:14) and the preservation of historic sites (101:7) resulted in sets issued between 1966 and 1971. The beautification of America was the subject of a stamp in 1966 (99:25) and a se-tenant block of four in 1969 (100:16). Concern with pollution resulted in a set of four in 1970 (100:33) and the Expo '74 commemorative carried an environmental slogan (101:36).

Humane treatment of animals, family planning, urban planning, the abuse of drugs (101:6), stamp collecting (101:20), the progress of electronics (101:29), the rehabilitation of the handicapped (1969) and retarded children (1974) were among the subjects of stamps focusing attention on matters of public concern.

Four diamond-shaped stamps of 1974 featured the mineral heritage of America (101:40) and were the first stamps released by the United States in this format. One of the three Christmas stamps of 1974 was issued pre-cancelled with self-adhesive gum. The stamp itself was imperforate and was issued in sheets of 50 on rouletted backing paper. The 1975 Christmas stamps were even more extraordinary in one respect – they were issued without any value expressed. The lack of face value reflected the prevailing uncertainty at the time of production, regarding the eventual postal rates that would be in force by the time of issue. Other issues of 1975 emphasised American space achievements and included stamps publicising the Pioneer and Mariner 10 probes to Jupiter and Mercury respectively, as well as a se-tenant pair (produced in conjunction with the USSR) honouring the Apollo–Soyuz link-up. Composite stamps honoured banking and commerce, and a symbolic motif was used for a stamp in honour of collective bargaining. Otherwise, the imminent celebrations of the bicentenary of independence continued to dominate American philately. A set of four paid tribute to 'contributors to the cause' and a single stamp commemorated the 200th anniversary of the battles of Lexington and Concord – a modest prelude to the 50-stamp flag series and 32-stamp composite design, reproducing the text of the *Declaration of Independence* of 1776. Other sets marked bicentenaries of the armed forces and the postal service (101:41).

Central America

British Honduras (Belize)
The birds series of 1962, was reprinted on paper with a sideways watermark in 1967, and the 15-cent stamp of this printing is known with polyvinyl gum instead of gum arabic. Fish and animals formed the subject of the series lithographed by De La Rue in 1968 (102:4). In June 1973, British Honduras was renamed Belize and the existing definitives were thus overprinted (102:1), pending the production of similar stamps with the inscription redrawn (102:2). The fourth definitive series in eighteen months, featuring butterflies, appeared towards the end of 1974 (102:3). Christmas sets and thematic series were issued from 1969 onwards, but the only commemorative issue celebrated the establishment of the new capital of Belmopan in 1971 (102:5).

Canal Zone
One of the world's least prolific countries, the Canal Zone produced only two issues in this decade; an airmail series in 1965, featuring an airliner and the government seal (102:6) and two ordinary definitives covering the letter rates current in 1968 and 1971 respectively. The small-format definitives featured the Goethals memorial at Balboa and Fort San Lorenzo (102:7).

Costa Rica
Costa Rica produced relatively few stamps in this decade. The archaeological discoveries set of 1963, was superseded in 1967 by a lengthy series featuring churches and cathedrals. This set was re-issued in new colours in 1973. Obligatory Christmas stamps were issued each year as before, raising money for the children's village, Ciudad de los Niños. Apart from the Kennedy commemoratives of 1965 (102:8) the majority of stamps had non-pictorial poster designs lithographed in primary colours (102:9) by De La Rue of Bogota or the local firm, Fotolit.

El Salvador
Lengthy thematic sets, featuring flowers (1965), butterflies (1969) and insects (1970) provided the definitive stamps of this decade. Several commemorative sets were issued in a wide range of denominations, though none approached the length of the sets prevalent in the 1940s and 1950s. Since 1970, most commemoratives have, in fact, consisted of singles or pairs concerned with local anniversaries or current events (102:10, 11). Triangles, diamonds and rhomboids have been used to vary the appearance of stamps since 1969.

Guatemala
An all-purpose airmail stamp featuring the state emblem, was introduced in 1966. Although the denomination – 5-centavos – remained the same, the colour of this stamp was altered twice yearly between 1966 and 1969, and four times in 1970 (102:13). Apart from this stamp, there were no definitive issues in this period, though frequent thematic sets made good the deficiency. Several commemorative sets also provided the definitive range of values (102:12). The International Telecommunications Union centenary set appeared in 1969 – four years after the actual anniversary (102:14). Guatemala's claim to neighbouring Belize was tacitly promoted in several sets whose principal motif was a map of the country, showing Belize within the frontiers of Guatemala (102:15, 16).

Honduras
Long commemorative sets took the place of definitives in this period, the stamp centenary series alone comprising seventeen denominations (102:18). Like Guatemala, Honduras had a habit of issuing commemoratives rather belatedly. The Subirana series – dated 1964 – was released eighteen months after the event (102:17) and the independence sesquicentennial series, scheduled for 1970, did not appear until May 1972. De La Rue of Bogota lithographed the majority of stamps up to 1970, but subsequent issues were produced by Litografia Maia of Oporto.

Mexico
The definitive designs introduce in 1953 remained in use throughout this period, fluorescent paper being introduced in 1970. New values and changes of colour were produced at various times between 1965 and 1974. Unwatermarked paper was adopted in 1974. Propaganda for the 1968 Olympic Games in Mexico City began three years earlier, with a series of large-format stamps depicting Aztec artifacts. Subsequent sets featured sporting events (102:20) and culminated in a set of eleven stamps that were issued when the

Games took place. The stamps of this period were printed in photogravure, with the exception of an intaglio stamp, honouring Dante, in 1965. Monochrome was used in the earlier years (*102*:19) and was followed by some rather garish combinations (*102*:20, 21) before multicolour designs became the rule. Colours were frequently bled off into the perforations (*102*:20, 21, 23) and the very large format that Mexico had used occasionally since 1938, was employed much more frequently (*102*:19, 23, 24).

The majority of commemoratives were issued as singles, but a notable exception was the set of five, honouring the centenary of the death of President Juarez (*102*:24).

Nicaragua
An airmail definitive series, featuring antiquities, was lithographed by De La Rue and released in March 1965 (*102*:25). Subsequent airmail sets featured butterflies, fruits, fish and national products (*102*:28, 30) before turning to more unusual subjects, including football's 'Hall of Fame' (1970) and 'the ten mathematical equations that changed the face of the Earth' (*102*:31). Lengthy sets commemorated the Latin-American writers, Andres Bello and Ruben Dario (*102*:26), but Nicaragua also honoured Sir Winston Churchill (*102*:27) and Franklin D. Roosevelt, in this way. Inevitably, American space exploits resulted in several sets (*102*:29), but the most interesting series was that honouring the 50th anniversary of Interpol in 1972, illustrating such fictional detectives as Philip Marlowe and Perry Mason. Nicaragua developed a penchant for rhetorical questions in stamps. A series of eight, in 1971, posed the question 'Is there a formula for peace?', and the 1973 Christmas series asked 'Does Santa Claus exist?' The answer was provided in explanatory English text on the reverse of each stamp.

Panama
Between 1965 and 1969, Panama produced about fifty sets, each consisting of several denominations and mainly relating to events and personalities of little direct relevance to the country. Religious paintings, Olympic medallists, Americana and space exploration were high on the list of subjects that were thoroughly exploited in this period. These 'band-wagon' issues were lithographed in multicolour by De La Rue of Bogota and were mostly the product of Professor Mosdossy's fertile genius (*102*:32, 34, 36). Thereafter, a more conservative policy was adopted, the number of issues was reduced and some attempt was made to relate the subjects to the needs and interests of Panama. Many of the stamps in the later period were produced at the Argentinian Mint in Buenos Aires (*102*:35).

South America

Argentina
The definitive series, inaugurated in 1961, remained current for much of this period, with new values produced in photogravure, lithography or intaglio between 1965 and 1968 (*103*:1). The RA in Sun watermark was superseded by a multiple watermark featuring the inscription 'Casa de Moneda de la Nacion' in 1969 and unwatermarked paper was used in 1970–71. The designs were redrawn in 1970–73, with values in the reformed currency (100 old pesos being equal to one new peso). At the same time, a small format was introduced for stamps portraying famous Argentinians (*103*:6). Watermarked paper was re-introduced in 1972. The design of the airmail series was redrawn in 1965–7, replacing 'Argentina' by 'Republica Argentina' (*103*:7).

Thematic sets, featuring famous writers, scientists and musicians, military uniforms and paintings were issued regularly from 1966 onwards. Throughout this period, semi-postals were issued annually for Child Welfare, and Christmas stamps were introduced in 1969 (*103*:8). Commemorative singles were mainly concerned with Argentinian events and personalities, though stamps honoured Dante and Sun Yat-sen in 1965–6 (*103*:3). Argentinian preoccupation with Antarctica continued to dominate the special issues,

from the propaganda series of 1965 (*103*:2) to the space stamp of 1966 and the South Polar Expedition issues of 1966–71 (*103*:4, 5).

Bolivia
No stamps appeared in 1965 and those released the following year, consisted of overprints or surcharges on obsolete postal or revenue stamps. The situation returned to normal in 1967 with a pair of stamps honouring Lions International, but it was well into 1968 before stamps were issued regularly, beginning with lengthy sets marking the 150th anniversary of the Battle of Tablada and the quatercentenary of Cochabamba (*103*:9). Even after that date, Bolivia's stamp-issuing programme tended to be erratic. The long series honouring the centenary of the first Bolivian stamp was erroneously inscribed '1867–1967' – though the centenary was in 1966 – and was not actually issued till 22nd December 1968. Moreover, the design used for several denominations of this series was that of the stamp commissioned in 1863 but never issued (*103*:10).

Brazil
The portrait definitives of 1963 remained in use until 1967, when a new series was issued, with values in the reformed currency of 1 cruzeiro equal to 1000 old cruzeiros (*103*:12). Denominations in this style were added until 1969, but a different portrait series was released in 1967–8 to cover the higher denominations (*103*:13). The portrait designs were supplemented by a numeral series, released in 1972 (*103*:22) and by a stamp featuring the Post Office symbol, issued earlier in the same year (*103*:23). Stamps of this series, as well as some of the commemorative issues, were produced on fluorescent paper. Three stamps depicting birds were recess-printed and issued in 1968–9 (*103*:14), but the first full-length thematic set was that issued in 1969 featuring scenes from the Carioca Carnival. Subsequent sets featured butterflies (*103*:16), mineral resources, aspects of industry (*103*:19), sports (*103*:24) and birds (*103*:26). Since 1971, there have been several interesting developments in the design of Brazilian stamps. Two stamps of July 1971, publicising the Trans–Amazon Highway project, were issued in a composite map design, in sheets of twenty-eight, each line consisting of *se-tenant* pairs (*103*:17). In 1972, the previous policy of naturalistic pictorial motifs was almost totally abandoned in favour of abstract designs (*103*:19, 24, 25) or the frankly surrealist, such as the series devoted to social development (*103*:21). One of the few issues to depart from this new policy, was the large series featuring ancient maps, released in 1972 to mark the Exfilbra Philatelic Exhibition (*103*:20).

In 1973, a system was adopted whereby all special issues bore the digits of the date prominently after the name of the country; this practice has continued ever since (*103*:24, 26, 27).

Chile
The 1960 definitives, for ordinary postage and inland airmail, remained current throughout this decade, new values being added between 1965 and 1969. Stamps portraying Jorge Montt and German Riesco were lithographed in 1966 and added to the permanent range (*103*:30) and stamps with floral motifs were introduced between 1965 and 1969 (*103*:29). Money, for the modernisation of the postal services was raised by means of tax stamps, whose use was compulsory on all correspondence from February 1970 onwards. At first, obsolete stamps were overprinted with the article and number of the law levying the tax, together with a 10-centavo surcharge (*103*:34), but subsequently, a small-format stamp featuring the national arms, was lithographed for this purpose. When the tax was raised to 15 centavos in September 1971 these stamps were surcharged at the new rate (*103*:38).

The majority of the commemorative issues were issued in pairs as before, one stamp being intended for ordinary postage (*103*:37) and the other for inland or overseas airmail. An inland air stamp, inscribed LAN (Linea Aereo Nacional) was released in 1967, to mark International Tourist Year (*103*:31). Among the stamps intended for foreign airmail, and inscribed 'Correo Aereo', were those marking the inauguration of Entel-Chile Satellite Ground Station (*103*:33) and the centenary of the birth of Paul Harris, founder of Rotary International (*103*:36). The 225th anniversary of the Chilean Mint was celebrated by four stamps in December

1968, reproducing the first stamp and coin produced there (*103*:32); the series was subsequently released in an ungummed miniature sheet. Stamp caption writers have been confused by the complexities of British titles on several occasions since 1911, and Chile issued two stamps in 1970 honouring Thomas Cochrane, Earl of Dundonald, describing him as 'Lord Cochrane' (*103*:35). Unlike neighbouring Argentina, Chile showed little interest philatelically, in her Antarctic claims during this decade, although two stamps were issued in 1972, belatedly celebrating the 10th anniversary of the Antarctic Treaty of 1961 (*103*:39).

Colombia

Although De La Rue's Bogota subsidiary was in operation by 1961, it was not until 1968 that the company secured a virtual monopoly of Colombian stamp production. Up to that time, occasional sets were printed elsewhere, in intaglio at the Spanish Mint in Madrid (*104*:1) or even in multicolour photogravure by the Japanese Government Printing Works in Tokyo (*104*:6). Imre Mosdossy designed the majority of the De La Rue stamps and, inevitably, the designs assumed a stereotyped nature, particularly evident in his penchant for ribbons of inscriptions across the stamp, bleeding into the perforations, even across clear margins (*104*:2, 11). In his later work he obviously tried to avoid this, but the arrangement of the lettering across the foot of the design remained a typical Mosdossy device (*104*:7, 13, 19, 20). Two other artists designed stamps for Colombia from 1966 onwards. T. N. Molina produced the Arboleda commemorative of 1966, the famous Colombians series of 1967 and the Philatelic Week Stamp of 1970 (*104*:3, 5, 10) and C. Alonso designed several issues in the same period, including the Choconta satellite station stamp of 1970 (*104*:8) and the stamp of 1972, featuring the Postal Administration emblem (*104*:15).

Thematic sets took the place of long-term definitives, beginning with sets devoted to the history of Colombian aviation and shipping (*104*:2, 4). Subsequent issues featured famous Colombians, folklore dances and costumes, and crafts and products (*104*:5, 16). The majority of the commemoratives were issued as singles (*104*:3, 8, 9, 11–13, 17, 18). Pairs of stamps marked the Seventh World Orchid Conference in 1972 (*104*:14) and the 350th anniversary of Javeriana University in 1973 (*104*:19). In the 1970s, a much lighter style of design was evolved by Mosdossy, using lightly toned backgrounds (*104*:17) or white backgrounds without any framework (*104*:12, 21).

Ecuador

The butterflies definitives of 1961–4 were superseded by a birds series in 1966, which, in turn, was replaced by another butterflies set in 1970. The 1970 series was lithographed, the 50- and 80-centavo stamps being additionally typographed (*104*:23). From 1970 onwards, long thematic sets appeared at more frequent intervals and featured civic arms (*104*:26), religious paintings and indigenous crafts. A wide range of printers was used in 1965–6, from De La Rue of Bogota to Litografia Nacional in Oporto and the German State Printing Works in Berlin (*104*:22) but thereafter, numerous sets, handled by an external agency, were produced by De La Rue. The contract with the agency was terminated in 1969 and from then onwards the output of stamps was greatly reduced and the stamps invariably lithographed locally, at the Military Geographical Institute in Quito (*104*:24–29). In the 1970s, the long thematic sets were interspersed among lengthy commemorative issues, with stamps for ordinary and airmail postage. Two sets of twelve stamps celebrated the sesquicentennial of the Battle of Pichincha in 1972 (*104*:27) and an equally long series marked the establishment of the Galapagos Islands as a province in 1973 (*104*:29). From the Allende commemoratives of 1971 onwards (*104*:25) all Ecuadorean stamps have borne a fluorescent security marking across their surface.

Guyana (British Guiana)

The only stamps issued by British Guiana in 1965–6, consisted of colonial omnibus sets (*103*:28) and a pair in honour of Sir Winston Churchill. In May 1966, the country became independent and assumed the name of Guyana. The definitive series was overprinted to denote this (*104*:30) and a set of four stamps was also issued to celebrate independence (*104*:31). Wildlife and flowering plants were the subjects of the definitives released in 1968 and 1971

respectively (*104*:37). After independence, the output of commemorative stamps was greatly increased. Guyana was one of the first Commonwealth countries to issue Christmas stamps, though they usually had secular subjects (*104*:34, 36). Guyana was a pioneer of Easter stamps, reproducing religious paintings from 1968 onwards (*104*:35) and subsequently both Hindu and Moslem festivals were similarly honoured. Stamps celebrated the first anniversary of independence in 1967 (*104*:33), but this did not become a regular series till 1970; since then, annual sets have marked Republic Day. Two stamps were issued in 1967 featuring the 'world's rarest stamp', the 1-cent black on magenta of 1856 (*104*:32), but most commemoratives since then, have consisted of sets of four or five stamps (*104*:38).

Paraguay

From 1962 until 1973, the stamps of Paraguay were largely controlled by an external agency and in the majority of cases these stamps were only available in Paraguay in token quantities. Between 1965 and the end of 1972 alone, more than sixty sets, often consisting of eight or ten stamps each, were issued, exploiting the philatelic fashions of the moment, from space exploration to religious paintings and sporting events (*105*:2). By contrast, barely a handful of stamps marked events of local interest, and even the series commemorating the centenary of the national anthem had to portray Sir Winston Churchill and John Kennedy for good measure (*105*:1).

Peru

The lithographed pictorial definitives, first issued in 1952, remained in use until 1970. In 1966, the contract passed from De La Rue to the Austrian State Press and subsequent printings bore the initials INA (Impresa Nacional Austriaca) in the margins. A shortage of certain denominations in 1969, was met by surcharging a series of un-issued Agrarian Reform stamps with various values (*105*:5). Since 1970, frequent thematic sets have taken the place of the pictorial definitive series. The archaeological excavations at Chan-Chan were financed from 1967 onwards by a tax on correspondence, denoted by 20-centavo stamps issued at annual intervals in various colour combinations (*105*:3). Although an increasing number of commemoratives were issued as singles (*105*:4) the traditional custom of lengthy sets of ordinary and airmail stamps continued, typified by the three sets of 1971, marking the sesquicentenary of independence (*105*:6).

Surinam

An airmail series, featuring scenery and landmarks, was introduced in 1965. Definitives for ordinary postage appeared in 1966 and 1972 and respectively featured birds and butterflies in multicolour photogravure by Enschedé. Surinam was the first country in the world to issue Easter stamps, beginning in 1966, and although the idea spread to neighbouring Guyana the following year, the practice did not become popular elsewhere until the 1970s. Child Welfare semi-postals were issued each November or December according to Dutch custom (*105*:8). Few of the commemoratives of this period referred to local anniversaries (*105*:10, 12) but were mainly concerned with international events and particularly those connected with the United Nations (*105*:7, 9, 11).

Uruguay

Although a few values of the 1954 definitive series remained in circulation in this decade, they were largely superseded by thematic sets. A provisional 1-peso surcharge on obsolete stocks of the 7-centesimo stamp was made in 1967 (*105*:21) and a 500-peso stamp, featuring the national flag, was released in 1970. Thematic sets were introduced in 1966 and at annual intervals thereafter featured aspects of cattle and sheep-breeding, archaeological discoveries, birds (*105*:23), fauna (*105*:25) and minerals. The very small format definitives portraying General Artigas – a feature of Uruguayan stamps between 1928 and 1954 – were revived in 1972 in denominations ranging from 20- to 1000-peso. This series, like the majority of the special issues, was lithographed at the National Press in Montevideo. A few stamps up to 1966 were lithographed by the firm of Barreiro and Ramos (*105*:13, 15).

The long commemorative sets that had characterised the earlier decades were replaced by single stamps or pairs in most instances, though the old custom of issuing stamps for either ordinary or airmail postage continued. Apart from the thematic issues, the longer sets of this period were confined to commemoration of John Kennedy (*105*:13), the Olympic Games and other sporting events, and the series of 1968 celebrating the 150th anniversary of the navy (*105*:22). Several sets of three or five stamps were issued with the same denomination, in honour of former presidents or war heroes (*105*:16), but otherwise, personal commemoratives were limited to pairs, portraying the statesmen Nardone and Acevedo (*105*:14, 19). The stamps marking historic anniversaries or current events usually had poster-style designs that were well suited to the flat lithography of the National Press (*105*:18, 24, 26–28). The same technique was extended to the few stamps portraying visiting heads of state or historic personalities, incorporated with stylised vignettes (*105*:17, 20).

Venezuela

A chronic shortage of stamps in 1965–6 led to the revalidation of numerous obsolete issues surcharged with new values from 5- to 75-centavo. At the same time, various revenue stamps were overprinted CORREOS for postal use. Subsequent lengthy thematic sets took the place of definitives, and featured national dances (*105*:32), insects, fish, orchids (*105*:34), nature conservation, flowers and provincial maps (*105*:35–37). Map stamps were also issued in 1965 to revive Venezuela's claim to neighbouring Guyana, then on the brink of independence (*105*:30) and further map stamps for this purpose appeared in 1970. Lengthy airmail sets of 1966–70 reproduced various portraits of Simon Bolivar. The original version of the first set was produced by the German State Printing Works in Berlin, but was reissued a year later in a version lithographed by Rosenbaum Brothers of Vienna; the respective versions may be identified by the marginal imprint (*105*:33). An entirely new series of Bolivar portraits appeared in 1969 and 1970. Christmas stamps, sometimes linked to the annual children's festival, were issued from 1965 onwards. Most of the commemoratives referred to national events and personalities, but stamps were also issued in honour of John Kennedy, Sir Winston Churchill, Dr. Martin Luther King and Mahatma Gandhi (*105*:29, 31).

American Offshore Islands

British American Islands

The island territories off the coasts of South and Central America, belonging to the British Commonwealth, formed a variegated group in this period. Before 1965, only two of them – Jamaica and Trinidad and Tobago – had attained full independent status (1962) and the others were all administered as British Crown Colonies or dependencies. Full independence was subsequently granted to Barbados in 1966 and the Bahamas in 1973 (*106*:16) and a compromise between colonial status and complete independence was reached in the case of five territories in 1967–8. Associated Statehood status was accorded to Antigua (*106*:3), Dominica (*106*:32), Grenada (*107*:3), St. Christopher–Nevis–Anguilla and St. Lucia and in each case the event was celebrated by commemorative stamps and overprinted definitives. The other territories remained as Crown Colonies, though new constitutions, permitting varying degrees of autonomy or ministerial government, were given to the Virgin Islands (1967), Bermuda (1968) and the Turks and Caicos Islands (1970). These constitutional changes were likewise commemorated philatelically.

It might have been expected that the output of stamp issues would rise in proportion to the degree of independence conferred, but this did not prove to be the case. With the exception of Bermuda and the British Virgin Islands, the fewest stamps were in fact issued by the oldest of the independent countries, both Jamaica and Trinidad producing an average of fourteen stamps a year in this decade. Montserrat and the Cayman Islands were well represented with almost 200 stamps each, but generally, the most prolific group were the countries with Associated Statehood, with Dominica and Grenada at their head.

Immediately after the grant of Associated Statehood to St. Christopher–Nevis–Anguilla, the last-named and smallest island of the group seceded and declared itself independent. Stamps of St. Christopher–Nevis–Anguilla were at first overprinted, but later, distinctive issues were prepared through the agency of a London stamp-dealer. Since 1967, Anguilla has issued its own stamps and has become one of the most prolific of the West Indian countries (*106*:1). Since 1971, stamp captions usually include a reference to the Commissioner appointed by the British government to supervise the administration.

Although not politically independent, the island of Barbuda, a dependency of Antigua, began issuing its own stamps in 1968, reviving a short-lived practice of the 1920s (*106*:22). These stamps, which were apparently valid for postage in Antigua itself, were discontinued in 1972, after a hectic burst of activity that included a series of thirty-seven stamps portraying every British ruler since William the Conqueror. Distinctive stamps, however, were revived in 1973. The latest of the philatelic 'splinters' to emerge were the Grenadines, a small archipelago administered partly by Grenada and partly by St. Vincent. In November to December 1973, the Grenadines of Grenada and St. Vincent both took part in the omnibus issue celebrating the royal silver wedding, and this proved to be but the curtain-raiser to a prolific career by both island groups (*107*:5, 25).

All the West Indian countries continued to issue orthodox definitive sets throughout this period, though the life of these sets became progressively shorter. In the case of Jamaica, the Cayman Islands and the Turks and Caicos Islands, the decimalisation of the currency in 1969 resulted in provisional surcharges and redrawn designs (*107*:10, 32). In the earlier years, intaglio was still used for sets issued by Antigua (*106*:2) and the Bahamas (*106*:7, 8) and for the existing series of the British Virgin Islands, to which provisional surcharged denominations were added in 1966 (*107*:34), but elsewhere, multicolour photogravure reigned supreme, though multicolour lithography became popular in the 1970s. The concept of the single-subject series was well-established by 1966 and remained the pattern for the rest of the period. Thus, Antigua's buildings series was superseded in 1970 by a series depicting shipping (*106*:6), a theme which was also adopted by the Virgin Islands and St. Christopher–Nevis–Anguilla in the same year (*107*:18, 35). Fish and marine life were popular subjects, being used for the definitives of the Bahamas (*106*:14), Barbados (*106*:18), Grenada (*107*:4) and St. Christopher–Nevis–Anguilla (*107*:17). Other aspects of fauna, especially birds, provided inspiration for the sets issued by Montserrat (*107*:16), St. Vincent (*107*:24) and the Turks and Caicos Islands (*107*:33). Flowers were the theme of sets issued by Bermuda (*106*:24), Jamaica (*107*:13) and Trinidad and Tobago (*107*:26). With the dependence on tourism for the principal source of revenue, it was inevitable that many West Indian countries should promote their scenic qualities by means of their stamps, and sets in this style were released by the Bahamas (*106*:11), Barbados (*106*:20), the Cayman Islands (*106*:31), Grenada (*107*:2), Jamaica (*107*:11), St. Lucia (*107*:21) and St. Vincent (*107*:22). Several countries issued stamps during International Tourist Year (*107*:15). Dominica's scenic series of 1969–72 is particularly noteworthy on account of the ingenious use of the island's initial in the style of a medieval illuminated capital, as a frame to the vignettes (*106*:33). Technically, there were several important developments in the definitive stamps of the West Indian group of this period. The Block CA watermark was used on the stamps of the Crown Colonies and most of the associated states. At the beginning of this period, an upright watermark was used, but between 1966 and 1970 the sideways watermark was adopted. Chalk-surfaced paper was used up to 1970, but since then, glazed ordinary paper has been employed. At the end of 1974, an entirely new watermark, designated by the Crown Agents as a Scroll CA design, was introduced on commemorative stamps and was scheduled to replace the Block CA watermark on definitives from then onwards. The independent countries varied in their use of watermarks. Whereas Trinidad continued to use the Block CA paper for its stamps, Jamaica used a distinctive pineapple watermark, and Dominica's 1969–72 series was printed on unwatermarked paper (low values) or paper with the scrolled 'S' watermark of Singapore.

It was in the commemorative and special issues, however, that the greatest changes were apparent in this decade. The West Indies became the most enthusiastic and prolific issuers of Christmas stamps (106:17) and followed Guyana's lead in introducing Easter stamps (106:5; 107:20). Up to 1969, the bulk of the commemoratives consisted of the colonial omnibus issues (107:1), and included a specifically West Indian series of 1966 marking the royal visit to the Caribbean. After that, however, each country began issuing stamps commemorating anniversaries in its political development (106:4, 25) and other historic events (107:9, 19, 27, 31). Current events accounted for most of the special issues, ranging from the international conferences (106:9, 26) and sporting events (107:6) held in their countries, to topical events of world-wide interest (106:13, 15, 19, 23; 107:7). Several territories issued stamps commemorating anniversaries of Caribbean importance (106:21; 107:30), and modern developments in each island were a fertile source of philatelic inspiration (106:29, 30; 107:10). A number of issues exploited global interest in certain personalities, such as Dr. Martin Luther King (107:23), but the majority of the portrait stamps commemorated local figures (106:16, 21; 107:8, 12).

Most territories embarked on a policy of short thematic sets in 1970, the subjects ranging from pirates and national heroes (107:12) to aspects of wildlife (107:28, 29). Among the more unusual stamps of the early 1970s, may be mentioned Grenada's 'Miss World' series of 1971, and the Bahamas set of four stamps of 1968, commemorating the issue of gold coins, which themselves commemorated the first general election under the new constitution. The latter stamps were recess-printed by De La Rue on gold metallic paper, with perforations surrounding the kidney-shaped stamps (106:10). Most examples of these stamps had to be cut from the surrounding paper with scissors, which rather defeated the object of having perforations, and the gimmick was not subsequently repeated.

South Atlantic Islands
The intaglio birds series was replaced by a photogravure flower series in the Falkland Islands in 1968 (106:35) and the latter was rapidly followed by provisional surcharges (February 1971) and redrawn designs (June 1972) as a result of decimalisation. British Antarctic Territory and South Georgia introduced decimal surcharges simultaneously and though the South Georgia provisionals remained current, British Antarctic Territory issued an entirely new series in 1973, with designs tracing the history of exploration in the Antarctic by expeditions of many nationalities. Although the series included Russian, American and European explorers as well as British, it is understandable that Chilean and Argentinian contributors to polar research were excluded. The series ranged historically from Captain Cook to John Rymill (106:28) and was lithographed by Questa. Apart from the two royal wedding omnibus issues, both the Antarctic territories issued a commemorative set in the early 1970s, for the 10th anniversary of the Antarctic Treaty and the 50th anniversary of Shackleton's expedition respectively (106:27, 36). The Falkland Islands issued very few commemoratives in this period, other than the omnibus sets. Sets of four stamps marked Human Rights Year (106:34), the anniversary of the Falklands air service and the centenary of the bishopric (both 1969), the golden jubilee of the defence forces and the restoration of the S.S. *Great Britain* (both 1970), but the only subsequent commemoratives were those celebrating the Queen's silver wedding and the marriage of Princess Anne. A set with the theme of tourism appeared in 1974.

Cuba
Although the small-format portrait definitives of 1954 remained current in this period, they were largely overshadowed by the lengthy thematic sets which were produced at two-monthly intervals. These sets covered a wide range of subjects, from the Cuban merchant fleet and the tobacco industry to aspects of agriculture and horse-breeding (108:1, 15). More than any other American country, Cuba was obsessed with the Art craze which swept the world in the late 1960s and this was reflected in numerous sets reproducing

paintings, either as pure thematic issues featuring the treasures of national museums (108:13, 16) or to illustrate commemorative stamps, such as the cave paintings shown on the series marking the 30th anniversary of the Spelaeological Society (108:9). Children's paintings were reproduced on a series publicising the Children's Art Exhibition in Havana in 1971 (108:11) and paintings were also used to promote tourism (108:10), Stamp Day and other events.

Two regular issues continued in this period. The Christmas stamps were produced in composite designs, featuring such subjects as birds and flowers (108:4) while the Stamp Day issues concentrated on historic aspects of the posts (108:5, 14). The majority of stamps commemorated current events, often of global importance, and invariably used modernistic designs that ranged from poster styles (108:2) to abstract and impressionist (108:3, 6, 8). Only in the case of international sporting events was there any concession to realism (108:7). Relatively few stamps of this period attempted to convey a political message, but they included a set of three, attacking American policies in Vietnam (1966) and a set publicising the third symposium on the Indo–China War (1972). Most of the political stamps referred to internal matters, commemorating anniversaries of the Castro régime or honouring such martyrs of the revolutionary movement as Che Guevara and Frank Pais. Stamps were issued occasionally to mark Guerrillas' Day or Labour Day (108:12).

Dominican Republic
The 1961 definitives, featuring coffee and cocoa plants, were replaced by a similar series in January 1967. The small-format ordinary and airmail stamps depicted the National Shrine and the double-sized special delivery stamp featured a stylised pigeon and letter (108:17). Throughout this decade, low-value stamps were issued to prepay the compulsory levy on correspondence raising funds for Civil Defence, the Postal and Telecommunications School (108:18) and the anti-tuberculosis campaign. Obligatory tax stamps for Child Welfare and education were issued between 1967 and 1972. In the original version, lithographed by Ferrua, the design had a solid background, but stamps issued in 1968 and 1971 were lithographed by Padilla of Santo Domingo using a screened background (108:20). Christmas stamps were introduced in 1971, the inaugural series showing shepherds and the Star of Bethlehem, or the Spanish bell brought by Columbus in 1493 (108:21).

Short thematic sets boosted the rather meagre range of definitives and featured butterflies and Taino arts and crafts. The longest sets were those marking international sporting events, from the Central American and Caribbean Games to the various Olympic Games. Other events were usually marked by single stamps or pairs (108:19, 21) and in the latter case stamps were often inscribed for ordinary and airmail postage respectively (108:23). All stamps of the Dominican Republic in this period were lithographed by one or other of the two local printers.

Haiti
The most prolific of the West Indian countries in this decade, Haiti entrusted her philatelic output to a succession of external agencies and this resulted in a flood of stamps, especially from 1967 onwards, devoted to all the more fashionable themes, such as American and Russian space exploits, the Olympic Games (both summer and winter games), flora and fauna. A relatively high proportion of the stamps honoured philatelic exhibitions in other countries and some ingenuity was shown in combining different themes for maximum sales. Thus the 1969 series devoted to winners of the Olympic marathon, reproduced stamps of the appropriate period and country in honour of each winner (108:31). The most notable feature of Haitian stamps, however, was the wide range of printers employed in their production, which included the State Printers of Japan, Germany, Austria and Israel (108:28), Harrison (108:25, 30), Enschedé (108:24, 26, 27), De La Rue of Bogota (108:31) and Giesecke and Devrient, formerly of Leipzig but reconstituted after the Second World War in Munich (108:29). Long thematic sets took the place of definitives (108:25) and many sets trumpeted the achievements of the dictator, 'Papa Doc' Duvalier (108:27). Even stamps ostensibly commemorating other events were used to promote the Duvalier image, such as the series of 1966 honouring the Caribbean Football Championships (108:26).

Netherlands Antilles

All stamps of this period were produced by Enschedé as before, though multicolour lithography was increasingly used in preference to photogravure. The two semi-postal sets, raising money for the cultural and social fund and Child Welfare respectively, were issued in July and November as in previous years. The 1958 pictorial definitives remained current throughout this decade, new values being added up to 1973. Short thematic sets were introduced in 1965 and concentrated on scenery, air transport and other subjects related to tourism. From 1967 onwards, occasional singles commemorated historic personalities of the islands (*108*: 32) and single stamps were released to mark the anniversaries of local interest (*108*: 34). Few international events, other than those connected with the Netherlands, were commemorated, exceptions being the centenaries of the International Telecommunications Union (1965), the jubilee of the International Labour Organisation in 1969 (*108*: 33) and the Universal Postal Union (1974).

Australasia

Australia

Several shillings or pence denominations were added to the multicoloured birds series in 1965. In February of the following year, however, Australia introduced a decimal system based on the dollar of 100 cents and the entire definitive series – intaglio explorers and photogravure birds – was reissued, with values expressed in the new currency (*109*: 4). At the same time, small-format designs portraying Queen Elizabeth II were issued at various times up to 1971, covering the lowest denominations. Originally recess-printed, the latest of these designs was photogravure-printed for use in coils in 1966–7. The 4- and 5-cent values of the portrait stamps were also issued in booklets and may be found with printed labels *se-tenant*. In 1968, Australia adopted a new policy towards stamp booklets, issuing them at regular intervals with small-format stamps covering the inland letter rate and portraying famous Australians. These booklets were reissued annually. The earlier issues were recess-printed on coloured paper (*109*: 11, 16) but subsequently, white paper was used (*109*: 26, 37) and the sets from 1973 onwards were printed in combined intaglio and lithography (*109*: 41). From 1968 onwards, the middle values of the definitive series were replaced by multicolour photogravure sets with various themes: the state floral emblems in 1968 (*109*: 9), primary industries in 1969 and 1972 (*109*: 14, 38), animals in 1971 (*109*: 30), the 6-cent stamp being additionally inscribed to commemorate the centenary of the Australian Royal Society for the Prevention of Cruelty to Animals. Thereafter, the frequency of thematic definitives increased. Later sets featured aboriginal art, the rehabilitation of the disabled, pioneer life, national development, wild animals and architecture, the last-named coinciding with the inauguration of the controversial Sydney Opera House (*109*: 24, 34, 35, 38, 39, 42, 45).

The first phase of a new definitive series consisted of five coil stamps with modified versions of the state floral emblems. These stamps were issued in semi-perforate coils in 1970–71 (*109*: 23). As a result of increases in postal rates in 1974, the 7-cent – Sturt's Desert Pea – stamp was reissued in January 1975 as a 10-cent stamp. New low value definitives in normal sheet form were released in July 1973 and featured marine life and gemstones (*109*: 44). The 8-cent stamp (Opals) was surcharged for use as a 9-cent stamp in October 1974 and a 10-cent stamp featuring sapphires, appeared the following month. The dollar stamps portraying explorers were replaced during 1974 by large-format stamps in multicolour photogravure, reproducing contemporary Australian paintings.

Stamps have been used twice in recent years in support of government campaigns. The conversion to the metric system in 1973 was publicised by a set of four 7-cent stamps, using cartoons to convey the message of metrication (*109*: 33). In 1975, a set of three 10-cent stamps highlighted the environmental dangers of road traffic, pollution and bushfires.

Christmas stamps and air letter sheets were issued each year but there was a swing away from traditional motifs and Old Master reproductions to contemporary interpretations of the Christmas theme, culminating in the series of seven stamps of 1971 with a stylised treatment of the three kings and star theme, printed on coloured backgrounds in various combinations, in the same sheet (*109*: 36). Modernistic renderings of religious paintings in 1970 and 1972 (*109*: 21) failed to do justice to the printing processes used and were greeted by storms of protest at the apparently poor quality of the production. Experimentation, in fact, has been the keynote of Australian stamp design in the past decade. Overlapping images or colour bands were favourite devices in the commemorative stamps of the late 1960s (*109*: 6, 7, 10, 17, 25, 27) and the Laurence Hargrave stamp of 1965 actually foreshadowed the designs of the dollar bank-notes of the following year (*109*: 2). Stylised elements on flat coloured backgrounds recurred throughout this period (*109*: 3, 5, 18). More complex backgrounds were employed occasionally (*109*: 1, 22, 40, 43). Unframed designs, with contrasting motifs, were used increasingly from 1965 onwards (*109*: 2, 4, 8, 10, 20, 27, 32, 35, 39) and this pattern eventually extended to the definitives (*109*: 23, 44). Relatively few stamps adopted purely pictorial designs. There was a return to more realistic motifs in 1969, with the stamps commemorating the Northern Territory, the Ports and Harbours Conference issue and the jubilee of the England–Australia flight (*109*: 12, 13, 15), but in more recent years, examples of naturalistic design or portraiture were comparatively rate (*109*: 25, 29, 31, 46) and the temptation to impose modern poster techniques could not be resisted, even in these few examples.

All Australian stamps of this decade were produced by the Note Printing branch of the Reserve Bank of Australia. Photogravure was used, except for the explorer definitives, the famous Australians booklet stamps and a single, commemorating the 150th anniversary of Macquarie Lighthouse, for which combined intaglio and lithography was used. Helecon-impregnated paper was used for many of the commemorative and definitive stamps released from 1965 onwards in connection with electronic sorting experiments. In some cases, helecon ink was used instead. In 1967, experimental printings were made of the 4-cent definitive, coated with helecon or a substance known as Derby Luminescent; these substances are invisible to the naked eye. Since 1972, experiments have been conducted with a very white chalky paper that has a strong fluorescence under ultra-violet light, and many of the commemoratives as well as the definitives have been printed on it.

Apart from the famous Australian booklets, there were few attempts at issuing stamps in *se-tenant* combinations. The 1971 Christmas, and the England–Australia air commemoratives (*109*: 15, 36) were notable exceptions. There was, however, one important example of a composite design. The bicentenary of Captain Cook's discovery of Australia's east coast, was marked in 1970 by a set of six stamps, five of which were 5-cent stamps, printed in a continuous strip to form a single picture. A team of four artists was involved in the design of the strip, which consisted of a montage of subjects symbolising various aspects of Cook's voyage (*109*: 19). A very large 30-cent stamp accompanied this strip and all six stamps were also released in an imperforate miniature sheet. Some of the sheets were subsequently overprinted, to commemorate the ANPEX philatelic exhibition, and this encouraged certain private individuals to produce their own overprints, for a variety of purposes. These overprints, together with private perforations or roulettes, were completely unauthorised.

Australian Antarctic Territory

A decimal pictorial definitive series was issued in 1966 and featured scientific activities in the polar regions (*109*: 47). A 5-cent denomination was added in 1968 when the letter rate was increased. This series was superseded in August 1973, by a set featuring wildlife and aircraft used on various historic expeditions since 1928. Pairs of stamps in 1971–2 commemorated the 10th anniversary of the Antarctic Treaty and the bicentenary of Cook's circumnavigation of Antarctica.

New Zealand

Chalky paper was introduced in 1965 and used for printings of the definitive series, with sterling denominations from then until 1967, when the currency was decimalised, and similar designs, with values in cents and dollars, were released. New designs, with the theme of natural products, were introduced in 1967–9 for the middle denominations, and the colours of the 15-cent and 2-dollar stamps were changed (*110*:11). An entirely new series was issued in 1970–71. The small-format low values (½- to 8-cent) featured butterflies and fish (*110*:22), and the double-sized higher denominations (15-cent to 2-dollar) featured Maori artifacts, scenery and technological achievements. The 10-cent stamp portrayed Queen Elizabeth II and the national arms, and was released to coincide with the royal visit in March 1970. As a result of increases in postal rates, the obsolescent 2½-cent stamp was surcharged 4 cents in 1971, by Harrison, using either photogravure or letterpress; the surcharges may be identified by the presence or absence of screening dots. A locally typographed version of the surcharge was made in 1973 and can be distinguished from the Harrison version by the thickness and position of the bars obliterating the original value. Since September 1973, unwatermarked paper has gradually replaced the NZ and star paper used for New Zealand stamps for the past hundred years.

The Health semi-postal stamps continued to appear in August–October of each year, in normal and miniature sheets. Birds were the subject of these stamps until 1966 (*110*:6) but thereafter, aspects of children's games were chosen (*110*:9, 24). A third stamp was released in 1969, portraying Dr. Elizabeth Gunn who founded the first health camp fifty years earlier. Single stamps reproducing Old Master paintings were issued for Christmas each year up to 1969 (*110*:7), but subsequently, sets of three stamps were released. In these sets, one stamp reproduced a religious painting as before, but the others featured a New Zealand church window and miscellaneous designs ranging from the architectural (*110*:26) to the purely symbolic.

Short thematic sets of three or four stamps were introduced in 1968, the first being dedicated to the armed forces (*110*:14). Subsequent sets featured wildlife of the Chatham Islands (*110*:27), alpine plants, vintage locomotives (*110*:36) and paintings by Frances Hodgkins (*110*:38). Multicolour stamps boosted the tourist industry from 1972 onwards, with vignettes featuring lake scenery (*110*:37) and mountains and islands and forest parks in 1975 (*110*:41) in successive years. A more thematic approach was applied to commemoratives in a few instances. In 1971, three stamps featuring roses were issued in connection with the World Rose Convention (*110*:34) and the International Vintage Car Rally later the same year was honoured by six stamps featuring veteran and vintage cars. Although separate sets were issued throughout this period, to commemorate historic anniversaries and current events, an attempt to reduce the number of such stamps was made from 1972 onwards, by grouping anniversaries into a single uniform series each year (*110*:35, 40). Hitherto, related anniversaries were grouped together; in 1971, two stamps designed by L. C. Mitchell, marked the jubilees of Rotary International and the Country Women's Institute (*110*:28) and subsequently, R. M. Conly designed three armorial stamps to celebrate the civic centenaries of Palmerston North, Auckland and Invercargill (*110*:30).

Unlike Australia, a high proportion of New Zealand stamps continued to be completely pictorial in concept, their designs often based on photographs (*110*:1, 4, 5, 10, 12, 16–18, 20, 29). Symbolism was originally confined to stamps commemorating anniversaries of international organisations (*110*:2, 15, 25, 31) or occasional current events of international significance (*110*:8). A more abstract style of design was pioneered by Mark Cleverley in 1970, in his stylised treatment of the scenic high values of the definitive series and continued in his designs for the Ross Dependency series of 1972 (*110*:43). His later work was characterised by symbolic elements on a plain white background (*110*:23) or the abstract motifs chosen for the Earth Satellite pair of 1971 and the 1972 Anniversaries set (*110*:32, 35), but after this intriguing interlude, New Zealand shied away from symbolism and returned to designs whose meaning would be readily apparent to the general public. Although he used more orthodox designs for the two stamps honouring Lord Rutherford in 1971 (*110*:33), Cleverley preferred a more stylised approach in the Commonwealth Games set of 1974 (*110*:39), in order to convey the feeling of movement. Nevertheless, these designs were much closer to photographic likenesses than, for example, Britain's Commonwealth Games stamps of 1970 (*72*:35).

New Zealand's first *se-tenant* stamps appeared in 1969. Four stamps of various denominations were issued in the normal sheet form, to mark the bicentenary of Captain Cook's landing in New Zealand and the four values were also issued in a miniature sheet (*110*:19). In 1974, five stamps, all of 4-cent value, were issued in miniature sheet form only, to mark New Zealand Day and celebrate the royal visit. Only one omnibus issue appeared in this period, a seven-pence stamp of 1965, honouring Sir Winston Churchill. This stamp, and a similar one for use in Australia were photogravure-printed by the Reserve Bank of Australia (*110*:3). Apart from this stamp, all New Zealand issues up to 1969 were produced by Harrison, De La Rue or Bradbury Wilkinson, as before, but subsequently, contracts for commemoratives and definitives were awarded to printers in other countries, including Courvoisier (*110*:21, 32, 34, 37, 38, 40), Enschedé and the Japanese Government Printing Works (*110*:20, 23, 27, 28, 30, 31).

The Government Life Insurance Department's definitives were reissued in 1967–8, with decimal currency surcharges, pending the release of a new series lithographed by Bradbury Wilkinson. The designs featured five New Zealand lighthouses (*110*:42). Decimalisation also affected the stamps of the Ross Dependency which were released in July 1967 in the original designs, but with the values re-engraved. An entirely new series, designed by Mark Cleverley as already noted, appeared in January 1972, the six stamps featuring stylised interpretations of life and work in the Antarctic (*110*:43).

Australian Dependencies

Both the Australian dependencies in the Indian Ocean had a change of currency in this decade, with different consequences in each case. Christmas Island continued to use Malay cents and dollars until 1968, when Australian money was substituted. A multicoloured series, depicting fish was issued in May 1968 with values in Australian currency (*111*:4) and new denominations were added in 1970. In 1972–3, a definitive series depicting historic ships connected with the island was issued (*111*:5). Appropriately, Christmas stamps of distinctive designs were issued from 1969 onwards. Both Christmas Island and Australia's other dependencies issued omnibus stamps in 1965 to mark the jubilee of the Gallipoli Landing (*111*:6). The Gallipoli commemorative was, in fact, the only stamp issued by the Cocos Islands in the early part of this decade. When decimal currency was introduced in 1966, the Cocos Islands ceased issuing their own stamps and reverted to ordinary Australian issues. Distinctive stamps were resumed, however in July 1969, a series of twelve featuring island wildlife being introduced (*111*:7). No other stamps have appeared since that date.

The decimalisation of the currency resulted in the definitives of Norfolk Island being surcharged in February 1966, but these provisionals were replaced a year later by a photogravure series, featuring historic ships (*112*:14). This and subsequent definitive sets were released in four phases, spread over a period of more than a year. The 1970–71 series featured island birds and the 1973–4 set depicted elevation drawings of historic buildings (*112*:16). Apart from Christmas stamps, Norfolk Island produced very few special issues, though three of these commemorated Captain Cook's voyages of discovery in the Pacific and Antarctica (*112*:15).

Several values with new designs were added to the birds series of Nauru in 1965 (*112*:1), but the pictorial definitives were reissued in 1966 with values inscribed in decimal currency. On 31st January 1968, the island became an independent republic and the existing series was overprinted to denote the change in status (*112*:2). Although independent, Nauru was subsequently admitted to membership of the British Commonwealth. Two stamps celebrating independence were issued belatedly in September 1968 (*112*:3), and the first distinctive definitive of the republic appeared on the first anniversary of independence (*112*:4). This stamp was later overprinted to celebrate the 5th anniversary of independence. A pictorial series featuring flowers and birds was released in 1973.

Papua New Guinea was granted internal self-government in December 1973, but continued under Australian aegis. A significant step in the progress towards nationhood, was the subtle change in the name of the territory. In 1972, as part of the constitutional development, the word 'and' was dropped from the title, to emphasise the unity of the two parts that had originally been administered by Britain and Germany, but which had been under Australian rule since the First World War. The first stamps to be thus inscribed, appropriately celebrated the 1972 constitutional changes (*112*:29).

Like Norfolk Island, the definitives of Papua New Guinea were issued in instalments. At the beginning of the decade, the final phase of the birds series was introduced, but following the introduction of Australian decimal currency in 1966, a series featuring butterflies was issued (*112*:17). Subsequent definitives depicted seashells, in 1968–9, and local customs and occupations in 1973–4 (*112*:21, 30). Ethnography was a fertile source of material for many of the short thematic sets issued in this period (*112*:19, 25, 27, 28), but insects, flowers and wildlife were also featured (*112*:18, 23, 26). All of the definitive, thematic and commemorative stamps of this period were printed in multicolour photogravure by Courvoisier, with the exception of a set of three in 1969, recess-printed by the Reserve Bank of Australia, to mark the Third South Pacific Games (*112*:22), a folklore series of the same year lithographed by Enschedé and a series of 1971 for the fourth Games, lithographed by De La Rue. Papua New Guinea became completely independent at the end of 1975.

British Pacific Islands

A series depicting flora, fauna and artifacts, was lithographed by De La Rue and issued in the British Solomon Islands in May 1965. Following the introduction of Australian decimal currency, the series was surcharged in cents and dollars (*111*:1). The surcharged series may be found with the watermark upright or sideways. A photogravure series by Harrison was introduced in 1968 (*111*:2); initially printed on chalk-surfaced paper, several values appeared in 1971 on glazed, ordinary paper. Questa lithographed a series featuring butterflies, issued in 1972–3. Short thematic sets depicting ships, navigators and musical instruments, were released between 1971 and 1974. Apart from the colonial omnibus issues of 1965–73, the Solomon Islands issued Christmas stamps from 1969 onwards (*111*:3) and a handful of commemoratives marking events and anniversaries of local interest.

Fiji's first co-ordinated definitive series for many years, appeared in July 1968. Although the designs were the prize-winning entries in an international design competition, they were adapted and standardised by Victor Whiteley and printed in multicolour photogravure by De La Rue (*111*:24). The same designs were used for decimal currency stamps issued in 1969–70. Birds and flowers were the subjects of a series lithographed by Questa in 1971–2. The original version had an upright Block CA watermark, but later printings (1972–3) had a sideways watermark (*111*:26). Fiji issued a considerable number of commemoratives in this decade, all of them printed by British companies but predominantly, in photogravure, by Harrison (*111*:23, 25, 27). No stamps celebrated the introduction of the legislative assembly in 1966, but the attainment of independence in 1970 was marked by four stamps. Oddly enough, Fiji even issued a set of stamps in 1974, to celebrate the centenary of annexation by the British – an unusual issue for a recently independent country to make.

The Gilbert and Ellice Islands issued a definitive series in 1965, lithographed by Bradbury Wilkinson and featuring occupations of the islanders. The series was surcharged in Australian decimal currency in the following year and in January 1968, was issued with the values redrawn (*111*:33). A multicoloured pictorial series, by Walsall Security Printers, appeared in May 1971 (*111*:34); the position of the watermark was changed in stamps reprinted in 1972–4. Christmas stamps were introduced in 1969 (*111*:36) and short thematic sets in 1972. In addition, there were several sets of four stamps from 1967 onwards, commemorating events of local or international interest (*111*:32, 35, 37). Pitcairn's 1964 definitives were surcharged in Australian decimal currency in July 1967, a device in the form of the *Bounty* anchor being used to obliterate the old denominations (*112*:31). The stamp designer, Jennifer Toombs, spent some time on the island in 1967 and subsequently designed the 1969–73 definitives (*112*:32) and all the commemorative or thematic sets from 1968 onwards, most of them in a highly distinctive style with the background colour bled into the perforations.

French Pacific Islands

All three French Pacific possessions continued to issue their own stamps, and increased their output from 1965 onwards. Instead of definitive sets, they chose short thematic issues, featuring wildlife, flowers, boats (*111*:28) and Polynesian art and artifacts. In common with France, the size of the stamps tended to increase in the late 1960s, a large horizontal format being popular for single stamps, commemorating important current events or local anniversaries (*111*:30; *112*:5, 43). The more traditional double-sized format, however, was still used occasionally, especially for recess-printed commemoratives (*111*:29; *112*:42). All of the stamps issued by French Polynesia (*111*:28–31), New Caledonia (*112*:5) and the Wallis and Futuna Islands (*112*:42, 43) were designed and produced in France, as before.

New Zealand Pacific Islands

Although the independence and autonomy granted to Samoa and the Cook Islands respectively, reduced the New Zealand dependencies to two, the output of stamps in the remaining territories, Niue and the Tokelau Islands, increased dramatically in this period. Niue had, in fact, issued no stamps at all in the previous decade and Tokelau had only produced one stamp, a provisional shilling surcharge in 1956. Niue's 1950 definitives were surcharged in decimal currency in 1967 as a prelude to a multicoloured flower series, lithographed by Enschedé (*112*:10) in 1969. The following year, a short set featuring edible crabs was issued (*112*:11) and subsequently, similar thematic sets appeared annually (*112*:13). At the same time, Christmas stamps were introduced in both Niue and the Tokelau group, at first following the New Zealand design, but using distinctive designs since 1973 (*112*:9). The Tokelau definitives of 1948 were likewise surcharged in decimal currency in 1966 (*112*:35), but since a larger range of denominations was felt to be necessary, undenominated 'arms' stamps of New Zealand were overprinted, first in sterling values (1966) and then in decimal currency (*112*:39), pending the introduction of a series featuring local handicrafts in 1971 (*112*:36). Like Niue, the Tokelau Islands began issuing thematic sets, beginning with a curious historical issue in 1969 (*112*:37) and subsequently issuing a set of four, featuring corals (*112*:40). Both Niue and the Tokelau Islands have issued sets in recent years, marking current events (*112*:12) or historic anniversaries (*112*:38).

Cook Islands

Autonomy was granted to the Cook Islands in September 1965 and since then, the output of stamps has risen drastically. Announcing a more liberal philatelic policy, soon after self-government was attained, the Cook Islands postmaster-general stated, naively, that it was intended to finance old-age pensions and social security from philatelic revenue. Thus warned, the stamp world watched pessimistically for a dramatic increase in issues, on the same lines as certain Arab sheikhdoms and Latin-American countries. Although there has been a significant increase in the number of stamps, the Cook Islands has never gone beyond the bounds of reason, and the stamps have been mainly confined to events and personalities relevant to the country. Even the various space issues could be justified on the grounds that the Cook Islands were within the splash-down zone of the Apollo flights. The 1963 definitives were overprinted in 1966 for airmail (*111*:8) and were subsequently surcharged in New Zealand decimal currency in 1967, prior to the introduction of a floral series later that year (*111*:10). The series was reissued from 1970 onwards, with fluorescent security markings applied across the face of the stamps. This form of security marking was extended to the commemoratives issued from October 1968 onwards. A new definitive series, depicting seashells, was released in 1974 (*111*:18).

Christmas stamps, invariably reproducing Old Master religious paintings, were introduced in 1966. One curious exception, was the series released in 1970, reproducing details from the illuminated manuscript known as the De Lisle Psalter. By an incredible coincidence, the same details were reproduced on the British Christmas stamps issued the same year (*111*:12). Although the Cook Islands have periodically overprinted obsolescent commemoratives, or stamps of the flower definitives, to mark other events (*111*:9, 15), the majority of the special issues have been designed for a specific event or anniversary and printed by Heraclio Fournier of Spain in a distinctive style which may be recognised by his fondness for metallic ink in frames and inscriptions (*111*:11, 14, 16, 17). In recent years, the Cook Islands have turned their attention to numismatics and have produced several sets of coins, commemorating such events as the Cook bicentenary, the royal silver wedding and the Churchill centenary; these coins have also been linked to issues of stamps, reproducing both obverse and reverse (*111*:14).

The most intriguing phenomenon in the recent philately of the Cook Islands, has been the fragmentation of the archipelago into separate stamp-issuing entities. There was ample historic precedent for this, since both Aitutaki and Penrhyn had issued their own stamps between 1902 and 1932. In August 1972, Aitutaki was declared a port of entry into the Cook Islands, though why this should have resulted in Aitutaki resuming separate issues of stamps is not clear. At first, Cook Islands definitives were overprinted in upper and lower case, but four months later, an overprint in an ornamental oval was introduced (*111*:19). Subsequently, Christmas and commemorative stamps were produced by Fournier, analogous to those of the Cook Islands (*111*:20). In October 1973, Penrhyn Island in the northern Cook group began issuing its own stamps. Again, the inaugural series consisted of Cook Island stamps overprinted (*111*:21), followed by distinctive pictorial definitives and commemoratives by Fournier (*111*:22).

New Hebrides
The definitive series instituted in 1963, remained current throughout this decade and new values and designs were added up to 1972. Two versions were produced, with inscriptions in English and French, as before, and the stamps were printed in photogravure by Harrison or intaglio by the French Government Printing Works. The same policy applied to the commemorative stamps, which included both French and British colonial omnibus issues and distinctive sets (*112*:6–8). A new series of pictorial definitives, photogravure-printed by the French Government Printing Works, was released in both language versions in 1972.

Samoa
The independence definitives of 1962 were reprinted in 1965–6 on paper with a watermark showing the kava bowl emblem, in place of the NZ and star watermark previously used. Between 1967 and 1969, a series featuring Pacific birds was issued, the low values (up to 1-dollar) being printed in photogravure by Harrison and the 2- and 4-dollar values, lithographed by Format International (*112*:33). A pictorial series featuring seashells was lithographed by Questa and issued in October 1972 (*112*:34). Christmas stamps were adopted in 1969 and thematic sets were issued annually to mark the anniversary of independence. In addition, Samoa increased its output of commemorative sets, mainly relating to anniversaries and current events of South Pacific interest.

Tonga
All the stamps issued by Tonga in this period were of the free-form, self-adhesive variety, either embossed on metal foil to simulate coins (*112*:41) or die-stamped and lithographed on specially treated paper. In most cases, even the shape of the stamps was related to the event commemorated, and the definitives of 1969, 1970 and 1972, were shaped respectively like bananas, coconuts and watermelons. All of these stamps were produced by Walsall Security Printers Limited.

1

2

3

4

5

6

7

8

9

10

11

12

13

14

15

16

17

18

19

20

21

22

23

24

25

26

27

28

29

30

31

32

33

34

35

36

37

38

1

2

3

4

5

6

7

8

9

10

11

12

13

14

15

16

17

18

19

20

21

22

23

24

25

26

27

28

29

30

31

32

33

34

35

36

37

38

39

1

2

3

4

5

6

7

8

9

10

11

12

13

14

15

16

17

18

19

20

21

22

23

24

25

26

27

28

29

30

31

32

33

34

35

36

37

38

39

40

41

42

1

2

3

4

5

6

7

8

9

10

11

12

13

14 15

16

17

18

19

20

21

22

23

24

25

26

27

28

29

30

31

32

33

34

35

36

37

38

39

40

41

42

43

44

45

46

47

48

49

50

51

70

1

2

3

4

5

6

8

9

11

12

13

14

15

16

17

18

19

20

21

22

23

24

25

26

27

28

29

30

31

32

33

34

35

36

37

BRITISH LEGION
50TH Anniversary
3p

3p
Coleg Prifysgol
Aberystwyth
University College

James Clark Ross 1800-1862
3p

2½p

Tutankhamun discovery 1922
3p

9p
Huish Episcopi Somerset

2½p

BBC 1922/1972
5p

SILVER WEDDING
20p

3p European Communities 1973

9p
Oak Quercus robur

Walter Raleigh c.1552-1618
7½p

3p
County Cricket 1873-1973

Sir Henry Raeburn
1756-1823
Rev R Walker
9p

10p

14 November 1973
20p

INIGO JONES 1573-1652
architect/designer
COURT MASQUE COSTUMES
INIGO JONES 1573-1652
architect/designer
ST PAUL'S COVENT GARDEN
3p

Good King Wenceslas
3½p

5½p
Prizewinning fire engine 1863

Universal Postal Union 1874/1974
8p
Airmail blue van and postbox 1930

Churchill centenary 5½p

4½+1½p for
health and
handicap
charities

7p
The Rows Chester

3p

7½p

5p

GUERNSEY
BAILIWICK
Edward III
3p

BAILIWICK OF GUERNSEY
1923-1973
WESTLAND WESSEX
3p

GUERNSEY
ROYAL MILITIA 1874
3p

JERSEY 2½p
THE ROYAL MACE

L'ARMÉE
DE LA LOIRE
AVIATION HISTORY
1870
JERSEY
3p

JERSEY
POTATO DIGGER (Trouthus a Digou)
Nineteenth Century Farming
3p

2½p

MANX GRAND PRIX GOLDEN JUBILEE
ISLE OF MAN
3p

ΘΕΟΤΟΚΟΠΟΥΛΟΣ 1541-1614
ΕΛΛΑΣ ΔΡ.2.50 **1**

ΕΛΛΑΣ ΔΡ. 3 **2**

ΕΛΛΑΣ ΛΕΠ 10 **3**

ΕΛΛΑΣ-HELLAS ΔΡ.4.50 **4**

ΕΛΛΑΣ-HELLAS ΔΡ.5 **5**

ΕΛΛΑΣ-HELLAS ΔΡ.1.50 **6**

ΕΛΛΑΣ HELLAS ΔΡ.4.50 OTE **7**

ΕΤΟΣ ΠΡΟΣΤΑΣΙΑΣ ΤΗΣ ΦΥΣΕΩΣ 1970 Capra Aegagrus Cretensis HELLAS ΕΛΛΑΣ 8 **8**

1821-1971 ΕΛΛΑΣ - HELLAS ΔΡ.2 **9**

EUROPA CEPT 1971 HELLAS ΕΛΛΑΣ ΔΡ.5 **10**

ΜΕΓΑΡΑ (ΓΕΩΡΓΙΝΗ) 1972 ΕΛΛΑΣ-Hellas ΔΡ.4.50 **11**

1972 ΕΚΚΛΗΣΙΑ ΔΑΦΝΙΟΥ ΕΛΛΑΣ HELLAS ΔΡ.1 **12**

ΕΛΛΑΣ-HELLAS ΔΡ.4,50 **13**

ΕΛΛΑΣ ΔΡ.4.50 **14**

EUROPA-CEPT ΕΛΛΑΣ HELLAS ΔΡ.3 **1**

A. NYIKOLAJEV 1962.VIII.11-15. P. POPOVICS 1962.VIII.12-15. 20 f MAGYAR POSTA **16**

30f MAGYAR POSTA ДУНАЙСКАЯ КОМИССИЯ · COMMISSION DU DANUBE **17**

MUNKA ÉRDEMREND BRONZ FOKOZATA 20f MAGYAR POSTA **18**

FELSZABADULÁSUNK 20f 20. ÉVFORDULÓJÁRA... 1985 MAGYAR POSTA **1**

LÉGIPOSTA 50f MAGYAR POSTA **20**

MAGYAR POSTA ACIPENSER RUTHENUS L. 20 KECSEGE MAGYAR POSTA **21**

40f GYERMEKBÉLYEGRAJZ 50 ÉVE KM MAGYAR POSTA **22**

1868 1968 100 ÉVES AZ ATHENAEUM NYOMDA 2f MAGYAR POSTA **23**

CIOLKOVSZKIJ ŰRÁLLOMÁS TERVE ~1903 60f LÉGIPOSTA MAGYAR POSTA **24**

BE A VÖRÖS HADSEREGBE! MAGYAR POSTA 40f **25**

MAGYAR POSTA 1,50 Ft LÉGIPOSTA CSEPEL 1902 **26**

3 MAGYAR MŰEMLÉKVÉDELEM 1872-1972 MAGYAR POSTA **27**

SURTSEY APRIL 1964 ÍSLAND 2.00 KR **28**

EUROPA Kr. 8,00 ÍSLAND **29**

LÖNDRANGAR ÍSLAND 2.50 KR **30**

HÆGRI UMFERÐ 26 MAÍ 1968 ÍSLAND 4 KR **31**

30 KR ÍSLAND **32**

LISTAHÁTÍÐ Í REYKJAVÍK 1970 ÞÓRARINN B. ÞORLÁKSSON 1867-1924 ÍSLAND 50 KR **33**

ÍSLAND 10 NORRÆNA HÚSIÐ REYKJAVÍK **34**

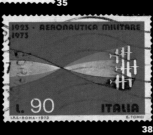

1

2

3

4

5

7

8

9

10

11

13

14

15

16

17

19

20

21

22

23

24

25

26

27

28

29

30

31

32

33

34

35

36

37

38

39

40

41

43

44

45

46

47

48

83

1

2

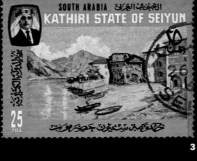

3

4

5

6

7

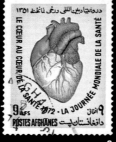

8

9

10

11

12

13

14

15

16

17

18

19

20

21

22

23

24

25

26

27

28

29

30

31

32

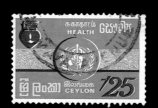

33

34

1

2

3

4

5

6

7

8

9

10

11

12

13

14

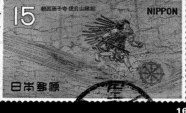
15

16

17

18

19

20

21

22

23

24

25

26

27

28

29

30

31

32

33

34

35

36

37

38

39

40

41

42

43

44

45

46

47

48

1

2

3

4

5

6

7

8

9

10

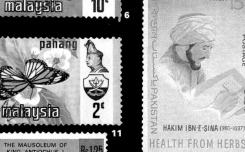

11

12

13

14

15

16

17

18

19

20

21

22

23

24

25

26

27

28

29

30

31

32

33

34

35

36

37

38

39

40

1

2

3

4

6

7

8

9

11

12

13

14

16

17

18

19

23

24

26

27

30

31

32

33

35

36

37

38

39

1

2

3

4

5

6

7

8

9

10

11

12

13

14

15

16

17

18

19

20

21

22

23

24

25

26

27

28

29

30

31

32

33

34

35

1

2

3

5

6

7

8

10

11

12

13

14

15

16

17

18

19

20

21

22

23

24

25

27

28

29

30

32

33

34

35

36

5F — RÉPUBLIQUE DE GUINÉE — 1

10F — RÉPUBLIQUE DE GUINÉE — 2

RÉPUBLIQUE DE GUINÉE — DÉCENNIE HYDROLOGIQUE — 100F UNESCO INTERNATIONALE 1965-1974 — 3

RÉPUBLIQUE DE GUINÉE — 4

RÉPUBLIQUE DE GUINÉE — 0.60F POSTES — 5

ESPAÑA — IFNI — CORREOS — 1'50 PTAS — DIA DEL SELLO 1965 — 6

IBIS IBIS — 75r POSTES — RÉPUBLIQUE DE CÔTE D'IVOIRE — 7

VERVET MONKEY — KENYA — 5/- — 8

5c — Pharaonella perna — KENYA — 9

LESOTHO — 25 CENTS — MALETSUNYANE FALLS, 630ft. — 10

LESOTHO — 50 CENTS — DIAMONDS — 11

JOHN F. KENNEDY ANNIVERSARY MEMORIAL — LIBERIA — LIBERIA · 20¢ — 12

AFRICAN MASK - BAMILÉKÉ — LIBERIA 15¢ — 13

OLYMPIC GAMES - MUNICH 1972 — LIBERIA 5¢ — 14

LIBYA — 1865-1965 centenaire 1965-1970 — de l'Union Internationale des TELECOMMUNICATIONS — 15

LAR — 35 — 16

LAR — 17

KINGDOM OF LIBYA — POSTAGE 35 MILLS — COURVOISIER S.A. — 18

REPOBLIKA MALAGASY — POSTES — 1F — CICINDELIDAE CHAETODERA ANDRIANA — 19

REPOBLIKA MALAGASY — POSTES 5F — CATHÉDRALE CATHOLIQUE DE TANANARIVE — 20

YELLOW BISHOP — 9d — MALAWI — 21

K1 — BUSHBUCK — MALAWI — 22

kalimba/thumb dulcitone — MALAWI — 3t — 23

CHARAXES BOHEMANI — MALAWI 3t — 24

MALAWI 3t — 25

CHRISTMAS 1972 — MALAWI 3t — ADORATION OF THE KINGS - ORCAGNA — 26

MALAWI 35th ANNIVERSARY — 3T — LARGEMOUTH BLACK BASS — 27

RÉPUBLIQUE DU MALI — POSTES — 5F — SYNCERUS CAFFER — 28

RÉPUBLIQUE DU MALI — POSTES — 4F — 29

RÉPUBLIQUE DU MALI — 5F POSTES — DE DION-BOUTON 1894 — 30

RÉPUBLIQUE DU MALI — BOUC 2F POSTES — 31

RÉPUBLIQUE DU MALI — 5F POSTES — CHELORRHINA POLYPHEMUS FAB. — 32

RÉPUBLIQUE ISLAMIQUE DE MAURITANIE — POSTE AÉRIENNE — 50F — PASTEUR MARTIN LUTHER KING · 1929-1968 — DELRIEU — 33

MAURITIUS — 5c — PARADISE FLYCATCHER — COQ des BOIS — 34

Mauritius — BATARDÉ — 2 CENTS — 35

1869-1969 — GANDHI AS A LAW STUDENT IN LONDON — 2 cents — MAURITIUS — CENTENARY OF THE BIRTH OF GANDHI — 36

INTERNATIONAL CO-OPERATION YEAR 1965
CANADA
5
ANNÉE DE LA COOPÉRATION INTERNATIONALE 1965

1

SIR WILFRED GRENFELL
5
CANADA
POSTES POSTAGE

2

CANADA
5
POSTES · POSTAGE

3

CHURCHILL
CANADA

4

INTER-PARLIAMENTARY UNION INTERPARLEMENTAIRE 1965
CANADA
5

5

CANADA
3c
CHRISTMAS NOËL

5

OTTAWA
1865 1965
5
CANADA

7

ALOUETTE II
5
CANADA POSTES · POSTAGE

8

CANADA
5
HIGHWAY SAFETY · SÉCURITÉ ROUTIÈRE

9

5
LONDON CONFERENCE CONFÉRENCE DE LONDRES 1866
MAY 28
CANADA

10

PEACEFUL USES · UTILISATIONS PACIFIQUES
CANADA 5

11

COMMONWEALTH PARLIAMENTARY ASSOCIATION
CANADA 5

1

CANADA
3
CHRISTMAS · NOËL

13

POSTES POSTAGE
6
CANADA

14

POSTES POSTAGE
$1
CANADA

15

CANADA
POSTES POSTAGE
expo67
5

16

VOTE FOR WOMEN · LA FEMME
5
5
1917-1967 CANADA POSTAGE

17

5 POSTES POSTAGE
RETURN ADDRESSES
1867 1967
CANADA
IMPORTANT

18

POSTES · POSTAGE 5
CANADA
1867 1967

19

PAN-AMERICAN GAMES
CANADA
5
JEUX PAN-AMERICAINS
WINNIPEG 1967

20

CANADA
5
ANNIVERSARY ANNIVERSAIRE
THE CANADIAN PRESS · LA PRESSE CANADIENNE

21

GOVERNOR-GENERAL 1959 1967 GOUVERNEUR GÉNÉRAL
CANADA 5

22

CHRISTMAS NOËL
3
CANADA

23

CANADA
5

2

CANADA METEOROLOGY
5
MÉTÉOROLOGIE
1768 1968

25

5
Narwhal Narval
Monodon monoceros
CANADA

26

CANADA
POSTES POSTAGE
5
HENRI BOURASSA
1868 1952

27

INTERNATIONAL HYDROLOGICAL DECADE 1965-1974 DÉCENNIE HYDROLOGIQUE INTERNATIONALE
5
CANADA

28

CANADA
5
1668
VOYAGE OF THE VOYAGE DU NONSUCH

2

The Globe
CANADA POSTES POSTAGE
5
HON. GEORGE BROWN 1818-1880

30

CANADA POSTAGE POSTES
5
JOHN M. CRAE 1872-1918

31

CHRISTMAS · NOËL
6
CANADA

32

Le curling Curling
CANADA
6

33

CANADA
15
1919
FIRST NON-STOP TRANSATLANTIC FLIGHT
LE PREMIER VOL TRANSATLANTIQUE SANS ESCALE

34

6
VINCENT MASSEY 1887-1967
GOVERNOR GOUVERNEUR GENERAL GÉNÉRAL 1952-1959
CANADA

35

CANADA 6
INTERNATIONAL LABOUR ORGANIZATION 1919 ORGANISATION INTERNATIONALE DU TRAVAIL
CANADA 6
1969

36

CANADA 6
CHRISTMAS · NOËL

37

CANADA
STEPHEN LEACOCK 1869-1944
POSTAGE POSTES
6

38

6
Canada
JEUX CANADIENS CANADA GAMES
6

200 ANNIVERSARY ANNIVERSAIRE
SIR ISAAC BROCK 1769-1812
CANADA
6

40

Canada
6

Canada
6
CENTENAIRE du MANITOBA CENTENNIAL 1870-1970

Canada
6
HENRY KELSEY
FIRST EXPLORER ON THE PLAINS
LE PREMIER EXPLORATEUR DES PRAIRIES

6
Louis Riel

UNITED NATIONS 25 ANNIVERSARY ANNIVERSAIRE DES NATIONS UNIES
Canada

Canada

1

2

3

4

5

6

7

8

9

10

1

12

13

14

15

16

17

18

19

20

21

22

23

24

25

26

27

28

29

30

31

32

33

34

35

36

37

38

39

40

41

42

43

44

ILLINOIS 1818 1968
6¢ U.S. POSTAGE
1

6¢
HEMISFAIR '68
2

6¢
LAW AND ORDER ★
UNITED STATES POSTAGE
3

Marquette EXPLORER
UNITED STATES
6
4

REGISTER & VOTE US 6
5

WALT DISNEY
UNITED STATES
6c
6

leif erikson
U.S. postage
6¢
7

UNITED STATES 6
POSTAGE
DANIEL BOONE 1734
8

UNITED STATES POSTAGE
5¢
ARKANSAS RIVER NAVIGATION
9

UNITED STATES 6¢
"BATTLE OF BUNKER'S HILL"
John Trumbull
AMERICAN ARTIST
10

CHEROKEE STRIP UNITED STATES
POSTAGE 6¢
11

WATERFOWL CONSERVATION
UNITED STATES 6¢
12

CHRISTMAS 6¢
JAN EYCK NATIONAL GALLERY OF ART
UNITED STATES
13

Chief Joseph–National Portrait Gallery
United States Postage 6¢
14

USA 20¢
UNITED STATES AIR MAIL
15

6¢
PLANT for more **BEAUTIFUL PARKS**
16

The American Legion
50 years
Veterans as Citizens
U.S. POSTAGE 6 CENTS
17

Grandma Moses
6¢ U.S. Postage
18

6¢
UNITED STATES
W.C. HANDY
Father of the Blues
19

JOHN WESLEY POWELL 1869 EXPEDITION
6¢ U.S. POSTAGE
20

In the beginning God...
APOLLO 8
SIX CENTS · UNITED STATES
21

ALABAMA 1819 1969
UNITED STATES 6¢
22

Pseudotsuga menziesii
XIth INTERNATIONAL BOTANICAL CONGRESS
6¢ UNITED STATES
BOTANICAL
23

U.S. 6¢ POSTAGE
DWIGHT D. EISENHOWER
24

1869 - 1969
UNITED STATES 6¢
PROFESSIONAL BASEBALL
25

10¢ AIR MAIL
UNITED STATES
FIRST MAN ON THE MOON
26

Christmas
UNITED STATES 6¢
27

UNITED STATES POSTAGE
SIX CENTS
AMERICAN PAINTING
WILLIAM M. HARNETT
28

FRESNO SEP 9
MAINE STATEHOOD
1820-1970
U.S. POSTAGE SIX CENTS
29

Stone Mountain Memorial
UNITED STATES 6 CENTS
30

GREAT NORTHWEST
1820 FORT SNELLING 1970
US 6¢
31

9¢
U.S. AIR MAIL
32

SAVE OUR SOIL
UNITED STATES · SIX CENTS
33

Christmas
6 U.S.
34

UNITED STATES POSTAGE 6 CENTS
UN
United Nations 25th Anniversary
35

NATIONAL CHILDREN'S
1620 THE LANDING OF THE PILGRIMS
U.S. POSTAGE 6 CENTS
36

UNITED STATES
TROUT
WILDLIFE CONSERVATION 8¢
37

6¢ US
DOUGLAS MacARTHUR
38

8 U.S.
ANTARCTIC TREATY 1961-1971
39

00

1

2

3

4

5

6

7

8

9

10

11

12

13

14

15

16

17

18

19

20

21

22

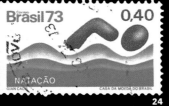

23

24

25

26

27

28

29

30

31

32

33

34

35

36

37

38

39

1

2

3

4

5

6

7

8

9

10

11

12

13

14

15

16

17

18

19

20

21

22

23

24

25

26

27

28

29

30

31

32

33

34

35

36

37

38

1

2

3

4

5

6

7

8

9

10

11

12

13

14

15

16

17

18

19

20

21

22

23

24

25

26

27

28

29

30

31

32

33

34

35

36

37

106

1

2

3

4

5

6

7

8

9

10

11

12

13

14

15

16

17

18

19

20

21

22

23

24

25

26

27

29

30

31

32

33

34

CUBA CORREOS
2
OMICRON
FLOTA PESQUERA
1965
1

CUBA CORREOS
2
EXPO67
EL HOMBRE COMO EXPLORADOR
6

1965
AÑOS
INTERNACIONALES
DE CALMA SOLAR
CUBA CORREOS
2
2

X JUEGOS CENTROAMERICANOS
Y DEL CARIBE
CUBA CORREOS / 1966
7
3

NAVIDAD 1966-67
CORREOS DE CUBA 1c
Cypripedium curlatlus
4

Cuba correos
Dia del Sello
3
1967
Victoria
5

Cuba CORREOS
XIX OLIMPIADA MUNDIAL · MEXICO · 1968
7

EXPO70
CUBA CORREOS
PLANEAMIENTO DE UNA VIDA MAS SATISFACTORIA
8

CUBA CORREOS 1970 2
30 ANIVERSARIO DE LA SOCIEDAD ESPELEOLOGICA DE CUBA
9

CUBA CORREOS 1970 3
TRINIDAD
TRINIDAD JORGE HERNANDEZ
CENTROS TURISTICOS INIT
10

CUBA CORREOS 1971 9
DIBUJOS INFANTILES
11

CUBA-CORREOS 1972 3
1o DE MAYO
VIVA LA ALIANZA OBRERO CAMPESINA
12

Cuba CORREOS 1972 13
ISABEL II FEDERICO MADRAZO
MUSEO DE LA CIUDAD DE LA HABANA
13

CUBA correos 3
DIA del SELLO 1973
14

1 CORREOS 1972 CUBA
RAZAS EQUINAS TARPAN
15

CUBA CORREOS 1972 5
P. Z. FABRE ELIZABETTA MASCAGNI
OBRAS DE ARTE DEL MUSEO NACIONAL
16

REPUBLICA DOMINICANA
Correos
ENTREGA ESPECIAL
25 CENTAVOS
17

REPUBLICA DOMINICANA 1c
PRO ESCUELA POSTAL Y TELEGRAFICA
COMUNICACIONES
18

CORREO AEREO REPUBLICA DOMINICANA 28c
1865 1965
CENTENARIO
DE LA UNION INTERNACIONAL
DE TELECOMUNICACIONES
19

REPUBLICA DOMINICANA
Por el hombre
del futuro
ayuda al
niño de Hoy
1c HOGAR ESCUELA
MES DE PROTECCION A LA INFANCIA
20

REPUBLICA DOMINICANA
CORREO AEREO 10c
Campana de la Navidad de América-1493
NAVIDAD 1971
21

REPUBLICA DOMINICANA
DIA MUNDIAL DE LA SALUD
CORREO AEREO
7c
EN EL CORAZON LATE LA SALUD
22

1ra EXPOSICION
FILATELICA NACIONAL
REPUBLICA DOMINICANA
1972
Santo Domingo
Junio 3-17
33c CORREO aereo
23

REPUBLIQUE D'HAITI
EXPOSITION UNIVERSELLE DE N.Y.
1964 1965
50 CENTIMES POSTES
I.K.NUHUIS ENSCHEDE
24

Republique D'HAITI
Culture Amulette
POSTE
AERIENNE
1·50
GOURDE
HARRISON AND SONS LTD 1965
25

REPUBLIQUE D'HAITI
COUPE DR. FRANÇOIS DUVALIER
22 JUIN
15 CENTIMES
CHAMPIONNAT DE FOOTBALL DES
CARAIBES DU 10 AU 22 JUIN 1966
26

REPUBLIQUE D'HAITI 0.25
GOURDE
POSTES
L'AN X
DE LA REVOLUTION DUVALIERISTE
27

REPUBLIQUE D'HAITI
L'EDUCATION PAR L'ALPHABETISATION
ABC
POSTE AERIENNE 0.50
28

REPUBLIQUE D'HAITI 60B 0.10
POSTES
L'EDUCATION PAR LA METHODE AUDIO-VISUELLE
29

REVOLTE GENERALE DES ESCLAVES DE
ST. DOMINGUE, NUIT DU 22 AOUT 1791
0.25 POSTES
REPUBLIQUE D'HAITI
HARRISON AND SONS LTD 1968
30

PARIS-1900
MARATHON
THEATO
FRANCE
REPUBLIQUE FRANÇAISE
2h. 59 45.0
0.10
DE GOURDE
RÉPUBLIQUE D'HAITI
31

NEDERLANDSE
ANTILLEN 30c
moises f.d.h. costegomez
1907-1966
32

NEDERLANDSE ANTILLEN 25 CENT
INTERNATIONALE
ARBEIDSORGANISATIE
1919-1969
33

ST. THERESIA PAROCHIE
ST.NICOLAAS ARUBA
1931-1971-40 JAAR 20c
NEDERLANDSE ANTILLEN
34

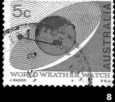

1

2

3

4

5

6

7

8

9

10

11

12

13

14

15

16

17

18

19

20

21

22

23

24

25

26

27

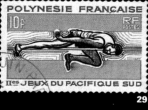

28

29

30

31

33

32

35

34

36

37

III

1

2

3

4

5

6

7

8

9

10

11

12

13

14

15

16

17

18

19

20

21

22

23

24

25

26

27

28

29

30

31

32

33

34

35

36

37

38

39

40

41

42

43

1965-1975
Captions to Plates 65-112

PLATE 65

ALBANIA:
1. 1965; Birds, 30q.
2. 1966; Luna 10, 20q.
3. 1969; Basketball, 25q.
4. 1973; Work and life, 3l.

ANDORRA (French):
5. 1974; Co-Princes, 1f.

ANDORRA (Spanish):
6. 1974; Europa, 8p.

AUSTRIA:
7. 1965; Reconstruction, 1s.80.
8. 1966; National Library, 2s.20.
9. 1966; Postal code, 1s.50.
10. 1965; Buildings, 1s.50.
11. 1966; Maria Ebner-Eschenbach, 3s.
12. 1965; University, 1s.50.
13. 1966; Wels Fair, 3s.
14. 1967; Ried Fair, 2s.
15. 1967; Brenner railway, 3s.50.
16. 1967; Trade Fairs, 2s.
17. 1968; Vorarlberg lace, 3s.50.
18. 1968; Silent Night, 2s.
19. 1968; Republic, 2s.
20. 1969; State Opera, 2s.
21. 1969; ILO, 2s.
22. 1969; Albertina art collection, 2s.
23. 1970; Antique clocks, 3s.50.
24. 1970; Famous operettas, 2s.
25. 1970; Carinthian Plebiscite, 2s.
26. 1971; Art treasures (second series), 1s.50.
27. 1972; Art exhibition, 2s.
28. 1971; Burgenland Province, 2s.
29. 1971; Nationalised industries, 2s.
30. 1972; Gurk diocese, 2s.
31. 1973; Drug abuse, 2s.
32. 1973; Aviation, 2s.
33. 1973; Franz Josef Land, 2s.50.
34. 1973; Trotting, 2s.
35. 1973; Scenery series, 5s.
36. 1973; Aqueduct, 2s.
37. 1974; Gendarmerie, 2s.
38. 1974; Fencing, 2s.50.

PLATE 66

BELGIUM:
1. 1965; Ghent flower show, 2f.
2. 1965; Belgian painters, 6f.
3. 1965; Belgian Farmers' Association, 50c.
4. 1965; Tourist publicity, 50c.
5. 1966; European chemical plant, 6f.
6. 1967; Nature conservation, 1f.
7. 1967; International Tourist Year, 6f.
8. 1968; National Interest, 3f.
9. 1968; Christmas, 1f.
10. 1969; Aulne Abbey, 3f.

11. 1969; Public education, 3f.
12. 1969; First man on the moon, 6f.
13. 1969; National war invalids' works, 1f.
14. 1969; Philately for the young, 1f.
15. 1969; National Credit Society, 3f.50.
16. 1970; Nature conservation, 7f.
17. 1970; Clock tower, Virton, 2f.50.
18. 1970; National Housing Society, 3f.50.
19. 1971; Royal Touring Club, 3f.50.
20. 1971; Automatic telephone service, 1f.50.
21. 1971; Tournai Cathedral, 7f.
22. 1971; World Telecommunications Day, 7f.
23. 1971; Antarctic Treaty, 10f.
24. 1971; King Baudouin, 9f.
25. 1971; Historic towns, 2f.50.
26. 1971; Celebrities, 3f.50.
27. 1971; Federation of Belgian industries, 3f.50.
28. 1972; Road Safety, 3f.50.
29. 1971; Persian Empire, 7f.
30. 1972; International Book Year, 7f.
31. 1971; Motor Show, 2f.50.
32. 1972; Tourist publicity (10th issue), 2f.50.
33. 1972; Stamp exhibition, 3f.50.
34. 1973; Stamp Day, 4f.50.
35. 1972; International Railways Union, 7f.
36. 1973; International Fair, 4f.50.
37. 1973; VAB motoring organisation, 5f.
38. 1972; Booklet definitive, 1f.50.
39. 1975; Ghent flower show, 5f.

PLATE 67

BULGARIA:
1. 1965; Agricultural products, 3st.
2. 1965; Civil aviation, 2st.
3. 1966; Ancient monuments, 1st.
4. 1966; April Uprising, 10st.
5. 1969; Stamp exhibition, 40st.
6. 1967; Tourism, 1st.
7. 1968; Air, 1l.
8. 1969; Stamp exhibition, 5st.
9. 1969; Children's Book Week, 1st.
10. 1966; Tourist resorts, 20st.
11. 1969; Silistra, 13st.
12. 1971; Industrial buildings, 2st.

CYPRUS:
13. 1966; Pictorial series, 10m.
14. 1970; Christmas, 25m.
15. 1971; 14th-century fresco, 40m.
16. 1971; Tourism, 25m.
17. 1974; Turkish zone of Cyprus, 10m.

CZECHOSLOVAKIA:
18. 1965; Spartacist Games, 30h.
19. 1965; Sports events, 60h.
20. 1965; Anniversaries and events, 60h.
21. 1965; Czech towns, 10h.
22. 1965; Prague Castle, 30h.
23. 1965; Medicinal plants, 60h.
24. 1966; North American Indians, 1k.40.
25. 1966; Game animals, 40h.

26. 1967; EXPO, 1k.
27. 1968; Commemorations series, 30h.
28. 1968; Cultural personalities, 40h.
29. 1969; Anniversaries, 60h.
30. 1969; Tatra National Park, 1k.60.
31. 1968; President Svoboda, 30h.
32. 1972; 30th anniversaries, 60h.
33. 1972; Cultural anniversaries, 40h.
34. 1971; Regional buildings, 5k.40.
35. 1974; Musical instruments, 30h.
36. 1971; Arms, 60h.
37. 1971; UNICEF, 80h.
38. 1974; Children's Day, 60h.
39. 1974; UPU, 1k.
40. 1974; Slovak national uprising, 30h.
41. 1974; Bratislava Music Academy, 30h.
42. 1974; Slovak collective, 30h.
43. 1975; International Women's Year, 30h.

PLATE 68

DENMARK:
1. 1966; Almshouses, 50ö.
2. 1967; EFTA, 80ö.
3. 1967; Copenhagen, 50ö.
4. 1967; Royal wedding, 50ö.
5. 1967; H. Sonne, 60ö.
6. 1968; Esbjerg harbour, 30ö.
7. 1968; Industries, 50ö.
8. 1969; Danish flag, 60ö.
9. 1969; Niels Stensen, 1k.
10. 1969; Abstract, 60ö.
11. 1970; North Schleswig, 60ö.
12. 1970; Giro, 60ö.
13. 1971; Women's association, 80ö.
14. 1971; Refugees, 60ö.
15. 1971; Hans Egede, 1k.
16. 1971; Sports, 90ö.
17. 1971; Georg Brandes, 90ö.
18. 1972; Meteorological Office, 1k.20.
19. 1972; King Frederick IX, 60ö.
20. 1972; Railways, 70ö.
21. 1972; Nature protection, 1k.
22. 1972; Homes for disabled, 70ö. + 10ö.
23. 1972; WHO, 2k.
24. 1972; Danish Theatre, 70ö.
25. 1972; Construction, 40ö.
26. 1972; Architecture, 60ö.
27. 1973; Johannes Jensen, 90ö.
28. 1973; Factory Act, 50ö.
29. 1973; Veterinary College, 1k.
30. 1973; Jutland Horticultural Society, 60ö.
31. 1973; Frescoes, 70ö.
32. 1974; Pantomime Theatre, 100ö.

FINLAND:
33. 1966; Red Cross, 15p. + 3p.
34. 1966; UNICEF, 15p.
35. 1967; Windmill, 40p.
36. 1967; Mannerheim statue, 40p.
37. 1967; Paper industry, 40p.

38. 1967; Martin Luther, 40p.
39. 1968; Wood-processing, 40p.
40. 1967; Independence, 40p.
41. 1968; WHO, 40p.
42. 1968; Saima Canal, 40p.
43. 1968; National defence, 40p.
44. 1968; Students' Union, 40p.
45. 1969; Schools Board, 40p.
46. 1970; Aurora Society, 50p.
47. 1972; Costumes, 50p.
48. 1973; President K. Kallio, 60p.
49. 1971; Post bus, 25p.
50. 1973; Paddling championships, 60p.
51. 1975; Definitive, 70p.

PLATE 69

FRANCE:
1. 1965; Youth clubs, 25c.
2. 1965; Friendship, 60c.
3. 1965; Philatelic Societies Congress, 40c.
4. 1965; Tourist publicity, 60c.
5. 1965; Reunion, 30c.
6. 1965; Aviation School, 25c.
7. 1965; French satellite, 30c. + 60c.
8. 1966; Chess festival, 60c.
9. 1966; History of France, 60c.
10. 1967; European Broadcasting Union, 40c.
11. 1967; Winter Olympics, 60c.
12. 1967; Trans-Atlantic flight, 40c.
13. 1967; R. Esnault-Pelterie, 60c.
14. 1967; Orleans Flower Show, 40c.
15. 1967; Marie Curie, 60c.
16. 1967; Lions International, 40c.
17. 1968; A. R. Le Sage, 40c.
18. 1968; Valréas, 60c.
19. 1968; Louis XV, 25c.
20. 1969; République, 40c.
21. 1969; Nuclear submarine, 70c.
22. 1970; Handball, 80c.
23. 1971; 'Marianne', 50c.
24. 1971; Oceanexpo, 80c.
25. 1971; Europa, 50c.
26. 1972; Tourist publicity, 1f.
27. 1972; Blood donors, 40c.
28. 1972; Postal code, 30c.
29. 1973; Masonic emblem, 90c.
30. 1974; French Art, 2f.
31. 1973; Radio link, 1f.
32. 1973; Molière, 1f.
33. 1974; Turbotrain, 60c.
34. 1974; Lifeboat, 90c.

UNESCO:
35. 1966; Open book, 60c.

PLATE 70

GERMANY (West):
1. 1965; Transport exhibition, 5pf.
2. 1964–9; German architecture, 10pf.
3. 1964–9; German architecture, 1Dm.
4. 1966; UNICEF, 30pf.
5. 1966; W. von Siemens, 30pf.
6. 1967; Europa, 30pf.
7. 1967; Churches Day, 30pf.
8. 1968; Scientific discoveries (third series), 10pf.
9. 1968; Sir Winston Churchill, 10pf.
10. 1968; Europa, 30pf.
11. 1968; Dr. Adenauer, 30pf.
12. 1968; Karl Marx, 30pf.
13. 1969; War graves, 30pf.

14. 1968; The Mastersingers, 30pf.
15. 1969; Airmail, 20pf.
16. 1969; Nature protection, 50pf.
17. 1969; Protestant Congress, 30pf.
18. 1969; Radio exhibition, 30pf.
19. 1969; Stamp centenary, 30pf.
20. 1969; Brine pipeline, 20pf.
21. 1970; Birth centenaries, 10pf.
22. 1970; Humanitarian relief funds, 10pf. + 5pf.
23. 1970; Stamp exhibition, 30pf.
24. 1970; Baron H. von Münchhausen, 20pf.
25. 1970; Tourism, 30pf.
26. 1970; Nord–Ostsee Canal, 20pf.
27. 1970; Voluntary relief services, 30pf.
28. 1970–73; President Heinemann, 30pf.
29. 1971; German Reich, 30pf.
30. 1971–3; Accident prevention, 100pf.
31. 1971; New Road traffic regulations, 5pf.
32. 1971; Albrecht Dürer, 30pf.
33. 1972; German postal museum, 40pf.
34. 1972; K. Schumacher, 40pf.
35. 1972; Book Year, 40pf.
36. 1972; Catholic synod, 40pf.
37. 1973; Stamp exhibition, 70pf. + 35pf.
38. 1972; Heinrich Heine, 40pf.
39. 1973; INTERPOL, 40pf.
40. 1973; World Meteorological Organisation, 30pf.
41. 1973; Europa, 40pf.
42. 1973; Environment, 25pf.
43. 1973; Broadcasting, 30pf.
44. 1973; Tourism, 40pf.
45. 1973; Humanitarian relief funds, 70pf. + 35pf.
46. 1975; Ice Hockey Championships, 50pf.

PLATE 71

GERMANY (West Berlin):
1. 1964–9; German architecture, 30pf.
2. 1967; Art treasures, 50pf.
3. 1969; Post office, 20pf.
4. 1969; Anniversaries, 50pf.
5. 1971; H. von Helmholtz, 25pf.
6. 1972; Youth Welfare, 60pf. + 30pf.
7. 1972; Stamp Day, 20pf.
8. 1972; Berlin lakes, 10pf.
9. 1973; J. Quantz, 40pf.
10. 1975; Sauerbruch centenary, 50pf.

GERMANY (East):
11. 1965; Putten war victims, 25pf.
12. 1965; International Brigade in Spain, 5pf.
13. 1966; Youth Movement, 20pf.
14. 1967; Socialist Unity Party, 25pf.
15. 1967; Children's Day, 20pf.
16. 1967; Dresden gallery paintings, 30pf.
17. 1967; Playing-cards, 10pf.
18. 1967; Cultural places, 20pf.
19. 1968; Provincial costumes (third series), 20pf.
20. 1967; Buildings, 15pf.
21. 1968; Small game, 30pf.
22. 1968; Walter Ulbricht, 20pf.
23. 1968; Celebrities' anniversaries, 15pf.
24. 1968; Dresden gallery paintings (second series), 15pf.
25. 1968; Dams, 25pf.
26. 1969; Dresden gallery paintings (third series), 20pf.
27. 1968; Young pioneers, 15pf.
28. 1971; Paris Commune, 20pf.
29. 1971; Art treasures, 30pf.
30. 1969; Aircraft, 30pf.
31. 1972; Monument, 25pf.

32. 1971; Fairy-tales (sixth series), 10pf.
33. 1973; Buildings, 40pf.
34. 1973; Cultural anniversaries, 5pf.
35. 1975; Children's Spartakiad, 35pf.

GIBRALTAR:
36. 1968; Christmas, 4d.
37. 1967; Ships series, 4d.
38. 1971; Scenery definitive, 3p.

PLATE 72

GREAT BRITAIN:
1. 1965; Sir Winston Churchill, 1s. 3d.
2. 1965; Parliament, 6d.
3. 1965; Salvation Army, 3d.
4. 1965; Joseph Lister, 4d.
5. 1965; Commonwealth Arts Festival, 6d.
6. 1965; Battle of Britain, 1s. 3d.
7. 1965; Post Office Tower, 3d.
8. 1965; UNO, 3d.
9. 1965; ITU, 1s. 6d.
10. 1966; Robert Burns, 4d.
11. 1966; Westminster Abbey, 3d.
12. 1966; Landscapes, 6d.
13. 1966; Football, 1s. 3d.
14. 1966; Technology, 1s. 6d.
15. 1966; Battle of Hastings, 1s. 3d.
16. 1967; EFTA, 1s. 6d.
17. 1967; Wild flowers, 9d.
18. 1967; Paintings, 9d.
19. 1967; *Gipsy Moth IV*, 1s. 9d.
20. 1967; Machin definitive, 8d.
21. 1967; Discoveries and inventions, 4d.
22. 1967; Christmas, 1s. 6d.
23. 1968; Bridges, 4d.
24. 1968; Anniversaries, 1s. 9d.
25. 1968; Christmas, 4d.
26. 1969; Ships, 5d.
27. 1969; Concorde, 1s. 6d.
28. 1969; Anniversaries, 1s. 9d.
29. 1970; Machin definitive, 20p.
30. 1969; Architecture, 1s. 6d.
31. 1969; Mahatma Gandhi, 1s. 6d.
32. 1969; Post office technology, 1s.
33. 1969; Christmas, 1s. 6d.
34. 1970; Anniversaries, 1s. 6d.
35. 1970; Commonwealth Games, 1s. 6d.
36. 1970; Rural architecture, 1s. 6d.
37. 1970; Philympia 70, 1s. 6d.
38. 1970; Christmas, 5d.
39. 1971; Paintings, 3p.
40. 1971; Literary anniversaries, 5p.
41. 1971; Postage due, 2p.

PLATE 73

GREAT BRITAIN:
1. 1971; Anniversaries, 3p.
2. 1971; Modern universities, 3p.
3. 1972; Polar explorers, 3p.
4. 1971; Christmas, 2½p.
5. 1972; Anniversaries, 3p.
6. 1972; Village churches, 9p.
7. 1972; Christmas, 2½p.
8. 1972; Broadcasting, 5p.
9. 1972; Silver wedding, 20p.
10. 1973; European communities, 3p.
11. 1973; Tree, 9p.
12. 1973; Explorers, 7½p.
13. 1973; County cricket, 3p.
14. 1973; Paintings, 9p.

15. 1973; Parliament, 10p.
16. 1973; Royal wedding, 20p.
17. 1973; Inigo Jones, 2 × 3p.
18. 1973; Christmas, 3½p.
19. 1974; Fire Service, 5½p.
20. 1974; UPU, 8p.
21. 1974; Sir Winston Churchill, 5½p.
22. 1974–5; Charity, 4½p. + 1½p.
23. 1974–5; European Architectural Heritage Year, 7p.

NORTHERN IRELAND:
24. 1971; Decimal currency, 3p.

SCOTLAND:
25. 1971; Elizabethan series, 7½p.

WALES AND MONMOUTHSHIRE:
26. 1971; Elizabethan definitive, 5p.

GUERNSEY:
27. 1971; Pictorial series, 3p.
28. 1973; Air, 3p.
29. 1974; Militia, 3p.

JERSEY:
30. 1971; Pictorial definitive, 2½p.
31. 1973; Aviation history, 3p.
32. 1975; Nineteenth-century farming, 3p.

ISLE OF MAN:
33. 1971; Queen Elizabeth definitive, 2½p.
34. 1973; Grand Prix, 3p.

PLATE 74

GREECE:
1. 1965; El Greco, 2d.50.
2. 1966; Art, 3d.
3. 1968; Exhibition, 10l.
4. 1969; NATO, 4d.50.
5. 1969; Athletics, 5d.
6. 1970; The Labours of Hercules, 1d.50.
7. 1970; Telecommunications, 4d.50.
8. 1970; Nature conservation, 8d.
9. 1971; War of Independence, 2d.
10. 1971; Europa, 5d.
11. 1972; Regional costumes, 4d.50.
12. 1972; Monasteries and churches, 1d.
13. 1972; Olympics, 4d.50.
14. 1972; Mythology (second series), 4d.50.
15. 1974; Europa, 3d.

HUNGARY:
16. 1966; Twin space flights, 20fi.
17. 1967; Danube Commission, 30fi.
18. 1966; Medals and orders, 20fi.
19. 1965; Liberation, 20fi.
20. 1966; Air, 50fi.
21. 1967; Angling, 20fi.
22. 1968; Communist Party, 40fi.
23. 1969; Athenaeum Press, 2fo.
24. 1969; Space, 60fi.
25. 1969; Hungarian Republic, 40fi.
26. 1970; Cars, 1fo.50.
27. 1972; Monuments, 3fo.

ICELAND:
28. 1965; Surtsey Island, 2k.
29. 1965; Europa, 8k.
30. 1966; Landscapes, 2k.50.
31. 1968; Right-hand traffic, 4k.
32. 1970; Manuscripts, 30k.

33. 1970; Arts Festival, 50k.
34. 1973; Nordic countries, 10k.

PLATE 75

IRELAND:
1. 1965; ITU, 3d.
2. 1966; Easter Rising, 5d.
3. 1967; Fenian Rising, 5d.
4. 1967; Canadian centennial, 5d.
5. 1968; Countess Markievicz, 3d.
6. 1969; Parliament, 6d.
7. 1970; Cork Yacht Club, 4d.
8. 1969–70; Stag, 9d.
9. 1970; Kevin Barry, 6d.
10. 1974; Winged Ox, 12p.
11. 1972; World Health Day, 2½p.
12. 1973; Irish Art, 5p.
13. 1973; Christmas, 3½p.
14. 1973; Ploughing, 5p.
15. 1975; Castletown Hunt, 7p.

ITALY:
16. 1965; Sailing, 70l.
17. 1965; Dante, 90l.
18. 1965; Night airmail, 40l.
19. 1966; Olive tree, 170l.
20. 1966; Republic, 90l.
21. 1966; Battle of Bezzecca, 90l.
22. 1966; Giotto, 40l.
23. 1967; Cycle race, 40l.
24. 1967; National parks, 20l.
25. 1967; Luigi Pirandello, 40l.
26. 1967; Francesco Borromini, 90l.
27. 1967; Oath of Pontida, 20l.
28. 1967; Two Worlds Festival, 40l.
29. 1967; U. Giordano, 20l.
30. 1968; Coin of Syracuse, 200l.
31. 1968; Cycling, 25l.
32. 1968; Victory, 90l.
33. 1970; United Nations, 90l.
34. 1972; Don Orione, 90l.
35. 1974; Coin of Syracuse, 125l.
36. 1971; Grazia Deledda, 50l.
37. 1971; UNICEF, 90l.
38. 1973; Military aviation, 90l.
39. 1973; 'Save Venice', 20l.
40. 1975; Holy Year, 40l.

PLATE 76

LIECHTENSTEIN:
1. 1967; Patrons of the Churches, 30r.
2. 1969; Pioneers of philately (second series), 80r.

LUXEMBOURG:
3. 1965; Grand Duke Jean, 3f.
4. 1967; NATO, 6f.
5. 1967; Pottery, 3f.
6. 1968; Olympic Games, 6f.
7. 1969; Joseph Kutter, 6f.
8. 1973; Europa, 8f.
9. 1969; Tourism, 3f.

MALTA:
10. 1965; Photogravure definitive, 1s.
11. 1965; Dante, 2d.
12. 1965; Great Siege, 2d.
13. 1965; Christmas, 1d.
14. 1966; Christmas, 4d.
15. 1967; George Cross, 2d.
16. 1967; Melchior Gafa, 2d.
17. 1967; Christmas 1d.

18. 1967; Royal visit, 2d.
19. 1968; Human Rights, 2d.
20. 1968; Grand Master La Valette, 1d.
21. 1968; Christmas, 1s. 4d.
22. 1969 International Labour Organisation, 2d.
23. 1969; Independence, 5d.
24. 1970; United Nations, 5d.
25. 1972; Decimal coins, 5m.
26. 1972; Christmas, 3c. + 1c.
27. 1973; Industry, 8m.
28. 1974; Air, 7c.5.
29. 1974; Europa, 7c.5.

MONACO:
30. 1960–71; Views, 40c.
31. 1967; Grand Prix, 1c.
32. 1967; Lions International, 60c.
33. 1970; Animals, 80c.
34. 1972; Christmas, 90c.
35. 1973; Europa, 90c.
36. 1973; Drugs campaign, 90c.
37. 1975; Flowers, 1.10fr.

PLATE 77

NETHERLANDS:
1. 1965; Resistance, 7c.
2. 1965; ITU, 40c.
3. 1965; Marine Corps, 18c.
4. 1966; Europa, 40c.
5. 1966; Child Welfare, 20c. + 10c.
6. 1967; Delft Technological University, 20c.
7. 1968; Postal cheque and clearing service, 20c.
8. 1968; National anthem, 20c.
9. 1968; Aviation, 45c.
10. 1969; Statute of the Kingdom, 25c.
11. 1969; BENELUX, 25c.
12. 1969; Desiderius Erasmus, 25c.
13. 1970; Civil Code, 25c.
14. 1970; Expo 70, 25c.
15. 1970; Inter-Parliamentary Union, 25c.
16. 1970; United Nations, 45c.
17. 1970; Child Welfare, 25c. + 10c.
18. 1971; 14th Netherlands census, 15c.
19. 1971; Child Welfare, 15c. + 10c.
20. 1969–73; Queen Juliana, 50c.
21. 1972; Delta Plan, 20c.
22. 1972; J. R. Thorbecke, 30c.
23. 1972; Olympic Games, 30c.
24. 1972; Netherlands flag, 20c.
25. 1972; Red Cross, 45c. + 25c.
26. 1972; Child Welfare, 25c. + 15c.
27. 1973; Tulips, 25c.
28. 1973; Events and anniversaries, 25c.
29. 1973; Queen Juliana, 40c.
30. 1974; Council of Europe silver jubilee, 45c.
31. 1975; Schweitzer centenary, 50c.

NORWAY:
32. 1965; Europa, 90ö.
33. 1967; EFTA, 90ö.
34. 1967; Johanne Dybwad, 60ö.
35. 1968; A. O. Vinje, 50ö.
36. 1968; Deaconess House, 65ö.
37. 1969–70; King Olav V, 1k.
38. 1968; Nobel prizewinners, 65ö.
39. 1969; Road Safety, 65ö.
40. 1971; Tønsberg, 100ö.
41. 1971; Hans Nielsen Hauge, 70ö.
42. 1971; Folk tales, 50ö.
43. 1972; Stamp centenary, 1k.
44. 1972; Unification relics, 80ö.
45. 1972; King Haakon VII, 1k.20.

46. 1972; Folk tales, 50ö.
47. 1973; King Olav V, 1k.
48. 1973; Mountain flowers, 1k.
49. 1973; Leprosy bacillus, 1k.

PLATE 78

POLAND:
1. 1965; Warsaw, 20g.
2. 1965; Forest animals, 50g.
3. 1966; European athletics, 90g.
4. 1966; Tourism, 1z.55.
5. 1967; Martyrdom and Resistance, 40g.
6. 1967; Protected plants, 4z.50.
7. 1972; Warsaw 60g. surcharged, 1z.50.
8. 1968; Paintings, 3z.40.
9. 1969; Pedigree dogs, 2z.50.
10. 1970; Olympic Academy, 60g.
11. 1971; Folk art, 20g.
12. 1968; Monument, 60g.
13. 1971; Ships, 60g.
14. 1971; UNICEF, 40g.
15. 1972; Olympics, 2z.50.
16. 1973; Copernicus, 1z.50.
17. 1973; Philatelic exhibition, 1z.

PORTUGAL:
18. 1965; Traffic, 1E.
19. 1965; ITU, 1E.
20. 1965; Gil Vicente, 1E.
21. 1966; Christian Congress, 1E.
22. 1966; National Revolution, 4E.
23. 1967; Lisnave shipyard, 3E.50.
24. 1967; Tombstones, 2E.
25. 1968; Stamp exhibition, 50c.
26. 1969; Pedro Alvares Cabral, 1E.
27. 1970; Porto oil refinery, 1E.
28. 1970; Expo 70, 5E.
29. 1970; Cities, centenaries, 1E.
30. 1970; Submarine telegraph cable, 1E.
31. 1970; Port wine industry, 3E.50.
32. 1971; Sculptors, 1E.
33. 1971; President Salazar, 1E.
34. 1972; World Heart Month, 1E.
35. 1972; Pictorial definitive 3E.
36. 1972; Camoëns, 1E.
37. 1973; For the child, 1E.
38. 1974; Europa, 1E.
39. 1974; UPU, 4E.50.

PLATE 79

ROMANIA:
1. 1965; Space achievements, 2l.40.
2. 1965; Botanical gardens, 30b.
3. 1966; Football, 55b.
4. 1966; Space achievements, 10b.
5. 1967; Cultural anniversaries, 10b.
6. 1968; Lakeside highway, 1l.75.
7. 1968; Paintings, 40b.
8. 1968; Fauna, 10b.
9. 1969; Frescoes, 10b.
10. 1971; Prince Neagoe Basarab, 60b.
11. 1970; Ancient coins, 60b.
12. 1973; Treasures, 6l.80.
13. 1973; Ceramics, 6l.80.
14. 1974; Ships, 4l.70.
15. 1974; Population, 2l.
16. 1974; Postage due, 2 × 50b.

RUSSIA:
17. 1966; Definitive, 3k.
18. 1965; 1905 Rebellion, 4k.

19. 1965; Schoolchildren's spartakiad, 4k.
20. 1967; Paintings, 16k.
21. 1967; Kremlin buildings, 12k.
22. 1965; Flowers, 1k.
23. 1967; October Revolution, 4k.
24. 1968; T. Antikainen, 6k.
25. 1969; I. Krylov, 4k.
26. 1970; Warships, 10k.
27. 1968; War Heroes, 4k.
28. 1972; Izhory factory, 4k.
29. 1972; Miners' Day, 4k.
30. 1973; Civil aviation, 6k.
31. 1974; Ice-skating, 6k.
32. 1974; Academy of Sciences, 10k.

PLATE 80

SAN MARINO:
1. 1966; Fish, 4l.
2. 1967; Flowers, 5l.
3. 1967; Fungi, 5l.
4. 1967; Gothic cathedrals, 40l.
5. 1970; Walt Disney, 1l.
6. 1972; Botticelli, 50l.

SPAIN:
7. 1965; Arms, 5p.
8. 1965; Tourist series, 25c.
9. 1966; World Stamp Day, 1p.
10. 1966; Forestry Congress, 1p.
11. 1967; Radiology Congress, 1p.50.
12. 1968; Famous Spanish women, 1p.20.
13. 1969; Rock of Gibraltar, 2p.
14. 1969; Explorers and colonisers of America (9th series), 6p.
15. 1969; Provincial costumes, 6p.
16. 1970; Stamp Day, 3p.50.
17. 1970; Spanish writers, 50c.
18. 1970; United Nations, 8p.
19. 1970; Ripoli monastery, 5p.
20. 1971; Fauna, 8p.
21. 1971; Airmail, 15p.
22. 1971; Christmas, 8p.
23. 1971; Holy Year of Compostella, 10p.
24. 1972; Spanish celebrities, 50p.
25. 1972; Int. Book Year, 2p.
26. 1972; Stamp Day, 7p.
27. 1972; Flora, 5p.
28. 1972; Olympic Games, 5p.
29. 1974; Fine Art Academy, 5p.
30. 1972; Castles (6th series), 5p.
31. 1972; Grand Lyceum Theatre, 8p.
32. 1972; Christmas, 8p.
33. 1973; Architects, 10p.
34. 1973; Europa, 2p.
35. 1973; World Stamp Day, 2p.
36. 1973; International High Dams Commission, 8p.
37. 1973; Tourist series, 8p.
38. 1973; Santo Domingo de Silos Monastery, 8p.
39. 1973; Christmas, 8p.

PLATE 81

SWEDEN:
1. 1965; Post-horns, 20ö.
2. 1965; ITU, 60ö.
3. 1965; F. Brëmer, 25ö.
4. 1965; Nobel prizewinners, 40ö.
5. 1966; Nathan Soderblom, 60ö.
6. 1966–7; Pictorial series, 3k.50.
7. 1967; EFTA, 70ö.

8. 1967–70; Pictorial set, 1k.
9. 1967; King Gustav VI Adolf, 70ö.
10. 1968; Wild flowers, 2 × 45ö.
11. 1968; Bank of Sweden, 45ö.
12. 1968; People's College, 45ö.
13. 1969; Warship Vasa, 55ö.
14. 1970; Seals, 3k.
15. 1970; Vita Vidder, 45ö.
16. 1970; United Nations, 55ö.
17. 1971; Royal Palace, 80ö.
18. 1970; Nobel prizewinners, 55ö.
19. 1971; Refugees Campaign, 55ö.
20. 1971; Art treasures, 2 × 25ö.
21. 1971; Mail coach, 1k.20.
22. 1971; Gotland stonemasons art, 5ö. and 10ö.
23. 1971; Road Safety, 65ö.
24. 1971; Goose, 65ö.
25. 1971; Women's suffrage, 1k.
26. 1971; Royal Academy of Music, 85ö.
27. 1972; Cultural celebrities, 35ö.
28. 1972; 'Lapponia', 1k.40.
29. 1972; 18th-century art, 75ö.
30. 1972; King Gustav VI Adolf, 75ö.
31. 1972; Christmas, 45ö.
32. 1972; Nobel prizewinners, 1k.
33. 1973; Royal Theatre, 1k.
34. 1973; Mail coaches, 70ö.
35. 1973; Gotland's picture stones, 10ö.
36. 1973; Landscapes, 50ö.
37. 1973; Trade Unions, 1k.40.
38. 1973; IMO–WMO centenary, 65ö.
39. 1973; Nordic museum centenary, 75ö.
40. 1973; King Gustav VI Adolf, 1k.
41. 1973; Christmas, 45ö.
42. 1974; Winter sports, 65ö.
43. 1974; Anniversaries, 75ö.
44. 1974; King Carl XVI Gustav, 75ö.
45. 1975; Rok Stone, 2k.

PLATE 82

SWITZERLAND:
1. 1965; Pro Juventute, 50c. + 10c.
2. 1966; Pro Patria, 20c. + 10c.
3. 1966; Swiss Alps, 10c.
4. 1966; Pro Juventute, 10c. + 10c.
5. 1967; Pro Patria, 50c. + 10c.
6. 1967; Pro Juventute, 10c. + 10c.
7. 1968; Pro Patria, 50c. + 20c.
8. 1968; Publicity, 10c.
9. 1968; Pro Juventute, 20c. + 10c.
10. 1969; Publicity, 20c.
11. 1969; Europa, 50c.
12. 1969; Publicity, 30c.
13. 1969; Pro Patria, 50c. + 20c.
14. 1969; Celebrities, 50c.
15. 1970; Publicity, 20c.
16. 1970; Publicity, 10c.
17. 1970; Pro Juventute, 50c. + 20c.
18. 1970; Coil, 10c.
19. 1971; Publicity, 10c.
20. 1971; Europa, 50c.
21. 1971; Pro Patria, 20c. + 10c.
22. 1971; Swiss Alps, 30c.
23. 1971; Famous physicians, 30c.
24. 1971; Pro Juventute, 40c. + 20c.
25. 1972; Publicity, 30c.
26. 1972; Europa, 30c.
27. 1972; Pro Patria, 40c. + 20c.
28. 1972; Celebrities, 80c.
29. 1972; Pro Juventute, 40c. + 20c.
30. 1973; Publicity, 30c.
31. 1973; Europa, 40c.

32. 1973; Pro Patria, 40c. + 20c.
33. 1973; Pictorial series, 30c.
34. 1973; Publicity, 40c.
35. 1973; Pro Juventute, 40c. + 20c.
36. 1974; Europa, 40c.
37. 1974; Publicity, 40c.
38. 1974; UPU, 30c.
39. 1974; UPU, 80c.
40. 1974; Pro Patria, 40c. + 20c.
41. 1975; International Women's Year, 30c.

UNITED NATIONS:
42. 1969–72; UN emblem, 60c.
43. 1972; United Nations art, 80c.
44. 1973; Namibia, 60c.
45. 1969–72; Geneva headquarters, 40c.
46. 1972; Non-proliferation of nuclear weapons, 40c.

PLATE 83

TURKEY:
1. 1964–5; Kemal Atatürk, 150k.
2. 1965; Cultural celebrities, 130k.
3. 1966; Kemal Atatürk, 100k.
4. 1967; Air, 60k.
5. 1967; Birds, 60k.
6. 1967; Kemal Atatürk booklet pair (50k and 10k).
7. 1972; Equestrian statue, 25k.
8. 1967; Greetings card stamp, 10k.
9. 1968; Kemal Atatürk, 50k.
10. 1968; Red Crescent, 60k. + 10k.
11. 1969; Turkish economy, 100k.
12. 1969; Folk dances, 60k.
13. 1970; Kemal Atatürk, 50k.
14. 1970; Nature Conservation Year, 60k. + 10k.
15. 1970; Turkish National Assembly, 60k.
16. 1970; Regional co-operation, 60k.
17. 1971; Kemal Atatürk, 250k.
18. 1972; Kemal Atatürk, 175k.

VATICAN CITY:
19. 1965; Dante, 40l.
20. 1966; Christmas, 55l.
21. 1967; Apostolic Congress, 130l.
22. 1968; Pope Paul's visit to Colombia, 220l.
23. 1972; Bramante celebrations, 90l.
24. 1971; Racial Equality Year, 20l.
25. 1973; Teresa of Lisieux, 220l.

YUGOSLAVIA:
26. 1966; Pictorial series, 85p.
27. 1966; Children's Week, 30p.
28. 1966; UNESCO, 85p.
29. 1966; Coins, 50p.
30. 1967; Medicinal plants, 30p.
31. 1967; World's Fair, Montreal, 30p.
32. 1967–72; President Tito, 1d.25.
33. 1967; International Tourist Year, 30p.
34. 1967; New Year, 30p.
35. 1968; Medieval icons, 1d.
36. 1968; Obligatory tax, 10p.
37. 1968; National heroes, 50p.
38. 1968; New Year, 20p.
39. 1969; Ptuj, 50p.
40. 1970; Mosaics, 3d.25.
41. 1970; Dogs, 50p.
42. 1971; Views series, 30p.
43. 1972; Olympic Games 50p.
44. 1974; President Tito, 50p.

PLATE 84

ABU DHABI:
1. 1967; Palace, 1d.
2. 1970; Airport entrance, 60f.

ADEN (Kathiri State of Seiyun):
3. 1966; Sir Winston Churchill's paintings, 25f.

ADEN (Qu'aiti State in Hadhramaut):
4. 1966; World Cup, 15f.

ADEN (Mahra Sultanate of Qishn and Socotra):
5. 1967; Flag, 65f.

AFGHANISTAN:
6. 1970; Tourist publicity, 2a.
7. 1971; Red Crescent Day, 8a.
8. 1972; World Health Day, 9a.
9. 1975; Independence Day, 16a.

AJMAN;
10. 1967; Photogravure series, 70d.
11. 1967; President Kennedy, 20d.

BAHRAIN:
12. 1966; Photogravure series, 30f.
13. 1973; UPU, 150f.

BANGLADESH:
14. 1971; 10p. Pakistan stamp, overprinted for use in Bangladesh.
15. 1972; In memory of the martyrs, 20p.
16. 1973; Official overprint on 1t.
17. 1973; Pictorial series, 50p.

BHUTAN:
18. 1966; Fortress, 20ch.
19. 1973; Roses, 3n.

BRUNEI:
20. 1971; View of Brunei town, 50c.
21. 1973; Royal wedding, 50c.

BURMA:
22. 1968; Birds (second series), 15p.

CEYLON:
23. 1965; Colombo Municipal Council, 25c.
24. 1967; Galle Municipal Council, 25c.
25. 1967; Poya holiday system, 60c.
26. 1967; Girl Guides, 3c.
27. 1968; Holy Quran, 25c.
28. 1969; ILO, 5c.
29. 1969; Educational centenary, 35c.
30. 1970; Wildlife conservation, 50c.
31. 1970; Asian Productivity Year, 60c.
32. 1970; Establishment of United Front government, 10c.
33. 1972; World Health Day, 25c.
34. 1972; ECAFE, 85c.

PLATE 85

CHINA (People's Republic):
1. 1965; Chingkiang mountains, 8f.
2. 1965; Games, 8f.
3. 1967; Third Five-Year-Plan, 8f.

CHINA (Taiwan):
4. 1965; Double carp, $10.
5. 1968; Olympic Games, $8.

6. 1968; Scroll paintings, $8.
7. 1972; Winter Olympics, $5.

DUBAI:
8. 1966; Telephone exchange opening, 40 n.p.
9. 1966; Oil exploration, 15 n.p.
10. 1967; Currency surcharge, 25d.

FUJEIRA:
11. 1967; Butterflies, 25d.
12. 1970; Football, 70d.

HONG KONG:
13. 1968; Definitive series, 65c.
14. 1973; Elizabethan definitive, $1.30.
15. 1974; Chinese New Year, $1.30.
16. 1973; Hong Kong Festival, $1.

INDIA:
17. 1965–8; Definitive, 5p.
18. 1966; Pacific area Travel Association Conference, 15p.
19. 1966; G. K. Gokhale, 15p.
20. 1968; Opening of 100,000th post office, 20p.
21. 1968; Birds, 50p.
22. 1969; Airmail, 20p.
23. 1971; Census centenary, 20p.
24. 1971; Obligatory tax, 5p.
25. 1972; Bertrand Russell, 1r.45.
26. 1973; Stamp exhibition, 1r.45.

INDONESIA:
27. 1967; Thomas Cup, 12r.
28. 1967; Musical instruments, 1r.
29. 1967; Paintings, 5r.
30. 1969; ILO, 25r.
31. 1968; Special delivery, 15r.
32. 1969; Five-Year Development Plan, 20r.

WEST IRIAN:
33. 1968; Flora and fauna, 50s.

IRAN:
34. 1966; Muhammed Riza Pahlavi, 50d.
35. 1966; WHO, 10r.
36. 1971; Shah, 6r.
37. 1972; International Literacy Day, 2r.

PLATE 86

IRAQ:
1. 1965; 1920 Rebellion, 5f.
2. 1967; Costumes, 15f.
3. 1967; Tourist Year, 50f.
4. 1967; Scouts and Guides, 15f.
5. 1969; ILO, 5f.
6. 1970; Iraqi press, 15f.
7. 1970; Flowers, 10f.
8. 1969; Hajeer Year, 15f.
9. 1971; Army Day, 40f.
10. 1973; Harp, 10f.

ISRAEL:
11. 1965; Civic arms, 15a.
12. 1965–73; Civic arms, I£3.
13. 1966; New Year, 80a.
14. 1967; Memorial Day, 55a.
15. 1968; Exports, 30a.
16. 1968; Independence Day, 40a.
17. 1968; New Year, 35a.
18. 1969; Eighth Maccabiah Games, 60a.
19. 1970; Immigration, 30a.
20. 1969; Israeli ports, 30a.

21. 1969; New Year, 15a.
22. 1969; Civic arms (second series), 15a.
23. 1969; King David, I£3.
24. 1970; Nature reserves, 3a.
25. 1970; Agricultural college, 40a.
26. 1970; New Year, 15a.
27. 1971; New Year, 18a.
28. 1971; Hapoel Games, 50a.
29. 1971; Israeli Theatre, 50a.
30. 1971; Landscapes, 18a.
31. 1972; Educational development, 40a.
32. 1972; Art, 55a.
33. 1972; Feast of the Passover, 45a.
34. 1973; Stained-glass windows, I£1.
35. 1973; Independence Day, I£1.
36. 1973; New Year, 65a.

PLATE 87

JAPAN:
1. 1965; Radar station, 10y.
2. 1965; Postal museum, 10y.
3. 1965; Aso National Park, 10y.
4. 1965; Blood donors, 10y.
5. 1965; Census, 10y.
6. 1965; Conference, 30y.
7. 1965; Antarctic expedition, 10y.
8. 1966; Definitive, 65y.
9. 1966; Amakusa bridges, 15y.
10. 1966; Cancer Congress, 7y. + 3y.
11. 1966; New Year's greetings, 7y.
12. 1967; Philatelic Week, 15y.
13. 1967; Road Safety, 15y.
14. 1967; New Year's greetings, 7y.
15. 1967; National parks, 15y.
16. 1968; National treasures, 15y.
17. 1968; Hokkaido centenary, 15y.
18. 1968; Postal codes campaign, 15y.
19. 1968; National parks, 7y.
20. 1968; Correspondence Week, 50y.
21. 1968; New Year's greetings, 7y.
22. 1968; Savings promotion, 15y.
23. 1969; National treasures, 15y.
24. 1969; Road Safety, 15y.
25. 1969; Postal codes, 15y.
26. 1969; National parks, 15y.
27. 1969; New Year's greetings, 7y.
28. 1970; World's Fair, Osaka, 15y.
29. 1970; National parks, 15y.
30. 1970; Postal codes, 7y.
31. 1970; Girl Scouts, 15y.
32. 1970; New Year's greetings, 7y.
33. 1971–3; Pictorial series, 10y.
34. 1971; Japanese Theatre, 15y.
35. 1971; Afforestation campaign, 7y.
36. 1971; Postal services, 15y.
37. 1971; Antarctic Treaty, 15y.
38. 1971; Postal codes, 15y.
39. 1971; Scout jamboree, 15y.
40. 1972; Japanese Theatre, 20y.
41. 1971; Family conciliation, 15y.
42. 1972; National parks, 20y.
43. 1972; Railways, 20y.
44. 1972; Philatelic Week, 20y.
45. 1972; National parks, 20y.
46. 1972; Education, 20y.
47. 1972; Railways (second series), 20y.
48. 1973; National parks, 10y.

PLATE 88

JOHORE:
1. 1971; Butterflies, 1c.

JORDAN:
2. 1966; King Hussein, 1f.
3. 1973; 50th anniversary, 5f.
4. 1973; Book Year, 30f.
5. 1974; Art series, 50f.
6. 1972; United Nations, 20f.
7. 1973; Iranian monarchy, 30f.
8. 1874; King Hussein, 2f.
9. 1971; Arab League, 30f.

KEDAH:
10. 1965; Orchids, 15c.
11. 1971; Butterflies, 10c.

KELANTAN:
12. 1971; Butterflies, 15c.

KHMER REPUBLIC:
13. 1971; Telecommunications, 8f.

KOREA (South):
14. 1968; Flag, 7w.
15. 1968; Republic, 7w.
16. 1972; Olympic Games, 20w.
17. 1969; Flag, 7w.

KOREA (North):
18. 1965; Flowers, 4ch.
19. 1970; Political programme, 2ch.
20. 1969; Poultry, 10ch.
21. 1970; Mount Paekdu-san, 10ch.

KUWAIT:
22. 1968; Palestine Day, 45f.

INTERNATIONAL COMMISSION IN INDO-CHINA:
23. 1964; Indian stamp, overprinted ICC for use in Laos and Vietnam, 15p.

LAOS:
24. 1965; Hophabang, 10k.
25. 1966; Folklore, 25k.

LEBANON:
26. 1965; Butterflies, 300p.
27. 1973; Flowers, 25p.
28. 1965; Cedars of Friendship, 40p.
29. 1966; Tourism, 5p.

MACAO:
30. 1968; Pedro Cabral, 70a.

MALACCA:
31. 1971; Butterflies, 10c.

MALAYSIA:
32. 1965; National mosque, 20c.
33. 1965; Airport, 30c.
34. 1965; Birds series, 75c.
35. 1965; SEAP Games, 25c.
36. 1971; UNICEF, 15c.
37. 1973; Social security, 15c.
38. 1973; 10th anniversary, 15c.

MALDIVE ISLANDS:
39. 1965; President Kennedy, 1r.
40. 1970; United Nations, 1r.
41. 1968; Boy Scouts, 24l.

PLATE 89

MONGOLIA:
1. 1966; Wrestling, 60m.
2. 1966; Prehistoric animals, 15m.
3. 1970; World Cup, 10m.

MUSCAT AND OMAN:
4. 1966; Definitive, 5b.

NEGRI SEMBILAN:
5. 1965; Orchids, 6c.
6. 1971; Butterflies, 10c.

NEPAL:
7. 1966; Red Cross, 50p.
8. 1970; Asian Productivity Year, 1r.

OMAN:
9. 1970; Muscat and Oman, overprinted 'Sultanate of Oman', 1r.

PAHANG:
10. 1965; Orchids, 15c.
11. 1971; Butterflies, 2c.

PAKISTAN:
12. 1966; Health from herbs, 15p.
13. 1965; Blind Welfare, 15p.
14. 1967; Independence, 15p.
15. 1973; Copernicus, 20p.
16. 1973; RCD, 1r.25.
17. 1973; Constitution Week, 20p.
18. 1973; Bank, 1r.

PENANG:
19. 1965; Orchids, 10c.
20. 1971; Butterflies, 6c.

PERAK:
21. 1965; Orchids, 5c.
22. 1971; Butterflies, 15c.

PERLIS:
23. 1971; Butterflies, 20c.

PHILIPPINE ISLANDS:
24. 1967; Presidential sayings, 10c.
25. 1969; Leyte landing, 40c.
26. 1968; Concordia College, 70c.
27. 1969; President Emilio Aguinaldo, 70c.
28. 1969; TB relief, 10c. + 5c.
29. 1971; Philatelic Week, 5c.
30. 1973; J. L. Escoda, 15c.
31. 1973; Pedro Paterno, 1p.50.
32. 1974; Central Bank, 1p.50.

QATAR:
33. 1972; Sheikh Khalifa bin Hamad al-Thani, 75d.

RAS AL KHAIMA:
34. 1971; Apollo XIV, 3r.

RYUKYU ISLANDS:
35. 1968; Library Week, 3c.
36. 1969; New Year, 1½c.

SABAH:
37. 1965; Orchids, 5c.

SARAWAK:
38. 1971; Butterflies, 5c.

SAUDI ARABIA:
39. 1966; King Faisal series, 6p.
40. 1968; Tourism, 10p.

PLATE 90

SELANGOR:
1. 1965; Orchids, 6c.
2. 1971; Butterflies, 5c.

SHARJAH:
3. 1965; Birds, 30 n.p.
4. 1965; Portrait of Sheikh Saqr, obliterated, 16 n.p.

SINGAPORE:
5. 1967; National Day, 6c.
6. 1968; Sword dance, 5c.
7. 1971; Commonwealth heads of government meeting, 15c.
8. 1973; Flowers series, 10c.
9. 1973; SEAP Games, 15c.

SOUTH ARABIAN FEDERATION:
10. 1965; Federal flag, 250f.

SOUTHERN YEMEN:
11. 1968; Independence, 100f.

SRI LANKA:
12. 1972; Republic, 15c.
13. 1973; Bandaranaike Memorial Hall, 15c.

SYRIA:
14. 1966; Astarte and Tyche, 60p.
15. 1970; Industry and graph, $22\frac{1}{2}$p.
16. 1973; Children's Day, 15p.

THAILAND:
17. 1965; UPU, 50s.
18. 1970; Heroes and heroines, 1b.
19. 1972; National costumes, 50s.
20. 1972; King Bhumibol, 5b.
21. 1973; King Bhumibol, 20s.
22. 1973; Stamp exhibition, 2b.

TIMOR:
23. 1965; Military uniforms, $4.50.

TRENGGANU:
24. 1965; Orchids, 2c.
25. 1971; Butterflies, 5c.

UMM AL QIWAIN:
26. 1967; World's Fair, Montreal, 25d.
27. 1968; Mexico Olympic Games, 5R.

UNITED ARAB EMIRATES:
28. 1973; Clock tower, Dubai, 1d.

VIETNAM (South):
29. 1965; ICY, 1p.
30. 1968; Farmers, 10p.
31. 1969; Mobile post office, 3p.
32. 1969; ILO, 20p.
33. 1970; Reconstruction, 16p.
34. 1969; Vietnamese women, 20p.

VIETNAM (North):
35. 1967; Vietnamese fish, 20x.
36. 1968; Production and fighting paintings, 40x.

YEMEN ARAB REPUBLIC:
37. 1972; 10th anniversary of revolution, 21b.

MUTAWAKELITE KINGDOM OF YEMEN:
38. 1965; Sir Winston Churchill, 4b.

PEOPLE'S DEMOCRATIC REPUBLIC OF YEMEN:
39. 1974; UPU, 5f.

PLATE 91

ALGERIA:
1. 1966; Boy Scouts, 30c.
2. 1967–71; Emir Abd el Kader, 5c.

3. 1968; Algerian carpets, 70c.
4. 1969; Aid for flood victims, 95c. + 25c.

ANGOLA:
5. 1968; National revolution, 1E.
6. 1967; Civil and military orders, 2E.50.
7. 1968; Pedro Cabral, 2E.50.
8. 1970; Marshal Carmona, 2E.50.

ASCENSION:
9. 1966; BBC relay station, 6d.
10. 1971; Royal naval crests (third series), 9p.

BIAFRA:
11. 1968; Independence, 4d. + 2d. surcharge.

BOTSWANA:
12. 1966; Independence, 35c.
13. 1967; Birds series, 50c.

BURUNDI:
14. 1967; African art, 24f.
15. 1967; Air, 17f.
16. 1969; Red Cross, 4f. + 1f.
17. 1971; Animals, 10f.
18. 1968; Olympic Games, 26f.

CAMEROUN:
19. 1967; Fruits, 6f.
20. 1973; St. Teresa of Lisieux, 100f.

CAPE VERDE ISLANDS:
21. 1970; Marshal Carmona, 2E.50.

CENTRAL AFRICAN REPUBLIC:
22. 1965; Plant protection, 2f.
23. 1967; Aircraft, 1f.
24. 1967; Female coiffures, 5f.

CHAD:
25. 1966; Official, 5f.
26. 1965; Musical instruments, 2f.
27. 1969; Fish, 2f.

COMORO ISLANDS:
28. 1971; Tropical plants, 1f.

CONGO (Kinshasha):
29. 1969; Arms, 15s.
30. 1971; Insects, 10s.

CONGO (Brazzaville):
31. 1970; Flora and fauna, 3f.
32. 1971; Caterpillars, 40f.

DAHOMEY:
33. 1970; United Nations, 40f.
34. 1967; Flowers, 3f.
35. 1970; Bariba horsemen, 2f.

PLATE 92

EAST AFRICA:
1. 1966; Tourism, 30c.
2. 1966; Commonwealth Games, 30c.
3. 1968; Olympic Games, 50c.
4. 1969; Water transport, 50c.
5. 1969; Pope Paul's visit, 1s.50.
6. 1970; Satellite Earth Station, 30c.
7. 1970; Commonwealth Games, 2s.50.
8. 1971; Metric system, 30c.
9. 1971; Railway transport, 30c.
10. 1971; Rinderpest campaign, 70c.
11. 1971; Tanzanaian Independence anniversary, 30c.

12. 1972; UNICEF, 30c.
13. 1973; Boy Scouts, 70c.
14. 1972; IMO/WMO, 40c.
15. 1973; Interpol, 40c.
16. 1973; Kenya's Independence anniversary, 40c.
17. 1973; Zanzibar's revolution anniversary, 40c.

EGYPT:
18. 1969; Kiosk, Sultan Hassan's mosque, 55m.
19. 1971; President Nasser, 20m.
20. 1972; Aerospace Education Conference, 30m.
21. 1973; Ramadan festival, 10m.
22. 1973; Attack on Libyan airliner over Sinai, 110m.

INDIAN UN FORCE IN GAZA:
23. 1965; Indian stamp overprinted UNEF, 15p.

EQUATORIAL GUINEA:
24. 1970; Independence anniversary, 1p.50.

ETHIOPIA:
25. 1965; National and commercial banks, 60c.
26. 1975; Koka Dam, 40c.

FRENCH SOUTHERN AND ANTARCTIC TERRITORIES:
27. 1969; French polar expedition, 25f.

FRENCH TERRITORY OF THE AFARS AND ISSAS:
28. 1967; Fauna, 10f.

GABON:
29. 1973; St. Teresa of Lisieux, 30f.

GAMBIA:
30. 1966; Birds definitive, 2s. 6d.
31. 1971; Fish series, 1d.25.
32. 1969; Pioneer air services, 1s. 6d.

GHANA:
33. 1965; 2d. stamp surcharged 2p.
34. 1967; Pictorial definitive, 8 n.p.
35. 1973; 13th January Revolution, 3p.
36. 1973; WHO, 5p.

PLATE 93

GUINEA:
1. 1965; Guinean dances, 5f.
2. 1966; Flora and female head-dresses, 10f.
3. 1966; International Hydrological Decade, 100f.
4. 1966; UNICEF, 10f.
5. 1967; Masks, 60c.

IFNI:
6. 1965; Stamp Day, 1p.50.

IVORY COAST:
7. 1965; Birds, 75f.

KENYA:
8. 1966; Animals definitive, 5s.
9. 1971; Seashells, 5c.

LESOTHO:
10. 1967; Photogravure series, 25c.
11. 1971; Diamonds, 50c.

LIBERIA:
12. 1966; President Kennedy, 20c.
13. 1971; Ceremonial masks, 15c.
14. 1972; Olympic Games, 5c.

LIBYA:
15. 1965; ITU, 10m.
16. 1971; World Telecommunications Day, 35m.
17. 1972; Libyan arms, 70dh.
18. 1971; Kingdom of Libya obliterated, 35m.

MALAGASY REPUBLIC:
19. 1966; Insects, 1f.
20. 1967; Religious buildings, 5f.

MALAWI:
21. 1968; Birds series, 9d.
22. 1971; Antelope definitive, 1k.
23. 1973; Musical instruments, 3t.
24. 1973; Butterflies, 3t.
25. 1973; David Livingstone, 3t.
26. 1972; Christmas, 3t.
27. 1973; Angling Society, 3t.

MALI REPUBLIC:
28. 1965; Animals, 5f.
29. 1966; River fishing, 4f.
30. 1968; Veteran bicycles and motor cars, 5f.
31. 1969; Domestic animals, 2f.
32. 1967; Insects, 5f.

MAURITANIA:
33. 1968; Apostles of Peace, 50f.

MAURITIUS:
34. 1965; Birds definitive, 5c.
35. 1969; Fish, 2c.
36. 1969; Mahatma Gandhi, 2c.

PLATE 94

MOROCCO:
1. 1968; King Hassan, 10f.
2. 1973; King Hassan, 70f.

MOZAMBIQUE:
3. 1967; Military uniforms, 3E.
4. 1970; Marshal Carmona, 5E.
5. 1973; Yachting, 3E.
6. 1970; Rocks, minerals and fossils series, 3E.
7. 1965; Charity tax, 1E.

NIGER REPUBLIC:
8. 1967; Birds, 2f.

NIGERIA:
9. 1965–6; Kingfishers, 1s.
10. 1970; Civil War, 1s.
11. 1972; Arts Festival, 1s. 9d.
12. 1973; Docks, 25k.
13. 1973; All-Africa Games, 18k.
14. 1973; OAU, 18k.
15. 1973; Leprosy, 5k. + 2k.

PORTUGUESE GUINEA:
16. 1965; ITU, 2E.50.

RÉUNION:
17. 1971; Marianne stamp surcharged, 25f.

RHODESIA:
18. 1966; Independence, $\frac{1}{2}$d.
19. 1966; Tobacco, 9d.
20. 1966; Central African Airways, 5s.
21. 1967; Famous Rhodesians, 1s. 6d.
22. 1970; Decimal currency series, 2$\frac{1}{2}$c.
23. 1971; Birds, 8c.
24. 1971; Famous Rhodesians (fifth series), 15c.

25. 1972; Prevent pollution, 2$\frac{1}{2}$c.
26. 1972; Christmas, 13c.
27. 1973; IMO/WMO, 3c.
28. 1973; Responsible government, 2$\frac{1}{2}$c.

RWANDA REPUBLIC:
29. 1970; Vatican Council, 20c.
30. 1970; Quinine, 20c.
31. 1972; Birds, 20c.

ST. HELENA:
32. 1968; Tristan da Cunha, 4d.
33. 1968; Hospital, 10s.
34. 1970; Charles Dickens, 4d.
35. 1970; Military equipment, 4d.
36. 1970; British Red Cross, 6d.
37. 1974; Sir Winston Churchill, 5p.

ST. THOMAS AND PRINCE:
38. 1969; Vasco da Gama, 2E.50.

PLATE 95

SENEGAL:
1. 1966; Flowers, 45f.
2. 1966; Arms, 30f.
3. 1968; Marine crustacea, 10f.
4. 1971; Scout jamboree, 65f.

SEYCHELLES:
5. 1966; Sir Winston Churchill, 5c.
6. 1969; Pictorial series, 10c.

BRITISH INDIAN OCEAN TERRITORY:
7. 1968–70; Sea creatures, 30c.

SIERRA LEONE:
8. 1970; Diamonds, self-adhesive, 3$\frac{1}{2}$c.
9. 1972; Siaka Stevens, 10c.

SOMALIA:
10. 1966; Art, 1s.50.
11. 1968; Antelope, 1s.50.

SOUTH AFRICA:
12. 1965; Dutch Reformed Church, 2$\frac{1}{2}$c.
13. 1966; Republic, *se-tenant*, 1c.
14. 1966; Dr H. F. Verwoerd, 3c.
15. 1967; Martin Luther, 2$\frac{1}{2}$c.
16. 1968; President Fouché, 2$\frac{1}{2}$c.
17. 1965; ITU, 2$\frac{1}{2}$c.
18. 1968; General Hertzog, 2$\frac{1}{2}$c.
19. 1969; Pictorial definitive, 1c.
20. 1969; Games, 2$\frac{1}{2}$c.
21. 1969; Heart transplant, 2$\frac{1}{2}$c.
22. 1970; Water 70, 2$\frac{1}{2}$c.
23. 1969; Stamp centenary, 2$\frac{1}{2}$c.
24. 1970; Bible Society, 2$\frac{1}{2}$c.
25. 1971; Stamp exhibition, 5c.
26. 1971; Antarctic Treaty, 12$\frac{1}{2}$c.
27. 1971; Landing of British settlers, 2c.
28. 1972; Cats, 5c.
29. 1972; Dam, 4c.
30. 1972; Sheep, 4c.
31. 1973; University, 4c.
32. 1973; Electricity, 4c.
33. 1973; Wolraad Woltemade, 5c.
34. 1973; C. J. Langenhoven, 15c.
35. 1973; World Communications Day, 15c.
36. 1974; Tulbagh, 4c.
37. 1974; Broadcasting, 4c.
38. 1974; British settlers, 5c.
39. 1974; Burgerspond, 9c.
40. 1974; UPU centenary, 15c.
41. 1974; Definitive, 10c.

PLATE 96

SOUTH WEST AFRICA:
1. 1968; Swart commemoration, *se-tenant*, 3c.
2. 1970; Bible Society, 12$\frac{1}{2}$c.

SPANISH SAHARA:
3. 1973; Child Welfare, 7p.

SUDAN:
4. 1974; UPU, 10$\frac{1}{2}$p.

SWAZILAND:
5. 1969; Animals definitive, 1r.
6. 1975; Animals, 2E.

TANZANIA:
7. 1965; Flag, 10c.
8. 1967; Scorpion fish, Official, 1s.
9. 1973; Butterflies definitive, 2s.50.

TOGO:
10. 1965; Astronauts in space, 25f.
11. 1969; Red Cross Societies, 90f.
12. 1971; 'Apollo 14', 200f.
13. 1971; Tourism, 20f.

TRISTAN DA CUNHA:
14. 1965; Elizabethan series, 5s.
15. 1967; 4$\frac{1}{2}$d. definitive surcharged, 4d.
16. 1972; Flowering plants, $\frac{1}{2}$p.

TUNISIA:
17. 1967; National Day at Montreal World's Fair, 65m.
18. 1967; Tunisian history, 25m.
19. 1967; Republic, 25m.
20. 1968; WHO, 25m.
21. 1968; Fauna, 25m.
22. 1970; Musical instruments, 25m.
23. 1973; UNESCO Save Carthage campaign, 40m.
24. 1973; Pan-African festival of youth, 40m.
25. 1973; Road Safety, 30m.
26. 1973; 11th Poetry Festival, 60m.

UGANDA:
27. 1965; Birds definitive, 5s.
28. 1967; Commonwealth Parliamentary Association Conference, 1s.30.
29. 1969; Flowers series, 1s.

UPPER VOLTA:
30. 1971; Butterflies, 5f.

ZAIRE REPUBLIC:
31. 1972; President Mobutu, 3k.

ZAMBIA:
32. 1966; WHO headquarters, 3d.
33. 1968; Decimal currency definitive, 2n.
34. 1972; Christmas, 9n.
35. 1973; Dr. Livingstone, 9n.

ZANZIBAR:
36. 1967; Voluntary Workers Brigade, 2s.50.

PLATE 97

CANADA:
1. 1965; ICY, 5c.
2. 1965; Sir W. Grenfell, 5c.
3. 1965; National flag, 5c.
4. 1965; Sir Winston Churchill, 5c.
5. 1965; Inter-parliamentary Union, 5c.

6. 1965; Christmas, 5c.
7. 1965; Ottawa, 5c.
8. 1966; Canadian satellite, 5c.
9. 1966; Highway Safety, 5c.
10. 1966; London Conference, 5c.
11. 1966; Atomic energy, 5c.
12. 1966; Commonwealth Parliamentary Association Conference, 5c.
13. 1966; Christmas, 3c.
14. 1967–72; Elizabethan definitive, 6c.
15. 1967; Oilfield, $1.
16. 1967; World's Fair, Montreal, 5c.
17. 1967; Women's franchise, 5c.
18. 1967; Royal visit, 5c.
19. 1967; Canadian centennial, 5c.
20. 1967; Pan-American Games, 5c.
21. 1967; Canadian press, 5c.
22. 1967; Governor-General Vanier, 5c.
23. 1967; Christmas, 3c.
24. 1968; Wildlife, 5c.
25. 1968; Meteorological readings, 5c.
26. 1968; Wildlife, 5c.
27. 1968; H. Bourassa, 5c.
28. 1968; International Hydrological Decade, 5c.
29. 1968; Voyage of the *Nonsuch*, 5c.
30. 1968; George Brown, 5c.
31. 1968; John McCrae, 5c.
32. 1968; Christmas, 6c.
33. 1969; Curling, 6c.
34. 1969; Transatlantic flight, 15c.
35. 1969; Vincent Massey, 6c.
36. 1969; ILO, 6c.
37. 1969; Christmas, 6c.
38. 1969; Stephen Leacock, 6c.
39. 1969; Canadian Games, 6c.
40. 1969; Sir Isaac Brock, 6c.
41. 1970; Northwest Territory, 6c.
42. 1970; Manitoba, 6c.
43. 1970; Henry Kelsey, 6c.
44. 1970; Louis Riel, 6c.
45. 1970; United Nations, 15c.
46. 1970; Sir Oliver Mowat, 6c.

PLATE 98

CANADA:
1. 1970; Sir Alexander Mackenzie, 6c.
2. 1970; 'Group of Seven' artists, 6c.
3. 1971; Emily Carr, 6c.
4. 1971; Insulin, 6c.
5. 1971; Maple leaf, 7c.
6. 1971; Louis-Joseph Papineau, 6c.
7. 1971; Pierre Laporte, 7c.
8. 1970; Christmas, 15c.
9. 1970; Sir Donald Alexander Smith, 6c.
10. 1971; Sir Ernest Rutherford, 6c.
11. 1971; Copper mine, 6c.
12. 1971; British Columbia, 7c.
13. 1971; Census, 6c.
14. 1971; Christmas, 7c.
15. 1972; Skating, 8c.
16. 1972; Pictorial definitive, 2c.
17. 1972–3; Pictorial series, $1.
18. 1972; World Health Day, 8c.
19. 1972; Canadian Indians, 8c.
20. 1972; Earth sciences, 15c.
21. 1972; Governor Frontenac, 8c.
22. 1972; Christmas, 8c.
23. 1972; Cornelius Krieghoff, 8c.
24. 1973; Monsignor de Laval, 8c.
25. 1973; Mounted police, 8c.
26. 1973; Jeanne Mance, 8c.
27. 1973; Prince Edward Island, 8c.

28. 1973; J. E. H. MacDonald, 15c.
29. 1975; Advance publicity for 1976 Olympic Games, 8c. + 2c.
30. 1973; Joseph Howe, 8c.
31. 1973; Nellie McClung, 8c.
32. 1973; Christmas, 6c.

GREENLAND:
33. 1967; Greenland legends, 90ö.
34. 1969; Greenland legends, 80ö.
35. 1969–73; Whale, 1k.

ST. PIERRE & MIQUELON:
36. 1970; Rowing, 20f.

UNITED NATIONS (New York):
37. 1966; WHO, 11c.
38. 1966; Coffee, 11c.
39. 1967; UN development, 11c.
40. 1967; Disarmament Campaign, 13c.
41. 1968; UN Secretariat, 13c.
42. 1970; UN Charter, 6c.
43. 1971; Refugees, 6c.
44. 1972; Non-proliferation of nuclear weapons, 8c.
45. 1972; Air, 17c.
46. 1974; UPU, 10c.

PLATE 99

UNITED STATES OF AMERICA:
1. 1965; New Orleans, 5c.
2. 1965; Physical fitness, 5c.
3. 1965; Cancer, 5c.
4. 1965; Sir Winston Churchill, 5c.
5. 1965; Salvation Army, 5c.
6. 1965; Magna Carta, 5c.
7. 1965; Dante, 5c.
8. 1965; ICY, 5c.
9. 1965; Robert Fulton, 5c.
10. 1965; Traffic Safety, 5c.
11. 1965; Herbert Hoover, 5c.
12. 1965; J. S. Copley, 5c.
13. 1965; ITU, 5c.
14. 1965; Adlai Stevenson, 5c.
15. 1965; Christmas, 5c.
16. 1965–8; Prominent Americans, $1.
17. 1966; Migratory birds, 5c.
18. 1966; Philatelic exhibition, 5c.
19. 1966; Indiana statehood, 5c.
20. 1966; National Park Service, 5c.
21. 1966; Bill of Rights, 5c.
22. 1966; Polish Millennium, 5c.
23. 1966; Marine Corps Reserve, 5c.
24. 1966; Women's clubs, 5c.
25. 1966; Beautification of America, 5c.
26. 1966; Great River Road, 5c.
27. 1966; US Savings Bonds, 5c.
28. 1966; Christmas, 5c.
29. 1966; Mary Cassatt, 5c.
30. 1967; Alaska Purchase, 5c.
31. 1967; National Grange, 5c.
32. 1967; Canadian centennial, 5c.
33. 1967; Erie Canal, 5c.
34. 1967; H. D. Thoreau, 5c.
35. 1967; Voice of America, 5c.
36. 1967; Search for peace, 5c.
37. 1967; Davy Crockett, 5c.
38. 1967; Space achievements, 2 × 5c.
39. 1967; Thomas Eakins, 5c.
40. 1967; Mississippi, 5c.
41. 1968; Youth, 6c.
42. 1968; Flag issue, 6c.

43. 1968; Air, 10c.
44. 1968; Historic flags, 6c.

PLATE 100

UNITED STATES OF AMERICA:
1. 1968; Illinois, 6c.
2. 1968; Hemisfair '68, 6c.
3. 1968; Law and order, 6c.
4. 1968; Marquette, 6c.
5. 1968; Register and vote, 6c.
6. 1968; Walt Disney, 6c.
7. 1968; Leif Erikson, 6c.
8. 1968; Daniel Boone, 6c.
9. 1968; Arkansas river navigation, 6c.
10. 1968; John Trumbull, 6c.
11. 1968; Cherokee Strip, 6c.
12. 1968; Waterfowl conservation, 6c.
13. 1968; Christmas, 6c.
14. 1968; The American Indian, 6c.
15. 1968; Air, 20c.
16. 1969; Beautification of America, 6c.
17. 1969; American Legion, 6c.
18. 1969; Grandma Moses, 6c.
19. 1969; W. C. Handy, 6c.
20. 1969; Colorado River, 6c.
21. 1969; Moon flight, 6c.
22. 1969; Alabama, 6c.
23. 1969; Botanical Congress, 6c.
24. 1969; President Eisenhower, 6c.
25. 1969; Baseball, 6c.
26. 1969; First man on the moon, 10c.
27. 1969; Christmas, 6c.
28. 1969; William H. Harnett, 6c.
29. 1970; Maine statehood, 6c.
30. 1970; Stone Mountain memorial, 6c.
31. 1970; Fort Snelling, 6c.
32. 1971; Air, 9c.
33. 1970; Prevention of pollution, 6c.
34. 1970; Christmas, 6c.
35. 1970; UN, 6c.
36. 1970; Pilgrim Fathers, 6c.
37. 1971; Wildlife conservation, 8c.
38. 1971; General MacArthur, 6c.
39. 1971; Antarctic Treaty, 8c.

PLATE 101

UNITED STATES OF AMERICA:
1. 1971; Postal service emblem, 8c.
2. 1971; John Sloan, 8c.
3. 1971; Space achievements, 8c.
4. 1971; Emily Dickinson, 8c.
5. 1971; San Juan, 8c.
6. 1971; Drug abuse, 8c.
7. 1971; Historic preservation, 8c.
8. 1972; Sidney Lanier, 8c.
9. 1972; Peace Corps, 8c.
10. 1972; National parks, 15c.
11. 1972; Colonial craftsmen, 8c.
12. 1972; Olympic Games, 15c.
13. 1972; Parents Teacher Association, 8c.
14. 1972; Wildlife conservation, 8c.
15. 1972; Osteopathic Association, 8c.
16. 1972; Mail Order, 8c.
17. 1972; Tom Sawyer, 8c.
18. 1972; Christmas, 8c.
19. 1972; Pharmaceutical Association, 8c.
20. 1972; Stamp-collecting, 8c.
21. 1973; Greetings stamp, 8c.
22. 1973; Copernicus, 8c.
23. 1973; American Revolution, 8c.
24. 1973; George Gershwin, 8c.

25. 1973; Postal service, 8c.
26. 1973; President Harry Truman, 8c.
27. 1973; Boston Tea Party, 8c.
28. 1973; Robinson Jeffers, 8c.
29. 1973; Electronics, 8c.
30. 1973; Willa Cather, 8c.
31. 1973; Rural America, 8c.
32. 1973; Jefferson memorial, 10c.
33. 1973; Flags, 10c.
34. 1973; President Lyndon B. Johnson, 8c.
35. 1973; Christmas, 8c.
36. 1974; EXPO 74, 10c.
37. 1974; Mail transport, 10c.
38. 1974; Air, 18c.
39. 1974; Veterans of foreign wars, 10c.
40. 1974; Gemstones, 10c.
41. 1975; 200 Years of Postal Serivce, 10c.

PLATE 102

BELIZE:
1. 1973; Dolphin, 15c.
2. 1974; Pictorial series, 25c.
3. 1974; Butterflies, $5.

BRITISH HONDURAS:
4. 1968; Fish and animals, $1.
5. 1971; New capital, 25c.

CANAL ZONE:
6. 1965; Air, 15c.
7. 1971; Fort San Lorenzo, 8c.

COSTA RICA:
8. 1965; President Kennedy, 55c.
9. 1972; American Tourist Year, 90c.

EL SALVADOR:
10. 1973; Lions International, 20c.
11. 1973; Music festival, 50c.

GUATEMALA:
12. 1966; Mario Montenegro, 5c.
13. 1966–70; Arms, 5c.
14. 1968; ITU, 21c.
15. 1971; Liberal reforms, 10c.
16. 1971; Central American independence, 9c.

HONDURAS:
17. 1965; Father Manuel de Jesus Subirana, 8c.
18. 1966; Stamp centenary, 4c.

MEXICO:
19. 1965; Andrés Manuel del Rio, 30c.
20. 1968; Olympic Games (4th issue), 2p.
21. 1969; Underground train, 40c.
22. 1972; Science and technology, 2p.
23. 1971; Conquest of space, 2p.
24. 1972; President Benito Juarez, 2p.

NICARAGUA:
25. 1965; Antiquities, 25c.
26. 1965; Andres Bello, 2cor.
27. 1966; Sir Winston Churchill, 35c.
28. 1967; Butterflies, 2cor.
29. 1970; Apollo 11 moon landing, 60c.
30. 1968; Fruit, 15c.
31. 1971; Scientific formulae, 2cor.

PANAMA:
32. 1966; Religious paintings, 21c.
33. 1966; Pope Paul's visit, 10c.
34. 1966; President Kennedy, 5c.

35. 1971; UPU, 30c.
36. 1968; Winter Olympics, 13c.

PLATE 103

ARGENTINE REPUBLIC:
1. 1961–8; Stag, 500p.
2. 1965; Tierra del Fuego, 4p.
3. 1965; Dante, 8p.
4. 1966; Rocket launch, 27p.50.
5. 1971; Expedition to South Pole, 20c.
6. 1970–73; José de San Martin, 50c.
7. 1970–73; Air, 45c.
8. 1973; Christmas, 1p.20.

BOLIVIA:
9. 1968; Cochabamba, 4p.
10. 1968; Stamp centenary, 30c.

BRAZIL:
11. 1965; Sir Winston Churchill, 200cr.
12. 1967; Portraits, 5c.
13. 1967–8; Portraits, 1cr.
14. 1968; Birds, 50c.
15. 1970; Marist students, 50c.
16. 1971; Butterflies, 20c.
17. 1971; Trans-Amazon Highway, 40c.
18. 1971; Children's Day, 60c.
19. 1972; Major industries, 45c.
20. 1972; Stamp exhibition, 70c.
21. 1972; Social development, 1cr.
22. 1972; Definitive, 30c.
23. 1972; Post Office symbol, 20c.
24. 1973; Sports, 40c.
25. 1973; Chamber of Commerce, 1cr.
26. 1973; Tropical birds and plants, 20c.
27. 1973; National Tourism Year, 70c.

BRITISH GUIANA:
28. 1965; ITU, 25c.

CHILE:
29. 1965–9; National flower, 20c.
30. 1966; Portraits, 50c.
31. 1967; International Tourist Year, 30c.
32. 1968; Chilean Mint, 1E.
33. 1969; Satellite communications, 2E.
34. 1970; Compulsory tax, 10c.
35. 1970; Capture of Valdivia, 40c.
36. 1970; Paul Harris, 1E.
37. 1971; State Maritime Corporation, 52c.
38. 1971; Compulsory tax, 15c.
39. 1972; Antarctic Treaty, 1E.15.

PLATE 104

COLOMBIA:
1. 1965; Manuel Mejia, 45c.
2. 1965; Air, 5c.
3. 1966; J. Arboleda, 5c.
4. 1966; Maritime mail, 20c.
5. 1967; Famous Colombians, 80c.
6. 1968; Eucharistic Congress, 1p.
7. 1969; Air, 3p.50.
8. 1970; Satellite earth station, 1p.
9. 1970; Territorial Credit Institute, 1p.
10. 1970; Philatelic Week, 2p.
11. 1970; National Games, 80c.
12. 1972; Leyva, 1p.10.
13. 1972; Korean War, 1p.20.
14. 1972; Orchid, 1p.30.
15. 1972; Postal administration, 1p.10.

16. 1973; Museum of Pre-Colombian Antiquities, 3p.50.
17. 1972; President G. L. Valencia, 1p.30.
18. 1973; Radio amateurs, 60c.
19. 1973; Javeriana University, 1p.50.
20. 1973; Battle of Bombona, 1p.30.
21. 1973; Child Welfare, 1p.10.

ECUADOR:
22. 1965; Stamp centenary, 4s.
23. 1970; Butterflies, 50c.
24. 1971; *El Universo* newspaper, 2s.50.
25. 1971; President Allende, 2s.
26. 1972; Arms, 3s.
27. 1972; Battle of Pichincha (second issue), 2s.30.
28. 1972; President Lanusse's visit, 5s.
29. 1973; Galapagos Islands, 1s.30.

GUYANA:
30. 1966; Independence, $5.
31. 1966; Independence, 25c.
32. 1967; Rarest stamp, 5c.
33. 1967; Independence anniversary, 6c.
34. 1967; Christmas, 25c.
35. 1968; Easter, 25c.
36. 1968; Christmas, 6c.
37. 1971; Flowering plants, 3c.
38. 1973; Red Cross, 8c.

PLATE 105

PARAGUAY:
1. 1965; Sir Winston Churchill, 12g.45.
2. 1966; Mexican Olympics, 10c.

PERU:
3. 1967; Obligatory tax, 20c.
4. 1967; Lions International, 1s.60.
5. 1967; Agrarian reform unissued stamp surcharged, 6s.50.
6. 1971; Precursors of Independence, 5s.50.

SURINAM:
7. 1968; WHO, 25c.
8. 1969; Child Welfare, 20c. + 10c.
9. 1970; United Nations, 25c.
10. 1971; First census, 15c.
11. 1974; UPU, 30c.
12. 1972; Airmail, 30c.

URUGUAY:
13. 1965; President Kennedy, 20c.
14. 1965; Benito Nardone, 40c.
15. 1966; Architects Association, 4c.
16. 1966; War heroes, 20c.
17. 1967; President Makarios, 6.60c.
18. 1967; Heads of State meeting, 10c.
19. 1967; Eduardo Acevedo, 40c.
20. 1967; Railways, 2p.
21. 1967; 7c. definitive, surcharged, 1p.
22. 1968; Navy, 2p.
23. 1968; Birds, 2p.
24. 1968; Football, 1p.
25. 1970; Fauna, 20p.
26. 1970; General Artigas' home, 15p.
27. 1970; Rheumatology Congress, 30p.
28. 1971; Secret vote, 10p.

VENEZUELA:
29. 1965; Alliance for Progress, 60c.
30. 1965; Guyana Claim, 75c.
31. 1965; Sir Winston Churchill, 1b.
32. 1966; National dances, 20c.
33. 1967; Simon Bolivar, 35c.

34. 1971; Orchids, 1b.
35. 1968; Nature conservation, 15c.
36. 1970; Flowers, 25c.
37. 1971; Provincial maps, 65c.

PLATE 106

ANGUILLA:
1. 1968; Girl Guides, 10c.

ANTIGUA:
2. 1966; Definitive series, $1.
3. 1967; Associated Statehood, 4c.
4. 1969; Parliament, 4c.
5. 1971; Easter, 35c.
6. 1970; Pictorial series, 5c.

BAHAMAS:
7. 1966; Decimal currency definitive, 15c.
8. 1967; Pictorial series, 8c.
9. 1968; Commonwealth Parliamentary Conference, 3c.
10. 1968; Gold coins, 15c.
11. 1969; Tourism, 15c.
12. 1970; Goodwill Caravan, 15c.
13. 1970; Red Cross, 15c.
14. 1971; Pictorial series, 15c.
15. 1972; Olympic Games, 10c.
16. 1973; Independence, 3c.
17. 1973; Christmas, 3c.

BARBADOS:
18. 1965; Photogravure series, 5c.
19. 1968; Human Rights, 4c.
20. 1970; Pictorial series, 15c.
21. 1973; University of West Indies, 5c.

BARBUDA:
22. 1968; Pictorial series, 15c.
23. 1968; Olympic Games, 75c.

BERMUDA:
24. 1970; Flowers series, 9c.
25. 1970; Parliament 18c.
26. 1971; Anglo–American talks, 18c.

BRITISH ANTARCTIC TERRITORY:
27. 1971; Antarctic Treaty, 10p.
28. 1973; Pictorial series, £1.

CAYMAN ISLANDS:
29. 1966; International telephone links, 4d.
30. 1966; Cayman jet service, 1s.
31. 1970; Decimal currency series, 40c.

DOMINICA:
32. 1968; Associated statehood, 60c.
33. 1969; Photogravure series, $1.20.

FALKLAND ISLANDS:
34. 1968; Human Rights Year, 2d.
35. 1968; Flowers, 2d.

SOUTH GEORGIA:
36. 1972; Sir Ernest Shackleton, 10p.

PLATE 107

GRENADA:
1. 1965; ICY, 1c.
2. 1966; Photogravure series, 50c.
3. 1967; Associated statehood, 25c.
4. 1968–71; Pictorial series, 8c.

GRENADINES OF GRENADA:
5. 1974; World Cup, 1c.

JAMAICA:
6. 1966; Commonwealth Games, 1s.
7. 1967; World's Fair, Montreal, 6d.
8. 1967; Sir Donald Sangster, 3d.
9. 1967; Constabulary, 3d.
10. 1969; Decimal currency, 3c.
11. 1972; Pictorial series, 15c.
12. 1970; National heroes, 1c.
13. 1973; Orchids, 5c.

MONTSERRAT:
14. 1965; Elizabethan series, 1c.
15. 1967; Tourist Year, 24c.
16. 1970; Birds series, 50c.

ST. CHRISTOPHER, NEVIS AND ANGUILLA:
17. 1969; Fish, 6c.
18. 1970; Pictorial series, 6c.
19. 1971; Siege of Brimstone Hill, 20c.

ST. LUCIA:
20. 1968; Easter, 35c.
21. 1970; Pictorial series, 10c.

ST. VINCENT:
22. 1965; Photogravure series, 10c.
23. 1968; Dr. Martin Luther King, 5c.
24. 1970; Birds definitive, $1.

GRENADINES OF ST. VINCENT:
25. 1974; UPU, $1.

TRINIDAD AND TOBABO:
26. 1969; Elizabethan series, 12c.
27. 1970; San Fernando, 3c.
28. 1971; Wildlife, 6c.
29. 1972; Butterflies, 10c.
30. 1973; Anniversaries, 10c.

TURKS AND CAICOS ISLANDS:
31. 1967; Stamp centenary, 1s.
32. 1971; Decimal currency series, $1.
33. 1973; Birds definitive, 20c.

VIRGIN ISLANDS:
34. 1966; 70c. definitive surcharged, 50c.
35. 1970; Boats series, 50c.

PLATE 108

CUBA:
1. 1965; Fishing fleet, 2c.
2. 1965; Quiet Sun Year, 2c.
3. 1966; Games, 7c.
4. 1966; Christmas, 1c.
5. 1967; Stamp Day, 3c.
6. 1967; EXPO 67, 2c.
7. 1968; Olympic Games, 1c.
8. 1970; EXPO 70, 3c.
9. 1970; Spelaeological Society, 2c.
10. 1970; Tourist centres, 3c.
11. 1971; Children's drawings, 9c.
12. 1972; Labour Day, 3c.
13. 1972; Paintings, 13c.
14. 1973; Stamp Day, 13c.
15. 1972; Horses, 1c.
16. 1973; Paintings, 5c.

DOMINICAN REPUBLIC:
17. 1967; Special delivery, 25c.
18. 1971; Obligatory tax, 1c.

19. 1966; ITU, 28c.
20. 1972; Obligatory tax, 1c.
21. 1971; Christmas, 10c.
22. 1972; World Health Day, 7c.
23. 1972; Philatelic exhibition, 33c.

HAITI:
24. 1965; New York World's Fair, 50c.
25. 1966; Culture, 1g.50.
26. 1966; Football, 15c.
27. 1967; Duvalieriste Revolution, 25c.
28. 1966; National education, 50c.
29. 1968; National education, 10c.
30. 1968; 'Revolt of the slaves', 25c.
31. 1969; Olympic marathon, 10c.

NETHERLANDS ANTILLES:
32. 1972; M. F. Da Costa Gomez, 30c.
33. 1969; ILO, 25c.
34. 1971; St Theresia Parish, Aruba, 20c.

PLATE 109

AUSTRALIA:
1. 1965; ITU, 5d.
2. 1965; Lawrence Hargrave, 5d.
3. 1965; ICY, 2s. 3d.
4. 1966; Decimal currency series, $2.
5. 1966; Life saving, 4c.
6. 1967; YWCA, 4c.
7. 1967; Gynaecology and obstetrics, 4c.
8. 1968; World Weather Watch, 5c.
9. 1968; State floral emblems, 20c.
10. 1968; Soil Science Congress, 5c.
11. 1968; Famous Australians, 5c.
12. 1969; Northern Territory, 5c.
13. 1969; Ports and harbours, 5c.
14. 1969; Primary industries, 25c.
15. 1969; England–Australia flight, 5c.
16. 1969; Famous Australians (second series), 5c.
17. 1970; Railway, 5c.
18. 1970; EXPO, 20c.
19. 1970; Captain Cook, 5 × 5c.
20. 1970; Commonwealth Parliamentary Association Conference, 6c.
21. 1970; Christmas, 6c.
22. 1970; United Nations, 6c.
23. 1970–71; Flowers, coil stamp, 6c.
24. 1970; National development, 8c.
25. 1970; QANTAS, 30c.
26. 1970; Famous Australians (third series), 6c.
27. 1971; Rotary International, 6c.
28. 1971; Aboriginal art, 20c.
29. 1971; RAAF, 6c.
30. 1971; Animals, 12c.
31. 1972; Country Women's Association, 7c.
32. 1972; Olympic Games, 7c.
33. 1973; Metric conversion, 7c.
34. 1973; National development (second series), 20c.
35. 1974; Animals, 30c.
36. 1971; Christmas, 7c.
37. 1972; Famous Australians (fourth series), 7c.
38. 1972; Primary industries, 30c.
39. 1972; Rehabilitation of the disabled, 18c.
40. 1972; Accountants Congress, 7c.
41. 1973; Famous Australians (fifth series), 7c.
42. 1972; Pioneer life, 40c.
43. 1973; Legacy, 7c.
44. 1973; Marine life and gemstones, 7c.
45. 1973; Architecture, 7c.
46. 1973; Radio, 7c.

AUSTRALIAN ANTARCTIC TERRITORY:
47. 1966–8; Pictorial definitive, 5c.

PLATE 110

NEW ZEALAND:
1. 1965; Gallipoli landing, 5d.
2. 1965; ITU, 9d.
3. 1965; Sir Winston Churchill, 7d.
4. 1965; Government centenary, 4d.
5. 1965; Commonwealth Parliamentary Conference, 2s.
6. 1965; Health, 4d. + 1d.
7. 1965; Christmas, 3d.
8. 1966; Scout jamboree, 4d.
9. 1967; Health, 3c. + 1c.
10. 1967; Post Office, 9d.
11. 1967–9; Pictorial definitive, $2.
12. 1967; Royal Society, 8c.
13. 1968; Maori Bible, 3c.
14. 1968; Armed forces, 28c.
15. 1969; ILO, 7c.
16. 1969; Law Society, 3c.
17. 1969; Otago University, 10c.
18. 1969; Kerikeri, 4c.
19. 1969; Captain Cook, 28c.
20. 1969; CORSO, 8c.
21. 1970; Cardigan Bay, 10c.
22. 1970; Pictorial series, 7½c.
23. 1970; World's Fair, 18c.
24. 1970; Health, 3c. + 1c.
25. 1970; United Nations, 10c.
26. 1970; Christmas, 10c.
27. 1970; Chatham Islands, 2c.
28. 1971; Country Women's Institute, 4c.
29. 1971; Yacht racing, 5c.
30. 1971; Civic centenaries, 5c.
31. 1971; Antarctic Treaty, 6c.
32. 1971; Satellite earth station, 10c.
33. 1971; Lord Rutherford, 7c.
34. 1971; Rose Convention, 2c.
35. 1972; Anniversaries, 10c.
36. 1973; Steam locomotive, 10c.
37. 1972; Lake scenes, 6c.
38. 1973; Francis Hodgkins, 5c.
39. 1974; Commonwealth Games, 4c.
40. 1974; Centenaries, 4c.
41. 1975; Forest parks, 18c.
42. 1969; Life Insurance, 3c.

ROSS DEPENDENCY:
43. 1972; Pictorial series, 8c.

PLATE 111

BRITISH SOLOMON ISLANDS:
1. 1966; Decimal currency, 25c.
2. 1968; Photogravure series, 35c.
3. 1969; Christmas, 8c.

CHRISTMAS ISLAND:
4. 1968; Fish, $1.
5. 1972–3; Ships series, 35c.
6. 1965; Gallipoli landing, 10c.

COCOS (KEELING) ISLANDS:
7. 1969; Pictorial series, 50c.

COOK ISLANDS:
8. 1966; Air, 1s.
9. 1965; Internal self-government, 4d.
10. 1967; Floral series, 30c.
11. 1969; South Pacific Conference, 30c.
12. 1970; Christmas, 20c.
13. 1972; Hurricane Relief, 10c. + 2c.
14. 1973; Silver wedding coinage, 50c.
15. 1973; Nuclear testing, 10c.
16. 1973; Maori exploration, 5c.
17. 1973; Royal wedding, 30c.
18. 1974; Shells definitive, 30c.

AITUTAKI:
19. 1972; Floral, 20c.
20. 1973; Easter, 10c.

PENRHYN ISLAND:
21. 1973; Floral, 8c.
22. 1973; Royal wedding, 50c.

FIJI:
23. 1968; Kingsford Smith, 1s.
24. 1969; Photogravure series, 3c.
25. 1970; Stamp centenary, 20c.
26. 1971–2; Birds and flowers series, 1c.
27. 1969; University of the South Pacific, 8c.

FRENCH POLYNESIA:
28. 1966; Polynesian boats, 19f.
29. 1966; South Pacific Games, 10f.
30. 1972; Port of Papeete, 28f.
31. 1973; Women's Union crèche, 28f.

GILBERT AND ELLICE ISLANDS:
32. 1967; Island family, 35c.
33. 1968; Decimal currency, 15c.
34. 1971; Pictorial series, 20c.
35. 1971; UNICEF, 10c.
36. 1971; Christmas, 35c.
37. 1972; South Pacific Commission, 35c.

PLATE 112

NAURU:
1. 1965; Reed warbler, 3s. 3d.
2. 1968; Republic, 10c.
3. 1968; Independence, 10c.
4. 1973; Independence, 15c.

NEW CALEDONIA:
5. 1972; New post office, 23f.

NEW HEBRIDES:
6. 1967; Pacific war, 1f.
7. 1968; Concorde, 25c.
8. 1973; New wharf, 70c.

NIUE:
9. 1969; Christmas, 2½c.
10. 1969; Flowers series, 30c.
11. 1970; Edible crabs, 30c.
12. 1972; Arts festival, 25c.
13. 1971; Portraits, 14c.

NORFOLK ISLAND:
14. 1967; Ships definitive, 15c.
15. 1967; Captain Cook, 10c.
16. 1970–71; Birds series, 20c.

PAPUA–NEW GUINEA:
17. 1966; Butterflies, 25c.
18. 1967; Beetles, 25c.
19. 1968; National heritage, 5c.
20. 1968; Universal suffrage, 20c.
21. 1968; Seashells, 30c.
22. 1969; South Pacific Games, 20c.
23. 1969; Orchids, 30c.
24. 1970; National heritage, 30c.
25. 1970; Native artifacts, 30c.
26. 1971; Fauna conservation, 30c.
27. 1971; Primary industries, 30c.
28. 1971; Native dances, 28c.
29. 1972; South Pacific Commission, 15c.
30. 1973; Pictorial series, 7c.

PITCAIRN ISLANDS:
31. 1967; Decimal currency, 30c.
32. 1969; Pictorial series, 15c.

SAMOA:
33. 1967; Birds series, 25s.
34. 1972; Triton shell, 10s.

TOKELAU ISLANDS:
35. 1967; Decimal currency surcharge, 10c.
36. 1971; Handicrafts, 25c.
37. 1969; History, 20c.
38. 1972; South Pacific Commission, 20c.
39. 1967; New Zealand arms stamp, overprinted, 20c.
40. 1973; Coral, 25c.

TONGA:
41. 1967; Coronation, 7s.

WALLIS AND FUTUNA ISLANDS:
42. 1971; President de Gaulle, 30f.
43. 1972; South Pacific Commission, 44f.

Appendices
Glossary of technical terms

Commemorative (stamp): Postage stamp intended specifically to commemorate an event or personality. The term is rather loosely applied to all postage stamps issued for special occasions or for a limited period.

Definitive (stamp): Stamp belonging to the ordinary postage series in regular use over a comparatively long period, as opposed to commemorative stamps, postage-due labels or semi-postal issues.

Die: The original or master engraving, from which the multiple impressions of the plate are taken.

Miniature sheet: Small sheet containing one or more stamps, often with a decorative margin. Stamps in miniature sheets may differ from those in normal large sheets by having different perforations or no perforations at all, or by being printed in different colours. Miniature sheets are produced mainly as collector's pieces and have a very limited postal usage.

Omnibus issue: Stamps released in uniform designs by a group of countries simultaneously. Stamps of this type usually differ only in the name of the country and the values expressed, although in more recent years there has been a tendency to inject some measure of variety into the designs of such related issues.

Overprint: Inscription added to stamps after the basic printing process or processes have been completed. An overprint, applied by hand or machine, is used to alter the scope of a stamp's validity (often the actual country in which it is intended to be used), or to convert a stamp from one purpose to another (e.g. a definitive to commemorative, or from ordinary postage to airmail, or from revenue to postal use). An overprint which alters the value of a stamp is known as a surcharge.

Postage-due label: Labels, often, though erroneously known as stamps, affixed to unpaid or underpaid mail to denote that a charge is to be payed by the recipient.

Semi-postal or **Charity stamp:** Stamp whose face value is composed partly of a postal fee and partly of a premium in aid of charity or some other fund-raising purpose.

Se-tenant: French term meaning side by side, used to describe stamps of different designs, colours or denominations, printed side by side in the same sheet.

Surcharge: Inscription overprinted on stamps to change their value. Such inscriptions may be in words or figures and usually incorporate bars or other forms of obliteration to cover the original value inscriptions. Surcharges are often necessitated by changes in postal rates, or by the temporary shortage of certain denominations.

The printing processes

Intaglio: Otherwise known as copperplate, *taille douce* or recess-printing and sometimes, though incorrectly, described as line-engraving, this is the oldest of stamp printing processes, having been used for the British Penny Black and Twopence Blue of 1840. In this method, the lines to be printed are engraved into the surface of the plate and the ink is then applied to the recesses or grooves. The surface of the plate is then wiped clean and polished. The paper, which is often dampened to make it more pliable, is then laid on the plate and forced under great pressure into the recesses of the plate where it absorbs the ink lying there. This gives stamps printed by intaglio their characteristic ridged surface.

Letterpress: Otherwise known rather inaccurately to philatelists as surface-printing or typography (although, strictly speaking, the latter term means the design and layout of type itself), this is the opposite process to intaglio. In this process the printing plate has raised lines and areas which pick up the ink from a roller and transfer it to the paper by surface pressure. Clichés or stereos (printing blocks cast in moulds or made by electrotype) are usually assembled in a forme to produce the multiple layout of the stamp printing plate. Stamps printed by this process have slight indentations visible on the back where the lines of the plate have pressed on to the paper. A variant of this is *type-setting* in which moveable type – letters, numerals, printer's rule and ornaments – are assembled to compose a design. In more recent years this has been mainly confined to overprints and surcharges.

Lithography: Literally, this means printing from stones, a reference to the original process which made use of a special form of limestone. A design was drawn directly on to the polished surface of the stone, using a special fat ink. The stone was then wetted and a roller inked over the stone. The fat ink on the roller was repelled by the wetted portion of the stone but taken up by the fat ink impression of the drawing. When the paper was placed on the stone it took up an impression from the inked area. Lithography has been modified and improved enormously in recent years, though the basic principle still relies on the mutually repellant properties of water and fat inks. Modern variants include offset lithography, duotone offset and Delacryl (the latter being a trade name of De La Rue). Lithography is characterised by its flat appearance, as compared to intaglio, and does not show any indentation or 'print-through', which is to be found on modern letterpress stamps. Modern multicolour offset lithography often exhibits screening dots, which the beginner is apt to confuse with photogravure, but in the latter process the screening is considerably finer.

Photogravure: Otherwise known as rotogravure or heliogravure, this is probably the most widely used process today. An image is transferred photographically on to a coated cylinder which is then immersed in an acid bath and the image is etched on to it. The original design is photographed, reduced photographically and then repeated the required number of times on the cylinder, using a 'step and repeat' machine. Photogravure is similar to intaglio in so far as the ink lies in the tiny dots or clusters of dots which pit the surface of the cylinder and, under pressure, the paper picks up the ink from these dots. The screening in photogravure is generally much finer than that found in half-tone book or magazine illustrations that reproduce a photographic image by the letterpress method.

In recent years, greater variety has been given to stamp production by combining two or more or the above processes. Modern multicolour photogravure or offset-lithography can produce very colourful results, but lack the depth and quality of intaglio. Intaglio on its own, however, cannot achieve the range and complexity of colours found in the other processes. Thus intaglio combined with photogravure or lithography will produce stamps with a rich texture as well as colour. Less frequently intaglio is combined with letterpress, or letterpress with lithography.

Index to the plates

160 | INDEX TO THE PLATES